Acting Out

CULTURE

Readings for Critical Inquiry

Fourth Edition

James S. Miller

University of Wisconsin–Whitewater

bedford/st.martin's
Macmillan Learning

Boston | New York

For Henry, Eliza, and Hope

For Bedford/St. Martin's

Vice President, Editorial, Macmillan Learning Humanities: Edwin Hill
Senior Program Director for English: Leasa Burton
Program Manager: John Sullivan
Executive Marketing Manager: Joy Fisher Williams
Director of Content Development: Jane Knetzger
Associate Editor: Lexi DeConti
Content Project Manager: Lidia MacDonald-Carr
Workflow Supervisor: Joe Ford
Production Supervisor: Robin Besofsky
Media Project Manager: Rand Thomas
Manager of Publishing Services: Andrea Cava
Project Management: Lumina Datamatics, Inc.
Composition: Lumina Datamatics, Inc.
Photo Researcher: Candice Cheesman, Lumina Datamatics, Inc.
Text Permissions/Text Permissions Researcher: Mark Schaefer, Lumina Datamatics, Inc.
Permissions Manager: Kalina Ingham
Senior Art Director: Anna Palchik
Cover Design: William Boardman
Cover Photo: DNY59/Getty Images
Printing and Binding: LSC Communications

2   1   0   9
f   e   d   c   b

For information, write: Bedford/St. Martin's, 75 Arlington Street, Boston, MA 02116

ISBN 978-1-319-05674-2

Acknowledgments

Text acknowledgments and copyrights appear at the back of the book on pages 558–563, which constitute an extension of the copyright page. Art acknowledgments and copyrights appear on the same page as the art selections they cover.

At the time of publication all Internet URLs published in this text were found to accurately link to their intended website. If you do find a broken link, please forward the information to english@macmillan.com so that it can be corrected for the next printing.

Preface for Instructors

A CRITICAL EYE

James Dean's leather jacket in *Rebel Without a Cause* and Katniss Everdeen's mockingjay pin in *The Hunger Games* have become symbols of rebellion in American popular culture. But what does it really mean to rebel? True rebellion can begin with a question, with taking another look at the traditions and rituals that form the fabric of society and asking, "Why?"

Acting Out Culture encourages students to train a critical eye on American culture, instructing them how to challenge the norms and rewrite the scripts society sets forth instead of simply accepting them at face value. It takes as a given that students have already internalized countless rules and are bombarded every day with media messages that dictate how they should think, feel, and behave. *Acting Out Culture* urges them to recognize these rules and prescriptions that they may adhere to unthinkingly, probe them, and imagine alternatives. Although scripts for their lives abound, the endings are not yet written. Working with the readings and assignments in *Acting Out Culture* gives students the opportunity to think critically about the norms and roles handed to or imposed on them and, as it were, devise their own scripts in response to what they discover. On the stage of a composition classroom where popular culture is the subject of inquiry, they have the chance to "act out" through writing that positions them as citizens making informed decisions about their world.

WHY THESE THEMES?

Because they start where students are and encourage them to move beyond their own comfort zones of belief and action. The thematic organization of *Acting Out Culture* focuses students' attention not only on *what* our culture tells us but also on *how* it establishes those rules and disseminates those norms. The chapter themes explore questions of what and how we believe, watch and listen, eat, learn, work, connect, and identify — questions that get to the heart of who students are and how they behave. Do they count themselves among the "we"s? As students evaluate, negotiate, and resist the roles and stances reflected in the chapters, their critical responses begin to emerge.

Moreover, the specific topics and readings within the chapters use students' own knowledge of popular culture as a springboard to deeper analysis. For example, Chapter 2, "How We Watch and Listen," covers several types of seeing and hearing, making connections between what it means to watch and be watched, to listen and to be heard. Students are asked to draw on *what* they know about such diverse topics as professional football, physical disabilities, and podcasts as a first step in considering broader questions of *how* this knowledge might connect to the culture at large.

Students today are highly culturally attuned. They are surrounded by marketing and are adept at paying attention to huge streams of competing cultural data. In order to help them translate these native skills to the college classroom, the fourth edition of *Acting Out Culture* provides extensive support for doing critical analysis in academic work. The Introduction, "How We Read and Write About Culture (and How We Ought To)," gives students a brief crash course in the vocabulary of cultural analysis with extended, real-life examples, offers a framework that models the process of critical reading, and provides an annotated professional essay that walks students step-by-step through performing cultural analysis. In addition, a complete student essay in MLA format in the Introduction makes it easier for students to see how to integrate cultural analysis into academic writing.

WHY THESE READINGS?

Because they are exceptional models of writing and thinking by contemporary writers who have important things to say about issues students care about. Each chapter includes longer pieces that support sustained reading and model in-depth critical analysis, as well as more popular pieces that go beyond trend spotting to tackle the question "How does America tick?" — with often surprising conclusions. The writers include academics such as Michael Eric Dyson (writing on the perception of African American patriotism), journalists such as Barbara Ehrenreich (who exposes the ways in which the American poor are victimized), and activists such as Bryan Stevenson (who calls for a wholesale reevaluation of our criminal justice system). Although the readings approach the book's main themes from different angles, the overall focus on making and breaking the sometimes unspoken rules that govern our everyday lives creates a dialogue that will challenge students' critical thinking skills.

WHY THESE FEATURES IN EACH CHAPTER?

Because they introduce a variety of approaches to thinking and writing about cultural norms and rules. To analyze culture, students need to notice what they often overlook or take for granted. For this reason, each chapter opens with a multimedia example (e.g., image, website, infographic, public service announcement) depicting the sort of cultural norm that often flies beneath students' radar. Calling out these norms for inspection and analysis, each chapter opener presents students with a set of prompts asking them to analyze and evaluate the key messages being promoted. Another recurring feature that makes the often-invisible visible is **"What is normal?"** which appears in the margins of the chapter introductions. These callouts list common rules that reflect conventional wisdom and invite students to move what's in the margins of their awareness to front and center, the better to unpack and examine the assumptions nested in the norms. Opportunities to conduct this kind of analysis recur throughout the book, as students are regularly invited to engage with and respond to a range of pop culture texts — from web pages to advertisements, television to news photos — as conductors of cultural messages.

Students also need to see that thinking critically about culture can serve as a powerful tool for rethinking and rewriting prevailing social scripts. Therefore, each chapter includes a box entitled **Rewriting the Script**, which showcases a particular effort to push back against conventional thinking on a current cultural issue. By looking at contradictions within the organic food industry or reconsidering the growing efforts to vocationalize public education, students learn first-hand some of the strategies cultural actors use to rethink and revise the instructions by which we are taught to think, talk, and act. Furthermore, by inviting them to write about these strategies, this feature also encourages students to engage in this process of cultural reflection and revision themselves.

The images in **Then and Now** depict popular thinking from the past to the present. Students can compare and contrast the images, but they can also use the accompanying contextual information to think further about what *hasn't* changed over time. In the "How We Believe" chapter, for example, a news photo of a Cold War–era duck-and-cover air raid drill is paired with a recent news photo showing bottles of shampoo and mouthwash being confiscated at the airport. Students are asked to consider, then and now, "What's more important? To feel safe or to be safe?" Do the images suggest similarly futile responses to overwhelming perils? If not, why not? If so, what are some alternatives?

Scenes and Un-Scenes track cultural norms in visual media by juxtaposing images on a central topic. These topics range from patriotic symbols in political speeches to the importance of victory as an American ideal. Students are encouraged to see the images as texts, composed to persuade audiences to interpret the world in a certain way. Discussion and writing prompts then direct students to think about how visual media portray, navigate, and reframe social rules and norms. What's in the pictures, and what's been left out?

WHY THESE WRITING ASSIGNMENTS?

Because writing is the best way for students to harness their own thinking and take control of what the culture wants them to believe. Writing is one of the most powerful tools we have for participating as active members of society, and the assignments in *Acting Out Culture* help students get a grip on the issues and construct sturdy arguments for action and change. After reading each selection, students are asked to identify the norms the piece addresses, think critically about the issues at hand, and take a stand on these topics by analyzing a writer's argument, examining the point of view, or evaluating the effectiveness of the language.

In particular, the **Acting Like a Citizen** assignment puts students in the driver's seat, asking them to explore the ways rules and norms affect actual people living in real communities, and to consider what actions might be taken in response. Often rooted in field research, these assignments urge students to also consider the social and civic consequences that arguments can have by more deeply examining the ways the issues in a chapter play out within their own communities and their own personal lives. For example, in the "How We Work" chapter, students are asked to research mean salaries for a range of jobs and write about why we value different types of work in different ways, using what they've discovered by reading the chapter selections to consider how we might act to change these particular social scripts.

Comparing Arguments, the discussion/writing prompt that accompanies each selection in every chapter, encourages students to think about two essays in relation to one another, assessing the different but complementary ways they address an issue or question related to the broader chapter theme. Putting two writers within a given chapter into dialogue, these prompts challenge students to compare the ways different writers argue about such issues as poverty, consumerism, or the relationship between education and work.

WHAT'S NEW IN THE FOURTH EDITION?

*Because American culture evolves at such a rapid pace, there are **thirty-five new readings about current and relevant issues.*** More than half of the reading selections are new, featuring up-and-coming and established voices that think through and challenge established rules and norms, whether these are online, on television, at the dinner table, or at the cash register. The new readings feature the brightest writers, educators, journalists, and activists who challenge our thinking on the issues that matter in America today. From Rebecca Traister's sharp-eyed analysis of our culture's evolving marriage norms, to Steve Almond's anguished meditation on the ethics of watching professional football, to Mac McClelland's journey into the dark world of warehouse fulfillment centers, each new reading addresses issues students encounter as they move through every role they play in life.

Whether through writing or social interaction, social norms play a formative role in shaping how we view and define ourselves. A new chapter, **"How We Identify,"** takes up just this question, exploring our complex relationship with the public roles we choose, and the norms that underlie them. Are we, this chapter asks, defined by the roles we play? What does it mean to identify with the social norms such roles reflect? By inviting students to consider these questions, "How We Identify" reinforces *Acting Out Culture*'s overall belief that writing and action give students the power to change not only their world but also themselves. The chapter addresses the theme of "identification" from a variety of vantages, covering topics as timely and engaging as transgender identity, sexuality on the web, and the threats to black bodies in public space.

SUPPORT FOR INSTRUCTORS AND STUDENTS

At Bedford/St. Martin's, providing support to teachers and their students who use our books and digital tools is our top priority. The Bedford/St. Martin's English Community is now our home for professional resources, including Bedford *Bits*, our popular blog with new ideas for the composition classroom. Join us to connect with our authors and your colleagues at **community.macmillan.com** where you can download titles from our professional resource series, review projects in the pipeline, sign up for webinars, or start a discussion.

In addition to this dynamic online community and book-specific instructor resources, we offer digital tools, custom solutions, and value packages to support both you and your students. We are committed to delivering the quality and value that you've come to expect from Bedford/St. Martin's, supported as always by the power of Macmillan Learning. To learn more about or to order any of the following products, contact your Bedford/St. Martin's sales representative or visit the website at **macmillanlearning.com**.

SELECT VALUE PACKAGES

Add value to your text by packaging one of the following resources with *Acting Out Culture*. To learn more about package options for any of the following products, contact your Bedford/St. Martin's sales representative or visit **macmillanlearning.com**.

Writer's Help 2.0 is a powerful online writing resource that helps students find answers whether they are searching for writing advice on their own or as part of an assignment.

- **Smart search.** Built on research with more than 1,600 student writers, the smart search in Writer's Help provides reliable results even when students use novice terms, such as *flow* and *unstuck*.

- **Trusted content from our best-selling handbooks.** Choose *Writer's Help 2.0, Hacker Version*, or *Writer's Help 2.0, Lunsford Version*, to ensure that students have clear advice and examples for all of their writing questions.

- **Diagnostics that help establish a baseline for instruction**. Assign diagnostics to identify areas of strength and areas for improvement on topics related to grammar and reading and to help students plan a course of study. Use visual reports to track performance by topic, class, and student as well as comparison reports that track improvement over time.

- **Adaptive exercises that engage students**. Writer's Help 2.0 includes LearningCurve, gamelike online quizzing that adapts to what students already know and helps them focus on what they need to learn.

Writer's Help 2.0 can be packaged with *Acting Out Culture* at a significant discount. For more information, contact your sales representative or visit **macmillanlearning.com/writershelp2**.

LaunchPad Solo for Readers and Writers allows students to work on whatever they need help with the most. At home or in class, students learn at their own pace, with instruction tailored to each student's unique needs. *LaunchPad Solo for Readers and Writers* features

- **pre-built units that support a learning arc.** Each easy-to-assign unit consists of a pretest check, multimedia instruction and assessment, and a posttest that assesses what students have learned about critical reading, writing process, using sources, grammar, style, and mechanics. Dedicated units also offer help for multilingual writers.

- **diagnostics that help establish a baseline for instruction.** Assign diagnostics to identify areas of strength and areas for improvement on topics related to grammar and reading and to help students plan a course of study. Use visual reports to track performance by topic, class, and student, as well as comparison reports to track improvement over time.

- **a video introduction to many topics.** Introductions offer an overview of the unit's topic, and many include a brief, accessible video to illustrate the concepts at hand.

- **twenty-five reading selections with comprehension quizzes.** Assign a range of classic and contemporary essays each of which includes a label indicating Lexile level to help you scaffold instruction in critical reading.

- **adaptive quizzing for targeted learning.** Most units include Learning-Curve, gamelike adaptive quizzing that focuses on the areas in which each student needs the most help.

- **the ability to monitor student progress.** Use our gradebook to see which students are on track and which need additional help with specific topics.

Students who rent or buy a used book can purchase access and instructors may request free access at **macmillanlearning.com/readwrite**.

MACMILLAN LEARNING CURRICULUM SOLUTIONS

Curriculum Solutions brings together the quality of Bedford/St. Martin's content with Hayden-McNeil's expertise in publishing original custom print and digital products. Developed especially for writing courses, our ForeWords for English program contains a library of the most popular, requested content in easy-to-use modules to help you build the best possible text. Whether you are considering creating a custom version of *Acting Out Culture* or incorporating our content with your own, we can adapt and combine the resources that work best for your course or program. Some enrollment minimums apply. Contact your sales representative for more information.

INSTRUCTOR RESOURCES

You have a lot to do in your course. Bedford/St. Martin's wants to make it easy for you to find the support you need — and to get it quickly.

The *Instructor's Manual for Acting Out Culture* is available as a PDF that can be downloaded from **macmillanlearning.com**. Visit the instructor resources tab for *Acting Out Culture*. In addition to chapter overviews and teaching tips, the instructor's manual includes sample syllabi and classroom activities.

ACKNOWLEDGMENTS

As befits its focus on "acting," this book owes its existence to the contributions of a truly ensemble cast. First of all, I would like to thank Alanya Harter and Leasa Burton, whose early insights and guidance several years ago helped get this project off the ground. Thanks as well to Joan Feinberg, Denise Wydra, Karen Henry, Steve Scipione, Adam Whitehurst, and Jane

Carter, whose combined wealth of experience and ideas added immeasurable depth and purpose to the book.

Once again, I'd like to extend my thanks to the countless students and instructors intrepid enough to have taken a chance on a new cultural studies reader. The anecdotes, reflections, and suggestions I have received over the last three years provided me with exactly the right foundation for thinking about what this book really needs to be. In particular, I would like to single out the contributions of my own students at University of Wisconsin–Whitewater, who never stinted in offering candid and constructive feedback about both what did and did not work. Thank you to the following instructors for their valuable input on the fourth edition:

Craig Bartholomaus, Metropolitan Community College–Penn Valley
Tamara Ponzo Brattoli, Joliet Junior College
Krista Callahan-Caudill, University of Kentucky
Kyndra Campbell, Gallatin College
Cornelius FitzPatrick, Colorado State University
Jacquelyn Geiger, Bucks County Community College
Deena Lynk, Carteret Community College
Carole Mackie, California State University, Fullerton
Paul Nagy, Clovis Community College
Stacey Parham, Judson College
Thomas Pfister, Idaho State University

This book would never have made it past manuscript without the careful work of Managing Editor Michael Granger, Manager of Publisher Services Andrea Cava, and Content Project Manager Lidia MacDonald-Carr. And there'd be very little in it without Kalina Ingham and Mark Schaefer to hammer out the text permissions and without Martha Friedman and Candice Cheesman applying their expert research skills to the visuals.

Of course *Acting Out Culture* would never have rounded the corner into a fourth edition were it not for the stalwart efforts of my editor, Jill Gallagher. Jill brought a degree of insight and enthusiasm to this project that reinvigorated this book precisely when it was needed most. Also, my gratitude to associate editor Lexi DeConti. My heartfelt thanks to you both. Additionally, thanks are due to Vice President of Editorial, Humanities, Edwin Hill; Program Manager John Sullivan; and Executive Marketing Manager Joy Fisher Williams. My continuing affection and gratitude, as well, go to the gang at EVP Coffee in Madison. When you're lucky enough to have discovered the perfect place for writing a book, why mess with a good thing? And finally, to Emily Hall, whose belief in and support for this project continues to make it all possible. My love and thanks.

Contents

CONTENTS

3 How We Eat:

CONTENTS

4 How We Learn:

What Kinds of Knowledge Are Most Valuable? How Are We Supposed to Go About Acquiring Such Knowledge?   235

5   How We Work:

What Do Our Jobs Say About Us?   329

CONTENTS

7 How We Identify:

Do The Roles We Play Reflect Who We Truly Are?   495

Introduction: How We Read and Write About Culture (and How We Ought To)

THESE ARE THE RULES

Why do you act differently at a job interview than on a night out with friends? Why do we so rarely see people wearing their pajamas out to dinner? What accounts for the fact that you're far more likely to be on a first-name basis with a classmate than with a professor? Why does your Thanksgiving dinner conversation with a grandparent sound so different from the texts you exchange with friends? Whether sitting in class or working an off-campus job, chatting with family on the phone or meeting a roommate for coffee, it's hardly a secret that different situations require different standards of behavior. This observation may seem obvious, but it also raises some important questions. Namely, why do we accept *these* standards instead of others? Why do we regard only certain ways of acting, talking, and dressing as acceptable, appropriate, *normal*? Who, or what, teaches us to be normal?

This book invites you to look at and think more deeply about the countless rules that operate in our world: where they come from; how they shape our actions and attitudes; and whether they can be ultimately questioned, challenged, or even rewritten. From the shopping mall to the classroom, from the jobs we hold to the parties we attend, from family holidays to first dates, our world abounds with an almost endless array of instructions: different collections of "dos" and "don'ts" that, while generally unspoken, nonetheless influence how we act. This book asks you to more deeply consider and question these instructions by writing more critically about the world around you. You can start by asking yourself the following questions:

- *What* is it that producers of popular culture want me to do?

- *How* do they use our common cultural beliefs, identities, or fears to persuade me to do it?

- How do I *really* want to do it, or do I want to do it at all?

Unlike other books that focus on popular culture, this book asks you to begin by examining the ordinary details of your daily life. Rather than exploring the texts and products of pop culture in isolation, you will be asked to uncover and make sense of the complex connections between this material and your personal actions. It is the goal of this book to direct your attention not just to what our popular culture *says* but to what it asks you to *do* (or *think* or *feel*) as well. You probably already know quite a bit about some of the ways that popular culture attempts to influence you. You're likely aware, for example, that commercial ads exist to sell you products, that political commentary aims to influence your vote, and that TV producers want you to

1

watch their programs. But deciding for yourself which pitches to tune in and which to tune out means looking deeper, beyond *what's* being sold to you to *how* it's being sold. How do writers, advertisers, politicians, and activists use common cultural ideas — shared assumptions about what is and is not normal — to influence what you believe and how you behave?

NORMS, SCRIPTS, ROLES, RULES: ANALYZING POPULAR CULTURE

Although you are surrounded by the messages of popular culture every day, the act of talking and writing about it can seem a little foreign. How do we talk about something we all experience but none of us experiences the same way? Because it explores how popular culture teaches us to "act," this book undertakes its analysis by using a set of terms borrowed from the theater as well as cultural studies. What happens, it asks, when we begin looking at our daily actions and choices as if they were highly choreo-graphed *performances*? When we begin thinking about the rules that define the different settings in our world as *scripts* to be followed? When we start redefining our own individual behavior as *roles* we have been assigned to play? What do we gain, in sum, by thinking about our world as a kind of *stage* on which we are encouraged to *act out* parts written for us in advance?

> ## Rule:
>
> **A spoken or unspoken directive for how people should or should not act in a given situation.**

To better understand what this approach looks like, let's examine one of those everyday situations as a case study. Imagine you're sitting in a college composition classroom on the first day of the semester. If you wanted to ana-lyze this setting in performative terms, you might begin by itemizing all of the different **rules** (spoken and unspoken) that govern within this environment: sit attentively, listen to the instructor, write down all the information you are told is important, agree to complete the readings, hand in assignments by the due dates, respond on point when questioned by the instructor, and restrict your conversation to topics and issues that fit the course themes. Listing these rules would help you see something about them that might otherwise escape your notice: namely, that they are instructions setting clear boundaries around how you are and are not allowed to *act*. Armed with this new perspective, you would then be in a position to begin asking some important questions. What educa-tional goals are being furthered when I agree to follow these rules? Do these goals truly serve my interests? And if they don't, how do I think they should be changed?

> ## Norm:
>
> **A widely held cultural belief about what is appropriate in a given situation.**

You could extend this investigation by next delving into the ideas these classroom rules invite us to accept as **norms**. A norm is a widely held cultural assumption about what is proper to think or do in a given situation. In this case, you might look at the norms underlying the rules restricting student speech, pinpointing the key assumptions that serve to make this instruction seem reasonable, fair, or normal. Such assumptions might include: "real" learning happens only when the power to speak is shared unequally within the classroom. Or: "quality" education requires instructors to lead and students to follow. Once again, conducting this kind of analysis could open up some critical questions. Does a classroom that so unequally delegates the authority to speak promote genuine learning? Is it helpful, or even fair, to define only certain forms of classroom speech as legitimate?

Social script:

A set of behavioral instructions reinforced by norms and rules.

You could build upon this performative analysis further by next examining these classroom rules as **social scripts**. A social script is a set of directions outlining the actions to take in order to put a particular rule into practice. Whenever you act out a social script, you are signalling that you find the rules governing a particular setting, as well as the norms underlying them, to be acceptable. In the case of the classroom, acting out a social script could include things like completing all of the assignments according to their exact specifications, or speaking only when invited to by the instructor. Thinking of these behaviors as the performance of a social script might, in turn, lead you to question them, to consider how they might be rewritten. You might ask yourself: Are there alternative ways to complete these class assignments? Should there be different opportunities for students to speak up in class?

Posing questions like these might then lead you to the final phase of a performative analysis: considering how rules, norms, and scripts create **roles**. A role is the public form our behavior takes whenever we agree to follow a specific rule or act out a particular social script. When you work to meet every assignment

Role:

How people act in relation to their standing or environment.

deadline or faithfully request permission from the instructor before speaking, you could be said to be playing the role of the "good" student. Of course, once you begin thinking of these behaviors as a role — mandated by rules and guided by scripts created by others — you are in a much better position to start questioning them. Looking more closely at the behaviors this role permits and those that it prohibits, in fact, might even lead you to consider adopting a different role, one that deviates from the accepted rules and approved script.

The relationship between these four terms can be applied to an analysis of any topic in this book, and the more you practice them in your writing, the more this analysis will become second nature.

EXERCISE:

Think of two or three roles you are often required to play in your life (e.g., student, sibling, friend, consumer) and write a paragraph for each in which you describe the scripts you follow as a part of performing these roles. What norms and rules do you think influence how effectively you play these roles?

How Culture Shapes Us: Rules of the Road

The classroom is far from an isolated example. Consider how many other settings in your life are defined and governed by a similar set of rules. Whether in the classroom or on the job, at our computers or riding on the bus, we constantly find ourselves in situations that call on us to navigate the boundary separating what is acceptable to do from what is not. We don't always think about our lives in these terms because, day to day, it's easier to take for granted the way the world works, the rules we are taught to follow, and the roles we are expected to play. But the truth is that these rules and roles are anything but timeless or universal. They are rather the product of extended, often contested, efforts to define what is normal. Norms, scripts, roles, and rules have been influenced and shaped over time, products of forces that we can learn to recognize and challenge ourselves.

Jeffrey Coolidge/Getty Images

To illustrate, let's choose an example from daily life to which we can all relate: seat belts. Have you ever known a time when you weren't aware that you are supposed to wear your seat belt every time you are inside a moving car? Don't most of us think of buckling up as a normal part of our driving? Wasn't it always this way? Among all the rules we (hopefully) follow when we drive — stop on red, go on green, obey the speed limit, use the turn signals — wearing a seat belt sits squarely among them as one of the most important. The 2014 U.S. average for seat belt use was 84 percent, according to the National Highway Traffic Safety Administration.

It might surprise you to learn that although seat belts were invented in the mid-1800s, they first appeared as standard equipment in the United States in 1958, in cars made by Swedish car manufacturer Saab. Only when a federal law was passed in 1968 did it become mandatory for car manufacturers to install seat belts in every car they sold.

At first, few people wore them. Seat belts were seen as uncomfortable and inconvenient. America's car culture has always used buzzwords like *freedom* to describe the experience of driving, and what feels less like being free than being — literally — restrained in your seat? Seat belt laws have always been left to states, and throughout the 1960s and 1970s, attempts to pass mandatory seat belt laws repeatedly failed in many states.

New York passed the first law requiring drivers to wear seat belts — after many defeated attempts — in 1984.

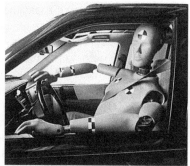

Steve Hathaway/Getty Images

But although seat belt use became the law of the land (currently New Hampshire, the "Live Free or Die" state, is the only one without a mandatory seat belt law for all passengers), penalizing drivers was not enough to make wearing seat belts seem like a normal thing to do. It would take the passage of time and a concerted public service campaign, including the popular 1980s campaign featuring Vince and Larry, two crash test dummies who walked away from accidents while a voice-over intoned, "You can learn a lot from a dummy. Buckle your safety belt."

In the time since seat belts first appeared in cars, many small changes to our car culture have made wearing them seem like a good thing to do. From the accident statistics cited in the evening news, to road signs telling us how many of our fellow drivers are similarly buckled in, to dashboard lights in our cars that blink and beep until we strap ourselves in, reminders to wear our seat belts shape our thinking and our actions every time we get into a car. Playing the role of good driver now makes wearing seat belts more than a rule we obey or a script we follow. It is a social norm.

This historical recap of Americans' seat belt habits highlights another important point about the relationship between rules and norms. It reminds us that the process by which a rule transforms itself into a norm is neither seamless nor quick. Rather, it happens gradually and is always the product of concerted, often contentious, effort. This is worth keeping in mind because it reminds us that these norms are actually subject to greater change and influence by us than at first might seem to be the case. As you hear or read debates about issues such as taxes, same-sex marriage, or the budget deficit, think about what messages each side is sending out. The more you practice, the better you'll become at understanding how these messages seep in and interact with our larger culture, as well as with our individual lives.

Martin Hospach/Getty Images

THE WORLD IN WORDS

While they surround us, the rules and norms produced and promoted by our pop culture are not set in stone. Indeed, one of the primary goals of this book is to underscore our own ability to examine, question, and (potentially) change the messages we encounter. The ways we think about and respond to popular culture are constantly changing, and these changes are often brought about by one common act: questioning the norm through writing. By learning to write critically, we learn to *talk back* to popular culture, to reconsider the dominant rules and roles, to revise the social scripts, and to challenge the embedded norms by which we are taught to live our daily lives. Through writing, we learn not only to question the attitudes and actions our popular culture promotes, but also to contemplate and construct alternatives. In a world that seems bent on making our choices for us, we can use writing to choose for ourselves.

To see examples of how writing helps us question and rewrite norms, you need look no further than the selections in this book. Only by reading and writing about the world we live in can we understand it and learn to navigate it on our own terms. The selections in this book are designed to challenge the ways many of us think about a wide range of topics. What they're *not* designed to do is to inspire you to agree with everything their authors say. Each of the authors in this book is using writing as a way to explore, influence, or protest against different aspects of our larger culture. By responding to their ideas with your own writing, you are entering a larger dialogue in which you begin to defend and define your place as part of that culture.

As you read these selections, remember that your ultimate goal is to talk back to these writers, to analyze and respond to their key ideas and claims, and to synthesize ideas from sources with ideas of your own. To do this, you will have to think critically about the rules, norms, scripts, and roles involved. You may also find it useful to analyze these selections in rhetorical terms. *Rhetoric*, in the most basic sense, refers to the strategies writers use to persuade an audience to accept their point of view. We can't effectively respond to the main point unless we fully grasp the persuasive strategies used to get this point across. One of the most effective ways to do this is to look at what is called the **rhetorical situation** — the context for a writer's argument that influences the form this argument ultimately takes. Here is a set of steps that will help you analyze the rhetorical situation:

- **Question the Author:** Who is this author? What is her level of expertise about this topic? What else has she written? Is she an academic, a journalist, an activist, a politician? How do those roles influence the way she communicates her opinions? What is the author's purpose? What prompted the author to write this piece? What is the author trying to say, and why is she trying to say it? What larger goal does she seem to have in mind? What is the author's attitude toward her topic or her readers, and what words or sentences convey this attitude?

- **Question the Audience (Including Yourself):** Toward whom is this piece directed? Which words or sentences help to create the overall tone or level of formality, and what do the tone and level tell me about the intended audience? What evidence or arguments were chosen to appeal to this audience? How do I react to this piece? Does it support or go against my own experience and exposure to this topic?

- **Question the Context:** What is the setting within which this argument is made? The classroom? The workplace? An online community? Through what medium is the writing created? If, for example, the selection is delivered online, what visuals or links are included, and how do these features affect the overall message?

- **Question the Genre:** What form does this argument take? An academic essay? A memo? A blog post? What are the conventions particular to this genre, and how might genre expectations have affected the form or content of the selection?

- **Question the Rules, Norms, and Scripts:** What rules, norms, or scripts is this author writing about? Is the author writing in support of or in opposition to them?

- **Question the Argument:** What are the main points of this piece? How does the author support this point of view? Are the examples scientific, derived from interviews, or part of the author's experience? What are the possible counterarguments? How does the author anticipate and refute them?

GUIDED READING: ANNE TRUBEK'S "STOP TEACHING HANDWRITING"

To figure out how to analyze this material most effectively, let's take a look at a sample essay. The classroom, as we have already seen, offers a perfect example of how forces beyond our immediate control can shape our actions and assumptions. In this setting, we are told to obey certain rules, asked to share certain norms, expected to follow certain scripts, and called on to play certain roles. Anne Trubek's "Stop Teaching Handwriting" challenges one of these norms and presents an impassioned plea for changing it. Seeking to question a long-standing classroom practice, Trubek asks: What are the goals this handwriting rule is designed to achieve? What broader assumptions about children and learning do these goals reflect? And are these assumptions valid? This essay is annotated with the sorts of questions you might ask while reading many of the essays in this book, questions about where an essay fits in relation to established norms and how it seeks to question them. As you review the annotations, think about how the questions and observations they raise help you put the essay in perspective. Once you've done this, take a look at the analysis of the rhetorical situation that follows the essay. How does this information help prepare you to analyze this essay more effectively? And how might you use it as a model for analyzing the rhetorical situation of other essays?

ANNE TRUBEK

Stop Teaching Handwriting

MY SON, WHO IS IN THIRD GRADE, SPENDS MUCH OF HIS SCHOOL day struggling to learn how to form the letter "G." Sometimes he writes it backwards. Sometimes the tail on his lowercase "T" goes the wrong way. His teachers keep telling him he may fail the state assessment standards. We have had several "interventions." Simon now fears taking up a pencil. Repeatedly being told his handwriting is bad (a fine-motor-skill issue) has become, in his mind, proof that he is a bad writer (an expression issue). He now hates writing, period.

This is absurd: I am a college professor and a freelance writer, and the only time I pick up a pen is to sign a credit-card receipt. Let's stop brutalizing our kids with years of drills on the proper formation of a cursive capital "S"—handwriting is a historical blip in the long history of writing technologies, and it's time to consign to the trash heap this artificial way of making letters, along with clay tablets, smoke signals, and other arcane technologies.

Many will find this argument hard to swallow because we cling to handwriting out of a romantic sense that script expresses identity. But only since the invention of the printing press has handwriting been considered a mark of self-expression. Medieval monks first worried that the invention of printing would be the ruin of books, as presses were more idiosyncratic and prone to human error than manuscripts produced in scriptoriums. And the monks never conceived of handwriting as a sign of identity: For them, script was formulaic, not self-expressive. That concept did not appear until the early 18th century. Still later came the notion that personality and individuality could be deduced by analyzing handwriting. All the while, print became widely available, and handwriting lost its primacy as a vehicle of mass communication.

The typewriter took handwriting down another notch. Henry James took up the then-new writing machine in the 1880s, most likely because he, like my son, had poor handwriting. By the 1890s, James was dictating all his novels to a secretary. And as novelists and businesses were putting down their pens, others started to valorize handwriting as somehow more pure and more authentic, infusing script with nostalgic romanticism. The philosopher Martin Heidegger was particularly guilty of this, writing in 1940 of the losses wrought by typewriters: "In handwriting the relation of Being to man, namely the word, is inscribed in beings themselves. . . . When writing was withdrawn from the origin of its essence, i.e. from the hand, and was transferred to the machine, a transformation occurred in the relation of Being to man."

Meanwhile, back in school, teachers were trying to get student papers to look like typewritten documents: letter characters, the students were told, should look like fonts.

The pattern doesn't change: As writing technologies evolve, we romanticize the old and adapt to the new. This will happen with keyboards, too — some contemporary novelists have ceased using them already. Richard Powers uses voice-recognition software to compose everything, including his novels. "Except for brief moments of duress, I haven't touched a keyboard for years," he says. "No fingers were tortured in producing these words — or the last half a million words of my published fiction." Powers is wonderfully free of technological nostalgia: "Writing is the act of accepting the huge shortfall between the story in the mind and what hits the page. . . . For that, no interface will ever be clean or invisible enough for us to get the passage right," he says to his computer.

That shortfall is exactly how my son describes his writing troubles: "I have it all in my memory bank and then I stop and my memory bank gets wiped out," he explains. Voice-recognition software — judging from the rapid-fire monologues he delivers at dinner about Pokémon and Yu-Gi-Oh! — would help.

No matter what we use to write, something will be lost between conception and execution. I have yet to be convinced that making a graphite stick go in certain directions enhances intellectual development. Let us teach our kids to use the best tools at our disposal: There are plenty of cool toys out there. Boys and girls, it is time to put down your pencils.

Why do people think that handwritten script is more personal than typewritten script? Trubek provides a quote that reinforces this point of view. Do I think that way? Why?

Why might a writer, and the mother of a struggling child, be in favor of these changing norms? What is the purpose of writing, according to Trubek or Powers?

Do I think of writing similarly?

Pokémon and Yu-Gi-Oh! are role-playing games that are very popular with children. What does this reference suggest about the audience Trubek is addressing?

She concludes using a play on words involving classroom rules. Why?

ANALYZING THE RHETORICAL SITUATION

- **Question the Author:** Anne Trubek is a professor of English and rhetoric at Oberlin College, where she teaches a range of courses on argumentation and persuasive writing. She is currently conducting research for her upcoming book, *The History and Uncertain Future of Handwriting*. She is also the mother of a child who struggles with penmanship.

- **Question the Audience (Including Yourself):** The intended audience here seems to be parents who have children currently learning these handwriting norms or those interested in educational reform. What are your own views about handwriting? Are these skills useful in your daily life? Did you struggle with handwriting as her son does? Did this struggle affect the way you think about writing?

- **Question the Context:** Trubek's essay first appeared in *Good*, a magazine published by a group that describes itself as "pragmatic idealists working toward individual and collective progress" on social, cultural, and political issues. What does this description suggest about the audience Trubek intends to reach? About how she views the issue of handwriting instruction?

- **Question the Genre:** This piece follows the format of an opinion piece that might be found on the editorial page of a newspaper or a selection in a mainstream magazine.

- **Question the Rules, Norms, and Scripts:** Trubek is directly challenging the rule that requires students to be taught proper handwriting. In this sense, she seems to be calling for a change in one of the key social scripts defining life in the elementary-school classroom.

- **Question the Argument:** Trubek's main argument revolves around whether or not traditional handwriting instruction fosters meaningful learning. Claiming that it doesn't, Trubek argues that we should "adapt to the new" and regard handwriting as an obsolete skill. Is she right? Is there really no value, in this day and age, to learning handwriting? Or is Trubek overlooking ways such instruction might still be useful?

A STUDENT'S RESPONSE TO TRUBEK

After reading Trubek's essay and considering the questions posed about her argument, you probably have your own reaction to it. Thinking about her argument in terms of rules, roles, scripts, and norms, as well as the rhetorical situation, can help you analyze the selection and come up with something to say about it. In order to convey your assessment as clearly and cogently as possible, make sure that your own written response includes several key elements:

- **Thesis:** One main claim stated clearly and directly, usually in one (or sometimes two) sentence(s); your thesis should be the conclusion you want your reader to draw or the point of view you want your reader to share. The thesis usually occurs at the end of the introduction, but it may be held back until the conclusion, and in some cases may be implied rather than stated directly (although this strategy is less common in academic writing).

- **Introduction:** A compelling opening paragraph or section that announces your topic, engages your intended audience, and prepares readers for what follows. An effective introduction often ends with the thesis, and in a response essay, the introduction often includes a brief summary of the reading selection, including its main point and key supporting points.

- **Supporting Paragraphs:** Paragraphs that provide the reasons and evidence needed to convince readers to accept the thesis. Supporting paragraphs usually include a topic sentence that states the main point of the paragraph (a point supporting the thesis) and also include reasons and evidence that support the topic sentence. They also usually include transitions, words or phrases (such as *however, therefore, for example, granted, at first, next, finally*) that show how previous or subsequent paragraphs or sentences connect with one another.

- **Concession and Rebuttal:** A concession acknowledges that opposing points of view may be valid, and a rebuttal shows how that position is flawed. Concessions often suggest to readers that the author is reasonable and has considered others' views, while rebuttals provide authors with an opportunity to respond.

- **Conclusion:** A final paragraph or section that reminds readers of your thesis and leaves them feeling that you have delivered what your thesis and introduction promised. An effective conclusion may summarize your argument (if it is lengthy or complex), may suggest why your position is important or relevant, or may encourage the audience to take action.

Let's look at a student response to Trubek's essay. Creating an effective response to an essay requires you to do a number of things: first, identify and summarize the basic argument the author is making; second, restate the author's main points one by one; and third, explain how and why you either agree or disagree with each of these points. As you read, pay special attention to the annotations included in the margins. How do these annotations help you identify the specific elements this writer uses to make his own argument?

JORDAN RADZIECKI
Don't Erase Handwriting

In "Stop Teaching Handwriting," Anne Trubek argues that it's time to stop teaching handwriting and to throw this "historical blip in the long history of writing technologies" on the "trash heap" (p. 8). According to Trubek, new technologies make handwriting instruction unnecessary. She thinks schools still teach it because of a "nostalgic

Identifies the selection by author and title; presents a summary of Trubek's argument

Summarizes Trubek's main argument, using quotations from the text to illustrate

11

romanticism" (p. 8) and a mistaken belief that "script expresses identity" (p. 8). While she is correct that handwriting has become less

Author's thesis statement (two sentences)

important in recent years, Trubek is wrong in her overall argument. It is only when one examines her argument in light of her roles as a freelance writer and professor, and also as the mother of a child who struggles with his handwriting because of poor fine-motor skills, that

Author's thesis statement (two sentences)

one begins to see that the roles she plays in her life limit her willingness to see the usefulness of handwriting to others.

Concession

While it may be true that Trubek only picks up a pen to "sign a credit-card receipt" (p. 8), she cannot assume that this is true of everyone. The ability to write is fundamental to our society's under-

Rebuttal
First supporting reason

standing of what it means to be an educated person. Students must often take quizzes, tests, and exams, and they need to be able to write legibly and with minimal effort. Moreover, how much valuable

Supporting evidence

teachers' time is wasted trying to decipher illegible handwriting? Many classes tend to focus on group work, papers, and projects. Trubek doesn't consider the reality that writing for students goes beyond work done outside of class.

Author restates one of Trubek's key claims

As a mother, Trubek sees her son struggle with writing and decides based on his difficulties that teaching handwriting is "brutal-izing our kids" (p. 8). She sees handwriting as a problem because it is

Author's second main point

not her son's strength in school. This doesn't automatically make handwriting useless. Of course, learning fundamental skills can be

Concession and rebuttal, with author's supporting reasons

difficult, and no one thinks "drills" are fun. Yet education at the elementary school level is mostly about mastering the basics. After all, you are not learning history, economics, or high-level math at that age. The subject matter is often secondary. Instead, in the third grade you are learning the rules and scripts of the educational process: you are learning how to learn inside a classroom and outside it, too. You are learning how to perform your role as a student. In a sense, knowing how to write is not much different than knowing how to sit still at your desk or knowing how to raise your hand to answer a question rather than just shouting out a response.

Transition sentence

When we get out of school or look for work as students, we still must be able to write, even though it's likely that most of our writing will be done on computers, BlackBerry devices, or iPads. Trubek's

Restatement of another of Trubek's main points (in a sentence responding to her claim)

argument that technology continually advances doesn't mean that we should willingly become dependent on it to do everything for us. For a long, long time, students have been required to learn the three Rs: "reading, 'writing, and 'rithmetic." Despite Trubek's belief that handwriting's time has passed, educated and capable people are still expected to be able to write legibly. As a professor, Trubek should understand that technology is still too expensive for many students to own. She might see a great advantage to using voice-recognition software, but students, especially in college, will always struggle to keep money in their pockets. Some of us cannot afford to have laptops with us every second, and we shouldn't be denied education because of costly technology.

Author uses his own experience as evidence

Like Trubek, I am among those lucky enough to be able to afford a laptop, and so do most of my writing on a computer, at least outside the classroom. Trubek argues that handwriting has long been viewed, incorrectly, as an expression of one's true self, but I was never taught that handwriting expresses my true identity, nor, as Trubek says, do I "romanticize the old" (p. 9). At the same time, I do like to send hand-written "Thank You" notes: nearly everyone agrees that they are more personal and show more thought. When I write a love note or Valentine to my girlfriend, I do it by hand. Who wants to receive a word-processed love letter? I appreciate the time and care put into such letters on special occasions. I like to know that her pen has pressed down and shaped each letter. But that doesn't mean that I am sentimental about handwriting in general or that I am romanticizing an old technology in a silly way. We all value handmade things, and I am sure that Trubek is no exception to that rule in some aspect of her life. In some respects, however, the argument she makes here leaves the impression that she doesn't value such traditional practices or values at all.

Concession

Rebuttal of Trubek's claim

Author's claim, rebutting Trubek; based on personal experiences

While I sympathize with Trubek's son's problems as a third grader and understand Trubek's own frustration as a parent, she takes her argument too far. The answer is for her young son to get the extra help he needs (don't many students struggle with some aspect of elementary school?) to learn a crucial and fundamental skill for school—and for life.

Author restates his thesis and highlights his key difference with Trubek

Work Cited

Trubek, Anne. "Stop Teaching Handwriting." *Acting Out Culture: Readings for Critical Inquiry*, 4th ed., edited by James S. Miller, Bedford/St. Martin's, 2018, pp. 8–9.

READING MULTIMODAL TEXTS

Of course, not all the information we consume takes the form of a printed essay. In today's multimedia environment, we are just as likely to encounter pop culture messages through texts that combine an array of features (written, visual, video, graphic, or audio) — whether these are news photos or a political cartoon, a public service announcement or a YouTube video, a tweet or an Instagram post. Because multimodal texts employ such a diverse array of elements, fully understanding them requires careful analysis.

What is Edudemic? Who are its organizers, what are its goals, who are its sponsors?

Think about how textual, visual, and video elements work together. How do they present a coherent message?

What do these headers suggest about the larger goals of Edudemic and the audience this website aims to address? Is there a connection between the issues raised here and the problem of school bullying?

edudemic

Featured Articles   Most Popular   Trending Topics

HOME   TOOLS   TRENDS   NEWS   HOW TO   ONLINE LEARNING   SOCIAL MEDIA   ADVERTISE   IPAD MAGAZINE   APP DIR

Do you think you're worthy of better grades?   ✓ote

← The Incredibly Risky Real Life Game of College Admissions [Infographic]

KnowU: Harrison College's Social Learning Network May Just Be The Future Of Education →

Wednesday, December 14, 2011 8:15 am, Posted by **Jeff Dunn** 💬 1 | VIDEOS

An Anti-Bullying PSA All Students Should See

Topics: anti-bullying, bullying, psa, schoolchildren, video, youtube

🐦 Tweet 40   👍 Like 12   in Share 9   Buffer 0   Submit +1 2   Pin it 35

This story is framed to seem like a news report, but it also conveys an opinion and includes an embedded public service announcement (PSA), a message disseminated by the media without charge to raise awareness of or change behavior regarding an important social issue. How do these three categories—news story, editorial, and PSA—help you make sense of the main message this website is presenting?

Over 6 million American schoolchildren have been bullied in the past six months. Whether you cheer on the bully, or silently watch, you are supporting the bully. The effects upon the victim can be devastating, and the effects can last a lifetime. Do something besides watching.

Try to diffuse the situation. Tell a teacher, or a principal. If you can, stand up to the bully and let them know that it's not okay. Support the victim. Let them know you care and you don't think what happened to them was fair or right.

The world is a dangerous place, not because of those who do evil, but because of those who look on and do nothing.

-Albert Einstein

Einstein was celebrated not only for his revolutionary theories of mathematics and physics, but also as one of the great humanists of the twentieth century. Why include a quote from such a renowned figure? How does his statement relate to bullying?

Anti-Bullying PSA: The Price of Silence   Share ⌄ More info

Who is the audience for this argument? What role do the statistics play? How does this text relate to the Einstein quotation?

This website allows users to comment on and share the article or video. How does this medium foster this organization's goal(s)? What audience feedback is the statement "An anti-bullying PSA all students should see" designed to evoke?

How does this visual relate to the textual elements of this website? Does the scenario depicted here illustrate or reinforce the Einstein statement above? Who is the target audience for the embedded PSA? How does the image of the playground appeal to the intended audience?

Information from http://smartgunlaws.org/gun-laws/policy-areas/firearms-in-public-places/guns-in-schools/

Consider, for example, the screenshot from Edudemic, a website dedicated to providing the latest educational research "by pulling back the curtains on the learning process."

As you look at this image, think back to the outline of the rhetorical situation presented earlier. How do these categories provide you with a framework for beginning your own analysis? Then take a look at the annotations included with the screenshot. How do these annotations help you read this multimodal text more rhetorically and critically?

Most of the multimodal texts in this book can be read independently or as part of a series. Just like with texts, considering images together can show you a larger picture about how our culture depicts any action or belief as normal. Take a look at this PSA, which details the dangers that bullying poses to school-age kids, side by side with the screenshot above calling for greater restrictions around gun possession at schools. Considering the images as a pair and thinking about the issue of school safety, how does looking at the second image influence how you read the first?

ALTERNATIVE FACTS

The multimodal nature of modern texts adds both complexity and responsibility to the task of analyzing their cultural messages. Immersed in a world of websites and blogs, posts and pronouncements, texts and tweets, we find ourselves living in a media moment where the line between what is true and what is false has become increasingly difficult to draw. Now more than ever we face an obligation to verify the credibility of the media we consume. In an environment where cultural producers have the tools to pur-vey (or even invent) any kind of information they wish, it is critical that we ask ourselves: How do we figure out whom and what to believe?

No recent development better captures how urgent these questions have become than the rise of "fake news." As the volume, variety, and velocity of media has continued to expand, so too has the number of stories, surveys, and reports that traffic in fabricated, falsified, or factually incorrect informa-tion. Whether it is a fringe blogger spreading unfounded rumors about a ter-rorist threat or a presidential tweet trumpeting inaccurate poll numbers, ours is an era in which the truth of the information we consume has been cast into considerable doubt. And yet while problematic, the spread of "fake news" also presents us with a valuable opportunity: namely, to develop a set of ana-lytical skills specifically designed to vet and verify media messages for their credibility, reliability, and truth.

To illustrate what this kind of analysis looks like, let's take a look at a recent example. In many ways, the election of Donald Trump to the presidency in 2016 marked a turning point in the evolution of "fake news." In the months following his election, the policies and pronouncements of the Trump administration became a flashpoint for a broader public debate over what is true in today's media environment. Throughout this period, spokes-people from the Trump administration were routinely called out by journalists for reporting inaccurate stories, advancing false theories, and citing bogus statistics. No figure garnered more critical scrutiny in this regard than presi-dential advisor Kellyanne Conway, who infamously asserted the prerogative of the new White House to present "alternative facts" to the general public. For many, this statement confirmed the worst suspicions about the new administration's commitment to objective fact.

These suspicions were reinforced when Conway made reference to the "Bowling Green Massacre," a terrorist attack that never took place, as evi-dence of Muslim violence to support the administration's ban on travel from certain Muslim-majority countries. As seen in her tweet, Conway used an invented story to sow fears about "terrorist refugees" by repeating unfounded allegations about Al Qaeda operatives in Kentucky.

This example captures exactly what is so dangerous about "fake news." By reporting a made-up incident as if it were fact, stories like this not only misrepresent the truth to the general public, but they also undermine the public's ability to participate in a meaningful dialogue over the issues they raise. By falsely alleging a connection between refugees and terrorism, Conway's tweet makes it harder for Americans to figure out what they actually think about these issues, or to make an informed decision about policies such as a proposed refugee ban. Thoughtful deliberation and informed consent — the cornerstones of a democratic

 **Kellyanne Conway** ✔
@KellyannePolls

 Follow ⌄

READ: Bowling Green Terrorists: Al Qaeda in KY: US May Have Let 'Dozens' of Terrorists Into Country as Refugees

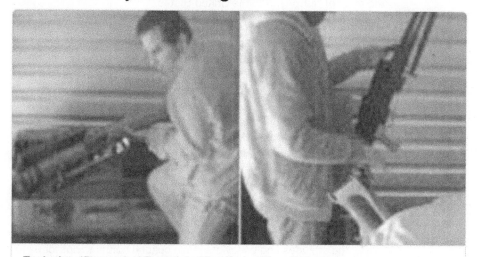

Exclusive: 'Dozens' of Terrorists May Be in US as Refugees

society — require an ironclad commitment to objective fact. When this commitment wavers, democracy itself suffers.

Fortunately, however, there are strategies we can employ to verify the relative truth of what we are told. Above all, this involves maintaining a critical, questioning attitude toward *all* media. Inundated with information, we need to make sure we ask pointed questions about where it all comes from, how it is generated and validated, and whether or not it is actually true.

Here are a few questions you may begin with to fact-check the "Bowling Green Massacre" story:

- What does the police record indicate actually took place at Bowling Green?

- Did the accused actually enter the country as refugees?
- Did they commit any act of violence?

Having challenged the facts of this story, we might then turn our attention to questioning the factual basis of the broader argument — about refugees, terrorists, and the need to restrict national immigration policy — this story was intended to prove:

- How many refugees have ever been convicted of a terrorist act?
- Where is the evidence that our current immigration policy has allowed the entry of "terrorists" to the United States?

With these questions answered, we could then begin analyzing this cultural text in relation to our four key terms: rules, norms, scripts, and roles. Once in possession of the facts, we would be able, for example, to clarify our understanding of the **rules** by which we expect responsible journalism to operate. Among them: news outlets should verify the factual truth of every story they report; all statements by public officials should be met with a demand for evidence or proof; any information disseminated through social media needs to be traced back to more objective sources. This, in turn, might lead us to question the assumptions or **norms** (i.e., about immigration, terrorism, and refugees) this type of "fake news" aims to promote. Do our current fears about global terrorism teach us to unfairly scapegoat immigrants or refugees? Does a focus on foreign enemies encourage us to overlook other threats to national security? Does restricting the entry of immigrants and refugees truly make us safer? Posing such questions might lead us next to reconsider the attitudes and behaviors these cultural norms **script** for us to follow. What would it be like to regard immigrants or refugees not as a threat, but as equal members of society? What different kinds of relationship, what different modes of social interaction, might this change make possible? And finally, all of this reflection and analysis might lead us to rethink what our proper **role** should be — whether as citizens, voters, or media consumers.

MAKING YOURSELF HEARD

The bulk of this book consists of readings from a range of writers who've accepted the task of analyzing the rules we live by. You will be familiar with many of these topics, but some may be new to you. Whether you've had any exposure to these topics or not, each selection is part of a chapter that examines one of the roles we all play: believers, watchers, eaters, learners, workers, and communicators. The writing assignments in this book will ask you to consider what you know about these topics side by side with these authors so that you can ultimately decide for yourself how *you* want to play life's roles.

Why should we care about analyzing popular culture? Consider the example of President Trump. From the moment he launched his longshot presidential bid, Trump has built a political movement and pursued a political agenda fueled in no small measure by his ability to harness the power of social media. In the eyes of many political observers, Trump's victory was directly attributable to the ways he cowed opponents, dictated the political conversation, and controlled the news cycle through memes and tweets. Whereas sites like Twitter, YouTube, and SnapChat were once designed for killing time, watching clips of strangers' home movies, or keeping in touch with friends, the power of popular culture has forced contenders for the biggest job in the United States to use the methods of dissemination perfected by popular culture to spread very serious promises about the future of America itself. By writing about popular culture, you become a part of the cultural conversation. This book will ask you to analyze and write about the world around you, but more importantly, it will ask you to analyze the world and to rewrite it on your own terms. You're not only about to read the writing of people who have used words as a way to navigate thousands of competing media messages. You're about to become one of them.

Alex Wong/Getty Images

Photos like this remind us that the strength and durability of cultural beliefs often depend on the public rituals designed to reinforce them. Take a closer look at this image. Then answer the following questions:

➲ What is the goal behind the Pledge of Allegiance?

➲ What particular belief is this ritual designed to reinforce or normalize?

➲ Should reciting the Pledge be mandatory for school-age kids?

➲ Why is the Pledge scripted as a public ritual?

➲ Would you alter or revise any part of the Pledge of Allegiance? In what way?

1 How We
BELIEVE
In What Way Does What We Know Shape Our Daily Actions?

Introduction

BELIEVING IN "BELIEF"

Imagine yourself as the central actor in the following scenarios:

- First-time voter contemplating the choice between candidates in the presidential election
- Pacifist member of the National Guard summoned to active military duty overseas
- Graduating senior considering employment offers from both the Peace Corps and Goldman Sachs
- Student in a college physics class who has happened on to the answers to an upcoming midterm exam
- Shopper deciding whether to spend rent money on a new outfit
- Pedestrian on a city street approached by a homeless person asking for money
- Journalist ordered by a judge to divulge a confidential news source

Although these examples touch on different issues, they are alike in one crucial way: Each situation requires you to make a value judgment, to choose between what matters more and what matters less. In other words, each choice hinges on *what you believe*.

The concept of belief turns our attention to what lies *underneath* the choices we make: to the embedded, unspoken, and often subconscious assumptions that make these choices feel normal. It's easy for most of us, given a set of circumstances, to say *what* we believe. But how often do any of us stop to think about *how* we came to hold the beliefs we take for granted? When we really stop to think about it, *how* do we make up our minds about what is right and wrong to do? Who or what teaches us to draw these kinds of distinctions? And how do these lessons come to feel so natural to us? Beliefs are not hypotheses. Grounded as they are in faith, in our intuitive or instinctive conviction that something is so, they require no recourse to empirical proof, factual data, or concrete evidence in order to stand in our minds as truth. Indeed, belief could be said to encompass everything in our lives we're convinced is true simply because it *feels* right.

Of course, this is also what makes explaining or defending our beliefs so tricky. If ultimately we can't prove the validity of our beliefs, then how can we ever hope to make others understand, accept, or share them? This dilemma may partly explain why our society is marked by so many disputes and controversies over what is and is not proper to believe. If beliefs are not hypotheses that can be proved but rather convictions that are "right" because they feel so to their believers, how can different members of society ever establish common ground?

Although it is often assumed to apply only to questions of religion, belief lies at the heart of some of our most urgent and intractable debates: from gay marriage to abortion to the war against terrorism. At the same time, belief is also part of the choices we make in our everyday lives: from how (or even whether) we vote to where we shop, from the work we perform to the money we earn, from the shows we watch to the books we read and the clothes we wear. Whatever the context, belief always boils down to the core ideas and values we hold because they just feel right.

But if we are not born already hardwired with these ingrained assumptions, how do our beliefs come to feel like second nature? By what process do we learn to regard only certain viewpoints and values as articles of faith?

PERSONAL BELIEFS, CULTURAL NORMS, AND SCRIPTING BELIEF

To pose these kinds of questions is to connect belief to the broader question of social *norms*, to consider how our own assumptions about right and wrong intersect with the standards scripted by our larger culture. To be sure, we are used to thinking of personal belief as something that belongs exclusively to us: values, ethics, and priorities that remain beyond the influence of our larger culture. Such a view is appealing because it reaffirms our

What is normal?

Sonda Dawes/The Image Works

What does this image ask us to believe? What are the ideas/values/ attitudes it asks us to accept as normal?

What is normal?
💬 A New World."

The official slogan of the 2016 Rio Olympic Games

rvlsoft/Shutterstock

Do you share this belief? Should we automatically accept it as normal?

23

faith in our individual *agency*: our ability to control and determine the choices we make. But while attractive, this view misrepresents our relationship to the larger culture. More than just the context or backdrop for our choices, culture plays an important role in shaping what we come to believe, suggesting that the values we consider to be our own private domain do not necessarily belong to us alone.

We do, after all, live in a world that promotes very specific messages about what is right and what is wrong, a world in which countless instructions get issued telling us what we should and should not care about. From political campaigns to our Facebook news feed, from *Cosmopolitan* magazine to the *New York Times* business section, our cultural landscape is littered with sources that tell us, often in very authoritative tones, which things truly matter and which things do not. Taking stock of these sources makes clear that belief is more than a matter of personal *choice*, that it also touches upon the ways our values can be scripted and normalized by the broader culture. In seeking to understand how this happens, our goal is less to pass judgment on different beliefs than to more deeply examine how they take shape in the first place, to better understand how certain ideas come to acquire this special status as unexamined and cherished norms.

What is normal?

"I believe in . . . an America that lives by a Constitution that inspires freedom and democracy around the world. An America with a big, open, charitable heart that reaches out to people in need around the world. . . . An America that is still the beacon of light to the darkest corner of the world."

Colin Powell, "The America I Believe In" from the National Public Radio series This I Believe

What kind of social script does this norm create? What would it feel like to act out this script in our personal lives?

"PLEDGING ALLEGIANCE": ACTING ON AND ACTING OUT OUR COMMITMENTS

An example from everyday life will clarify the kind of work this involves, as well as the implications for us in undertaking it. Virtually all of us are familiar with reciting the Pledge of Allegiance. The Pledge offers a useful case study because it illustrates how closely tied to social scripts and role-playing belief can be. Whether it involves the solemn pose we are supposed to maintain toward the flag, the obligatory "hand-over-the-heart" gesture, or the words of the Pledge we are expected to recite, the rules through which we are taught to express our "allegiance" couldn't be more specific. To better understand the norms underlying this public ritual, we might start by asking what goal these rules are designed to accomplish. Why have schoolchildren been required to recite the Pledge as a daily part of their school lives? What lesson or idea is this ritual supposed to teach them? These questions, in turn, might lead us to take a deeper look into the role patriotism plays within our educational system. Why does the Pledge include a loyalty oath? Why are children required to memorize and recite this oath in unison? What would be different if the words of the Pledge were different, if students were allowed to recite the oath silently or even to opt out from it altogether?

It is precisely this kind of cultural questioning that each of the chapter's selections invites us to conduct. Referencing a wide range of contemporary issues — from patriotism to consumerism, environmentalism to race — these readings show how com-

What is normal?

"That's something that this country stands for — freedom, liberty, and justice for all. And it's not happening for all right now."

NFL quarterback Colin Kaepernick in 2016 explaining his decision to kneel during the playing of the national anthem before football games.

Can social scripts be rewritten? What alternative to our culture's dominant patriotic norms does this quotation promote?

plex and overlapping the connection between personal beliefs and cultural norms can be. The first two essays take a closer look at the some of the beliefs underlying current economic orthodoxy. Michael Sandel starts us off by testing the limits of our faith in markets, drawing a distinction between the kinds of things money can and cannot buy. Andi Zeisler, on the other hand, traces the long history of efforts to use feminism to promote commercial products. The next two selections direct our attention to cultural beliefs around the issue of race. Michael Eric Dyson complicates our received ideas about patriotism, detailing how racial difference can shape the various ways "love-of-country" gets expressed. Debra Dickerson, meanwhile, shares her thoughts on what it means to be nonwhite, issuing a challenge to our historically rooted assumptions of what constitutes "race" altogether. The next pair of essays shifts our attention to the criminal justice system. Bryan Stevenson takes a closer look at the social and racial norms that teach us to view convicted criminals as the "other," while Amitava Kumar contemplates an alternative to the ways we typically punish criminals, making a powerful case for forgiveness through the concept of "restorative justice." Our final two selections engage beliefs around environmentalism. Naomi Klein turns a critical eye toward current debates over global warming, arguing for an environmental politics that seeks to change capitalism from the inside out. Tom Jacobs, by contrast, explores environmentalism through the lens of gender, using a focus on green politics to question cultural stereotypes of masculinity.

MICHAEL SANDEL
Markets and Morals

In a world marked by an ever-growing penchant for privatization, one in which services and opportunities formerly considered part of the public domain are increasingly auctioned for sale, it is now an open question whether there still exist things in our culture that cannot be bought and sold. Taking stock of this situation, noted philosopher Michael Sandel offers a few cautionary thoughts about embracing a belief in money as the sole arbiter of value. Michael Sandel is the Anne T. and Robert M. Bass Professor of Government at Harvard University. His books include *Liberalism and the Limits of Justice* (1982), *Democracy's Discontent* (1996), *Public Philosophy: Essays on Morality in Politics* (2005), and *The Case against Perfection: Ethics in the Age of Genetic Engineering* (2007). His most recent book is *What Money Can't Buy: The Moral Limits of Markets* (2012). The essay below is excerpted from the book's introduction.

Before You Read

How pervasive are "monetary values" in our culture? Do you think Americans are taught to measure the value of things in terms of their financial cost?

THERE ARE SOME THINGS MONEY CAN'T BUY, BUT THESE DAYS, NOT many. Today, almost everything is up for sale. Here are a few examples:

- *A prison cell upgrade: $82 per night.* In Santa Ana, California, and some other cities, nonviolent offenders can pay for better accommodations—a clean, quiet jail cell, away from the cells for nonpaying prisoners.
- *Access to the car pool lane while driving solo: $8 during rush hour.* Minneapolis and other cities are trying to ease traffic congestion by letting solo drivers pay to drive in car pool lanes, at rates that vary according to traffic.
- *The services of an Indian surrogate mother to carry a pregnancy: $6,250.* Western couples seeking surrogates increasingly outsource the job to India, where the practice is legal and the price is less than one-third the going rate in the United States.
- *The right to immigrate to the United States: $500,000.* Foreigners who invest $500,000 and create at least ten jobs in an area of high unemployment are eligible for a green card that entitles them to permanent residency.
- *The right to shoot an endangered black rhino: $150,000.* South Africa has begun letting ranchers sell hunters the right to kill a limited number

of rhinos, to give the ranchers an incentive to raise and protect the endangered species.

- *The cell phone number of your doctor: $1,500 and up per year.* A growing number of "concierge" doctors offer cell phone access and same-day appointments for patients willing to pay annual fees ranging from $1,500 to $25,000.
- *The right to emit a metric ton of carbon into the atmosphere: €13 (about $18).* The European Union runs a carbon emissions market that enables companies to buy and sell the right to pollute.
- *Admission of your child to a prestigious university:?* Although the price is not posted, officials from some top universities told *The Wall Street Journal* that they accept some less than stellar students whose parents are wealthy and likely to make substantial financial contributions.

Not everyone can afford to buy these things. But today there are lots of new ways to make money. If you need to earn some extra cash, here are some novel possibilities:

- *Rent out space on your forehead (or elsewhere on your body) to display commercial advertising: $777.* Air New Zealand hired thirty people to shave their heads and wear temporary tattoos with the slogan "Need a change? Head down to New Zealand."
- *Serve as a human guinea pig in a drug safety trial for a pharmaceutical company: $7,500.* The pay can be higher or lower, depending on the invasiveness of the procedure used to test the drug's effect, and the discomfort involved.
- *Fight in Somalia or Afghanistan for a private military company: $250 per month to $1,000 per day.* The pay varies according to qualifications, experience, and nationality.
- *Stand in line overnight on Capitol Hill to hold a place for a lobbyist who wants to attend a congressional hearing: $15–$20 per hour.* The lobbyists pay line-standing companies, who hire homeless people and others to queue up.
- *If you are a second grader in an underachieving Dallas school, read a book: $2.* To encourage reading, the schools pay kids for each book they read.
- *If you are obese, lose fourteen pounds in four months: $378.* Companies and health insurers offer financial incentives for weight loss and other kinds of healthy behavior.
- *Buy the life insurance policy of an ailing or elderly person, pay the annual premiums while the person is alive, and then collect the death benefit when he or she dies: potentially, millions (depending on the policy).* This form of

betting on the lives of strangers has become a $30 billion industry. The sooner the stranger dies, the more the investor makes.

We live at a time when almost everything can be bought and sold. Over the past three decades, markets—and market values—have come to govern our lives as never before. We did not arrive at this condition through any deliberate choice. It is almost as if it came upon us.

As the Cold War ended, markets and market thinking enjoyed unrivaled prestige, understandably so. No other mechanism for organizing the production and distribution of goods had proved as successful at generating affluence and prosperity. And yet, even as growing numbers of countries around the world embraced market mechanisms in the operation of their economies, something else was happening. Market values were coming to play a greater and greater role in social life. Economics was becoming an imperial domain. Today, the logic of buying and selling no longer applies to material goods alone but increasingly governs the whole of life. It is time to ask whether we want to live this way.

> **We live at a time when almost everything can be bought and sold.**

THE ERA OF MARKET TRIUMPHALISM

5 The years leading up to the financial crisis of 2008 were a heady time of market faith and deregulation—an era of market triumphalism. The era began in the early 1980s, when Ronald Reagan and Margaret Thatcher proclaimed their conviction that markets, not government, held the key to prosperity and freedom. And it continued in the 1990s, with the market-friendly liberalism of Bill Clinton and Tony Blair, who moderated but consolidated the faith that markets are the primary means for achieving the public good.

Today, that faith is in doubt. The era of market triumphalism has come to an end. The financial crisis did more than cast doubt on the ability of markets to allocate risk efficiently. It also prompted a widespread sense that markets have become detached from morals and that we need somehow to reconnect them. But it's not obvious what this would mean, or how we should go about it.

Some say the moral failing at the heart of market triumphalism was greed, which led to irresponsible risk taking. The solution, according to this view, is to rein in greed, insist on greater integrity and responsibility among bankers and Wall Street executives, and enact sensible regulations to prevent a similar crisis from happening again.

This is, at best, a partial diagnosis. While it is certainly true that greed played a role in the financial crisis, something bigger is at stake. The most fateful change that unfolded during the past three decades was not an increase in greed. It was the expansion of markets, and of market values, into spheres of life where they don't belong.

To contend with this condition, we need to do more than inveigh against greed; we need to rethink the role that markets should play in our society. We need a public debate about what it means to keep markets in their place. To have this debate, we need to think through the moral limits of markets. We need to ask whether there are some things money should not buy.

The reach of markets, and market-oriented thinking, into aspects of 10 life traditionally governed by nonmarket norms is one of the most significant developments of our time.

Consider the proliferation of for-profit schools, hospitals, and prisons, and the outsourcing of war to private military contractors. (In Iraq and Afghanistan, private contractors actually outnumbered U.S. military troops.)

Consider the eclipse of public police forces by private security firms — especially in the United States and Britain, where the number of private guards is more than twice the number of public police officers.

Or consider the pharmaceutical companies' aggressive marketing of prescription drugs to consumers in rich countries. (If you've ever seen the television commercials on the evening news in the United States, you could be forgiven for thinking that the greatest health crisis in the world is not malaria or river blindness or sleeping sickness, but a rampant epidemic of erectile dysfunction.)

> *Paying kids to read books might get them to read more, but also teach them to regard reading as a chore rather than a source of intrinsic satisfaction.*

Consider too the reach of commercial advertising into public schools; the sale of "naming rights" to parks and civic spaces; the marketing of "designer" eggs and sperm for assisted reproduction; the outsourcing of pregnancy to surrogate mothers in the developing world; the buying and selling, by companies and countries, of the right to pollute; a system of campaign finance that comes close to permitting the buying and selling of elections.

These uses of markets to allocate health, education, public safety, 15 national security, criminal justice, environmental protection, recreation, procreation, and other social goods were for the most part unheard of thirty years ago. Today, we take them largely for granted.

EVERYTHING FOR SALE

Why worry that we are moving toward a society in which everything is up for sale?

For two reasons: one is about inequality; the other is about corruption. Consider inequality. In a society where everything is for sale, life is harder for those of modest means. The more money can buy, the more affluence (or the lack of it) matters.

If the only advantage of affluence were the ability to buy yachts, sports cars, and fancy vacations, inequalities of income and wealth would not matter very much. But as money comes to buy more and more—political influence, good medical care, a home in a safe neighborhood rather than a crime-ridden one, access to elite schools rather than failing ones—the distribution of income and wealth looms larger and larger. Where all good things are bought and sold, having money makes all the difference in the world.

> *In a society where everything is for sale, life is harder for those of modest means.*

This explains why the last few decades have been especially hard on poor and middle-class families. Not only has the gap between rich and poor widened, the commodification of everything has sharpened the sting of inequality by making money matter more.

20   The second reason we should hesitate to put everything up for sale is more difficult to describe. It is not about inequality and fairness but about the corrosive tendency of markets. Putting a price on the good things in life can corrupt them. That's because markets don't only allocate goods; they also express and promote certain attitudes toward the goods being exchanged. Paying kids to read books might get them to read more, but also teach them to regard reading as a chore rather than a source of intrinsic satisfaction. Auctioning seats in the freshman class to the highest bidders might raise revenue but also erode the integrity of the college and the value of its diploma. Hiring foreign mercenaries to fight our wars might spare the lives of our citizens but corrupt the meaning of citizenship.

Economists often assume that markets are inert, that they do not affect the goods they exchange. But this is untrue. Markets leave their mark. Sometimes, market values crowd out nonmarket values worth caring about.

Of course, people disagree about what values are worth caring about, and why. So to decide what money should—and should not—be able to buy, we have to decide what values should govern the various domains of social and civic life. . . .

[W]hen we decide that certain goods may be bought and sold, we decide, at least implicitly, that it is appropriate to treat them as commodities, as instruments of profit and use. But not all goods are properly valued in this way. The most obvious example is human beings. Slavery was appalling because it treated human beings as commodities, to be bought and sold at auction. Such treatment fails to value human beings in the appropriate way — as persons worthy of dignity and respect, rather than as instruments of gain and objects of use.

Something similar can be said of other cherished goods and practices. We don't allow children to be bought and sold on the market. Even if buyers did not mistreat the children they purchased, a market in children would express and promote the wrong way of valuing them. Children are not properly regarded as consumer goods but as beings worthy of love and care. Or consider the rights and obligations of citizenship. If you are called to jury duty, you may not hire a substitute to take your place. Nor do we allow citizens to sell their votes, even though others might be eager to buy them. Why not? Because we believe that civic duties should not be regarded as private property but should be viewed instead as public responsibilities. To outsource them is to demean them, to value them in the wrong way.

These examples illustrate a broader point: some of the good things 25 in life are corrupted or degraded if turned into commodities. So to decide where the market belongs, and where it should be kept at a distance, we have to decide how to value the goods in question — health, education, family life, nature, art, civic duties, and so on. These are moral and political questions, not merely economic ones. To resolve them, we have to debate, case by case, the moral meaning of these goods and the proper way of valuing them.

This is a debate we didn't have during the era of market triumphalism. As a result, without quite realizing it, without ever deciding to do so, we drifted from *having* a market economy to *being* a market society.

The difference is this: A market economy is a tool — a valuable and effective tool — for organizing productive activity. A market society is a way of life in which market values seep into every aspect of human endeavor. It's a place where social relations are made over in the image of the market.

The great missing debate in contemporary politics is about the role and reach of markets. Do we want a market economy, or a market society? What role should markets play in public life and personal relations? How can we decide which goods should be bought and sold, and which should be governed by nonmarket values? Where should money's writ not run?...

RETHINKING THE ROLE OF MARKETS

Even if you agree that we need to grapple with big questions about the morality of markets, you might doubt that our public discourse is up to the task. It's a legitimate worry. Any attempt to rethink the role and reach of markets should begin by acknowledging two daunting obstacles.

30   One is the persisting power and prestige of market thinking, even in the aftermath of the worst market failure in eighty years. The other is the rancor and emptiness of our public discourse. These two conditions are not entirely unrelated.

The first obstacle is puzzling. At the time, the financial crisis of 2008 was widely seen as a moral verdict on the uncritical embrace of markets that had prevailed, across the political spectrum, for three decades. The near collapse of once-mighty Wall Street financial firms, and the need for a massive bailout at taxpayers' expense, seemed sure to prompt a reconsideration of markets. Even Alan Greenspan, who as chairman of the U.S. Federal Reserve had served as high priest of the market triumphalist faith, admitted to "a state of shocked disbelief" that his confidence in the self-correcting power of free markets turned out to be mistaken. The cover of *The Economist*, the buoyantly pro-market British magazine, showed an economics textbook melting into a puddle, under the headline WHAT WENT WRONG WITH ECONOMICS.

The era of market triumphalism had come to a devastating end. Now, surely, would be a time of moral reckoning, a season of sober second thoughts about the market faith. But things haven't turned out that way.

The spectacular failure of financial markets did little to dampen the faith in markets generally. In fact, the financial crisis discredited government more than the banks. In 2011, surveys found that the American public blamed the federal government more than Wall Street financial institutions for the economic problems facing the country—by a margin of more than two to one.

The financial crisis had pitched the United States and much of the global economy into the worst economic downturn since the Great Depression and left millions of people out of work. Yet it did not prompt a fundamental rethinking of markets. Instead, its most notable political consequence in the United States was the rise of the Tea Party movement, whose hostility to government and embrace of free markets would have made Ronald Reagan blush. In the fall of 2011, the Occupy Wall Street movement brought protests to cities throughout the United States and around the world. These protests targeted big banks and corporate power, and the rising inequality of income and wealth. Despite their different ideological orientations, both the Tea Party and Occupy Wall Street activists gave voice to populist outrage against the bailout.

35   Notwithstanding these voices of protest, serious debate about the role and reach of markets remains largely absent from our political life. Democrats and Republicans argue, as they long have done, about taxes, spending, and budget deficits, only now with greater partisanship and little ability to inspire or persuade. Disillusion with politics has deepened as citizens grow frustrated with a political system unable to act for the public good, or to address the questions that matter most.

This parlous state of public discourse is the second obstacle to a debate about the moral limits of markets. At a time when political argument consists mainly of shouting matches on cable television, partisan vitriol on talk radio, and ideological food fights on the floor of Congress, it's hard to imagine a reasoned public debate about such controversial moral questions as the right way to value procreation, children, education, health, the environment, citizenship, and other goods. But I believe such a debate is possible, and that it would invigorate our public life.

Some see in our rancorous politics a surfeit of moral conviction: too many people believe too deeply, too stridently, in their own convictions and want to impose them on everyone else. I think this misreads our predicament. The problem with our politics is not too much moral argument but too little. Our politics is overheated because it is mostly vacant, empty of moral and spiritual content. It fails to engage with big questions that people care about.

The moral vacancy of contemporary politics has a number of sources. One is the attempt to banish notions of the good life from public discourse. In hopes of avoiding sectarian strife, we often insist that citizens leave their moral and spiritual convictions behind when they enter the public square. But despite its good intention, the reluctance to admit arguments about the good life into politics prepared the way for market triumphalism and for the continuing hold of market reasoning.

In its own way, market reasoning also empties public life of moral argument. Part of the appeal of markets is that they don't pass judgment on the preferences they satisfy. They don't ask whether some ways of valuing goods are higher, or worthier, than others. If someone is willing to pay for sex or a kidney, and a consenting adult is willing to sell, the only question the economist asks is, "How much?" Markets don't wag fingers. They don't discriminate between admirable preferences and base ones. Each party to a deal decides for himself or herself what value to place on the things being exchanged.

This nonjudgmental stance toward values lies at the heart of market 40 reasoning and explains much of its appeal. But our reluctance to engage in moral and spiritual argument, together with our embrace of markets, has exacted a heavy price: it has drained public discourse of moral and civic energy, and contributed to the technocratic, managerial politics that afflicts many societies today.

A debate about the moral limits of markets would enable us to decide, as a society, where markets serve the public good and where they don't belong. It would also invigorate our politics, by welcoming competing notions of the good life into the public square. For how else could such arguments proceed? If you agree that buying and selling certain goods corrupts or degrades them, then you must believe that some ways of valuing these goods are more appropriate than others. It hardly makes sense to speak of corrupting an activity—parenthood, say, or citizenship—unless you think that some ways of being a parent, or a citizen, are better than others.

Moral judgments such as these lie behind the few limitations on markets we still observe. We don't allow parents to sell their children or citizens to sell their votes. And one of the reasons we don't is, frankly, judgmental: we believe that selling these things values them in the wrong way and cultivates bad attitudes.

Thinking through the moral limits of markets makes these questions unavoidable. It requires that we reason together, in public, about how to value the social goods we prize. It would be folly to expect that a morally more robust public discourse, even at its best, would lead to agreement on every contested question. But it would make for a healthier public life. And it would make us more aware of the price we pay for living in a society where everything is up for sale.

When we think of the morality of markets, we think first of Wall Street banks and their reckless misdeeds, of hedge funds and bailouts and regulatory reform. But the moral and political challenge we face today is more pervasive and more mundane—to rethink the role and reach of markets in our social practices, human relationships, and everyday lives.

FOR A SECOND READING

1. Why do you think Sandel chooses this title ("Markets and Morals") for his essay? How does it summarize or preview the argument his essay makes about the role ethics should play in assessing and/or regulating the commercial marketplace? Do you agree with this argument? In your view, is the marketplace in need of greater moral oversight? If so, what kind?

2. According to Sandel, we live at a cultural moment where commercial values are increasingly coming to "crowd out nonmarket values" (p. 30). What are the "nonmarket values" Sandel seems to have in mind? How does his definition of this term compare to your own?

3. "Markets," Sandel tells us, "don't wag fingers. They don't discriminate between admirable preferences and base ones" (p. 33). Do you agree with this assessment? Do you think markets should "wag fingers"? If so, what kinds of actions or attitudes should be discouraged? Why?

PUTTING IT INTO WRITING

4. Sandel opens this essay by listing some of the services that are now for sale on the open market. Choose one. Then write a short essay

in which you argue either for or against the merits of treating this service as a purchasable commodity. In your view, what is or is not valid about putting this service up for sale? What rules would you establish for how this transaction should unfold?

5. According to Sandel, there are two reasons why we should worry about the societal trend toward treating everything as if it were up for sale: "inequality" and "corruption." Choose an example of a good or service that is possible to buy or sell on the open market. In an essay, analyze the particular ways this product raises questions or risks having to do with "inequality" or "corruption." In order to conduct this analysis, you need to make sure you are clear about what each of these terms means, and how each applies to the example you choose.

COMPARING ARGUMENTS

6. How does Sandel's discussion here compare to the argument about feminism and commercial culture advanced by Andi Zeisler (p. 36)? In your view, does Zeisler's historical account of efforts to use this political movement to market commercial products offer convincing evidence to support Sandel's argument about the encroachment of "nonmarket values" into arenas of public life where they don't belong? Do you think her account confirms or challenges Sandel's thesis?

ANDI ZEISLER
The Corridors of Empower

There is a long tradition in American consumer culture of using ads to promote broader social messages. But what happens to these messages when they are subordinated to the goal of selling commercial products? Taking up these questions, Andi Zeisler recounts the long, complicated history of efforts by advertisers to use the idea of "female empowerment" to market products. In doing so, she offers a bracing reminder about the limits of using things like cigarettes, credit cards, and deodorant as vehicles for promoting "symbolic liberation." Andi Zeisler is a cofounder and creative/editorial director of Bitch Media, a nonprofit feminist media organization based in Portland, Oregon. She is also the author of the book *We Were Feminists Once: From Riot Girrl to CoverGirl®, the Buying and Selling of a Political Movement* (2016), from which this selection is excerpted.

Before You Read

Do you think there is a fundamental difference between promoting a political viewpoint and marketing a commercial product? How or how not?

> "In a village chapel in upstate new york, 150 years ago, the initial bold steps in a revolution that would ensure women the right to vote were taken at the first women's rights celebration at Seneca Falls. And now you can celebrate the anniversary of this milestone in women's rights, and the strength and conviction of the courageous suffragettes involved whenever you use your First USA Anniversary Series Platinum Mastercard®. Celebrate women's rights. Apply today."

IT WASN'T THE FIRST TIME THAT WOMEN'S LIBERATION HAD BEEN connected to our power to spend money we didn't have, and it wouldn't be the last. But First USA's linking of women's enfranchisement and their freedom to go into debt, in the form of a 1998 credit card come-on, was an almost admirably shameless co-option of the language of feminism in the service of capitalism. (The bank even promised to send a free "women's almanac" to cardholders after their first purchase.)

One of the many preliberation factoids that regularly makes the rounds to illustrate just how far women have come is that, up until the mid-1970s, women were unable to get credit cards in their own names. Married women needed a male cosigner—a husband or father—in order to use a card that was then issued in his name; single, divorced, and even widowed women were denied altogether. (Very often both of these standards applied to library cards as well.) So when 1974's Equal Credit Opportunity Act was passed, it was a marker of liberation realized: marital status was no longer a bank's business where credit was concerned, and women were granted the right to buy whatever, whenever, with money that was theirs, and to go into debt right alongside men.[1] But the idea that purchasing itself was a feminist act became a key tenet of emerging marketplace feminism. . . .

It wasn't the first time that women's liberation had been connected to our power to spend money we didn't have, and it wouldn't be the last.

SUBTEXT AND THE SINGLE GIRL

For decades, advertisers had spoken to women chiefly by emphasizing their roles in relation to others. Early ads for Listerine warned women that their "poor hygiene"—malodorous breath or, worse, genitals—would cost them their marriages, and tartly reprimanded mothers for not treating their baby's butts with only the best diaper creams and disposable nappies. The 1990s brought ads that served as a departure, explicitly acknowledging not only that women can be happily single, but that many women, in fact, choose that status, and, as consumers, revel in it. In a 1999 *Village Voice* article titled "Women Are Easy: Why TV Ad Agencies Take Female Viewers for Granted," journalist Mark Boal mused, "Today's marketer or media buyer may well be a woman in Prada, reflecting the profound shift in gender roles that is also being acted out on the tube. The stay-at-home wife in *Bewitched* has been replaced by Buffy the weapon-wielding go-getter." Yet his piece went on to surmise that even this brave new adscape was pulling from an outdated playbook in targeting women, one in which their identities are still built around love and romance.

To anyone with a pop culture habit, this wasn't exactly news. Even flat- 5 tering consumer appeals to single women served to underscore their status as outliers. One 1999 ad for Diet Coke featured a woman filling out a video-dating profile, telling the matchmaker that she has "great friends" and a "great job." "Sounds like you have a pretty good life," responds the matchmaker. The would-be bachelorette takes a swig of her low-cal beverage as those words sink in, and then zips out of the joint before wasting any more of her abundant singleton time. Who needs a man when you've got this artificially sweetened and caffeinated soda in your life? The ad was part of a series that emphasized "empowerment," with a tagline ("Live Your Life") conceived as a 180-degree turn from Diet Coke's previous appeal, whose smirky tagline ("You are what you drink") prioritized physical appearance.

A 2000 ad for De Beers' diamond solitaire necklace, meanwhile, cast the single woman as looking for Mr. Goodbar in a sparkler form. The ad copy invoked the language of a bar pickup, reading, "It beckons me as

I pass the store window. . . . We look at each other. And though I'm not usually that kind of girl, I take it home." Neither the Diet Coke nor the De Beers ad seemed entirely comfortable representing a single women; it seemed as though their makers were so hamstrung by not being able to depend on the old wife-and-mom prompts that they had to hammer home exactly what these women weren't to define what they were. But as more brands began marketing to single women, they realized that the language of liberation from just those old ideals was the right pitch.

"Your left hand says 'we.' Your right hand says 'me.' Your left hand loves candlelight. Your right hand loves the spotlight. Your left hand rocks the cradle. Your right hand rules the world. Women of the world, raise your right hand."

With its 1947 "A Diamond Is Forever" ad, De Beers had single-handedly created the market for engagement rings, turning diamonds into as crucial a symbol of wedded bliss as the white dress or floral bouquet. But by the early 2000s, the company was looking to expand its market, and the proliferation of unmarried female consumers aged thirty to fifty was its target. The right-hand ring was born: a line of fanciful designs meant for that formerly lesser ring finger, and an ad campaign that set out to flatter their would-be wearers. In the language of the right-hand ring's sales pitch, marriage was for unimaginative yes-women who were sweet, traditional, and, let's face it, pretty boring. Why would you want to wear a plain old diamond solitaire given to you by some chump when you could pick out your own, even fancier model?

For a time, the campaign was a smash: "Nonbridal" ring sales increased 15 percent in 2004, and in 2005 the campaign won the Gold EFFIE award from the New York American Marketing Association for "exceeding its objectives of bringing ring growth into line with total diamond jewelry growth."[2] The founder of consumer behavior–tracking organization America's Research Group told NBC News in January 2004 that the key to the rings' success was the sense of empowered entitlement among female consumers. "The days of getting permission are really over, and that's what's really expanded the buying power of women over the last 10 years."[3]

10   It turned out to be a short run. The brisk trade in right-hand rings was slowed down in part by the rising awareness of the blood-diamond scourge in Angola, Sierra Leone, Zimbabwe, and the Democratic Republic of Congo, where children as young as five were forced into mining labor in order to fund civil wars in those countries. But stateside, things had changed as well: in the years after 9/11, there was a new emphasis on stability and domesticity, much of which envisioned a re-centering of traditional gender roles. Magazines theorized that the terrorist attacks had been a wake-up call for men emasculated by American culture, and

declared the return of the cowboy as heartthrob; George W. Bush played at comic-book fortitude with his florid references to "evildoers" and chest-pounding entreaties to "Bring 'em on!" Publishing houses and women's magazines were suddenly all about the "art of domesticity"; sleek scouring tools and aromatic floor cleaners became stars of a new prestige-housekeeping category of consumer goods. Marriage was on the country's mind: the Bush administration, egged on by conservative-Christian advocacy groups, dedicated $1.5 million toward encouraging low-income couples to marry, but was quick to note that the push was for straight couples only. At the other end of the spectrum, splashy celebrity nuptials like those of Jennifer Lopez and Marc Anthony, David and Victoria Beckham, and Ben Affleck and Jennifer Garner were obsessively chronicled in a glut of new wedding-industry media, and even credited for bumping up the overall marriage rate. And despite Bush's fierce "protection" of heterosexual marriage, the wedding-industrial complex welcomed gay marriage with open arms and a slew of rainbow-themed product. By 2014, the new trend in "nonmarital" rings, according to Vogue, was single women wearing wedding band–esque baubles on their left-hand ring finger for a psychological sense of belonging. So much for upending tradition.

· · ·

SELL IT, BUT DON'T YELL IT

Advertising's pitch to feminists has changed over time, from "liberated" versions of feminine standbys (the personal douche, the pushup bra, the low-cal frozen food) to the liberation inherent in consumer choice itself. But recently, the pitch has become a bit more nebulous. Two thousand fourteen introduced a new breed of empowertising with an ad for Verizon called "Inspire Her Mind." In it, a girl in various stages of child- and teenhood is discouraged at every juncture by an offscreen voice—when she's stomping through a creek ("Don't get your dress dirty!"), when she's examining marine life in tidepools ("You don't want to mess with that"), when she's building a rocket in the garage ("Why don't you hand that [drill] to your brother?"). The final scene finds the girl stopping in front of a science-fair poster in a school hall-way, pausing, and then dejectedly using the window's reflection for that most stereotypically girly act: applying lip gloss. The voice-over: "Our words can have a big impact. Isn't it time we told her she's pretty brilliant, too?" appeared as statistics on how girls are often steered away from STEM (science, technology, engineering, and math) fields bloomed on the screen.

Another ad, for Always menstrual products, involved filmmaker and longtime girl-culture chronicler Lauren Greenfield asking adults to pan-tomime running, fighting, and throwing "like a girl." They did so with exaggerated, simpering steps and rubber-wristed movements. Greenfield then asked actual girls to do the same activities, and they followed directions with a fierceness untainted by stereotype—throwing, running, and fighting with their entire bodies engaged and their faces full of intent. Afterward, Greenfield followed up with both the kids, who were genuinely confused by the idea that doing things "like a girl" was meant to be an insult, and the adults, who were well aware. The text in the ad then noted that girls' self-confidence drops dramatically at puberty, and urged viewers to redefine what "like a girl" means.

The "Inspire Her Mind" ad centered on drawing more girls to STEM fields, an issue that's gained a lot of cultural traction, outreach, and funding in the past decade. For the campaign, Verizon partnered with MAKERS, the digital initiative aimed at showcasing the stories of women globally; its voice-over was done by Reshma Saujani, founder of the organization Girls Who Code. A section of Verizon's Web site called "Responsibility" elaborates on the company's efforts to raise awareness about girls' STEM education and showcases its partnerships with women's-and-girls' advocacy organizations. It's hard not to be moved by the evocative photos and videos of young, multicultural GWC graduates on the Web site—one holds a hand-lettered sign that reads "Great ideas STEM from diversity"—and it helps that nothing in either the Web site or the ad itself is explicitly selling a product to its audience. The unspoken message is, "Hey, we're the carrier who cares about your (or your daughter's) potential, so choose us."

> *[T]here's a vast difference between using the language of empowerment to suggest that being able to choose between three different kinds of diet frozen pizza is a radical accomplishment and helping to create a world where diet frozen pizza isn't something that needs to exist in the first place.*

Likewise, Always's "Like a Girl" spot wasn't pegged to any new product in the brand's line, but seemed simply to have been created to position the brand itself as one that's conscious of how stereotypes and beliefs about girls and women affect their lives. A section of the Always Web site titled "Fighting to empower girls everywhere" focuses on the brand's partnership with organizations like the Girl Scouts of America (for its #BanBossy campaign, a partnership with the Lean In Foundation launched in 2014) and UNESCO, with which

Always works to deliver products to rural areas in Nigeria and Senegal where lack of access to pads equates to missed school days and decreased opportunities for girls.

Here's the thing we all know about advertising to women: the products aimed their way, from household cleaners to cosmetics to personal-care products, are pitched to solve a problem that in many cases the consumer might not ever know she had until she was alerted to and/or shamed for it. (Wait, I didn't *know* my armpits were supposed to be sexier!) What this new slate of commercials announced was that, finally, it seemed possible for the ad industry to reach women without making them feel totally awful about themselves. In 2014, after decades of women's movements, that was advertising's big breakthrough: don't make women feel like shit and they're more likely to buy your product. An incredibly low bar had been cleared, and everyone rushed to pat themselves on the back for it. Suddenly, there was a name for the phenomenon: "femvertising"—or, excuse me, #Femvertising. It was a hot topic on ad-industry trade sites, and panels on how to do this astonishing new thing of not insulting women became a draw for conference slates and seminars. A 2015 *AdWeek* roundup was titled "These Empowering Ads Were Named the Best of #Femvertising"; and that year's BlogHer—a yearly convening of lifestyle and brand-friendly women's media—featured a #Femvertising awards ceremony.

It is worth wondering what made the likes of Verizon and Always suddenly turn to the empowerment and well-being of women and girls as a strategy. After all, Always had been content to coast on its products' wings for years, with such bland, cheery taglines as "Have a happy period. Always!" and copy that focused on Dri-weave technology and "quick-wrap" packaging. Previous to 2014, Verizon's claim to fame was the cute, bespectacled "Can you hear me now?" guy. It probably sounds overly cynical to question the motives of a brand when their end result seems as genuine as the "Inspire Her Mind" and "Like a Girl" campaigns. But given the emphasis on the brands themselves and not the products, it's tempting to think that their pitches were, in a way, for feminism itself.

For a second, anyway. Empowertising can suck you in that way, and because there are so few commercials that celebrate, say, the athletic skill of preteen girls, of course they're going to stand out. But looking closer, it's the same old pitch—in Always's case, one that does everything it can to decouple girls' lack of confidence from the shame they're still taught to feel about their menstruating and developing bodies. ("Have a happy period, Always!" at least *mentioned* the word "period.") The ad seemed especially reticent in the context of a feminine-products market that has in recent years successfully

15

harnessed humor and absurdism to send up the earnestness of the period-marketing past: Kotex, for example, marketed its U by Kotex line with commercials in which women mused, "When I have my period . . . I want to hold really soft things, like my cat . . . sometimes I like to run on the beach . . . I like to twirl . . . in slow motion." By the end, the spot just comes right out with it: "Why are tampon ads so ridiculous?" The upstart menstrual-product subscription service HelloFlo, meanwhile, has managed to make menstrual products downright delightful: their long-form ads incorporate nods to how young girls actually *feel* about their periods—excitement, fear, embarrassment, pride—and, as a bonus, dare to use the word "vagina" in pitching their service.

The Internet, social media, and the rise of rapid-response media criticism have undoubtedly played a substantial role in getting corporations to understand that even if a brand's bottom line is solid, it has to at least appear to care what its customers think. It used to be that a print ad or commercial that insulted women—think of those that wound up in *Ms.* magazine's "No Comment" section—might garner a stack of strongly-worded letters to a brand's corporate HQ, but there was little to keep the ad from continuing to run. More recently, it's a wildly different story: the same ad would very likely be the basis for well-placed blog posts at Forbes, the *Wall Street Journal*, and Copyranter, callouts on Feministing and Clutch and Autostraddle and Bitch, an untold number of pointed tweets, and very possibly an online petition at Ultra Violet or Change.org. It's depressing that responses like this are consistently necessary, but public shaming has turned out to be an incredibly effective way—and, in the case of ads offensive to women, perhaps the only way—to get brands thinking about the impact of their messages and imagery.

And at a time when audiences are choking on consumer choice, marketing with a purpose is no longer just a value-add for companies, but a crucial part of brand identity. In September 2014, a few months after both the Always "Like a Girl" and the Verizon "Inspire Her Mind" ads premiered, *Ad Age* reported on their effects as measured by the Advertising Benchmark Index. It found "that not only do a majority of consumers feel the ads promote a positive message for women, [but] they have a strong, positive impact on the brands' reputation. 'Given the subject matter, the call-to-action scores were higher than might be expected,' said ABX president Gary Getto."[4]

20   Advertising has one job to do, and it's not to reflect the nuances of social movements. But the staggering growth and spread of the medium in just the past two decades—from its slow creep into new physical spaces (shopping-cart handles, sports leaderboards, public-transit

tickets) to its primacy in the digital realm (sponsored Tweets and Instagram posts, responsive Facebook ads) to its sneaky guerrilla and viral manifestations—has meant an attendant growth in power. If, as media scholars like Jean Kilbourne and Sut Jhally have spent decades arguing, advertising's power is both cumulative and unconscious, it will absolutely continue to play a crucial role in the ongoing project of gender equality.

Still, there's a vast difference between using the language of empowerment to suggest that being able to choose between three different kinds of diet frozen pizza is a radical accomplishment and helping to create a world where diet frozen pizza isn't something that needs to exist in the first place. (Or, at least, isn't something marketed solely to women.) And the difference between feminism and marketplace feminism is just as vast, which is why the designation of femvertising is useful, if not necessarily in the way it was supposed to be. Empowering and femvertising are both ways to talk about the business of selling to women without conflating examples of that business with actual feminism. They're a gateway toward learning more about specific issues that impact women and girls; maybe they're a way to discover alternatives to mainstream products. But celebrating the ads themselves simply celebrates advertisers' skill at co-opting women's movements and selling them back us—and then rewards us for buying in.

NOTES

[1]In theory, at least. Since then, there's plenty of evidence that banks continue to discriminate on the basis of race.

[2]http://marketing-case-studies.blogspot.com/2008/07/raise-your-right-hand-campaign.html

[3]"The Alluring Right-Hand Diamond Ring," NBCnews.com, January 20, 2004.

[4]http://adage.com/article/cmo-strategy/marketers-soft-feminism/294740/

FOR A SECOND READING

1. Zeisler suggests that feminist marketing strategies play as much on notions of female insecurity as the idea of female empowerment. Choose one of the ad campaigns profiled in this essay, and discuss how it either confirms or challenges this view. What product does this campaign market? What messages about empowerment does it attempt to promote? To what extent do these messages foster insecurity?

2. Zeisler situates her argument within a broader historical account of the advertising industry. How effective do you find this

strategy to be? What does this history teach us about the relationship between feminism and consumerism we might not otherwise see?

3. "For decades," writes Zeisler, "advertisers had spoken to women chiefly by emphasizing their roles in relation to others." To what extent, in your view, has this strategy changed? Do advertisers nowadays depict independent roles for women? Do you find these roles to be empowering? Why or why not?

PUTTING IT INTO WRITING

4. As Zeisler notes, a central tenet behind current efforts to use feminist ideas to market commercial products is that consumer choice is power. Do you agree with the proposition that consumer choice—the prerogative to choose one product over another—is genuinely empowering? If so, what kind of power does this choice represent for women in particular? Do you think it is valid to term this type of power "feminist"? Why or why not?

5. At the conclusion of this piece, Zeisler expresses the hope that the next generation of ads might help viewers "learn more about specific issues that impact women and girls . . . [even] to discover alternatives" (p. 43). Create your own example of what this type of ad might look like. What "product" would it showcase? What message(s) would it promote? And what strategies would you use to get these messages across?

COMPARING ARGUMENTS

6. In his essay, "Markets and Morals" (p. 26), Michael Sandel argues that market values have the potential to "corrupt" civic values. In your view, does the history Zeisler recounts here offer support for his thesis? What types of "corruption" is her essay drawing our attention to? Do you agree with Sandel that such corruption poses a threat to the "public good"?

Rewriting the Script: **Buy Nothing Christmas**

❝ *As the year-end approaches keep in mind that an object will never make you happy. It might for a few minutes, maybe even days, but in the end your experiences are all you've got. So this year why not get your family together and do something wildly different. Ignore Black Friday. Try buying almost nothing for Christmas and you might experience the most joyous holiday season you've ever had. Buy nothing and experience everything.*

Since the early 1990s, Buy Nothing Day has inspired worldwide personal and collective action against consumerism. Buy Nothing Day isn't just about changing your habits for one day it is about rediscovering what it means to live freely.

Join millions of us in over 60 countries on November 27/28 for Buy Nothing Day and see what it feels like to take a stand against corporate domination. Then, as we enter the holiday season, consider what it might mean to celebrate a holiday that isn't driven by commercial forces. If you are going to buy, make a choice and go local, independent, or make something. Let's take back our lives and stop buying into the consumerist machine.

And why not get playful while you're at it!? . . . Put up posters, organize a credit card cut up, pull off a Whirl–mart, or a Christmas Zombie walk through your local mall."

— BUY NOTHING CHRISTMAS
HOMEPAGE,
ADBUSTERS.ORG, 2015

Buy Nothing Christmas

Every year, it seems, brings with it an even earlier start to the traditional holiday shopping season. Long before the last leaves have fallen or the Thanksgiving turkey has been carved, Americans find themselves inundated with countless commercial messages urging them to "get a jump" on the holidays by purchasing this year's must-have gifts. The visual above, excerpted from the Adbusters' "Buy Nothing Day Initiative," offers an example of how this seemingly inevitable consumer trend can be challenged and rethought. On the next page the image of a meditating Santa Claus hovers above the picture of a typical shopping mall, as the accompanying quote invites viewers to "rise above it." What does this example tell you about the ways our culture's consumerist scripts can be rewritten? What specific beliefs are being called into question here?

IDENTIFY THE SCRIPT: Make a list of the holiday shopping habits this example seems to be challenging. Then write a paragraph in which you identify and discuss the cultural norms that underlie these scripts. What attitude toward consumerism do these habits serve to reinforce?

CHALLENGE THE SCRIPT: Write a brief essay in which you assess the merits and shortcomings of this attempt to challenge this script. What aspect of this script does this example critique most effectively? Least effectively? How convinced are you to share its viewpoint? Why?

WRITE YOUR OWN SCRIPT: Write a 500- to 750-word essay in which you make the case for what our attitude toward holiday shopping ought to be. How would you characterize the "proper" attitude we should have toward holiday shopping? What makes your view of this issue compelling? What reasons, factors, or evidence can you cite as support? How do your views compare to those expressed in the image and quote? To what extent can the points raised be used to support the thesis you are advancing here?

This year, rise above it.

MICHAEL ERIC DYSON
Understanding Black Patriotism

What are the acceptable forms for expressing one's love of country? And do these boundaries establish different standards for the way people of different races are allowed to voice these views? Taking up this provocative question, noted public intellectual Michael Eric Dyson maps the contours of what he calls "black patriotism." Given the history that defines the African American experience, he argues, we shouldn't be surprised to discover that nationalistic feelings skew along racial lines. Nor, he adds, should we shrink from confronting what these differences tell us about what it means to accept conventional patriotic ideals as a universal norm. Dyson is the University Professor of Sociology at Georgetown University. He is the author of numerous books, among them: *I May Not Get There with You: The True Martin Luther King, Jr.* (2000), *The Black Presidency?* (2016), and *Holler If You Hear Me: Searching for Tupac Shakur* (2006). The essay below was published by *Time* in 2008.

Before You Read

Can dissent be patriotic? Should "love of country" preclude any effort to critique American society?

TIME
From the Pages of TIME

MAINSTREAM AMERICA HAS SHOWN LITTLE UNDERSTANDING lately of the patriotism that a lot of black people practice. Black love of country is often far more robust and complicated than the lapel-pin nationalism some citizens swear by. Barack Obama hinted at this when he declared in Montana a few weeks ago, "I love this country not because it's perfect but because we've always been able to move it closer to perfection. Because through revolution and slavery . . . generations of Americans have shown their love of country by struggling and sacrificing and risking their lives to bring us that much closer to our founding promise."

> **Mainstream America has shown little understanding lately of the patriotism that a lot of black people practice.**

That's a far cry from the "My country, right or wrong" credo, which confuses blind boosterism with a more authentic, if sometimes questioning, loyalty. At their best, black folk offer critical patriotism, an exacting devotion that carries on a lover's quarrel with America while they shed blood in its defense.

It is easy to see why the words of black critics and leaders, taken out of context, can be read as cynical renunciations of country. Abolitionist and runaway slave Frederick Douglass gave a famous oration on the meaning of Independence Day, asking "What, to the American slave, is your Fourth of July? I answer, a day that reveals to him, more than all other days in the year, the gross injustice and cruelty to which he is the constant victim." But instead of joining the chorus of black voices swelling with nostalgia to return to their African roots, Douglass stayed put. Poet Langston Hughes grieved in verse that "(America never was America to me) . . . (There's never been equality for me, / Nor freedom in this 'homeland of the free')." But his lament is couched in a poem whose title, like its author, yearns for acceptance: Let America Be America Again.

Even Martin Luther King Jr. was branded a traitor to his country because he opposed the war in Vietnam. When King announced his opposition in 1967, journalist Kenneth Crawford attacked him for his "demagoguery," while black writer Carl Rowan bitterly concluded that King's speech had created "the impression that the Negro is disloyal." Black dissent over war has historically brought charges of disloyalty despite the eagerness among blacks to defend on foreign soil a democracy they couldn't enjoy back home. Since the time of slavery, blacks have actively defended the U.S. in every war it has waged, from the Civil War down to the war on terrorism, a loyalty to the Federal Government conceived by black leaders as a critical force in gaining freedom. W. E. B. Du Bois argued in World War I that blacks should "forget our special grievances and close our ranks . . . with our white fellow citizens." Some 380,000 soldiers answered the call even as they failed to reap the benefits of their sacrifice when they came home.

5   Even the angry comments of Jeremiah Wright have to be read as the bitter complaint of a spurned lover. Like millions of other blacks, Wright was willing to serve the country while suffering rejection. He surrendered his student deferment in 1961, voluntarily joined the Marines and, after a two-year stint, volunteered to become a Navy corpsman. He excelled and became valedictorian, later a cardiopulmonary technician, and eventually a member of the President's medical team. Wright cared for Lyndon B. Johnson after his 1966 surgery, earning three White House letters of commendation.

> **Since the time of slavery, blacks have actively defended the U.S. in every war it has waged, from the Civil War down to the war on terrorism.**

Dick Cheney, born in the same year as Wright, received five deferments—four while an undergraduate or graduate student and one as a prospective father. Both Bill Clinton and George W. Bush used their student deferments to remain in college until 1968. Clinton did not serve, and Bush was on active duty in the National Guard for two years. If time in uniform is any measure, Wright, much more than Cheney, Clinton, or Bush, embodies Obama's ideal of "Americans [who] have shown their love of country by struggling and sacrificing and risking their lives to bring us that much closer to our founding promise."

Wright's critics have confused nationalism with patriotism. Nationalism is the uncritical support of one's country regardless of its moral or political bearing. Patriotism is the affirmation of one's country in light of its best values, including the attempt to correct it when it's in error. Wright's words are the tough love of a war-tested patriot speaking his mind—one of the great virtues of our democracy. The most patriotic thing his nation can do now is extend to him the same right for which he was willing to die.

FOR A SECOND READING

1. "At their best," writes Dyson, "black folk offer critical patriotism, an exacting devotion that carries on a lover's quarrel with America while they shed blood in its defense" (p. 47). Evaluate the language Dyson chooses here. Why do you think he describes the patriotic feelings of African Americans as a "lover's quarrel with America"? How does this definition of a "critical patriotism" challenge or rewrite the social scripts through which love of country typically gets expressed? In your view, are these changes for the better? Why or why not?

2. Dyson describes conventional forms of patriotism as "lapel-pin nationalism." What does he mean by this phrase? What definition of patriotism does it suggest to you? Do you think it accurately captures the form patriotic feeling conventionally takes in our culture?

3. To support his argument, Dyson cites numerous examples of prominent African Americans (e.g., W. E. B. Du Bois, Martin Luther King, Jeremiah Wright) whose patriotic declarations have included expressions of dissent or criticism. How effective do you find this strategy to be? In your view, does it help support Dyson's larger argument? Can you think of an example of dissent that served simultaneously as an expression of patriotism?

PUTTING IT INTO WRITING

4. Those who have criticized black patriots for voicing dissent, Dyson contends, "have confused nationalism with patriotism. Nationalism is the uncritical support of one's country regardless of its moral or political bearing. Patriotism is the affirmation of one's country

in light of its best values, including the attempt to correct it when it's in error" (p. 49). First, describe in your own words the distinction Dyson is drawing here. What, according to Dyson, are the key differences between "nationalism" and "patriotism"? Then choose a recent debate that you think illustrates this distinction: Who is part of this debate? What issue or controversy does it concern? And which view do you find most compelling or persuasive?

5. Quoting a speech by then–presidential candidate Barack Obama, Dyson draws a distinction between stereotypical expressions of patriotism and those that, in his view, capture the kind of nationalism often expressed by African Americans: "'I love this country not because it's perfect but because we've always been able to move it closer to perfection. Because through revolution and slavery . . . generations of Americans have shown their love of country by struggling and sacrificing and risking their lives to bring us that much closer to our founding promise.' That's a far cry from the 'My country, right or wrong' credo, which confuses blind boosterism with a more authentic, if sometimes questioning, loyalty" (p. 47). In a three- to five-page essay, describe, analyze, and assess the distinction Dyson is drawing here. What are the basic differences—in attitude, assumption, and viewpoint—between these contrasting expressions of patriotism? What factors, in Dyson's estimation, account for these differences? Do you agree with Dyson's characterization of each? How or how not?

COMPARING ARGUMENTS

6. How does Dyson's explication of a "critical" black patriotism compare with the argument about "whiteness" presented by Debra Dickerson (p. 51)? Based on his argument here, how do you think Dyson would respond to Dickerson's analysis of race as a system for establishing "hierarchy and privilege"? And what are your own views on this question? What does Dyson's emphasis on African American "dissent" and "critique" suggest to you about the state of race relations in America?

DEBRA J. DICKERSON
The Great White Way

In this book review, Debra Dickerson questions the status of "whiteness" as our culture's preeminent racial and social norm, the standard against which all other racial and ethnic identity is defined as "different." Challenging the hegemony this term has long exerted over American thought, she offers a succinct historical overview of the ways the boundaries dividing white from nonwhite have shifted in America. Dickerson's work has appeared in many publications, including the *New Republic*, *Slate*, and *Vibe*. Her memoir, *An American Story* (2001), describes her move from the rough St. Louis neighborhood where she grew up to her success as a Harvard Law School–trained, award-winning journalist. Her most recent book is *The End of Blackness: Returning the Souls of Black Folk to Their Rightful Owners* (2005). The following book review discusses *Working Toward Whiteness: How America's Immigrants Became White* (2005) by David R. Roediger and *When Affirmative Action Was White: An Untold History of Racial Inequality in Twentieth-Century America* (2005) by Ira Katznelson. It was originally published in the September/October 2005 issue of *Mother Jones*.

Before You Read

How does racial difference get reinforced in our culture? What societal forces or factors lead Americans to perceive differences in race or ethnicity as "natural" when in fact they are not?

WHEN SPACE ALIENS ARRIVE TO COLONIZE US, RACE, ALONG WITH the Atkins diet and Paris Hilton, will be among the things they'll think we're kidding about. Oh, to be a fly on the wall when the president tries to explain to creatures with eight legs what blacks, whites, Asians, and Hispanics are. Race is America's central drama, but just try to define it in 25 words or less. Usually, race is skin color, but our visitors will likely want to know what a "black" person from Darfur and one from Detroit have in common beyond melanin. Sometimes race is language. *Sometimes* it's religion. Until recently, race was culture and law: Whites in the front, blacks in the back, Asians and Hispanics on the fringes. Race governed who could vote, who could murder or marry whom, what kind of work one could do and how much it could pay. The only thing we know for sure is that race is not biology: Decoding the human genome tells us there is more difference within races than between them.

Hopefully, with time, more Americans will come to accept that race is an arbitrary system for establishing hierarchy and privilege, good for little more than doling out the world's loot and deciding who gets to kick whose butt and then write epic verse about it. A belief in the immutable nature of race is the only way one can still believe that socioeconomic outcomes in America are either fair or entirely determined by individual effort. [David Roediger's *Working Toward Whiteness* and Ira Katznelson's *When Affirmative Action Was White*] should put to rest any such claims.

If race is real and not just a method for the haves to decide who will be have-nots, then all European immigrants, from Ireland to Greece, would have been "white" the moment they arrived here. Instead, as documented in David Roediger's excellent *Working Toward Whiteness*, they were long considered inferior, nearly subhuman, and certainly not white. Southern and eastern European immigrants' language, dress, poverty, and willingness to do "nigger" work excited not pity or curiosity but fear and xenophobia. Teddy Roosevelt popularized the term "race suicide" while calling for Americans to have more babies to offset the mongrel hordes. Scientists tried to prove that Slavs and "dagoes" were incapable of normal adult intelligence. Africans and Asians were clearly less than human, but Hungarians and Sicilians ranked not far above.

It gives one cultural vertigo to learn that, until the 1920s, Americans from northern Europe called themselves "white men" so as not to be confused with their fellow laborers from southern Europe. Or that 11 Italians were lynched in Louisiana in 1891, and Greeks were targeted by whites during a 1909 Omaha race riot. And curiously, the only black family on the Titanic was almost lost to history because "Italian" was used to label the ship's darker-skinned, nonwhite passengers.

5   Yet it was this very bureaucratic impulse and political self-interest that eventually led America to "promote" southern and eastern Europeans to "whiteness." The discussion turned to how to fully assimilate these much-needed, newly white workers and how to get their votes. If you were neither black nor Asian nor Hispanic, eventually

> **Race is an arbitrary system for establishing hierarchy and privilege.**

you could become white, invested with enforceable civil rights and the right to exploit—and hate—nonwhites. World War II finally made all European Americans white, as the "Americans All" banner was reduced to physiognomy alone: Patriotic Japanese Americans ended up in internment camps while fascist-leaning Italian Americans roamed free. While recent European immigrants had abstained from World War I–era race riots, racial violence in the 1940s was an equal-opportunity affair. One Italian American later recalled the time he and his friends "beat up some niggers" in Harlem as "wonderful. It was new. The Italo-American stopped being Italo and started becoming American."

While European immigrants got the racial stamp of approval, the federal government was engaged in a little-recognized piece of racial rigging that resulted in both FDR's New Deal and Truman's Fair Deal being set up largely for the benefit of whites. As Ira Katznelson explains in *When Affirmative Action Was White*, these transformative public programs, from Social Security to the GI Bill, were deeply—and intentionally— discriminatory. Faced with a de facto veto by Southern Democrats, throughout the 1930s and 1940s Northern liberals acquiesced to calls for "states' rights" as they drafted the landmark laws that would create a new white middle class. As first-generation white immigrants cashed in on life-altering benefits, black families who had been here since Revolutionary times were left out in the cold.

Disbursement of federal Depression relief was left at the local level, so that Southern blacks were denied benefits and their labor kept at serf status. In

> **Race is America's central drama.**

parts of Georgia, no blacks received emergency relief; in Mississippi, less than 1 percent did. Agricultural and domestic workers were excluded from the new Social Security system, subjecting 60 percent of blacks (and 75 percent of Southern blacks) to what Katznelson calls "a form of policy apartheid" far from what FDR had envisioned. Until the 1950s, most blacks remained ineligible for Social Security. Even across the North, black veterans' mortgage, education, and housing benefits lagged behind whites'. Idealized as the capstone of progressive liberalism, such policies were as devastatingly racist as Jim Crow.

To remedy this unacknowledged injustice, Katznelson proposes that current discussions about affirmative action refer to events that took place seven, rather than four, decades ago, when it wasn't called affirmative action but business as usual. He's frustrated by the anemic arguments of his liberal allies, who rely on the most tenuous, least defensible of grounds—diversity—while their opponents invoke color blindness, merit, and the Constitution. In short, affirmative action can't be wrong now when it was right—and white—for so long.

Together, these two books indict the notion of race as, ultimately, a failure of the American imagination. We simply can't imagine a world in which skin color does not entitle us to think we know what people are capable of, what they deserve, or their character. We can't imagine what America might become if true affirmative action—not the kind aimed at the Huxtable kids[1] but at poverty and substandard education—was enacted at anywhere near the level once bestowed on those fortunate enough to be seen as white.

NOTE

[1]The Huxtables are the fictional family that appeared on the popular sitcom *The Cosby Show* in the 1980s and 1990s.

FOR A SECOND READING

1. Dickerson opens her essay with a hypothetical scenario in which space aliens are faced with the task of understanding how Americans have perceived and sought to deal with race. Why do you think she chooses to begin her discussion on race by focusing on it from an "alien" perspective? What kind of commentary on race does this particular strategy imply?

2. Dickerson refers to race as the "central drama" of American history. Why do you think she uses the term *drama*? Does her discussion of racial politics and racialist violence invite us in any way to think about this history in terms of role-playing, performance, or social and cultural scripts? If so, how?

3. According to Dickerson, race is best understood as a question of power. "Hopefully, with time," she writes, "more Americans will come to accept that race is an arbitrary system for establishing hierarchy and privilege" (p. 51). What do you make of this claim? To what extent do you share Dickerson's conviction about the arbitrariness of racial categories and racial difference?

PUTTING IT INTO WRITING

4. The dominant ways of thinking about race in America, argues Dickerson, are more the product of social fantasy than a reflection of objective reality. In a brief essay, evaluate the validity of this thesis. To what extent is it valid to think of the racial scripts that get taught in our culture as fantastic or fictional? Does this possibility diminish or accentuate the power they can wield?

5. One of the goals of this essay is to denaturalize the racial differences we've been taught to accept. Write a three- to five-page essay in which you analyze and evaluate this goal. Choose an example from our popular culture (for example, a television show, an advertisement, or a news story) that, in your view, encourages us to accept a view about race and racial difference that you consider artificial. First identify, describe, and analyze the views this example invites its audience to share: What is the main point this text attempts to convey? How does it represent this false view as right or normal? What are the particular strategies it uses to persuade readers to accept this view? Then evaluate the consequences you believe follow from accepting the argument being advanced. In your view, what is problematic, counterproductive, or just plain wrong about taking at face value the view advanced here?

COMPARING ARGUMENTS

6. Debra Dickerson shares with Michael Eric Dyson (p. 47) a concern about public attitudes about race as well as the implications of accepting these attitudes uncritically. How do you think Dickerson would respond to the arguments about "black patriotism" or religion in African American life advanced by Dyson? In your view, would Dickerson find his arguments to be in line with her own conclusions about race, power, and hierarchy? How or how not?

Then and Now: **Feeling (In)Secure**

Certainly belief touches on those things we've been taught to value and embrace, but it also concerns those things we've been taught to fear. When it comes to the threats we are told are most dangerous, what exactly are we supposed to believe? How are we taught to define these threats? What instructions are we issued for how to deal with them? These days, no danger looms more ominously or ubiquitously in our lives than the threat of terrorism. From nightly news broadcasts to political speeches, terrorist "watchlists" to made-for-TV dramas, it is made clear to us in countless ways that the world is full of shadowy enemies who despise "our way of life" and are therefore intent on doing us harm. So ingrained has this belief in the omnipresent terrorist threat become, in fact, that we have reorganized major swaths of our public behavior to accommodate it. There is no more vivid illustration of this fact than in the changes that have reshaped modern air travel. For the millions of Americans who travel by plane, things like long lines at security checkpoints, constantly changing restrictions on what may and may not be brought on board, random body searches, and full body image scanners have come to be regarded as established facts of life. Less clear,

American Stock Archive/Getty Images

though, are the particular anxieties and fears that these new security rituals have simultaneously normalized. Indeed, it could be argued that all of these precautions and prohibitions have served to make air travel itself into a kind of extended tutorial in how and what we are supposed to fear. Every time we remove our shoes at the security check-in or dispose of our contraband toothpaste before getting on board, we are acting on (and thereby reinforcing) a particular definition of who and what our enemies are.

When framed as an example of cultural instruction, our modern-day preoccupation with terrorist threats starts to look less new than it first appears. The twentieth century in America was marked by a series of "scares" — from the Palmer Raids fears about alien immigrants in the 1920s to the anti-communist "Red Menace" hysteria of the 1950s — which taught Americans to define and fear the threats to the nation in very specific ways. During the Cold War, for instance, which most historians believe started soon after the end of World War II, these fears revolved largely around the twin specters of Soviet communism and nuclear weapons. Anticipating in many ways the media coverage we see today, television broadcasts and newspaper headlines of this era were replete with warnings about the "enemies" who might be lurking "in our midst"; politicians regularly enjoined audiences to remain vigilant against "sneak attacks," which, they cautioned, could happen at any time. As a result, countless Americans became convinced that their highest civic duty was to prepare against a Soviet missile attack, digging bomb shelters or stocking

Pool/Getty Images

basements with canned goods. In contrast to the airport restrictions of today, the rituals through which people acted out these fears centered on the classroom. For elementary schoolchildren of the 1950s, air-raid alerts and "duck and cover" drills came to stand as the norm, the mid-century equivalent to the metal detectors and bomb-sniffing dogs of today.

When we place these two sets of security rituals side by side, what (if any) differences do we see? On the basis of the roles scripted for us in these respective eras, does it seem that we've learned to define and deal with the threats confronting us in new and different ways? Or does it seem instead that we've simply carried old attitudes and anxieties forward?

PUTTING IT INTO WRITING

1. Compare the ways that each image demonstrates the concept of safety. How are the rituals depicted in these photos designed to make us *feel* about our own safety?

2. While they may seem at first glance merely to be objective portraits, the images can also be read as depicting *public performances* in which people are shown acting out social scripts that have been written for them. It is from this perspective that such activities can start to seem like tutorials in security, scenarios designed to teach us what and how to fear. For each set of activities shown in the photographs, create instructions that lay out the steps for the safety rituals depicted and state why Americans should perform these steps.

BRYAN STEVENSON
Higher Ground

Studies have consistently shown that the United States incarcerates a greater percentage of its population than any other developed country, a percentage that spikes dramatically for African American men. With these statistics as a backdrop, Bryan Stevenson recounts the story of his first encounter as a young defense attorney with a prisoner on death row. What he learns from this encounter not only confounds virtually every cultural stereotype about convicted criminals, but also challenges the very premise on which our entire criminal justice system is based. Bryan Stevenson is a lawyer, social justice activist, a clinical professor of law at New York University, and the founder/executive director of the Equal Justice Initiative, a nonprofit organization that provides legal representation to prisoners who may have been wrongly convicted of crimes. He is also the author of *Just Mercy: A Story of Justice and Redemption* (2014), from which the essay below is excerpted.

Before You Read

What stereotype(s) of the "convicted criminal" does our culture create? What image does this phrase evoke in your mind?

I DROVE THROUGH FARMLAND AND WOODED AREAS OF RURAL Georgia, rehearsing what I would say when I met this man. I practiced my introduction over and over.

"Hello, my name is Bryan. I'm a student with the . . ." No. "I'm a law student with . . ." No. "My name is Bryan Stevenson. I'm a legal intern with the Southern Prisoners Defense Committee, and I've been instructed to inform you that you will not be executed soon." "You can't be executed soon." "You are not at risk of execution anytime soon." No.

I continued practicing my presentation until I pulled up to the intimidating barbed-wire fence and white guard tower of the Georgia Diagnostic and Classification Center. Around the office we just called it "Jackson," so seeing the facility's actual name on a sign was jarring—it sounded clinical, even therapeutic. I parked and found my way to the prison entrance and walked inside the main building with its dark corridors and gated hallways, where metal bars barricaded every access point. The interior eliminated any doubt that this was a hard place.

I walked down a tunneled corridor to the legal visitation area, each step echoing ominously across the spotless tiled floor. When I told the visitation officer that I was a paralegal sent to meet with a death row prisoner, he looked at me suspiciously. I was wearing the only suit I owned, and we could both see that it had seen better days. The officer's eyes seemed to linger long and hard over my driver's license before he tilted his head toward me to speak.

"You're not local."   5

It was more of a statement than a question.

"No, sir. Well, I'm working in Atlanta." After calling the warden's office to confirm that my visit had been properly scheduled, he finally admitted me, brusquely directing me to the small room where the visit would take place. "Don't get lost in here; we don't promise to come and find you," he warned.

The visitation room was twenty feet square with a few stools bolted to the floor. Everything in the room was made of metal and secured. In front of the stools, wire mesh ran from a small ledge up to a ceiling twelve feet high. The room was an empty cage until I walked into it. For family visits, inmates and visitors had to be on opposite sides of the mesh interior wall; they spoke to one another through the wires of the mesh. Legal visits, on the other hand, were "contact visits"—the two of us would be on the same side of the room to permit more privacy. The room was small and, although I knew it couldn't be true, it felt like it was getting smaller by the second. I began worrying again about my lack of preparation. I'd scheduled to meet with the client for one hour, but I wasn't sure how I'd fill even fifteen minutes with what I knew. I sat down on one of the stools and waited. After fifteen minutes of growing anxiety, I finally heard the clanging of chains on the other side of the door.

The man who walked in seemed even more nervous than I was. He glanced at me, his face screwed up in a worried wince, and he quickly averted his gaze when I looked back. He didn't move far from the room's entrance, as if he didn't really want to enter the visitation room. He was a young, neatly groomed African American man with short hair—clean-shaven, medium frame and build—wearing bright, clean prison whites. He looked immediately familiar to me, like everyone I'd grown up with, friends from school, people I played sports or music with, someone I'd talk to on the street about the weather. The guard slowly unchained him, removing his handcuffs and the shackles around his ankles, and then locked eyes with me and told me I had one hour. The officer seemed to sense that both the prisoner and I were nervous and to take some pleasure in our discomfort, grinning at me before turning on his heel and leaving the room. The metal door banged loudly behind him and reverberated through the small space.

The condemned man didn't come any closer, and I didn't know what   10 else to do, so I walked over and offered him my hand. He shook it cautiously. We sat down and he spoke first.

"I'm Henry," he said.

The condemned man didn't come any closer, and I didn't know what else to do, so I walked over and offered my hand. He shook it cautiously.

"I'm very sorry" were the first words I blurted out. Despite all my preparations and rehearsed remarks, I couldn't stop myself from apologizing repeatedly.

"I'm really sorry, I'm really sorry, uh, okay, I don't really know, uh, I'm just a law student, I'm not a real lawyer. . . . I'm so sorry I can't tell you very much, but I don't know very much."

The man looked at me worriedly. "Is everything all right with my case?"

15   "Oh, yes, sir. The lawyers at SPDC sent me down to tell you that they don't have a lawyer yet. . . . I mean, we don't have a lawyer for you yet, but you're not at risk of execution anytime in the next year. . . . We're working on finding you a lawyer, a real lawyer, and we hope the lawyer will be down to see you in the next few months. I'm just a law student. I'm really happy to help, I mean, if there's something I can do."

The man interrupted my chatter by quickly grabbing my hands.

"I'm not going to have an execution date anytime in the next year?"

"No, sir. They said it would be at least a year before you get an execution date." Those words didn't sound very comforting to me. But Henry just squeezed my hands tighter and tighter.

"Thank you, man. I mean, really, thank you! This is great news." His shoulders unhunched, and he looked at me with intense relief in his eyes.

20   "You are the first person I've met in over two years after coming to death row who is not another death row prisoner or a death row guard. I'm so glad you're here, and I'm so glad to get this news." He exhaled loudly and seemed to relax.

"I've been talking to my wife on the phone, but I haven't wanted her to come and visit me or bring the kids because I was afraid they'd show up and I'd have an execution date. I just don't want them here like that. Now I'm going to tell them they can come and visit. Thank you!"

I was astonished that he was so happy. I relaxed, too, and we began to talk. It turned out that we were exactly the same age. Henry asked me questions about myself, and I asked him about his life. Within an hour we were both lost in conversation. We talked about everything. He told me about his family, and he told me about his trial. He asked me about law school and my family. We talked about music, we talked about prison, we talked about what's important in life and what's not. I was completely absorbed in our conversation. We laughed at times, and there were moments when he was very emotional and sad. We kept talking and talking, and it was only when I heard a loud bang on the door that I realized I'd stayed way past my allotted time for the legal visit. I looked at my watch. I'd been there three hours.

The guard came in and he was angry. He snarled at me, "You should have been done a long time ago. You have to leave."

He began handcuffing Henry, pulling his hands together behind his back and locking them there. Then he roughly shackled Henry's ankles. The guard was so angry he put the cuffs on too tight. I could see Henry grimacing with pain.

I said, "I think those cuffs are on too tight. Can you loosen them, please?" 25

"I told you: You need to leave. You don't tell me how to do my job."

Henry gave me a smile and said. "It's okay, Bryan. Don't worry about this. Just come back and see me again, okay?" I could see him wince with each click of the chains being tightened around his waist.

I must have looked pretty distraught. Henry kept saying "Don't worry, Bryan, don't worry. Come back okay?"

As the officer pushed him toward the door, Henry turned back to look at me.

I started mumbling, "I'm really sorry. I'm really sor—" 30

"Don't worry about this, Bryan" he said, cutting me off. "Just come back."

I looked at him and struggled to say something appropriate, something reassuring, something that expressed my gratitude to him for being so patient with me. But I couldn't think of anything to say. Henry looked at me and smiled. The guard was shoving him toward the door roughly. I didn't like the way Henry was being treated, but he continued to smile until, just before the guard could push him fully out of the room, he planted his feet to resist the officer's shoving. He looked so calm. Then he did something completely unexpected. I watched him close his eyes and tilt his head back. I was confused by what he was doing, but then he opened his mouth and I understood. He began to sing. He had a tremendous baritone voice that was strong and clear. It startled both me and the guard, who stopped his pushing.

> I'm pressing on, the upward way
> New heights I'm gaining, every day
> Still praying as, I'm onward bound
> Lord, plant my feet on Higher Ground.

It was an old hymn they used to sing all the time in the church where I grew up. I hadn't heard it in years. Henry sang slowly and with great sincerity and conviction. It took a moment before the officer recovered and resumed pushing him out the door. Because his ankles were shackled and his hands were locked behind his back, Henry almost stumbled when the guard shoved him forward. He had to waddle to keep his balance, but he kept on singing. I could hear him as he went down the hall:

Lord lift me up, and let me stand
By faith on Heaven's tableland
A higher plane, that I have found
Lord, plant my feet on Higher Ground.

I sat down, completely stunned. Henry's voice was filled with desire. I experienced his song as a precious gift. I had come into the prison with such anxiety and fear about his willingness to tolerate my inadequacy. I didn't expect him to be compassionate or generous. I had no right to expect anything from a condemned man on death row. Yet he gave me an astonishing measure of his humanity. In that moment, Henry altered something in my understanding of human potential, redemption, and hopefulness.

35   I finished my internship committed to helping the death row prisoners I had met that month. Proximity to the condemned and incarcerated made the question of each person's humanity more urgent and meaningful, including my own. I went back to law school with an intense desire to understand the laws and doctrines that sanctioned the death penalty and extreme punishments. I piled up courses on constitutional law, litigation, appellate procedure, federal courts, and collateral remedies. I did extra work to broaden my understanding of how constitutional theory shapes criminal procedure. I plunged deeply into the law and the sociology of race, poverty and power. Law school had seemed abstract and disconnected before, but after meeting the desperate and imprisoned, it all became relevant and critically important. Even my studies at the Kennedy School took on a new significance. Developing the skills to quantify and deconstruct the discrimination and inequality I saw became urgent and meaningful.

> **Proximity to the condemned and incarcerated made the question of each person's humanity more urgent and meaningful, including my own.**

My short time on death row revealed that there was something missing in the way we treat people in our judicial system, that maybe we judge some people unfairly. The more I reflected on the experience, the more I recognized that I had been struggling my whole life with the question of how and why people are judged unfairly.

I grew up in a poor, rural, racially segregated settlement on the eastern shore of the Delmarva Peninsula, in Delaware, where the racial history of this country casts a long shadow. The coastal communities that stretched from Virginia and eastern Maryland to lower Delaware were unapologetically Southern. Many people in the region insisted on a racialized hierarchy that required symbols, markers, and constant reinforcement, in part because of the area's proximity to the North.

Confederate flags were proudly displayed throughout the region, baldly and defiantly marking the cultural, social, and political landscape.

African Americans lived in racially segregated ghettos isolated by railroad tracks within small towns or in "colored sections" in the country. I grew up in a country settlement where some people lived in tiny shacks; families without indoor plumbing had to use outhouses. We shared our outdoor play space with chickens and pigs.

The black people around me were strong and determined but marginalized and excluded. The poultry plant bus came each day to pick up adults and take them to the factory where they would daily pluck, hack, and process thousands of chickens. My father left the area as a teenager because there was no local high school for black children. He returned with my mother and found work in a food factory; on weekends he did domestic work at beach cottages and rentals. My mother had a civilian job at an Air Force base. It seemed that we were all cloaked in an unwelcome garment of racial difference that constrained, confined, and restricted us.

My relatives worked hard all the time but never seemed to prosper. 40 My grandfather was murdered when I was a teenager, but it didn't seem to matter much to the world outside our family.

My grandmother was the daughter of people who were enslaved in Caroline County, Virginia. She was born in the 1880s, her parents in the 1840s. Her father talked to her all the time about growing up in slavery and how he learned to read and write but kept it a secret. He hid the things he knew—until Emancipation. The legacy of slavery very much shaped my grandmother and the way she raised her nine children. It influenced the way she talked to me, the way she constantly told me to "Keep close."

When I visited her, she would hug me so tightly I could barely breathe. After a little while, she would ask me, "Bryan, do you still feel me hugging you?" If I said yes, she'd let me be; if I said no, she would assault me again. I said no a lot because it made me happy to be wrapped in her formidable arms. She never tired of pulling me to her.

"You can't understand most of the important things from a distance, Bryan. You have to get close," she told me all the time.

The distance I experienced in my first year of law school made me feel lost. Proximity to the condemned, to people unfairly judged; that was what guided me back to something that felt like home.

FOR A SECOND READING

1. Stevenson begins this account by describing how unprepared he felt before his first meeting with a death row prisoner, admitting to feelings of "panic" and worrying that he might be "over my head." Why do you think Stevenson chooses to open his essay this way? What view toward convicted criminals does this preface reflect? How does this view change over the course of the essay?

2. Review the section of the essay where Stevenson describes the meeting with his client, Henry (pp. 60–62). How would you characterize this portrait of Henry? What details do you find most striking? In what ways does this depiction counter the stereotypical image of a death row inmate?

3 . In addition to telling the story of his encounter with Henry, Stevenson also recounts his own childhood as an African American growing up during the pre–civil rights era. Why do you think Stevenson chooses to include both of these stories? What do we see about Henry's incarceration when it is placed in the context of Stevenson's personal history that we otherwise would not? What do we see about Stevenson's life when it is placed in the context of Henry's incarceration that we otherwise would not?

PUTTING IT INTO WRITING

4. As he acknowledges, Stevenson's vision of a reformed criminal justice system is quite different from the model that predominates in today's society. Use Stevenson's vision as the starting point for creating your own definition of an ideal criminal justice system. What does this system look like? What social scripts does it reflect? What roles does it create? What underlying norms does it represent? Then indicate the specific ways your model challenges or revises the roles, scripts, and norms that define the "typical" model.

5. "Proximity to the condemned and incarcerated," writes Stevenson, "made the question of each person's humanity more urgent and meaningful, including my own" (p. 62). In a 500-word response, analyze and evaluate the point Stevenson is making here. Why would "proximity" to "condemned and incarcerated" prisoners make the question of their "humanity more urgent"? Why, furthermore, would such "proximity" raise for Stevenson the question of his own "humanity"? What larger point do you think Stevenson is trying to make—about the ways we are taught to think about and punish "criminals"—through this statement?

COMPARING ARGUMENTS

6. Like Stevenson, Amitava Kumar (p. 65) wants to reexamine the cultural norms governing how we think about crime and punishment. How do you think Stevenson would respond to the model of "restorative justice" Kumar describes in his essay? Do you think Stevenson would find the practice of public "forgiveness" applicable to the criminal cases he discusses? What details from Stevenson's essay make you think so?

AMITAVA KUMAR
The Restoration of Faith

In many ways, our contemporary legal system encourages us to define justice in terms of punishment. Advocates for stricter penalties and harsher sentences for criminals often speak of the "closure" such treatment brings to victims. But might this conventional wisdom have it wrong? Is it possible that resolution happens more through forgiveness and understanding than vengeance and punishment? This is the possibility Amitava Kumar contemplates here. Sketching a compelling portrait of "restorative justice," he raises important questions about the ways we have been taught to think about crime and punishment. Amitava Kumar is a writer and professor of English at Vassar College. His books include *Husband of a Fanatic* (2005) and *A Foreigner Carrying in the Crook of His Arm a Tiny Bomb* (2010). This essay was published in *Caravan* magazine in 2013.

Before You Read

In your view, does our criminal justice system promote the goal of "rehabilitation"? Should it?

ON A RECENT WEEKEND I PICKED UP THE NEW YORK TIMES THAT IS delivered in a blue polythene bag outside my door each morning, and read a story about a young man who had fatally shot his girlfriend during a fight. The young man's name was Conor McBride and the victim's name was Ann Margaret Grosmaire. Both were 19 when this happened, in March 2010, in Tallahassee, Florida.

The reporter, Paul Tullis, introduced an early note about what made the story unusual. Ann's father, Andy Grosmaire, standing next to his "intubated and unconscious" daughter in hospital, heard her say before her death, "Forgive him." Conor, when he was booked, was asked to provide the names of five people who could visit him in jail. He included the name of Ann's mother, Kate Grosmaire.

Talking to the reporter who had written the story, Kate explained her desire to go and see Conor in prison, "Before this happened, I loved Conor. I knew that if I defined Conor by that one moment—as a murderer—I was defining my daughter as a murder victim. And I could not allow that to happen."

> **The significance of restorative justice [lies] in "community-based processes that hold people who harm directly accountable to the people that they've harmed."**

The state attorney's office had charged Conor McBride with first-degree murder; this meant that he was likely to spend the rest of his life in prison. (As the case didn't have any aggravating circumstances, like prior convictions or the victim being a child, the prosecutors were probably not likely to seek the death penalty.) But Ann's parents told the assistant state attorney that they didn't want Conor to spend the rest of his life in prison. The concept that the Grosmaires had embraced, together with Conor's parents, Julie and Michael McBride, was that of "restorative justice," a not very widely known practice based on the idea of victim–offender dialogue.

Where the report took a turn for me is that the lawyer they hired to facilitate this process was a woman named Sujatha Baliga. The reporter had mentioned that Baliga was born in Shippensburg, Pennsylvania, the child of Indian immigrants. As I read her name and then a few more lines about her, I wanted to ask Baliga a question about India.

5 Baliga told me that the significance of restorative justice lay in "community-based processes that hold people who harm directly accountable to the people that they've harmed." There was great faith invested there in face-to-face dialogue and participatory decision-making. Paraphrasing Howard Zehr, a pioneer in the field of restorative justice, Baliga said that rather than asking the traditional justice system questions of "What law was broken? Who broke it? How should we punish them?" the approach she was advocating asked instead, "What harm has been done? What needs have arisen? Whose obligation is it to meet those needs?" Evidence of this shift was present in the actions of the Grosmaires and the McBrides. They had each sought to honor the memory of Ann Grosmaire.

Even approaching Baliga couldn't have been easy for the Grosmaires and the McBrides. Restorative justice cases have usually involved burglaries or property disputes — not violent crimes, and certainly not homicides. To add to this, Florida is considered a law-and-order state with a strong leaning toward punitive justice. But Baliga facilitated a meeting in June 2011 in the jail where Conor was incarcerated. At that conference, Ann's parents spoke first, talking of the young woman's childhood and her dreams.

> **[T]he Grosmaires said that they didn't forgive Conor for his sake, but their own.**

They told the young man who had killed their daughter about the pain he had caused. Then, Conor told them the story of how he and Ann had been fighting for 38 hours. Conor told the group, "What I did was inexcusable. There is no why, there are no excuses, there is no reason."

Earlier, while reading the report in the *New York Times* I had been struck by the fact that Conor had made such an honest and open admission at the meeting. But it wasn't until I had my exchanges with Baliga that I learned that Conor's statement had not—rather, *could* not—have been a spontaneous process. Baliga told me that helping Conor remember the details of the crime so that he would be prepared to answer the Grosmaires' questions had been "heartbreaking." The young man appeared to be experiencing what Baliga called "participatory traumatic stress" and he "couldn't remember many of the details of Ann's last moments." At the conference meeting, however, he came clean, telling Ann's parents the story of how he and Ann had been fighting for two days; in person, by text, and over the phone. Ann was on her knees, her hand raised to stop him, when he fired. It had been difficult, and understandably painful, for the dead woman's parents to hear this account. In fact, everyone involved in the process found it difficult, including the lawyers. Baliga said that it was "always challenging to get people in the traditional system to understand what we are doing—explaining it to jail staff, to the prosecutor, to the defense attorney."

When the meeting was over, Baliga asked the Grosmaires what they wanted. Ann's mother said that he should get a five- to 15-year term, and her father said ten to 15 years. Conor's parents agreed. The assistant state attorney was asked to speak. He didn't suggest a punishment, pointing out that even a statement like that required consideration. Later, he wrote to the Grosmaires and said that he was going to offer Conor a choice: 20 years in prison plus ten years probation, or 25 years in prison. Conor has chosen the former.

In the *New York Times*, Tullis had written that the Grosmaires said that they didn't forgive Conor for his sake, but their own. Ann's mother told Tullis, "Forgiveness for me was self-preservation." For his part, Conor told Tullis, "With the Grosmaires' forgiveness, I could accept the responsibility and not be condemned." If he had simply been turned into an enemy, he could have escaped the human contract, but by accepting him, the Grosmaires had drawn him into the circle of obligation. He was going to have to do good enough for two.

In my discussion with Baliga, I came to the question I had been 10 meaning to ask her the moment I finished reading the piece by Tullis. I asked Baliga about the recent gang rape of the young woman in a moving bus in Delhi. The entire society had been galvanized and was demanding justice. The victim's family has demanded that the perpetrators be hanged. In such circumstances, would Baliga still want to advocate restorative justice?

Baliga's answer was a forthright no. She explained that "restorative justice is a voluntary process, and is best when driven by the desires of the victims. The victims in this case have been clear—the woman from her deathbed, and her father now—that they want the death penalty. The family has said they don't want to see the young men who did this. So this is not an appropriate case for restorative justice."

Having said that, Baliga added that she was opposed to the death penalty. And that more information was needed about the men involved before a recommendation could be made about how long they ought to remain inside prison. She doubted that the penal system had the capacity to "rehabilitate this level of sexualized violence," in part because she believes that such behavior "comes from either some mental health issues or a history of unthinkable trauma that is being passed on to others." What was key now, far greater than simply wanting to hang the men now, was "to get to the roots of how these horrors happened."

Tullis's report in the *New York Times* had introduced Baliga by telling readers that she was a former public defender who was now the director of the restorative justice project at the National Council on Crime and Delinquency. Tullis had also written that "from as far back as Baliga can remember, she was sexually abused by her father." As a teen, she was dyeing her hair and cutting herself. Later, while studying at Harvard, she wanted to become a prosecutor and lock up child molesters. During a visit to India, she got a chance to meet the Dalai Lama, from whom she sought advice about how she could go on with her work on the behalf of the oppressed without having anger as her motivating force. The Dalai Lama advised Baliga to meditate and then asked her to align herself with the enemy. Baliga wasn't prepared to follow the second part of his advice, but after checking into a meditation course she found herself freed from rage and a desire for revenge.

FOR A SECOND READING

1. What do you make of the term "restorative justice"? What specifically does this approach to crime "restore"? And what about this approach is supposed to be more "just"? Do you agree? Why or why not?

2. Kumar quotes the victim's mother as saying that "forgiveness for me was self-preservation" (p. 67). What do you think she means by this? Does it make sense to you that forgiving someone who has harmed you can actually "preserve" you?

3. This essay draws a firm distinction between a willingness to forgive and a desire for vengeance. In your view, should vengeance play any role in the criminal justice system? And if so, what role specifically?

PUTTING IT INTO WRITING

4. In interviewing one of the lawyers involved, Kumar highlights the key difference between traditional notions of justice and restorative justice: "[Rather] than asking the traditional justice system questions of 'What law was broken? Who broke it? How should we

punish them?' the approach [the lawyer] was advocating asked instead, 'What harm has been done? What needs have arisen? Whose obligation is it to meet those needs?' " (p. 66). In an essay, discuss what you see as the key differences between these two types of questions. What attitude toward crime and criminals does each set of questions imply? How does each set of questions define the concept of justice differently? And which definition do you find more valid? Why?

5. Kumar describes restorative justice as a "practice based on the idea of victim–offender dialogue" (p. 66). Write an essay in which you lay out the rules by which you think a dialogue between a victim and an offender should unfold. What types of statements or questions should each party be allowed to make? What (if any) limits should be placed around what each party is allowed to say? And how would these rules help achieve a "just" outcome?

COMPARING ARGUMENTS

6. Bryan Stevenson's essay (p. 58) amounts to an extended argument that the criminal justice system needs to be made more ethical and empathetic. How do you think Kumar would respond to the story about the "condemned convict" that Stevenson tells? Given what he has to say about the value of "forgiveness," what aspects of this story do you think he would find most compelling? And why?

NAOMI KLEIN

One Way or Another, Everything Changes

Few issues pit more diametrically opposed beliefs against each other than global warming. Despite the overwhelming scientific consensus that man-made climate change is real and dangerous, debates continue to rage over whether we should regard and respond to it as a genuine threat. Weighing forcefully into this discussion, Naomi Klein pushes back against climate change denial by arguing for nothing short of a political and economic revolution. Klein, a writer and activist, was born into a political family in Montreal, Quebec, and currently lives in Toronto. She has worked as the editor of *THIS Magazine* and as a weekly columnist for the *Toronto Star*, and she is currently a columnist for the *Nation* and the *Guardian*. Her books include *No Logo* (2000), *Fences and Windows* (2002), *The Shock Doctrine: The Rise of Disaster Capitalism* (2007), and *This Changes Everything: Capitalism vs. Climate Change* (2015), from which this excerpt is taken.

Before You Read

What do you know about the current science on "global warming"? Based on this knowledge, how urgent do you think this issue is?

"Most projections of climate change presume that future changes—greenhouse gas emissions, temperature increases and effects such as sea level rise—will happen incrementally. A given amount of emission will lead to a given amount of temperature increase that will lead to a given amount of smooth incremental sea level rise. However, the geological record for the climate reflects instances where a relatively small change in one element of climate led to abrupt changes in the system as a whole. In other words, pushing global temperatures past certain thresholds could trigger abrupt, unpredictable and potentially irreversible changes that have massively disruptive and large-scale impacts. At that point, even if we do not add any additional CO_2 to the atmosphere, potentially unstoppable processes are set in motion. We can think of this as sudden climate brake and steering failure where the problem and its consequences are no longer something we can control."

—Report by the American Association for the Advancement of Science, the world's largest general scientific society, 2014[1]

"I love that smell of the emissions."

—Sarah Palin, 2011[2]

A VOICE CAME OVER THE INTERCOM: WOULD THE PASSENGERS OF FLIGHT 3935, scheduled to depart Washington, D.C., for Charleston, South Carolina, kindly collect their carry-on luggage and get off the plane.

They went down the stairs and gathered on the hot tarmac. There they saw something unusual: the wheels of the US Airways jet had sunk into the black pavement as if it were wet cement. The wheels were lodged so deep, in fact, that the truck that came to tow the plane away couldn't pry it loose. The airline had hoped that without the added weight of the flight's thirty-five passengers, the aircraft would be light enough to pull. It wasn't. Someone posted a picture: "Why is my flight cancelled? Because DC is so damn hot that our plane sank 4" into the pavement."[3]

Eventually, a larger, more powerful vehicle was brought in to tow the plane and this time it worked; the plane finally took off, three hours behind schedule. A spokesperson for the airline blamed the incident on "very unusual temperatures."[4]

The temperatures in the summer of 2012 were indeed unusually hot. (As they were the year before and the year after.) And it's no mystery why this has been happening: the profligate burning of fossil fuels, the very thing that US Airways was bound and determined to do despite the inconvenience presented by a melting tarmac. This irony—the fact that the burning of fossil fuels is so radically changing our climate that it is getting in the way of our capacity to burn fossil fuels—did not stop the passengers of Flight 3935 from reembarking and continuing their journeys. Nor was climate change mentioned in any of the major news coverage of the incident.

I am in no position to judge these passengers. All of us who live high consumer lifestyles, wherever we happen to reside, are, metaphorically, passengers on Flight 3935. Faced with a crisis that threatens our survival as a species, our entire culture is continuing to do the very thing that caused the crisis, only with an extra dose of elbow grease behind it. Like the airline bringing in a truck with a more powerful engine to tow that plane, the global economy is upping the ante from conventional sources of fossil fuels to even dirtier and more dangerous versions—bitumen from the Alberta tar sands, oil from deepwater drilling, gas from hydraulic fracturing (fracking), coal from detonated mountains, and so on.

Meanwhile, each supercharged natural disaster produces new irony-laden snapshots of a climate increasingly inhospitable to the very industries most responsible for its warming. Like the 2013 historic floods in Calgary that forced the head offices of the oil companies mining the Alberta tar sands to go dark and send their employees home, while a train carrying flammable petroleum products teetered on the edge of a disintegrating rail bridge. Or the drought that hit the Mississippi River one year earlier, pushing water levels so low that barges loaded with oil and coal were unable to move for days, while they waited for the Army Corps of Engineers to dredge a channel (they had to appropriate funds allocated to

5

rebuild from the previous year's historic flooding along the same water-
way). Or the coal-fired power plants in other parts of the country that were
temporarily shut down because the waterways that they draw on to cool
their machinery were either too hot or too dry (or, in some cases, both).

Living with this kind of cognitive dissonance is simply part of being
alive in this jarring moment in history, when a crisis we have been studi-
ously ignoring is hitting us in the face—and yet we are doubling down on
the stuff that is causing the crisis in the first place.

10   I denied climate change for longer than I care to admit. I knew it was
happening, sure. Not like Donald Trump and the Tea Partiers going on
about how the continued existence of winter proves it's all a hoax. But I
stayed pretty hazy on the details and only skimmed most of the news
stories, especially the really scary ones. I told myself the science was too
complicated and that the environmentalists were dealing with it. And I
continued to behave as if there was nothing wrong with the shiny card in
my wallet attesting to my "elite" frequent flyer status.

> *A great many of us engage in this kind of climate denial. We look for a split second then we look away. Or we look but then turn it into a joke . . . . Which is another way of looking away.*

A great many of us engage in this
kind of climate change denial. We look
for a split second and then we look away.
Or we look but then turn it into a joke
("more signs of the Apocalypse!"). Which
is another way of looking away.

Or we look but tell ourselves comforting stories about how humans are
clever and will come up with a technological miracle that will safely suck the
carbon out of the skies or magically turn
down the heat of the sun. Which, I was to
discover while researching this book, is
yet another way of looking away.

Or we look but try to be hyper-rational about it ("dollar for dollar it's
more efficient to focus on economic development than climate change,
since wealth is the best protection from weather extremes")—as if having
a few more dollars will make much difference when your city is underwater.
Which is a way of looking away if you happen to be a policy wonk.

Or we look but tell ourselves we are too busy to care about something
so distant and abstract—even though we saw the water in the subways
in New York City, and the people on their rooftops in New Orleans, and
know that no one is safe, the most vulnerable least of all. And though
perfectly understandable, this too is a way of looking away.

15   Or we look but tell ourselves that all we can do is focus on ourselves.
Meditate and shop at farmers' markets and stop driving—but forget trying
to actually change the systems that are making the crisis inevitable

because that's too much "bad energy" and it will never work. And at first it may appear as if we are looking, because many of these lifestyle changes are indeed part of the solution, but we still have one eye tightly shut.

Or maybe we do look—really look—but then, inevitably, we seem to forget. Remember and then forget again. Climate change is like that; it's hard to keep it in your head for very long. We engage in this odd form of on-again-off-again ecological amnesia for perfectly rational reasons. We deny because we fear that letting in the full reality of this crisis will change everything. And we are right.[5]

We know that if we continue on our current path of allowing emissions to rise year after year, climate change will change everything about our world. Major cities will very likely drown, ancient cultures will be swallowed by the seas, and there is a very high chance that our children will spend a great deal of their lives fleeing and recovering from vicious storms and extreme droughts. And we don't have to do anything to bring about this future. All we have to do is nothing. Just continue to do what we are doing now, whether it's counting on a techno-fix or tending to our gardens or telling ourselves we're unfortunately too busy to deal with it.

All we have to do is *not* react as if this is a full-blown crisis. All we have to do is keep on denying how frightened we actually are. And then, bit by bit, we will have arrived at the place we most fear, the thing from which we have been averting our eyes. No additional effort required.

There are ways of preventing this grim future, or at least making it a lot less dire. But the catch is that these also involve changing everything. For us high consumers, it involves changing how we live, how our economies function, even the stories we tell about our place on earth. The good news is that many of these changes are distinctly un-catastrophic. Many are downright exciting. But I didn't discover this for a long while.

I remember the precise moment when I stopped averting my eyes to 20 the reality of climate change, or at least when I first allowed my eyes to rest there for a good while. It was in Geneva, in April 2009, and I was meeting with Bolivia's ambassador to the World Trade Organization (WTO), who was then a surprisingly young woman named Angélica Navarro Llanos. Bolivia being a poor country with a small international budget, Navarro Llanos had recently taken on the climate portfolio in addition to her trade responsibilities. Over lunch in an empty Chinese restaurant, she explained to me (using chopsticks as props to make a graph of the global emission trajectory) that she saw climate change both as a terrible threat to her people—but also an opportunity.

A threat for the obvious reasons: Bolivia is extraordinarily dependent on glaciers for its drinking and irrigation water and those white-capped mountains that tower over its capital were turning gray and brown at an alarming rate. The opportunity, Navarro Llanos said, was that since countries like hers had done almost nothing to send emissions soaring, they were in a position to declare themselves "climate creditors," owed money and technology support from the large emitters to defray the hefty costs of coping with more climate-related disasters, as well as to help them develop on a green energy path.

She had recently given a speech at a United Nations climate conference in which she laid out the case for these kinds of wealth transfers, and she gave me a copy. "Millions of people," it read, "in small islands, least-developed countries, landlocked countries as well as vulnerable communities in Brazil, India and China, and all around the world—are suffering from the effects of a problem to which they did not contribute. . . . If we are to curb emissions in the next decade, we need a massive mobilization larger than any in history. We need a Marshall Plan for the Earth. This plan must mobilize financing and technology transfer on scales never seen before. It must get technology onto the ground in every country to ensure we reduce emissions while raising people's quality of life. We have only a decade."[6]

Of course a Marshall Plan for the Earth would be very costly—hundreds of billions if not trillions of dollars (Navarro Llanos was reluctant to name a figure). And one might have thought that the cost alone would make it a nonstarter—after all, this was 2009 and the global financial crisis was in full swing. Yet the grinding logic of austerity—passing on the bankers' bills to the people in the form of public sector layoffs, school closures, and the like—had not yet been normalized. So rather than making Navarro Llanos's ideas seem less plausible, the crisis had the opposite effect.

Climate change has never received the crisis treatment from our leaders, despite the fact that it carries the risk of destroying lives on a vastly greater scale than collapsed banks or collapsed buildings.

We had all just watched as trillions of dollars were marshaled in a moment when our elites decided to declare a crisis. If the banks were allowed to fail, we were told, the rest of the economy would collapse. It was a matter of collective survival, so the money had to be found. In the process, some rather large fictions at the heart of our economic system were exposed (Need more money? Print some!). A few years earlier, governments took a similar approach to public finances after the September 11 terrorist attacks. In many Western countries, when it came to constructing the security/surveillance state at home and waging war abroad, budgets never seemed to be an issue.

25   Climate change has never received the crisis treatment from our leaders, despite the fact that it carries the risk of destroying lives on a vastly greater scale than collapsed banks or collapsed buildings. The cuts

to our greenhouse gas emissions that scientists tell us are necessary in order to greatly reduce the risk of catastrophe are treated as nothing more than gentle suggestions, actions that can be put off pretty much indefinitely. Clearly, what gets declared a crisis is an expression of power and priorities as much as hard facts. But we need not be spectators in all this: politicians aren't the only ones with the power to declare a crisis. Mass movements of regular people can declare one too.

Slavery wasn't a crisis for British and American elites until abolitionism turned it into one. Racial discrimination wasn't a crisis until the civil rights movement turned it into one. Sex discrimination wasn't a crisis until feminism turned it into one. Apartheid wasn't a crisis until the anti-apartheid movement turned it into one.

In the very same way, if enough of us stop looking away and decide that climate change is a crisis worthy of Marshall Plan levels of response, then it will become one, and the political class will have to respond, both by making resources available and by bending the free market rules that have proven so pliable when elite interests are in peril. We occasionally catch glimpses of this potential when a crisis puts climate change at the front of our minds for a while. "Money is no object in this relief effort. Whatever money is needed for it will be spent," declared British prime minister David Cameron—Mr. Austerity himself—when large parts of his country were underwater from historic flooding in February 2014 and the public was enraged that his government was not doing more to help.[7]

Listening to Navarro Llanos describe Bolivia's perspective, I began to understand how climate change—if treated as a true planetary emergency akin to those rising flood waters—could become a galvanizing force for humanity, leaving us all not just safer from extreme weather, but with societies that are safer and fairer in all kinds of other ways as well. The resources required to rapidly move away from fossil fuels and prepare for the coming heavy weather could pull huge swaths of humanity out of poverty, providing services now sorely lacking, from clean water to electricity. This is a vision of the future that goes beyond just surviving or enduring climate change, beyond "mitigating" and "adapting" to it in the grim language of the United Nations. It is a vision in which we collectively use the crisis to leap somewhere that seems, frankly, better than where we are right now.

After that conversation, I found that I no longer feared immersing myself in the scientific reality of the climate threat. I stopped avoiding the articles and the scientific studies and read everything I could find. I also stopped outsourcing the problem to the environmentalists, stopped telling myself this was somebody else's issue, somebody else's job. And through conversations with others in the growing climate justice movement, I began to see all kinds of ways that climate change could become a catalyzing force for positive change—how it could be the best argument progressives have ever had to demand the rebuilding and reviving of local economies; to reclaim our democracies from corrosive corporate influence; to block harmful new free trade deals and rewrite old ones; to invest in starving public infrastructure like mass transit and affordable housing; to take back ownership of essential services like energy and water; to remake our sick agricultural system into something much healthier; to open borders to migrants whose displacement is linked to climate impacts; to finally respect Indigenous land rights—all of which would help to end grotesque levels of inequality within our nations and between them.

30   And I started to see signs—new coalitions and fresh arguments—hinting at how, if these various connections were more widely understood, the urgency of the climate crisis could form the basis of a powerful mass movement, one that would weave all these seemingly disparate issues into a coherent narrative about how to protect humanity from the ravages of both a savagely unjust economic system and a destabilized climate system. I have written this book because I came to the conclusion that climate action could provide just such a rare catalyst.

NOTES

[1]Mario Malina et al., "What We Know: The Reality, Risks and Response to Climate Change," AAAS Climate Science Panel, American Association for the Advancement of Science, 2014, pp. 15–16.

[2]"Sarah Palin Rolls Out at Rolling Thunder Motorcycle Ride," Fox News, May 29, 2011.

[3]Martin Weil, "US Airways Plane Gets Stuck in 'Soft Spot' on Pavement at Reagan National," Washington Post, July 7, 2012; "Why Is My Flight Cancelled?" Imgur, http://imgur.com.

[4]Weil, "US Airways Plane Gets Stuck in 'Soft Spot' on Pavement at Reagan National."

[5]For important sociological and psychological perspectives on the everyday denial of climate change, see: Kari Marie Norgaard, Living in Denial: Climate Change, Emotions, and Everyday Life (Cambridge, MA: MIT Press, 2011); Rosemary Randall, "Loss and Climate Change: The Cost of Parallel Narratives," Ecopsychology 1.3 (2009): 118–29; and the essays in Sally Weintrobe, ed., Engaging with Climate Change (East Sussex: Routledge, 2013).

[6]Angelica Navarro Llanos, "Climate Debt: The Basis of a Fair and Effective Solution to Climate" Change," presentation to Technical Briefing on Historical Responsibility, Ad Hoc Working Group on Long-term Cooperative Action, United Nations Framework Convention on Climate Change, Bonn, Germany, June 4, 2009.

[7]"British PM Warns of Worsening Floods Crisis," Agence France-Presse, February 11, 2014.

FOR A SECOND READING

1.   Klein opens her essay by recounting a story about airline passengers being forced to disembark because "the wheels of the . . . jet had sunk into the black pavement as if it were wet cement" (p. 71). How persuasive do you find this anecdote to be? How effectively does it preview the broader argument about climate change Klein goes on to present?

2. Klein describes the experience of living in the era of global warming as an exercise in "cognitive dissonance." What do you think she means by this term? What is she trying to say about the particular beliefs that surround discussions of global climate change?

3. Klein fills her essay with facts and statistics designed to support her case about the need for dramatic action regarding climate change. Choose one such example that you find especially noteworthy or effective. What information does it convey? How does this information serve to support the larger argument about acting upon climate Klein is making?

PUTTING IT INTO WRITING

4. Klein lists a number of possible explanations for why "climate change denial" is so prevalent: We "tell ourselves comforting stories about how humans are clever and will come up with a technological miracle"; we tell ourselves "it's more efficient to focus on economic development than climate change"; "we tell ourselves we are too busy to care about something so distant and abstract"; "we tell ourselves that all we can do is focus on ourselves" (p. 72). In a 500-word essay, identify, analyze, and evaluate the belief that underlies and supports each of these rationalizations. In each case, what assumption or idea makes this explanation seem reasonable? Do you agree? Why or why not?

5. "Clearly," writes Klein, "what gets declared a crisis is an expression of power and priorities as much as hard facts. But we need not be spectators in all this: politicians aren't the only ones with the power to declare a crisis. Mass movements of regular people can declare one too" (p. 75). Write an essay in which you take up Klein's invitation here. How would you define the "crisis" of global climate change? In your view, what "priorities" should guide our efforts to respond to this crisis? What kind of public action do you think would most effectively articulate these priorities?

COMPARING ARGUMENTS

6. Like Klein, Tom Jacobs (p. 78) focuses on the beliefs that underlie our culture's current environmental thinking. And as does Klein, Jacobs also uses statistical evidence to frame his discussion. Notwithstanding these similarities, what would you say are the key differences (e.g., language, tone, organization) in how each writer examines this question? Which discussion do you find more compelling and persuasive? Why?

TOM JACOBS
It's Not Easy Being Green—and Manly

The cultural norms around environmentalism have changed dramatically over the last generation. Where a basic activity like recycling may have been regarded as a curiosity twenty-five years ago, today it is largely accepted as a given in everyday life. And yet, according to Tom Jacobs, there still remain pockets of resistance to these "green" ways of thinking — resistance, he argues, that is surprisingly connected to gender. Tom Jacobs is a regular contributor to *Pacific Standard*, an online journal about culture and politics, where this essay was published in 2015.

Before You Read

Can you think of any way that your gender affects your views on environmentalism? If you can, does this surprise you?

> *Taking the bus, eating less meat, even turning down the thermostat can conflict with traditionally masculine notions of power and self-reliance.*

LET'S FACE IT: MULCHING ISN'T manly. Neither are most environmentally conscious behaviors. Taking the bus, eating less meat, even turning down the thermostat can conflict with traditionally masculine notions of power and self-reliance.

This helps explain why men are less likely than women to think and act in Earth-friendly ways. The mental association of caring for the Earth with femininity can "motivate men to avoid green behaviors in order to preserve a macho image," writes a research team led by Aaron Brough of Utah State University. It's just a guy thing.

But their new study suggests there are effective ways to defuse this dynamic. In the *Journal of Consumer Research*, the researchers offer evidence that "men's inhibitions about engaging in green behavior can be mitigated through masculine affirmation, and masculine branding."

They begin by describing four studies that show people really do link green behavior with femininity. In one, 194 university students were given a list of words, and asked which best described a shopper leaving a grocery store.

5   If the person (man or woman) was carrying their purchases in a canvas bag, participants were less likely to use such terms as "macho" or

"aggressive," but more likely to suggest ones like "gentle" and "sensitive." And this stereotyping didn't just apply to other people: A follow-up study found recalling "green" behaviors led both men and women to think of themselves in more feminine terms.

Another set of studies examines ways to break this linkage. The first featured 472 participants (roughly half of them male) recruited online, who began by giving a writing sample. Half were told that an instant analysis "strongly indicated that they write more like a man than a woman," while the others were given no feedback.

They then read about "a new household drain cleaner," which was described as being either "better for the environment" or "better at dissolving grease." Afterwards, all participants rated the product on a one-to-nine scale (definitely prefer it to definitely do not).

The result: Men who had just been told their handwriting was manly preferred the "green" product more than those who did not receive that information.

Men who had just been told their handwriting was manly preferred the "green" product more than those who did not receive that information.

"These results suggest that while men typically prefer green products less than females," the researchers write, "affirming their masculinity can increase preference for green products to be similar to that of women."

In another study, 322 people recruited online examined one of two 10 versions of a fund-raising pitch from an environmental organization. Half saw a version in which "the organization was named Friends of Nature, the logo was green and light tan with a tree symbol, the font was frilly, and the mission was described in terms of preserving nature areas." Pretty typical, in other words. The other half saw a version in which "the organization was named Wilderness Rangers, the logo was black and dark blue with a howling wolf symbol, the font was bold and lacked frills, and the mission was described in terms of preserving wilderness areas."

The key result: Male participants "were less likely to donate to the conventional-branded green nonprofit than females." However, "men and women were similarly likely to donate to the masculine-branded green nonprofit."

A major reason for this was suggested in another finding: "Participants reported they would feel more masculine wearing a t-shirt featuring the masculine-branded logo" than one with the more standard image of a tree.

It all indicates "that men avoid green behaviors, at least in part, to maintain a macho image," Brough and his colleagues conclude, "and that masculine branding can increase men's likelihood to donate to green organizations."

So, Sierra Club, Nature Conservatory, and the rest: Keep these results in mind during your next re-design. In the end, saving the environment may require convincing Americans that real men recycle.

FOR A SECOND READING

1. Jacobs begins his essay this way: "Let's face it. Mulching isn't manly. Neither are most environmentally conscious behaviors. Taking the bus, eating less meat, even turning down the thermostat can conflict with traditionally masculine notions of power and self-reliance" (p. 78). Do you accept Jacob's contention here that "environmentally conscious behaviors" are in "conflict" with "traditional" masculinity? If so, why is this an important observation to make? What do we learn by uncovering the gendered implications behind so-called green activities?

2. Jacobs concludes his essay with the following statement: "In the end, saving the environment may require convincing Americans that real men recycle" (p. 80). How effective an environmental slogan do you find this phrase to be? Do you think environmentally conscious behavior would increase if the general public believed that "real men recycle"?

3. Jacobs's argument depends upon cultural stereotypes about both men and women, in particular upon what he calls "the mental association of caring for the Earth with femininity" (p. 78). Are you persuaded by this tactic? Do you agree with Jacobs our culture tends to "feminize" a concern for the environment? If so, why do you think this is the case?

PUTTING IT INTO WRITING

4. For Jacobs, cultural attitudes about environmentalism are inseparable from cultural stereotypes about gender. To test this hypothesis, make a list of all the words that come to mind when you hear the phrase "going green." Look over this list closely. Then write a quick analysis of the stereotypical assumptions or associations these terms raise.

5. Jacobs cites the following study to support his claim: "322 people recruited online examined one of two versions of a fund-raising pitch from an environmental organization. Half saw a version in

which 'the organization was named Friends of Nature, the logo was green and light tan with a tree symbol, the font was frilly, and the mission was described in terms of preserving nature areas.'. . . The other half saw a version in which 'the organization was named Wilderness Rangers, the logo was black and dark blue with a howling wolf symbol, the font was bold and lacked frills, and the mission was described in terms of preserving wilderness areas' " (p. 79). In an essay, describe how you interpret these results. What point does this study prove? How important is this point? Does it change your own views about environmentalism?

COMPARING ARGUMENTS

6. For Naomi Klein (p. 70), the threat of global warming is so dire that it demands a complete transformation of our economic and political system. Do you think Klein would consider Jacobs's essay to be a useful tool in this effort? Do you think she would find the argument Jacobs makes about environmentalism and gender, or the studies he cites to support this argument, particularly helpful? Why or why not?

Scenes and Un-Scenes: *Political Protest*

There is a long and storied tradition in America of robust social protest. From the Boston Tea Party to the women's suffrage movement, antisegregation campaigns to abortion rights rallies, civil rights demonstrations to Black Lives Matter and the Women's March, our national history is replete with efforts to challenge the practices and beliefs that, at one time or another, have stood as unexamined norms. But how do these public demonstrations actually succeed — if indeed they do — in rewriting beliefs that, for any given era, have become so embedded and entrenched? The short answer, of course, is that these beliefs were never quite as universal as they may have appeared. Bringing together people who felt marginalized or oppressed by a given societal norm, these demonstrations were designed to challenge the beliefs on which such norms rested, to offer up for scrutiny the embedded practices and unspoken assumptions that justified the status quo. For each of the following examples, how fully would you say this objective is achieved? What particular beliefs does each put on display? What social scripts does each attempt to rewrite?

CNP/Contributor/Getty Images

▲▲ *Even today, the civil rights movement led by Martin Luther King Jr. in the 1960s still stands as a model for how Americans think about social or political protest. The tradition of public, nonviolent protest that King pioneered persists within the public imagination as the blueprint for how "the people" can affect not only tangible changes in public policy but also meaningful shifts in social attitude. The famous 1963 March on Washington, for example, marks a watershed both for efforts to create new civil rights legislation and for the struggle to challenge and undo long-standing public attitudes about race.*

David McNew/Getty Images

▲▲ *The Black Lives Matter movement sought to carry forward King's standard of public, nonviolent protest into the present day. At the same time, though, such spectacles make evident how much has changed over the last forty plus years. In updating King's messages for our contemporary media-driven age, for example, it reminds us how different the tactics of public protest have become. Availing itself of the same tools we might find at a sporting event or rock concert, this image shows how deeply shaped by our media culture political protest is these days.*

Justin Sullivan/Getty Images

≪ Over the years, in fact, King's legacy has moved well beyond the realm of racial politics, coming to underlie and inform all manner of different causes. His tradition of public, nonviolent protest as well as his rhetoric of civil and social rights have long been adopted by a variety of other constituencies and used to advance a host of other interests. Not surprisingly, this has led to the marriage of these tactics to a number of seemingly unlikely causes. We might well wonder, for example, what particular "right" a celebrity-studded, Scientology-sponsored demonstration against the use of antidepressants is meant to advance. When you compare this spectacle to the March on Washington, how much commonality do you discern?

The legacy of the civil rights ≫ movement extends even to the financial realm, informing recent efforts to challenge and critique the role the financial industry played in causing the global recession. This image captures a moment from the Occupy Wall Street protests. To what extent does the Occupy movement reflect the core values of King's legacy?

Stan Honda/Getty Images

Alex Wong/Getty Images

▲▲ *Another arena in which King's tradition of public demonstration and civil rights protest has been taken up in recent years is gay rights — in particular, the much-publicized issue of gay marriage. In ways large and small, proponents of this movement have sought to model their efforts along the lines of the African American struggle for justice and equality before the law. Deploying some of the same rhetoric, many have framed the demand for legalized marriage as a natural extension of King's work. Do you agree with this analogy?*

FOR A SECOND READING

1. Which of these protests raises an issue that most resonates with your personal experience? Which one touches on an issue or conflict in which you feel a personal stake? To what extent does its critique reflect your own views?

2. Choose one of the previous examples. In what ways does this protest seem designed to affect or alter a fundamental cultural belief?

3. What political or social controversy does this collection leave out? What protest would you add to this list, and what in your view would make it worthy of inclusion?

PUTTING IT INTO WRITING

4. Choose something from our popular culture (e.g., website, a television show, a commercial, a movie, or the like) that shows an example of a political or social protest challenging a particular societal rule. Describe how this protest gets depicted. How are the protesters presented? What specific issues or ideas are offered up for critique? How do the symbols match or differ from the images you've viewed in this feature? How compelling or convincing do you find this depiction? Why?

5. Choose one of the images above that offers a blueprint for social protest that you yourself would not follow. Identify and evaluate the particular aspects of this protest that you find problematic, inadequate, or otherwise ineffective. Then use this critique to create a model of the kind of protest you would endorse. What different sorts of tactics would your model utilize? What different objectives would it attempt to achieve? And finally, what, in your estimation, makes this alternative more preferable?

6. The role of social protest in our culture has gone a long way toward normalizing certain issues. In what ways can Bryan Stevenson's discussion of the criminal justice system (p. 58) or Michael Sandel's reflections on the marketplace (p. 26) be read as their own forms of social protest? To what extent do their arguments challenge prevailing social scripts or underlying cultural norms?

Acting Like a Citizen: **Re-Scripting Belief**

The chapter selections above do more than simply present views on particular issues. Each addresses its issue with an expectation that readers will not only be persuaded by the argument presented, but also be motivated to *act*. Determining what action an argument asks us to take, and considering whether such action is reasonable, beneficial, or ethical, is critical to playing our role as a citizen. The following exercises give you an opportunity to play this role. Focusing on a setting in which a particular set of cultural beliefs gets scripted, each activity invites you to take action by reconsidering and revising the values these beliefs promote as the normal.

SURVEYING OURSELVES   How do you think "normal" Americans think? Visit the Gallup Poll website (www.galluppoll.com) and look at the home page. Choose two or three topics from the toolbar at the top of the page and decide how you would answer the survey questions posed. Write an essay in which you compare your beliefs to those of the American majority. Are you "normal" or are you "different"? How do you respond to being categorized in either of those groups?

MARKETING BELIEF   Choose some venue or organization that you think actively works to promote or market a set of beliefs to the general public (e.g., a church, a military recruitment center, a campus activist group, or a similar group). Research the ways that this group advertises itself to the larger community. Write an essay in which you explore what tactics the group uses to court new members. What symbols does it use in its advertising? What language do these ads include that is designed to inspire new believers?

SELL IT   Try combining the two activities above. Choose one of the survey topics you wrote about in the first assignment and design an ad you think would be effective in appealing to nonbelievers. This ad could be anything from a speech to a commercial or billboard. What images or language do you believe is most important in convincing others to follow the particular belief you've chosen?

NYC Girls Project

PRINTER FRIENDLY   EMAIL A FRIEND   TRANSLATE PAGE   TEXT SIZE: A A A

GO

Home

About NYC Girls Project

The Issues

The Campaign

Public Service Announcement

Additional Resources

Welcome to NYC Girls Project

I'M A GIRL

I'M A LEADER, ADVENTUROUS, OUTGOING, SPORTY, UNIQUE, SMART AND STRONG.

I'M BEAUTIFUL THE WAY I AM

This fall, New York City becomes the first major city in the nation to tackle the issue of girls' self-esteem and body image. Recognizing that girls as young as 6 and 7 are struggling with body image and self-esteem, New York City is launching a self-esteem initiative to help girls believe their value comes from their character, skills, and attributes – not appearance.

Partner Agencies

» The Human Resources Administration
» The Center for Economic Opportunity
» The NYC Commission on Women's Issues
» The Administration for Children's Services
» The Department of Youth and Community Development
» The Department of Education

Founded in 2013, the NYC Girls Project is an initiative dedicated to "tackling the issue of girls' self-esteem and body image." Take a closer look at this screenshot of the NYC Girls Project website. Then answer the following questions:

⊃ What cultural messages do young girls receive about how to view their bodies?

⊃ In what ways does the NYC Girls Project challenge these messages?

⊃ Does this website create a different script for how girls can view their own bodies?

⊃ What specific elements in this website would you point to as evidence of this?

2 How We
WATCH AND LISTEN
Does What We See and Hear Depend On How We're Looking and Listening?

Introduction

PAYING ATTENTION

We hear over and over these days that we live in an era of "distraction." Burying our heads in our digital devices, furiously skipping from one link, post, or site to another, Americans seem to have lost the ability to pay close, sustained attention to the world around them. But these worried commentaries often overlook the fact that our new ways of processing the world — new ways of absorbing all that we see and hear — represent less the loss of attention than its redirection into different channels. Today we are more likely to get our information from an online video or an Instagram post, a Twitter feed or a favorite podcast, than from the 6 o'clock evening news or the morning newspaper. And while the rivers of information flooding our senses can sometimes feel overwhelming, this doesn't mean that our ability to navigate them has been washed away.

For all its volume, variety, and velocity, our modern communications environment is still governed by certain standards and expectations — unspoken rules that guide how we are supposed to process all that we see and hear. Take, for example, reality television. Chief among the rules in place here is the expectation that viewers will treat these shows as a snapshot of reality, a glimpse into the personal lives of real people in real situations feeling real emotions. And yet at the same time we know that the version of reality being presented has been carefully orchestrated, scripted, and edited. We know, in other words, that by the rules of reality TV, not everything counts as equally "real." As viewers, we learn to expect only certain character types, certain relationships, and certain kinds of conflict. We learn that performing our expected role involves accepting as "reality" only what these shows tells us is important. We learn to view *selectively*.

This same experience applies to a good deal more than reality television. Indeed, few things are more selectively scripted than the ways we are taught to watch and listen. Whether it is the selfies that pop up on our phones, the billboards we drive past on the highway, the music we stream, or the podcasts we download, we are encouraged to consume our society's vast cultural output in very particular ways. So natural have such acts of consumption come to feel, however, that we sometimes miss the larger implication: at the same time we are being taught how to *watch and listen*, we are also being taught how to *think* — about ourselves and the wider world around us.

Imagine, for example, a commercial for a luxury car. Because we have grown so accustomed to this type of promotion, we don't need any explicit instructions reminding us how we are supposed to respond to the visual imagery, interpret the voice-over narration, or react to the accompanying soundtrack. Through our repeated exposure to examples just like it, we have internalized this form of cultural consumption. And because we have learned this role so well, we also know exactly what this commercial wants us to think. We know, for example, that eye-catching footage of the car's lush interior is our invitation to imagine a specific type of person sitting behind the wheel — a person with a certain kind of look (young, fit, fashionable); a certain kind of lifestyle (yuppie professional); a particular circle of friends (similarly young, fit, and fashionable); and a certain level of income (comfortably upper middle class). And we further know that, by imagining this hypothetical driver, we are also expected to admire the ideals of attractiveness and wealth, status and success, he symbolizes.

This same formula underlies countless of our encounters across the cultural spectrum, turning the ever-expanding universe of shows and songs, websites and videos, into a virtual classroom where we are told to focus our attention selectively so that we learn to tell the difference between what really matters and what actually doesn't. Whether we are catching the tail end of a presidential press conference or watching footage of a natural disaster, streaming the latest political spoof on YouTube or retweeting photos from the Academy Awards, we are always navigating cultural expectations about what is and isn't worthy of our attention. As we do so, however, we want to give thought to the kinds of value judgments these expectations encourage us to pass. Which ways of looking and listening get scripted as normal? And how do these scripts, in turn, shape the conclusions we are taught to draw about each other?

It is this connection — between how we are taught to look and listen on the one hand, and how we are taught to think and feel on the other — that each of the selections in this chapter invites you to consider. The first set of paired readings takes up this connection by focusing on the scripts that teach us how to view and judge each other's bodies. In recounting her debate with famed medical ethicist Peter Singer,

What is normal?

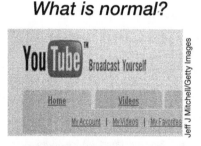

Jeff J Mitchell/Getty Images

What does this logo ask you to believe? What are the ideas/values/ attitudes it asks you to accept as normal?

What is normal?

Tabloids like *US Weekly* tell us, "Stars are just like us!"

Alo Ceballos/Getty Images

Do you share this belief? Should we automatically accept it as normal?

What is normal?

"Their hope is not to be condemned to live in loneliness, excluded from one of civilization's oldest institutions. They ask for equal dignity in the eyes of the law. The Constitution grants them that right."

U.S. Supreme Court Justice Anthony Kennedy, ruling on the constitutionality of same-sex marriage in a 2015 decision.

AFP/Getty Images

What kind of social script does this quotation advocate? What would it feel like to act out this script in our personal lives?

What is normal?

"Under observation, we act less free, which means we effectively are less free."

Former national security worker Edward Snowden on US government surveillance programs.

Bryan Bedder/Getty Images

Can social scripts be rewritten? What alternative norms does this quotation promote?

Harriet McBryde Johnson, an American with disabilities, offers a startlingly blunt and thought-provoking meditation on what it means to be viewed — and stereotyped — as the "token cripple." Deepening this focus on our culture's visual norms, Lindy West looks back on her childhood experiences being viewed and stigmatized as a "big girl." The second set of paired readings examine the gendered implications of our culture's visual norms by exploring them within the context of our modern media. Heather Havrilesky looks at the increasing use of the term *girl* to describe female characters on television. In what ways, she asks, does this term frame and/or limit our understanding of female experience and female power? Steve Almond, meanwhile, takes a closer look at the hypermasculinity underlying the role of the sports fan, making a passionate argument about the moral pitfalls of watching professional football. Shifting gears, the next two writers, Amanda Hess and Tiffanie Wen, present essays that take up the question of how we are taught to listen. Taking note of a prevalent hostility among some podcast and radio listeners toward women's voices, Hess speculates whether this phenomenon might be related to the increasing prospect of female power. Wen, on the other hand, explores what we might think of as the flip side of this phenomenon: the ways that podcasts can provide listeners with an enhanced sense of emotional well-being. And finally, Tom Vanderbilt and Kevin Fallon round out our paired selections by exploring the question of cultural consumption more generally. Vanderbilt takes stock of the powerful, if often invisible, cultural forces that shape our personal taste, while Fallon attempts to make sense of the growing popularity of "binge-watching."

HARRIET McBRYDE JOHNSON
Unspeakable Conversations

What does it mean to be tokenized, to have the stereotypes based on how we look become the scripts by which others think about and define us? In recounting her two-day experience playing the role of what she calls the "token cripple" on a Princeton University visit, Harriet McBryde Johnson raises a series of provocative questions about the ways in which our physical appearance comes to stand as definitive proof of who and what we are. Johnson practiced law in Charleston, South Carolina. She earned a BS in history from Charleston Southern University (1978), a master's in public administration from the College of Charleston (1981), and a JD from the University of South Carolina (1985). She wrote about political and disability issues for a number of publications, such as *South Carolina Lawyer* and *Review of Public Personnel Administration.* She also wrote a novel titled *Accidents of Nature* (2006). Johnson died on June 4, 2008. This piece was first published in the *New York Times* in 2003.

Before You Read

What stereotypes about the physically disabled would you say our culture reinforces? How do these stereotypes teach us to see people with physical disabilities? How do you think these visual scripts should be rewritten?

HE INSISTS HE DOESN'T WANT TO KILL ME. HE SIMPLY THINKS IT would have been better, all things considered, to have given my parents the option of killing the baby I once was, and to let other parents kill similar babies as they come along and thereby avoid the suffering that comes with lives like mine and satisfy the reasonable preferences of parents for a different kind of child. It has nothing to do with me. I should not feel threatened.

Whenever I try to wrap my head around his tight string of syllogisms, my brain gets so fried it's . . . almost fun. Mercy! It's like *Alice in Wonderland.*

It is a chilly Monday in late March, just less than a year ago. I am at Princeton University.

My host is Prof. Peter Singer, often called—and not just by his book publicist—the most influential philosopher of our time. He is the man who wants me dead. No, that's not at all fair. He wants to legalize the killing of certain babies who might come to be like me if allowed to live. He also says he believes that it should be lawful under some circumstances to kill, at any age, individuals with cognitive impairments so severe that he doesn't consider them "persons." What does it take to be a person? Awareness of your own existence in time. The capacity to harbor preferences as to the future, including the preference for continuing to live.

5   At this stage of my life, he says, I am a person. However, as an infant, I wasn't. I, like all humans, was born without self-awareness. And eventually, assuming my brain finally gets so fried that I fall into that wonderland where self and other and present and past and future blur into one boundless, formless all or nothing, then I'll lose my personhood and therefore my right to life. Then, he says, my family and doctors might put me out of my misery, or out of my bliss or oblivion, and no one count it murder.

> ### *My host is Prof. Peter Singer. . . . He is the man who wants me dead.*

I have agreed to two speaking engagements. In the morning, I talk to 150 undergraduates on selective infanticide. In the evening, it is a convivial discussion, over dinner, of assisted suicide. I am the token cripple with an opposing view.

I had several reasons for accepting Singer's invitation, some grounded in my involvement in the disability rights movement, others entirely personal. For the movement it seemed an unusual opportunity to experiment with modes of discourse that might work with very tough audiences and bridge the divide between our perceptions and theirs. I didn't expect to straighten out Singer's head. But maybe I could reach a student or two. Among the personal reasons: I was sure it would make a great story, first for telling and then for writing down.

By now I've told it to family and friends and colleagues, over lunches and dinners, on long car trips, in scads of e-mail messages and a couple of formal speeches. But it seems to be a story that just won't settle down. After all these tellings, it still lacks a coherent structure; I'm miles away from a rational argument. I keep getting interrupted by questions like these:

Q: Was he totally grossed out by your physical appearance?

A: He gave no sign of it. None whatsoever.

Q: How did he handle having to interact with someone like you?

A: He behaved in every way appropriately and treated me as a respected professional acquaintance and was a gracious and accommodating host.

Q: Was it emotionally difficult for you to take part in a public discussion of whether your life should have happened?

A: It was very difficult. And horribly easy.

Q: Did he get that job at Princeton because they like his ideas on killing disabled babies?

A: It apparently didn't hurt. But he's most famous for animal rights. He's the author of *Animal Liberation*.

Q: How can he put so much value on animal life and so little value on human life?

That last question is the only one I avoid. I used to say I don't know; it doesn't make sense. But now I've read some of Singer's writing, and I admit it does make sense—within the conceptual world of Peter Singer. But I don't want to go there. Or at least not for long.

So I will start from those other questions and see where the story 10 goes this time.

That first question, about my physical appearance, needs some explaining.

It's not that I'm ugly. It's more that most people don't know how to look at me. The sight of me is routinely discombobulating. The power wheelchair is enough to inspire gawking, but that's the least of it. Much more impressive is the impact on my body of more than four decades of a muscle-wasting disease. At this stage of my life, I'm Karen Carpenter thin, flesh mostly vanished, a jumble of bones in a floppy bag of skin. When, in childhood, my muscles got too weak to hold up my spine, I tried a brace for a while, but fortunately a skittish anesthesiologist said no to fusion, plates, and pins—all the apparatus that might have kept me straight. At 15, I threw away the back brace and let my spine reshape itself into a deep twisty S-curve. Now my right side is two deep canyons. To keep myself upright, I lean forward, rest my rib cage on my lap, plant my elbows beside my knees. Since my backbone found its own natural shape, I've been entirely comfortable in my skin.

I am in the first generation to survive to such decrepitude. Because antibiotics were available, we didn't die from the childhood pneumonias that often come with weakened respiratory systems. I guess it is natural enough that most people don't know what to make of us.

> *It's not that I'm ugly. It's more that most people don't know how to look at me.*

Two or three times in my life—I recall particularly one largely crip, largely lesbian cookout halfway across the continent—I have been looked at as a rare kind of beauty. There is also the bizarre fact that where I live, Charleston, S.C., some people call me Good Luck Lady: they consider it propitious to cross my path when a hurricane is coming and to kiss my head just before voting day. But most often, the reactions are decidedly negative. Strangers on the street are moved to comment:

I admire you for being out; most people would give up.
God bless you! I'll pray for you.
You don't let the pain hold you back, do you?
If I had to live like you, I think I'd kill myself.

15   I used to try to explain that in fact I enjoy my life, that it's a great sensual pleasure to zoom by power chair on these delicious muggy streets, that I have no more reason to kill myself than most people. But it gets tedious. God didn't put me on this street to provide disability awareness training to the likes of them. In fact, no god put anyone anywhere for any reason, if you want to know.

But they don't want to know. They think they know everything there is to know, just by looking at me. That's how stereotypes work. They don't know that they're confused. That they're really expressing the discombobulation that comes in my wake.

So. What stands out when I recall first meeting Peter Singer in the spring of 2001 is his apparent immunity to my looks. His apparent lack of discombobulation, his immediate ability to deal with me as a person with a particular point of view.

Then, 2001. Singer has been invited to the College of Charleston, not two blocks from my house. He is to lecture on "Rethinking Life and Death." I have been dispatched by Not Dead Yet, the national organization leading the disability-rights opposition to legalized assisted suicide and disability-based killing. I am to put out a leaflet and do something during the Q and A.

On arriving almost an hour early to reconnoiter, I find the scene almost entirely peaceful; even the boisterous display of South Carolina spring is muted by gray wisps of Spanish moss and mottled oak bark.

20   I roll around the corner of the building and am confronted with the unnerving sight of two people I know sitting on a park bench eating veggie pitas with Singer. Sharon is a veteran activist for human rights. Herb is South Carolina's most famous atheist. Good people, I've always thought—now sharing veggie pitas and conversation with a proponent of genocide. I try to beat a retreat, but Herb and Sharon have seen me. Sharon tosses her trash and comes over. After we exchange the usual courtesies she asks, "Would you like to meet Professor Singer?"

She doesn't have a clue. She probably likes his book on animal rights. "I'll just talk to him in the Q and A."

But Herb, with Singer at his side, is fast approaching. They are looking at me, and Herb is talking, no doubt saying nice things about me. He'll be saying that I'm a disability rights lawyer and that I gave a talk against assisted suicide at his secular humanist group a while back. He didn't agree with everything I said, he'll say, but I was brilliant. Singer appears interested, engaged. I sit where I'm parked. Herb makes an introduction. Singer extends his hand.

I hesitate. I shouldn't shake hands with the Evil One. But he is Herb's guest, and I simply can't snub Herb's guest at the college where Herb teaches. Hereabouts, the rule is that if you're not prepared to shoot on sight, you have to be prepared to shake hands. I give Singer the three fingers on my right hand that still work. "Good afternoon, Mr. Singer. I'm here for Not Dead Yet." I want to think he flinches just a little. Not Dead Yet did everything possible to disrupt his first week at Princeton. I sent a check to the fund for the 14 arrestees, who included comrades in power chairs. But if Singer flinches, he instantly recovers. He answers my questions about the lecture format. When he says he looks forward to an interesting exchange, he seems entirely sincere.

It is an interesting exchange. In the lecture hall that afternoon, Singer lays it all out. The "illogic" of allowing abortion but not infanticide, of allowing withdrawal of life support but not active killing. Applying the basic assumptions of preference utilitarianism, he spins out his bone-chilling argument for letting parents kill disabled babies and replace them with nondisabled babies who have a greater chance at happiness. It is all about allowing as many individuals as possible to fulfill as many of their preferences as possible.

As soon as he's done, I get the microphone and say I'd like to discuss 25 selective infanticide. As a lawyer, I disagree with his jurisprudential assumptions. Logical inconsistency is not a sufficient reason to change the law. As an atheist, I object to his using religious terms ("the doctrine of the sanctity of human life") to characterize his critics. Singer takes a note pad out of his pocket and jots down my points, apparently eager to take them on, and I proceed to the heart of my argument: that the presence or absence of a disability doesn't predict quality of life. I question his replacement-baby theory, with its assumption of "other things equal," arguing that people are not fungible. I draw out a comparison of myself and my nondisabled brother Mac (the next-born after me), each of us with a combination of gifts and flaws so peculiar that we can't be measured on the same scale.

He responds to each point with clear and lucid counterarguments. He proceeds with the assumption that I am one of the people who might rightly have been killed at birth. He sticks to his guns, conceding just enough to show himself open-minded and flexible. We go back and forth for 10 long minutes. Even as I am horrified by what he says, and by the fact that I have been sucked into a civil discussion of whether I ought to exist, I can't help being dazzled by his verbal facility. He is so respectful, so free of condescension, so focused on the argument, that by the time the show is over, I'm not exactly angry with him. Yes, I am shaking, furious, enraged—but it's for the big room, 200 of my fellow Charlestonians who have listened with polite interest, when in decency they should have run him out of town on a rail.

My encounter with Peter Singer merits a mention in my annual canned letter that December. I decide to send Singer a copy. In response, he sends me the nicest possible e-mail message. Dear Harriet (if he may) . . . Just back from Australia, where he's from. Agrees with my comments on the world situation. Supports my work against institutionalization. And then some pointed questions to clarify my views on selective infanticide.

I reply. Fine, call me Harriet, and I'll reciprocate in the interest of equality, though I'm accustomed to more formality. Skipping agreeable preambles, I answer his questions on disability-based infanticide and pose some of my own. Answers and more questions come back. Back and forth over several weeks it proceeds, an engaging discussion of baby killing, disability prejudice, and related points of law and philosophy. Dear Harriet. Dear Peter.

Singer seems curious to learn how someone who is as good an atheist as he is could disagree with his entirely reasonable views. At the same time, I am trying to plumb his theories. What has him so convinced it would be best to allow parents to kill babies with severe disabilities, and not other kinds of babies if no infant is a "person" with a right to life? I learn it is partly that both biological and adoptive parents prefer

Imagine a disabled child on the beach, watching the other children play.

healthy babies. But I have trouble with basing life-and-death decisions on market considerations when the market is structured by prejudice. I offer a hypothetical comparison: "What about mixed-race babies, especially when the combination is entirely nonwhite, who I believe are just about as unadoptable as babies with disabilities?" Wouldn't a law allowing the killing of these undervalued babies validate race prejudice? Singer agrees there is a problem. "It would be horrible," he says, "to see mixed-race babies being killed because they can't be adopted, whereas white ones could be." What's the difference? Preferences based on race are unreasonable. Preferences based on ability are not. Why? To Singer, it's pretty simple: disability makes a person "worse off."

30   Are we "worse off"? I don't think so. Not in any meaningful sense. There are too many variables. For those of us with congenital conditions, disability shapes all we are. Those disabled later in life adapt. We take constraints that no one would choose and build rich and satisfying lives within them. We enjoy pleasures other people enjoy, and pleasures peculiarly our own. We have something the world needs.

Pressing me to admit a negative correlation between disability and happiness, Singer presents a situation: imagine a disabled child on the beach, watching the other children play.

It's right out of the telethon. I expected something more sophisticated from a professional thinker. I respond: "As a little girl playing on the beach, I was already aware that some people felt sorry for me, that I wasn't frolicking with the same level of frenzy as other children. This annoyed me, and still does." I take the time to write a detailed description of how I, in fact, had fun playing on the beach, without the need of standing, walking, or running. But, really, I've had enough. I suggest to Singer that we have exhausted our topic, and I'll be back in touch when I get around to writing about him.

He responds by inviting me to Princeton. I fire off an immediate maybe.

Of course I'm flattered. Mama will be impressed.

But there are things to consider. Not Dead Yet says—and I com- 35
pletely agree—that we should not legitimate Singer's views by giving them a forum. We should not make disabled lives subject to debate. Moreover, any spokesman chosen by the opposition is by definition a token. But even if I'm a token, I won't have to act like one. Anyway, I'm kind of stuck. If I decline, Singer can make some hay: "I offered them a platform, but they refuse rational discussion." It's an old trick, and I've laid myself wide open.

My invitation is to have an exchange of views with Singer during his undergraduate course. He also proposes a second "exchange," open to the whole university, later in the day. This sounds a lot like debating my life—and on my opponent's turf, with my opponent moderating, to boot. I offer a counterproposal, to which Singer proves amenable. I will open the class with some comments on infanticide and related issues and then let Singer grill me as hard as he likes before we open it up for the students. Later in the day, I might take part in a discussion of some other disability issue in a neutral forum. Singer suggests a faculty-student discussion group sponsored by his department but with cross-departmental membership. The topic I select is "Assisted Suicide, Disability Discrimination, and the Illusion of Choice: A Disability Rights Perspective." I inform a few movement colleagues of this turn of events, and advice starts rolling in. I decide to go with the advisers who counsel me to do the gig, lie low, and get out of Dodge.

I ask Singer to refer me to the person who arranges travel at Princeton. I imagine some capable and unflappable woman like my sister, Beth, whose varied job description at a North Carolina university includes handling visiting artists. Singer refers me to his own assistant, who certainly seems capable and unflappable enough. However, almost immediately Singer jumps back in via e-mail. It seems the nearest hotel has only one wheelchair-accessible suite, available with two rooms for $600 per night. What to do? I know I shouldn't be so accommodating, but I say I can make do with an inaccessible room if it has certain features. Other logistical issues come up. We go back and forth. Questions and answers. Do I really need a lift-equipped vehicle at the airport? Can't my assistant assist me into a conventional car? How wide is my wheelchair?

By the time we're done, Singer knows that I am 28 inches wide. I have trouble controlling my wheelchair if my hand gets cold. I am accustomed to driving on rough, irregular surfaces, but I get nervous turning on steep slopes. Even one step is too many. I can swallow purées, soft bread, and grapes. I use a bedpan, not a toilet. None of this is a secret; none of it cause for angst. But I do wonder whether Singer is jotting down my specs in his little note pad as evidence of how "bad off" people like me really are.

I realize I must put one more issue on the table: etiquette. I was criticized within the movement when I confessed to shaking Singer's hand in Charleston, and some are appalled that I have agreed to break bread with him in Princeton. I think they have a very good point, but, again, I'm stuck. I'm engaged for a day of discussion, not a picket line. It is not in my power to marginalize Singer at Princeton; nothing would be accomplished by displays of personal disrespect. However, chumminess is clearly inappropriate. I tell Singer that in the lecture hall it can't be Harriet and Peter; it must be Ms. Johnson and Mr. Singer.

40   He seems genuinely nettled. Shouldn't it be Ms. Johnson and Professor Singer, if I want to be formal? To counter, I invoke the ceremonial low-country usage, Attorney Johnson and Professor Singer, but point out that Mr./Ms. is the custom in American political debates and might seem more normal in New Jersey. All right, he says. Ms./Mr. it will be.

I describe this awkward social situation to the lawyer in my office who has served as my default lunch partner for the past 14 years. He gives forth a full-body shudder.

"That poor, sorry son of a bitch! He has no idea what he's in for."

Being a disability rights lawyer lecturing at Princeton does confer some cachet at the Newark airport. I need all the cachet I can get. Delta Airlines has torn up my power chair. It is a fairly frequent occurrence for any air traveler on wheels.

When they inform me of the damage in Atlanta, I throw a monumental fit and tell them to have a repair person meet me in Newark with new batteries to replace the ones inexplicably destroyed. Then I am told no new batteries can be had until the morning. It's Sunday night. On arrival in Newark, I'm told of a plan to put me up there for the night and get me repaired and driven to Princeton by 10 A.M.

45   "That won't work. I'm lecturing at 10. I need to get there tonight, go to sleep, and be in my right mind tomorrow."

"What? You're lecturing? They told us it was a conference. We need to get you fixed tonight!"

Carla, the gate agent, relieves me of the need to throw any further fits by undertaking on my behalf the fit of all fits.

Carmen, the personal assistant with whom I'm traveling, pushes me in my disabled chair around the airport in search of a place to use the bedpan. However, instead of diaper-changing tables, which are functional though far from private, we find a flip-down plastic shelf that doesn't look like it would hold my 70 pounds of body weight. It's no big deal; I've restricted my fluids. But Carmen is a little freaked. It is her first adventure in power-chair air travel. I thought I prepared her for the trip, but I guess I neglected to warn her about the probability of wheelchair destruction. I keep forgetting that even people who know me well don't know much about my world.

We reach the hotel at 10:15 P.M., four hours late.

I wake up tired. I slept better than I would have slept in Newark with   50
an unrepaired chair, but any hotel bed is a near guarantee of morning crankiness. I tell Carmen to leave the TV off. I don't want to hear the temperature.

I do the morning stretch. Medical people call it passive movement, but it's not really passive. Carmen's hands move my limbs, following my precise instructions, her strength giving effect to my will. Carmen knows the routine, so it is in near silence that we begin easing slowly into the day. I let myself be propped up to eat oatmeal and drink tea.

> **I keep forgetting that even people who know me well don't know much about my world.**

Then there's the bedpan and then bathing and dressing, still in bed. As the caffeine kicks in, silence gives way to conversation about practical things. Carmen lifts me into my chair and straps a rolled towel under my ribs for comfort and stability. She tugs at my clothes to remove wrinkles that could cause pressure sores. She switches on my motors and gives me the means of moving without anyone's help. They don't call it a power chair for nothing.

I drive to the mirror. I do my hair in one long braid. Even this primal hairdo requires, at this stage of my life, joint effort. I undo yesterday's braid. Fix the part and comb the hair in front. Carmen combs where I can't reach. I divide the mass into three long hanks and start the braid just behind my left ear. Section by section, I hand it over to her, and her unimpaired young fingers pull tight, crisscross, until the braid is fully formed.

A big polyester scarf completes my costume. Carmen lays it over my back. I tie it the way I want it, but Carmen starts fussing with it, trying to tuck it down in the back. I tell her that it's fine, and she stops.

On top of the scarf, she wraps the two big shawls that I hope will substitute for an overcoat. I don't own any real winter clothes. I just stay out of the cold, such cold as we get in Charleston.

We review her instructions for the day. Keep me in view and earshot.   55
Be instantly available but not intrusive. Be polite, but don't answer any questions about me. I am glad that she has agreed to come. She's strong, smart, adaptable, and very loyal. But now she is digging under the shawls, fussing with that scarf again.

"Carmen. What are you doing?"

"I thought I could hide this furry thing you sit on."

"Leave it. Singer knows lots of people eat meat. Now he'll know some crips sit on sheepskin."

The walk in is cold but mercifully short. The hotel is just across the street from Princeton's wrought-iron gate and a few short blocks from the building where Singer's assistant shows us to the elevator. The elevator doubles as the janitor's closet—the cart with the big trash can and all the accouterments is rolled aside so I can get in. Evidently, there aren't a lot of wheelchair people using this building.

60 We ride the broom closet down to the basement and are led down a long passageway to a big lecture hall. As the students drift in, I engage in light badinage with the sound technician. He is squeamish about touching me, but I insist that the cordless lavaliere is my mike of choice. I invite him to clip it to the big polyester scarf.

The students enter from the rear door, way up at ground level and walk down stairs to their seats. I feel like an animal in the zoo. I hadn't reckoned on the architecture, those tiers of steps that separate me from a human wall of apparent physical and mental perfection, that keep me confined down here in my pit.

It is 5 before 10. Singer is loping down the stairs. I feel like signaling to Carmen to open the door, summon the broom closet, and get me out of here. But Singer greets me pleasantly and hands me Princeton's check for $500, the fee he offered with apologies for its inadequacy.

So. On with the show.

My talk to the students is pretty Southern. I've decided to pound them with heart, hammer them with narrative, and say "y'all" and "folks." I play with the emotional tone, giving them little peaks and valleys, modulating three times in one 45-second patch. I talk about justice. Even beauty and love. I figure they haven't been getting much of that from Singer.

65 Of course, I give them some argument too. I mean to honor my contractual obligations. I lead with the hypothetical about mixed-race, nonwhite babies and build the ending around the question of who should have the burden of proof as to the quality of disabled lives. And woven through the talk is the presentation of myself as a representative of a minority group that has been rendered invisible by prejudice and oppression, a participant in a discussion that would not occur in a just world.

I let it go a little longer than I should. Their faces show they're going where I'm leading, and I don't look forward to letting them go. But the clock on the wall reminds me of promises I mean to keep, and I stop talking and submit myself to examination and inquiry.

Singer's response is surprisingly soft. Maybe after hearing that this discussion is insulting and painful to me, he doesn't want to exacerbate my discomfort. His reframing of the issues is almost pro forma, abstract, entirely impersonal. Likewise, the students' inquiries are abstract and fairly predictable: anencephaly, permanent unconsciousness, eugenic abortion. I respond to some of them with stories, but mostly I give answers I could have e-mailed in.

I call on a young man near the top of the room.

"Do you eat meat?"

"Yes, I do." 70

"Then how do you justify—"

"I haven't made any study of animal rights, so anything I could say on the subject wouldn't be worth everyone's time."

The next student wants to work the comparison of disability and race, and Singer joins the discussion until he elicits a comment from me that he can characterize as racist. He scores a point, but that's all right. I've never claimed to be free of prejudice, just struggling with it.

Singer proposes taking me on a walk around campus, unless I think it would be too cold. What the hell? "It's probably warmed up some. Let's go out and see how I do."

He doesn't know how to get out of the building without using the 75 stairs, so this time it is my assistant leading the way. Carmen has learned of another elevator, which arrives empty. When we get out of the building, she falls behind a couple of paces, like a respectful chaperone.

In the classroom, there was a question about keeping alive the unconscious. In response, I told a story about a family I knew as a child, which took loving care of a nonresponsive teenage girl, acting out their unconditional commitment to each other, making all the other children, and me as their visitor, feel safe. This doesn't satisfy Singer. "Let's assume we can prove, absolutely, that the individual is totally unconscious and that we can know, absolutely, that the individual will never regain consciousness."

I see no need to state an objection with no stenographer present to record it; I'll play the game and let him continue.

"Assuming all that," he says, "don't you think continuing to take care of that individual would be a bit—weird?"

"No. Done right, it could be profoundly beautiful."

"But what about the caregiver, a woman typically, who is forced to 80 provide all this service to a family member, unable to work, unable to have a life of her own?"

"That's not the way it should be. Not the way it has to be. As a society, we should pay workers to provide that care, in the home. In some places, it's been done that way for years. That woman shouldn't be forced to do it, any more than my family should be forced to do my care."

Singer takes me around the architectural smorgasbord that is Princeton University by a route that includes not one step, unramped curb, or turn on a slope. Within the strange limits of this strange assignment, it seems Singer is doing all he can to make me comfortable.

He asks what I thought of the students' questions.

"They were fine, about what I expected. I was a little surprised by the question about meat eating."

85 "I apologize for that. That was out of left field. But—I think what he wanted to know is how you can have such high respect for human life and so little respect for animal life."

"People have lately been asking me the converse, how you can have so much respect for animal life and so little respect for human life."

"And what do you answer?"

"I say I don't know. It doesn't make a lot of sense to me."

"Well, in my view—"

90 "Look, I have lived in blissful ignorance all these years, and I'm not prepared to give that up today."

"Fair enough," he says and proceeds to recount bits of Princeton history. He stops. "This will be of particular interest to you, I think. This is where your colleagues with Not Dead Yet set up their blockade." I'm grateful for the reminder. My brothers and sisters were here before me and behaved far more appropriately than I am doing.

A van delivers Carmen and me early for the evening forum. Singer says he hopes I had a pleasant afternoon.

Yes, indeed. I report a pleasant lunch and a very pleasant nap, and I tell him about the Christopher Reeve Suite in the hotel, which has been remodeled to accommodate Reeve, who has family in the area.

"Do you suppose that's the $600 accessible suite they told me about?"

95 "Without doubt. And if I'd known it was the Christopher Reeve Suite, I would have held out for it."

"Of course you would have!" Singer laughs. "And we'd have had no choice, would we?"

We talk about the disability rights critique of Reeve and various other topics. Singer is easy to talk to, good company. Too bad he sees lives like mine as avoidable mistakes.

I'm looking forward to the soft vegetarian meal that has been arranged; I'm hungry. Assisted suicide, as difficult as it is, doesn't cause the kind of agony I felt discussing disability-based infanticide. In this one, I understand, and to some degree can sympathize with, the opposing point of view—misguided though it is.

My opening sticks to the five-minute time limit. I introduce the issue as framed by academic articles Not Dead Yet recommended for my use. Andrew Batavia argues for assisted suicide based on autonomy, a principle generally held high in the disability rights movement. In general, he says, the movement fights for our right to control our own lives; when we need assistance to effect our choices, assistance should be available to us as a matter of right. If the choice is to end our lives, he says, we should have assistance then as well. But Carol Gill says that it is differential treatment—disability discrimination—to try to prevent most suicides while facilitating the suicides of ill and disabled people. The social-science literature suggests that the public in general, and physicians in particular, tend to underestimate the quality of life of disabled people, compared with our own assessments of our lives. The case for assisted suicide rests on stereotypes that our lives are inherently so bad that it is entirely rational if we want to die.

100   I side with Gill. What worries me most about the proposals for legalized assisted suicide is their veneer of

The case for assisted suicide rests on stereotypes.

beneficence—the medical determination that, for a given individual, suicide is reasonable or right. It is not about autonomy but about nondisabled people telling us what's good for us.

In the discussion that follows, I argue that choice is illusory in a context of pervasive inequality. Choices are structured by oppression. We shouldn't offer assistance with suicide until we all have the assistance we need to get out of bed in the morning and live a good life. Common causes of suicidality—dependence, institutional confinement, being a burden—are entirely curable. Singer, seated on my right, participates in the discussion but doesn't dominate it. During the meal, I occasionally ask him to put things within my reach and he competently complies.

I feel as if I'm getting to a few of them, when a student asks me a question. The words are all familiar, but they're strung together in a way so meaningless that I can't even retain them—it's like a long sentence in Tagalog. I can only admit my limitations. "That question's too abstract for me to deal with. Can you rephrase it?"

He indicates that it is as clear as he can make it, so I move on.

A little while later my right elbow slips out from under me. This is awkward. Normally I get whoever is on my right to do this sort of thing. Why not now? I gesture to Singer. He leans over, and I whisper, "Grasp this wrist and pull forward one inch, without lifting." He follows my instructions to the letter. He sees that now I can again reach my food with my fork. And he may now understand what I was saying a minute ago, that most of the assistance disabled people need does not demand medical training.

A philosophy professor says, "It appears that your objections to   105 assisted suicide are essentially tactical."

"Excuse me?"

"By that I mean they are grounded in current conditions of political, social, and economic inequality. What if we assume that such conditions do not exist?"

"Why would we want to do that?"

"I want to get to the real basis for the position you take."

110   I feel as if I'm losing caste. It is suddenly very clear that I'm not a philosopher. I'm like one of those old practitioners who used to visit my law school, full of bluster about life in the real world. Such a bore! A once-sharp mind gone muddy! And I'm only 44—not all that old.

The forum is ended, and I've been able to eat very little of my puréed food. I ask Carmen to find the caterer and get me a container. Singer jumps up to take care of it. He returns with a box and obligingly packs my food to go.

When I get home, people are clamoring for the story. The lawyers want the blow-by-blow of my forensic triumph over the formidable foe; when I tell them it wasn't like that, they insist that it was. Within the disability rights community, there is less confidence. It is generally assumed that I handled the substantive discussion well, but people worry that my civility may have given Singer a new kind of legitimacy. I hear from Laura, a beloved movement sister. She is appalled that I let Singer provide even minor physical assistance at the dinner. "Where was your assistant?" she wants to know. How could I put myself in a relationship with Singer that made him appear so human, even kind?

I struggle to explain. I didn't feel disempowered; quite the contrary, it seemed a good thing to make him do some useful work. And then, the hard part: I've come to believe that Singer actually is human, even kind in his way. There ensues a discussion of good and evil and personal assistance and power and philosophy and tactics for which I'm profoundly grateful.

I e-mail Laura again. This time I inform her that I've changed my will. She will inherit a book that Singer gave me, a collection of his writings with a weirdly appropriate inscription: "To Harriet Johnson, So that you will have a better answer to questions about animals. And thanks for coming to Princeton. Peter Singer. March 25, 2002." She responds that she is changing her will, too. I'll get the autographed photo of Jerry Lewis she received as an M.D.A. poster child. We joke that each of us has given the other a "reason to live."

115   I have had a nice e-mail message from Singer, hoping Carmen and I and the chair got home without injury, relaying positive feedback from my audiences—and taking me to task for a statement that isn't supported by a relevant legal authority, which he looked up. I report that we got home exhausted but unharmed and concede that he has caught me

in a generalization that should have been qualified. It's clear that the conversation will continue.

I am soon sucked into the daily demands of law practice, family, community, and politics. In the closing days of the state legislative session, I help get a bill passed that I hope will move us one small step toward a world in which killing won't be such an appealing solution to the "problem" of disability. It is good to focus on this kind of work. But the conversations with and about Singer continue. Unable to muster the appropriate moral judgments, I ask myself a tough question: Am I in fact a silly little lady whose head is easily turned by a man who gives her a kind of attention she enjoys? I hope not, but I confess that I've never been able to sustain righteous anger for more than about 30 minutes at a time. My view of life tends more toward tragedy.

The tragic view comes closest to describing how I now look at Peter Singer. He is a man of unusual gifts, reaching for the heights. He writes that he is trying to create a system of ethics derived from fact and reason, that largely throws off the perspectives of religion, place, family, tribe, community, and maybe even species—to "take the point of view of the universe." His is a grand, heroic undertaking.

But like the protagonist in a classical drama, Singer has his flaw. It is his unexamined assumption that disabled people are inherently "worse off," that we "suffer," that we have lesser "prospects of a happy life." Because of this all-too-common prejudice, and his rare courage in taking it to its logical conclusion, catastrophe looms. Here in the midpoint of the play, I can't look at him without fellow-feeling.

I am regularly confronted by people who tell me that Singer doesn't deserve my human sympathy. I should make him an object of implacable wrath, to be cut off, silenced, destroyed absolutely. And I find myself lacking an argument to the contrary.

I am talking to my sister Beth on the phone. "You kind of like the monster, don't you?" she says.   120

I find myself unable to evade, certainly unwilling to lie. "Yeah, in a way. And he's not exactly a monster."

"You know, Harriet, there were some very pleasant Nazis. They say the SS guards went home and played on the floor with their children every night."

She can tell that I'm chastened; she changes the topic, lets me off the hook. Her harshness has come as a surprise. She isn't inclined to moralizing; in our family, I'm the one who sets people straight.

When I put the phone down, my argumentative nature feels frustrated. In my mind, I replay the conversation but this time defend my position.

"He's not exactly a monster. He just has some strange ways of look-   125
ing at things."

"He's advocating genocide."

"That's the thing. In his mind, he isn't. He's only giving parents a choice. He thinks the humans he is talking about aren't people, aren't 'persons.'"

"But that's the way it always works, isn't it? They're always animals or vermin or chattel goods. Objects, not persons. He's repacking some old ideas. Making them acceptable."

"I think his ideas are new, in a way. It's not old-fashioned hate. It's a twisted, misinformed, warped kind of beneficence. His motive is to do good."

130 "What do you care about motives?" she asks. "Doesn't this beneficent killing make disabled brothers and sisters just as dead?"

"But he isn't killing anyone. It's just talk."

"Just talk? It's talk with an agenda, talk aimed at forming policy. Talk that's getting a receptive audience. You of all people know the power of that kind of talk."

"Well, sure, but—"

"If talk didn't matter, would you make it your life's work?"

135 "But," I say, "his talk won't matter in the end. He won't succeed in reinventing morality. He stirs the pot, brings things out into the open. But ultimately, we'll make a world that's fit to live in, a society that has room for all its flawed creatures. History will remember Singer as a curious example of the bizarre things that can happen when paradigms collide."

"What if you're wrong? What if he convinces people that there's no morally significant difference between a fetus and a newborn, and just as disabled fetuses are routinely aborted now, so disabled babies are routinely killed? Might some future generation take it further than Singer wants to go? Might some say there's no morally significant line between a newborn and a 3-year-old?"

"Sure. Singer concedes that a bright line cannot be drawn. But he doesn't propose killing anyone who prefers to live."

"That overarching respect for the individual's preference for life—might some say it's a fiction, a fetish, a quasi-religious belief?"

"Yes," I say. "That's pretty close to what I think. As an atheist, I think all preferences are moot once you kill someone. The injury is entirely to the surviving community."

140 "So what if that view wins out, but you can't break disability prejudice? What if you wind up in a world where the disabled person's 'irrational' preference to live must yield to society's 'rational' interest in reducing the incidence of disability? Doesn't horror kick in somewhere? Maybe as you watch the door close behind whoever has wheeled you into the gas chamber?"

"That's not going to happen."

"Do you have empirical evidence?" she asks. "A logical argument?"

"Of course not. And I know it's happened before, in what was considered the most progressive medical community in the world. But it won't happen. I have to believe that."

Belief. Is that what it comes down to? Am I a person of faith after all? Or am I clinging to foolish hope that the tragic protagonist, this one time, will shift course before it's too late?

FOR A SECOND READING

1. Johnson devotes a good deal of time acquainting her readers with the facts about her disability, itemizing the various things that, as a result of her physical condition, she can and cannot do. Why do you think she does this? How does this tactic help her advance her argument about the ways disabled people are seen in our culture?

2. Based on Johnson's descriptions of her physical appearance, what do you think she looked like? How do you think she was perceived by the general public? In what ways does our popular culture encourage us both to see and *not* see people with disabilities? That is to say, how do the images of and stories about disability we typically see teach us to judge people with disabilities in particular ways?

3. To what extent is it valid to think of Johnson's account as expanding or enlarging the scope of the ways disabled people are conventionally seen? What quotes can you find from her essay to support your opinion?

PUTTING IT INTO WRITING

4. Spend some time reflecting on the specific language Johnson uses to describe her physical condition. Then write a 300-word essay in which you analyze the ways this language is designed to challenge the way people with physical disabilities are viewed. What specific cultural norms do you think this description is intended to challenge? How does Johnson's language differ from the kind typically used to describe one's physical appearance? What larger point about the way we are taught to "see" disabled people do you think this description is designed to convey? Make sure to include quotations from Johnson's essay to support your analysis.

5. Have you ever felt "tokenized" because of your physical or external appearance? When people first meet you, what assumptions do

you think they make about you based on your appearance? Write a personal essay (500 words) in which you recount what the experience of being seen in this particular way was like. What perceptions of you did people have? What conclusions did they draw? And in what ways were they inaccurate, unfair, or otherwise limiting? Use quotes from Johnson's essay to pinpoint both the parallels and the key differences between your own experience and what Johnson recounts in her essay.

COMPARING ARGUMENTS

6. Johnson and Lindy West (p. 111) share an interest in cultural stereotyping. Each of their essays acknowledges the ways people can be mislabeled or misread by the public at large, and how this experience can lead to disenfranchisement or marginalization. Write an essay in which you compare and contrast the ways these two writers explore this question. Despite their shared concern over stereotyping, where do their discussions diverge?

LINDY WEST
Bones

When it comes to our bodies, how big is "too big"? Who is given the power to draw these boundaries? And what happens when we find ourselves on the other side of this line? Taking up these questions, Lindy West recounts her own experiences growing up as a so-called big girl. Taking aim at the misguided and destructive assumptions behind this label, West makes a powerful argument for living outside of our culture's pernicious body norms. Lindy West is a journalist, author, and activist. A former staff writer for the feminist website Jezebel, her work has also appeared in *The Guardian*, *The New York Daily News*, and *Vulture*. She is also the author of *Shrill: Notes from a Loud Woman* (2016), from which this essay is excerpted.

Before You Read

Why does "bigness" get stigmatized in our culture? Why is transgressing this particular body norm considered so unacceptable?

I'VE ALWAYS BEEN A GREAT BIG PERSON. IN THE MONTHS AFTER I WAS born, the doctor was so alarmed by the circumference of my head that she insisted my parents bring me back, over and over, to be weighed and measured and held up for scrutiny next to the "normal" babies. My head was "off the charts," she said. Science literally had not produced a chart expansive enough to account for my monster dome. "Off the charts" became a West family joke over the years—I always deflected, saying it was because of my giant brain—but I absorbed the message nonetheless. I was too big, from birth. Abnormally big. Medical-anomaly big. Unchartably big.

There were people-sized people, and then there was me.

So, what do you do when you're too big, in a world where bigness is cast not only as aesthetically objectionable, but also as a moral failing? You fold yourself up like origami, you make yourself smaller in other ways, you take up less space with your personality, since you can't with your body. You diet. You starve, you run till you taste blood in your throat, you count out your almonds, you try to buy back your humanity with pounds of flesh.

I got good at being small early on—socially, if not physically. In public, until I was eight, I would speak only to my mother, and even then, only in whispers, pressing my face into her leg. I retreated into fantasy novels, movies, computer games, and, eventually, comedy—places where I could feel safe, assume any personality, fit into any space. I preferred tracing to drawing. Drawing was too bold an act of creation, too presumptuous.

5   In third grade I was at a birthday party with a bunch of friends, playing in the backyard, and someone suggested we line up in two groups—the girls who were over one hundred pounds and the girls who were still under. There were only two of us in the fat group. We all looked at each other, not sure what to do next. No one was quite sophisticated enough to make a value judgment based on size yet, but we knew it meant something.

My dad was friends with Bob Dorough, an old jazz guy who wrote all the songs for *Multiplication Rock, Schoolhouse Rock's* math-themed sibling. He's that breezy, froggy voice on "Three Is a Magic Number"—you'd recognize it. "A man and a woman had a little baby, yes, they did. They had three-ee-ee in the family . . ." Bob signed a vinyl copy of *Multiplication Rock* for me when I was two or three years old. "Dear Lindy," it said, "get big!" I hid that record, as a teenager, afraid that people would see the inscription and think, "She took *that* a little too seriously."

I dislike "big" as a euphemism, maybe because it's the one chosen most often by people who mean well, who love me and are trying to be gentle with my feelings. I don't want the people who love me to avoid the reality of my body. I don't want them to feel uncomfortable with its size and shape, to tacitly endorse the idea that fat is shameful, to pretend I'm something I'm not out of deference to a system that hates me. I don't want to be gentled, like I'm something wild and alarming. (If I'm going to be wild and alarming, I'll do it on my terms.) I don't want them to think that I need a euphemism at all.

"Big" is a word we use to cajole a child: "Be a big girl!" "Act like the big kids!" Having it applied to you as an adult is a cloaked reminder of what people really think, of the way we infantilize and desexualize fat people. (Desexualization is just another form of sexualization. Telling fat women they're sexless is still putting women in their sexual place.) Fat people are helpless babies enslaved to their most capricious cravings. Fat people do not know what's best for them. Fat people need to be guided and scolded like children. Having that awkward, babyish word dragging on you every day of your life, from childhood into maturity, well, maybe it's no wonder that I prefer hot chocolate to whiskey and substitute Harry Potter audiobooks for therapy.

> **I was too big, from birth. Abnormally big. Medical-anomoly big. Unchartably big.**

Every cell in my body would rather be "fat" than "big." Grown-ups speak the truth.

10   Please don't forget: I am my body. When my body gets smaller, it is still me. When my body gets bigger, it is still me. There is not a thin woman inside me, awaiting excavation. I am one piece. I am also not a uterus riding around in a meat incubator. There is no substantive difference between the repulsive campaign to separate women's bodies from

their reproductive systems—perpetuating the lie that abortion and birth control are not healthcare—and the repulsive campaign to convince women that they and their body size are separate, alienated entities. Both say, "Your body is not yours." Both demand, "Beg for your humanity." Both insist, "Your autonomy is conditional." This is why fat is a feminist issue.

All my life people have told me that my body doesn't belong to me.

As a teenager, I was walking down the street in Seattle's International District, when an old woman rushed up to me and pushed a business card into my hand. The card was covered in characters I couldn't read, but at the bottom it was translated: "WEIGHT LOSS/FAT BURN." I tried to hand it back, "Oh, no thank you," but the woman gestured up and down at my body, up and down. "Too fat," she said. "You call."

In my early twenties, I was working a summer job as a cashier at an "upscale general store and gift shop" (or, as it was known around my house, the Bourgeois Splendor Ceramic Bird Emporium & Money Fire), when a tan, wiry man in his sixties strode up to my register. I remember him looking like the infamous Silver Lake Walking Man, if anyone remembers him, or if Jack LaLanne fucked a tanning bed and a Benjamin Button came out.

"Do you want to lose some weight?" he asked, with no introduction.

I laughed uncomfortably, hoping he'd go away: "Ha ha, doesn't every- 15 one? Ha ha."

He pushed a brochure for some smoothie cleanse pyramid scheme over the counter at me. I glanced at it and pushed it back. "Oh, no thank you."

He pushed it toward me again, more aggressively. "Take it. Believe me, you need it."

"I'm not interested," I insisted.

He glared for a moment, then said, "So you're fine looking like that and getting the cancer?"

My ears roared. "That's rude," was all I could manage. I was still small 20 then, inside. He laughed and walked out.

Over time, the knowledge that I was too big made my life smaller and smaller. I insisted that shoes and accessories were just "my thing," because my friends didn't realize that I couldn't shop for clothes at a regular store and I was too mortified to explain it to them. I backed out of dinner plans if I remembered the restaurant had particularly narrow aisles or rickety chairs. I ordered salad even if everyone else was having fish and chips. I pretended to hate skiing because my giant men's ski pants made me look like a smokestack and I was terrified my bulk would tip me off the chairlift. I stayed home as my friends went hiking, biking, sailing, climbing, diving, exploring—I was sure I couldn't keep up, and what if we got into a scrape? They couldn't boost me up a cliff or lower me down an embankment or squeeze me through a tight fissure or hoist me from the hot jaws of a bear. I never revealed a single crush, convinced that the idea of my disgusting body as a sexual being would send people—even people who loved me—into fits of projectile vomiting (or worse, pity). I didn't go swimming for a fucking decade.

As I imperceptibly rounded the corner into adulthood—fourteen, fifteen, sixteen, seventeen—I watched my friends elongate and arch into these effortless, exquisite things. I waited. I remained a stump. I wasn't jealous, exactly; I loved them, but I felt cheated.

We each get just a few years to be perfect. That's what I'd been sold. To be young and smooth and decorative and collectible. I was missing my window, I could feel it pulling at my navel (my obsessively hidden, hated navel), and I scrabbled, desperate and frantic. Deep down, in my honest places, I knew it was already gone—I had stretch marks and cellulite long before twenty—but they tell you that if you hate yourself hard enough, you can grab just a tail feather or two of perfection. Chasing perfection was your duty and your birthright, as a woman, and I would never know what it was like—this thing, this most important thing for girls.

I missed it. I failed. I wasn't a woman. You only get one life. I missed it.

25   There is a certain kind of woman. She is graceful. She is slim. Yes, she would like to go kayaking with you. On her frame, angular but soft, a baggy T-shirt is coded as "low-maintenance," not "sloppy"; a ponytail is "sleek," not "tennis ball on top of a mini-fridge." Not only can she pull off ugly clothes, like sports sandals, or "boyfriend jeans," they somehow make her beauty thrum even more clearly. She is thrifted J.Crew. She can put her feet up on a chair and draw her knees to her chest. She can hold an ocean in her clavicle.

People go on and on about boobs and butts and teeny waists, but the clavicle is the true benchmark of female desirability. It is a fetish item. Without visible clavicles you might as well be a meatloaf in the sexual marketplace. And I don't mean Meatloaf the person, who has probably gotten laid lotsa times despite the fact that his clavicle is buried so deep as to be mere urban legend, because our culture does not have a creepy sexual fixation on the bones of meaty men.

Only women. Show us your bones, they say. If only you were nothing but bones.

America's monomaniacal fixation on female thinness isn't a distant abstraction, something to be pulled apart by academics in women's studies classrooms or leveraged for traffic in

> **Please don't forget. I am my body. When my body gets smaller, it is still me. When my body gets bigger, it is still me. There is not a thin woman inside me, awaiting excavation. I am one piece.**

shallow "body-positive" listicles ("Check Out These Eleven Fat Chicks Who You Somehow Still Kind of Want to Bang—Number Seven Is Almost Like a Regular Woman!")—it is a constant, pervasive taint that warps every single woman's life. And, by extension, it is in the amniotic fluid of every major cultural shift.

Women matter. Women are half of us. When you raise every woman to believe that we are insignificant, that we are broken, that we are sick, that the only cure is starvation and restraint and smallness; when you pit women against one another, keep us shackled by shame and hunger, obsessing over our flaws rather than our power and potential; when you leverage all of that to sap our money and our time—that moves the rudder of the world. It steers humanity toward conservatism and walls and the narrow interests of men, and it keeps us adrift in waters where women's safety and humanity are secondary to men's pleasure and convenience.

I watched my friends become slender and beautiful, I watched them 30 get picked and wear J.Crew and step into small boats without fear, but I also watched them starve and harm themselves, get lost and sink. They were picked by bad people, people who hurt them on purpose, eroded their confidence, and kept them trapped in an endless chase. The real scam is that being bones isn't enough either. The game is rigged. There is no perfection.

I listened to Howard Stern every morning in college. I loved Howard. I still do, though I had to achingly bow out as my feminism solidified. (In a certain light, feminism is just the long, slow realization that the stuff you love hates you.) When I say I used to listen to Stern, a lot of people look at me like I said I used to eat cat meat, but what they don't understand is that *The Howard Stern Show* is on the air for hours and hours every day. Yes, there is gleeful, persistent misogyny, but the bulk of it, back when I was a daily obsessive, at least, was Howard seeking validation for his neuroses; Robin cackling about her runner's diarrhea; Artie detailing the leviathan sandwich he'd eaten yesterday in a heroin stupor, then weeping over his debasement; Howard wheedling truth out of cagey celebrities like a surgeon; Howard buoying the news with supernatural comic timing; a Sagrada Familia of inside jokes and references and memories and love and people's lives willingly gutted and splayed open and dissected every day for the sake of good radio. It was magnificent entertainment. It felt like a family.

Except, for female listeners, membership in that family came at a price. Howard would do this thing (the thing, I think, that most non-listeners associate with the show) where hot chicks could turn up at the studio and he would look them over like a fucking horse vet—running his hands over their withers and flanks, inspecting their bite and the sway of their back, honking their massive horse jugs—and tell them, in intricate detail, what was wrong with their bodies. There was literally always something. If they were 110 pounds, they could stand to be too. If they were 90, gross. ("Why'd you do that to your body, sweetie?") If they were a C cup, they'd be hotter as a DD. They should stop working out so much—those legs are too muscular. Their 29-inch waist was subpar—come back when it's a 26.

Then there was me: 225, 40-inch waist, no idea what bra size because I'd never bothered to buy a nice one because who would see it? Frumpy miserable, cylindrical. The distance between my failure of a body and perfection stretched away beyond the horizon. According to Howard, even girls who were there weren't there.

If you want to be a part of this community that you love, I realized—this family that keeps you sane in a shitty, boring world, this million-dollar enterprise that you fund with your consumer clout, just as much as male listeners do—you have to participate, with a smile, in your own disintegration. You have to swallow, every day, that you are a second-ary being whose worth is measured by an arbitrary, impossible standard, administered by men.

35   When I was twenty-two, and all I wanted was to blend in, that rejec-tion was crushing and hopeless and lonely. Years later, when I was finally ready to stand out, the realization that the mainstream didn't want me was freeing and galvanizing. It gave me something to fight for. It taught me that women are an army.

When I look at photographs of my twenty-two-year-old self so con-vinced of her own defectiveness, I see a perfectly normal girl and I think about aliens. If an alien came to earth—a gaseous orb or a polyamorous cat person or whatever—it wouldn't even be able to tell the difference between me and Angelina Jolie, let alone rank us by hotness. It'd be like, "Uh, yeah, so those ones have the under-the-face fat sacks, and the other kind has that dangly pants nose. Fuck, these things are gross. I can't wait to get back to the omnidirectional orgy gardens of Vlaxnoid 7."[1]

The "perfect body" is a lie. I believed in it for a long time, and I let it shape my life, and shrink it—my real life, populated by my real body. Don't let fiction tell you what to do.

In the omnidirectional orgy gardens of Vlaxnoid 7, no one cares about your arm flab.

NOTE

[1]This is also the rationale that I use to feel better every time there's a "horse meat in your IKEA meatballs" scandal. Do you think an alien could tell the difference between a horse and a cow? Please.

FOR A SECOND READING

1.   Why do you think West chooses to title this essay "Bones"? How does this term relate to, or help advance, her argument about the way female bodies are judged, ranked, and stigmatized?

2. "What do you do," West asks, "when you're too big, in a world where bigness is cast not only as aesthetically objectionable, but also as a moral failing?" (p. 111). How effectively do you think West answers her own query? Does her essay provide a convincing answer to the challenge of being "too big" in a world that scripts "bigness" as a "failing?"

3. "America's monomaniacal fixation on female thinness isn't a distant abstraction," West declares, "it is a constant, pervasive taint that warps every single woman's life" (p. 115). Analyze the language West uses here. Why does she use phrases like "monomaniacal fixation" and "pervasive taint" to critique cultural norms around women's bodies? How persuasive do you find this kind of language to be? Why?

PUTTING IT INTO WRITING

4. West writes: "I dislike 'big' as a euphemism, maybe because it's the one chosen by people who mean well, who love me and are trying to be gentle with my feelings. I don't want the people who love me to avoid the reality of my body. I don't want them to feel uncomfortable with its size and shape, to tacitly endorse the idea that fat is shameful, to pretend I'm something I'm not out of deference to a system that hates me. . . . I don't want them to think I need a euphemism at all" (p. 112). In a 500-word essay, analyze and respond to the argument West is making here. What is her critique of terms like "big" to describe her body? What does she find problematic, even harmful, about such euphemistic language? Do you share her view? Can you think of other "euphemisms" used to describe different body sizes that, intentionally or not, reinforce harmful cultural stereotypes?

5. West concludes her essay by offering readers some pointed advice: "The 'perfect body' is a lie. I believed in it for a long time, and let it shape my life, and shrink it—my real life, populated by my real body. Don't let fiction tell you what to do" (p. 116). In an essay (300–500 words), explain how you might go about following this advice. What actions could you take to ensure that the "lie" of the "perfect body" doesn't dictate "what you do"?

COMPARING ARGUMENTS

6. "When I was finally ready to stand out," writes West, "the realization that the mainstream didn't want me was freeing and galvanizing. It gave me something to fight for" (p. 116). To what extent do you think this declaration could also be applied to Harriet McBryde Johnson (p. 93)? Based on her essay, would you say that Johnson finds a similarly liberating power in confronting inaccurate and alienating cultural stereotypes based on her appearance? Can her essay, like West's, be read as an effort to "fight for" herself? How, specifically?

Rewriting the Script: **Reality Television**

> ❝ It's all real. There's nothing fixed and nothing staged. Literally those deals go from just 30 minutes for just stupid-ass ones to 2.5 hours for some."
>
> — MARK CUBAN, BILLIONAIRE BUSINESSMAN AND CO-HOST OF THE
> REALITY SHOW, *SHARK TANK*
>
> QUOTED IN INTERVIEW WITH NEXTSHARK.COM, MARCH 15, 2014

HOW REAL IS REALITY TV?

Is what we are shown on reality television, in fact, *real*? It depends on whom you ask. For those who create and produce these shows, the answer could quite easily be yes. They might acknowledge that aspiring participants are put through a rigorous screening process or that specific story lines are tailored and polished in the editing room, but such producers would likely still maintain that these shows nonetheless bring viewers into contact with real people simply being *themselves*. Those on the other side of the camera, however, might easily argue that reality TV is less an opportunity to showcase the "real you" than a job: one that requires you to conform to a role you had no direct hand in creating. Every reality show has its villain, its crybaby, its average Joe, and those who aspire to be on these shows work hard to conform themselves to these pre-made categories.

Michael Stewart/Getty Images

IDENTIFY THE SCRIPT: Choose a reality television show and write a profile of it. More specifically, summarize the goals of the show, analyze its participants, and evaluate the story lines it creates for them.

CHALLENGE THE SCRIPT: Write a brief essay in which you assess the merits and shortcomings of the rules that the reality show producer and the reality show actors attempt to promote. Which set of rules do you find more compelling? Which set are you more inclined to accept as normal? And why?

MAKE YOUR OWN SCRIPT: Imagine that you are creating a reality television show that must be 100 percent real. In a brief essay, describe what this show would look like. What would be the show's format? Its setting and characters? Explain how this "100 percent real" show would rewrite the rules and norms by which reality television shows are conventionally created.

HEATHER HAVRILESKY
Some "Girls" Are Better Than Others

Our world abounds with examples of culturally loaded language: words or phrases that carry powerful but unspoken connotations, positive or negative. How do we respond to such language? To what extent do unspoken connotations shape our own assumptions, values, and views? Using these questions as her frame, Heather Havrilesky tries to make sense of the growing ubiquity of the term *girl* in popular culture. What particular assumptions, she asks, stand behind this term? And what portrait of contemporary female life do these assumptions create? Havrilesky, a former TV critic for Salon.com, is the author of *Disaster Preparedness: A Memoir* (2010) and *How to Be a Person in the World* (2016), a compilation of her "existential" advice column, "Ask Polly." This essay appeared in the *New York Times* in April 2012.

Before You Read

To what extent do you think fictional characters on TV and in the movies serve as role models for the broader public? How much power do such cultural figures have to write the scripts the rest of us are expected to follow?

AH, TO BE A GIRL AGAIN! NOT A CHILD, OF COURSE, BUT AN inhabitant of that rarefied, pH-balanced zone of romance and optimism where you might flirt and flounce and be easily bruised by a pea. Girls can put on a dress and twirl in a circle and others will clap and say, "How pretty!" Girls never question whether the attention they get is well-meaning. They skip through the forest with a basket full of treats for Grandma, happily telling every Big Bad Wolf they encounter exactly where they're headed.

Sooner or later, of course, some of us wise up. A combination of skepticism and feminist indignation sets in, and it becomes harder to wink coyly at strangers or to marvel innocently at Grandma's sharp and pointy teeth.

But for those of us who retain some sense memory of twirling and hearing someone coo, spotting the word *girl* in every other title these days (*2 Broke Girls, New Girl, The Girl with the Dragon Tattoo*, and, of course, *Girls*) or just hearing it in a line of dialogue (think *Sex and the City*, conspiratorial clinking of cosmopolitans, etc.) can bring on a faintly nostalgic twinge. Or is it a shudder? We recall that privileged but exasperating era when we were transfixing and special but also a little doomed. As a girl, you are a delicate glass vase, waiting to be broken. You are a sweet-smelling flower, waiting for life's hobnailed boots to trample you. That built-in suspense is part of your appeal.

119

"How will you make it on your own?" the theme song for *The Mary Tyler Moore Show* asks, hinting that the slightest pothole in the road might ruin everything for our hopeful heroine, peering worriedly from behind her steering wheel. When modern TV shows use the word *girl* in their titles, it's this state of uncertainty they're hoping to conjure. Forget that Mary Richards herself was done with twirling, if not hat tossing, well before she stepped into Mr. Grant's newsroom. Ever since she (and *That Girl* Marlo Thomas before her) turned the world on with her smile, we've been offered coquettish creatures who mimic her second-guessing and nervous tics but curiously lack her complexity and gravitas.

5   With their forced laughs and their preening and those heavy bangs resting straight on their eyeballs, our current batch of TV ingénues seems designed to conjure the childlike poutiness of America's onetime sweetheart Ally McBeal. You can afford to be a little sassy and street smart when you have big doll eyes and the frame of a preteen.

> *Witnessing the female characters on TV comedies today, I find it hard not to marvel at the effortful overcompensation at play here, as adult women are transformed into something lighter, perkier, less frightening.*

Aside from a few exceptions—Tina Fey's Liz Lemon on *30 Rock*, Amy Poehler's Leslie Knope on *Parks and Recreation*, both farcical enough to have more in common with *S.N.L.* personas than actual characters—we've largely been spared confident, complicated, single comedic heroines for a few decades now. Each week on *2 Broke Girls*, the spunky leads flee confrontation, seek solace in each other's "You go, girl!" clichés, and then stride out from their hidey hole to shake a finger in someone's face (only to be rewarded with more humiliation). For all of the single-girl bluster of *Whitney*, our heroine seems to have few interests outside of her live-in boyfriend, whether turning him on, manipulating him, or distracting him from ogling another girl's assets. Even Jess (Zooey Deschanel) of *New Girl*, the least insipid of the lot, tends to go all bashful and pigeon-toed a few times per episode, forsaking weightier goals in favor of trotting out her oddball charms for the adoration of her male roommates.

After prolonged exposure to these smoldering doll-babies, it's hard not to long for some of the stubbornness of Lucy Ricardo (Lucille Ball), the insatiability and bad temper of Samantha Jones (Kim Cattrall), or the nerve and self-possession of Mary Richards. When Mary and Rhoda go to a party amid young hippies and Mary notices that they are the only ones wearing eyeliner, we understand Mary and Rhoda as real human beings, complex entities capable of layered reactions to their surroundings.

If this were *2 Broke Girls*, Mary and Rhoda would dash off to the bathroom to giggle behind their hands, then wipe off their makeup and re-emerge, anxious to blend in with the crowd. Or Rhoda, after resolving to tell those nutty hippie kids a thing or two, would end up being humiliated by them in the process.

Witnessing the female characters on TV comedies today, I find it hard not to marvel at the effortful overcompensation at play here, as adult women are transformed into something lighter, perkier, less frightening. Each character is outfitted with charming tics ("What an adorable sneeze!") and inoffensive mediocrities ("She's so clumsy!") and toothless yuppie righteousness ("You tell that snippy barista the customer is always right!") Our culture chooses the naïve audacity of girlhood over more robust concepts of femininity—even Madonna has taken to waving sparkly pompoms. If watching shows like *2 Broke Girls* and *Whitney* and *New Girl* brings on a certain nausea and dizziness, it's most likely a result of seeing the same grown women twirl and twirl and twirl endlessly for an imagined audience each week. Even Carrie Bradshaw, in all of her attention-seeking wishy-washiness, at least had the courage of conviction to dress like an extra in the Ziegfeld Follies.

It's against this backdrop that we encounter Lena Dunham's new HBO comedy, *Girls*, in which Dunham tosses the basket of cupcakes aside and rolls out the Big Bad Wolf instead. It's no mistake that we meet our lead, Hannah (played by Dunham), while she's slurping up pasta on her parents' dime. Just a few scenes later, she's having awkward sex on the couch with a guy who rarely returns her texts. The deliberately jarring juxtaposition of these images, one of an overgrown infant, the other of a sexually submissive woman, is at once horrifying and hilariously caustic.

> *This discord between how vehemently we're told to believe in ourselves as young girls and how dismissively we're treated as young women . . . is part of what fuels the shudder brought on by that word, "girl."*

Caught in that bewildering nowhereland between childhood and adulthood, Hannah demonstrates how easy it is to experience a loss of directional cues, if not a total shutdown of onboard instrument panels. The show's use of that ubiquitous term *girl* is less about offering up another candidate for America's sweetheart than it is about charting that unnerving intersection of giggly specialness and self-consciousness, coyness and skepticism, flirtation and feminist indignation. Hannah herself appears to have marched straight from a Take Back the Night rally to a booty call with a guy who wants her to pretend she's a lost girl on the

10

street with a Cabbage Patch Kids lunchbox. She plays along, limply—"Yeah, I was really scared." But a few minutes later, when the guy calls her friend's abortion a "heavy situation," she asserts that it's less a tragic affair than a pragmatic concern. "What was she gonna do, like, have a baby and then take it to her baby-sitting job? It's not realistic."

If *Girls* has been heralded as game-changing television, there's a reason for that: the stuttered confessions, half-smiles, hissed warnings, and quiet shared confidences between Hannah and her friends make the empty sassing and high-fiving of existing girlie comedies look like the spasms of a bygone era. But what's most riveting about Hannah and her friends is not their wisdom, their righteousness, or their backbone—as we might imagine would be the antidote to the frothy pap of other girlie comedies—but their confusion, their vulnerability, and their ambivalence. Instead of clamoring for attention like Whitney or Jess, Hannah's roommate, Marnie (Allison Williams), who is beautiful and has a devoted boyfriend, is bored by his sensitivity, bored by his affection (she complains that "his touch now feels like a weird uncle putting his hand on my knee at Thanksgiving") but can't muster the resolve to dump him. This is not how the candy-coated ingénue of American imagining, poised on the doorstep of womanhood, is supposed to react to male attention.

Hannah, meanwhile, almost never takes a stand. She asks her boss at her publishing internship to give her a paid job, and he politely bids her farewell in that passive-aggressive professional way that's difficult to counter. After trading quips with a potential employer at an interview, she says something off-color and is summarily dismissed for her insensitivity. (She's baffled but doesn't protest.) Worst of all, she lets her sort-of-not-really-boyfriend call her a dirty little whore and smash her face into the mattress. Afterward, he asks her if she wants a Gatorade. "What flavor?" she asks. "Orange," he answers. "Um, no thanks, I'm good," she replies, politely.

Hannah, like so many women walking the line between the coddling of girlhood and the realities of adulthood, doesn't hoot or cackle or tell it like it is. Most young women, even if they're assertive and determined, still find themselves, in those forlorn in-between years, apologizing for themselves, blurting some muddled, half-finished thought, and, finally, resolving to take up less space.

This discord between how vehemently we're told to believe in ourselves as young girls and how dismissively we're treated as young women—captured so heartbreakingly in *Girls*—is part of what fuels the shudder brought on by that word, "girl." As vivid as our culture's fantasy of this magical juncture between childhood and adulthood might be, it's hardly a carefree time occupied by effusive pixies, let alone a period to which most of us would happily return. Because one day, we wake up ready—not to wag our fingers in someone's face (which is just another way of twirling when you get right down to it) but to present our true selves without apology. This is the trajectory that Lena Dunham and her collaborators have set out to portray, with humor and subtlety and realism. You can turn the world on with your smile for only so long before it gets a little dull. Or as Hannah tells her parents, trying to remain calm despite the fact that her extended childhood is suddenly in peril: "I have work, and then I have a dinner thing, and then I am busy, trying to become who I am."

Eventually, we learn to explain, calmly, who we are and what we will 15 and won't accept. That's how you make it on your own, as Mary Richards often demonstrated, though her voice sometimes trembled and her hands sometimes shook. That's the reason that scene of Mary throwing her hat in the air still feels exhilarating, 42 years later. No, that girl didn't break. But she was never all that fragile to begin with.

FOR A SECOND READING

1. What is your personal response to the term *girl*? What specific assumptions or stereotypes does it evoke? Do you think they are fair or accurate? Why or why not?

2. Havrilesky writes about the "discord between how vehemently we're told to believe in ourselves as young girls and how dismissively we're treated as young women" (p. 122). What does she mean by this? What specific gap between personal self-regard and public treatment is Havrilesky calling out? And do you agree it exists?

3. "Most young women," Havrilesky declares, "even if they're assertive and determined, still find themselves, in those forlorn in-between years, apologizing for themselves, blurting some muddled, half-finished thought, and, finally, resolving to take up less space" (p. 122). What kind of social script for "young women" does this passage describe? Is it one you have either encountered or experienced yourself?

PUTTING IT INTO WRITING

4. "As a girl," Havrilesky writes, "you are a delicate glass vase, waiting to be broken. You are a sweet-smelling flower, waiting for life's hobnailed boots to trample you. That built-in suspense is part of your appeal" (p. 119). Write a short essay in which you describe and analyze the description Havrilesky offers here. What portrait of "girlhood" does this passage create? What images or associations does her specific language evoke? In your view, does it create a social script worth following? How or how not?

5. Havrilesky cites numerous examples of pop culture shows (both past and present) that put the title *girl* front and center. Choose a pop culture example of your own (an ad, TV show, website, song, etc.) that does this same thing. Then write a three- to five-page essay in which you summarize, analyze, and evaluate the ways this text utilizes the term *girl*. What portrait of "girlhood" does this text present? What specific language and/or images does it use to create this portrait? In your view, is this a valid or appropriate portrait for our times? How or how not?

COMPARING ARGUMENTS

6. Havrilesky shares with Steve Almond (p. 125) a concern over the ways our entertainment media can shape public attitudes regarding social issues. What aspects of Havrilesky's essay do you think Almond would most likely endorse? Where might the two writers part ways? Offer a response to Havrilesky's argument that, in your view, Almond himself would write, using quotes from both writers to support your argument.

STEVE ALMOND

Is It Immoral to Watch the Super Bowl?

Over the last several years, public concern over violence in professional football has grown dramatically. As the data about the dangers pro football players face has accumulated, a growing number of fans has begun calling for a wholesale reevaluation of America's favorite sport. The essay below offers a case in point. Written by author and long-time football fan Steve Almond, it makes the case for turning away from football. Steve Almond is the author of many books, most recently, *Against Football: One Fan's Reluctant Manifesto* (2014). This essay appeared in the *New York Times* in 2014.

Before You Read

Is it possible to separate the popularity of professional football from its violence? In your view, how central is such violence to the sport's appeal?

IN THE SUMMER OF 1978, DURING A PRESEASON GAME, A WIDE receiver for the New England Patriots named Darryl Stingley lunged for a pass just out of his reach. Before he could regain his balance, he was hit by Jack Tatum, an Oakland Raiders defensive back. It was clear at once that Stingley was, in gridiron parlance, "shaken up on the play." Team doctors rushed to his side.

I was 11, a devout Raiders fan. I knew I was supposed to feel bad for Stingley, and I did in some minor, dutiful way. Mostly I was proud of Tatum, of the destructive capacities central to his mystique. The whole point of being Jack Tatum—a.k.a. the Assassin—was to level wide receivers in this manner.

The problem was that Stingley wasn't moving. The doctors kept tapping at his knees with reflex hammers. The longer Stingley lay on the chalked grass, the more ashamed I grew. Because I knew, even then, that part of my attraction to football was the thrill of such violent transactions.

What I remember most of all is the thought that dogged me in the days afterward, as it became clear that a star player had been rendered quadriplegic on national television: Surely the game of football would now be outlawed.

5   Obviously that never happened. Instead, Stingley wound up taking a desk job with the Patriots and being honored in the manner of a war hero. Tatum continued to terrorize opposing players. The N.F.L. juggernaut rolled on, solidifying its place atop America's Athletic Industrial Complex. And I kept right on watching, often devoting entire Sunday afternoons to football in my bachelor years.

Recently, though, medical research has confirmed that football can cause catastrophic brain injury—not as a rare and unintended consequence, but as a routine byproduct of how the game is played. That puts us fans in a morally queasy position. We not only tolerate this brutality. We sponsor it, just by watching at home. We're the reason the N.F.L. will earn $5 billion in television revenue alone next year, three times as much as its runner-up, Major League Baseball.

Never is this sponsorship more overt than next Sunday, for the Super Bowl has become an event of such magnitude that it ranks as a secular holiday at this point, as much a celebration of the sport's ability to draw multimillion-dollar ads as the contest itself. More than 100 million people will watch the game. Most of my friends will be parked in front of their TVs. For the first time in 35 years, I won't be among them.

• • •

Just so we're clear on this: I still love football. I love the grace and the poise of the athletes. I love the tension between the ornate structure of the game and its improvisatory chaos, and I love the way great players find opportunity, even a mystical kind of order, in the midst of that chaos.

What I remember most of all is the thought that dogged me in the days afterward, as it became clear that a star player had been rendered quadriplegic on national television: Surely the game of football would now be outlawed.

The problem is that I can no longer indulge these pleasures without feeling complicit. It was easier years ago, when injuries like Stingley's could be filed away as freakish accidents. TV coverage was relatively primitive, the players hidden under helmets and pads, obscured by fuzzy reception, more superheroes than men. Today we see the cruelty of the game in high definition. Slow-motion replays show us the precise angle of a grotesquely twisted ankle and a quarterback's contorted face at the exact moment he is concussed.

10   The sport's incredible popularity has turned players into national celebrities and has made their mental and physical deterioration front-page news. In 2012, the former All-Pro linebacker Junior Seau killed

himself. The autopsy confirmed that he had chronic traumatic encepha-lopathy, or C.T.E., the cause of the dementia that is increasingly prevalent among former players. A whole new crop of retired stars, including Tony Dorsett and Brett Favre, are just beginning to report symptoms like mem-ory loss and depression.

There are two basic rationalizations for fans like myself. The first is that the N.F.L. is working hard to make the game safer, which is flimsy at best. The league spent years denying that the game was causing neurological damage. Now that the medical evidence is incontrovertible, it has sought to reduce high-speed collisions, fining defenders for helmet-to-helmet hits and other flagrantly violent play. Its most significant response has been to offer $765 million to settle a class-action lawsuit brought by more than 4,500 former players, but a judge recently blocked the settlement. It simply wasn't enough money.

The second argument is that players choose to incur the game's risks and are lavishly compensated for doing so. This is technically true. N.F.L. players are members of an elite fraternity that knowingly places self-sacrifice, valor and machismo above ethical or medical common sense. But most start out as kids with limited options. They may love football for its inherent virtues. But they also quickly come to see the game as a path to glory and riches. These rewards aren't inherent. They arise from a cul-ture of fandom that views players as valuable only so long as they can perform.

But if I'm completely honest about my misgivings, it's not just that the N.F.L. is a negligent employer. It's how our worship of the game has blinded us to its pathologies.

• • •

Pro sports are, by definition, monetized arenas for hypermasculinity. Football is nowhere near as overtly vicious as, say, boxing. But it is the one sport that most faithfully recreates our childhood fantasies of war as a winnable contest.

Over the past 12 years, as Americans have sought a distraction from 15 the moral incoherence of the wars in Afghanistan and Iraq, the game has served as a loyal and satisfying proxy. It has become an acceptable way of experiencing our savage impulses, the cultural lodestar when it comes to consuming violence. What differentiates it from the glut of bloody films and video games we devour is our awareness that the violence in football, and the toll of that violence, is real.

The struggle playing out in living rooms across the country is that of a civilian leisure class that has created, for its own entertainment, a caste of warriors too big and strong and fast to play a child's game without grievously injuring one another. The very rules that govern our perceptions of them might well be applied to soldiers: Those who exhibit impulsive savagery on the field are heroes. Those who do so off the field are reviled monsters.

The civilian and the fan participate in the same basic transaction. We offload the mortal burdens of combat, mostly to young men from the underclass, whom we send off to battle with cheers and largely ignore when they wind up wounded.

No single episode speaks to this twisted dynamic more pointedly than the death of Pat Tillman, an idealistic N.F.L. star who enlisted in the Army after the Sept. 11 attacks. In 2004, Tillman was killed by friendly fire in a bungled ambush in Afghanistan. His superiors orchestrated an elaborate cover-up that included burning his uniform and recast the circumstances of his death as a heroic charge into enemy territory.

But suppose Tillman had survived, returned to play in the N.F.L. and wound up with brain damage at age 50. Would we see him as a victim of friendly fire? Would we acknowledge our role in his demise? Or would we construct our own personal cover-ups?

. . .

20   The N.F.L. and the bloated media cult that feeds off it rely on fans not to connect the dots between our consumption of football and brain-damaged human beings. But to an even larger extent, we rely on one another.

I had a number of difficult conversations with friends in the course of writing this, none more so than with my neighbor Sean. He stood in my kitchen listening to all of my self-righteous bullet points. When I was done, he looked at me and said, in a quiet, imploring voice, "Please don't take this away from me."

I knew exactly what he meant—or thought I did. For the past five years, he and I have sought refuge from our grinding family duties by sneaking out to watch games together. I assumed he was referring to this camaraderie.

But Sean's fandom is far more elemental than mine. He grew up in rural West Virginia, hard-core football country. He was a natural from early on, a kid with the size, speed and agility to play at least college ball. When I asked him why he quit, he told me this story:

> *The civilian and the fan participate in the same basic transaction. We offload the mortal burdens of combat, mostly to young men from the underclass, whom we send off to battle with cheers and largely ignore when they wind up wounded.*

When he was about 11, his team played a rival with the best running back in the league. It was Sean's role, as the star of the defense, to make sure the kid didn't break through the line. On one play, Sean met the running back just as he was about to burst through a gap. The running back lowered his head, in the same instinctual way Darryl Stingley had, and their helmets collided at full speed. The kid fell and lay motionless.

The boy's coaches, and later his parents, ran onto the field. Smelling 25 salts wouldn't revive him. Eventually, an ambulance appeared. Sean was convinced that he'd killed the boy. He began to cry. But what Sean remembers most vividly was the way, right after the tackle, his teammates kept slapping his helmet, as if he'd just done the most heroic thing ever, which, in a purely football sense, he had. He also recalls trying to walk away from his teammates, because he didn't want them to see that he was crying. Even three decades later, recounting this episode shook Sean up.

The running back was not paralyzed. That's not the point of the story. It was the tremendous anguish Sean felt over his power to harm another boy. Having walked away from football—despite his passion for the game and his obvious gifts—Sean hardly needed to hear a lecture about the evils of being a fan. I felt like (and probably am) a moralizing jerk.

Don't we turn to football precisely to escape such ethical complexities, to experience the joy of watching bodies at play, to pretend, however briefly, that life is just a fearless game? After all, I, too, recognize the desperate ardor that Frederick Exley captures in his novel "A Fan's Notes": "Whatever it was, I gave myself up to the Giants utterly. The recompense I gained was the feeling of being alive."

Still, I can't help thinking about something else Sean told me, which was how, in the hours and days after he delivered his big hit, he kept asking the same question of his coaches: "I didn't do anything wrong, did I?"

FOR A SECOND READING

1. Almond opens his essay by recounting a childhood experience watching a pro football player suffer a paralyzing injury on national television. Why do you think he chooses to begin this way? In what ways does this recollection preview the larger argument Almond goes on to make?

2. Almond describes the relationship between football players and football fans as a "violent transaction." What does he mean by this term? According to Almond, what specifically is exchanged or "transacted" in the relationship between players and fans? And how is this exchange related to violence?

3. According to Almond, it is our "worship of football" that has "blinded us to its pathologies" (p. 127). How do you respond to the language Almond uses here? What do words like "worship" and "blindness" suggest about the role of the typical football fan? What point do you think Almond is trying to make by using a term like "pathologies" to describe football?

PUTTING IT INTO WRITING

4. Almond cites one of the "rationalizations" often used to justify the violence of pro football: that "players choose to incur the game's risk" (p. 127). Write a 300–500-word essay in which you evaluate how persuasive you find this argument to be. In your view, is it logical to cite "player choice" as a justification for football violence? Does this strategy raise any questions for you? Do you see any flaws or contradictions in this argument? What do you find persuasive about this logic?

5. In the most fundamental terms, this essay can be read as an invitation to confront the "ethical complexities" inherent in playing the role of the pro football fan. In a 500-word essay, take up this invitation by arguing for what you see as the ethical obligations of playing this role. What degree of responsibility does the football fan hold for the dangers of this sport? To what extent is the fan obligated to address these dangers? And why?

COMPARING ARGUMENTS

6. From very different vantages, Almond and Heather Havrilesky (p. 119) invite us to reflect more deeply on the role gender plays in shaping our consumption of popular culture. How do their respective treatments of this question compare? Do you see any common threads between Almond's critique of football violence and Havrilesky's examination of female representation?

AMANDA HESS

Why Old Men Find Young Women's Voices So Annoying

Are there gendered differences in how we listen to each other? According to prevailing cultural norms, are all voices truly created equal? These are the questions Amanda Hess considers here. Surveying the landscape of radio journalism, Hess notes a striking disparity in the ways the vocal styles of male and female broadcasters are evaluated. Citing recent social science research into this question, she wonders what these differing standards tell us about the general public's willingness to respect and heed women's voices. Amanda Hess is a staff writer for *Slate* who has also written for *Elle*, *ESPN*, and *Wired*. This piece appeared in *Slate* in 2013.

Before You Read

How would you define the ideal "professional voice"? What image of a speaker does this phrase evoke in your mind?

LAST WEEK, SLATE LEXICON VALLEY PODCASTER (AND NPR ON THE *Media* host) Bob Garfield lamented a frightening tic invading American speech. It appears "almost exclusively among women, and young women at that." As these women form sentences, Garfield explains, "something happens to their voice, as if they have a catch in their throat." He summons his 11-year-old daughter Ida to the microphone to mimic the speech pattern. "Ida," he instructs her, "be obnoxious."

The affect of which Garfield speaks is known as "creaky voice" or "vocal fry," a gravelly lowering of the voice that conjures the sounds of "a door creaking or a hinge that needs oiling." Over the course of the 26-minute podcast, Garfield describes the speech pattern as "vulgar," "repulsive," "mindless," "annoying," and "really annoying." "I want the oil to stop frying," Garfield says. "I want someone to wave a magic wand over a significant portion of the American public"—you know, women—"and have the frying come to an end."

For years, women have been criticized for *raising* their voices at the end of sentences. This "Valley Girl lift," as Hofstra fine arts professor Laurie Fendrich maligns it, "reveals an unexplainable lack of confidence in one's opinions and a radical uncertainty about one's place in the world." Raising our voices makes women sound like "an empty-headed clotheshorse for whom the mall represents the height of culture," she writes.

So we're wrong when we raise our voices, and we're wrong when we lower them. (Lest you think Garfield's fix to the vocal fry "problem" is that we all just revert back to Valleyspeak—that register also strikes him as "frightful," and he repeatedly mocks both voices throughout the podcast.) Just as Valley Girls are perceived as overly feminine and submissive, Creaky Girls may be seen as overly masculine and derisive. Lexicon Valley co-host Mike Vuolo notes that a woman's voice is, on average, an octave higher than a man's. Lowering into a gravelly creak puts men and women on the same wavelength. "Vulgar!"

5   Of course, young women could work to flatten their speech patterns to conform to Garfield's own NPRish affectation, which one commenter describes as "Richard Pryor making fun of WASPs." So why do we instead insist on speaking in ways that older men find so objectionable? Vuolo valiantly meets Garfield's annoyance with some research into how the vocal creak actually functions among young women. ("I don't have any data," Garfield counters. "I simply know I'm right.") One study recorded a college-aged woman's voice while speaking in an even tone, and then again when employing the creak. When both samples were played for students in Berkeley and Iowa, those peers viewed the affectation as "a prestigious characteristic of contemporary female speech," characterizing the creaky woman as "professional," "urban," "looking for her career," and most tellingly: "not yet a professional, but on her way there."

> **For years, women have been criticized for raising their voices at the end of sentences. . . . So we're wrong when we raise our voices, and we're wrong when we lower them.**

"You mean there were positive associations among her demographic?" Garfield asks incredulously. "It's so repulsive, and yet it's deemed sophisticated by our next generation of leaders?"

That's right, Bob. And a 2011 *Science* investigation into vocal fry confirms that the vocal creak is not a universally-reviled tic. *Science* cites a study conducted by speech scientist Nassima Abdelli-Beruh of Long Island University, who observed the creak in two-thirds of the college women she sampled. She also found that "young students tend to use it when they get together," with the speech pattern functioning as a "social link between members of a group." One of the most prominent vocal creakers of my generation, Britney Spears, actually digitally modifies her voice to creak more impressively when delivering lines like, "It's Britney, bitch."

Garfield may be satisfied to learn that Abdelli-Beruh "does not hear vocal fry on National Public Radio, which targets an older audience." But if an older white guy like Garfield did creak, would Garfield be annoyed? Linguist Mark Liberman has documented the rise of the Valley Girl lift, which he describes as American "uptalk," among even the manliest of men. He's noticed it in the speech of a python wrangler, a NASA official, and George W. Bush. (The "uptalk" is also a common feature in much non-American English speech, where it does not hold the same sissy connotations.) The sounds of the Valley have traveled so far, they've entered into the vocal patterns of Pat Robertson, who once said: "I really believe I'm hearing from the Lord it's going to be, like, a blowout election in 2004." In some discourse communities, Liberman documents, "final rises" have actually been used by men and women to "assert dominance and control" over the conversation "by holding the floor, by exerting pressure on the hearer to respond, or by reminding the hearer(s) of common ground." Only when young women employ it is the speech pattern so vilified.

As women gain status and power in the professional world, young women may not be forced to carefully modify totally benign aspects of their behavior in order to be heard.

I suspect that the spread of "creaky voice" makes Garfield so mad because it represents the downfall of his own mode of communication, which is swiftly being replaced by the patterns and preferences of 11-year-old girls like Ida and her peers. As women gain status and power in the professional world, young women may not be forced to carefully modify totally benign aspects of their behavior in order to be heard. Our speech may not yet be considered professional, but it's on its way there. Once, an anxious parent wrote into Liberman's blog to complain that a Ph.D. daughter populates her speech with uptalks, as do her doctor/lawyer peers. Could Liberman point to any research proving the "negative effects" of this feminine affectation? "You're certainly entitled to your crotchets and irks, just as your adult daughter is entitled to her prosodic preferences," Liberman responded. "But in order for the two of you to get along, something's going to have to give. And realistically, it's you."

FOR A SECOND READING

1. Here is a partial list of the language one critic cited in this piece uses to deride the speaking style known as vocal fry: "vulgar," "repulsive," "mindless," and "annoying." To what extent do these words strike you as gendered descriptors? In your view, are these terms that would more likely be used to denigrate female speakers than male speakers? Why or why not?

2. To support her thesis, Hess cites recent social science research documenting a difference in the ways male and female listeners react to broadcasts featuring women's voices. How effective do you find this strategy to be? In your view, does it help strengthen Hess's argument about female voice and female power?

3. Running beneath Hess's discussion of "masculine" and "feminine" voices is the idea that vocal style is an instrument for navigating and expressing social power. How would you characterize the message about voice and power Hess is trying to get across in this essay? And how persuasive do you find this argument to be?

PUTTING IT INTO WRITING

4. "[Women's] speech may not yet be considered professional," (p. 133) writes Hess, "but it's on its way there." In a 300-word essay, respond to this statement. Do you accept the premise that female voices are not yet considered fully "professional"? If so, what factors or forces are responsible for this situation? And, finally, what specific steps could be taken to help increase a recognition of the "professionalism" of female voices?

5. As Hess observes, the counterpoint to the gravelly, lower-register tone of "vocal fry" is the "Valley Girl lift": a style in which women "rais[e] their voices at the end of sentences" (p. 131). Write a 300-word essay in which you analyze and evaluate the differences between these two vocal styles along gender lines. What gender norms are associated with each vocal style? What do these norms suggest about the authority of the speaker who employs each style?

COMPARING ARGUMENTS

6. Like Hess, Tiffanie Wen (p. 135) is interested in exploring the emotional dynamics of how we listen. In what ways does this interest overlap? In what ways does it differ? Does the information Wen presents about the neuroscience of listening to podcasts help bolster the case Hess makes about the voice and gender? How?

TIFFANIE WEN

Inside the Podcast Brain: Why Do Audio Stories Captivate?

The last several years have witnessed an explosion in the popularity of podcasts. From current events shows like *Serial* and the *TED Radio Hour* to comedies like *Judge John Hodgman* and the *Adam Carolla Show*, there is hardly a topic or question that has failed to find its own podcast audience. But what accounts for this outsized popularity? Why have podcasts emerged as one of this era's most ubiquitous and preeminent cultural outlets? Seeking to answer these questions, Tiffanie Wen introduces us to what might be called the neuroscience of listening, guiding readers through a discussion of what really happens in our brains when we plug into this particular aural medium. Tiffanie Wen is a freelance writer whose work has appeared in such publications as *The Atlantic* and *The Daily Beast*. This piece was published in *The Atlantic* in 2015.

Before You Read

What are some of the different ways you consume stories? Do spoken stories have a greater capacity to engage your interest than stories you experience in written form?

IN MY ALL-TIME FAVORITE EPISODE OF RADIOLAB, "FINDING EMILIE," a young art student named Emilie Gossiaux gets into a terrible accident while riding her bike and, rendered blind and deaf, is unable to communicate with her loved ones until she makes an incredible breakthrough. Listening to it on my drive home only got me to the middle of the episode, so I sat in my parked car staring at the garage until it was over. I was captivated by the voices of Emilie and her family. I've been an audio convert ever since.

It's likely that thousands, if not millions, of others had the same experience last year when they discovered *Serial*, the *This American Life* spinoff considered to be the most successful podcast of all time (5 million downloads and counting) that launched the medium back into the spotlight.

As a *New York* magazine piece noted last year, the increasing popularity of audio storytelling owes a lot to technology, as smartphones allow people to consume shows on demand anywhere, and cars increasingly come equipped with satellite radio and Internet-friendly dashboards. A recent report by Edison Research estimated that 64 percent of 12- to 24-year-olds and 37 percent of 25- to 54-year-olds in the United States listened to online radio weekly in 2014. The same year, 30 percent of respondents reported that they had listened to a podcast at least once, with 15 percent indicating that they had listened to a podcast within the last month.

Beyond the obvious convenience factor of listening on the go, what is it that makes some audio storytelling so engaging? And what happens in the brain when someone hears a really compelling story?

5   "A good story's a good story from the brain's perspective, whether it's audio or video or text. It's the same kind of activation in the brain," says Paul Zak, the director of the Center for Neuroeconomics Studies at Claremont Graduate University. Zak has studied how watching and listening to stories influence our physiology and behavior.

In a study published in *The Annals of the New York Academy of Science* in 2009, Zak and his colleagues had participants watch short video clips featuring an emotional or unemotional scene. Afterwards, they filled out a survey about their emotions, played a game designed to test their level of generosity toward a stranger, and had their blood drawn. Those who reported feeling empathy for the characters in the clip were found to have 47 percent more of the neurochemical oxytocin in their body than those who didn't feel empathetic toward the characters.

> **[T]he increasing popularity of audio storytelling owes a lot to technology, as smartphones allow people to consume shows on demand anywhere, and cars increasingly come equipped with satellite radio and Internet-friendly dashboards.**

The researchers reason that experiencing tension in a story makes people feel stressed, which makes their bodies release the hormone and neurotransmitter oxytocin. Since oxytocin has been shown to increase empathy in some experiments, when things get tense while listening to a story, reading a book, or watching a TV show or movie, you may begin to empathize with the characters and get "transported" into the story.

Which means, according to Zak, that the best stories will always have an increasing level of tension, and that there exists a type of universal story structure—one in which a protagonist faces some sort of stressful challenge or conflict—that draws attention because it's engaging emotionally and intellectually.

"What we have found in our research is that people require some sort of stressor, some sort of arousal response in the brain to have this type of narrative transportation where we begin to share the emotions of the characters in a story," Zak says. "It makes sense that we need some sufficient reason to have that response. Our brain is trying to save resources and energy and having this arousal response is costly. Therefore we only want to give attention to something when it matters, when there's something going on."

He describes transporting into a story as a "neuro ballet" in which the reader, viewer, or listener knows she's not physically part of the story, and yet she still physically responds to it in a way that can change her behavior in the future.

Since oxytocin has been shown to make people more sensitive to social cues, Zak says that stories that keep people's attention have to be character-driven. "You can tell a war story or something with a lot of action that will grab your attention," he says, "but you still need a personal story, someone to empathize with. We need to have that social aspect for it to resonate with us."

Podcasts and audiobooks benefit from the advantages of any character-based story. But some research, like a recent study conducted at the University of Waterloo, has shown that people who listen to the narration of a passage, like the audio storytelling found in traditional audiobooks, remember less information, are less interested in the content, and are more likely to daydream than those who read the same book out loud or silently to themselves.

But anyone who has gotten hooked on a podcast knows that audio can be much more than just narration. Emma Rodero, a communications professor at the Pompeu Fabra University in Barcelona, studies how audio productions retain people's attention. Her work has shown that a dramatized audio structure, using voice actors who tell the story exclusively through dialogue, stimulate listeners' imagination more than a typical "voice of God" narration. Participants who listened to the dramatized structure reported that they generated more vivid images in their minds, and conjured the images more quickly and easily than those in the narration condition. They also reported being more emotionally aroused and interested in the story.

> *Our brain is trying to save resources and energy and having this arousal response is costly. Therefore we only want to give attention to something when it matters, when there's something going on.*

Another study illustrates the importance of using sound effects, sounds that represent objects and/or environments and sound shots, an effect that gives the listener a sense of space by recording a sound that's far away. Rodero found that the use of sound effects and sound shots in an audio drama increased the level of mental imagery that listeners reported, and also caused listeners to pay more attention.

15   Audiobook producers are catching on, and have started rolling out new types of "audio entertainment." A novel by best-selling crime writer Jeffrey Deaver, called *The Starling Project*, has only been released as an audiobook, and features characters brought to life by 29 voice actors. Adapted by famed sci-fi author Orson Scott Card, *Ender's Game Alive*, released by Audible in 2013, tells the *Ender's Game* story entirely through the use of dialogue and sound effects. And companies like Graphic Audio are creating audio dramas exclusively in the style, calling it "a movie in your mind."

The tagline captures one of the best things about audio storytelling, according to Rodero. She says that, like reading, listening to audio allows people to create their own versions of characters and scenes in the story. But she thinks listening, unlike looking at a written page, is more active, since the brain has to process the information at the pace it is played.

"Audio is one of the most intimate forms of media because you are constantly building your own images of the story in your mind and you're creating your own production," Rodero says. "And that of course, is something that you can never get with visual media."

FOR A SECOND READING

1. For cultural observers, why is it useful to focus on the neuroscience of podcasts? What does the brain research Wen profiles here tell us about the social scripts and cultural norms that define this particular type of media?

2. According to one study cited in this essay, participants "reported that [audio stories] generated more vivid images in their minds, and conjured the images more quickly and easily" (p. 137) than narratives read in conventional written form. What does this fact suggest about the difference between listening to and reading stories? Is this a significant difference in the way you personally consume narrative?

3. Another study cited in this essay shows "that people who listen to the narration of a passage, like the audio storytelling found in traditional audiobooks, remember less information, are less interested in the content, and are more likely to daydream than those who read the same book out loud or silently to themselves." (p. 137). What does this result suggest may be the limit or downside to consuming narrative aurally?

PUTTING IT INTO WRITING

4. One of the studies Wen cites in her essay is the following: "[P]articipants watch short video clips featuring an emotional or unemotional scene. Afterwards, they filled out a survey about their emotions, played a game designed to test their level of generosity toward a stranger, and had their blood drawn. Those who reported feeling empathy for the characters in the clip were found to have 47 percent more of the neurochemical oxytocin in their body than those who didn't feel empathetic toward the characters." (p. 136). Write a 300-word essay in which you evaluate the usefulness of this study. What hypothesis is this experiment designed to test? How successfully do the results support this hypothesis? And how important, in your view, are these results?

5. According to one of the experts Wen interviews in this essay, "[a]udio is one of the most intimate forms of media because you are constantly building your own images of the story in your mind and you're creating your own production" (p. 138). Write a 300-word essay in which you argue for the value of this particular form of storytelling. Why is it important for stories to be "intimate"? As readers, what do we gain by virtue of "building our own images of the story in our minds"? How is this way of consuming narrative better than reading it in conventional form?

COMPARING ARGUMENTS

6. How do you think Amanda Hess (p. 131) would respond to the scientific data Wen presents in this essay? Based on the argument she makes, do you think Hess would look for gendered differences in the ways listeners respond to audio storytelling? Is there anything in the data Wen cites here to support this kind of conclusion?

Then and Now: **Wearing Your Identity on Your Sleeve**

Merchandisers have long sought to sell their goods by appealing to our sense of personal style: by flattering our desire to make an impression or cultivate an image that reflects our unique individuality. For years, this goal revolved around a strategy known as niche marketing, a tactic designed to associate a given product with the interests, hobbies, or "look" of a particular group. To wear a specific brand of clothing, drive a certain model of car, drink a particular variety of soda was (according to this formulation) to demonstrate your membership within a cohort of people who wear, drive, and drink the same thing — in effect, to make a statement about the *type* of person you truly are. Niche marketing, in other words, has long encouraged us to treat commercial marketing as a viable blueprint for *self*-marketing. When you think of 1950s fashion, one word that might first come to mind is *conformity*, and indeed the

Donald Uhrbrock/Getty Images

picture at the left shows a group of teenage girls wearing more or less the teenage girl uniform of the 1950s.

Fashions are often designed to appeal to members of a certain group, even as we talk about fashion as a way to express individual identity. These days, however, niche marketing is giving way to a new sales strategy, one that seems at first glance to resolve this contradiction. No longer content with associating their goods with a consumer type, many merchandisers nowadays promote products that they claim are tailored to nonconformist consumers. A website like Threadless.com, for example, allows artists to create designs that are then voted on by Threadless members, with the most popular designs being printed and sold by the company. For many, this change not only heralds the demise of niche marketing but also signals a movement beyond the outmoded ideas of self-marketing and image creation. With the advent of customized marketing, we are told, it is now possible for shopping to serve as a truly legitimate means of self-expression, a vehicle for defining and displaying our true individuality.

WHAT'S A DESIGN CHALLENGE?

 + + 🎲 = 💰

Come up with an idea
First, get inspired! Come up with the most creative design idea ever created.

Submit your design
Place your design on a template, give it a sweet title, and upload it.

The community scores it
Watch the comments and scores roll in while you promote your design all over the interwebs.

Win cash, prizes & fame!
If your design is chosen for print, you'll get mad cash and the world gets to buy your art!

But how much has *really* changed? Just because merchandisers now market customized products doesn't necessarily mean they've gotten out of the business of creating and marketing different images. No matter how personalized the messages on these design-your-own T-shirts, they are still logos. Indeed we could well ask whether all of this so-called customized design is simply a different, admittedly more sophisticated, form of branding. At the end of the day, after all, customers who wear these products are still engaging in the same operation that customers always have, one in which they use brand images and logos to make statements about the types of people they are. Do we find ourselves drawn to these kinds of products because they really do help us showcase our genuine selves? Or do we respond to this come-on for the same old reasons — because these products promise to supply us with a genuine self that is made for us?

PUTTING IT INTO WRITING

1. In a brief essay, compare the different directions each image lays out for how and why we should shop. What role for the average consumer does each example seem to create? What parallels or similarities do you note? What differences? Which is a more effective way to market clothing? Why?

2. Tom Vanderbilt (p. 142) explores the dynamics of consumerism, exploring the ways that commercial culture influences some of our personal preferences and tastes. Put yourself in the position of Vanderbilt for a moment and write a description of the ways you think he would evaluate or respond to the notion of "personalized marketing." On which aspects of this promotional campaign do you think Vanderbilt would focus most attention? How would he evaluate the way this campaign works to create and guide consumer taste?

TOM VANDERBILT

How Predictable Is Our Taste?

We all likely have had some experience with the kinds of computer algorithms that can predict the next song we want to hear, recommend the next book we should read, or introduce us to "friends" we might like to meet. But how many of us stop to ponder what all this advice says about where our tastes and preferences actually come from? When we really start to think about it, how do we end up liking the stuff we like? Taking up just this question, Tom Vanderbilt takes a deeper look at the ways that smart technology and Big Data are measuring — and in many cases actively shaping — our cultural tastes. Tom Vanderbilt is a journalist and the author of the best-selling book *Traffic: Why We Drive the Way We Do* (2008) and *You May Also Like: Taste in an Age of Endless Choice* (2016) from which this essay is excerpted.

Before You Read

How would you characterize your own cultural tastes? To what extent do you think these tastes make a larger statement about the kind of person you are?

WHAT SORT OF MUSIC DO YOU LIKE?

Is there a question that at once seems so reductionist yet so open-ended, so banal yet so freighted with meaning?

But it comes up: In studies of "zero acquaintance," where people were meant to try to get to know one another, music was the first topic broached (granted, they were college students). It is not just small talk: People's music preferences are potent in drawing accurate inferences about their personality, or at least the personality they are trying to project.

> *Being a snob could actually be socially counterproductive, lessening one's ability to move across different social networks.*

Likes seem easier to discuss than dislikes. Likes are public, Hugo Liu[1] had told me. A person's clothes reveal his likes, but not necessarily his dislikes. Dislikes — even though they are so crucial to taste — tend to be private. . . . Talking about likes might be a good way to find out if someone could be a possible friend. But discussing dislikes is generally reserved for those already in your social network; Liu compared dislikes to gossip you exchange with friends, a way to groom relationships. Simply expressing your musical preferences depend on any number of factors: who's asking, what you've listened to lately, where you are, what you can remember.

These kinds of questions animate the Echo Nest, a "music intelli-   5
gence" company in Cambridge, Massachusetts, that is a kind of mash-up between the neighbors MIT and the Berklee College of Music, data geeks playing with music geeks. The essential job of the Echo Nest, owned by Spotify, is to help solve the dilemma of matching people to music in an age when the latter is in virtually inexhaustible supply.

When I arrived at its offices one afternoon, it probably should not have come as a surprise that the very first interaction I had was about musical taste. As I sat down with Glenn McDonald, the company's principal engineer, I asked what was playing on the stereo. In an office where everyone must be bristling with opinions, how could they decide *what* to play? "The rule is 'anything but Coldplay,'" he said sardonically. There it was, that line in the sand, delivered half in jest but still able, in one cutting thrust, to divide the population into those who liked Coldplay, those who did not, and those who did not feel strongly either way—but could still perhaps get the joke. Coldplay may be a particularly good litmus test for taste. Type in "Coldplay is," and Google autocompletes, in this order, "Coldplay is the best band ever" and "Coldplay is the worst band ever." Much of the venom for Coldplay is no doubt driven by that very adoration. Whatever the reason, people are taking sides. Take enough of these sides, and you begin to locate "your music"—and *yourself*—on the taste graph. . . .

What does the music you like say about you? Before coming to the Echo Nest, I had partaken in one of its playful experiments called "What's Your Stereotype?" You enter a few of your favorite musical acts and are profiled as a "Manic Pixie Dream Girl" or "Vengeance Dad." ("Based upon your affinity for artists like: Iron Maiden.") I was dubbed a "Hipster Barista," which, given that much of my music listening these days occurs in Brooklyn coffee shops, seemed predictive enough. Brian Whitman, the bearded, laid-back co-founder of the Echo Nest, sounded like a latter-day Bourdieu[2] when he told me nothing is more predictive of a person than his music preference. "If all I knew about you was the last five books you read, I probably wouldn't know much," he says. "But if I knew the last five songs you listened to on a streaming service, I'd probably know a lot about you."

Films, he suggested, are less predictive. There are fewer of them and fewer consumption opportunities. Genres matter, but there is not the same hairsplitting as with music. "They're more directly social things," he said. "Your wife will make you watch a movie." Music is what people do on their own: in the car, with their headphones, via their playlists and customized stations. Preferences for it are strongly personal, and people will talk about "my music" in a way they do not about "my movies." When people broadcast the bands they like on a social network like Facebook, research indicates they will not necessary influence someone else to like that band. They may in fact do the opposite.

In an age in which, as the Echo Nest engineer Paul Lamere described it, you can carry "almost all of recorded music in your pocket," the question of *what to play next* has grown increasingly complex. Many of the people who sign up for trials on music-streaming services, Whitman said, never actually listen to anything. "They see a blank search box. What do you do?" Some people, McDonald suggested, might "listen to that Dave Matthews album, the CD of which is in a box somewhere they haven't unpacked from the last move." They are happy for forty-two minutes.

10   And then what? Call it "Search Fright." You sign up for a service that has everything you could ever want to listen to, and suddenly the prospect of listening to any *one* thing becomes overwhelming. The goal of music "discovery," as it is called, is to steer listeners through the morass, navigating within the boundaries of the acceptable and through the shoals of disaffection. "How would you distinguish between the ten million songs you're never going to like, either because they're terrible or because they're something that has no context for you," McDonald said, "and one of the ten million songs that might be your favorite thing, if only you knew it existed?"

Located on the other side of the computer screen, the Echo Nest faces the "cold start problem" that bedevils all recommendation enterprises: What is the first song I should play for this person whom I do not really know much about? Figuring out what kind of listener you are, the Echo Nest believes—rather than simply knowing what you listened to—is the key to keeping you engaged. It models attributes like "mainstreamness"—how far out do your tastes go compared with those of other services' listeners? Is Radiohead thrillingly experimental for you or about as popular a band as you will listen to?

The Echo Nest began as an effort to understand, through data and machine learning, the vast world of music by merging its two central qualities: how it sounds, and how we talk about it. . . .

The way we talk about music is, it turns out, fairly predictable. "We see people talking about its context related to everything else they know," he said. "That's exactly the kind of text you want." Musicological detail is relatively unimportant; knowing the key or pitch of a song does not help guide listeners to the next song, Whitman suggested. You want to know where a band is from, what its influences are.

The Echo Nest's other co-founder, Tristan Jehan, meanwhile, was toiling in the world of "Music Information Retrieval," a wide-ranging discipline that seeks to turn music into data so it can be better understood. Trying to assign an emotional valence to songs can baffle machines. . . .

Computers are also not very good—sonically, at least—at under- 15
standing the human classificatory system known as genre. In a sprawling project called "Every Noise at Once," McDonald was using the Echo Nest's semantic engines to map the world's corpus of musical genres—everything from "Romanian pop" to "Finnish hip-hop" to "Polish reggae." Curiously, he does not rely at all on what the genres *sound* like to identify them as genres (where a computer might struggle, humans can recognize a genre faster than we can say the word "genre").

Genres, to paraphrase the music critic Simon Frith, are as much social distinctions as musical distinctions. To human ears, there may indeed be Polish reggae; McDonald described a "Polish polka-folk melody to some of it." And the lyrics are in Polish. To a computer, however, the distinction is murkier. There are reggae bands from Bulgaria to Omaha that would sound, in terms of audio signal, fairly similar. "But 'Polish reggae' is clearly a thing," McDonald said, "and bands from Bulgaria to Omaha aren't part of it, no matter what they sound like." The Echo Nest's computers help tell us something about music: We say we like the way it sounds, but, often as not, what we really like is what it means. And something else: Knowing what to *call* something helps us like it.

Lamere gave the example of Miley Cyrus, whom his then-fifteen-year-old daughter was into a few years back. Acoustically, he suggested, you could line Cyrus up with "a few indie singer-songwriters." On paper, they sounded pretty similar. But you would not want to play, on a music service, one of those indie singer-songwriters after you had played Miley Cyrus. "The cultural impedance mismatch would just be too bad," he said.

What he was talking about, of course, in the wonky language of a software engineer, was perhaps the greatest machine learning challenge of all: human taste. It is humans who decide that Miley Cyrus is not appropriate to play among a group of other similar-sounding singer-songwriters. It is humans who decide what genre an artist belongs in or whether something is a genre; those genres are endlessly shifting.

The singer Lucinda Williams tells the story that when she was shopping around an early demo tape, she was turned down by the record labels. "At Sony records here in L.A., it's too country for rock, and so we sent it to Nashville." In Nashville, they said, "It's too rock for country." As it happens, her album was eventually released by an English record company known more for punk, and it became a touchstone in the emerging "alt-country" genre, "whatever that is," in the famous refrain of the movement's chronicling magazine, *No Depression*. Her song "Passionate Kisses" eventually charted in Nashville, but only when sung by Mary Chapin Carpenter, in a version that the Echo Nest's computers would probably have trouble distinguishing.

20   Whitman confessed that while the company's algorithms had gotten pretty good at automatically making sense of music itself—based on more than a trillion data points covering over thirty-five million songs and over 2.5 million artists—they had less of a grip "on understanding how listeners relate to that music." So when I visited, the company was testing its "Taste Profile" technology. At its furthest horizon, this is about using music to understand people's other affinities. In one Bourdieu-style exercise, the Echo Nest correlated people's listening preferences in the United States with their political affiliations. As Whitman asked, "Can we tell if someone is a Republican just from his or her iTunes collection?" There were some obvious findings: Republicans more often liked country; Democrats more often liked rap.

But other correlations were more unexpected. Pink Floyd, it turns out, is one of the bands most liked primarily by Republicans (even if the band's members seem to be rather liberal in outlook). Whitman speculated this was mostly about the changing demographics of an aging fan base. But Pink Floyd itself changed with age, musically, and so Whitman was able to identify a split in which fans of the earlier, more psychedelic, Syd Barrett–helmed Pink Floyd tilted more Democratic. Data mining revealed other tendencies: Democrats liked more music genres (ten) than Republicans (seven); and liking for the Beatles pretty much predicted nothing in the way of political preference.

Curiously, the least predictive of all musical genres when it came to political affiliation was metal. Loud and rebellious apparently cuts all kinds of ways. . . .

Bourdieu had proposed that one reason music was so predictive of people's class, historically, was that it was hard to acquire, for example, the ability to play a "noble instrument." Easier, less costly "cultural capital" could be found in galleries or theaters. This argument collapsed with the arrival of the phonograph. "One can hear famous pieces of music," the composer Claude Debussy noted, not kindly, "as easily as one can buy a glass of beer."

Now the cost of reproduction has dwindled to virtually nothing. There is so much to listen to on Spotify that, as the Forgotify Web site illustrated, circa 2013, some four million of the service's twenty-million-odd tracks had *never been played* (whatever the virtues of Desperation Squad's "I Need a Girl [with a Car]," the world was deaf). What happens to taste in an age when most people have equal access to much of the music that has ever been recorded? As the sociologist Richard Peterson writes, "The appreciation of classical music, rock, techno, and country can hardly be expected to retain their status-making value if they are increasingly commodified and easy to acquire." Is there anything *less* scarce these days than access to music?

Of course, Bourdieu had always hinted that what you did *not* listen to said as much about you as what you did. Your love of opera precluded a liking of country and western. But in the early 1990s, Peterson and his colleague Albert Simkus, poring over Census Bureau data on the arts, discovered an interesting trend: From 1982 to 1992, so-called highbrows began listening to—and liking—more kinds of music, including "lowbrow" genres like country and blues. . . . 25

Being a snob could actually be socially counterproductive, lessening one's ability to move across different social networks. The culture of the MP3 playlist—where nothing was physically owned—was less about having the right music than having the most eclectic; less about rejecting music genres outright than having "interesting" reasons for adding them to the mix (as Bourdieu put it, "liking the same things differently"). . . .

It was not, suggests the sociologist Omar Lizardo, that omnivores really *loved* all that new music but that they could maintain a weak, wide-ranging appreciation, a number of small pots on a low boil. After all, liking things takes time. Not only do people consume music, notes the sociologist Noah Mark, but "musical forms consume people." The more you like one genre, the less time and energy you have to like others. At the Echo Nest, Whitman found flickers of omnivorousness: "We modeled listeners where we have a rich taste profile, and then compared their behavior for a week to station profiles for the top 12 radio formats. In a given week, the average on-demand listener went across 5.6 listening formats." Of course, there is probably self-selection going on here: The most omnivorous people are going to want the huge variety offered by online services. Most people still seem to want the hits: By one analysis, 1 percent of artists accounted for 77 percent of all income from recorded music. . . .

The flip side of the omnivore is the so-called univore, those people who listen to the fewest genres and express the most disliking for other music genres. Univores tend to be lower-educated people in groups with lesser cultural status; curiously, Peterson suggested there may be "highbrow univores," similarly restrictive but for different reasons. In a neat symbiosis, univores tend to inhabit the very same genres that are liked least by the omnivores. The Echo Nest has found some evidence of this in a metric it has dubbed the "passion index." Which artists, they wanted to know, "dominate the playlists of their fans"? Metal bands, that scourge of the omnivore, made up much of the list. Metal fans want to hear metal—to the exclusion of other music—more than fans of other genres want to hear their own music. In their own way, univores are drawing their own, more powerful cultural lines of exclusion, perhaps, in some ways, as a reaction against the symbolic (and real) exclusion they face. . . .

People label music; music labels people. The way those labels match up or do not between particular people and music is interesting. As always, however, the more revealing action is in what people say they do not like, rather than in what they do.

THE PANDORA'S BOX OF TASTE: HOW CAN WE LIKE WHAT WE DON'T KNOW?

30 . . . In the early days of Pandora, the popular online music service, one of its founders, Tim Westergren, proposed something radical: What if the listener were shown no information about what was playing?

"The idea," he told me, "was that our appreciation of music is so deeply affected by our preconceived notions of what an artist stands for, what a genre means. You don't listen to music objectively. People have a knee-jerk reaction to an artist based on something that's not musical." This had helped inspire Pandora's Music Genome Project, the vast web of hand-coded musicological attributes driving what it plays for you. "The idea of the genome was to strip that down, to make choices based on musicology," he said. Like using DNA to locate distant relatives, the genome could point you to music that shared secret bloodlines. "Getting rid of the names and pictures of the artist would be a way of making the listener do the same." The idea, he said, "was deemed stupid."

Before starting Pandora, Westergren worked as a film composer. His job was to find the right musical style for a film but also to discern the director's taste. "I would play someone a bunch of songs and get their feedback," he said. "I was trying to map their preferences." He compares it to the children's game Battleship. "It is literally like that, feeling around for what the shape of their taste was." This was the spirit of Pandora: trying to codify that taste-mapping process by playing you a bunch of songs and registering your feedback.

Something else haunted him. He had read an article about the singer Aimee Mann and her struggles to get her music distributed. "This is a woman who has a fan base," he said. "There must be some way to more cost-effectively connect them with her." Perhaps there were people who might like Aimee Mann—because she shared certain musical attributes with other artists they already knew and liked—if they could only hear her. Think about how many times artists have been lifted from obscurity by their placement in a film soundtrack, such as the Proclaimers' song "I'm Gonna Be (500 Miles)." A movie is a place where, like Westergren's early idea, music comes at us rather blind, without preconceptions. You do not know what it is or who is singing it. You *have* to listen to it.

The most fundamental factor in liking a song is whether you have heard it before. Exposure, as with food, is key: The more you hear something, the more you will like it (there are exceptions I will return to). There is a huge body of literature about the effects of exposure. In one typical study, when groups of English children and college students were played samples of unfamiliar Pakistani folk music, they liked it more the more they heard it. This is how DJs help make hits. The Echo Nest's Whitman admitted he was jealous of radio in that it had no "skip button." "Maybe some DJ out there did have insight into the fact that if you heard 'Bohemian Rhapsody' twenty times," he said, "that operatic thing got wired in your brain and became something you liked."

Many psychologists argue that as we are repeatedly exposed to a [35] stimulus—like music, or shapes, or Chinese ideograms—our "perceptual fluency" increases, and we learn to process that thing more easily. We translate this ease of processing, which itself feels good, into feelings for the thing itself. As the psychologist Elizabeth Hellmuth Margulis puts it, we do not necessarily think, seeing a triangle for the fourth time, "I've seen that triangle before, that's why I know it." Instead, people think, "Gee, I like that triangle. It makes me feel clever." The more "prototypical" things are, the easier they are to process. People in studies have tended to find digitally morphed composites of faces (or birds or cars or shapes) more attractive than any single face or bird or car, because in that averageness lies a greater chance for the thing to look like what a person thinks that thing should look like. . . .

Exposure contains a hidden peril: We begin to like some things *less* the more we are exposed to them—especially the things we disliked before. There is no exact formula to this, but one leading theory, offered by the psychologist Daniel Berlyne, is that our liking for things like music follows an inverted U-shaped graph, based on the factor of "complexity."

We like things less the more simple or complex they are. The sweet spot, for most people, is somewhere in the middle.

Each time we listen to that music, however, it gets less complex. So the infectious pop song built around a simple beat that tears up the charts one summer might quickly fall off the liking cliff. Another song, more intricately arranged, full of deeper melodies and meanings, might slowly ascend in our estimation. Nick Drake's *Pink Moon*, with its densely poetic lyrics and complex chords, missed the 1972 English pop charts by a mile. Yet you are far more likely to have heard the album's title song in the past few years—in films, in commercials, on the radio—than one of the *top* songs of that year: Donny Osmond's "Puppy Love" or Chuck Berry's "My Ding-a-Ling." It is as if it took longer to like Nick Drake. When the Beatles' catalog is arranged by complexity, note the music scholars Adrian North and David Hargreaves, albums such as *Please Please Me*, chart toppers in their day, have enjoyed less lasting popularity than more musically and lyrically complex works such as *Abbey Road*. . . .

Complexity aside, why do we seem to prefer what is familiar? With food, the familiar is evolutionarily adaptive: What did not kill you last time is good for you this time. We face Paul Rozin's "omnivore's dilemma": Like rats, we are not restrictive in our food choices, but as a consequence, writes Michael Pollan, "a vast amount of brain space and time must be devoted to figuring out which of all the many potential dishes nature lays on are safe to eat." In music, and with taste in general, we face a similar omnivore's dilemma: more songs than you can listen to in a lifetime. The early promise of the digital music revolution was, as the musician Peter Gabriel noted, freedom to choose. As hard drives overflowed and the cloud began to burst with music, we suddenly needed freedom *from* choice.

> **Pink Floyd, it turns out, is one of the bands most liked primarily by Republicans.**

So we fall back on exposure: Why should we not like what we know (even if there might be something we would like more)? It saves us time and energy, versus foraging in the great musical wilderness for things that are difficult to process. This may be why people seem to most like the music that they heard during "a critical period of maximum sensitivity," as research by Morris Holbrook and Robert Schindler has shown—an age they peg at 23.5 years. This too could be familiarity. It would be strange for people in their 70s to *not* prefer the Mills Brothers' "Smoke Rings" to Peter Gabriel's "Sledgehammer," if only because they will be more familiar with the former.

There may be more than mere exposure and familiarity, however, to explain why we hold a special place in our hearts for the music of our early adult years. Holbrook and Schindler raise the idea of some kind of Lorenzian imprinting, a "biologically fixed" period in which we form parental attachments or learn language (although the long-held idea of an age-based "critical period" for language acquisition has been more recently challenged).

I think something simpler is also going on. The college-age years are 40 when we typically have the most time to search out and consume music. I still feel a vestigial crick in my neck from hunching over record bins. Now I barely have time to scroll through a playlist.

During a period of life when most of us do not have fancy watches or cars, music becomes a cheap, socially important signal of distinction. We are trying on, like silk-screened T-shirts, various identities. My high-school notebooks were filled with band logos, while an old cigar box held countless concert ticket stubs, like fetish objects, clues to my soul. Arguments over bands were arguments over who we wanted (and did not want) to be. How could these fierce attachments survive the transition to adulthood? In the documentary film *Rush: Beyond the Lighted Stage*, Matt Stone, the creator of *South Park*, talks about being the sort of person who would try in vain to impress upon his skeptical peers—whose taste ran to more "critically accepted" acts like Elvis Costello—the virtues of the Canadian progressive rock trio. "Now it's like we're all so old," he said, "even if you hated Rush in the '70s and '80s, you've just got to give it up for them. You've just got to."

And indeed, when I now hear a song like Rush's "Spirit of Radio," damned if I do not derive a certain pleasure from it. Was I wrong about Rush all those years ago? Is my new appreciation itself unadulterated or leavened with a dash of ironic distance? Or is it that not only do I not have time to figure out what music to like (all over again), I do not *even have time to maintain my dislikes*.[3] I am "losing my edge." I am suffering "taste freeze." What is the opportunity cost of hunting down the latest band when it sounds to your ears like some rough derivative of a band you heard in your youth? It is hard to escape what has been called the "reminiscence peak," described as follows: "The events and changes that have maximum impact in terms of memorableness occur during a cohort's adolescence and young adulthood."

By this analysis, one suspects the reason Woodstock loomed so large in the culture is not the music itself but an almost *statistical* outcome of the largest birth cohort in American history suddenly hitting that age bracket of maximum impact. But why do we all—and not just *The Big Chill* generation—seem to insist that the music of our youth was *better*? As Carnegie Mellon's Carey Morewedge points out, because everyone basically has this experience, it cannot be objectively true. He suggests that in the same way we tend to remember positive life events more strongly than negative events, only the "good" music from our past tends to survive in our memory. In the raw and unpolished present, meanwhile, we hear music we think we like *and* music we know we do not like. Memory, as he describes it, is like a radio station that only plays what we want to hear. Given that we had devoted so much time to thinking about the music, it is no surprise that it still so easily fills our memory and that we seem to have a hedonic soft spot for it.

So how do we move beyond the safe perimeter of our typical foraging ground into promising, if terrifying, new vistas, filled with new, unknown pleasures? We look for someone to take us there. As Westergren had joked to me, "We allow the lazy middle-age man to get back in the game.". . .

45   And there is the idea that like food, music may comprise basic "tastes"—instead of saltiness or sweetness, think of syncopation or vocal breathiness or drum snare—but it is the "flavors" we learn to like and discern. A few years ago, Pandora listeners seemed to be lodging particularly negative feedback in the electronic dance music genre. "We had analyzed about forty-five thousand tracks, and we realized a lot of the club dance music was indiscriminately mixing together," Hogan said. "To the genome, they all have the same 'boosh boosh boosh' beat." But fans were hearing techno on their trance stations. Techno, says Eric Bieschke, "means something very specific if you're into electronic music. If you're my dad, everything I've ever listened to is techno." So Pandora, Bieschke said, added a dozen or so new "attributes" into the genome. "How much reverb and ambience is on there? What sort of eq'ing effects or filter sweeps are being used?"

Even an individual band can represent many different pathways of taste. Sometimes it's the people who change, while the song remains the same. Take the hit song "We Are Young" by Fun. The year prior, Conrad told me, Fun was "just one of the countless kind of semi-faceless bands that put out a record and get a review on *Pitchfork* and no one in any mass scale hears about them." The song, he noted, had been on Pandora "for years," played by a "core of people who felt like they had discovered this band." Then, suddenly, the song appeared on the soundtrack to the popular television show *Glee*. "Overnight this song had a huge new audience, who I think had a different set of expectations when they came to listen to it on Pandora. They wanted to hear other songs that had been on *Glee*."

The whole world of recorded music, Zapruder had suggested to me, is like an ocean. "Every recording is an entry point. So you might get into the water at the Beatles, and once you're in the water, you can end up anywhere." Some people hug the shore; others brave the open ocean. At its most incisive, Pandora might make a serendipitous connection, the way a free-form DJ might, following the Beatles with, say, "Lemons Never Forget" by the Bee Gees. The sound is quite Beatles-esque. But for many people, their mental model of the Bee Gees as a disco act would not permit them this connection. Bieschke says the "holy trinity" at Pandora is "variety, discovery, familiarity." It has a mathematical model of where you sit on that axis—from "active" to "passive" listening. The stations you create are shorthand for the breadth of your taste. "If you've ever created a jazz station, you probably have stations all over the map," he said. "If you ever typed in 'Coltrane,' you're likely to have a very wide umbrella of interested listening habits."

In the end, the thumb rules. In early 2015, someone's up or down vote was the fifty billionth thumb on Pandora. The thumb is the clearest signal it has, stronger than the skip button. But even here there is room for ambiguity. Are you saying you do not want to hear that right now? Do you not like that band, or is it not quite right for this station? "We actually ran a test," Bieschke said. "We took half of a percent of people listening to Pandora. When they hit thumb up or thumb down, we'd ask why." Listeners could list reasons why in a text box. "The tricky part was that the things people wrote in were all over the map. They would write things like 'I thumbed this up because it was the first dance at my daughter's wedding.' As an algorithm guy, I was like, what the hell am I going to do with that?" The feature was scuttled, and that particular Pandora's box—trying to learn why people liked or disliked something—was closed.

"They say there's no accounting for taste," Hogan told me. "But we can account for it, en masse. We can say there's an 84 percent chance that this song is going to work for people listening to Rolling Stones radio. It's a good bet; we've accounted for the taste of this big group of people." He paused, looked briefly into space, then added, "Maybe there's no accounting for why they *didn't* like it."

NOTES

[1]Hugo Liu is an artificial intelligence researcher and the founder of art tech startup, ARTADVISOR.

[2]Pierre Bourdieu (1930–2002) was a French sociologist and philosopher who theorized that taste was liked with power.

³In the film *While We're Young*, Ben Stiller's highbrow Gen X character, upon being played, with seemingly pure appreciation, Survivor's "Eye of the Tiger" by a hip young omnivore, says with wonder, "I remember when this was just supposed to be bad."

FOR A SECOND READING

1. "People's music preferences," writes Vanderbilt, "are potent in drawing accurate inferences about their personality, or at least the personality they are trying to project" (p. 142). Why does Vanderbilt draw this distinction? What is the difference between having a personality and "projecting" a personality? And how is this difference important to the larger point about cultural taste Vanderbilt is trying to make in this essay?

2. Central to a cultural product's appeal, notes Vanderbilt, is familiarity. "Why," he asks, "do we seem to prefer what is familiar?" (p. 150). How would you answer this question? Do your own experiences as a cultural consumer confirm this observation? And if so, what is it about "familiar" cultural fare that makes it more appealing?

3. Take a moment to reflect upon your own experiences with music streaming sites like Pandora and Spotify. How effective are these sites in predicting your musical tastes? If you were in charge, how would you change the algorithms used to make these predictions? What additional information would you program them to factor in?

PUTTING IT INTO WRITING

4. Citing the observation of a noted music critic, Vanderbilt declares that "genres are as much social distinctions as musical distinctions" (p. 145). In a 300-word essay, use your personal experiences as a music consumer to test the validity of this statement. Which musical genres do you like the most? Which genres do you like the least? In what specific ways would you say musical preferences serve to differentiate you socially from other musical consumers? And, finally, are these social distinctions important to you? Why or why not?

5. In the early days of Pandora, notes Vanderbilt, one of the founders "proposed something radical: What if the listener were shown no information about what was playing?" (p. 148). In a 300-word essay, offer your own response to this hypothetical. How do you think listeners would react to a song if they knew no additional information about it? On what basis would they evaluate its appeal?

Do you think this kind of experience might change a listener's musical tastes more broadly? How?

COMPARING ARGUMENTS

6. How would you apply the research about "cultural taste" Vanderbilt discusses here to the phenomenon of "binge-watching" Kevin Fallon (p. 156) explores in his essay? Do you think it's possible to use data about binge-watching preferences to classify viewers according to different types? Do you group or define people based on the kind of TV shows they watch?

KEVIN FALLON
Why We Binge-Watch Television

Commentators of all stripes have long deplored America's fascination with excess, pointing to such things as Big Gulps and supersized fast food, eight-lane highways and Monster Truck rallies, as evidence of the country's cultural decline. Adopting a decidedly different point of view, Kevin Fallon offers a deeper investigation and spirited defense of one particular pop culture excess: television binge-watching. Kevin Fallon is the senior entertainment reporter for *The Daily Beast*, where this piece was published in 2013.

Before You Read

How much experience do you have binge-watching? How does it differ from other, more traditional, ways of watching television? In what ways do you consider it to be an improvement over these more traditional ways of watching television? Why?

WE CORRESPOND WITH EACH OTHER IN 140-CHARACTER BURSTS. We consume news in sound bites and blog posts. We're, by all accounts, an increasingly distracted society, with the attention span of a house fly sipping on Red Bull in a room lit by a strobe light while dubstep plays. Knowing that, it makes absolutely no sense that we are also a society that enjoys binge-watching TV.

But we do. Oh, for the love of Walter White, we do.

According to a new study by Harris Interactive on behalf of Netflix, 61 percent of us binge-watch TV regularly, which is to say that we watch at least 2–3 episodes of a single series in one sitting. Or, some of us (many of us), devour 14 in a row with breaks just for bathroom and answering the door for the delivery man. Almost three-quarters of us view binge-watching as a positive experience, and nearly 80 percent say that feasting on a show actually makes it better.

Given how many times we've heard people use the word "binge-watch" this past year and how many times we've alarmed our friends by disappearing from society for a week to marathon a show, it shouldn't be surprising that the practice is quickly becoming the new normal when it comes to consuming television. But it is remarkable that such a highly fragmented world is actively seeking out—and even preferring—longer form, more complex storytelling at the same time we want everything else in life easy and breezy.

5   It shouldn't compute. So why does it?

All of the elements of a perfect storm brewed at the same time, explains Grant McCracken, a cultural anthropologist who worked on the study. More accurately, it's a storm cycle: TV has gotten better, making viewers smarter, making TV even more complex, making binge-watching more fun. And because we're living in a world where too many things are constantly competing for our attention, developing a habit of binge-watching is like seeking shelter in the calm eye of that storm.

"I was illuminated to hear people say, 'Look, it's precisely because there's so much distraction that this is a special pleasure,'" McCracken says of the 1,500 streamers he interviewed as part of the study. While TV marathons have always been events, the rise of binge-watching is a by-product of necessary and sufficient conditions that have only surfaced in recent years, with the easy availability of streaming, season DVDs, and TiVos compounded with the rise in quality of the shows available.

Plus, there's the undeniably fun appropriation of the word "binge."

"You hear that people are slightly embarrassed to spend four or five hours watching TV, that there's something reckless or indulgent or ill-advised about it," McCracken says. "That was the origin of the research project: to find out if 'binge' is the right metaphor, and if not then what is."

As it turns out, the entire connotation of "binge"—a word tinged   10 with the shame of eating an entire roll of cookie dough—has changed into something prideful and brag-worthy. "Finally some people get that there's something ironic about the term," McCracken says. "People aren't watching *Dukes of Hazard*. They're watching great TV, not bad TV."

Indeed, the successive-episode viewing couldn't be as popular as it is—especially, again, in the age where people discuss everything and anything on social media and attempting to avoid a major plot spoiler online is a fool's errand—if the series being binged weren't as creatively evolved and dra-

According to a new study by Harris Interactive on behalf of Netflix, 61 percent of us binge-watch TV regularly, which is to say that we watch at least 2–3 episodes of a single series in one sitting.

matically complex as *Breaking Bad*, *The Wire*, *Game of Thrones*, *Orange Is the New Black*, and other popular binging series are.

"Remember on *Dallas* when somebody shot J.R.?" says McCracken. "If you found out who did it after the fact, what would be the point of going back and watching that season? But with something like *The Wire*, even if a friend accidentally let a key character's death slip it doesn't really destroy the point of watching the show." There's so much more to pick apart, dissect, and become emotionally and intellectually engaged with that watching it, despite the unintended spoiler, is still enjoyable.

The late-in-its-run success of *Breaking Bad* is the perfect example of that. The show's final season premiered to double the series' previous ratings high and almost four times the ratings for the show's debut in 2008. The five years in between saw hordes of people finally caving to the "you *have* to watch *Breaking Bad!*" pressure of their colleagues, thanks to the availability of the entire series for streaming on Netflix.

"I think Netflix kept us on the air," Vince Gillian, *Breaking Bad*'s creator, said after his show won the Emmy for Best Drama Series in September. "Not only are we standing up here [with the Emmy], I don't think our show would have lasted beyond Season Two. It's a new era in television and we've been very fortunate to reap the benefits."

15   Netflix is notorious for keeping its data locked away in that same bunker where the UFOs and the still-alive Elvis Presley are kept, but the company does confirm that binging is more popular than ever with its subscribers. "Our viewing data shows that the majority of streamers would actually prefer to have a whole season of a show available to watch at their own pace," said Ted Sarandos, Chief Content Officer of Netflix.

> **[B]ecause we're living in a world where too many things are constantly competing for our attention, developing a habit of binge-watching is like seeking shelter in the calm eye of that storm.**

The habits even shape its original programming choices, including *House of Cards* and *Orange Is the New Black*. "Netflix has pioneered audience choice in programming and has helped free consumers from the limitations of linear television. Our own original series are created for multi-episodic viewing, lining up the content with new norms of viewer control for the first time."

The result, not just because of strides in original programming from Netflix but because of the "binging" now becoming a legitimate alternative to most first-run broadcast airings, is that we are rejecting, in at least one crucial aspect of our lives—entertainment—the idea of instant gratification. It's what McCracken calls the "in case of emergency, break glass" phenomenon. And we all can identify with it.

There's a new series that you're excited about. You can't wait to try it out. "Then there's a small tension," McCracken says. "Do you watch it right away or do you set it aside for some eventuality like a terrible flu or a terrible snowstorm?" Anyone who just snuggled under a blanket with Olivia Pope during Snowstorm Hercules to watch an entire season of *Scandal* and gasped because OMG HE'S HER FATHER!? knows exactly what he means. "You have a great show on hand. You're protected in event of emergency. And then there's something delicious about having a great show on standby, in reserve."

Binging, as we used to do it, was a hindsight act of embarrassment, an action realized only after its completion when staring at an empty Doritos bag. Now we're planning to do it. In a world moving faster than ever and our focus more split than ever, who would have thought that it would be the medium of television, once called "a vast wasteland" by former FCC Chairman Newton Minow, that would finally slow us down.

FOR A SECOND READING

1. "[T]he entire connotation of 'binge,'" writes Fallon, "—a word tinged with the shame of eating an entire roll of cookie dough—has changed into something prideful and brag-worthy" (p. 157). Do you agree? How do you respond to the term "binge-watching"? Does it suggest passionate interest or slothful excess?

2. Fallon offers the following formula to explain the growing popularity of binge-watching: "TV has gotten better, making viewers smarter, making TV even more complex, making binge-watching more fun" (p. 157). How accurate do you find this formula to be? In your view, does it adequately explain the root causes behind the rise of binge-watching?

3. According to Fallon, many broadcasters keep the data about their customers' viewing habits "locked away." Why do you think companies adhere to this practice? What do you think we would learn about the public's viewing habits if this information were made public?

PUTTING IT INTO WRITING

4. Fallon writes: "We correspond with each other in 140-character bursts. We consume news in sound bites and blog posts. We're, by all accounts, an increasingly distracted society, with the attention span of a house fly sipping on Red Bull in a room lit by a strobe light while dubstep plays. Knowing that, it makes absolutely no sense that we are also a society that enjoys binge-watching TV" (p. 156). Write a 300-word essay in which you examine Fallon's statement. Given the state of our current communications culture, do you agree that the rise of "binge-watching" is an anomaly? If so, what do you think explains its unexpected popularity? And if not, how is this phenomenon similar to other contemporary forms of cultural consumption?

5. Fallon concludes his essay this way: "Binging, as we used to do it, was a hindsight act of embarrassment, an action realized only after its completion when staring at an empty Doritos bag. Now we're planning to do it. In a world moving faster than ever and our focus more split than ever, who would have thought that it would be the medium of television . . . that would finally slow us down?" (p. 159). Choose a TV show that you have binge-watched yourself. Then write a 500-word essay in which you discuss the ways your experience watching this show either confirms or challenges the claim Fallon makes here. First, describe your experience of binge-watching. What did this form of cultural consumption feel like? Was it easy or difficult to keep track of the plot, different characters, etc.? Then use this description as a way to respond to Fallon. Did you "plan" to binge-watch this show? Did the experience of binge-watching increase your attention or "slow you down"? How or how not?

COMPARING ARGUMENTS

6. According to Tom Vanderbilt (p. 142), cultural tastes are important in part because they are central to our effort to "project a public personality." Do you think the same hypothesis applies to binge-watching? Do our binge-watching preferences similarly make a public statement about who we are? And if not, what makes binge-watching different from other forms of cultural consumption?

Scenes and Un-Scenes: **Picturing Climate Change**

Whether it is a television commercial or a news broadcast, a web image or a blockbuster movie, virtually everything we see has been selectively shaped for our inspection. While it may purport to show us "the way things are," the truth is that every image bears traces of some slant or bias, intentional or not. And yet while it may be inevitable, this doesn't mean it is automatically excusable — that such bias doesn't warrant our attention, doesn't deserve to be challenged, critiqued, or changed. Certainly when it comes to something as consequential, even potentially catastrophic, as global climate change, it is no small matter to know whether the images we are shown tell the whole story. The images that follow offer an overview of the ways that media coverage shaped, perhaps even skewed, the public's understanding of this phenomenon: what is causing it, whom it affecting, who is most responsible for addressing it.

NOAA

▲▲ *One of the debates around climate change concerns the role that "man-made" forces have played in contributing to a spike in global temperatures. Despite the overwhelming scientific consensus that human activity is the primary cause behind global warming, some skeptics continue to maintain that such extreme climactic events superstorms and glacial melting are the result of natural, cyclical trends. Satellite photos like the one above, for example, would seem to offer support for both views. Tracking the movements a recent superstorm, this photo could be read on the one hand as evidence that "man-made" carbon emissions are having a drastic effect on the environment. Recording this event from the supposedly objective view of outer space, however, it could also be read as proof that such extreme weather events are the result of entirely "natural" forces.*

Scott J. Ferrell/Getty Images

Bloomberg/Getty Images

Not surprisingly, the question of who or what is responsible for global climate change has become the subject of intense political debate. Over the last decade, countless climate change experts have testified before Congress, presenting the scientific data about global warming, and urging legislators to address the growing threat this phenomenon poses. A number of these elected officials, however, have pushed back against such testimony, reframing the climate change question as less a debate about science than a debate about jobs. The two pictures featured here illustrate this divide. In the first, representatives from the Union of Concerned Scientists present evidence of polar ice cap melt before a congressional committee. In the second, Oklahoma senator James Inhoff presides over a Senate hearing on the threat global warming legislation poses to American workers.

Another hallmark of global warming coverage involves what we might call the "sympathetic celebrity" feature, in which a famous person offers a personal testimony about importance of addressing this issue. The photo here, which depicts former President Barack Obama and Hollywood star Leonardo DiCaprio attending a global climate panel, offers one such example. What is the effect of casting global climate change as a celebrity testimonial? What kind of reaction does it seem designed to elicit from viewers?

Pool/Getty Images

Another type of global warming coverage involves depictions of natural disasters presumed to be the result of climate change. Coverage of events like the 2012 Superstorm Sandy tends to be informed by a far more immediate sense of suffering and emergency. How does this perspective differ from that modeled in other examples? What attitude toward or action regarding global climate change does it encourage?

RICHARD B. LEVINE/Newscom/Levine Roberts Photography/ NEW YORK/NY/USA

FOR A SECOND READING

1. How would you characterize the bias that each of the images above reflects? In what ways does this bias shape your views about global climate change?

2. What factors (i.e., gender, race, social class, age, work history, region, etc.) do you think might affect the way viewers respond to these images? What different conclusions about this issue might different members of the general public draw? Why?

3. Is the coverage of climate change an isolated or idiosyncratic example of media bias, or do you think it reflects a more wide-ranging pattern? Can you think of another news event or controversy that ended up being defined by such contrasting sorts of images?

PUTTING IT INTO WRITING

4. This portfolio makes clear that bias is a question not only of (mis)representation but also of omission. That is, it shows how bias reveals itself not simply in terms of what an image shows, but also by virtue of what it leaves out. Choose one of the images showcased in the preceding pages and write a one-page assessment of the things it does not show. What key aspects of its portrait are left out? How do these omissions influence the conclusions viewers are encouraged to draw?

5. As discussed throughout this chapter, our culture's visual rules teach us not only how to watch but also how to think. Choose one of the images from the preceding pages and write a one-page script for how the image is supposed to make us think about the politically loaded issue of federal disaster relief. What sorts of ideas concerning the responsibility of the government to aid those in need does it encourage viewers to adopt?

COMPARING ARGUMENTS

6. As her essay suggests, Harriet McBryde Johnson (p. 93) was someone interested in the ways that people's personal experiences and struggles can be misunderstood by the public at large. Choose three of the images previously listed and in two or three sentences write the kind of caption you think Johnson would create for each. What aspect of each image would she focus on? What specific sort of bias or slant would she identify? Then, write a second set of captions you think accurately describes what is happening in the photos you've chosen. How does your perspective compare to Johnson's?

Acting Like a Citizen: **Keeping an Eye Out**

As the chapter selections above make clear, it isn't enough simply to identify the ways we are taught to process, visually and aurally, the world around us. We also need to consider whether or not it is right to act out these instructions in our own lives. How do these kinds of scripts teach us to evaluate the world around us? What sorts of value judgments do they invite us to make? And are these judgments accurate, beneficial, or fair? The following exercises give you an opportunity to answer these questions, and in the process gain more firsthand experience in learning to think and act "like a citizen."

WINDOW SHOPPING   Pay a visit to the retail website of your choice. Based on the marketing images it includes, what sort of customer do you think it is trying to attract? How do the site's layout, links, and icons stereotype this customer? Imagine that you are creating a website of your own, designed to attract a certain type of person, whether it is the soccer mom, macho guy, or hipster. Describe what your customer looks like, and then decide what sorts of elements and images you would use to draw the customer to your site.

RATING THE HEADLINES   In television news, stories are typically covered in the order that news producers deem most important to least important. Watch a broadcast of the national evening news and keep a running record of the order in which the stories of the day are covered. What characterizing images stand out in your mind for each story? Write a brief essay in which you discuss why you think certain stories are given more weight or are broadcast earlier than others, and be sure to include examples from the broadcast you've just watched. If you were a news producer, in what order would you broadcast the same stories? Why?

THE REAL YOU   Create a playlist of the songs you think express facets of your identity: your cultural tastes, your personal values, and/or your social views. In class, exchange playlists with a peer and write a brief characterization of him or her based on the musical selections you've been given. Based on your playlist, what do your classmates have to say about you? How closely does their description of you match your personality or identity? How might you have altered your playlist to get them to describe you more accurately?

No One Can Thrive on an Empty Stomach

42 million people face hunger in the U.S. today — including nearly 13 million children and more than five million seniors. Hunger knows no boundaries — it touches every community in the U.S., including your own.

Learn more about the facts, and the impact of hunger in the U.S. ›

Working Together to End Hunger

The Feeding America network is the nation's largest domestic hunger-relief organization, working to connect people with food and end hunger. Donors, staff, and volunteers all play an important role in our efforts to end hunger in the United States.

Learn more about our work ›

This screenshot is taken from the website for Feeding America, a nonprofit organization that oversees a network of 200 food banks nationwide, responsible for feeding over 45 million people annually. As you look over this infographic, consider what it says to you about the current state of hunger in America. Then answer the following questions:

➲ How important an issue is childhood hunger to you?

➲ What kinds of stereotypes get associated with childhood hunger?

➲ How can these particular norms be challenged?

➲ What specific action would you take to address the issue of childhood hunger in America?

3 How We
EAT

Which Rules Dictate the Foods We Put in Our Bodies?

Introduction

SCRIPTING THE PERFECT MEAL

Few choices, at first glance, seem as straightforward as what to eat. You're hungry. You eat. What's so complicated about that? Some people like Chicken McNuggets while others prefer sushi; some of us are die-hard vegetarians while others fall into the meat-and-potatoes camp. Whichever way we slice it, the underlying assumption remains the same: How and what we eat is, in every sense of the phrase, a matter of personal taste.

And yet, we might want to pause before too quickly accepting this premise. True, we live in a world that offers us a seemingly endless array of food-related choices. But we also live in a world that provides a lot of instruction in how we are supposed to make these choices. From diet books to FDA guidelines, fast-food commercials to gourmet magazines, we are surrounded by images, messages, and advice — all of it designed, in one way or another, to fix our "proper" relationship to food. There are cultural rules telling us what types of foods we are supposed to eat, as well as in what amounts. There are cultural rules that dictate how different meals should be prepared or consumed, as well as ones decreeing how much they are expected to cost. Indeed the sheer volume of cultural rules around eating makes one basic fact inescapable: No matter how personal they may feel, our food choices are framed long before we ever set foot in the kitchen, the grocery store, or the restaurant.

What is normal?

> ❝ **Atkins Diet: The Rules of Induction**
>
> **Rule 4. Eat nothing that isn't on the Acceptable Foods list. And that means absolutely nothing. Your 'just this one taste won't hurt' rationalization is the kiss of failure during this phase of Atkins."**
>
> *Atkins Nutritional Approach*

What does this diet advice ask you to believe? What are the ideas, values, or attitudes it asks you to accept as normal?

FOOD FOR THOUGHT

Such cultural instruction does not only govern how we *act*. Just as importantly, it also shapes how we *think*. Whether or not we are fully aware of it, every time we elect to follow one of our culture's food-related instructions we are simultaneously endorsing the idea or value (i.e., the norm) that underlies it. To illustrate, let's compare two representative, if distinct, eating experiences: a Thanksgiving dinner and a McDonald's meal. In each case, there are well-established and universally recognized rules for how these two meals are supposed to unfold. We know, for example, to expect only a few select items on the menu for each. We are far more likely to come across turkey and cranberry sauce at the Thanksgiving table than veggie kabobs or tuna salad, and burgers and fries at the fast-food counter rather than tofu stir-fry. We also know that, in each case, very different dress codes apply. Cut-off jeans are far more appropriate when we are sitting in a plastic booth at McDonald's than when we are sitting at a holiday dinner table. And we know, finally, that there exist very different social rituals as well. Napkins go on laps and pleases and thank-yous accompany requests for food at a Thanksgiving gathering, while at McDonald's it is OK to eat with your hands and to throw away plates, containers, and napkins once the meal is finished.

What is normal?

U.S. Department of Agriculture

Do you share the attitude toward eating presented here? Should we automatically accept it as normal?

Listing these different rules isn't especially difficult. A bit trickier, however, is uncovering the ideas or assumptions these instructions simultaneously *normalize*. When we live up to the more formal expectations of a traditional Thanksgiving dinner, we are doing more than playing the role of a particular kind of diner. In donning this costume and adhering to this script, we are just as firmly giving our assent to a number of related notions: about the importance of tradition, about the special role that home and family should play in commemorating national holidays, even about which version of American history to accept as right. Similarly, when we assume the role of the typical fast-food consumer, our performance registers our tacit acceptance of a number of unspoken priorities: processed over "whole" foods, speed and efficiency over patience, convenience over nutrition.

This particular relationship — between the eating roles we take on and the eating rules we follow on the one hand and the social norms that underlie them on the other — links all of the readings in this chapter. Because our eating habits offer such a sensitive barometer of our current ideals and anxieties, each of the following selections uses its portrait of eating as a jumping-off point for investigating a larger issue, question or controversy to which food is connected.

Kim Bosch and Sophie Egan initiate this inquiry by taking a closer look at the forces (cultural, social, economic) that alternately enable or constrain our individual eating choices. Focusing on the gendered dimension of this question, Bosch begins by exploring what it means for women to "eat alone," arguing for the power of this unorthodox eating experience to challenge and revise prevailing social scripts. Egan, on the other hand, examines the issue of choice from a commercial perspective, chronicling the way that the rise of "customization" within the food industry is reshaping how we think about and engage in consumer choice.

The second set of paired readings focuses on some of the social and ethical norms that undergird our contemporary food system. Nicholas Kristof poses hard questions about our current food-stamp policy, calling legislative leaders to task for what he considers to be the government's callous "cruelty" toward poor Americans. Nathanael Johnson, meanwhile, delves more deeply into the debate over carnivorism, questioning whether a moral case can be made for "eating meat."

The next two writers turn their attention to cultural attitudes and taboos that shape the ways we think about our own bodies. Surveying the cultural history of "gluttony," Francine Prose indicts our contemporary society for its long-standing demonization of overeating, a tradition that has led many of us to stigmatize our overweight population as victims of food, social misfits, or pariahs. Exploring this question from a more personal vantage, Harriet Brown tells the story her own life long effort to navigate our culture's destructive norms around body image.

The final set of paired writers, Lily Wong and Brendan Buhler, rounds out our selections by considering the ways that individual or idiosyncratic eating practices can help to redefine cultural norms. Exploring how food choices intersect with ethnic/national identity, Wong reflects on what it means to eat like a Chinese American. Outlining the parameters of another eating practice deemed to lie outside the cultural mainstream, Buhler offers a surprising defense of "roadkill" as a viable food alternative.

What is normal?

"How do I prepare my TOMBSTONE FOR ONE Pizza? Toaster Oven/ Conventional Oven Cooking Directions: Preheat the oven to 400 degrees Fahrenheit. Remove pizza from box and overwrap. Discard silver cooking circle. Place pizza directly on oven rack in Center Position (8 to 10 inches from bottom of oven). Bake according to the table below, or until the cheese is melted and edges are golden brown. Oven temperatures vary, so adjust baking time and oven temperature as necessary. Supreme: 12 to 16 minutes. Extra Cheese: 9 to 12 minutes. Pepperoni: 9 to 12 minutes. CAUTION: Do not use silver circle in toaster oven or conventional oven."

Frequently Asked Questions,
www.kraftfoods.com

What kind of social script do these instructions write? What would it feel like to act out this script in our own lives? And can this kind of social script be rewritten?

KIM BOSCH

The Things We Eat Alone

For women, solitary eating has long suffered a checkered reputation, stigmatized by many as something suspicious, even illicit. But is this reputation, asks Kim Bosch, truly deserved? When we take into account the intense pressures women confront regarding their choices about food, can the decision to "eat alone" become a strategy for empowerment? Kim Bosch is a Canadian writer whose work has appeared in such publications as *The National Post* and *The* (Toronto) *Globe and Mail*. This essay appeared in 2015 in *GUTS*, an online Canadian feminist magazine.

Before You Read

Do you think eating can be understood as a public performance? If so, how does this act get scripted by our larger culture? What particular role(s) are we expected to play?

IT STARTS WITH BUTTER—A SOLID CHUNK, ROUGHLY A LARGE tablespoon in size and easily retrieved from the door of the fridge. It is melted in a small bowl in the microwave on high heat for forty seconds. Next comes the sugar. I forgo the accessible sugar bowl on top of the stove as there's rarely enough in it for this project. Instead, I drag a chair over to the pantry and snatch the bag of sugar off the top shelf (along with the bag of white flour). I spoon the sugar into the melted butter. I don't count the scoops. I keep adding and stirring and adding and stirring until a gritty paste reveals itself. I know what it's supposed to look like. Then I add about a tablespoon of flour, a little bit at a time, until a sort of dry dough ball starts to form. I prepare and eat this only when I am alone. It is immensely satisfying.

When I mention it to people, I call it "the shame ball." A self-deprecating title which I feel allows me to erase any real sense of shame in it at all. Like preemptively making a joke about myself. The more people, women especially, I talk to about my snack, the more they share their own indulgent recipes (and secret snacking rituals) with me. Raw butter, entire packs of gum, Kraft Singles, the crystalized lumps of brown sugar that you can easily pick out and pop into your mouth. The snacks are as varied as they are simple; however, it is not just the food itself that invokes such pleasure, it's the ritual associated with the snack, too. One friend explains how something as mundane as popcorn becomes even more satisfying when eaten a specific way. "I take as much popcorn as my hand will hold, unhinge my jaw, and shove the entire handful into my mouth. Once my mouth is full, I take a small sip of pop or juice and let the popcorn melt away. Delish! Repeat, repeat, repeat."

171

The creation of a ritual for eating these snacks personalizes the act of eating, and each woman I talk to has a unique snacking ritual that contradicts how a "snacking woman" is often portrayed. A quick Google image search of "snacking woman" curates ladies smiling at the camera while gingerly biting down on a carrot stick or apple, women in mock orgasm with chocolate at their mouths, women with a bowl of potato chips or can of frosting in front of her shushing the viewer with a single finger to her lips. These representations categorize women as specific types of eaters: healthy, sexy, naughty. On the contrary, secret snacking rituals are more visceral. One woman I spoke with remarked how her secret snack eating is "nothing like eating pretty bonbons while taking a bubble bath." Instead, the snacking routine is created out of comfort and convenience. The adoption of one's own system of eating therefore rejects these stereotypical categorizations of feminine eating, and arguably allows more focus to be placed on the pleasure of eating itself.

> *For women, eating has always been a keenly observed and heavily scrutinized public act.*

Of course ingesting a large amount of pure-form fat, sugar, or salt is also bound to feel satisfying, but there is more to this pleasure than a bodily rush. "I'm just basically giving into all my whims in one moment," explained Erica Hess, a fellow indulger in secret snacks, "it's that type of freedom." She told me about a secret foods party she was once invited to, a potluck-style get-together that encouraged guests to bring "a food that they would only eat in secret." She was really excited about it and prepared her then go-to secret food—a box of Bisquick mixed with milk, uncooked, served in a generic mixing bowl with spoons on the side. But when she arrived at the party, she was surprised how many of the snacks were just "regular foods." She was disappointed because, "I just think there are so many aspects to day-to-day life that people don't share—some women share with others, but I don't think it's really put out there."

5   This potluck-scenario exposes the inherent lack of trust among people in their shared eating habits, which is most often due to concerns about being judged. The "regular foods" Erica mentions are a reflection of the commodification of the guilty pleasure, specifically the marketization of "cheat foods." This phenomenon is exemplified in numerous articles found in women's magazines and health websites with titles like "8 Cheat Foods That Won't Ruin Your Diet" and that promote eating anticlimactic "treats" such as real cream in your coffee, veggie chips, or a handful of pistachios. Articles like these set forth a ranking system for the snacking woman—there are sanctioned snacks, with pretty

packaging and shame-free advertising ("indulge yourself with a 100-calorie yogurt!"), and there are unsanctioned snacks which should never be eaten, probably not spoken about, and definitely not shared.

Many of the women I've talked to seem to agree: there are unspoken rules about the indulgences in such treats. Most do not desire to share their snack (and/or their ritual or eating of it) with another person, others downright hide their snacks from partners, family, friends. Some explained that it is the fear of judgment that stops them from sharing, while others simply said that it is more enjoyable to eat by themselves. Other women told me that certain snacks could only be shared with certain people. One woman described how her secret snack—"Scrapey-Scrapey" (or "Scratchy-Scratchy"), the hardened chicken fat that fills the bottom of a pan after being cooked, and that must be "scratched" up in order to eat it—started as something shared with her brother when they were kids. She noted that when she is with her brother she feels no judgment in eating Scrapey-Scrapey, but in her own home, she sneaks it "so as not to be considered a weirdo for scraping the pan with my bare hands." She continued, "For me it's like, why is it okay when my brother is around? Because he is a man and he does it so suddenly it's not weird? Or if it is weird, it's like endearing weird, not gross fatty-fat weird."

Considering the pressures placed on women to eat well and to be healthy (read: thin), the act of eating, even in its most simple form, is gendered. For women, eating has always been a keenly observed and heavily scrutinized public act. Take for example the somewhat recent stranger shaming phenomenon of "Women Who Eat on Tubes"—a Tumblr that displays photos of women (and only women) eating everyday foods on the London Underground. The rightful outcry against the site focused primarily on issues of voyeurism, specifically that women on the site were photographed without their knowledge. However, Nell Frizzell of the *Guardian* rightfully points out that the larger issue lies in the fact "that women eating on the tube is even seen as noteworthy, [and that] to enjoy food alone and to eat without shame are vital parts of becoming self-sufficient." In a society that continuously scolds and infantilizes women for their eating habits—not unlike a child caught with their hand in the cookie jar—what then is the value, if any, of women choosing to eat poorly and in secret?

All too often, eating alone is seen as a symptom of loneliness, misbehavior, and so on. The act of eating alone implies guilt. In an article on the rise of secret female snackers, Cathy Kapica states flatly, "if [women] were eating snacks like they should be, they wouldn't be worried about doing it in secret." As Women Eating on Tubes implies, women who eat are specimens to be observed. Therefore, the creation of a private space for oneself to simply eat can be liberating for women. As Erica explains,

In a society that continuously scolds and infantilizes women for their eating habits—not unlike a child caught with their hand in the cookie jar—what then is the value, if any, of women choosing to eat poorly and in secret?

the pleasure of eating her secret food is not just in the food itself but also, and importantly, "being home alone, [because] no one's watching." Eating alone takes away the audience, so that the act is no longer a performance for women which like the ritual, allows women to focus more on the pleasure of eating instead of the performance. Considering also that historically the preparation of food has been an all too frequent duty assigned to women, the stripped down methods of making these snacks (eating out of simple bowls, using one's hands instead of linen tablecloths and fine china) further reject the decorum typically associated with women and food preparation. Eating becomes less about performance when we disregard pretty presentation.

Choosing snacks that actively reject the nutritional value of food is also rebellious; eating non-nutritionally is a rejection of productivity. For women, nutrition is often aligned with the concept of "balance"—a balanced diet, a balanced skin tone, the work-life balance. Everything in moderation, ladies. But in reality, the concept of "balance" means control. That is, "balance" as a term doesn't simply reflect caring for oneself, but instead indicates a state of perpetual unease: eight glasses of water a day, seven servings of fruits and vegetables, high protein, low fat, no sugar—our diets are a constant juggling act. Balance is work, and in the context of health, it has come to represent self-denial more than self-respect (balance never implies one should have fries, it always implies one should have salad). Much like "cheat foods," "balance" controls women, it makes us uncomfortable, and constantly reminds us of what we should and shouldn't eat. This often results in "balance" being flaunted as a means to achieving what in reality is an unattainable body. When women choose to eat the crappy food they love whenever they want, they are rejecting the rules, the unrealistic goals, the balance—instead, they take pleasure in eating, even if it is just for the amount of time it takes to enjoy their snack.

10   "Society expects you to be a certain way and for you to fit a certain standard, so I think pigging out is a statement," said one women I spoke to. I couldn't agree more. With that, I take the bowl containing my shame ball, huddle into the corner of my couch, and spoon it into my mouth in small wedges, slowly chipping away. The privacy, the ritual, and the

personal decision to make and ingest this thing, which provides me such pure and immediate pleasure, makes me feel content. In that moment, I am truly satisfied.

FOR A SECOND READING

1. Bosch opens this essay by detailing how she prepares her own "private snack." Why do you think she chooses to begin this way? How does it preview the larger argument she makes in this essay about the gendered nature of our culture's eating scripts?

2. According to Bosch, women routinely face the prospect of being "judged" and "stigmatized" for the eating choices they make. Do you agree? Which of the "secret snacks" Bosch describes in this essay do you think best illustrates this point?

3. Quoting one of the women she interviews, Bosch writes: "Society expects you to be a certain way and for you to fit a certain standard, so I think pigging out is a statement" (p. 174). How do you respond to this claim? What type of "statement" do you think "pigging out" makes? What kind of commentary about our culture's food norms and eating scripts does it offer?

PUTTING IT INTO WRITING

4. As Bosch notes, our popular culture is rife with images that slot women into specific eating roles: "A quick Google image search of 'snacking woman' curates ladies smiling at the camera while gingerly biting down on a carrot stick or apple, women in mock orgasm with chocolate at their mouths, women with a bowl of potato chips or can of frosting in front of her shushing the viewer with a single finger to her lips. These representations categorize women as specific types of eaters: healthy, sexy, naughty" (p. 172). Go online and conduct your own search into "representations" that "categorize women as specific types of eaters." Based on what you find, write a 500-word essay in which you identify and analyze the particular eating scripts for women created by these images. What messages do these representations promote about how women should and should not eat? In your view, are these messages helpful or harmful? Why?

5. Because judgment and guilt so often attach to women's eating choices, Bosch argues for "the creation of a private space" in which women have the power to choose for themselves. "Eating alone," she writes, "takes away the audience, so that the act is no longer a performance for women which . . . allows women to focus more on the

pleasure of eating instead of the performance" (p. 174). In a 500-word essay, respond to this argument. Do you share Bosch's view that the act of eating is typically scripted for women as a public "performance"? Do you agree that "tak[ing] away the audience" by "eating alone" can create a liberating space for women? Why or why not?

COMPARING ARGUMENTS

6. Bosch and Sophie Egan (p. 177) both examine how our food choices can be scripted by the larger culture. How do their respective arguments compare? Which writer, in your view, makes a more convincing case for how these scripts can be challenged or rewritten? Why?

SOPHIE EGAN
Having It Our Way

As twenty-first-century consumers, we are told that we live in an era of limitless choice. Perhaps nowhere is this more true than in relation to what we eat. Surveying the landscape of our contemporary food culture, Sophie Egan offers a snapshot of how the rise of "customization" is reshaping how we choose, consume, and even think about food. Sophie Egan is a food writer and a program director for the Culinary Institute of America. She is also the author of *Devoured: From Chicken Wings to Kale Smoothies—How What We Eat Defines Who We Are* (2016), from which this essay is excerpted.

Before You Read

As a consumer, do you feel your eating choices are truly individualized? How much does the question of individual choice matter to you?

DID YOU KNOW THERE ARE EIGHTY-SEVEN *THOUSAND* DIFFERENT drink combinations at Starbucks? The company has bragged about this at public appearances, on its website, and in full-page ads in *The Wall Street Journal* and *The New York Times*. It's as if they're saying: No two individuals are the same, so neither are their Frappuccinos. Just like . . . snowflakes. (Sigh.)

Nowadays, there's a Starbucks on every corner, a Chipotle in every strip mall. Each diner designs her own burrito or bowl or tacos exactly to her liking. From 500 flavors of individual-size Keurig cups of coffee and tea to the countless assembly-line style restaurant chains, we are living in the Era of Infinite Choice. Americans are hardwired to personalize and individualize our eating experiences. Customization, it seems, is our birthright.

HAVING IT OUR WAY, AT A RESTAURANT

. . . The desirability of uniqueness is part of the broader American cultural context in which we all live. It is so second nature to value individualism that we don't even realize that it affects how we think and act—especially about food.

Ohhh, but it does. Every time you step up to that restaurant counter, you are committing an act of intentionally and joyously deviating from a prescribed box.

"If a person orders a decaffeinated cappuccino with nonfat milk in a 5 café in San Francisco, he or she can feel good about having a preference that is not exactly regular," write Kim and Markus in the *Journal of*

Personality and Social Psychology. "The best taste is one's individualized taste," they say, yet in a café in Seoul, a person "may feel strange about being the only person who is getting this specialized beverage."

They go on: "Ordering a cup of coffee is a social act saturated with culture-specific meanings. Liking and ordering a cup of decaffeinated cappuccino with nonfat milk is a result of being in a cultural context where individuality is valued and the communication of one's individuality is required."

Think about what all those different Starbucks orders might say about who you are.

Venti Caramel Cocoa Cluster Frappuccino, soy, half-caff, extra whip. This says, *What I really wanted was an ice cream sundae, but I'm out running errands, and what if I run into that guy I've been eying at the gym?* This satisfies a craving you have but looks more dainty when sipped from a straw.

> **Americans are hardwired to personalize and individualize our eating experiences. Customization, it seems, is our birthright.**

Short, nonfat, no-foam latte, quad, 120 degrees. You're a purist. A very amped-up purist. Ordering four shots of espresso, in a cup so small it's not even on the menu, below the normal temperature says, *I have to give an important presentation in an hour, and I don't have time to mess around. All I need is a splash of milk to wash this down so I'll be on my game.*

10   So while you may think nothing of your order, think again. In the United States, conformity is unpatriotic.

HAVING IT OUR WAY, AT A RESTAURANT 2.0: FAST CASUAL

Food marketers have taken our desire to reduce the effort and time spent on meal preparation and consumption to such extreme levels that the hassle of sorting through all the options has gotten "out of control," says University of Pennsylvania food psychologist Paul Rozin. Now, Rozin laments, you can't even find the fish sandwich, or the shake, that was the reason you went to a given fast-food joint in the first place.

At last check, McDonald's—once a destination for four simple choices: French fries, hamburgers, milkshakes, and soft drinks—had 107 items on the menu. There you stand, beneath panels and panels of menu items in tiny print, eyes scanning up, down, side-to-side, unable to make up your mind, until you're ready to just throw a dart at the thing.

This speaks to the now-famous "Paradox of Choice," the situation explained by Swarthmore College psychology professor Barry Schwartz that having more choices can actually make us feel *less* satisfied.

Paralyzed even. Many consumers simultaneously say they are satisfied by having personalized choices when eating out, *and* that there is an excessive amount of choice at many places.

"I think there's going to be a response to these menus that take fifteen minutes to read," Rozin told me in the spring of 2014.

He turned out to be right. Recent figures from Datassential Menu 15 Trends show that, basically, Americans don't like to read. Er, when it comes to the menu-as-textbook, they're over it. And in the last several years, restaurants have been responding. New restaurants classified as "fast casual" have been offering fewer items to start with, on average about forty items fewer. Instead, they emphasize quality: both in the food (often made in-house that day, with seasonal and/or local ingredients), and in the experience (often more upscale décor, with more gentle lighting). Existing chains—including McDonald's but also others like Olive Garden and IHOP—have been paring down the number of items on their menus.

Some places, such as The Cheese Board Collective and Sliver in Berkeley, California, have just one option on the menu each day. If, on Wednesday, December 10, you don't like pizza with citrus zest, garlic olive oil, Emmentaler, baby chard, and roasted kabocha squash, you will be dining elsewhere. Come back and see what they have the next day.

For decades, many restaurants gave us customization in the sense of providing an ever larger number of permutations of mood × price × dietary restriction × taste preference. For example: feeling guilty about this morning's bear claw × no restraints on cost × lactose intolerant × picky eater might lead to the Grilled Chicken Sandwich at Chick-fil-A, which is a marinated, boneless chicken breast on a toasted multigrain bun that's only 320 calories. It comes with lettuce and tomato but no cheese, and you skip the Honey Roasted BBQ Sauce, but make it a meal by adding a large fruit cup and a large diet lemonade. This classic system meant greater odds that during a given visit, every customer would fall into one of the buckets generated by those permutations. But now, we want to build our own damn bucket.

According to food industry research experts, customized dining options are now more available to us than ever before. A major driver is the growth in fast-casual restaurants. Your Paneras and your Baja Freshes, your Shake Shacks and your Noodles & Companys. And don't you dare call them fast food. The number of diners visiting fast-casual restaurants grew at ten times the rate of traffic to fast-food restaurants from 1999 through 2014. Double-digit growth is expected to continue through 2022, compared to an increase of just half a percentage point for the rest of the restaurant industry. Sales at numerous fast-food chains have been dropping.

Fast casual is all around us, yet a mere 5 percent of consumers are familiar with the term. So let me take a stab.

20   Think of fast casual as the Goldilocks of restaurant-going.

Wendy's, Burger King, KFC, Pizza Hut—those places sell ungodly quantities of low-quality food from a menu of scripture-length choices that are highly processed, prepared far away, in bulk. The food is made using standardized, mechanized cooking methods to ensure transportability and uniformity, sold at rock-bottom prices, served within so little time you can keep your engine running. On the other end, fine dining sells teensy quantities of the best-quality food from a menu of single-digit choices that are prepared on the premises, by humans trained in culinary excellence. The food is prepared from scratch to ensure optimal flavor and presentation, sold at sticker-shock prices, served within so much time it's worth having a pimply teenager valet park your car in a lot somewhere.

Fast casual, however, sells reasonable quantities of reasonable quality food from a menu listing a reasonable number of choices. The food is prepared partly far away and partly on-site, to ensure adequate freshness and temperature, sold at decent prices, served within enough time to gather your napkins and beverage and secure a booth.

In other words, for many, fast casual is *juuuust* right.

About one in seven Americans received a Starbucks gift card during the 2014 holiday season. That's 46 million people.

Plus, fast-casual restaurants tend to appeal to environmental and social responsibility concerns you might have, or at least feel you're supposed to have—from their locally sourced ingredients and compostable cutlery to the reclaimed wood beams that line the booths.

25   Part of why fast-casual menus feel approachable and infinite at the same time is that many follow the create-your-own-meal concept. For example, at Blaze Pizza, Custom Fuel Pizza, and that one with the funny name, &Pizza, you can pick your dough and cheese, point to your favorite toppings, and have your personal pizza baked in just minutes. At the DC-based Mediterranean spot Cava Mezze Grill—which Zagat calls a "Greek spin on the Chipotle model"—you start with a base of anything from salad to mini pitas to a rice bowl, choose up to three dips or spreads, from harissa to "crazy feta," throw in a "hearty protein" and some toppings, and finish it off with a dressing. Everyone from the vegetarian yogi to the carnivorous football player is happy.

At the Encinitas Fish Shop in Southern California, you pick your type of fish, your marinade, whether to have it grilled or fried, and whether to have it as a sandwich, taco, salad, or plate with sides. The Counter gives diners a clipboard with an order sheet to "Build Your Own Burger." The chain, which boasts 312,120 possible burger concoctions, urges customers on its website to "Create something special. Show us what you've got."

Whether it's salads or rice bowls, wraps or noodle bowls, at Sweetgreen or Asian Box or Tava Indian Kitchen, you're given a set of starting blocks, and you construct your masterpiece. At all of these places, you can add a little flair, take up the heat, or go wild and combine sauces.

And because you work your way through different menu choices one batch at a time, the decision as a whole doesn't feel as daunting.

Not only do these restaurants not reprimand you for making special requests, they *require* that you be a participant in the process. That's a long way from don't you dare hold the pickle!

It's not only Chipotlified restaurants that are successful, though. To make sure we don't lose sight of this fact amid the landscape of next-generation have-it-your-way concepts, consider these two stats: 30

1. 80 percent of Americans live within twenty miles of a Starbucks. (For fun: Over 70 percent of married Americans live within thirty miles of their mother or mother-in-law. Awww.)

2. About one in seven Americans received a Starbucks gift card during the 2014 holiday season. That's 46 million people.

Clearly, the harbinger of the customized consumption craze is still wildly popular.

FOR A SECOND READING

1. Egan refers to the current moment in our food history as the "Era of Infinite Choice." How do you interpret this descriptor? What does it suggest about the role of food consumer in today's culture? Does it accurately describe your own role as a food consumer? How or how not?

2. "The desirability of uniqueness," writes Egan, "is part of the broader American cultural context in which we all live" (p. 177). Do you agree? In cultural terms, are we taught to regard "uniqueness" as a personal ideal? Where, in our "broader cultural context" do you think this message is most directly promoted?

3. As Egan's discussion suggests, it's not entirely clear that today's food culture offers consumers genuine individual choice or just the illusion of it. How would you answer this question? As a food consumer, do you feel that your true individuality is recognized in the marketplace?

PUTTING IT INTO WRITING

4. According to Egan, more and more restaurants are choosing to provide customers with a "create-your-own-meal" option. Write a 500-word essay in which you do the following. First, describe your ideal "create-your-own-meal." What foods does it include? In what amounts? Next, explain why you chose this particular meal as your ideal. What standards did you use to make these selections? What makes these standards preferable to others? And finally, analyze how your choices and standards compare to those scripted by the larger culture. Is your own ideal meal in line or at odds with the culture's ideal(s)?

5. Here is a partial list of the words Egan uses to characterize the growing trend in "fast casual" dining: *approachable, reasonable, decent.* Here is a partial list of the words she uses to characterize the fast-food model this trend is displacing: *standardized, mechanized, uniform.* Write an essay in which you compare these two sets of terms, and use this comparison to make a broader argument about how our cultural norms and social scripts around eating are changing. What portrait of the typical eating experience does the fast-food terminology suggest? How does this differ from the portrait evoked by the terms used to describe "fast casual" dining?

COMPARING ARGUMENTS

6. The essays by Egan and Kim Bosch (p. 171) can both be read as efforts to define what it truly means to eat as an *individual*, to make one's eating choices apart from the cultural norms and social scripts that so often proscribe them. Write an essay in which you compare how these two writers address this particular question. What does each have to say about the possibility of exercising free choice when it comes to food? Which discussion do you find more persuasive? Why?

Rewriting the Script: **Organic Food**

> ❝ The organic movement, as it was once called, has come a remarkably long way in the last thirty years, to the point where it now looks considerably less like a movement than a big business. . . . So is an industrial organic food chain finally a contradiction in terms? It's hard to escape the conclusion that it is. . . . As in so many other realms, nature's logic has proven no match for the logic of capitalism.❞
>
> — MICHAEL POLLAN,
> AUTHOR OF THE OMNIVORE'S DILEMMA

THE CONTRADICTION OF BIG ORGANIC

Since the 1960s and 1970s, the organic food industry has played a major role in reshaping how millions of Americans think about, shop for, and (of course) eat their food. Pioneered by a small cadre of local farmers, grocery co-op proprietors, and eco-conscious consumers, the organic movement cast itself in its early years as a revolutionary alternative to what was often termed the "corporate" or "industrial" food economy, a system typified by the giant, chain grocery store, with its row after row of frozen TV dinners, pesticide-coated oranges, canned vegetables, and potato chips. And yet, as such popular and profitable stores like Whole Foods and Trader Joe's have become national chains, many have begun to wonder whether any meaningful differences still exist between industrial and organic food. In a world where even Wal-Mart has begun marketing organic selections to its shoppers, does it still make sense to talk about this movement as a kind of anticorporate revolution? For observers like noted food author Michael Pollan, the answer is "not really." Questioning the script we have long used to celebrate "going organic" as a genuine alternative, Pollan wonders whether we have reached a point where we need to speak of Big Organic as a corporate enterprise in its own right.

IDENTIFY THE SCRIPT: Next time you're at the grocery store, take notes on the way the store markets its "organic" products. How do the product labels and nutritional information for organic and nonorganic items compare? The price? Next, use these observations as the basis for writing a 300–500 word essay in which you describe the way this store defines the "typical" organic food shopper. What assumptions are being made about who organic shoppers are? What they want? What they most care about?

CHALLENGE THE SCRIPT: In a 500-word essay, identify what you find to be questionable or inaccurate about these assumptions. What conclusions about organic food and organic food shoppers do they encourage us to draw? What, in your view, is potentially problematic about these conclusions?

WRITE YOUR OWN SCRIPT: In a 300–500 word essay, propose a different model for how to define the ideal organic food consumer. What assumptions about or attitudes toward food define this consumer? What kind of shopping scenario would best cater to this consumer's interests?

Portland Press Herald/Getty Images

NICHOLAS KRISTOF
Prudence or Cruelty?

While it can often feel like an entirely personal activity, the truth is that eating is connected to some of the most pressing political, economic, and ethical questions of our day. It shapes not only how we approach health and nutrition but also how we think about such overtly political issues as poverty, social class, and social justice. It is this insight that underlies Nicholas Kristof's unsparing assessment of our federal food-stamp policy. Calling out congressional leaders for their callous indifference to the plight of hungry children, Kristof's essay highlights the social, economic, and moral issues our debates over food often involve. Kristof is a two-time Pulitzer Prize–winning columnist for the *New York Times*. He is also the coauthor of two books: *China Wakes: The Struggle for the Soul of a Rising Power* (1994) and *Thunder from the East: Portrait of a Rising Asia* (2000). This essay appeared in the *New York Times* in 2013.

Before You Read

To what extent do you regard food as political issue? In your eyes, what political issues or questions does a focus on food raise?

WHEN MEMBERS OF CONGRESS DEBATE WHETHER TO SLASH THE food stamp program, they should ask if they really want more small children arriving at school having skipped breakfast.

As it is, in the last few days of the month before food stamps are distributed, some children often eat less and have trouble focusing, says Kisha Hill, a teacher in a high-poverty prekindergarten school in North Tulsa, Okla.

"Kids can't focus on studying when their stomachs are grumbling," Hill told me.

Some 47 million Americans receive food stamps, including some who would otherwise go hungry—or hungrier. A recent government study found that about 5 percent of American households have "very low food security," which means that food can run out before the end of the month. In almost a third of those households, an adult reported not eating for an entire day because there wasn't money for food.

> *In almost a third of those households, an adult reported not eating for an entire day because there wasn't money for food.*

Meanwhile, 14 percent of American toddlers suffer iron deficiency. Malnutrition isn't the only cause, but

5

it's an important one—and these children may suffer impaired brain development as a result. This kind of malnutrition in America is tough to measure, because some children are simultaneously malnourished and overweight, but experts agree it's a problem. We expect to find malnourished or anemic children in Africa and Asia, but it's dispiriting to see this in a country as wealthy as our own.

Let me take that back. It's not just dispiriting. It's also infuriating.

"The cutback in food stamps represents a clear threat to the nutritional status and health of America's children," says Dr. Irwin Redlener, the president of the Children's Health Fund and a professor of pediatrics at Columbia University. Dr. Redlener said that one result of cutbacks will be more kids with anemia and educational difficulties.

Food stamp recipients already took a cut in benefits this month, and they may face more. The Senate Democratic version of the farm bill would cut food stamps by $4 billion over ten years, while the House Republican version would slash them by $40 billion.

More than 90 percent of benefits go to families living below the poverty line, according to federal government data, and nearly two-thirds of the recipients are children, elderly, or disabled.

10   Let's remember that the government already subsidizes lots of food. When wealthy executives dine at fancy French restaurants, part of the bill is likely to be deducted from taxes, which amounts to a subsidy from taxpayers. How is it that food subsidies to anemic children are more controversial than food subsidies to executives enjoying coq au vin?

> **We expect to find malnourished or anemic children in Africa and Asia, but it's dispiriting to see this in a country as wealthy as our own.**

Meanwhile, the same farm bill that is hotly debated because of food stamps includes agricultural subsidies that don't go just to struggling farmers but also, in recent years, to 50 billionaires or companies they are involved in, according to the Environmental Working Group, a Washington research group.

Among the undeserving people receiving farm subsidies has been a New York Times columnist. Yes, I have been paid $588 a year not to grow crops on wooded land I own in Oregon (I then forward the money to a maternity hospital in Somaliland). When our country pays a New York journalist not to grow crops in an Oregon forest, there's a problem with the farm bill—but it's not food stamps.

Granted, safety-net spending is more about treating symptoms of poverty than causes, and we may get more bang for the buck when we chip away at long-term poverty through early education, home visitation for infants, job training, and helping teenagers avoid unwanted pregnancies.

That said, food stamps do work in important ways. For starters, they effectively reduce the number of children living in extreme poverty by half, according to the Center on Budget and Policy Priorities in Washington.

By improving nutrition of young children, food stamps also improve 15 long-term outcomes. In recent years, mounting scholarship has found that malnutrition in utero or in small children has lasting consequences. One reason seems to be that when a fetus or small child is undernourished, it is programmed to anticipate food shortages for the remainder of its life. If food later becomes plentiful, the metabolic mismatch can lead to diabetes, obesity, and heart disease.

An excellent study last year from the National Bureau of Economic Research followed up on the rollout of food stamps, county by county, between 1961 and 1975. It found that those who began receiving food stamps by the age of 5 had better health as adults. Women who as small children had benefited from food stamps were more likely to go farther in school, earn more money, and stay off welfare.

So slashing food stamp benefits—overwhelmingly for children, the disabled, and the elderly—wouldn't be a sign of prudent fiscal management by Congress. It would be a mark of shortsighted cruelty.

FOR A SECOND READING

1. How do you understand the juxtaposition within the title between the terms "prudence" and "cruelty"? Why do you think Kristof uses these two terms to frame his discussion of food stamps?

2. In calling out the widespread effects of "malnutrition," Kristof also makes an argument for supporting the "social safety net." How do you think a member of Congress would respond to this argument? Do you think s/he would be persuaded by what Kristof says about the importance of the "social safety net"? Why or why not?

3. Kristof repeatedly uses the word "slash" to describe the proposed cuts to food-stamp benefits Congress is currently considering. Why do you think he uses this particular term? How does it differ from a word like "reduce" or "cut"?

PUTTING IT INTO WRITING

4. Much of Kristof's critique here revolves around the statistics about childhood malnutrition he presents. Write an essay in which you analyze and evaluate the role this type of data plays in advancing Kristof's larger argument. What sort of connection between malnutrition and food-stamp policy is Kristof asserting here? Is it a connection that makes his call for changes to food-stamp legislation more credible or persuasive? How or how not?

5. Create a proposal that outlines what you believe should be the proper government policy concerning food stamps. How much support for this program should the government provide? What particular needs should it address? What limits should it establish? Then write a quick assessment of the ways your proposal compares to Kristof's. What are the key similarities and differences?

COMPARING ARGUMENTS

6. Like Kristof, Nathanael Johnson (p. 189) also invites readers to consider the ethical implications behind our food choices. In a brief essay, compare the ethical arguments each essay presents. What specific moral questions does each writer raise? How, in each case, are these questions related to food and eating? Which ethical concern do you think is more important? Why?

NATHANAEL JOHNSON
Is There a Moral Case for Eating Meat?

What does the widespread willingness in our culture to eat meat tell us about the ethical guidelines we use to make our food-related choices? When we look at these choices through an ethical lens, do they continue to seem defensible? Taking up these questions, Nathanael Johnson walks his readers through the moral arguments against "eating meat." Johnson is a food writer for *Grist*, an online magazine that examines environmental questions and issues. He is also the author of *All Natural: A Skeptic's Quest to Discover. If the Natural Approach to Diet, Children, Healing, and the Environment Really Makes Us Healthier and Happier* (2013). This piece was published in *Grist* in 2015.

Before You Read

How much time do you spend considering the ethical implications of what you eat? Would giving more thought to these implications affect or alter the food-related choices you make?

WHERE ARE THE PHILOSOPHERS ARGUING THAT EATING MEAT IS moral?

When I started researching this piece, I'd already read a lot of arguments against meat, but I hadn't seen a serious philosophical defense of carnivores. So I started asking around. I asked academics, meat industry representatives, and farmers: Who was the philosophical counterweight to Peter Singer?

In 1975, Singer wrote *Animal Liberation*, which launched the modern animal rights movement with its argument that causing animal suffering is immoral. There are plenty of other arguments against eating animals besides Singer's, going back to the ancient Greeks and Hindus. There are even arguments that Christianity contains a mandate for vegetarianism. Matthew Scully's *Dominion* argues against animal suffering; Scully rejects Singer's utilitarian assertion that humans and animals are equal but says that, since God gave people "dominion over the fish of the sea and the fowl of the air, and over the cattle, and over all the earth," so we have a responsibility to care for them and show them mercy.

The arguments against eating animals are pretty convincing. But surely, I thought, there were also intellectuals making convincing counterarguments. Right? Nope. Not really.

There is the Cartesian idea that animals are unfeeling machines, incapable of suffering—but I just wasn't buying that. It's clear that animals have an aversive response to pain, and careful, well-respected scientists are saying that animals are probably capable of feeling and

5

189

consciousness. Once we admit even the possibility that animals are sentient, the ethical game is on: It doesn't matter that an animal is *just an animal*; if you're against suffering and you agree animals can feel pain, it's pretty hard to justify eating them. (Of course, the further you get from humans the harder it is to judge—plants may be sentient in a totally alien way! Singer says we can stop caring somewhere between a shrimp and oyster.)

My enquiries didn't turn up any sophisticated defense of meat. Certainly there are a few people here and there making arguments around the edges, but nothing that looked to me like a serious challenge to Singer. In fact, the lack of philosophical work to justify meat eating is so extreme that people kept referring me not to scholarly publications, but to an essay contest that the *New York Times* held back in 2012. Ariel Kaminer organized that contest after noticing the same gaping hole in the philosophical literature that I'd stumbled upon. Vegetarians have claimed the ethical high ground with book after book and, Kaminer wrote:

In response, those who love meat have had surprisingly little to say. They say, of course, that, well, they love meat or that meat is deeply ingrained in our habit or culture or cuisine or that it's nutritious or that it's just part of the natural order . . . But few have tried to answer the fundamental ethical issue: Whether it is right to eat animals in the first place, at least when human survival is not at stake.

The winner of that contest, Jay Bost, didn't take it much farther than that, basically arguing that "meat is just part of the natural order," because animals are an integral part of the food web. That's a start, but I'd want a lot more than a 600-word essay to flesh out the idea and respond to the obvious criticisms—since almost all the animals we eat are far removed from natural food webs, it's still basically a prescription for veganism. Plus, where do you draw the line on what's natural?

The arguments against eating animals are pretty convincing. But surely, I thought, there were also intellectuals making convincing counterarguments. Right? Nope. Not really.

I found several beginnings of arguments like this—no real philosophical shelter for a meat eater, but a few foundational observations that you might build something upon if you carefully thought through all the implications.

10   Animal welfare expert Temple Grandin offered one potential plank for building a defense of meat eating. "We've gotta give animals a life worth living," she told me. Later in the interview, she reminded me that

most farm animals wouldn't have a life at all if no one ate meat. Combine these points and you could argue that it's better to have a life worth living than no life at all—even if it ends with slaughter and consumption.

When I bounced this argument off the ethicist Paul Thompson, he said, "That may be a defensible position, but a philosopher should also be prepared to apply it to humans."

Right. It's hard to limit the "a life worth living is better than no life at all" argument to farm animals. Using the same argument we might raise children for the purpose of producing organs: As long as they were well cared for, ignorant of their fate, and painlessly slaughtered, you could say they had a life worth living. The clone gets a (short) life, a dying girl get a new heart, everyone wins! It's rationally consistent, but certainly doesn't feel right to me.

Perhaps some brilliant philosopher will develop these points, but, since I am not one of those, I was left with the conclusion that the vegans were right. Oddly, however, that didn't make me think twice about laying sliced turkey on my sandwich the next day. I was convinced on a rational level, but not in an embodied, visceral way.

"*Animal Liberation* is one of those rare books that demand that you either defend the way you live or change it," Michael Pollan once wrote. I know what he means—when I first read it, I felt battered and stupefied by the horrors of animal suffering that Singer paraded before me. Nevertheless, despite my inability to muster a defense for my meat eating, I didn't change my way of life. Pollan didn't, either: His piece is set up as a stunt—he's reading *Animal Liberation* while eating rib-eye in a steakhouse. And, though Pollan finds himself agreeing with Singer, he has no problem finishing his steak.

I tend to think of rational argument as a powerful force, certainly   15
more powerful than the trivial pleasure of eating meat. But it turns out that's backwards: Rational morality tugs at us with the slenderest of threads, while meat pulls with the thick-twined chords of culture, tradition, pleasure, the flow of the crowd, and physical yearning—and it pulls at us three times a day. Thousands, convinced by Singer and the like, become vegetarians for moral reasons. And then most of those thousands start eating meat again. Vaclav Smil notes: "Prevalence of all forms of 'vegetarianism' is no higher than 2–4 percent in any Western society and that long-term (at least a decade) or life-long adherence to solely plant-based diets is less than 1 percent." As the psychologist Hal Herzog told Grist's Katie Herzog in this podcast, "It's the single biggest failure of the animal rights movement."

How do we deal with this? Some people just shrug and say, "Whatever, animals are different, it's OK to kill them." I can't quite bring myself to do that, because I value rational consistency. And yet, I don't feel immoral when I eat meat—I actually feel pretty good.

Whenever you have lots of people agreeing in principle to a goal that is impossible for most to achieve in practice, you have something resembling religion. Religions are all about setting standards that most people will never live up to. And Thompson thinks they have something to teach us on this issue.

Thompson's solution is to treat vegetarianism the way religious traditions treat virtues. Christians strive to love their neighbors, but they don't say that people who fail to reach Jesus-level self-sacrifice are immoral. Buddhists strive for detachment, but they don't flagellate themselves when they fail to achieve it.

Thompson suggests that we should strive to do better by animals, but that doesn't mean we should condemn ourselves for eating meat. There are lots of cases like this, he told me. "Some people are going to take these issues up in a way that other people would find really difficult," Thompson said. "For instance, we all respect Mother Theresa for taking on amazing burdens, but we don't say that you are evil for not doing it."

20   This makes sense to me. Louis CK can make a pretty solid argument that people who have enough money to buy a nice car (or to spend time reading long essays about meat philosophy) should be donating 90 percent of their income to the poor.

And yet most of us don't give up our luxuries. By Thompson's reasoning, that doesn't make us immoral. In fact, he says, it's just wrong to condemn people who eat meat. When people rise out of extreme poverty, that is, when they start earning $2.60 a day, they almost invariably spend that newfound money on animal protein: milk, meat, or eggs. Now, you might roll your eyes and say that *of course* the desperate should be excused from the moral obligation—but wait. As Thompson writes in his book, *From Field to Fork: Food Ethics for Everyone*:

> [T]his response misses my point. Excuses apply in extenuating circumstances, but the logic of excuses implies that the action itself is still morally wrong. A poor person might be excused for stealing a loaf of bread. Theft might be excused when a poor person's situation takes a turn for the worse, but in the case at hand, their situation has taken a turn toward the better. Under modestly improved circumstances, the extremely poor add a little meat, milk, or eggs into their diet. My claim is that there is something curious with a moral system that reclassifies legally and traditionally sanctioned conduct of people at the utter margins of society as something that needs to be excused.

Is it morally wrong for a hungry child in India to eat an egg? This isn't just a thought experiment—it's a real controversy. It's not enough to wave it off by saying it's easy to provide vegan alternatives, because those alternative just don't exist for many people. Often, the cheapest high-quality protein available to the poor comes from animals.

Thompson's point is that allowing people to access that protein should be *moral*, not just an excusable lapse.

If we accept Thompson's formulation (and I'm inclined to), it lets us stop wringing our hands over our hypocrisy and strive to improve conditions for animals. That's what Temple Grandin does. She didn't have much patience for

[I]f you're against suffering and you agree animals can feel pain, it's pretty hard to justify eating them.

my philosophical questions. Instead, she is focused on the realistic changes that will give animals better lives. And as I talked to her, she served up surprise after surprise. Many of the elements in confined animal feeding operations (CAFOs) that people find most abhorrent, she said, may be fine from the animal's perspective. For instance, consider egg-laying hens: What's better for them—an open barn or stacked cages? Small battery cages, with several hens packed inside each, are bad news, according to Grandin, but enriched cages are a really good alternative.

"There are objective ways to measure a hen's motivation to get   25
something she wants—like a private nest box," Grandin told me. "How long is she willing to not eat to get it, or how heavy a door will she push to get it? How many times will she push a switch to get it? A private nest box is something she wants, because in the wild she has an instinct to hide in the bushes so that a fox doesn't get [her eggs]. Give her some pieces of plastic to hang down that she can hide behind. Give her a little piece of Astroturf to lay [her eggs] on. Give her a perch, and a piece of plastic to scratch on, and at least enough cage height so she can walk normally. I'm gonna call that apartment living for chickens. Do they need natural elements? Being outside? Science can't answer that. I mean, there are people in New York that hardly go outside."

I pressed her: Can't you use those same objective measurement techniques to see how badly the hens want to go outside and scratch for bugs?

"Well you can," Grandin said, "and the motivation is pretty weak compared to something like the nest box, which is hardwired. Take dust bathing. For a hen dust bathing is nice to do, but it's kind of like, yes, it's nice to have a fancy hotel room, but the EconoLodge will do too."

And in fact, the free-range system that I would instinctively choose for chickens may be worse than an enriched cage—because the birds get sick and injured a lot more. And laying hens, unlike meat chickens, are pretty nasty about setting up pecking orders. As Thompson observes in his book, "This is well and good in the flocks of 10 to 20 birds, as might be observed among wild jungle fowl, and it is probably tolerable in a flock of 40 to 60 birds that might have been seen on a typical farmstead in 1900.. . . But a cage-free/free-range commercial egg barn will have between 150,000 to 500,000 hens occupying the same space. If you are a hen at the bottom end of the pecking order in an environment like that, you are going to get pecked. A lot."

Even small farms with pastured hens that produce $9-a-dozen eggs often have hundreds of birds, which means the most submissive hens are going to get beat up. I certainly prefer Joel Salatin's 400-bird Eggmobile on lush grass, because to my human eyes it's beautiful—and chicken cages look horrible. But I have real doubt as to what's better from the chicken's perspective.

30   There are a lot of counterintuitive things like this when it comes to animal farming. So I asked Grandin how we should feel about animal agriculture in the United States as it's currently practiced: Do these animals really have a life worth living?

It varies greatly, she said, but some CAFOs really are good. "I think cattle done right have a decent life," she said. I couldn't get her to give a simple thumbs up or down to chicken or pork CAFOs.

Talking to Grandin didn't make me want to go stock up on corn-fed beef, but it did significantly soften my (negative) feelings about industrial animal production. And talking to Thompson made me realize that I was willing to compromise the needs of animals for the needs of humans if they come into direct conflict. In that way I'm a speciesist—I have an unshakeable favoritism for humans. Perhaps it's irrational, but I really want that little girl in India to get her egg, even if it means hens suffer, even if there's a good vegan alternative for a slightly higher cost.

Perhaps there's a philosophical argument to be made in defense of killing animals, but no one has spelled that out in a way that I found convincing. Does this mean that we should join the vegans?

I think the answer is yes, but in a very limited way—in the same way that we all *should* take vows of poverty and stop thinking impure thoughts. Ending deaths and suffering is a worthy moral goal for those of us who have the wealth to make choices. But saying that it's wrong and immoral to eat meat is just too absolutist. I mean, even the Dalai Lama, who says vegetarianism is preferable, eats meat twice a week.

35   The binary, good-or-evil view of meat is pragmatically counterproductive—the black and white strategy hasn't gotten many people to become vegan. Instead, let's focus on giving farm animals a life worth living.

FOR A SECOND READING

1. "Perhaps there's a philosophical argument to be made in defense of killing animals," Johnson writes, "but no one has spelled that out in a way that I found convincing. Does this mean that we should

join the vegans?" (p. 194). How do you answer Johnson's question? After reading this essay, do you believe there is a moral "defense" for "killing animals"?

2. Johnson chooses to organize this essay as an overview of the arguments other people have made about the moral implications of eating meat. How effective do you find this organizational strategy to be? What are its strengths? Its limitations?

3. In Johnson's view, the American public's reluctance to stop eating meat uncovers an important paradox: "Whenever you have lots of people agreeing in principle to a goal that is impossible for most to achieve in practice, you have something resembling religion" (p. 192). What do you make of the parallel Johnson draws here? Do you agree that our attitudes toward meat-eating border on the religious? Does this analogy help you understand our cultural resistance to embracing vegetarianism?

PUTTING IT INTO WRITING

4. One of the arguments in support of meat eating that Johnson considers is the economic argument: "Is it morally wrong for a hungry child in India to eat an egg? This isn't just a thought experiment—it's a real controversy. It's not enough to wave it off by saying it's easy to provide vegan alternatives, because those alternative just don't exist for many people. Often, the cheapest high-quality protein available to the poor comes from animals. . . . [The] point is that allowing people to access that protein should be *moral*, not just an excusable lapse" (pp. 192–93). In a 500-word essay, respond to this argument. Is it valid to use one's economic circumstances as the basis for determining the morality of our eating choices? Do you agree that, for people living in poverty, it is moral to eat meat? Why or why not?

5. In seeking to explain why vegetarianism is not more widespread, Johnson makes the following claim: "Rational morality tugs at us with the slenderest of threads, while meat pulls with the thick-twined chords of culture, tradition, pleasure, the flow of the crowd, and physical yearning—and it pulls at us three times a day" (p. 191). Write a 500-word essay in which you analyze and evaluate the argument Johnson is making here. How would you characterize the distinction Johnson is drawing here between "rational morality" on the one hand, and the "chords of culture, tradition, pleasure . . . and physical yearning" on the other? How is he using this distinction to explain why so many people choose to eat meat? And how persuasive do you find this explanation to be?

COMPARING ARGUMENTS

6. In his own investigation into contemporary food culture, Nicholas Kristof (p. 185) uses the term "cruelty" to characterize the nature of certain eating-related scripts. In your view, how useful is this term in understanding the moral arguments against meat-eating that Johnson profiles here? In what ways do these ethical objections rest on the supposed "cruelty" of eating meat? Is there an alternative term you would use to characterize these arguments?

FRANCINE PROSE
The Wages of Sin

When it comes to eating, how much is too much? And who teaches us where to draw this line? Taking aim at our current fixation on food, dieting, and body image, Francine Prose contemplates whether ours has become a culture in which overeating now stands as the preeminent sign of our moral and physical failure. Prose graduated from Radcliffe College in 1968 and currently lives and writes in New York City. She is the author of nine novels, including *Blue Angel* (2000), a finalist for the National Book Award, and *A Changed Man* (2005), which won the Dayton Literary Peace Prize. She has also published several nonfiction books, including *Gluttony* (2003), from which the following is excerpted, and *Reading Like a Writer* (2006). Her most recent works are the novel *Lovers at the Chameleon Club, Paris, 1932* (2014), the nonfiction book *Anne Frank: The Book, the Life, the Afterlife* (2009), and the memoir *My New American Life* (2011).

Before You Read

Does our culture encourage us to regard overeating as a moral issue? What, in your view, are the implications of accepting this view as a cultural norm?

MORE AND MORE OFTEN, WE READ ARTICLES AND HEAR TV commentators advocating government intervention to protect us from the greed of a corporate culture that profits from our unhealthy attraction to sugary and fatty foods. Legal experts discuss the feasibility of mounting class action suits—on the model of the recent and ongoing litigation against so-called big tobacco companies—against fast-food restaurants, junk-food manufacturers, and advertisers who target children with ads for salty fried snacks and brightly colored candy masquerading as breakfast cereal.

What's slightly more disturbing is the notion that not only do fat people need to be monitored, controlled, and saved from their gluttonous impulses, but that we need to be saved from them—that certain forms of social control might be required to help the overweight resist temptation. Writing in the *San Francisco Chronicle*, essayist Ruth Rosen has suggested that such actions might be motivated by compassion for such innocent victims as the parents of a child whose overweight helped lead to diabetes, or the child of a parent who died from weight-related causes. Of course the bottom line is concern for our pocketbooks, for the cost—shared by the wider population—of treating those who suffer from obesity-related ailments. As a partial remedy, Rosen proposes that schools and employers might forbid the sale of junk food on campus and in offices. Finally, she suggests that, in a more glorious future, the host who serves his guests greasy potato chips and doughnuts will incur the same horrified disapproval as the smoker who lights up—and blows smoke in our faces.

Rosen is not alone in her belief that legislation may be required to regulate the social costs of overeating. A recent item on CBS worriedly considered the alarming growth in the number of overweight and obese young people—a group that now comprises 14 percent of American children. According to the news clip, overweight was soon expected to surpass cigarette smoking as the major preventable cause of death: each year, 350,000 people die of obesity-related causes. Thirteen billion dollars is spent annually on food ads directed at children, and four out of five ads are for some excessively sugary or fatty product. The problem is undeniable, but once more the projected solution gives one pause; several interviewees raised the possibility of suing the purveyors of potato chips and candy bars. How far we have come from Saint Augustine and John Cassian and Chrysostom, taking it for granted that the struggle against temptation would be waged in the glutton's heart and mind—and not, presumably, in the law courts.

5 You're so fat when they pierced your ears, they had to use a harpoon.
   You're so fat you've got to put on lipstick with a paint roller.

In studies that have examined the causes and motives behind the stigmatization of the overweight, such prejudice has been found to derive from the widely accepted notion that fat people are at fault, responsible for their weight and appearance, that they are self-indulgent, sloppy, lazy, morally lax, lacking in the qualities of self-denial and impulse control that our society (still so heavily influenced by the legacy of Puritanism) values and rewards. In a 1978 book, *The Seven Deadly Sins: Society and Evil*, sociologist Stanford M. Lyman takes a sociocultural approach to the reasons why we are so harsh in our condemnation of the so-called glutton.

> The apparently voluntary character of food gluttony serves to point up why it is more likely to seem "criminal" than sick, an act of moral defalcation rather than medical pathology. Although gluttony is not proscribed by the criminal law, it partakes of some of the social sanctions and moral understandings that govern orientations toward those who commit crimes.... Gluttony is an excessive *self*-indulgence. Even in its disrespect for the body it overvalues the ego that it slavishly satisfies.[1]

Most of us would no doubt claim that we are too sensible, compassionate, and enlightened to feel prejudice against the obese. We would never tell the sorts of cruel jokes scattered throughout this chapter. But let's consider how we feel when we've taken our already cramped seat in coach class on the airplane and suddenly our seatmate appears—a man or woman whose excessive weight promises to make our journey even more uncomfortable than we'd anticipated. Perhaps, contemplating a trip of this sort, we might find ourselves inclined to support Southwest Airline's discriminatory two-seats-per-large-passenger rule. Meanwhile, as we try not to stare at our sizable traveling companion, we might as well be the medieval monks glaring at the friar who's helped himself to an extra portion. For what's involved in both cases is our notion of one's proper share, of surfeit and shortage—not enough food in one case, not enough space in the other.

"The glutton is also noticeable as a defiler of his own body space. His appetite threatens to engulf the spaces of others as he spreads out to take more than one person's ordinary allotment of territory. If he grows too large, he may no longer fit into ordinary chairs . . . and require special arrangements in advance of his coming".[2] The glutton's "crime" is crossing boundaries that we jealously guard and that are defined by our most primitive instincts: hunger, territoriality—that is to say, survival.

So we come full circle back to the language of crime and innocence, 10 sin and penance, guilt and punishment—a view of overweight frequently adopted and internalized by the obese themselves. "Many groups of dieters whom I studied," writes Natalie Allon, "believed that fatness was the outcome of immoral self-indulgence. Group dieters used much religious language in considering themselves bad or good dieters—words such as sinner, saint, devil, angel, guilt, transgression, confession, absolution, diet Bible—as they partook of the rituals of group dieting."[3] Nor does the association between gluttony and the language of religion exist solely in the minds of dieters, the obese, and the food-obsessed. In fact it's extremely common to speak of having overeaten as having "been bad"; rich, fattening foods are advertised as being "sinfully delicious"; and probably most of us have thought or confessed the fact that we've felt "guilty" for having eaten more than we should have.

> **The glutton's "crime" is crossing boundaries that we jealously guard and that are defined by our most primitive instincts: hunger, territoriality—that is to say, survival.**

Like the members of other Twelve-Step programs, and not unlike the medieval gluttons who must have felt inspired to repent and pray for divine assistance in resisting temptation, the members of Overeaters Anonymous employ the terminology of religion. *Lifeline*, the magazine of Overeaters Anonymous, is filled with stories of healing and recovery, first-person accounts in which God was asked to intercede, to provide a spiritual awakening, and to remove the dangerous and destructive flaws from the recovering overeater's character.

Routinely, the capacity to achieve sobriety and abstinence—which for OA members means the ability to restrict one's self to three healthy and sensible meals a day—is credited to divine mercy and love, and to the good effects of an intimate and sustaining relationship with God. In one testimonial, a woman reports that coming to her first meeting and identifying herself as a recovering compulsive eater was more difficult for her than to say that she was a shoplifter, a serial killer, or a prostitute. Only after admitting that she was powerless over food and asking for the help of a higher power was she at last able to end her unhappy career as a "grazer and a binger."

For perhaps obvious reasons, the term "gluttony" is now rarely used as a synonym for compulsive eating. Yet Stanford Lyman conflates the two to make the point that our culture's attitude toward the obese is not unlike an older society's view of the gluttonous sinner:

> Societal opposition to gluttony manifests itself in a variety of social control devices and institutional arrangements. Although rarely organized as a group, very fat individuals at times seem to form a much beset minority, objects of calculating discrimination and bitter prejudice. Stigmatized because their addiction to food is so visible in its consequences, the obese find themselves ridiculed, rejected, and repulsed by many of those who do not overindulge. Children revile them on the streets, persons of average size refuse to date, dance, or dine with them, and many businesses, government, and professional associations refuse to employ them. So great is the pressure to conform to the dictates of the slimness culture in America that occasionally an overweight person speaks out, pointing to the similarities of his condition to that of racial and national minorities.[4]

15   Indeed, the overweight have found a forum in which to speak out, at the meetings, conventions, and in the bimonthly newsletter sponsored by NAAFA—the National Association to Advance Fat Acceptance. A recent issue of the newsletter, available on the internet, calls for readers to write to the government to protest the National Institutes of Health's ongoing studies of normal-sized children to find out if obesity might have a metabolic basis. There are directions for giving money and establishing a living trust to benefit NAAFA, reviews of relevant new books, a report on the Trunk Sale at a NAAFA gathering in San Francisco, an update on the struggle to force auto manufacturers to provide seat belts that can save the lives of passengers who weigh over 215 pounds, and an article on the problems—the fear of appearing in public in a bathing suit, the narrow ladders that often provide the only access to swimming pools—that make it more difficult for the overweight to get the exercise that they

need. There is a brief discussion of how obesity should be defined, and another about the effectiveness of behavioral psychotherapy in helping patients lose weight. Finally, there are grateful letters from readers whose lives have been improved by the support and sustenance they gain from belonging to NAAFA.

Equally fervent—if somewhat less affirmative and forgiving—are the gospel tracts, also available on-line. One of the most heartfelt and persuasive is the work of a preacher identified only as George Clark:

> After conducting healing campaigns and mailing out thousands of anointed handkerchiefs—since 1930—I have learned that the greatest physical cause of sickness among the people of God is coming from this lust for overindulgence in eating.... Tens of thousands of truly converted people are sick and are suffering with heart trouble coming from high blood pressure and other ailments which result from overeating.... Did you ever wonder why artists have never depicted any of Jesus' disciples as being overweight or of the fleshy type? No one could have followed Jesus very long and remained overweight.... If eating too much has brought on high blood pressure, heart trouble, or many of the other diseases which come from being overweight, then God requires a reduction in your eating.

Given our perhaps misguided sense of living in a secular society, it's startling to find that our relationship with food is still so commonly translated directly into the language of God and the devil, of sin and repentance. But why should we be surprised, when we are constantly being reminded that our feelings about our diet and our body can be irrational, passionate, and closer to the province of faith and superstition than that of reason and science?

BIBLIOGRAPHY

Albala, Ken. *Eating Right in the Renaissance.* Berkeley: University of California Press, 2002.

Augustine, Saint. *The Confessions of Saint Augustine,* trans. Edward B. Pusey, D. D. New York: The Modern Library, 1949.

Bell, Rudolph M. *Holy Anorexia.* Chicago: University of Chicago Press, 1985.

Chaucer, Geoffrey. *The Works of Geoffrey Chaucer,* ed. F. N. Robinson. Boston: Houghton Mifflin, 1957.

Chernin, Kim. *The Obsession.* New York: Harper Perennial, 1981.

Chesterton, G. K. *Saint Thomas Aquinas.* New York: Image Books, Doubleday, 2001.

Fielding, Henry. *Tom Jones.* New York: The Modern Library, 1994.

Fisher, M. F. K. *The Art of Eating.* New York: Vintage, 1976.

Lyman, Stanford M. *The Seven Deadly Sins: Society and Evil.* New York: St. Martin's Press, 1978.

Petronius. *The Satyricon,* trans. William Arrowsmith. New York: Meridian, 1994.

Pleij, Herman. *Dreaming of Cockaigne,* trans. Diane Webb. New York: Columbia University Press, 2001.

Rabelais, François. *Gargantua and Pantagruel,* trans. Burton Raffel. New York: W. W. Norton, 1991.

Roth, Geneen. *When Food Is Love.* New York: Plume, 1991.

Schwartz, Hillel. *Never Satisfied: A Cultural History of Fantasies and Fat.* New York: The Free Press, 1986.

Shaw, Teresa M. *The Burden of the Flesh: Fasting and Sexuality in Early Christianity.* Minneapolis: Fortress Press, 1996.

Spenser, Edmund. *The Faerie Queene.* New York: E. P. Dutton & Company, 1964.

Wolman, Benjamin, ed., with Stephen DeBerry, editorial associate. *Psychological Aspects of Obesity: A Handbook.* New York: Van Nostrand Reinhold, 1982.

NOTES

[1]Stanford M. Lyman, *The Seven Deadly Sins: Society and Evil* (New York: St. Martin's Press, 1978), 220.

[2]Ibid., 223.

[3]Benjamin Wolman, ed., *Psychological Aspects of Obesity: A Handbook* (New York: Van Nostrand Reinhold, 1982), 148.

[4]Lyman, *Seven Deadly Sins,* 218.

FOR A SECOND READING

1. Elsewhere Prose writes, "The so-called glutton is a walking rebuke to our self-control, our self-denial, and to our shaky faith that if we watch ourselves, then surely death cannot touch us." What exactly does she mean by this? Do you think she is right? In what ways do we use the images and examples of those body types that are regarded in our culture as deficient or abnormal as role models for what *not* to be ourselves?

2. From diet books to exercise videos, there is no shortage of material that scripts the ways we are and are not supposed to eat. Choose one such example from our current culture and describe the specific steps it itemizes. What does this list imply is the right attitude we should have toward food? How does it endeavor to get readers to adopt this view? What incentives does it offer? What punishments does it threaten?

3. There is, according to Prose, a close and complex connection between gluttony and guilt. Whether in the form of FDA warnings or ad copy for "sinfully delicious desserts," overeating is regularly associated in our culture with some kind of misbehavior or even moral failing. What do you make of this connection? Choose an example from our pop culture that you think is designed to teach this kind of guilt.

PUTTING IT INTO WRITING

4. Choose some venue (e.g. a fast-food restaurant, health club, doctor's office, or similar place) that in your view endeavors to teach us specific attitudes about overeating. Spend a couple of hours there. First, write out as comprehensive a description of this place as you can. What kind of people do you observe? What sorts of equipment or décor are present? Next, write a short essay in which you speculate about the rules for eating that this venue attempts to instill. What relationship to food are people here encouraged to form? How does this relationship get presented or packaged as the norm?

5. One of the hallmarks of our contemporary culture, according to Prose, is that overeating is no longer viewed as a vice or sin but as an illness. Do you agree? What are some of the ways this change in thinking is communicated in popular culture or in the media? Write an essay in which you argue for or against gluttony as a moral issue.

COMPARING ARGUMENTS

6. Prose and Harriet Brown (p. 204) address the relationship between eating and body image in similar ways. Write an essay in which you compare the arguments these two writers make. How does each define the connection between the eating scripts our culture creates and the messages about body image our culture promotes? What does each writer find problematic or harmful about this connection? And what (if any) solution to this problem does propose?

HARRIET BROWN
How My Life Changed with One Sentence

Can cultural concerns over body type and body image become so pervasive that they rise to the level of a national obsession? Can the norms around eating and bodies become so harmful as to constitute a national crisis? These are the provocative questions Harriet Brown poses here. Tracing her own personal struggle living under the oppressive and destructive weight of the eating scripts that dominate daily life, she makes a powerful case for repudiating our culture's widespread celebration of thinness. Harriet Brown is a professor of journalism at the S.I. Newhouse School of Public Communication at Syracuse University. She is the author, most recently, of *Body of Truth: How Science, History, and Culture Drive Our Obsession with Weight* (2015), from which this essay is excerpted.

Before You Read
What role do cultural messages and images play in shaping how you think and feel about your own body?

ON A STICKY SUMMER EVENING BACK IN THE 1990S, I SIT IN A CHAIR in a therapist's office and cry. My body, I tell her, is too fleshy, too hungry, too uncontained. It doesn't look like the bodies I see five hundred times a day[1] online, on TV, in magazines, and on billboards. It doesn't look the way it's supposed to, the way I want it to. There have been years when it did, when I weighed and measured and wrote down everything I ate, worked out twice a day, pummeled my body into shape. Inevitably, though, it reverts to its natural state. Like now, when it's thirty or forty pounds heavier than I want it to be. Than it should be.

I'm here because I want someone to fix me. Specifically, to tell me how to regain control of my body (and, yes, the brain that goes with it). This therapist runs a ten-week program that's supposed to help people with eating issues. I hope she's going to teach me how to control my appetite again, something I was better at in my twenties. Now, more than a decade later, after three pregnancies and a whole lot of living, I just can't seem to do it anymore. So I sit in the chair, leaking tears of self-pity, and wait for the therapist to break out the Kleenex and reassure me that yes, it's OK, she'll help me lose weight, we will take care of this together.

She does hand me a box of tissues. But she doesn't murmur soothingly. Instead, she leans back in her chair and looks at me. This woman in her fifties with spiky dark hair, a soft stomach, and stocky legs bridges the space between us with an expression I can't quite read. Pity? Sorrow? Judgment? Sweat slides down the back of my neck as I wait for her to save me. A long moment goes by, and then she says something unimaginable, something that will change my life, though I don't know it yet.

"What if you were OK with your body the way it is right now?" she asks.

I stare at her. What I *want* to say is "Are you fucking nuts?" I mean, 5
that's why I'm here, because I'm *not* OK with it. Does she want me to have a heart attack or stroke or get diabetes because I'm too fat? Does she know how much time I've wasted crying in front of the mirror? Does she think I want to *look like her* for the rest of my life?

Of *course* I've never considered the possibility of being OK with this body. This unacceptable body. And I'm not *going* to consider it. That would be letting myself go, as my grandmother used to say, shaking her head, about any woman who'd gained a few pounds. Even as a child I knew what she meant: they'd stopped caring about themselves, and they'd stopped *taking* care of themselves. And now they deserved exactly what they got from my grandmother and every other woman in their social circle—censure, gossip, and pity.

I will never let myself go. I will never, ever, *ever* be the sloppy, lazy, dull, fat friend or mother or relative people like my grandmother shake their heads about.

This therapist must understand how hard it is to be a woman in this time and place and not have the right kind of body. After all, she's not exactly thin herself. She must have experienced the nasty comments and patronizing remarks directed at any woman who's considered too big. She must have felt the same shame at having a body that won't behave, can't be reined in, and doesn't look the way it should. How can she possibly ask me such a question?

I consider leaving now, mid-session, and never coming back. But something keeps me in the chair. I have the sense that if I walk out, I'll be missing something big, something important. So I sit and I rock and I stutter through the rest of the session. I don't ask any questions because I don't want to hear that I'm unfixable, that I'd better get used to living this way for the rest of my almost-certainly-shortened life. By the time I get home I'm furious with her for suggesting that I'm the kind of person who would let go of the thing I want most in the world. I might be fat; I'm not a quitter.

But her words stay with me. They haunt me as I brush my teeth and 10
talk to my daughters and put dinner on the table. I'm in my late thirties, and it's actually never occurred to me before that some people might be OK with not being thin. Some *women.* It's as if her words revealed a huge blind spot in my vision, one I didn't know I had.

So over the next few weeks, without meaning or wanting to, I do consider them. Actually, I think about them night and day. I think about what it would be like to live in this body for the rest of my life. I also start panic-dieting, though not very successfully, swearing off carbs, then cutting out desserts, then declaring myself strictly vegan. It's all futile and ridiculous, because I can't keep up any of these new regimens for more than a day. I find myself jolting awake at night, drenched in sweat, adrenaline burning through my veins, the words *I'm fat I'm fat I'm fat* beating time in my head. I'm smart, disciplined, hardworking. By any standards I'm a successful woman. And I just can't do this anymore.

We're in the midst of an epidemic, one that's destroying both the quality and the longevity of our lives. It affects not just us but our children, and likely their children, too. And while this epidemic has been around a while, it's growing at an alarming rate, not just here but around the world. You'd be hard-pressed to find a twenty-first-century culture that *didn't* struggle with it.

I'm not talking about overweight or obesity. I'm talking about our *obsession* with weight, our never-ending quest for thinness, our relentless angst about our bodies. Even the most self-assured of us get caught up in body anxiety: 97 percent of young women surveyed by *Glamour* magazine in 2011 said they felt hatred toward their bodies at least once a day and often much more. Ninety-seven percent—that's pretty much everyone. Another eight out of ten women say they're unhappy with their reflection.

> **Of course, I've never considered the possibility of being OK with this body. This unacceptable body. . . . That would be letting myself go, as my grandmother used to say, shaking her head, about any woman who had gained a few pounds.**

I've interviewed hundreds of women about weight and body image over the last few years, and every one of them says she has struggled with body hatred, or continues to struggle, to one degree or another. Too many of us waste our time, our emotional energy, our very sanity trying to meet the ever-more-rigid rules about what size and shape our bodies are supposed to be. Even for women who get it, who know intellectually that the quest to be thin is ultimately both fruitless and pointless, it's unbelievably tough to challenge the cultural norms around weight.

15 The barrage of prescriptive messages starts early. Several studies have shown that three- and four-year-olds are afraid of getting fat, and no wonder: They're primed to absorb and internalize the lessons we teach them, which in this case means shame about their bodies and

self-loathing. Even if they don't hear it at home, they get it from TV shows, books, teachers, doctors, games, and other children. Even the most confident women struggle to navigate a daily gauntlet of images and messages warning us of the psychological, social, and physical perils of not meeting society's unattainable body ideals. And this isn't just a women's issue, either; men and boys are increasingly caught up in their own variation of body anxiety (in fact, 18 percent of men say they feel fat every day)[2]: Women want to be thin; men want to be buff. Women want thigh gaps; men want six-packs.

This obsession isn't new, of course; my friends and I spent many miserable hours in front of the mirror as teens in the 1970s. What is new is how encompassing the issue has become. It comes at us from all directions—from the media, from doctors and medical professionals, from school administrators, from politicians, from *environmentalists*, for pity's sake. Practically every modern problem from the recession to climate change has at some point been blamed on fat. We're told that we're undisciplined, gluttonous, lazy, that our children will be the first modern generation whose lives will be shorter than their parents' because of obesity. That weight issues rack up an extra $66 billion a year in healthcare costs, contribute to global warming, strain the world's food resources as much as an extra five hundred million people living on the planet.

Obsessing about weight has become a ritual and a refrain, punctuating and shaping every relationship, including our relationships with ourselves. It's become social currency not just for women but for teens and even children. My younger daughter was fifteen when she told me (with a great deal of exasperation at my naïveté), "Mom, fat-bashing is how girls bond with each other. I *have* to say bad things about my body if I want to have any friends." And saying those "bad things" to others reinforces our own inner critics, the ones that pick apart every outfit, that assess every inch of flesh, every blemish, every choice we make. We're so used to that constant inner judgment, we don't even think to question it.

The words we use to talk about our bodies have changed, too. We're no longer plump or chubby, stocky or stout or husky; now we're overweight or obese, words that connote facts and figures, illness rather than aesthetics. You're considered overweight with a BMI over 25 and obese with a BMI over 30. (According to the American Medical Association, with a BMI over 30 you're also diseased.) These words influence the way other people—including our doctors—relate to us. And, most devastatingly, they change the way we think about ourselves and others. The word *overweight*, for instance, suggests there's one acceptable weight, and everything above that is too much. It's "over" what it should be. The word *obesity* has become a diagnosis rather than a description, shorthand for a boatload of undesirable qualities: gluttony, lack of self-discipline, laziness, sloppiness, grotesqueness.

If you're reading this and thinking *wait a minute, that's not what's going on*, cast your mind back to the last TV news story or web article you saw about obesity. I bet it was illustrated with photos of extremely heavy people shown from the neck down, an faces, plodding along or overflowing a chair or scarfing down French fries or ice cream—what British psychotherapist Charlotte Cooper has described as "headless fatty" images.[3] It's tough to empathize with or relate to a faceless, fleshy blob, which is, of course, the point. (And maybe, too, there's also an element of "It's too embarrassing to show someone this fat, so we'll hide her identity." Which is equally offensive.)

20   I prefer the word *fat*, which is based in description rather than judgment. We have fat on our bodies, all of us; you can't be alive without it. More than half your brain is made of fatty acids;[4] without enough fat, your brain deteriorates, leaving you vulnerable to ailments from depression and anxiety to fatigue and cognitive decline.

But some people fear the word almost as much as the condition. At Syracuse University, where I'm a professor, I created a class on body diversity, in part because I've watched my students struggle with body issues over the years. They practically fall out of their chairs the first time I use the word in class. To call someone *fat* in this culture is beyond offensive; it's unforgiveable. Even Lance Armstrong wouldn't do it.

What was once a source of personal anxiety and distress has morphed into an ongoing public dialogue. Just ten years ago, a Google search for the word "obesity" returned about 217,000 hits. A similar search in just the first six months of 2014 turned up nearly twenty-seven million hits. Not that Google searches represent a scientific standard, but they do reflect a culture's preoccupations—in this case, the reality that we're more freaked out than ever about how much we weigh and what our bodies look like. Many of us believe, as the Duchess of Windsor so famously said, that we can *never* be thin enough—and that if we're not thin, we can never be successful, desirable, lovable, of worthwhile, either.

In Fall 2013, former *Good Morning America* host Joan Lunden joked on the *Today Show* that one of the benefits of having triple negative breast cancer, and going through several rounds of aggressive chemotherapy, was losing weight. I know this was gallows humor, meant to help defuse a terribly painful situation. But no one would have laughed if there wasn't some truth to the idea that thinness is prized even if it comes from battling a potentially fatal illness.

The way we talk about weight has become a kind of code. "I need to lose five pounds!" we complain to a friend, meaning *Tell me I'm OK the way I am*, meaning *I don't think I'm better than you are*, meaning *I feel inadequate*. "I just can't find a way to lose this weight," we say in despair, meaning *I can't find love, or work, or success, and it's all because of this one enormous thing wrong with me.*

Every January, for instance, when the whole country engages in its 25 annual post–New Year's self-flagellation, the media run countless stories on resolutions and diets, bikini bodies and love handles. And those stories make us feel worse, not better. They reinforce the idea that we're supposed to have Michelle Obama's arms, Jennifer Aniston's stomach, Joe Manganiello's six-pack, but they offer no useful resources.

If all this body angst made people healthier and happier, maybe we could argue that the end justified the means. But it doesn't. Instead, many of us spend a lot of our waking hours on a hamster wheel of self-loathing. We're screwed up about food, too; one recent survey found 75 percent of American women report disordered eating behaviors.[5] I believe it. I've heard my students boast about eating only once a day, seen grown women stare at a piece of bread with a heartbreaking mixture of fear and longing. We bounce between depriving ourselves and then "eating with disinhibition," a fancy way to say overeating.

And we're paying the price. Many prices, actually. When we focus on the size of Hillary Clinton's ankles rather than on her voting record, we miss the chance to make a meaningful political choice. When we can't skip a day working out at the gym, we sacrifice the chance to get a graduate degree, learn a language, acquire career skills, develop relationships, do volunteer work—to spend that time more productively in so many other ways. When we nag our children about their weight or what they eat, we're telling them they're not good enough and damaging our authentic relationships with them.

Over the years I've seen my body as an enemy to be conquered, deprived, and beaten into submission—that is, into the smallest possible shape and size. Occasionally I felt proud of its strength and curviness. But more often I saw it as a symbol of my personal weakness and shame, an outward manifestation of my inadequacies and failures. Catching sight of myself in a mirror—an experience I tried to avoid—could send me into a dark place for hours. I spent years wallowing in self-hatred because of the size of my thighs. My weight went up and down over those decades, from the low side of "normal" to mildly obese, but my level of despair and self-loathing stayed sky-high.

The worst part was that I knew better. I'd read Simone de Beauvoir, Gloria Steinem, Naomi Wolf. I understood intellectually that the more freedoms and power women achieve, the more insistent and damaging the social pressures that squeeze us (and, increasingly, men) into a certain shape, size, and attitude.

But when it came to my own body, everything I *knew* evaporated and 30 what I *felt* became overwhelming. So while I understood that in reality I was a reasonable-looking woman, with a loving husband, beloved daughters, and good friends, I still felt freakish and ugly. I felt like I took up way too much space; I imagined myself lumbering rather than walking,

> **We're in the midst of an epidemic, one that's destroying both the quality and the longevity of our lives. . . . I'm not talking about overweight or obesity. I'm talking about our obsession with weight, our never-ending quest for thinness, our relentless angst about our bodies.**

bulging where I should be taut. I got so used to thinking of myself as enormous that sometimes I was surprised when I caught sight of myself in a mirror and thought, for a second, *She looks normal.* I could argue a friend off a ledge of body hatred, but I couldn't feel good about my own body. Some days I wished I could just wear a plastic bag and be done with it.

Each of us thinks our obsession with weight and body image is ours alone. We blame ourselves for not being thin enough, sexy enough, shaped just the right way. We believe we're supposed to fit the standards of the day. And if we're not in the 1 percent of the population born with the body du jour, we feel its our fault. We believe we can get there if only we eat less, eat differently, work out more, go vegan, throw up what we eat, give up gluten, lake laxatives, fast, give up sugar, fill in the blank.

But the reality couldn't possibly get any clearer: *This is not a personal issue.* This is not about your weakness or my laziness or her lack of self-discipline. This obsession is bigger than all of us. It's become epidemic, endemic, and pandemic. It comes from all around us, but it's dug its way deep under our skins, and it festers there. It's a pain that involves our deepest sense of who we are in the world. We experience the world through our bodies, our skin and neurons and nerves. Other people see us only and always in the context of our flesh and hone and blood. How can you feel good about your essential self when you hate what contains it?

You can't, as it turns out. That's how I wound up in the therapist's chair, staring at her in disbelief, wondering if she'd lost her mind. And that's how I started on a journey that's put me into a completely different place. Along the way, my relationship with food started to shift, and so did my physical sense of myself.

It look years for my perspective to evolve, years of thinking and knowing before the feelings began to change. While I still occasionally react to food as if it were an enemy to be conquered, most of the time now I focus on what feels good—physically and mentally—rather than on weight. I eat well and enjoy what I eat. I take long walks and go for bike rides because doing those things makes me feel good, not because they burn calories.

And I see the beginnings of change in other people, too. There's 35 evidence that fewer American women are dieting now than in previous years.[6] We're starting to talk about *health* rather than *weight*—at least occasionally. We pay lip service to the fact that bodies naturally come in all shapes and sizes even if many of us don't believe it, especially when it comes to ourselves. I think we're smart enough to be confused by the hall-truths and mis-conceptions, to know there's a lot we don't yet understand about weight and health, about how metabolism works and why "calories in, calories out" may not always hold true. We're beginning to separate facts from fictions and, each of us, make decisions about what's best for our health.

Because contrary to what you hear in the media, the relationship between weight and health isn't simple or straightforward. It's terrifically complex, as multidimensional and complicated and elegant as the human body itself. We automatically conflate fat with being unhealthy, and praise thinness as a model of health. But in reality, that's *never* been the whole truth, or even most of it. People naturally come in a range of shapes and sizes. We might be short or tall, lanky or curvy, athletic or clumsy.

> *[W]hen it came to my own body, everything I knew evaporated, and what I felt became overwhelming.*

We might feel wretched at a weight the doctor says is fine and comfortable at a weight society deplores. We might be actively engaged in taking care of ourselves or not. There's no one-size-fits-all approach (so to speak). We each have our own physical and emotional realities, which, along with all the social and cultural baggage we carry, shape our experiences and reactions.

I still have occasional moments when I look in the mirror and feel a little zing of panic, when I find myself thinking I *won't ever eat any more bread! Or sugar! Or fat!* Luckily, I've learned to deflect and redirect the inner monologue that still sometimes runs on a continuous loop in my head, commenting viciously about the size of my thighs, my waist, my chins, my appetite.

I know I'm not the only one who's fed up with this obsession, who's tired of seeing weeks and years of my life go down the drain of self-loathing and self-denial. Over the last decade I've interviewed hundreds of women about how they feel about their bodies. I came away from those conversations with a profound sense of sadness at the real suffering this obsession creates and perpetuates. And eventually I got mad. Mad enough to spend years immersed in the research so I didn't *have* to believe everything I read, so I could understand the facts for myself. Mad enough to talk to many of the scientists who study obesity and eating disorders, to ask them the tough questions and know enough to contextualize their answers.

What I've learned from this process has been shocking and enlightening, enraging and empowering. It has forever changed the way I look at myself and others, how I think about weight and health and food. There's no question that we need a different kind of conversation, one rooted in science and evidence and reality rather than blame and fantasies, our own and others'. . . .

40   When I give lectures on this subject, audiences often react with disbelief—at first. Our intellectual perspectives and emotional comfort zone around weight and body size have developed over years, and are reinforced constantly by much of what we see and hear. It takes time to understand things differently. And it can be scary to shift the paradigm; many of us have a lot invested in seeing things the way we've always seen them.

NOTES

[1] In 2007, a marketing research firm estimated that people living in cities saw up to five thousand ads a day; some advertising executives and commentators question that number. Considering the continuing proliferation of ads over the last eight years, five hundred ads a day seems a conservative estimate.

[2] Body image issues are clearly on the rise for boys and men, but there are few statistics on the subject yet, maybe because men are far less open about such concerns than women.

[3] Charlotte Cooper, "Headless Fatties," 2007, accessed on October 23, 2014, www.charlottecooper.net.

[4] C. Y. Chang, D. S. Key, and J. Y. Chen, "Essential Fatty Acids and Human Brain," *Acta Neurologica Taiwanica* 18, no. 4 (2009): 231–241.

[5] According to a 2008 survey done by *Self* magazine and the University of North Carolina at Chapel Hill. See www.med.unc.edu/www/newsarchive/2008/april/survey-finds-disordered-eating-behaviors-among-three-out-of-four-american-women.

[6] According to an NPR story, "Skinny Isn't All That: Survey Finds Fewer American Women Are Dieting," aired January 7, 2013.

FOR A SECOND READING

1.   According to Brown, scrutinizing and judging our own bodies has come to feel so natural that it no longer seems remarkable. "We're so used to that constant inner judgment, we don't even think to question it" (p. 207). What is your view? Do you agree studying and judging our own bodies has become an unexamined norm? If so, what can be done to challenge it?

2.   Brown characterizes our cultural preoccupation with bodies and body weight in epidemiological terms: "It's become epidemic, endemic, and pandemic." How do you respond to this language?

In your view, is it helpful or accurate to describe cultural attitudes in the language of disease? Why or why not?

3. "While I still occasionally react to food as if it were an enemy to be conquered," Brown writes, "most of the time now I focus on what feels good—physically and mentally—rather than on weight" (p. 210). In today's eating culture, how difficult do you think this is to do? In light of the norms and scripts around eating and bodies, how challenging is it to focus on "what feels good" rather than on "weight"?

PUTTING IT INTO WRITING

4. Our cultural obsession with thinness, writes Brown, comes from an array of sources: "from the media, from doctors and medical professionals, from school administrators, from politicians, from *environmentalists*, for pity's sake" (p. 207). Choose one of the groups Brown calls out here. Then write a short essay (500 words) in which you explain how you believe this group contributes to our cultural "obsession with thinness." What messages about being think does this group promote? In what particular ways are these messages harmful?

5. Brown focuses a good deal on the language we use in today's culture to characterize our body type or body weight. "We're no longer plump or chubby, stocky or stout or husky; now we're overweight or obese, words that connote facts and figures, illness rather than aesthetics" (p. 207). In a 500–750 word essay, respond to Brown's claim here. What kind of distinction is she making between the language of "illness" and the language of "aesthetics"? Do you agree that a shift from the one to other represents a problem in the way we are being taught to talk and think about our bodies? Why or why not?

COMPARING ARGUMENTS

6. After interviewing hundreds of women about how they view their own bodies, Brown writes, she "eventually got mad." "Mad enough to spend years immersed in the research so I didn't *have* to believe everything I read, so I could understand the facts myself" (p. 211). How do you think Francine Prose (p. 197) would respond to this statement? Given the argument she makes about "gluttony," do you think Prose would welcome the kind of "research" Brown discusses here? Which particular "facts" do you think would best help to bolster Prose's argument?

Then and Now: **How to Make Meatloaf**

Far more than a list of ingredients and steps, each of these recipes offers a quick snapshot of the sorts of attitudes toward eating that, at two different moments in our food culture's recent history, passed for the norm. Meatloaf is a classic American dish that first became popular on family dinner tables during the Great Depression. It's a dish families could make on a budget because the recipe relied on cheaper cuts of meat and included bread or cracker crumbs as a way to create more servings. The first recipe is a classic meatloaf recipe from the Heinz ketchup company. Looking at it, we may learn more about what the prevailing food attitudes were by focusing on what the recipe does *not* say — that is, on the things it simply takes for granted. The instructions are much less explicit than what we're used to today: no temperature setting for the oven, no specifications for the size of baking dish, and no order for the ingredients added. The recipe also omits nutritional information — no discussion of calories or cholesterol here or references to recommended daily allowances of fiber or calcium. These omissions stem in part from ingrained assumptions about eating that people of this era simply regarded as *common sense.* To put it mildly, any dish whose list of ingredients goes no further than pepper, ground beef, and bologna didn't achieve popularity at a historical moment that placed a terribly high premium on physical health. The point of eating, this recipe all but says out loud, is not to make us live longer; it is to put things into our bodies that conform to a particular standard of good taste or smart spending — a standard that in this case appears to have revolved primarily around adding flavor using the least expensive ingredients possible.

> ### *Circa 1956*
> #### HEINZ KETCHUP MEATLOAF RECIPE
>
> 2 lbs. ground beef
> ½ lb. bologna
> 1 tablespoon grated onion
> 1 cup moist cracker crumbs
> 1 egg
> 1 teaspoon salt
> ½ cup Heinz Tomato Ketchup
> Pepper
>
> Chop bologna finely and add to the meat. Add other ingredients, adding Tomato Ketchup last, and bake in a moderate oven, basting frequently.

Contrast the second recipe, which transforms the all-American dish. The tofu meatloaf recipe carefully acquaints its readers with the particular facts about the ingredients it assembles, a tactic exemplified in its references to "light miso," "tahini," and "dried dill." This difference underscores how much more diversified our culture's prevailing definitions of American cuisine have grown since the Depression era. But perhaps even more important, it suggests how much more worried we are about what we put into our bodies.

This recipe is meat free and includes all-natural ingredients and exotic flavors. Indeed, if this Moosewood Restaurant recipe is a reliable guide, we could well argue that ours has become a food culture in which concerns over physical health (as well as its corollary, physical appearance) and ideology now supplant expense as the primary standard by which we judge the quality of our food.

These recipes may represent night and day in terms of what goes in them, but both represent a certain anxiety over eating. The first recipe includes just a few inexpensive ingredients (and relies on ketchup to provide the zing), while the second includes numerous fresh and healthy ingredients that are tough to find in some areas and cost considerably more than a bottle of ketchup. While the first recipe's author is conscious of the cook's pocketbook, the second is conscious of his or her health and lifestyle. Each recipe provides a revealing glimpse into how meatloaf can reflect our cultural concerns.

PUTTING IT INTO WRITING

1. How does each recipe seem to define "good" eating? What does each recipe seem to define its standards of good eating against? Why? Write a one-page essay in which you analyze and evaluate the key differences between these two scripts. In what ways have the norms around eating changed since the first recipe was popular?

2. Nicholas Kristof (p. 185) writes about the economics of food. What do you think he would have to say about these meatloaf recipes? Do they seem to confirm the kinds of connections between food and social class that Kristof identifies? How or how not?

2001
TOFU MEATLOAF RECIPE

Serves 8
Prep time: 30 minutes
Baking time: 25–30 minutes
2 cakes firm tofu (16 ounces each)
2 tablespoons vegetable oil
2 cups diced onions
1 cup peeled and grated carrots
1 cup diced bell peppers
1 teaspoon dried oregano
1 teaspoon dried basil
1 teaspoon dried dill
$^2/_3$ cup chopped walnuts
1 cup bread crumbs
2 tablespoons tahini
2 tablespoons light miso
2 tablespoons soy sauce
1–2 tablespoons Dijon mustard

Press the tofu between two plates and rest a heavy weight on the top plate. Press for 15 minutes, then drain the liquid.

Meanwhile, heat the oil in a frying pan and sauté the onions, carrots, peppers, oregano, basil, and dill for about 7 minutes, until the vegetables are just tender. Crumble the pressed tofu into a large bowl, or grind it through a food processor. Stir in the walnuts, bread crumbs, tahini, miso, soy sauce, and mustard. Add the sautéed vegetables and mix well.

Preheat the oven to 350 or 375 degrees. Press the mix into an oiled casserole dish, and bake for about 30 minutes, until lightly browned.

— *Reprinted from* Moosewood Restaurant New Classics, *Copyright © 2001 by the Moosewood Collective, Clarkson N. Potter, New York, publishers.*

LILY WONG
Eating the Hyphen

Can eating different types of food make us more or less "American"? Pondering the implications of this question, Lily Wong recounts the history of her own complicated relationship to Chinese and American traditions of eating. Along the way, she offers readers food for thought about the relationship between eating and identity. Lily Wong is a food writer whose work was featured in *The Best Food Writing of 2013*. This piece was published in 2013 in *Gastronomica*, an academic journal that explores issues of food and culture.

Before You Read

How do you understand the relationship between eating and identity? What does how we eat say about who we are?

FORK? CHECK. KNIFE? CHECK. CHOPSTICKS? CHECK. IT MAY SEEM odd to have all three of these eating utensils side by side for the consumption of a single meal, but for me, there's just no other way. Oh, and ketchup, that's key. Definitely need to have the ketchup, pre-shaken to avoid an awkward first squirt of pale red water. There's no place for that on my plate, not when I'm eating dumplings. Yes, that is what I said: I need a fork, a knife, a pair of chopsticks, and ketchup before I eat my dumplings.

Now I've just looked up "dumpling" on the online *Oxford English Dictionary* and discovered that it is "a kind of pudding consisting of a mass of paste or dough, more or less globular in form, either plain and boiled, or enclosing fruit and boiled or baked." I am definitely not talking about whatever unappetizing-sounding food that dumpling is supposed to be. I'm talking about Chinese dumplings, pot stickers, Peking ravioli, *jiaozi*, whatever you want to call them. Do you know what I mean yet? Maybe you've gotten a vague idea, but let me explain, because I am *very* picky about my dumplings.

To begin with, the skin has to be thick. I mean really thick. Thick and chewy and starchy and the bottom should be a bit burnt and dark golden brown from the pan-frying. Have you ever had *gyoza*, the Japanese dumplings? Yes, those thin, almost translucent skins just won't do it for me. Hands-down, no question, until my dying day, I will vouch that the skin is the make-or-break feature of a dumpling. Bad skin equals bad dumpling. Those boiled dumplings that are also a type of Chinese dumplings? The skin is too thin, too soggy, and frankly, rather flavorless. If I had to call it names, I'd say it was limp and weak and characterless. The thick-skinned dumplings that I know and love absorb more of the meaty-flavored goodness inside the dumplings. Also, because they are pan-fried (a key aspect of delicious dumplings), the bottom gets its own texture—a slightly charred crispiness to add that perfect smidgen of crunch. So, if you were to eat just the skin of the dumpling, it would be simultaneously chewy and crispy, with a bit of savory meat flavor mixed in with a burnt taste off the bottom—a wonderfulness that the words of the English language are hard-pressed to capture.

> *Yes, that is what I said: I need a fork, a knife, a pair of chopsticks, and ketchup before I eat my dumplings.*

But what about the filling? To me, it's a bit peripheral. The dumplings I'm talking about have a standard pork filling with "Chinese vegetables." I've never been entirely sure what these elusively named Chinese vegetables actually are, but I imagine that they are some combination of leeks and Chinese cabbage. They're not too salty and they don't have cilantro. These dumplings also have enough savory broth secretly sequestered inside the skin so that when you cut them open, you get some oil spatterings, pretty much all over your clothes, plate, and table. That's the sign of a good, moist, and juicy meat section.

I should mention before you envision me slaving away in a kitchen 5 to create the perfect dumpling that the ones I like come out of the freezer. In plastic bags of fifty each. Imported to my house from Boston's Chinatown. It's strange, considering that most days I like the homegrown version of foods more than the store-bought version, but these are the exception. Even though I know they're hand made by a small company, so you get that same small-batch feel as if you made them at home, they're still store-bought and frozen rather than fresh.

But enough about finding the right dumplings; you're probably still confused as to why it's so imperative that I have a fork, knife, chopsticks, and ketchup. Here is your step-by-step guide to an entirely new dumpling eating experience.

1. On a large white plate, place six or seven dumplings (or more if you're particularly ravenous) and add some broccoli or beans for color and nutrition.

2. Squirt a glop of ketchup in one of the empty white spaces on your plate (as in not touching the broccoli or the dumplings). This is where it's key that the ketchup has been shaken a bit, otherwise that red ketchup juice runs all over your plate ruining everything.

3. Take that fork and knife on the side and cut each dumpling in half width-wise. Make sure to cut completely through the skin and meat.

4. Take the backside of your fork and push down on the top of each dumpling half until the meat abruptly pops out in a pool of brothy juice.

5. Once you've finished systematically cutting and squishing, you'll have lots of skins and meat pieces separated and you can put that knife and fork away. Grab the chopsticks.

6. Pick up a piece of the meat (just the meat now, no trying to get some skin in on this too) and dip it into the ketchup. Eat and repeat. If at any point you want to indulge in that steamed broccoli, it's a good idea. You wouldn't want to leave it all to the end. But don't dip it in ketchup. That's weird.

7. Now this is the best part. Use your chopsticks to one-by-one eat every last half dumpling's worth of skin. Savor every part because this is what it's all really been about. No ketchup or meat to obscure the flavor and chewiness, just pure starchy goodness.

I'm not sure why I often think that to be a Chinese American means that you relish authentic Chinese food—and by authentic I mostly mean strictly what your grandmother cooks for you—but I do.

And that's how it goes. Every single time. Confused? So was I the first time I really sat down to think about how I eat dumplings. It sounds a little like a grand mutilation of how a dumpling should be eaten for it to be "authentic" (using only chopsticks and with the dumpling left whole and dipped in black vinegar, no ketchup in sight). And I have unabashedly criticized and ridiculed Americanized Chinese food for being fake and something of a disgrace to "authentic" Chinese food. Yet here I am, still eating my dumplings with ketchup and a fork unceremoniously and quite literally butchering my dumplings before I eat them. My grandmother meanwhile takes small bites out of whole dumplings, careful not to lose any of that broth from inside (with a face only three-quarters filled with disgust as I rush from the table to grab my ketchup from the fridge).

Bottled up in this entirely strange ritual is my status as a Chinese American. It is unclear to me where I ever came up with the idea that dumplings should be cut in half, or that the meat would taste better with ketchup (particularly since this is literally the only time that I use ketchup). Perhaps this combination has something to do with the fact that since both my parents grew up in the States, we've embraced many American traditions while abandoning or significantly modifying many

Chinese ones. But even so, I have always embraced my Chinese culture and heritage. It gives me something larger to cling to when I'm feeling ostracized by American culture for looking "different." The suburb I grew up in is mostly white, but it's not as if I didn't have Chinese people around me; after all, there was always Chinatown. But Chinatown was full of people who spoke the language—whether Cantonese or Mandarin—who somehow just seemed so much more Chinese than I ever could be. And perhaps that's true. Maybe that's why I feel so gosh-darned American when I eat my dumplings with ketchup while holding my chopsticks "incorrectly." The notion that this somehow takes away from my ability to identify with Chinese culture is, I rationally understand, flawed. But in my pursuit to try and discover who I am, it's taken an oddly large place.

I'm not sure why I often think that to be a Chinese American means that you relish authentic Chinese food—and by authentic I mostly mean strictly what your grandmother cooks for you—but I do. I've told friends that they don't know what real Chinese food is because all they know is Panda Express. I pride myself on my Cantonese background, which leads me to look favorably on pig's ears and fungus of all shapes and sizes. My innate territorialism regarding my particular definition of what Chinese food is makes the choice to continue eating my dumplings in such a strange fashion slightly fraught. I'm not even sure that anyone besides my family knows that this is how I eat dumplings. In part, I think my reticence derives precisely from a fear that it would make me "less" Chinese.

Somehow, I've come to strange terms with these contradictions. 10 Somewhere along the way, dumplings, cut in half with ketchup on the meat and the skin separated as a special entity of its own, have become my comfort food. So whether or not it perverts some thousand-year-old tradition of the "proper" way to eat dumplings, this is what makes me happy. Although I sometimes catch myself overcompensating with extra delight in Chinese delicacies involving jellyfish and sea cucumber that cause most Americans to squirm, eating dumplings in my own style has become the hyphen between Chinese and American in my identity.

FOR A SECOND READING

1. Take a moment to reflect on the title of this essay. What does Wong mean by "eating the hyphen"? How do you define what this phrase means? And how does this title preview the larger argument Wong is making in this essay?

2. Wong devotes significant time in this essay to detailing the specific qualities she most prizes in her favorite kind of dumpling. Why do you think she does this? What does this discussion tell us about Wong's broader attitude toward food? How does this discussion

relate to the larger point(s) she is making in this essay about our culture's eating scripts?

3. Reflecting on what she sees as the "contradictions" within her own experiences as an eater, Wong wrestles with the question of how to define truly "authentic" Chinese or American food? How do you answer this question? Do you have a standard for measuring the "authenticity" of a given food? Do you think such a standard is necessary? Why or why not?

PUTTING IT INTO WRITING

4. After walking readers through a "step-by-step guide to an entirely new dumpling experience," Wong declares that her "status as a Chinese American" is "bottled up" in this "strange ritual" (p. 218). Take a closer look at this guide. Then write a short essay (250–500 words) in which you analyze these steps as an effort to redefine stereotypes defining the "typical" American meal or the "typical" American eater.

5. Wong uses words like "confusing" and "contradictory" to describe her relationship to American food traditions. Write an essay (500–750 words) in which you describe and reflect upon your own relationship to American food traditions. What terms best capture this relationship? What examples from your own experience can you cite that best illustrate this relationship?

COMPARING ARGUMENTS

6. Wong is interested in examining how our eating practices are related to our identity. What, she wonders, does how we eat say about who we are? How do you think Brendan Buhler (p. 221) would answer this question? And what do you think the practice of "eating roadkill" might say about a person?

BRENDAN BUHLER

On Eating Roadkill

For most of us, our connection to the food we eat extends no further than the container in which it is packaged or the label with which it is affixed. For those in what has come to be known as the locavore movement, however, the connection goes all the way back to our food's former existence as a living thing. Offering an unexpected twist on this idea, Brendan Buhler makes a provocative case for roadkill as the ultimate locavore fare. And in doing so, he invites readers to think more deeply and more critically about where exactly our food comes from. Buhler is a freelance writer and former reporter for the *Las Vegas Sun*. This article appeared in *Modern Farmer* in 2013.

Before You Read

How important to you is knowing where your food comes from? How much does this knowledge factor into the eating choices you make day to day?

ETHICALLY SPEAKING, WE SHOULD ALL BE EATING ROADKILL. Not just us carnivores, either. It is the perfect meat for vegetarians and vegans, too, provided their objections to meat are its murder or its environmental implications and not because it's icky-gross. The animal was not raised for meat, it was not killed for meat; it is just simply and accidentally meat—manna from minivans.

Practical, culinary, and even legal considerations make it hard for many to imagine cooking our vehicular accidents, but that needn't be the case. If the roadkill is fresh, perhaps hit on a cold day and ideally a large animal, it is as safe as any game. Plus, not eating roadkill is intensely wasteful: last year,

> **The animal was not raised for meat, it was not killed for meat; it is just simply and accidentally meat—manna from minivans.**

State Farm Mutual Automobile Insurance Company estimated that some 1,232,000 deer were hit by cars in the United States. Now imagine that only a third of that meat could be salvaged. That'd be about 20 million pounds of free-range venison, perhaps not much compared to the 23 billion pounds of beef produced in the United States in 2011 but significant.

(*Nota bene*: Deer are the important edible roadkill category for two reasons: money and physics. Insurance companies keep statistics on roadkill deer because hitting a deer messes up a car in a way a jackrabbit can't—State Farm estimates the average cost of collision with a deer is just over $3,300. The reporting of all other roadkill is sporadic and anecdotal. But what you really care about is that deer are large animals and more likely to remain edible. Their height means they're unlikely to be mashed under a car but thrown over or around it. Their mass means their guts are less likely to rupture and contaminate the surrounding meat. That's not to say there's never an edible Thumper or Flower lying by the roadside, but the star attraction remains Bambi.)

5   Roadkill arrived with the age of the automobile. The first study of roadkill was probably published by New England naturalist James Raymond Simmons, author of 1938's *Feathers and Fur on the Turnpike*—a rare book, for knowledge of which we are grateful to Roger Knutson's more recent work, *Flattened Fauna*. While little hard data exists in the critically understudied field of eating roadkill, it's probably safe to say people have been eating it as long as it's been around. Wisconsin, for instance, started issuing roadkill salvage tags for deer in the 1950s, and there was already a demand. Culturally, roadkill foraging is largely a rural practice, because that's where you find farmers and hunters accustomed to butchering animals, and that's where you find more animals—animals that haven't been hit multiple times and animals that aren't either pets or sewer-dwelling vermin.

> **While little hard data exists in the critically understudied field of eating roadkill, it's probably safe to say people have been eating it as long as it's been around.**

For those new to eating roadkill, the best advice (other than trusting your eyes and nose) can be found in wild game cookbooks. Avoid roadkill-specific cookbooks, which tend to be jokey, like, you might be a redneck if you own this book.

The legal ramifications of eating roadkill are a bit dicey, though. In West Virginia, the roadkill must simply be reported to the state within 12 hours of its collection. Tennessee considered a similar law, but withdrew it under ridicule. In Massachusetts, you must obtain a permit after the fact and submit your roadkill to inspection by the state. In Illinois, the chain of title is somewhat complicated, and no one delinquent in child support may claim a dead deer. Alaska practices roadside socialism: all roadkill belongs to the state, which then feeds it to human families in need.

On the other hand, Texas, California, and Washington may not agree on much, but they are three of the very few states that agree that possession of roadkill is illegal. Apparently, they worry it will lead to poaching.

Carrie Wilson, a marine biologist with California's Department of Fish and Wildlife who writes a question and answer column for the state agency, said she's had to address the topic of roadkill a couple of times. She tells readers that even if they have a hunting license, smacking a deer with a Volvo does not constitute a legal method of taking game.

Now, I've been a passenger in a car that hit a deer. The deer bounded 10 off in who knows what condition and the car limped home with shaken passengers and several hundred dollars worth of damage. It is not an experience I would repeat on purpose. I asked Wilson if she thought there was anyone out there who would try to run a deer down for meat.

"There are people who will do it, unfortunately," she said.

Facts don't really back up that fear, though. In Wisconsin, a state that has issued salvage tags since the '50s, officials say poaching is not an issue. Scott Roepke, an assistant big game ecologist with the state's Department of Natural Resources, notes the state issued 4,400 roadkill deer salvage tags in 2011—up about 1,000 from the previous three years' totals, but nowhere near the almost 14,000 deer salvaged in 1998.

"We have prosecuted a few people at least who do try and run down deer with their cars. There is a sizable fine associated with it," Roepke said. "We definitely wouldn't want to encourage people to try and run down a deer with their trucks and take it home for meat."

It's worth noting here that in the woodsy states of the Northeast, the states with the most deer and the most deer dead alongside the road—Pennsylvania, Michigan, New York, Ohio, and Wisconsin—it's legal to collect and eat roadkill deer.

The most recent state to legalize roadkill collection is Montana, with 15 a bill introduced by Republican Representative Steve Lavin, a highway patrol sergeant in northwest Montana, near Glacier National Park. At first, Lavin says he laughed off the suggestion of one of his troopers that the meat be legalized, but the more he thought about it, the more it made sense. There is a lot of roadkill in the area; some of it's getting eaten, even taken to food banks. "What's happening is people are taking them already—essentially what this will do is legalize the process," he says.

Lavin's law will allow any peace officer to issue a permit for the salvage of roadkill antelope, deer, elk, or moose. (Bears, bighorn sheep, and other animals with valuable body parts are intentionally excluded from the statute, Lavin said.)

There are times, of course, when roadkill is not collected for human culinary purposes. In Wisconsin, and other states worried about the spread of a deer pathogen known as Chronic Wasting Disease, the deer are collected by contractors and hauled to nearby landfills. It's a patch-work system in California, Carrie Wilson said. If the state roads agency finds the animals, they tend to drag the carcasses off into the bushes for non-human scavengers. Some cities either have their own animal control agencies or hire animal shelters to collect carcasses. The carcasses are then either fed to rescued carnivores or taken to a rendering plant, from which they eventually exit as ingredients for pet food, glue, soap, phar-maceuticals, and gelatin.

So for those on the fence (or outright repelled) by the concept, con-sider this: because gelatin ends up in everything from marshmallows to gummy bears to ice cream, there's a good chance that you've already consumed, legally, some accidental meat.

FOR A SECOND READING

1. What are some of the associations you bring to the term *roadkill*? And are any of these associations compatible with the idea of eating roadkill? Why or why not?

2. Take a moment to consider the claim implied by the essay's title. Do you agree that roadkill could very well constitute one of our most ethical eating choices? How or how not?

3. What would happen if eating roadkill were to become a more widely accepted social norm? What rules would you suggest for how this practice should be carried out? What guidelines? What limitations? And why?

PUTTING IT INTO WRITING

4. Buhler spends a good deal of time reviewing the different state laws that regulate and restrict treatment of roadkill. Write an assessment of this decision. Why do you think Buhler chooses to include this information? What is his larger goal in doing so? Did reading these descriptions affect your views about eating roadkill in any way?

5. Buhler concludes his essay with these thoughts: "[F]or those on the fence (or outright repelled) by the concept, consider this: because gelatin ends up in everything from marshmallows to gummy bears to ice cream, there's a good chance that you've already consumed, legally, some accidental meat" (p. 224). Write an essay in which you analyze the rhetorical strategy at work here. Why does Buhler conclude by pointing out the likelihood that we all have already consumed "accidental meat"? How does this statement relate to the larger argument he is trying to make?

COMPARING ARGUMENTS

6. Buhler's essay, like Lily Wong's (p. 216), explores what it means to follow eating practices perceived to fall outside the boundaries of mainstream cultural norms. In a 500-word essay, discuss the ways each of these essays can be read as an attempt to redefine these cultural norms. What food-specific attitudes or behaviors do these two writers seem most directly to be questioning?

Scenes and Un-Scenes: **Giving Thanks**

Thanksgiving stands out as one of our few genuinely American holidays. Its rituals are rooted in American myth, one that is separate from religious doctrine. Regardless of who we are, where we come from, or what we do, virtually all Americans celebrate this holiday in one way or another. Of course, this doesn't mean we all share the same view of how this meal should go or what it means. We may all be familiar with the classic Thanksgiving stereotype (the harmonious and homogeneous nuclear family gathered around the well-stocked dinner table), but this doesn't mean our own holiday experiences conform to this template. It is precisely this question of difference, in fact, that the portraits assembled here highlight. Representing Thanksgiving dinner from a range of vantage points, the following images underscore various ways Americans observe and think about this national holiday. In each case, we can pose two related sets of questions. First, what vision of the typical holiday meal does it present? What typical ways of eating? What typical American family? What typical American values? And second, how does this depiction serve either to challenge or reinforce those traditional ideals this meal is supposed to symbolize?

Painted at the height of World War II, Norman Rockwell's Freedom from Want *remains arguably the most well-known and influential depiction of Thanksgiving dinner ever created. For decades, its old-fashioned, homespun portrait has succeeded in setting the boundaries around how we are supposed to think about this particular holiday. Connecting this meal to one of the nation's core freedoms, it has encouraged countless Americans over the years to regard Thanksgiving as a celebration of the values (such as comfort, security, and abundance) universally available to all Americans. Given how this picture defines the typical American family and the typical American meal, however, do these values seem as universal as they are intended?*

© John Currin. Courtesy Gagosian Gallery and Sadie Coles HQ, London

▲▲ *Created over a half century later, John Currin's* Thanksgiving *rewrites Rockwell's portrait in dramatic ways. Replacing* Freedom's *vision of comfort and plenitude with a darker and more anxiety-ridden image of thwarted desire and unfulfilled appetite, Currin makes this holiday meal into an occasion for critiquing our long-standing emphasis on excessive consumption. As one reviewer puts it, "We've come a long way from Norman Rockwell."*

John Holyfield

For artists of color, the effort to revise the Rockwell Thanksgiving vision has frequently revolved around challenging its assumptions about who gets to count as a typical American — a definition that treats being white as an unexamined given. Seeking to enlarge the boundaries of this definition, John Holyfield's *Blessing II* does more than merely recapitulate the basic terms of the Thanksgiving myth; it also subtly alters them. What sorts of messages (about comfort and security, about family and tradition) would you say this image conveys? And to what extent do they either resemble or rework the messages discernible in the Rockwell portrait?

The stereotypical Thanksgiving scene is so familiar to most Americans that it has become shorthand for visual artists seeking to comment on current events. This cartoon by Pat Oliphant adopts the traditional Thanksgiving scene in order to make a satirical point about paranoia surrounding recent news reports about possible bird flu outbreaks in the United States.

ARMEND NIMANI/Getty Images

▲▲ *Not every modern portrayal of Thanksgiving, of course, adopts such an ironic, a skeptical, or a dismissive perspective. Take for example this image, which depicts U.S. soldiers stationed overseas sitting down to a Thanksgiving meal in 2015. Commemorations of this holiday have regularly included media stories about soldiers sharing turkey dinner in some distant country, a tradition that joins the observance of Thanksgiving to patriotic support for "our troops." How do you respond to such stories? Does this portrait depict what you would consider a typical Thanksgiving meal?*

Rick Friedman/Getty Images

◀◀ *Another long-standing Thanksgiving tradition involves serving meals to fellow Americans who have found themselves homeless. Politicians and celebrities of all stripes are regularly pictured celebrating this holiday meal with one or another group of "regular" Americans — a ritual designed to promote the same vision of America that we see in Norman Rockwell's painting. How well would you say the photo here, which depicts New England Patriots quarterback Tom Brady serving Thanksgiving dinner, accomplishes this goal? Does it offer a similarly convincing portrait of community?*

FOR A SECOND READING

1. Which of these portraits most closely resembles your typical Thanksgiving experience? Which least resembles your experience? Why?

2. What does each of these images define its portrait of Thanksgiving against? In your view, which of these visions (ideal or anti-ideal) strikes you as more legitimate? How so?

3. As these pictures make clear, our eating attitudes and habits can serve as revealing metaphors for the other kinds of things we think and care about. Based on the preceding portfolio, which cultural issues and debates would you say eating gets connected to most often in our culture?

PUTTING IT INTO WRITING

4. First, focus on how eating is being represented in one of the images you've just reviewed. What stands out? What seems most important or noteworthy? And what, by contrast, seems noticeably absent? Then, analyze the ways you think this image uses its dining portrait to define the typical or ideal American family. What behaviors and attitudes does it seem to present as normal? And what values, beliefs, or ideas does this portrait seem to endorse as right?

5. Taken together, the images assembled here make clear what boundaries exist around how we are and are not allowed to think about eating. On the basis of what this portfolio includes, where do these boundaries seem to get drawn? Write an essay in which you speculate about the kinds of activities, attitudes, assumptions, and values that this collection of images implies lie outside the norm. Make sure you argue either in favor of or against drawing the boundary in these particular ways, using details from these images and your own experience to reinforce your point of view.

COMPARING ARGUMENTS

6. Choose one of the preceding examples. How does its depiction of the typical meal compare to the eating practices described by Lily Wong (p. 216) or Brendan Buhler (p. 221)? In a page, evaluate how the norms promoted by this image compare to those profiled in one of these two essays. What are the similarities? The differences? To what extent do you think either Wong or Buhler would subscribe to or choose to emulate them? Why do you think this?

Acting Like a Citizen: **Consumer Profiling**

By surveying the ways our food culture's scripts can be questioned and reimagined, this chapter invites us to connect our role as eaters to our role as citizens. While this might not always seem like an obvious connection, the truth is that the choices we make around food can have a much wider (social, cultural, and political) impact than we think. The following exercises give you a chance to gauge this kind of impact. Showcasing some of the settings in which our food choices often get scripted, they provide an opportunity to evaluate and revise the effect these food scripts can have.

FOOD JOURNAL   For one week, keep a written account of all your meals, including what you eat, what time you eat, where you eat, how healthy you believe your meal is, and how much it costs. At the end of the week, write a brief essay in which you reflect on the reasons or motives behind *why* you made these particular choices. Identify and evaluate the different scripts, rules, and norms you think may have played a part in your eating habits. How many of your choices were simply prompted by cravings and how many by nutritional concerns? How much did your physical appearance influence your choices? How much was determined by non-food-related factors (such as your time constraints or budget)? Do any of your decisions line up with the topics discussed by the authors in this chapter? How?

LOCAL CONTEXTS, LOCAL TASTES   What and how we eat are greatly influenced by context. The cultural traditions in which we are raised, the neighborhood in which we live, and the social class to which we belong play significant roles in determining the particular eating practices we follow. Choose one of these factors (i.e., culture, geography, class) and research the ways it shapes the eating customs of a particular group. Within this group, what foods are most popular? How are they eaten? In what settings do meals take place? Then write a brief essay in which you discuss how the particular factor you chose influences these outcomes. Be sure to cite your research in your discussion.

WHOLESALE MESSAGES   For this exercise, find some examples of the ways that food and eating are advertised: how restaurants, food brands, or diet gurus try to sell you on their products and on the idea that consuming them will be a positive experience. What elements of these products seem to have the most weight in terms of marketing? Taste? Fitness? Fun? Family? Write an essay in which you discuss which key elements seem to occur most often. Why do you think that is? Do you feel like food and eating are sold as part of a larger package? That is, when you are being sold the idea of eating, what other norms are you also buying, according to these advertisers?

RJ Matson

By calling attention to the problem of student debt, this cartoon reminds us that there are always factors that can obstruct even our most cherished educational norms. Indeed, so widespread has the problem of student debt become, we might even wonder whether the financial barriers undermining the ideal of "education for all" have become cultural norms in their own right. With this in mind, take a closer look at this visual. Then, answer the following questions:

⊃ How significant a problem is student debt? To what extent is such debt a barrier to obtaining an education?

⊃ How does this cartoon depict the problem of student debt? What message does it convey about "debt," "student loans," and "education"?

⊃ What action does this cartoon invite viewers to take to address this problem?

⊃ What action do *you* think should be taken?

4 How We
LEARN
What Kinds of Knowledge Are Most Valuable? How Are We Supposed to Go About Acquiring Such Knowledge?

Introduction

SCHOOL RULES

If you were to create your own school, what would it look like? What kinds of courses would get taught? What type of work would get assigned, and how would it be evaluated? What sorts of activities and routines would organize daily classroom life? What roles would you script for teachers and students? As you consider all this, think too about what such a school would *not* look like: what sorts of lessons would never get taught, what rules would never get written, what kinds of teachers and students you would never see. Now ask yourself one final question: How much of your own experience at school has ever measured up to this ideal?

It is difficult to think of an environment in contemporary life more rule bound than school. From firsthand experience, we know that once we walk into the classroom, there are very few decisions we get to make entirely on our own. We face rules dictating the kinds of homework we have to complete and the kinds of tests we have to take; rules that decree which courses are mandatory and which ones are optional; rules that mandate the number of hours per week and the number of weeks per semester we need to spend at school; there are even, in some cases, rules that set standards for what we can wear or how we can talk. And as with every set of cultural rules, these classroom requirements are underwritten and justified by an equally clear set of norms: that the rigid organization of school life is indispensable and nonnegotiable; that it is an essential component of a quality education; that without things like homework and pop quizzes, standardized testing and attendance policies, graduation requirements and semester schedules, P.E. and recess, "real" learning simply wouldn't happen.

But what exactly is *real* learning? And who should be given the authority to decide this? Do all the rules we are called on to follow at school really turn us into better-educated people? While school is one of the few genuine touchstones in our lives — one of only a handful of institutions with which we all have had some degree of personal experience — it remains one of the most problematic as well. Because

What is normal?

Jim West/Alamy

Detroit, Michigan, rules posted on a classroom door at Guyton Elementary School, part of the Detroit public school system

What do these rules ask you to believe? What actions and attitudes do they ask you to accept as normal?

so many of the day-to-day decisions are taken out of our hands, it doesn't always feel as if the education we spend so many years pursuing actually belongs to us. We may wonder whether there is a logical connection between the tests we take and the grades we receive or between our personal opinions about a poem or short story and the views espoused by a professor in lecture, but given the way school is typically set up, there isn't a whole lot we can do about it. We may have our own ideas about what rules should govern our school experience, but we also know that subordinating these ideas to somebody else's is part of our job.

To illustrate, take the example of grading. Grades are absolutely essential, so goes the conventional thinking, because they alone offer educators a reliable and verifiable way of assessing students' work. Without grades, how would we ever know if students were measuring up? But notice the unspoken assumptions that lie beneath this anxious query, foremost among them the belief that grades are accurate barometers of student ability and achievement. To believe in the validity and necessity of grading, we also have to believe that the standards on which they rest — the standards that differentiate, say, A-grade work from C-grade work — are grounded in a fair and universally applicable understanding of what good work involves. If we wanted to question this assumption, we might consider the fact that — from classroom to classroom and teacher to teacher — the standards for how the grading system gets applied can vary widely. Indeed, we might push back against these grading norms even further by questioning the educational value of a system that so conspicuously emphasizes competition and rank. Does an arrangement that compels students to focus so much attention on the external markers of achievement really offer the best way to encourage meaningful learning? This type of questioning might, in turn, lead us next to rethink the kinds of authority that typically get vested in teachers. Should teachers enjoy such exclusive authority not only to grade student work, but also to evaluate, assess, and judge more generally? Such questions not only help us rewrite prevailing educational scripts, they initiate the even more fundamental process of *relearning* what a worthwhile education might actually include.

What is normal?

a. The Honor Code is an undertaking of the students, individually and collectively:

1. that they will not give or receive aid in examinations; that they will not give or receive unpermitted aid in class work, in the preparation of reports, or in any other work that is to be used by the instructor as the basis of grading;

2. that they will do their share and take an active part in seeing to it that others as well as themselves uphold the spirit and letter of the Honor Code.

From the Stanford University Honor Code

Do you share the attitudes and values scripted here? Should we automatically accept them as normal?

What is normal?

"Charter schools are another choice—a very valid choice. As we work to help provide parents with more educational choices, it is always with the assumption that charter schools are part of the equation. We think of the educational choice movement as involving many parts: vouchers and tax credits, certainly, but also virtual schools, magnet schools, homeschooling, and charter schools."

Secretary of Education Betsy DeVos in remarks delivered at a Philanthropy Roundtable

What kind of script do these remarks write? How do these scripts play a role in your own life?

In many ways, this relearning process is already taking place. Education is one of the most contentiously debated issues of our time. We argue over the merits of public versus private schooling, over the limits of free speech on campus, over the place of religious belief in the classroom, over how to best utilize the educational resources of the Internet. Educational issues anchor our debates about multiculturalism, about economic and social class, about free speech. Whether it involves a political debate over public funding for charter schools or a state initiative to require school uniforms, a dispute over online university accreditation or protests regarding a college's financial ties to companies that exploit their workers, school-related issues and controversies remain at the very center of our national life.

Taken together, the readings assembled in this chapter provide a sense of how richly diverse and broadly encompassing the issue of education is. The first two writers, Alfie Kohn and Kristina Rizga, explore how deeply held assumptions about school can cause us to fundamentally misunderstand how genuine learning actually happens. Kohn does this by calling into question the conventional wisdom regarding grades and grading, arguing that our reliance on this system does more damage than good. Rizga, meanwhile, talks back to the myths and stereotypes that teach us to overlook the real reasons why schools "fail."

The next pair of selections, by bell hooks and Jonathan Kozol, directs our attention to the ways educational scripts can create and reinforce social barriers, especially those around race and class. In a personal comment on the educational system, hooks recounts her experiences navigating the educational and social boundaries she encountered as a working-class student of color. Looking at the experiences of many students of color today, Kozol describes how a vocational logic and language is increasingly (and narrowly) defining their elementary school education as little more than job skills training.

Shifting our focus to college admissions, Frank Bruni and Ben Casselman offer pointed reassessments of the social scripts used to determine access to and eligibility for higher education. Bruni turns a skeptical eye toward the college ranking system, arguing that these widely touted "best of" lists are profoundly unreliable measures of educational value. In a similar vein, Casselman decries our cultural fixation on so-called elite schools, demonstrating how this narrow focus skews public understanding of and public policy toward colleges and universities.

The final two readings take up one of the most topical and controversial educational issues today: censorship and free speech on college campuses. Aaron Hanlon examines this issue within the context of current debates over "trigger warnings," detailing the ways such notifications can serve to promote rather than stifle student speech. Addressing this issue from a different vantage, Ferentz Lafargue contends that policies around "safe spaces" and "micro-aggressions" are useful tools in preparing students to confront prejudice and inequity in the wider world.

What is normal?

"America's kids deserve to learn about climate change as part of a 21st century science education."

Excerpt from the "Climate Science Students' Bill of Rights," issued by the National Center for Science Education, 2017

Can social scripts be rewritten?

ALFIE KOHN

From Degrading to De-Grading

Are grades really necessary? Do they truly offer us an accurate, meaningful measure of student ability or achievement? Couldn't we have a quality education without them? Answering this final question with an emphatic yes, Alfie Kohn makes the case that grades are not only irrelevant but actually antithetical to learning. Kohn has published fifteen books on education and parenting, including *No Contest: The Case against Competition* (1986), *Unconditional Parenting: Moving from Rewards and Punishments to Love and Reason* (2005), *The Homework Myth: Why Our Kids Get Too Much of a Bad Thing* (2006), *Feel-Bad Education* (2011), and most recently, *Schooling Beyond Measure* (2015). His articles have appeared in the *Boston Globe*, the *Journal of Education*, the *Nation*, and the *Harvard Business Review. Time* magazine has called him "perhaps the country's most outspoken critic of education's fixation on grades [and] test scores." He has also appeared on the *Today* show and the *Oprah Winfrey Show*. The essay that follows was originally published in *High School Magazine* in 1999.

Before You Read

What are your own personal experiences with grading? Can you think of a moment when a grade measured your academic work inaccurately?

YOU CAN TELL A LOT ABOUT A TEACHER'S VALUES AND PERSONALITY just by asking how he or she feels about giving grades. Some defend the practice, claiming that grades are necessary to "motivate" students. Many of these teachers actually seem to enjoy keeping intricate records of students' marks. Such teachers periodically warn students that they're "going to have to know this for the test" as a way of compelling them to pay attention or do the assigned readings—and they may even use surprise quizzes for that purpose, keeping their grade books at the ready.

Frankly, we ought to be worried for these teachers' students. In my experience, the most impressive teachers are those who despise the whole process of giving grades. Their aversion, as it turns out, is supported by solid evidence that raises questions about the very idea of traditional grading.

THREE MAIN EFFECTS OF GRADING

Researchers have found three consistent effects of using—and especially, emphasizing the importance of—letter or number grades:

1. Grades tend to reduce students' interest in the learning itself. One of the best-researched findings in the field of motivational psychology is that the more people are rewarded for doing something, the more they tend to lose interest in whatever they had to do to get the reward (Kohn 1993). Thus, it shouldn't be surprising that when students are told they'll need to know something for a test—or, more generally, that something they're about to do will count for a grade—they are likely to come to view that task (or book or idea) as a chore.

While it's not impossible for a student to be concerned about getting 5 high marks and also to like what he or she is doing, the practical reality is that these two ways of thinking generally pull in opposite directions. Some research has explicitly demonstrated that a "grade orientation" and a "learning orientation" are inversely related (Beck, Rorrer-Woody, and Pierce 1991; Milton, Pollio, and Eison 1986). More strikingly, study after study has found that students—from elementary school to graduate school, and across cultures—demonstrate less interest in learning as a result of being graded (Benware and Deci 1984; Butler 1987; Butler and Nisan 1986; Grolnick and Ryan 1987; Harter and Guzman 1986; Hughes, Sullivan, and Mosley 1985; Kage 1991; Salili et al. 1976). Thus, anyone who wants to see students get hooked on words and numbers and ideas already has reason to look for other ways of assessing and describing their achievement.

2. Grades tend to reduce students' preference for challenging tasks. Students of all ages who have been led to concentrate on getting a good grade are likely to pick the easiest possible assignment if given a choice (Harter 1978; Harter and Guzman 1986; Kage 1991; Milton, Pollio, and Eison 1986). The more pressure to get an A, the less inclination to truly challenge oneself. Thus, students who cut corners may not be lazy so much as rational; they are adapting to an environment where good grades, not intellectual exploration, are what count. They might well say to us, "Hey, you told me the point here is to bring up my GPA, to get on the honor roll. Well, I'm not stupid: The easier the assignment, the more likely that I can give you what you want. So don't blame me when I try to find the easiest thing to do and end up not learning anything."

3. Grades tend to reduce the quality of students' thinking. Given that students may lose interest in what they're learning as a result of grades, it makes sense that they're also apt to think less deeply. One series of studies, for example, found that students given numerical grades were significantly less creative than those who received qualitative feedback but no grades. The more the task required creative thinking, in fact, the worse the performance of students who knew they were going to be graded. Providing students with comments in addition to a grade didn't help: The highest achievement occurred only when comments were given *instead* of numerical scores (Butler 1987; Butler 1988; Butler and Nisan 1986).

In another experiment, students told they would be graded on how well they learned a social studies lesson had more trouble understanding the main point of the text than did students who were told that no grades would be involved. Even on a measure of rote recall, the graded group remembered fewer facts a week later (Grolnick and Ryan 1987). And students who tended to think about current events in terms of what they'd need to know for a grade were less knowledgeable than their peers, even after taking other variables into account (Anderman and Johnston 1998).

MORE REASONS TO JUST SAY NO TO GRADES

The preceding three results should be enough to cause any conscientious educator to rethink the practice of giving students grades. But there's more.

10 **4. Grades aren't valid, reliable, or objective.** A B in English says nothing about what a student can do, what she understands, where she needs help. Moreover, the basis for that grade is as subjective as the result is uninformative. A teacher can meticulously record scores for one test or assignment after another, eventually calculating averages down to a hundredth of a percentage point, but that doesn't change the arbitrariness of each of these individual marks. Even the score on a math test is largely a reflection of how the test was written: what skills the teacher decided to assess, what kinds of questions happened to be left out, and how many points each section was "worth."

Moreover, research has long been available to confirm what all of us know: Any given assignment may well be given two different grades by two equally qualified teachers. It may even be given two different grades by a single teacher who reads it at two different times (for example, see some of the early research reviewed in Kirschenbaum, Simon, and Napier 1971). In short, what grades offer is spurious precision—a subjective rating masquerading as an objective evaluation.

5. Grades distort the curriculum. A school's use of letter or number grades may encourage a fact- and skill-based approach to instruction because that sort of learning is easier to score. The tail of assessment thus comes to wag the educational dog.

A B in English says nothing about what a student can do, what she understands, where she needs help.

6. Grades waste a lot of time that could be spent on learning. Add up all the hours that teachers spend fussing with their grade books. Then factor in the (mostly unpleasant) conversations they have with students and their parents about grades. It's tempting to just roll our eyes when confronted with whining or wheedling, but the real problem rests with the practice of grading itself.

7. Grades encourage cheating. Again, we can either continue to blame and punish all the students who cheat—or we can look for the structural reasons this keeps happening. Researchers have found that the more students are led to focus on getting good grades, the more likely they are to cheat, even if they themselves regard cheating as wrong (Anderman, Griesinger, and Westerfield 1998; Milton, Pollio, and Eison 1986).

8. Grades spoil teachers' relationships with students. Consider this 15 lament, which could have been offered by a teacher in your district:

> I'm getting tired of running a classroom in which everything we do revolves around grades. I'm tired of being suspicious when students give me compliments, wondering whether or not they are just trying to raise their grade. I'm tired of spending so much time and energy grading your papers, when there are probably a dozen more productive and enjoyable ways for all of us to handle the evaluation of papers. I'm tired of hearing you ask me, 'Does this count?' And, heaven knows, I'm certainly tired of all those little arguments and disagreements we get into concerning marks which take so much fun out of the teaching and the learning.... (Kirschenbaum, Simon, and Napier 1971, p. 115)

9. Grades spoil students' relationships with one another. The quality of students' thinking has been shown to depend partly on the extent to which they are permitted to learn cooperatively (Johnson and Johnson 1989; Kohn 1992). Thus, the ill feelings, suspicion, and resentment generated by grades aren't just disagreeable in their own right; they interfere with learning.

The most destructive form of grading by far is that which is done "on a curve," such that the number of top grades is artificially limited: No matter how well all the students do, not all of them can get an A. Apart from the intrinsic unfairness of this arrangement, its practical effect is to teach students that others are potential obstacles to their own success. The kind of collaboration that can help all students to learn more effectively doesn't stand a chance in such an environment. Sadly, even teachers who don't explicitly grade on a curve may assume, perhaps unconsciously, that the final grades "ought to" come out looking more or less this way: a few very good grades, a few very bad grades, and the majority somewhere in the middle.

The competition that turns schooling into a quest for triumph and ruptures relationships among students doesn't only happen within classrooms, of course. The same effect is witnessed schoolwide when kids are not just rated but ranked, sending the message that the point isn't to learn, or even to perform well, but to defeat others. Some students might be motivated to improve their class rank, but that is completely different from being motivated to understand ideas. (Wise educators realize that it doesn't matter how motivated students are; what matters is *how* students are motivated. It is the type of motivation that counts, not the amount.)

EXCUSES AND DISTRACTIONS

20   Most of us are directly acquainted with at least some of these disturbing consequences of grades, yet we continue to reduce students to letters or numbers on a regular basis. Perhaps we've become inured to these effects and take them for granted. This is the way it's always been, we assume, and the way it has to be. It's rather like people who have spent all their lives in a terribly polluted city and have come to assume that this is just the way air looks—and that it's natural to be coughing all the time.

Oddly, when educators are shown that it doesn't have to be this way, some react with suspicion instead of relief. They want to know why you're making trouble, or they assert that you're exaggerating the negative effects of grades (it's really not so bad—cough, cough), or they dismiss proven alternatives to grading on the grounds that our school could never do what other schools have done.

> *It's rather like people who have spent all their lives in a terribly polluted city and have come to assume that this is just the way air looks.*

The practical difficulties of abolishing letter grades are real. But the key question is whether those difficulties are seen as problems to be solved or as excuses for perpetuating the status quo. The logical response to the arguments and data summarized here is to say: "Good heavens! If even half of this is true, then it's imperative we do whatever we can, as soon as we can, to phase out traditional grading." Yet, many people begin and end with the problems of implementation, responding to all this evidence by saying, in effect, "Yeah, yeah, yeah, but we'll never get rid of grades because . . ."

It is also striking how many educators never get beyond relatively insignificant questions, such as how many tests to give, or how often to send home grade reports, or what number corresponds to what letter. Some even reserve their outrage for the possibility that too many students are ending up with good grades, a reaction that suggests stinginess with A's is being confused with intellectual rigor.

COMMON OBJECTIONS

Let's consider the most frequently heard responses to the above arguments—which is to say, the most common objections to getting rid of grades.

First, it is said that students expect to receive grades and even seem   25
addicted to them. This is often true; I've taught high school students who
reacted to the absence of grades with what I can only describe as existential vertigo. (*Who am I if not a B+?*) But as more elementary and even
some middle schools move to replace grades with more informative (and
less destructive) systems of assessment, the damage doesn't begin until
students get to high school. Moreover, elementary and middle schools
that *haven't* changed their practices often cite the local high school as the
reason they must get students used to getting grades regardless of their
damaging effects—just as high schools point the finger at colleges.

Even when students arrive in high school already accustomed to
grades, already primed to ask teachers, "Do we have to know this?" or
"What do I have to do to get an A?," this is a sign that something is very
wrong. It's more an indictment of what has happened to them in the past
than an argument to keep doing it in the future.

Perhaps because of this training, grades can succeed in getting students to show up on time, hand in their work, and otherwise do what
they're told. Many teachers are loath to give up what is essentially an
instrument of control. But even to the extent this instrument works
(which is not always), we are obliged to reflect on whether mindless compliance is really our goal. The teacher who exclaims, "These kids would
blow off my course in a minute if they weren't getting a grade for it!" may
be issuing a powerful indictment of his or her course. Who would be more
reluctant to give up grades than a teacher who spends the period slapping transparencies on the overhead projector and lecturing endlessly at
students about Romantic poets or genetic codes? Without bribes (A's) and
threats (F's), students would have no reason to do such assignments. To
maintain that this proves something is wrong with the kids—or that
grades are simply "necessary"—suggests a willful refusal to examine
one's classroom practices and assumptions about teaching and learning.

"If I can't give a child a better reason for studying than a grade on a
report card, I ought to lock my desk and go home and stay there." So
wrote Dorothy De Zouche, a Missouri teacher, in an article published in
February . . . of 1945. But teachers who *can* give a child a better reason for
studying don't need grades. Research substantiates this: When the curriculum is engaging—for example, when it involves hands-on, interactive learning activities—students who aren't graded at all perform just as
well as those who are graded (Moeller and Reschke 1993).

Another objection: It is sometimes argued that students must be
given grades because colleges demand them. One might reply that "high
schools have no responsibility to serve colleges by performing the sorting
function for them"—particularly if that process undermines learning
(Krumboltz and Yeh 1996, p. 325). But in any case the premise of this
argument is erroneous: Traditional grades are not mandatory for admission to colleges and universities.

MAKING CHANGE

30 A friend of mine likes to say that people don't resist change—they resist being changed. Even terrific ideas (like moving a school from a grade orientation to a learning orientation) are guaranteed to self-destruct if they are simply forced down people's throats. The first step for an administrator, therefore, is to open up a conversation—to spend perhaps a full year just encouraging people to think and talk about the effects of (and alternatives to) traditional grades. This can happen in individual classes, as teachers facilitate discussions about how students regard grades, as well as in evening meetings with parents, or on a website—all with the help of relevant books, articles, speakers, videos, and visits to neighboring schools that are further along in this journey.

The actual process of "de-grading" can be done in stages. For example, a high school might start by freeing ninth-grade classes from grades before doing the same for upperclassmen. (Even a school that never gets beyond the first stage will have done a considerable service, giving students one full year when they can think about what they're learning instead of their GPAs.)

Another route to gradual change is to begin by eliminating only the most pernicious practices, such as grading on a curve or ranking students. Although grades, per se, may continue for a while, at least the message will be sent from the beginning that all students can do well, and that the point is to succeed rather than to beat others.

Anyone who has heard the term *authentic assessment* knows that abolishing grades doesn't mean eliminating the process of gathering information about student performance—and communicating that information to students and parents. Rather, abolishing grades opens up possibilities that are far more meaningful and constructive. These include narratives (written comments), portfolios (carefully chosen collections of students' writings and projects that demonstrate their interests, achievements, and improvement over time), student-led parent-teacher conferences, exhibitions, and other opportunities for students to show what they can do.

Of course, it's harder for a teacher to do these kinds of assessments if he or she has 150 or more students and sees each of them for forty-five to fifty-five minutes a day. But that's not an argument for continuing to use traditional grades; it's an argument for challenging these archaic remnants of a factory-oriented approach to instruction, structural aspects of high schools that are bad news for reasons that go well beyond the issue of assessment. It's an argument for looking into block scheduling, team teaching, interdisciplinary courses—and learning more about schools that have arranged things so each teacher can spend more time with fewer students (e.g., Meier 1995).

Administrators should be prepared to respond to parental concerns, 35 some of them completely reasonable, about the prospect of edging away from grades. "Don't you value excellence?" You bet—and here's the evidence that traditional grading *undermines* excellence. "Are you just trying to spare the self-esteem of students who do poorly?" We are concerned that grades may be making things worse for such students, yes, but the problem isn't just that some kids won't get A's and will have their feelings hurt. The real problem is that almost all kids (including yours) will come to focus on grades and, as a result, their learning will be hurt.

If parents worry that grades are the only window they have into the school, we need to assure them that alternative assessments provide a far better view. But if parents don't seem to care about getting the most useful information or helping their children become more excited learners—if they demand grades for the purpose of documenting how much better their kids are than everyone else's—then we need to engage them in a discussion about whether this is a legitimate goal, and whether schools exist for the purpose of competitive credentialing or for the purpose of helping everyone to learn (Kohn 1998; Labaree 1997). Above all, we need to make sure that objections and concerns about the details don't obscure the main message, which is the demonstrated harm of traditional grading on the quality of students' learning and their interest in exploring ideas.

> **The real problem is that almost all kids . . . will come to focus on grades and, as a result, their learning will be hurt.**

High school administrators can do a world of good in their districts by actively supporting efforts to eliminate conventional grading in elementary and middle schools. Working with their colleagues in these schools can help pave the way for making such changes at the secondary school level.

IN THE MEANTIME

Finally, there is the question of what classroom teachers can do while grades continue to be required. The short answer is that they should do everything within their power to make grades as invisible as possible for as long as possible. Helping students forget about grades is the single best piece of advice for those who want to create a learning-oriented classroom.

When I was teaching high school, I did a lot of things I now regret. But one policy that still seems sensible to me was saying to students on the first day of class that, while I was compelled to give them a grade at the end of the term, I could not in good conscience ever put a letter or number on anything they did during the term—and I would not do so.

I would, however, write a comment—or, better, sit down and talk with them—as often as possible to give them feedback.

40   At this particular school I frequently faced students who had been prepared for admission to Harvard since their early childhood—a process I have come to call "Preparation H." I knew that my refusal to rate their learning might cause some students to worry about their marks all the more, or to create suspense about what would appear on their final grade reports, which of course would defeat the whole purpose. So I said that anyone who absolutely had to know what grade a given paper would get could come see me and we would figure it out together. An amazing thing happened: As the days went by, fewer and fewer students felt the need to ask me about grades. They began to be more involved with what we were learning, because I had taken responsibility as a teacher to stop pushing grades into their faces, so to speak, whenever they completed an assignment.

What I didn't do very well, however, was to get students involved in devising the criteria for excellence (what makes a math solution elegant, an experiment well designed, an essay persuasive, a story compelling) or in deciding how well their projects met those criteria. I'm afraid I unilaterally set the criteria and evaluated the students' efforts. But I have seen teachers who were more willing to give up control, more committed to helping students participate in assessment and turn that into part of the learning. Teachers who work with their students to design powerful alternatives to letter grades have a replacement ready to go when the school finally abandons traditional grading—and are able to minimize the harm of such grading in the meantime.

ADDENDUM: MUST CONCERNS ABOUT COLLEGE DERAIL HIGH SCHOOL LEARNING?

Here is the good news: College admissions practices are not as rigid and reactionary as many people think. Here is the better news: Even when that process doesn't seem to have its priorities straight, high schools don't have to be dragged down to that level.

Sometimes it is assumed that admissions officers at the best universities are eighty-year-old fuddy-duddies peering over their spectacles and muttering about "highly irregular" applications. In truth, the people charged with making these decisions are often just a few years out of college themselves, and after making their way through a pile of interchangeable applications from 3.8-GPA, student-council-vice-president, musically accomplished hopefuls from high-powered traditional suburban high schools, they are desperate for something unconventional. Given that the most selective colleges have been known to accept homeschooled children who have never set foot in a classroom, secondary schools have more latitude than they sometimes assume. It is not widely known, for example, that hundreds of colleges and universities don't require applicants to take either the SAT or the ACT.

Admittedly, large state universities are more resistant to unconventional applications than are small private colleges simply because of economics: It takes more time, and therefore more money, for admissions officers to read meaningful application materials than it does for them to glance at a GPA or an SAT score and plug it into a formula. But I have heard of high schools approaching the admissions directors of nearby universities and saying, in effect, "We'd like to improve our school by getting rid of grades. Here's why. Will you work with us to make sure our seniors aren't penalized?" This strategy may well be successful for the simple reason that not many high schools are requesting this at present and the added inconvenience for admissions offices is likely to be negligible. Of course, if more and more high schools abandon traditional grades, then the universities will have no choice but to adapt. This is a change that high schools will have to initiate rather than waiting for colleges to signal their readiness.

At the moment, plenty of admissions officers enjoy the convenience 45
of class ranking, apparently because they have confused being better than one's peers with being good at something; they're looking for winners rather than learners. But relatively few colleges actually insist on this practice. When a 1993 survey by the National Association of Secondary School Principals asked eleven hundred admissions officers what would happen if a high school stopped computing class rank, only 0.5 percent said the school's applicants would not be considered for admission, 4.5 percent said it would be a "great handicap," and 14.4 percent said it would be a "handicap" (Levy and Riordan 1994). In other words, it appears that the absence of class ranks would not interfere at all with students' prospects for admission to four out of five colleges.

> *It takes more time . . . for admissions officers to read meaningful application materials than it does for them to glance at a GPA or an SAT score. . . .*

Even more impressive, some high schools not only refuse to rank their students but refuse to give any sort of letter or number grades. Courses are all taken pass/fail, sometimes with narrative assessments of the students' performance that become part of a college application. I have spoken to representatives and all assure me that, year after year, their graduates are accepted into large state universities and small, highly selective colleges. *Even the complete absence of high school grades is not a barrier to college admission*, so we don't have that excuse for continuing to subject students to the harm done by traditional grading.

REFERENCES

Anderman, E. M., T. Griesinger, and G. Westerfield. 1998. "Motivation and Cheating During Early Adolescence." *Journal of Educational Psychology* 90: 84–93.

Anderman, E. M., and J. Johnston. 1998. "Television News in the Classroom: What Are Adolescents Learning?" *Journal of Adolescent Research* 13: 73–100.

Beck, H. P., S. Rorrer-Woody, and L. G. Pierce. 1991. "The Relations of Learning and Grade Orientations to Academic Performance." *Teaching of Psychology* 18: 35–37.

Benware, C. A., and E. L. Deci. 1984. "Quality of Learning with an Active Versus Passive Motivational Set." *American Educational Research Journal* 21: 755–65.

Butler, R. 1987. "Task-Involving and Ego-Involving Properties of Evaluation: Effects of Different Feedback Conditions on Motivational Perceptions, Interest, and Performance." *Journal of Educational Psychology* 79: 474–82.

Butler, R. 1988. "Enhancing and Undermining Intrinsic Motivation: The Effects of Task-Involving and Ego-Involving Evaluation on Interest and Performance." *British Journal of Educational Psychology* 58: 1–14.

Butler, R., and M. Nisan. 1986. "Effects of No Feedback, Task-Related Comments, and Grades on Intrinsic Motivation and Performance." *Journal of Educational Psychology* 78: 210–16.

De Zouche, D. 1945. "'The Wound Is Mortal': Marks, Honors, Unsound Activities." *The Clearing House* 19: 339–44.

Grolnick, W. S., and R. M. Ryan. 1987. "Autonomy in Children's Learning: An Experimental and Individual Difference Investigation." *Journal of Personality and Social Psychology* 52: 890–98.

Harter, S. 1978. "Pleasure Derived from Challenge and the Effects of Receiving Grades on Children's Difficulty Level Choices." *Child Development* 49: 788–99.

Harter, S., and M. E. Guzman. 1986. "The Effect of Perceived Cognitive Competence and Anxiety on Children's Problem-Solving Performance, Difficulty Level Choices, and Preference for Challenge." Unpublished manuscript, University of Denver.

Hughes, B., H. J. Sullivan, and M. L. Mosley. 1985. "External Evaluation, Task Difficulty, and Continuing Motivation." *Journal of Educational Research* 78: 210–15.

Johnson, D. W., and R. T. Johnson. 1989. *Cooperation and Competition: Theory and Research.* Edina, Minn.: Interaction Book Co.

Kage, M. 1991. "The Effects of Evaluation on Intrinsic Motivation." Paper presented at the meeting of the Japan Association of Educational Psychology, Joetsu, Japan.

Kirschenbaum, H., S. B. Simon, and R. W. Napier. 1971. *Wad-Ja-Get?: The Grading Game in American Education.* New York: Hart.

Kohn, A. 1992. *No Contest: The Case Against Competition.* Rev. ed. Boston: Houghton Mifflin.

Kohn, A. 1993. *Punished by Rewards: The Trouble with Gold Stars, Incentive Plans, A's, Praise, and Other Bribes.* Boston: Houghton Mifflin.

Kohn, A. 1998. "Only for My Kid: How Privileged Parents Undermine School Reform." *Phi Delta Kappan,* April: 569–77.

Krumboltz, J. D., and C. J. Yeh. 1996. "Competitive Grading Sabotages Good Teaching." *Phi Delta Kappan*, December: 324–26.

Labaree, D. F. 1997. *How to Succeed in School Without Really Learning: The Credentials Race in American Education*. New Haven, Conn.: Yale University Press.

Levy, J., and P. Riordan. 1994. *Rank-in-Class, Grade Point Average, and College Admission*. Reston, Va.: NASSP. (Available as ERIC Document 370988.)

Meier, D. 1995. *The Power of Their Ideas: Lessons for America from a Small School in Harlem*. Boston: Beacon.

Milton, O., H. R. Pollio, and J. A. Eison. 1986. *Making Sense of College Grades*. San Francisco: Jossey-Bass.

Moeller, A. J., and C. Reschke. 1993. "A Second Look at Grading and Classroom Performance: Report of a Research Study." *Modern Language Journal* 77: 163–69.

Salili, F., M. L. Maehr, R. L. Sorensen, and L. J. Fyans Jr. 1976. "A Further Consideration of the Effects of Evaluation on Motivation." *American Educational Research Journal* 13: 85–102.

FOR A SECOND READING

1. Kohn has some pointed things to say about the connection often presumed to exist between traditional grading and student motivation. More specifically, he questions the long-standing educational norm that says students who do not receive grades have no incentive to work. What do you think of this claim? Is it valid? How does your own view compare to Kohn's?

2. Kohn's critique of conventional grading practices rests in part on his assertion that, no matter how minutely calculated, every letter or number grade is a subjective and arbitrary assessment. Do you agree? Can you think of an example from your own school experiences that either confirms or confounds this argument?

3. "Perhaps," Kohn speculates, "we've become inured to [the] effects [of grades] and take them for granted. This is the way it's always been, we assume, and the way it has to be. It's rather like people who have spent all their lives in a terribly polluted city and have come to assume that this is just the way air looks—and that it's natural to be coughing all the time" (p. 244). What do you make of this analogy? To what extent does it seem valid to think of our contemporary approach to grading as a kind of pollution? Does this analogy capture any aspect of your own educational experiences?

PUTTING IT INTO WRITING

4. Write a personal essay in which you either support or refute Kohn's argument about grading, using anecdotes from your own experience as a student. Do you view grading in a negative or positive light? Why or why not? Make sure to structure your argument by addressing Kohn's multiple points directly.

5. Kohn writes about the need to move a school "from a grade orientation to a learning orientation" (p. 246). What do you think he means? How, according to Kohn, does grading make it harder to focus on learning? Write an essay in which you discuss the characteristics of these two orientations. Do you think it's possible to have an educational system that emphasizes both?

COMPARING ARGUMENTS

6. Write an essay in which you discuss how Kohn might use Kristina Rizga's observations about "failing schools" (p. 253) to support his argument against grading. Do you think Kohn would find Rizga's descriptions of the "secret successes" in school to be compatible with his own vision of a grade-free classroom?

KRISTINA RIZGA
Everything You've Heard About Failing Schools Is Wrong

We hear a lot these days about the crisis in public education. But how many discussions of this crisis are grounded in firsthand knowledge of what actually goes on in school? Seeking to provide just such a perspective, journalist Kristina Rizga takes a closer look at life in one school officially deemed to be "failing." What results is a surprising, enlightening, and complex portrait — one that challenges our received ideas about what is and isn't working in contemporary education. Kristina Rizga covers education for *Mother Jones* magazine. Her writing has appeared in the *Nation*, *Global Post*, Grist.com, and the *Bay Citizen*. This piece was published by *Mother Jones* in 2012.

Before You Read

In your view, what does a "successful" school look like? To what degree does your own school live up to this ideal?

"SPEEK EENGLISH, TACO," THE GIRL WITH THE GIANT BACKPACK yelled when Maria asked where to find a bathroom. The backpack giggled as it bounced down the hall. It had been hours since Maria began looking for a bathroom. Anger boiled inside her, but she didn't know any English words to yell back. That was the hardest part. Back in El Salvador she'd always had something to say.

The bell rang. A flood of shoulders and sneakers swirled around Maria, and she couldn't see much until the sea of strangers streamed back into classrooms. Then she stood alone in the hallway.

It was Maria's first day at school, her first week in the United States. Her middle school in San Francisco was the biggest building she'd ever seen. It was bigger than the entire Best Buy store she'd walked through in awe on her first day in the city.

Eventually, Maria found her way to class, a special setting for Spanish-speaking newcomers. There she would practice English words for colors and numbers, learn how to introduce herself and how to say thank you. By eighth grade she was moved into mainstream classes, where she struggled. It didn't help that her math teacher started each class by saying, "Okay, my little dummies." He spoke really fast. Maria never raised her hand in his class.

One day Maria stopped by the administrative office, looking for 5 someone to help her with multiplication. She took her spot in line behind a middle-aged woman who chatted with her in Spanish as they waited.

Maria said school was really hard for her. The woman told her not to worry. "Latinas usually don't finish high school," she said. "They go to work or raise kids."

The woman was right, statistically speaking, and Maria's middle-school experience all but ensured she'd join the 52 percent[1] of foreign-born Latinos who drop out of high school. She graduated from eighth grade without learning to speak English. She had a hard time writing in Spanish and didn't know how to multiply.

And then everything changed. At Mission High, the struggling school she'd chosen against the advice of her friends and relatives, Maria earned high grades in math and some days caught herself speaking English even with her Spanish-speaking teachers. By 11th grade, she wrote long papers on complex topics like desegregation and the war in Iraq. She became addicted to winning debates in class, despite her shyness and heavy accent. In her junior year, she became the go-to translator and advocate for her mother, her aunts, and for other Latino kids at school. In March, Maria and her teachers were celebrating acceptance letters to five colleges and two prestigious scholarships, including one from Dave Eggers' writing center, 826 Valencia.[2]

But on the big state tests—the days-long multiple-choice exams that students in California take once a year—Maria scored poorly. And these standardized tests, she understood, were how her school was graded. According to the scores, Mission High is among the lowest-performing 5 percent[3] of schools in the country, and it has consistently failed to meet the ever-rising benchmarks set by the federal No Child Left Behind Act.[4] The law mandates universal "proficiency" in math and reading by 2014—a deadline that weighs heavily on educators around the nation, since schools that don't meet it face stiff penalties.

It was with these penalties on his mind that Mission High principal Eric Guthertz got ready for work one morning in 2010. It was his wife's birthday, and also the day California was supposed to release its list of "persistently low-performing" schools—schools that the state deemed as urgently in need of improvement. As he put on his tie, he recalls, "I told my wife, 'I hope we dodged that bullet!' But I was kidding, because I was convinced we wouldn't be on that list. And on my ride to school, I was feeling bad for the principals who would."

10   It wasn't long after he got to the office that the phone rang. It was the district. Mission was on the list.

Guthertz was in shock. His teachers had been working so hard, he thought. What would they say? How about the parents, the students? Where would he get extra resources to bring up the numbers? Mission's test scores and college acceptance rates had been going up. But for purposes of the list, that didn't matter.

A few months later, Guthertz got another call from the district. This one was of the good news/bad news variety: As a low-performing school, Mission qualified for additional funding—but only if it agreed to undergo a major restructuring.[5] Options included replacing the principal and either revamping the curriculum or replacing half the staff; closing the school; or turning it into a charter. Guthertz had been promoted to his job less than two years earlier, and the district was allowed to report this change to the federal government—a loophole that bought Mission some time. But San Francisco's oldest comprehensive public high school,[6] founded in 1890, would still have to show dramatic growth in scores by 2014 or face more interventions, including possible closure.

Judging from what I'd read about "troubled" schools, I'd expected noisy classrooms, hallway fights, and disgruntled staff. Instead I found a welcoming place that many students and staff called "family."

Around the same time that Guthertz was digesting this news, I was calling education officials in search of a school that would let me spend time inside its classrooms. I was looking for a grassroots view of America's latest run at school reform: How do we know when schools are failing, and why is it so hard to turn them around? Is the close to $4.4 billion spent on testing since 2002—with scores now used for everything from deciding teacher pay to allocating education budgets—getting results? Is all that data helping us figure out what really works, or seducing us into focusing only on what the tests can measure?

If you wonder why you haven't read many accounts of how these questions are playing out in real life, there's a reason: It's easier for a journalist to embed with the Army or the Marines than to go behind the scenes at a public school. It took months to find one that would let me play fly on the wall. Once Guthertz opened the door at Mission, it took months more for some teachers, wary of distortion and stereotyping, to warm to me. In the end, I'd spend more than 18 months in Mission's classrooms, cafeterias, and administrative offices, finally watching the Class of 2012—including a beaming Maria—show off their diplomas.

The surprises began almost right away. Judging from what I'd read about "troubled" schools, I'd expected noisy classrooms, hallway fights, and disgruntled staff. Instead I found a welcoming place that many students and staff called "family." After a few weeks of talking to students, I failed to find a single one who didn't like the school, and most of the parents I met were happy too. Mission's student and parent satisfaction surveys rank among the highest in San Francisco.

One of the most diverse high schools in the country, Mission has 925 students holding 47 different passports. The majority are Latino, African American, and Asian American, and 72 percent are poor. Yet even as the school was being placed on the list of lowest-performing schools, 84 percent of the graduating class went on to college, higher than the district average; this year, 88 percent were accepted. (Nationally, 32 percent of Latino and 38 percent of African American students[7] go to college.) That same year, Mission improved Latinos' test scores more than any other school in the district. And while suspensions are skyrocketing across the nation, they had gone down by 42 percent at Mission. Guthertz had seen dropout rates fall from 32 percent to 8 percent. Was this what a failing school looked like?

When Maria turned three, she stopped hearing the voice of her mother in the mornings. No one explained where she'd gone, but when Maria was seven, her grandmother explained that her mom had crossed three borders to find work in California. Maria and her older brother were raised by her grandparents in the village of San Juan Las Minas in El Salvador. Their aunt Angelica came to visit when she could.

Maria doesn't remember much from those days except for her auntie's soft, soothing voice. Angelica had two children of her own, but she didn't mind when Maria started calling her "mom." When Angelica left, Maria kept to herself. Her grandparents were busy growing vegetables, raising cows and chickens, and looking after Maria, her brother, and four cousins.

Angelica ran a corner liquor store in San Salvador, two hours away. To stay in business, she had to pay off the MS-13 gang each month. They left her alone most of the time, except the day they shot one of her customers in the store. Maria was there. A piece of the man's head dropped on her foot.

20 Angelica loved escaping the city for Las Minas. "I'm like you, Maria. Like a little girl," she used to say when they played soccer together or climbed the mango trees.

Maria remembers everything about the day of her auntie's funeral. Angelica's tall body in a light wooden coffin beside the kitchen table, surrounded by candles. The scent of wax giving way to the smell of beer and sticky sweat as the day wore on. The 20 strangers in the house, their shiny, shirtless bodies covered in tattoos of letters, numbers, and devil's horns: symbols for MS-13. As the house got hotter, the men's voices grew louder. They started playing poker, roaring at their own jokes.

Maria, now 12, was praying near the coffin. She could see her auntie's dark hair through the white lace covering her face. It had been a week since she'd last heard from her. "Don't worry," Angelica had said. "I'll take care of everything. I'll pay off MS-13."

But she couldn't. She didn't have enough money. Three days after that call, she was found at the entrance of a San Salvador hospital, naked and barely alive. The doctors said she'd been raped and tortured for days. There was nothing they could do to save her.

Maria tried to focus on praying, but the men who'd invaded her grandparents' house got louder, throwing cards across the table and spitting on the floors. Maria gathered her courage and walked toward them. "Be respectful or get out of my house!" she shouted. The men's heads turned. For a few moments, the house was quiet. Then the men started laughing.

They left only after Angelica was buried, and they'd taken all of   25
Maria's grandparents' money.

"Why don't you come to America?" Maria's mother asked her on the phone a week after the funeral. She had been talking to her about coming to the States since she was seven. "I'd always say no," Maria recalls. "I loved my auntie more than anything. I didn't want to be in any other country but mine. But when my auntie died, I had no one close left."

Maria was the youngest passenger on the bus crossing El Salvador, Guatemala, and Mexico toward California. Her mom had paid the coyote $3,000, and Maria's ride was easy. No wandering through the desert. The coyote bought them chicken for dinner every night. At home, her grandparents cooked chicken only when relatives came over on Sunday.

The first time Maria set foot in Mission High, she thought it looked like a church. The facade and doorway were decorated with intricate Spanish Baroque moldings. Heavy iron chandeliers adorned the ornate ceiling above the entrance hall. The light glittered on spotless yellow linoleum. As Maria and her middle-school classmates toured the library, courtyards, and cafeteria, she noticed that people seemed friendly. Even the security guards were cracking jokes. Principal Guthertz regaled students with the school's history and famous alumni: Carlos Santana, Maya Angelou. There were after-school programs—the Latino student club, soccer, creative writing. Maria asked a few students if they liked Mission. To her surprise, all of them did.

Everyone Maria knew outside of Mission told her not to go there. Her mother's friends said she should pick a better school. Maria's friends said Mission had gangs.

Guthertz introduced Maria to Amadis Velez, who spoke to her in   30
Spanish. He told her that he'd be her English teacher. On the wall, Maria noticed Velez's diploma from the University of California-Berkeley, surrounded by photos of Frida Kahlo, César Chávez, and Salvador Dalí. "He was so welcoming," Maria remembers. "He kept making jokes about our English, making us laugh. After I met Mr. Velez, I knew I'll be going to Mission."

257

"She didn't speak a lick of English when she started in my ninth-grade English class," Velez recalls. "That year, there were only two students whose English was worse than Maria's." Velez also noticed that Maria's Spanish grammar was about two years behind her Latino classmates'. Maria was 5 feet tall and weighed about 80 pounds. "She was tiny," Velez remembers, "but very spunky, and her leadership and popularity among students stood out to me right away."

Maria loved that she had a class with Velez every day. He taught her English and geography in the 9th grade, and history in the 10th. He often checked in with her in the afternoon. All kinds of worries kept pouring out in their conversations. Could Velez explain the word *tariffs*? What's this thing, *analysis*? Who could teach Maria how to multiply?

"I thought of myself as a really bad student back then," she recalls. "I didn't believe in myself. But Mr. Velez always told me not to give up, to keep going, keep pushing."

One day, Velez sat her down, took out a piece of paper, and started charting her path to college. He said that she needed to transfer into regular English classes as soon as possible to prepare for college. He also explained that California was one of 12 states[8] that allow undocumented students like her to pay resident tuition rather than out-of-state rates, which can be twice as much. Velez said that Maria was not eligible for any government grants or student loans, but there were private scholarships, and he'd help her get them. All of this was possible, he said, if Maria kept her grades up, did all of her homework, and worked twice as hard as her classmates who already knew English. He said he'd be there for her no matter what. He told her to have fun and to laugh a lot.

> *Overall, the last 10 years have revealed that while Big Data can make our questions more sophisticated, it doesn't necessarily lead to Big Answers.*

35 Most days Maria did well and felt good about her progress. She met with Velez after class to review her grammar and plan for college. He urged her to write more complex sentences. By the end of 10th grade, she was writing essays that didn't fit on one page. She earned an A in Mr. Velez's modern world history class.

Then one morning, over breakfast, she found an envelope on her mother's kitchen table. Inside were the results of the standardized tests she'd taken a few months before. Her stomach tilted. She'd done much worse than she'd anticipated. In history her score was "far below basic," the lowest ranking.

What Maria didn't know was that only 19 percent[9] of Mission High's Latino students scored "proficient or above" in history. The vast majority of Latinos, at Mission High and statewide,[10] scored similar to Maria.

She knew that Velez thought she was smart. But this was the first grade she'd gotten from people outside of Mission, and it made her wonder. Was Mr. Velez wrong?

Every spring across the nation, students in 3rd to 11th grade sit down to take standardized tests required by the federal No Child Left Behind Act (NCLB). Each state comes up with its own tests, based on its own list of curriculum standards students have to master in each grade. In most states, standardized tests consist primarily[11] of multiple-choice questions.

People who fought for these tests wanted to raise expectations for all 40 students. They knew that for decades students of color, the learning disabled, and poor students weren't challenged, often stuck in segregated and underfunded schools and shuffled into vocational training. Education historian Larry Cuban pins the beginning of the move toward high-stakes testing to the passage of the Elementary and Secondary Education Act of 1965,[12] which sent significant extra funding to low-income schools neglected by local school boards.

The policies were also designed to find out which reforms were improving achievement. "Class size reduction, whole language instruction, everything under the sun has been tried in our schools," Arun Ramanathan, the executive director of the Oakland think tank Education Trust-West,[13] told me. "But how could we assess if there are any returns without reliable data? How could we know what we can scale up?"

As more states started using standardized testing, urban education reformers in the '70s and '80s were able to flag the outliers[14]: schools that were reducing the achievement gap between white, middle-class students and students of color and the poor. Cuban believes that this data helped to dismantle the idea that poor, minority, immigrant, or disabled students couldn't learn.

By 2001, when the Bush administration was pushing No Child Left Behind through Congress, testing had undergone

Closures or mass firings at low-performing schools, bonuses for high-scoring teachers, and an expansion of charter schools were supposed to disrupt a system that, in the reformers' view, had failed students and the companies for which they would one day work.

a political transformation: Now it was at the core of a business-inspired approach championed by a loose coalition of corporate leaders like Bill Gates,[15] idealists like Wendy Kopp[16] of Teach for America, and maverick education officials like Washington, DC, schools chief Michelle Rhee,[17] the heroine of the documentary *Waiting for "Superman."* Standardized tests, many of these reformers believed, could bring hard-and-fast metrics—and hardcore sanctions—to a complacent world of bureaucrats and teachers' unions. Closures or mass firings at low-performing schools, bonuses for high-scoring teachers, and an expansion of charter schools were supposed to disrupt a system that, in the reformers' view, had failed students and the companies for which they would one day work.

No Child Left Behind was animated by this faith in metrics. It mandated that states use test scores to determine whether schools were succeeding or failing, with the latter required to improve or accept punitive measures. NCLB passed with bipartisan support, and many civil rights groups were behind it.

45   Ten years later, a growing number[18] of education advocates say they didn't anticipate how high-stakes testing would change instruction for the worse. Among the converts is education historian Diane Ravitch, who served as assistant secretary of education in George H. W. Bush's administration and was an ardent champion of NCLB. "Accountability turned into a nightmare for American schools," she wrote in a 2010 *Wall Street Journal* op-ed,[19] "producing graduates who were drilled regularly on the basic skills but were often ignorant about almost everything else . . . This was not my vision of good education." In his studies, Cuban has also found that an increasing proportion of lesson time is spent preparing students for tests, and the curriculum is being narrowed to what is on those tests—even though many researchers agree that cramming for multiple-choice, a.k.a. "bubble," tests contributes very little[20] to actual learning.

The overwhelming emphasis on testing has led some schools and districts to cheat. An investigation[21] by the state of Georgia last year found widespread test-tampering in Atlanta, and the *Atlanta Journal-Constitution*[22] has identified similar patterns in hundreds of districts nationwide. Some schools have also cranked up discipline and school-based arrests, leading struggling students to drop out[23]—and thus improving scores.

Overall, the last 10 years have revealed that while Big Data can make our questions more sophisticated, it doesn't necessarily lead to Big Answers. The push to improve scores has left behind traditional assessments that, research indicates, work better to gauge performance: classroom work and homework,[24] teachers' grades and quizzes, the opinions of students and parents about a school. In his recent book *The Social Animal*, conservative columnist and veteran education commentator

David Brooks identifies this bias[25]—to emphasize and reward what we can measure, and ignore the rest—as a key reason why technocratic promises in social policy have largely failed to materialize. Research, Brooks notes, shows that the key to success is more often found in realms that resist quantification—relationships, emotions, and social norms.

Even the godfather of standardized testing, the cognitive psychologist Robert Glaser,[26] warned in 1987 about the dangers of placing too much emphasis on test scores. He called them "fallible and partial indicators of academic achievement" and warned that standardized tests would find it "extremely difficult to assess" the key skills people should gain from a good education: "resilience and courage in the face of stress, a sense of craft in our work, a commitment to justice and caring in our social relationships, a dedication to advancing the public good."

It was eight in the morning, and the lights were off in Mr. Roth's history class as winter rain tapped on the windowsills and warm moisture filled the room. In the flickering light of a television screen, Maria could see her friend Brianna breaking small pieces from a muffin and dropping them into her mouth. Maria lowered her chin into her hands. Her right leg, sheathed in dark blue jeans, bounced on the linoleum floor.

On the TV, Paula Crisostomo was waving a protest sign in the face of a police officer and arguing with her father, a Filipino immigrant wearing a blue work shirt. "I told you to stay away from these agitators!" he yelled at Paula. Based on a true story, *Walkout* captures the 1968 school protests[27] in East Los Angeles. About 22,000 Latino students participated, inspired by a teacher named Sal Castro. (One of them—Antonio Villaraigosa, né Antonio Villar—is now mayor of LA.) Back then, most Latinos were forbidden from speaking Spanish in class. Curricula largely ignored Mexican American history, and Latinos were steered toward menial labor.

In the film, students could be seen shaking the metal gate of their school, locked shut by officials to prevent them from walking out. The students rattled the bars chanting *"Viva la Raza!"* while police stood on the other side. The gate broke. Maria's entire class erupted in applause as the teens flooded into the street.

After the film ended, Robert Roth switched on the lights and turned to a class sitting in motionless silence. "Any thoughts, anyone?"

"It's incredible to see how courageous Paula was," said a student from Nicaragua named Catharine. "She lost confidence so many times, but whenever she lost it, her friends were there to support her."

"In middle school I was told to speak only English at home," Maria said next. "I think that's wrong. I already do at school. They shouldn't tell me how to live my life."

261

55   "I can relate to Paula, how people don't believe Latinos are smart enough for college," Yessenia added. "These stereotypes make me want to prove them wrong."

"Speaking of stereotypes," Brianna said, "I was in the bathroom with five other black girls, and we were fixing our hair. Two Asian American girls come in and they run out right away, thinking that we are going to bully them. I want to fix that. I'm a nice person!"

Roth jumped in, "Rebecca, you were talking to me about this kind of stereotype the other day. Do you mind sharing what you said?"

"When we moved to St. Louis from China," Rebecca said, "we went to an all African American school. My parents were telling me to stay away from black students. They said don't trust them, run away. But they were all really nice to us. A lot of times it's coming from parents, but they just don't know."

At the end of class, Brianna and her friend Destiny came up to Maria. "What's 'Viva la Raza'?"

60   "It kind of means being proud to be Latino," Maria explained.

"How do you say it?" Brianna asked, and Maria told them. "Viva la Raza! Viva la Raza! Viva la Raza!" the three chanted out loud, fists in the air, laughing.

As students shuffled out, Roth reminded them, "A short reflection on this film is due next time. And please! Don't summarize, analyze. Why is this important? How does it connect to other things we learned?"

The following Monday, Roth passed back his students' homework essays. On Maria's he'd written, "It's a B this time! See me about this, OK?"

Maria showed up at his office the next day. "Some of the stuff you've been writing is so powerful. You are really getting there, Maria," Roth said, lowering his reading glasses and putting down a folder.

65   "Why isn't it an A then?" Maria half-smiled, and pulled out her homework. "Is it because of bad grammar?" She pointed at Roth's corrections on her paper.

"Look, writing is primarily about ideas," Roth told her. "Language, grammar, and style are important tools to express those ideas. But don't start by focusing on a few grammar mistakes, or you'll get stuck and ignore the bigger issues." He explained why he made certain corrections, but he spent most of the time talking to Maria about the elements he deems essential "to getting your thoughts out": thesis, evidence, analysis, and conclusion. "Did you organize your thoughts in a way that made sense?" he asked her. "Did you back up your opinions with evidence? Did you go deep enough?"

Roth explained to Maria that she'd summarized and discussed *Walkout* really well, but when it came to analysis and conclusion, her writing seemed rushed. "What are the connections between these protests and the African American struggle for civil rights?" Maria gave a few examples. Roth suggested that she think more about why these efforts were successful. "How did these walkouts change things? Why are we studying this?"

A few weeks later, Maria presented a research paper on equal access to education. While rewriting her essay about *Walkout*, she'd discovered that some Latino parents were organizing school boycotts even before the onset of the civil rights movement. "Did you know that *Mendez v. Westminster*[28] happened eight years before *Brown v. Board*?" Maria announced to her class. In the 1946 case, Latino parents won the first-ever anti-segregation lawsuit in federal courts. "It helped the *Brown v. Board* attorneys to win their arguments before the Supreme Court," she explained. "The *Mendez* case was the beginning of the end for *Plessy v. Ferguson*, which said that 'separate but equal' is fine."

"Listen! One more day before the big bad test," Roth announced one spring day as he passed out a test that included some practice questions from the California STAR test—the final exam in US history as far as the state was concerned.

Maria and her classmates had been working with their teachers for a month to prepare for the state exams. Principal Guthertz, who has been known to eat live worms in front of students as a reward for higher test scores, promised to get a famous chef to cook a free meal for the entire school if scores went up again, as they had in the past three years.   70

"All I'm asking you to do is to take it seriously. Do it for the school," Roth said as he passed out the test. "Let's do a quick review together."

"Who was the first Catholic president? Give me three things about the New Deal!" Dozens of students shouted out answers. "You are going to *nail* this test!"

As Roth retreated to his desk, Maria stared at the rows of empty bubbles. A sharp, pounding pain filled her head. She picked up a pencil and read the first question:

> During the late 19th and 20th centuries, urban immigrants generally supported local political machines that:
> (a) discouraged the new immigrants from participating in civic affairs.
> (b) were usually supported by urban reformers.
> (c) provided essential services to the immigrants.
> (d) reminded immigrants of political practices in their homelands.

As always, Maria started translating the words into Spanish. Then she got to *discouraged*. She'd seen the word many times before, but it was usually in a context where she could guess the meaning of the passage without knowing every term. In this short sentence, though, there were no hints.

She tried to remember the word's meaning for a few minutes. Nothing.   75

263

Affairs was another word she'd heard before but couldn't remember. She translated the rest of the sentence—*new immigrants from participating*—but that didn't help. She took a deep breath and translated the rest of the answers. B was a possibility, she thought, but something felt off. C seemed right. But what about A? What if that was really the answer? There was no way of knowing. She filled in C for now.

"Five more minutes, everyone!" Roth interrupted. An ambulance siren wailed outside. Maria had spent too much time on the first five questions, and now she had to rush. She translated another page and randomly bubbled in the rest.

When she switched to the written section of the test, her leg stopped bouncing. When the bell rang, Maria kept writing, and didn't stop until Roth collected the pages from her.

Roth waited until the last student had left the room, and we looked over Maria's test together. She got almost all the answers wrong on the practice multiple-choice section, the only one that would have counted for the state. On Roth's essay question, she got an A+.

80   In 2010, Latinos made up the majority[29] of California's public school students for the first time. At Mission High, more than half the students are immigrants, and Guthertz says 20 percent have been in the United States for less than two years.

> **At Mission High, many teachers told me that there was simply no way to cover all of the standards while also maintaining a rich curriculum and actual research projects.**

After just one year in the country, Maria had to take the same test as native speakers, even though studies show[30] that immigrant teens take at least four years to become proficient in English—and that's with constant focus. Maria scored "proficient" in history for the first time in the 11th grade.

A look at Maria's schoolwork, on the other hand, is a glimpse at a learner's progress. In the quizzes and tests designed by her teachers, in her research papers, essays, art projects, class discussions, and presentations, what you see is an intellect battling to find its voice: developing research and analytical skills, the ambition and empathy to immerse herself in worlds beyond her own, and the tenacity and confidence to tackle challenging problems and keep rewriting her papers even as she wrestled with the basics of her new language.

Roth has been teaching in inner-city schools for 24 years. He has been able to find ways to cover most of the core standards for the high-stakes testing without neglecting courage, craft, intellectual curiosity, and justice. But he struggles to keep the balance, and study after study shows that's true for many teachers. At Mission High, many teachers told me that there is simply no way to cover all of the standards while also maintaining a rich curriculum and actual research projects.

Yet despite a mountain of evidence that standardized tests reveal a very narrow slice[31] of information, in most states they still determine a school's fate. In some, such as New York,[32] students' scores on the standardized tests also play a major role in grade promotion and high school placement. And in several states,[33] up to 50 percent of the evaluations that determine teachers' job security and sometimes pay are based on a week's worth of tests rather than a year's worth of learning.

In the broader context of education reform, standardized testing 85
data has been seen as absolute proof of specific policies' effectiveness. Pick up almost any news story on education—whether it is about charter schools, teacher bonuses, class sizes, or teacher unions—and the go-to evidence is gains or losses on the tests without regard for other measures, even easily available quantitative data such as dropout rates, student attendance, teacher attrition, or college enrollment rates.

It's not that reporters are blind to the other factors. Just like overworked school administrators, they simply use the data everyone talks about. And while the perspective of actual teachers and students might provide more nuance, there are few opportunities for exploring them. *Washington Post* reporter Paul Farhi noted in an essay for the *American Journalism Review*[34] that access to schools has been greatly constrained as administrators, fearful of sanctions, increasingly seek to control the message. It doesn't help that most of today's newsrooms simply can't afford to let a reporter spend time in a school for a month, let alone a year, as I did for *Mother Jones*. It's more efficient to look up scores online and make a few phone calls.

Given all that, it's no surprise that much of the debate is reduced to stereotypes. *Waiting for "Superman"* is a perfect distillation of education clichés, pitting charter schools run by enthusiastic reformers against sclerotic unions and incompetent administrators.

"I have seen about 20 rounds of classroom reform in my teaching career," Roth told me recently. "You know what I haven't seen? Serious dialogue with teachers, students, and parents. They can identify successful teaching, but they are rarely a part of the discussion."

Seeking alternatives to high-stakes testing doesn't mean giving ineffective teachers a pass, Roth added. "With all of that testing money floating around, I hope education reformers can spend some of it on finding a more holistic instrument"—one that would include a wide range of hard data as well as a deep look at student work.

One day as we sat on a curb near her mother's apartment, Maria told me 90
she'd learned more in her years at Mission than ever before. "I'm shy," she

said. "I don't speak that much in other classes, but Mr. Roth teaches me how to do it. He taught me that it's okay to argue even when I still have a lot of questions. As long as I give examples, support my point, and stay with it. Before, I would give up easily and not defend my point of view." Beaming, she added, "Now I argue, and I love winning."

But while debating was one of Maria's favorite things about school, she spent most of her time in Roth's class researching and writing papers. "That's how I prepare for the debates and learn how to express myself clearly."

"Mr. Roth tells me that I will get an A, if I am dedicated to working on my weaknesses," she told me. "What I really like is that he shows me exactly how I improve each time. In the past two years, I've seen Mr. Roth probably a thousand times to discuss each written assignment."

Maria told me that she used the textbooks to make an outline of important dates, names, and events, and to look up definitions of new words like "laissez-faire." She used the outlines to write papers. But Maria didn't remember many of these facts from year to year. What she did recall were her research papers, presentations, and art posters.

She plugged a small memory card into my laptop to show me what she'd learned.

95   "Oh, I really liked this one," she exclaimed, opening a paper titled "Latinos in the 1920s." As her class focused on the Roaring '20s, Maria found that Latino dances like the bolero, rumba, and tango were entering mainstream American culture. This led her to research Hollywood, where she made her favorite discovery. "Dolores del Río was the first Mexican movie star to gain interest to white audiences," she wrote in her paper. "Dolores showed the world that height does not matter at all if you want to be an actor, because she was very famous and beautiful even though she was very short like me!"

"Last year, I became really interested in African American history and their struggles," she explained, clicking through presentation files on Ida B. Wells, Frederick Douglass, Ella Baker, and W. E. B. Du Bois. "Learning about this motivates me not to give up." She opened a "Reconstruction Defeated" paper from the previous year. "I wanted to find out how did government justify treating African Americans unfairly with Jim Crow even though the Constitution said that all men and women were equal," she told me. "Through this paper, I became really interested in the 14th and 15th Amendment."

As I handed the memory card back to her, Maria said that as a sophomore she'd been determined to go back to her middle school to find the woman who'd told her that she'd never go to college. With her senior year under way, there was simply no time for that. She'd soon be filling out college applications and had recently been elected Latino student club president. She helped new immigrants at school. She also volunteered at a senior housing project through the Latino club, helping older neighbors. "And in my free time, I babysit my little cousins," she told me. "From now on, I only have time to talk with you over lunch at school."

One day this past spring as I lingered in Roth's room after class, a young teacher rushed in. "Robert, I've been teaching for years, but I'm really struggling this semester." Her students' grades were not showing any progress, she said, and they seemed to be losing interest. As the two looked over her grading book together, they realized she was attaching most of the grade to homework assignments and wasn't giving significant points on the work students did in her class. Those assignments showed that they were learning, but since her struggling students only saw the Fs on their homework, their engagement was dropping.

Roth's colleague, Pirette McKamey, has been teaching English and history for 24 years and is now the instructional reform facilitator at Mission High. She calls this kind of one-on-one mentoring "mucking in the dirt." "Every day, there are hundreds of small intellectual conversations all over the school about student work," explains McKamey. Along with Roth, she also co-leads a committee focused on improving achievement for kids of color, in which faculty review student work and grading policies and read the latest research. "What did the kid write? What did the kid produce?" McKamey says. "That's all that should matter."

An ample body of research shows that this kind of mentoring and   100
peer review helps teachers figure out ways for struggling students to improve. But it doesn't show up in standardized tests—and for many, it's pushed aside by the constant battle to ratchet up scores.

Before NCLB there was a movement[35] in many states, including California, to come up with reliable, unified rubrics for using classroom work to measure achievement—to move toward a mix of standardized tests and teacher assessments, something shared by most of the world's top-performing school systems, from Finland to Hong Kong. But that effort got largely steamrolled by NCLB's focus on high-stakes testing.

"I'm a history teacher," Roth says. "I believe in systemic change and macro-level conversations. But when it comes to schools, what most people don't realize is that it's about work at the micro level. The biggest reform at schools lives at the micro level, and it has to do with improving the craft of teaching."

There are some signs of a shift at the macro level. In 2009, President Obama asked[36] states to "develop standards and assessments that don't simply measure whether students can fill in a bubble on a test, but whether they possess 21st-century skills like problem-solving and critical thinking and entrepreneurship and creativity." The federal government has allocated $330 million for developing tests for a new set of standards, known as Common Core,[37] that will hit classrooms in 2015.

Supporters say that while the new tests will still include multiple-choice questions, they will also offer some opportunities for writing, and the lists of standards will be shorter, leaving teachers more freedom.

But many education experts are skeptical. A recent Brookings Institution study[38] finds no correlation at all between the testing standards and student achievement. Even Common Core advocates such as Ramanathan concede that there's a disconnect. "California has long been considered to have some of the best standards in the nation," he says, "but we also have some of the worst student outcomes."

105 Roth, who has been coaching fellow teachers for two decades, told me that standards can act as a "political security blanket" and a general guideline, but they can't help teachers with the more important tasks: figuring out how to apply the material in the classroom and gathering evidence to measure real understanding. Roth's filing cabinets are filled with different lesson plans. But every year, he creates another folder for each class, and approximately 50 percent of the material is new. He then adjusts everything throughout the year based on what works with his students.

I observed the same in other successful classrooms at Mission. "I adjust my lessons and tests every day," says a popular young math teacher named Taica Hsu. "The student body changes every semester, and what worked last year most likely won't work next year."

The Obama administration has softened some of NCLB's impact, granting waivers[39] to more than half of the states from the law's most punitive section, which calls for all students to score "proficient" in math and English by 2014. But even in the waiver states, standardized tests[40] remain the dominant measure for schools.

Midway through Maria's senior year in 2012, she was watching *Waiting for "Superman"* in Mr. Velez's college expository writing class. They were learning about achievement gaps, test scores, teacher unions, charter schools, and different solutions offered to "fix" schools like Mission. In one scene, DC's Michelle Rhee was shown firing the principal of a low-scoring school, and then the film cut to scenes of teachers and parents protesting school closures.

"Which facts in the movie shocked you?" Velez probed as the movie ended.

110 "What we spend on prison inmates," one student called out.

"Why is it so hard to fire a bad teacher?" said another, visibly upset.

"I was shocked how low test scores[42] are in California and DC," added a student with big headphones around his neck.

"California test scores are low, but the movie didn't mention we have the most immigrants here," countered a classmate. "Our English scores are bad, but that doesn't mean our school is bad."

"What would you do to fix schools?" Velez asked. Students took turns calling out responses as Velez wrote down their suggestions on a white-board: Make the tests more meaningful . . . Allow our teachers to write these tests . . . Don't test immigrant students in the first two years . . . Give more money to public schools in California . . . Make it easier to fire bad teachers . . . Ask students which schools are good and bad . . .

"Will they close Mission like those schools in DC?" Maria asked. 115
The shouting stopped.

"We won't let them," another kid responded, and the class burst out laughing. Velez kept writing.

NOTES

[1] blog.chron.com/immigration/2010/05/52-percent-of-adult-latino-immigrants-are -drop-outs/

[2] 826valencia.org/

[3] www.cde.ca.gov/ta/ac/pl/tier2.asp

[4] thomas.loc.gov/cgi-bin/bdquery/z?d107:HR00001:@@@D&summ1&

[5] data.ed.gov/grants/school-improvement-grants

[6] mhs-sfusd-ca.schoolloop.com/aboutmhs

[7] www.pewhispanic.org/2011/08/25/hispanic-college-enrollment-spikes -narrowing-gaps-with-other-groups/

[8] www.ncsl.org/issues-research/immig/in-state-tuition-and-unauthorized -immigrants.aspx

[9] star.cde.ca.gov/star2010/ViewReport.asp?ps=true&1stTestYear=2010& 1stTestType=C&1stCounty=38&1stDistrict=68478-000& 1stSchool=3834082&1stGroup=5&1stSubGroup=78

[10] star.cde.ca.gov/star2010/ViewReport.asp?ps=true&1stTestYear=2010& 1stTestType=C&1stCounty=&1stDistrict=&1stSchool=& 1stGroup=5&1stSubGroup=78

[11] www.motherjones.com/documents/406650-gao-nclb-report

[12] www.motherjones.com/documents/406651-esea-of-1965

[13] www.edtrust.org/west

[14] www.motherjones.com/documents/406652-history-of-testing

[15] online.wsj.com/article/SB10001424052970204485304576641123767006518.html

[16] www.theatlantic.com/national/archive/2012/04/how-micromanaging -educators-stifles-reform/255543/#

[17] www.huffingtonpost.com/michelle-rhee/why-im-proud-of-student-a_b_848560. html

[18] www.reuters.com/article/2012/06/12/us-usa-education-testing -idUSBRE85B0EO20120612

[19] online.wsj.com/article/SB10001424052748704869304575109443305343962.html

[20] edpolicy.stanford.edu/sites/default/files/publications/beyond-basic-skills-role -performance-assessment-achieving-21st-century-standards-learning_4.pdf

[21] gov.georgia.gov/00/press/detail/0,2668,165937316_172445682_173112104,00.html

[22]www.ajc.com/news/cheating-our-children-suspicious-1397022.html

[23]advancementproject.org/sites/default/files/Federal%20Policy%20ESEA%20
Reauthorization%20and%20the%20School-to-Prison%20Pipeline%20-%2003%
2009%2011.pdf

[24]educationnext.org/portfolio-assessment/

[25]www.npr.org/2011/03/07/134329412/david-brooks-defines-the-new-social-animal

[26]www.nytimes.com/2012/02/16/us/robert-glaser-cognitive-psychologist-and
-expert-on-student-testing-dies-at-91.html

[27]www.pomona.edu/magazine/PCMSP08/FSmaninthemiddle.shtml

[28]library.fullcoll.edu/friends/pdfs/Aguirre-MendezvWestminster.pdf

[29]www.sfgate.com/education/article/Latino-kids-now-majority-in-state-s-public
-schools-3166843.php

[30]steinhardt.nyu.edu/scmsAdmin/uploads/004/297/AERJ%202008.pdf

[31]dissentmagazine.org/online.php?id=156

[32]www.nytimes.com/schoolbook/2012/05/23/more-parents-are
-saying-no-to-pearsons-field-tests/

[33]www.nctq.org/p/publications/docs/nctq_stateOfTheStates.pdf

[34]www.ajr.org/Article.asp?id=5280

[35]edpolicy.stanford.edu/sites/default/files/publications/beyond-basic-skills-role
-performance-assessment-achieving-21st-century-standards-learning_3.pdf

[36]www.whitehouse.gov/the-press-office/fact-sheet-race-top

[37]www.corestandards.org/about-the-standards

[38]www.brookings.edu/~/media/newsletters/0216_brown_education_loveless.pdf

[39]www.ed.gov/news/press-releases/26-more-states-and-dc-seek-flexibility-nclb
-drive-education-reforms-second-round

[40]www.educationnews.org/education-policy-and-politics/nclb-waivers
-could-signal-attempts-by-obama-to-undermine-law/

[41]nces.ed.gov/nationsreportcard/pdf/main2011/2012457.pdf

FOR A SECOND READING

1. As Rizga notes, there exist very entrenched assumptions about what a "failing school" looks like. What images come to mind when you hear this phrase? What portrait of classroom life? What profile of students and teachers?

2. Rizga devotes a lot of attention in this essay to the experiences of students outside the classroom: their personal histories, family lives, economic circumstances. Why do you think Rizga chooses to include this information? In your view, is this helpful? How or how not?

3. "It is no surprise," writes Rizga, "that much of the debate [about schools] is reduced to stereotypes" (p. 265). Do you agree? What are the particular stereotypes we are taught to use in such debates?

What kind of attitude toward public education do such stereotypes script?

PUTTING IT INTO WRITING

4. According to Rizga, the primary factor responsible for designating a school as "failing" is our current reliance upon standardized tests. Write an essay in which you evaluate the validity or usefulness of using standardized tests to rank the performance of schools. Do such tests offer a fair, accurate, or helpful measure of a school's performance or not? How? If you were charged with revamping the system for evaluating school performance, what kind of standardized test (if any) would you utilize? Why?

5. Here is how Rizga characterizes the work of one student at Mission High School: "In the quizzes and tests designed by her teachers, in her research papers, essays, art projects, class discussions, and presentations, what you see is an intellect battling to find its voice: developing research and analytical skills, the ambition and empathy to immerse herself in worlds beyond her own, and the tenacity and confidence to tackle challenging problems" (p. 264). Write an essay in which you describe and analyze the model of learning this passage outlines. What are the key abilities and skills Rizga highlights? What makes these abilities and skills so valuable? In your experience, is this learning model representative of the typical classroom experience? How or how not?

COMPARING ARGUMENTS

6. For Alfie Kohn (p. 240), one of the main reasons contemporary schools are failing can be summed up in a single word: "grades." How do you think Rizga would respond to this charge? Given her portrait of life at Mission High School, how serious a problem do you think Rizga would consider the conventional grading system to be? What other problems does her essay highlight? In your view, are these problems more or less serious than grades? Why?

Rewriting the Script: **Job Skills in the Classroom**

❝ *Is this, really, what it all comes down to? Is future productivity, from this point on, to be the primary purpose of the education we provide our children? Is this to be the way in which we decide if teachers are complying with their obligations to their students and society? . . . [T]here must be something more to life as it is lived by six-year-olds or ten-year-olds, or by teenagers for that matter, than concerns about 'successful global competition.'"*

JONATHAN KOZOL, EDUCATION WRITER AND ACTIVIST

JeffG/Alamy

▲▲ *Miami, Florida, Little Haiti Edison Park Elementary School Career Day student uniforms*

Over the last several years, the national conversation about the direction of public schooling has focused more and more on the vocational purpose of education. For a growing cohort of politicians, pundits, and advocates, the goal of schooling is to prepare students to become productive workers and contributors to America's market-driven economy. As the above quotation makes clear, however, not everyone accepts or endorses this proposition. For those challenging this script, the true purpose of education is to make students into critical thinkers, to foster a familiarity with a diverse range of viewpoints, and to instill an appreciation for how varied and complex the world around us truly is. Envisioning school as a site for developing job skills, they argue, drains education of its more essential and intrinsic value. These two opposed educational visions invite us to consider fundamental questions about what learning is for, and what a "quality" education should include.

IDENTIFY THE SCRIPT: Write a brief essay in which you list all the ways you normally hear education described — in the news, in your classes, in your personal relationships with friends and families. What kind of educational script does this conversation create? To what extent does it define the basic purpose of education in vocational terms?

CHALLENGE THE SCRIPT: Write an essay in which you evaluate the relative benefits and drawbacks of a vocational model of education. What specific advantages to education does this model bring? What particular challenges or downsides does it pose?

WRITE YOUR OWN SCRIPT: Write an essay in which you replace this vocational model of education with one of your own. What kind of alternative script would this model follow? What different educational goals would it seek to accomplish? And what, in your view, would make this alternative script preferable?

BELL HOOKS

Learning in the Shadow of Race and Class

How does one's race and class affect one's experience of school? To what extent is modern education shaped by the unspoken norms connected to these two questions? Recounting her own experiences at one of America's elite institutions of higher education, bell hooks examines some of the core assumptions, ideals, and double standards that go into scripting the ideal "minority" student. As a cultural critic, feminist theorist, poet, and writer, hooks focuses on the intersections of race, class, and gender. She is the author of over thirty books, including *Talking Back: Thinking Feminist, Thinking Black* (1989), *Teaching to Transgress* (1994), *Rock My Soul: Black People and Self-Esteem* (2002), and *Outlaw Culture: Resisting Representations* (2006). hooks's most recent book is *Writing Beyond Race: Living Theory and Practice* (2013). She was born Gloria Jean Watkins in Hopkinsville, Kentucky. In 2014, she founded the bell hooks Institute at Berea College. Currently, hooks is a Distinguished Professor of English at City College in New York. The following essay first appeared in the November 17, 2000, issue of the *Chronicle of Higher Education*.

Before You Read

How wide is the racial and class divide among students on your campus? What ideas do you have about how this divide might be bridged?

AS A CHILD, I OFTEN WANTED THINGS MONEY COULD BUY THAT MY parents could not afford and would not get. Rather than tell us we did not get some material thing because money was lacking, mama would frequently manipulate us in an effort to make the desire go away. Sometimes she would belittle and shame us about the object of our desire. That's what I remember most. That lovely yellow dress I wanted would become in her storytelling mouth a really ugly mammy-made thing that no girl who cared about her looks would desire. My desires were often made to seem worthless and stupid. I learned to mistrust and silence them. I learned that the more clearly I named my desires, the more unlikely those desires would ever be fulfilled.

I learned that my inner life was more peaceful if I did not think about money, or allow myself to indulge in any fantasy of desire. I learned the art of sublimation and repression. I learned it was better to make do with acceptable material desires than to articulate the unacceptable. Before I knew money mattered, I had often chosen objects to desire that were costly, things a girl of my class would not ordinarily desire. But then I was still a girl who was *unaware of class*, who did not think my desires were stupid and wrong. And when I found they were, I let them go. I concentrated on *survival*, on making do.

> ## I was still a girl who was unaware of class, who did not think my desires were stupid and wrong.

When I was choosing a college to attend, the issue of money surfaced and had to be talked about. While I would seek loans and scholarships, even if everything related to school was paid for, there would still be transportation to pay for, books, and a host of other hidden costs. Letting me know that there was no extra money to be had, mama urged me to attend any college nearby that would offer financial aid. My first year of college, I went to a school close to home. A plain-looking white woman recruiter had sat in our living room and explained to my parents that everything would be taken care of, that I would be awarded a full academic scholarship, that they would have to pay nothing. They knew better. Still they found this school acceptable.

After my parents dropped me at the predominately white women's college, I saw the terror in my roommate's face that she was going to be housed with someone black, and I requested a change. She had no doubt also voiced her concern. I was given a tiny single room by the stairs—a room usually denied a first-year student—but I was a first-year black student, a scholarship girl who could never in a million years have afforded to pay her way or absorb the cost of a single room. My fellow students kept their distance from me. I ate in the cafeteria and did not have to worry about who would pay for pizza and drinks in the world outside. I kept my desires to myself, my lacks, and my loneliness; I made do.

I rarely shopped. Boxes came from home, with brand-new clothes 5 mama had purchased. Even though it was never spoken, she did not want me to feel ashamed among privileged white girls. I was the only black girl in my dorm. There was no room in me for shame. I felt contempt and disinterest. With their giggles and their obsession to marry, the white girls at the women's college were aliens. We did not reside on the same planet. I lived in the world of books. The one white woman who became my close friend found me there reading. I was hiding under the shadows of a tree with huge branches, the kinds of trees that just seemed to grow effortlessly on well-to-do college campuses. I sat on the "perfect" grass reading poetry, wondering how the grass around me could be so lovely, and yet, when daddy had tried to grow grass in the front yard of

Mr. Porter's house, it always turned yellow or brown and then died. Endlessly, the yard defeated him, until finally he gave up. The outside of the house looked good, but the yard always hinted at the possibility of endless neglect. The yard looked poor.

Foliage and trees on the college grounds flourished. Greens were lush and deep. From my place in the shadows, I saw a fellow student sitting alone weeping. Her sadness had to do with all the trivia that haunted our day's classwork, the fear of not being smart enough, of losing financial aid (like me she had loans and scholarships, though her family paid some), and boys. Coming from an Illinois family of Czechoslovakian immigrants, she understood class.

When she talked about the other girls who flaunted their wealth and family background, there was a hard edge of contempt, anger, and envy in her voice. Envy was always something I pushed away from my psyche. Kept too close for comfort, envy could lead to infatuation and on to desire. I desired nothing that they had. She desired everything, speaking her desires openly, without shame. Growing up in the kind of community where there was constant competition to see who could buy the bigger better whatever, in a world of organized labor, of unions and strikes, she understood a world of bosses and workers, of haves and have-nots.

White friends I had known in high school wore their class privilege modestly. Raised, like myself, in church traditions that taught us to identify only with the poor, we knew that there was evil in excess. We knew rich people were rarely allowed into heaven. God had given them a paradise of bounty on earth, and they had not shared. The rare ones, the rich people who shared, were the only ones able to meet the divine in paradise, and even then it was harder for them to find their way. According to the high-school friends we knew, flaunting wealth was frowned upon in our world, frowned upon by God and community.

The few women I befriended my first year in college were not wealthy. They were the ones who shared with me stories of the other girls flaunting the fact that they could buy anything expensive—clothes, food, vacations. There were not many of us from working-class backgrounds; we knew who we were. Most girls from poor backgrounds tried to blend in, or fought back by triumphing over wealth with beauty or style or some combination of the above. Being black made me an automatic outsider. Holding their world in contempt pushed me further to the edge. One of the fun things the "in" girls did was choose someone and trash their room. Like so much else deemed cute by insiders, I dreaded the thought of strangers entering my space and going through my things. Being outside the in crowd made me an unlikely target. Being contemptuous made me first on the list. I did not understand. And when my room was trashed, it unleashed my rage and deep grief over not being able to protect my space from violation and invasion. I hated the girls who had so much, took so much for granted, never considered that those of us who did not have mad money would not be able to replace broken things, perfume poured out, or talcum powder spread everywhere—that we did not know everything could be taken care of at the dry cleaner's, because we never took our clothes there. My rage fueled by contempt was deep, strong, and long lasting. Daily it stood as a challenge to their fun, to their habits of being.

Nothing they did to win me over worked. It came as a great surprise. 10
They had always believed black girls wanted to be white girls, wanted to possess their world. My stony gaze, silence, and absolute refusal to cross the threshold of their world was total mystery; it was for them a violation they needed to avenge. After trashing my room, they tried to win me over with apologies and urges to talk and understand. There was nothing about me I wanted them to understand. Everything about their world was overexposed, on the surface.

One of my English professors had attended Stanford University. She felt that was the place for me to go—a place where intellect was valued over foolish fun and games and dress up, and finding a husband did not overshadow academic work. I had never thought about the state of California. Getting my parents to agree to my leaving Kentucky to attend a college in a nearby state had been hard enough. They had accepted a college they could reach by car, but a college thousands of miles away was beyond their imagination. Even I had difficulty grasping going that far away from home. The lure for me was the promise of journeying and arriving at a destination where I would be accepted and understood.

All the barely articulated understandings of class privilege that I had learned my first year of college had not hipped me to the reality of class shame. It still had not dawned on me that my parents, especially mama, resolutely refused to acknowledge any difficulties with money because her sense of shame around class was deep and intense. And when this shame was coupled with her need to feel that she had risen above the low-class backwoods culture of her family, it was impossible for her to talk in a straightforward manner about the strains it would put on the family for me to attend Stanford.

All I knew then was that, as with all my desires, I was told that this desire was impossible to fulfill. At first, it was not talked about in relation to money, it was talked about in relation to sin. California was an evil place, a modern-day Babylon where souls were easily seduced away from the path of righteousness. It was not a place for an innocent young girl to go on her own. Mama brought the message back that my father had absolutely refused to give permission.

I expressed my disappointment through ongoing unrelenting grief. I explained to mama that other parents wanted their children to go to good schools. It still had not dawned on me that my parents knew nothing about "good" schools. Even though I knew mama had not graduated from high school, I still held her in awe.

15 When my parents refused to permit me to attend Stanford, I accepted the verdict for awhile. Overwhelmed by grief, I could barely speak for weeks. Mama intervened and tried to change my father's mind, as folks she respected in the outside world told her what a privilege it was for me to have this opportunity, that Stanford University was a good school for a smart girl. Without their permission, I decided I would go. And even though she did not give her approval, mama was willing to help.

My decision made conversations about money necessary. Mama explained that California was too far away, that it would always "cost" to get there, that if something went wrong, they would not be able to come and rescue me, that I would not be able to come home for holidays. I heard all this, but its meaning did not sink in. I was just relieved I would not be returning to the women's college, to the place where I had truly been an outsider.

There were other black students at Stanford. There was even a dormitory where many black students lived. I did not know I could choose to live there. I went where I was assigned. Going to Stanford was the first time I flew somewhere. Only mama stood and waved farewell as I left to take the bus to the airport. I left with a heavy heart, feeling both excitement and dread. I knew nothing about the world I was journeying to. Not knowing made me afraid, but my fear of staying in place was greater.

I had no idea what was ahead of me. In small ways, I was ignorant. I had never been on an escalator, a city bus, an airplane, or a subway. I arrived in San Francisco with no understanding that Palo Alto was a long drive away—that it would take money to find transportation there. I decided to take the city bus. With all my cheap overpacked bags, I must have seemed like just another innocent immigrant when I struggled to board the bus.

This was a city bus with no racks for luggage. It was filled with immigrants. English was not spoken. I felt lost and afraid. Without words the strangers surrounding me understood the universal language of need and distress. They reached for my bags, holding and helping. In return, I told them my story—that I had left my village in the South to come to Stanford University and that, like them, my family were workers.

20 On arriving, I called home. Before I could speak, I began to weep as I heard the faraway sound of mama's voice. I tried to find the words to slow down, to tell her how it felt to be a stranger, to speak my uncertainty and longing. She told me this is the lot I had chosen. I must live with it. After her words, there was only silence. She had hung up on me—let me go into this world where I am a stranger still.

Stanford University was a place where one could learn about class from the ground up. Built by a man who believed in hard work, it was to have been a place where students of all classes would come, women and men, to work together and learn. It was to be a place of equality and communalism. His vision was seen by many as almost communist. The fact that he was rich made it all less threatening. Perhaps no one really believed the vision could be realized. The university was named after his son, who had died young, a son who had carried his name but who had no future money could buy. No amount of money can keep death away. But it could keep memory alive.

Everything in the landscape of my new world fascinated me, the plants brought from a rich man's travels all over the world back to this place of water and clay. At Stanford University, adobe buildings blend with Japanese plum trees and leaves of kumquat. On my way to study medieval literature, I ate my first kumquat. Surrounded by flowering cactus and a South American shrub bougainvillea of such trailing beauty it took my breath away, I was in a landscape of dreams, full of hope and possibility. If nothing else would hold me, I would not remain a stranger to the earth. The ground I stood on would know me.

Class was talked about behind the scenes. The sons and daughters from rich, famous, or notorious families were identified. The grown-ups in charge of us were always looking out for a family who might give their millions to the college. At Stanford, my classmates wanted to know me, thought it hip, cute, and downright exciting to have a black friend. They invited me on the expensive vacations and ski trips I could not afford. They offered to pay. I never went. Along with other students who were not from privileged families, I searched for places to go during the holiday times when the dormitory was closed. We got together and talked about the assumption that everyone had money to travel and would necessarily be leaving. The staff would be on holiday as well, so all students had to leave. Now and then the staff did not leave, and we were allowed to stick around. Once, I went home with one of the women who cleaned for the college.

Now and then, when she wanted to make extra money, mama would work as a maid. Her decision to work outside the home was seen as an act of treason by our father. At Stanford, I was stunned to find that there were maids who came by regularly to vacuum and tidy our rooms. No one had ever cleaned up behind me, and I did not want them to. At first I roomed with another girl from a working-class background—a beautiful white girl from Orange County who looked like pictures I had seen on the cover of *Seventeen* magazine. Her mother had died of cancer during her high-school years, and she had since been raised by her father. She had been asked by the college officials if she would find it problematic to have a black roommate. A scholarship student like myself, she knew her preferences did not matter and, as she kept telling me, she did not really care.

25   Like my friend during freshman year, she shared the understanding of what it was like to be a have-not in a world of haves. But unlike me, she was determined to become one of them. If it meant she had to steal nice clothes to look the same as they did, she had no problem taking these risks. If it meant having a privileged boyfriend who left bruises on her body now and then, it was worth the risk. Cheating was worth it. She believed the world the privileged had created was all unfair—all one big cheat; to get ahead, one had to play the game. To her, I was truly an innocent, a lamb being led to the slaughter. It did not surprise her one bit when I began to crack under the pressure of contradictory values and longings.

Like all students who did not have seniority, I had to see the school psychiatrists to be given permission to live off campus. Unaccustomed to being around strangers, especially strangers who did not share or understand my values, I found the experience of living in the dorms difficult. Indeed, almost everyone around me believed working-class folks had no values. At the university where the founder, Leland Stanford, had imagined different classes meeting on common ground, I learned how deeply individuals with class privilege feared and hated the working classes. Hearing classmates express contempt and hatred toward people who did not come from the right backgrounds shocked me.

To survive in this new world of divided classes, this world where I was also encountering for the first time a black bourgeois elite that was as contemptuous of working people as their white counterparts were, I had to take a stand, to get clear my own class affiliations. This was the most difficult truth to face. Having been taught all my life to believe that black people were inextricably bound in solidarity by our struggles to end racism, I did not know how to respond to elitist black people who were full of contempt for anyone who did not share their class, their way of life.

I did not know how to respond to elitist black people who were full of contempt for anyone who did not share their class, their way of life.

At Stanford, I encountered for the first time a black diaspora. Of the few black professors present, the vast majority were from African or Caribbean backgrounds. Elites themselves, they were only interested in teaching other elites. Poor folks like myself, with no background to speak of, were invisible. We were not seen by them or anyone else. Initially, I went to all meetings welcoming black students, but when I found no one to connect with, I retreated. In the shadows, I had time and books to teach me about the nature of class—about the ways black people were divided from themselves.

Despite this rude awakening, my disappointment at finding myself estranged from the group of students I thought would understand, I still looked for connections. I met an older black male graduate student who also came from a working-class background. Even though he had gone to the right high school, a California school for gifted students, and then to Princeton as an undergraduate, he understood intimately the intersections of race and class. Good in sports and in the classroom, he had been slotted early on to go far, to go where other black males had not gone. He understood the system. Academically, he fit. Had he wanted to, he could have been among the elite, but he chose to be on the margins, to hang with an intellectual artistic avant-garde. He wanted to live in a world of the mind where there was no race or class. He wanted to worship at the throne of art and knowledge. He became my mentor, comrade, and companion.

Slowly, I began to understand fully that there was no place in academe for folks from working-class backgrounds who did not wish to leave the past behind. That was the price of the ticket. Poor students would be welcome at the best institutions of higher learning only if they were willing to surrender memory, to forget the past and claim the assimilated present as the only worthwhile and meaningful reality.

Students from nonprivileged backgrounds who did not want to forget often had nervous breakdowns. They could not bear the weight of all the contradictions they had to confront. They were crushed. More often than not, they dropped out with no trace of their inner anguish recorded, no institutional record of the myriad ways their take on the world was assaulted by an elite vision of class and privilege. The records merely indicated that, even after receiving financial aid and other support, these students simply could not make it, simply were not good enough.

At no time in my years as a student did I march in a graduation ceremony. I was not proud to hold degrees from institutions where I had been constantly scorned and shamed. I wanted to forget these experiences, to erase them from my consciousness. Like a prisoner set free, I did not want to remember my years on the inside. When I finished my doctorate, I felt too much uncertainty about who I had become. Uncertain about whether I had managed to make it through without giving up the best of myself, the best of the values I had been raised to believe in—hard work, honesty, and respect for everyone no matter their class—I finished my education with my allegiance to the working class intact. Even so, I had planted my feet on the path leading in the direction of class

30

privilege. There would always be contradictions to face. There would always be confrontations around the issue of class. I would always have to reexamine where I stand.

FOR A SECOND READING

1. Take a few moments to consider the title of this piece. What are the shadows that, according to hooks, most directly affect or shape her experiences of school? To what extent do these shadows operate in her life as powerful, unspoken scripts, drawing the lines around the particular role she felt allowed to play?

2. As hooks relates, she became familiar with the standards and expectations being placed on her in college largely by indirection and inference. The norms and scripts to which she was expected to conform, she makes clear, remained invisible and unspoken. How would you put some of these norms and scripts into words? What script would you write?

3. For hooks, the prospect of succeeding in school revolved around the experience of loss: giving up connections and relationships that had formerly defined how she viewed herself. In your experience, has anything similar defined your relationship to school?

PUTTING IT INTO WRITING

4. Race and class, hooks argues, are the unspoken norms that structure everyday college life, the invisible scripts that set the boundaries around what different types of students are encouraged or allowed to expect from school. Write an essay in which you analyze how hooks makes this argument. How does she present her own experience as a student as an example? What unspoken (or spoken) scripts about schooling, education, race, or class does hooks expose in her writing?

5. For hooks, there is a complicated relationship between education and desire. Write an essay in which you analyze how this relationship works, according to hooks. Describe the particular role imposed on hooks as a black working-class student, and assess the particular ways this role seems designed to set boundaries around the educational designs and desires she was allowed to have.

COMPARING ARGUMENTS

6. Jonathan Kozol (p. 283) makes a strenuous argument against the increasing vocationalization of education. How do you think hooks would respond to Kozol's critique? Do you think she would add what Kozol decries as a "work-themed" curriculum to her list of factors responsible for creating insiders and outsiders in school?

JONATHAN KOZOL
Preparing Minds for Markets

Whether or not we want to admit it, many of our public schools play a formative role in shaping how children come to see themselves as workers. Presenting an eye-opening account of the ways that corporate logos and workplace terminology have permeated the modern classroom, Jonathan Kozol offers a spirited critique of the work-related scripts children today are often compelled to take up. Kozol is a writer and educator best known for his works on inequality in American education. He graduated from Harvard University and was awarded a Rhodes Scholarship to study at Magdalen College, Oxford. Rather than finishing at Oxford, however, he moved to Paris to work on a novel. When he returned to the United States, he began teaching in the Boston public schools, but he was fired for teaching a Langston Hughes poem that was not in the curriculum. His experiences in Boston's segregated classrooms led to his first book, *Death at an Early Age* (1967), which won the National Book Award. His other books include *Savage Inequalities* (1991), *Amazing Grace* (1995), *Letters to a Young Teacher* (2007), *Fire in the Ashes: Twenty-Five Years Among the Poorest Children in America* (2012), and most recently, *The Theft of Memory: Losing My Father One Day at a Time* (2015). The following selection is from *The Shame of the Nation*, published in 2005.

Before You Read

How much do vocational concerns factor into the ways you think about your own education? In your view, should the principal goal of education be to prepare students to be workers? Why or why not?

THREE YEARS AGO, IN COLUMBUS, OHIO, I WAS VISITING A SCHOOL in which the stimulus-response curriculum that Mr. Endicott was using in New York had been in place for several years.[1] The scripted teaching method started very early in this school. ("Practice Active Listening!" a kindergarten teacher kept repeating to her children.) So too did a program of surprisingly explicit training of young children for the modern marketplace. Starting in kindergarten, children in the school were being asked to think about the jobs that they might choose when they grew up. The posters that surrounded them made clear which kinds of jobs they were expected to select.

"Do you want a manager's job?" the first line of a kindergarten poster asked.

"What job do you want?" a second question asked in an apparent effort to expand the range of choices that these five-year-olds might wish to make.

But the momentary window that this second question seemed to open into other possible careers was closed by the next question on the wall. "How will you do the manager's job?" the final question asked.

5   The tiny hint of choice afforded by the second question was eradicated by the third, which presupposed that all the kids had said yes to the first. No written question asked the children: "Do you want a lawyer's job? a nurse's job? a doctor's job? a poet's job? a preacher's job? an engineer's job? or an artist's job?" Sadly enough, the teacher had not even thought to ask if anybody in the class might someday like to be a teacher.

In another kindergarten class, there was a poster that displayed the names of several retail stores: JCPenney, Wal-Mart, Kmart, Sears, and a few others. "It's like working in a store," a classroom aide explained. "The children are learning to pretend that they're cashiers."

Work-related themes and managerial ideas were carried over into almost every classroom of the school. In a first grade class, for instance, children had been given classroom tasks for which they were responsible. The names of children and their tasks were posted on the wall, an ordinary thing to see in classrooms everywhere. But in this case there was a novel twist: All the jobs the kids were given were described as management positions!

There was a "Coat Room Manager" and a "Door Manager," a "Pencil Sharpener Manager" and a "Soap Manager," an "Eraser, Board, and Marker Manager," and there was also a "Line Manager." What on earth, I was about to ask, is a "Line Manager"? My question was answered when a group of children filing in the hallway grew a bit unruly and a grown-up's voice barked out, "Who is your line manager?"

In the upper grades, the management positions became more sophisticated and demanding. In a fourth grade, for example, I was introduced to a "Time Manager" who was assigned to hold the timer to be sure the teacher didn't wander from her schedule and that everyone adhered to the prescribed number of minutes that had been assigned to every classroom task.

10   Turning a corner, I encountered a "HELP WANTED" sign. Several of these signs, I found, were posted on the walls at various locations in the school. These were not advertisements for school employees, but for children who would be selected to fill various positions as class managers. "Children in the higher grades are taught to file applications for a job," the principal explained—then "go for interviews," she said, before they can be hired. According to a summary of school-wide practices she gave me, interviews "for management positions" were intended to teach values of "responsibility for . . . jobs."

> **"Children in the higher grades are taught to file applications for a job."**

In another fourth grade class, there was an "earnings chart" that had been taped to every child's desk, on which a number of important writing skills had been spelled out and, next to each, the corresponding earnings that a child would receive if written answers he or she provided in the course of classroom exercises such as mini-drills or book reports displayed the necessary skills.

"How Much Is My Written Answer Worth?" the children in the class were asked. There were, in all, four columns on the "earnings charts" and children had been taught the way to fill them in. There was also a Classroom Bank in which the children's earnings were accrued. A wall display beneath the heading of the Classroom Bank presented an enticing sample of real currency—one-dollar bills, five-dollar bills, ten-dollar bills—in order to make clear the nexus between cash rewards and writing proper sentences.

Ninety-eight percent of children in the school were living in poverty, according to the school's annual report card; about four-fifths were African-American. The principal said that only about a quarter of the students had been given preschool education.

At another elementary school in the same district, in which 93 percent of children were black or Hispanic, the same "HELP WANTED" posters and the lists of management positions were displayed. Among the positions open to the children in this school, there was an "Absence Manager," a "Form-Collector Manager," a "Paper-Passing Manager," a "Paper-Collecting Manager," a "Paper-Returning Manager," an "Exit Ticket Manager," even a "Learning Manager," a "Reading Manager," a "Behavior Manager," and a "Score-Keeper Manager." Applications for all management positions, starting with the second graders, had to be "accompanied by references," according to the principal.

On a printed application form she handed me—"Consistency 15 Management Manager Application"[2] was its title—children were instructed to fill in their name, address, phone number, teacher, and grade level, and then indicate the job that they preferred ("First job choice. . . . Why do you want this job? Second job choice. . . . Why do you want this job?"), then sign and date their application. The awkwardly named document, the principal explained, originated in a program aimed at children of minorities that had been developed with financial backing from a businessman in Texas.

The silent signals I'd observed in the South Bronx and Hartford were in use in this school also. As I entered one class, the teacher gave his students the straight-arm salute, with fingers flat. The children responded quickly with the same salute. On one of the walls, there was a sign that read "A Million Dollars Worth of Self-Control." It was "a little incentive thing," the teacher told me when I asked about this later in the afternoon.

As I was chatting with the principal before I left, I asked her if there was a reason why those two words "management" and "manager" kept popping up throughout the school. I also summoned up my nerve to tell her that I was surprised to see "help wanted" signs within an elementary school.

"We want every child to be working as a manager while he or she is in this school," the principal explained. "We want to make them understand that, in this country, companies will give you opportunities to work, to prove yourself, no matter what you've done."

I wasn't sure of what she meant by that—"no matter what you've done"—and asked her if she could explain this. "Even if you have a felony arrest," she said, "we want you to understand that you can be a manager someday."

20   I told her that I still did not quite understand why management positions were presented to the children as opposed to other jobs—being a postal worker, for example, or construction worker, or, for that matter, working in a field of purely intellectual endeavor—as a possible way to earn a living even if one once had been in trouble with the law. But the principal was interrupted at this point and since she had already been extremely patient with me, I did not believe I had the right to press her any further. So I left the school with far more questions in my mind than answers.

When I had been observing Mr. Endicott at P.S. 65, it had occurred to me that something truly radical about the way that inner-city children are perceived was presupposed by the peculiar way he spoke to students and the way they had been programmed to respond. I thought of this again here in these classes in Ohio. What is the radical perception of these kids that underlies such practices? How is this different from the way most educated friends of mine would look at their own children?

"Primitive utilitarianism"—"Taylorism in the classroom"—were two of the terms that Mr. Endicott had used in speaking of the teaching methods in effect within his school. "Commodification"—"of the separate pieces of the learning process, of the children in themselves"—is the expression that another teacher uses to describe these practices. Children, in this frame of reference, are regarded as investments, assets, or productive units—or else, failing that, as pint-sized human deficits who threaten our competitive capacities. The package of skills they learn, or do not learn, is called "the product" of the school. Sometimes the educated child is referred to as "the product" too.

These ways of viewing children, which were common at the start of the last century, have reemerged over the past two decades in the words of business leaders, influential educators, and political officials. "We must start thinking of students as workers . . . ," said a high official of one of the nation's teachers unions at a forum convened by *Fortune* magazine in 1988.[3] I remember thinking when I read these words: Is this, really, what it all comes down to? Is future productivity, from this point on, to be the primary purpose of the education we provide our children? Is this to be the way in which we will decide if teachers are complying with their obligations to their students and society? What if a child should grow ill and die before she's old enough to make her contribution to the national economy? Will all the money that our government has spent to educate that child have to be regarded as a bad investment?

Admittedly, the economic needs of a society are bound to be reflected to some rational degree within the policies and purposes of public schools. But, even so, most of us are inclined to ask, there must be *something* more to life as it is lived by six-year-olds or ten-year-olds, or by teenagers for that matter, than concerns about "successful global competition." Childhood is not merely basic training for utilitarian adulthood. It should have some claims upon our mercy, not for its future value to the economic interests of competitive societies but for its present value as a perishable piece of life itself.

Listening to the stern demands we hear for inculcating worker ideologies in the mentalities of inner-city youth—and, as we are constantly exhorted now, for "getting tough" with those who don't comply—I am reminded of a passage from the work of Erik Erikson, who urged us to be wary of prescriptive absoluteness in the ways we treat and think about our children. "The most deadly of all possible sins" in the upbringing of a child, Erikson wrote, derive too frequently from what he called "destructive forms of conscientiousness."[4] Erikson's good counsel notwithstanding, the momentum that has led to these utilitarian ideas about the education of low-income children has been building for a long, long time and, at least in public discourse as it is presented in the press and on TV, has not met with widespread opposition. Beginning in the early 1980s and continuing with little deviation right up to the present time, the notion of producing "products" who will then produce more wealth for the society has come to be embraced by many politicians and, increasingly, by principals of inner-city schools that have developed close affiliations with the representatives of private business corporations. 25

"Dismayed by the faulty products being turned out by Chicago's troubled public schools," the *Wall Street Journal* wrote in 1990, "some 60 of the city's giant corporations have taken over the production line themselves," a reference to the efforts that these corporations had invested in creation of a model school in

> **The notion of producing "products" who will then produce more wealth for the society has come to be embraced by many politicians and . . . principals.**

a predominantly black neighborhood that was intended to embody corporate ideas of management and productivity. "I'm in the business of developing minds to meet a market demand," the principal of the school announced during a speech delivered at "a power breakfast" of the top executives of several of these corporations. "If you were manufacturing Buicks, you would have the same objectives," said a corporate official who was serving as the school's executive director.[5]

Business jargon has since come to be commonplace in the vocabularies used within the schools themselves. Children in the primary grades are being taught they must "negotiate" with one another for a book or toy or box of crayons or a pencil-sharpener—certainly not a normal word for five- or six-year-olds to use. In many schools, young children have been learning also to "sign contracts" to complete their lessons rather than just looking up and telling Miss O'Brien they will "try real hard" to do what she has asked.

Learning itself—the learning of a skill, or the enjoying of a book, and even having an idea—is now defined increasingly not as a process or preoccupation that holds satisfaction of its own but in proprietary terms, as if it were the acquisition of an object or stock-option or the purchase of a piece of land. "Taking ownership" is the accepted term, which now is used both by the kids themselves and also by their teachers. Most people like to think they "get" ideas, "understand" a process, or "take pleasure" in the act of digging into a good book. In the market-driven classroom, children are encouraged to believe they "own" the book, the concept, the idea. They don't *engage* with knowledge; they possess it.

In the Columbus schools, as we have seen, children are actively "incentivized" (this is another term one hears in many inner-city schools) by getting reimbursements for the acquisition of a skill in terms of simulated cash. At P.S. 65 in the South Bronx, I was shown another Classroom Bank, out of which a currency called "Scholar Dollars" was disbursed. Some of these things may be dismissed as little more than modern reembodiments of ordinary rituals and phrases known to schoolchildren for decades. We all got gold stars in my elementary school if we brought in completed homework; many teachers give their students sticky decals with a picture of a frog or mouse or cat or dog, for instance, as rewards for finishing a book report or simply treating one another with politeness. Most Americans, I think, would smile at these innocent and pleasant ways of giving children small rewards. But would they smile quite so easily if their own children were provided earnings charts to calculate how much they will be paid for learning to write sentences?

30   Some of the usages that I have cited here ("ownership," "negotiate," for instance) have filtered into the vocabularies of suburban schools as well, but in most of these schools they are not introduced to children as the elements of acquisitional vocabulary and are more likely to be used,

unconsciously perhaps, as borrowings from language that has come to be familiar in the world of pop psychology—"learning to 'take ownership' of one's emotions," for example. It is a different story when they are incorporated into a much broader package of pervasive corporate indoctrination.

Very few people who are not involved with inner-city schools have any idea of the extremes to which the mercantile distortion of the purposes and character of education have been taken or how unabashedly proponents of these practices are willing to defend them. The head of a Chicago school, for instance, who was criticized by some for emphasizing rote instruction which, his critics said, was turning children into "robots," found no reason to dispute the charge. "Did you ever stop to think that these robots will never burglarize your home?" he asked, and "will never snatch your pocket books. . . . These robots are going to be producing taxes. . . ."[6]

> *These ways of speaking about children and perceiving children are specific to the schools that serve minorities.*

Would any educator feel at ease in using terms like these in reference to the children of a town like Scarsdale or Manhasset, Glencoe or Winnetka, or the affluent suburban town of Newton, Massachusetts, in which I attended elementary school and later taught? I think we know this is unlikely. These ways of speaking about children and perceiving children are specific to the schools that serve minorities. Shorn of unattractive language about "robots" who will be producing taxes and not burglarizing homes, the general idea that schools in ghettoized communities must settle for a different set of goals than schools that serve the children of the middle class and upper middle class has been accepted widely. And much of the rhetoric of "rigor" and "high standards" that we hear so frequently, no matter how egalitarian in spirit it may sound to some, is fatally belied by practices that vulgarize the intellects of children and take from their education far too many of the opportunities for cultural and critical reflectiveness without which citizens become receptacles for other people's ideologies and ways of looking at the world but lack the independent spirits to create their own.

Perhaps the clearest evidence of what is taking place is seen in schools in which the linkage between education and employment is explicitly established in the names these schools are given and the work-related goals that they espouse. When badly failing schools are redesigned—or undergo "reconstitution," as the current language holds—a fashionable trend today is to assign them names related to the world of economics and careers. "Academy of Enterprise" or "Corporate

Academy" are two such names adopted commonly in the renaming of a segregated school. Starting about ten years ago, a previously unfamiliar term emerged to specify the purposes these various academies espouse. "School-to-work" is the unflinching designation that has since been used to codify these goals, and "industry-embedded education" for the children of minorities has now become a term of art among practitioners.

Advocates for school-to-work do not, in general, describe it as a race-specific project but tend instead to emphasize the worth of linking academic programs to the world of work for children of all backgrounds and insisting that suburban children too should be prepared in school for marketplace demands, that children of all social classes ought to have "some work experience" in high school, for example. But the attempt at even-handedness in speaking of the ways that this idea might be applied has been misleading from the start. In most suburban schools, the school-to-work idea, if educators even speak of it at all, is little more than seemly decoration on the outer edges of a liberal curriculum. In many urban schools, by contrast, it has come to be the energizing instrument of almost every aspect of instruction.

35 Some business leaders argue that this emphasis is both realistic and humane in cases, for example, where a sixteen-year-old student lacks the skills or motivation to pursue a richly academic course of study or, indeed, can sometimes barely write a simple paragraph or handle elementary math. If the rationale for this were so defined in just so many words by the administrators of our schools, and if it were not introduced until the final years of secondary education at a point when other options for a student may appear to be foreclosed, an argument could certainly be made that school-to-work is a constructive adaptation to the situation many teenage students actually face.

But when this ethos takes control of secondary education almost from the start, or even earlier than that, before a child even enters middle school, as is the case in many districts now, it's something very different from an adaptation to the needs of students or the preferences they may express. It's not at all an "adaptation" in these cases; it's a prior legislation of diminished options for a class of children who are not perceived as having the potential of most other citizens. It's not "acceding" to their preferences. It's manufacturing those preferences and, all too frequently, it's doing this to the direct exclusion of those options other children rightly take as their entitlement.

There are middle schools in urban neighborhoods today where children are required, in effect, to choose careers before they even enter adolescence. Children make their applications to a middle school when they're in the fifth grade. . . . [A] South Bronx middle school [bears] Paul Robeson's name. "Robeson," however, as I subsequently learned, wasn't the complete name of this school. "The Paul Robeson School for Medical Careers and Health Professions" was the full and seemingly enticing designation that it bore; and, sadly enough, this designation and the way the school described itself in a brochure that had been given to the fifth grade students in the local elementary schools had led these girls into believing that enrolling there would lead to the fulfillment of a dream they shared: They wanted to be doctors.

"An understanding and embracement of medical science and health," said the brochure in a description of the school's curriculum, "is developed through powerful learning opportunities. . . . To be successful at the Paul Robeson School . . . , a student is expected to be highly motivated to broaden their horizons." Not many ten-year-olds in the South Bronx would likely know that this description represented an outrageous overstatement of the academic offerings this middle school provided. Unless they had an older sibling who had been a student there, most would have no way of knowing that the Robeson School, perennially ranking at the lowest level of the city's middle schools, sent very few students into high schools that successfully prepared a child for college and that any likelihood of moving from this school into a medical career, as these girls understood the term, was almost nonexistent.

"It's a medical school," another child, named Timeka, told me when I asked her why she had applied there. "I want to be a baby doctor," she explained, a goal that a number of the girls had settled on together, as children often do in elementary school. But the program at the Robeson School did not provide the kind of education that could lead her to that goal. A cynic, indeed, might easily suspect it was designed instead to turn out nursing aides and health assistants and the other relatively low-paid personnel within a hospital or nursing home, for instance, all of which might be regarded as good jobs for children with no other options, if they continued with their education long enough to graduate; but even this was not the usual pattern for a child who had spent three years at Robeson.

Timeka went from Robeson to another of those "industry-embedded" 40 schools,[7] a 97 percent black and Hispanic school called "Health Opportunities," in which only one in five ninth graders ever reached twelfth grade and from which Timeka dropped out in eleventh grade.[8] I had known Timeka since she was a jubilant and energetic eight-year-old. I used to help her with her math and reading when she was in the fourth grade. She was smart and quick and good with words, and very good in math. If she had gone to school in almost any middle-class suburban district in this nation, she'd have had at least a chance of realizing her dream if she still wanted to when she completed high school. And if she changed her mind and settled on a different dream, or many different dreams, as adolescents usually do, she would have been exposed to an array of options that would have permitted her to make a well-informed decision. The choice of a career means virtually nothing if you do not know what choices you may actually have.

The choice of a career means virtually nothing if you do not know what choices you may actually have.

"In recent years, business has taken ownership of school-to-work . . . ," according to an advocate for these career academies.[9] National and regional industry associations, he reports, are "linking students" to "standards-driven, work-based learning opportunities while they are in school" and then, he says, providing students with job offers from participating businesses. One such program has taken place for several years at a high school in Chicago where an emphasis on "Culinary Arts" has been embedded in curriculum.[10] A teacher at the school, where 98 percent of students are black or Hispanic (many of Mexican descent), told me of a student she had grown attached to when she taught her in eleventh grade. The student, she said, showed academic promise—"I definitely thought that she was capable of going on to college"—so she recommended her to be admitted to a senior honors class.

It was a big school (2,200 students) and the teacher said she didn't see this girl again until the following September when she happened to run into her during a class break on an escalator in the building, and she asked her if she'd been admitted to the honors class. The student told her, "No," she said. "I couldn't figure out why." Then, she said, "I realized she'd been placed in Culinary Arts."

Students, she explained, were required "to decide on a 'career path' at the end of freshman year," and "once you do this, your entire program is determined by that choice." Technically, she said, a student could select a college education as "career path," but this option, she reported, wasn't marketed to many of the students at the school as forcefully as were the job-related programs. The career programs in the upper-level grades, moreover, were blocked out "as a double period every day," the teacher said, which made it harder for the students in these programs who so wished to take an honors class or other academic classes that appealed to them.[11]

The program in culinary arts, in which the students were prepared to work in restaurant kitchens, had been set up in coordination with Hyatt Hotels, which offered jobs or internships to students on completion of their education.[12] The program was promoted to the students so effectively that many who initially may have had academic goals "appear to acquiesce in this"—"they will defend it, once they've made the choice," she said—even though some recognize that this will lead them to a relatively lower economic role in later years than if they somehow found the will to keep on and pursue a college education. "If you talk with them of college options at this point," and "if they trust you," said the teacher, "they will say, 'Nobody ever told me I could do it.' If you tell them, 'You could do it,' they will say, 'Why didn't someone tell me this before?'"

She told me she felt torn about expressing her concern that college   45
education as a possible career path for such students was, in her words, either "not presented" or else "undersold," because she said there were outstanding teachers in the work-related programs and she did not want to speak of them with disrespect or compromise their jobs. At the same time, she clearly was upset about this since she spoke with deep emotion of the likelihood that "we may be trapping these young ones" in "low-paying jobs."

The teacher's story of her brief encounter with her former student reminded me of the disappointment I had felt about Timeka. The teacher seemed to blame herself to some degree, wishing, I guess, that she could have remained in closer touch with this bright student in the months since she had been a pupil in her class, perhaps believing that she might have intervened somehow on her behalf. The teacher didn't speak of a career in cooking in a restaurant, or work in a hotel, with any hint of condescension or disparagement. She was simply cognizant of other possibilities her student might have entertained; and she was saddened by this memory.

NOTES

[1] I visited these schools in November 2002, following a preliminary visit in October 2001.

Poverty and racial data for both schools described: School Year Report Cards, Columbus City School District, 2003–2004 (race and poverty data from 2002–2003).

[2] This document, part of a self-described "comprehensive classroom management program" known as "Consistency Management and Cooperative Discipline," is published by Project Grad USA, based in Houston, Texas.

[3] Albert Shanker, American Federation of Teachers, cited in *Fortune*, November 7, 1988.

[4] *Young Man Luther*, by Erik Erikson (New York: Norton, 1962).

[5] *Wall Street Journal*, February 9, 1990.

[6] "Learning in America," a MacNeil/Lehrer Production, PBS, April 3, 1989.

[7] Clara Barton High School for Health Professionals (95 percent black and Hispanic) had 633 ninth graders and 301 twelfth graders in 2002–2003. Graphic Arts Communications High School (94 percent black and Hispanic) had 1,096 ninth graders and 199 twelfth graders. Metropolitan Corporate Academy (98 percent black and Hispanic) had 90 ninth graders and 55 twelfth graders, of whom 34 graduated in 2003. Metropolitan Corporate Academy was conceived as a partnership with the financial firm Goldman Sachs, which provided mentors and internships for students. A school's reliance on resources from the private sector carries risks of instability, however. After serious layoffs at Goldman Sachs in 2002, according

to Insideschools, an online service of Advocates for Children, "the number of mentors was cut in half." (Annual School Reports for all three schools, New York City Public Schools, 2002–2003 and 2003–2004; Insideschools 2002.)

[8]Of 294 ninth graders in the fall of 1999, only 60 remained as twelfth graders in 2003. White students made up 1.6 percent of the school's enrollment of 665. (Annual School Report for Health Opportunities High School, New York City Public Schools, 2002–2003; Common Core of Data, National Center for Education Statistics, U.S. Department of Education, 1999–2000 and 2002–2003.)

[9]Tim Barnicle, director of the Workforce Development Program at the National Center on Education and the Economy, Washington, D.C., in a letter to *Education Week*, February 3, 1999. "The most viable school-to-work partnerships," Mr. Barnicle writes, are "tied to high academic standards . . . , supported by business and industry partners that provide students with technical skills needed to succeed in a job. . . ." He concedes that "too often school-to-work" has not been "viewed as being connected to higher academic performance in the classroom," but nonetheless believes that career-embedded schools, if properly conceived, can improve retention and increase "access to postsecondary education."

[10]The program is sited at the Roberto Clemente High School. For racial demographics, see Illinois School Report Card for Roberto Clemente Community High School, 2002, and Roberto Clemente Community High School Profile 2003–2004, Chicago Public Schools, 2004.

[11]Interview with teacher (unnamed for privacy concerns), July 2003, and subsequent correspondence in 2004 and 2005.

[12]"Project Profile, Roberto Clemente Community Academy," Executive Service Corps of Chicago, 2002–2003. An early evaluation of the program is provided in "The Millennium Breach: The American Dilemma, Richer and Poorer," a report by the Milton S. Eisenhower Foundation and the Corporation for What Works, Washington, D.C., 1998.

FOR A SECOND READING

1. For many minority or low-income children in the United States today, school is primarily a dress rehearsal for one's future life on the job—what Kozol refers to as "vocational" or "utilitarian" learning. What do you think of this educational model? Are the market-driven roles Kozol describes the ones best for children to practice and master in school?

2. What do you make of the phrase "school-to-work"? In your view, does it suggest an approach to education that is legitimate or useful? Does it reflect the way we're usually taught to think about education? Can you think of an alternative term that would suggest an educational approach that is preferable?

3. Kozol describes visiting one kindergarten classroom in which posters of different retail stores (JCPenney, Wal-Mart, Kmart, Sears) were displayed. "'It's like working in a store,' a classroom aide explained. 'The children are learning to pretend that they're cashiers'" (p. 284). What, in your opinion, is either good or bad about this kind of educational setting? This particular lesson? Are these types of roles worth modeling?

PUTTING IT INTO WRITING

4. Here is a list of the job titles to which the students in the classroom Kozol observes can aspire: coat room manager; door manager; pencil sharpener manager; soap manager; eraser, board, and marker manager; and line manager. Write an essay in which you assess the particular kind of learning environment this classroom seems to offer. What rules and what roles are present for students and teachers alike? Do you find anything redeeming about this classroom model? Why or why not?

5. "A fashionable trend today," Kozol writes, "is to assign [schools] names related to the world of economics and careers"—names like "Academy of Enterprise" or "Corporate Academy" (p. 289). Write an essay in which you analyze how this practice might or might not represent a shift in the way we think about the purposes of education. How would you go about arguing in favor of this market-oriented approach to education? What advantages or benefits of this model would you play up?

COMPARING ARGUMENTS

6. From very different perspectives, Kozol and bell hooks (p. 274) invite readers to take a closer look at cultural stereotypes that inhibit genuine or meaningful learning. Write an essay in which you assess how these writers' respective commentaries compare. What particular stereotypes does each writer identify? What argument does each make about how these stereotypes undermine or inhibit learning? What conclusion or solution (if any) does each offer? And which do you find more convincing or compelling? Why?

FRANK BRUNI

Why College Rankings Are a Joke

Over the last two decades, *US News and World Report*'s annual release of its "Best Of" college rankings has become one of the most anticipated events on the academic calendar. But how much useful information do these lists actually provide? And perhaps even more importantly, what does our growing obsession with them say about the ways we've been taught to measure the value of our education? Taking up these questions, Frank Bruni argues that our current reliance on college rankings has led us astray. Guiding readers through a quick tour of nonelite schools, Bruni challenges the assumption that academic selectiveness and academic quality are one and the same. Frank Bruni is a longtime columnist for the *New York Times*. He is also the author of several books, including: *Ambling into History: The Unlikely Odyssey of George W. Bush* (2002); *Born Round: The Secret History of a Full-Time Eater* (2009); and *Where You Go Is Not Who You'll Be: An Antidote to the College Admissions Mania* (2015). The following piece originally appeared in the *New York Times* in 2015.

Before You Read

How much do rankings factor into your own thinking about college? In your view, do such rankings offer a valid measure of a school's true value?

SHORTLY BEFORE THE NEWEST *U.S. NEWS & WORLD REPORT* COLLEGE rankings came out last week, I got a fresh glimpse of how ridiculous they can be—and of why panicked high school seniors and their status-conscious parents should *not* spend the next months obsessing over them.

I was reporting a column on how few veterans are admitted to elite colleges and stumbled across a *U.S. News* sub-ranking of top schools for veterans. Its irrelevance floored me. It merely mirrored the general rankings—same institutions, same order—minus the minority of prominent schools that don't participate in certain federal education benefits for veterans.

It didn't take into account whether there were many—or, for that matter, *any*—veterans on a given campus. It didn't reflect what support for them did or didn't exist.

It was just another way to package and peddle the overall *U.S. News* rankings, illustrating the extent to which they're a marketing ploy. No wonder so many college presidents, provosts and deans of admissions express disdain for them. How sad that they participate in them nonetheless.

The rankings nourish the myth that the richest, most selective 5 colleges have some corner on superior education; don't adequately recognize public institutions that prioritize access and affordability; and do insufficient justice to the particular virtues of individual campuses.

Consider a school I visited this month, in conjunction with its 50th birthday: the University of Maryland, Baltimore County.

At the Starbucks in the middle of campus, I met a senior majoring in film. He has the usual Hollywood dreams but more than the usual optimism about making them come true. After all, a short movie that he wrote and directed as a sophomore got a showing at the Cannes Film Festival.

Later I spoke with a renowned mathematics professor, Manil Suri, who is also the openly gay author of an acclaimed sequence of novels set in India, where he was born, and who has contributed frequently to The Times. His conversations with undergraduates range far beyond algorithms.

I slipped into the arts center, completed just two years ago, where there's a stunning music hall with sumptuous acoustics and a theater of eye-popping technical sophistication.

I dropped in on Michael Summers, a biochemist who has done 10 pioneering research into retroviruses and H.I.V. He said that he'd never trade his faculty position here for one elsewhere, though he has been wooed, because of U.M.B.C.'s almost unrivaled record for guiding African-American undergraduates toward doctorates and other postgraduate degrees in STEM fields (science, technology, engineering and math).

"We're doing something that nobody else is doing," Summers told me. In a conversation with another journalist years ago, he put it this way: "If you see a group of black students walking together on a college campus, your first thought might be, 'Oh, there goes the basketball team.' Here you think, 'There goes the chemistry honors club, or the chess team.' It's just a different attitude."

The U.M.B.C. chess team has won the national college chess championship six times over the last 13 years. But Summers's remarks also reflect something else: In 1988, the school started the Meyerhoff Scholars Program, designed to address the paucity of minorities in STEM fields by giving generous financial aid and extensive mentorship to talented African-American students.

More than 1,100 men and women of all races have been through the program, typically going on to extraordinary careers. Summers and I chatted about one graduate we both knew, Isaac Kinde, who said no to Stanford in order to attend U.M.B.C. He recently completed a combined medical degree and doctorate at Johns Hopkins and is now at a biotech start-up.

"He has found a way to detect ovarian cancer with a Pap smear," Summers said. "That guy is going to revolutionize health care for women."

15   Four former Meyerhoff Scholars are on the faculty of Duke University's medical school, including Damon Tweedy, who wrote the 2015 best seller "Black Man in a White Coat: A Doctor's Reflections on Race and Medicine."

Duke is where Tweedy himself went to medical school, and he told me that although most of his classmates there were from colleges more selective than U.M.B.C. and families with more money than his, "I scored in the top 20 percent of my class during that first year of basic science classes, which are the toughest part of med school." U.M.B.C. had prepared him well, not just academically but also, he said, by making him feel that he was "part of something more than just your individual attainment."

> **The rankings nourish the myth that the richest, most selective colleges have some corner on superior education.**

He recalled that before he decided to go there, several Ivy League colleges tried to recruit him—for basketball. In contrast, he first came on to U.M.B.C.'s radar because of his aptitude for science.

More than one in four U.M.B.C. undergraduates qualifies for federal Pell grants, meant to serve low-income families. About 45 percent are white, while 18 percent are Asian-American and 16 percent are African-American.

From the ceiling of the student commons hang flags of countries from which students have come. There are more than 100. It's a kind of kaleidoscope, and as I walked under it with Freeman Hrabowski, U.M.B.C.'s dynamic president, he stressed the school's determination to "connect students to people different from themselves and lives different from their own." The young men and women who ate, talked or studied at almost every one of the tables around us were a mix of colors, and I couldn't map the room in terms of any obvious tribes or cliques.

20   Diversity, socioeconomic or otherwise, doesn't factor much into *U.S. News* rankings, though a broadening of perspectives lies at the heart of the best education. U.M.B.C., with its acceptance rate of nearly 60 percent, places 159th among national universities.

One of the main factors in a school's rank is how highly officials at peer institutions and secondary-school guidance counselors esteem it. But they may not know it well. They're going by its reputation, established in no small part by previous *U.S. News* evaluations. A lofty rank perpetuates itself.

Another main factor is the percentage of a school's students who graduate within six years. But this says as much about a school's selectiveness—the proven achievement and discipline of the students it admits—as about its stewardship of them.

Schools try to game the system and score better on additional criteria that go into their rank, though Robert Morse, the chief data strategist for *U.S. News*, told me in an email that the methodology had evolved so that "you cannot make a meaningful rise in the rankings by tweaking one or two numbers."

> **The rankings elevate clout above learning, which isn't as easily measured.**

He also noted, rightly, that the copious information that *U.S. News* collects about the student bodies and academic tracks at hundreds of schools produces a mother lode of useful facts and figures that go far beyond the numerical rankings.

But those rankings are front and center, fostering the idea that 25 schools are brands in competition with one another. The rankings elevate clout above learning, which isn't as easily measured.

Intentionally or not, they fuel a frenzy to get into the most selective schools. They can't adjust for how well certain colleges serve certain ambitions.

And they err. For the newest rankings, in what was obviously meant as an improvement, the sub-list for veterans included only schools at which 20 or more students were using G.I. Bill benefits.

But those benefits flow to *dependents* of veterans—their children, for example—as well as to veterans themselves. They're a fatally flawed metric. So M.I.T. is ranked second though it knows of only four veterans among its undergraduates. (I checked.) Duke is tied for third though it knows of only two.

These colleges' best-for-veterans triumphs still have no real relevance. There's a larger lesson in that.

FOR A SECOND READING

1. Bruni refers to the *U.S. News* college rankings as a "marketing ploy," which the magazine "packages and peddles" to its readers. How do you respond to this characterization? What does Bruni's language here suggest about how he views the magazine's motives for creating this type of list? Do you agree?

2. One of the major deficiencies of the current college ranking lists, Bruni writes, is that "they don't adequately recognize public

institutions that prioritize access and affordability" (p. 297). Do you agree? How important do you feel issues of "access" and "affordability" are in determining the suitability or overall value of a given school?

3. According to Bruni, "competition" is one of the key cultural norms underwriting our current college ranking system. Is this, in your view, a good thing? Should students be encouraged to view the college application process as a "competition" to be admitted by the so-called best school? Why or why not?

PUTTING IT INTO WRITING

4. "Diversity," writes Bruni, "socioeconomic or otherwise, doesn't factor much into *U.S. News* rankings, though a broadening of perspectives lies at the heart of the best education" (p. 298). In a 500-word essay, respond to the claims Bruni makes here. Do you agree that "a broadening of perspectives lies at the heart of the best education"? Why or why not? In your view, how much emphasis should college rankings place on "diversity"?

5. Bruni's critique of the college ranking system rests on his view that such lists underestimate or overlook the educational value of the schools they omit. Create a college ranking system that, in your view, would do a better job of accurately representing the educational value of different schools. What factors would this ranking system consider? Which of these metrics would be given the most emphasis? Which the least? Then, in an additional paragraph, explain why you feel this revised system would represent an improvement over the script that traditionally guides such rankings.

COMPARING ARGUMENTS

6. Bruni and Ben Casselman (p. 301) both make arguments that can be read as critiques of "elite" education. In a 500-word essay, discuss how these respective critiques compare. According to each, how is an "elite" education defined in our culture? What problems does this definition raise? What solution to these problems does each writer ultimately propose? And which solution, finally, do you find more persuasive? Why?

BEN CASSELMAN

Shut Up About Harvard

From academic brochures to Hollywood movies, we're all familiar with the classic vision of college life: stately brick buildings, leafy quads, unhurried and untroubled students. But how, asks Ben Casselman, do we deal with the fact that this deeply embedded stereotype gets the truth about college life so dramatically wrong? Offering readers a more realistic portrait of the schools most of today's college students actually attend, Casselman brings to light the issues and questions that our prevailing myths about college life encourage us to overlook. A former writer for the *Wall Street Journal*, Ben Casselman is a senior editor and chief economics correspondent for *FiveThirtyEight*, a website that features writing about politics, economics, and sports. This essay was published in *FiveThirtyEight* in 2016.

Before You Read

How do your own college experiences compare to the ways college life is typically portrayed in the media? Which differences strike you as most important?

IT'S COLLEGE ADMISSIONS SEASON, WHICH MEANS IT'S TIME ONCE again for the annual flood of stories that badly misrepresent what higher education looks like for most American students—and skew the public debate over everything from student debt to the purpose of college in the process.

"How college admissions has turned into something akin to 'The Hunger Games,'" screamed a *Washington Post* headline Monday. "What you need to remember about fate during college admission season," wrote *Elite Daily* earlier this month. "Use rejection to prepare teens for college," advised *The Huffington Post*.

Here's how the national media usually depicts the admissions process: High school seniors spend months visiting colleges; writing essays; wrangling letters of recommendation; and practicing, taking and retaking an alphabet soup of ACTs, SATs and AP exams. Then the really hard part: months of nervously waiting to find out if they are among the lucky few (fewer every year, we're told!) with the right blend of academic achievement, extracurricular involvement and an odds-defying personal story to gain admission to their favored university.

Here's the reality: Most students never have to write a college entrance essay, pad a résumé or sweet-talk a potential letter-writer. Nor are most, as *The Atlantic* put it Monday, "obsessively checking their mailboxes" awaiting acceptance decisions. (Never mind that for most schools, those decisions now arrive online.) According to data from the Department of Education,[1] more than three-quarters of U.S. undergraduates[2] attend colleges that accept at least half their applicants; just 4 percent attend schools that accept 25 percent or less, and hardly any—well under 1 percent—attend schools like Harvard and Yale that accept less than 10 percent.

5   Media misconceptions don't end with admission. "College," in the mainstream media, seems to mean people in their late teens and early 20s living in dorms, going to parties, studying English (or maybe pre-med) and emerging four years later with a degree and an unpaid internship. But that image, never truly representative, is increasingly disconnected from reality. Nearly half of all college students attend community colleges;[3] among those at four-year schools, nearly a quarter attend part time and about the same share are 25 or older. In total, less than a third of U.S. undergraduates are "traditional" students in the sense that they are full-time, degree-seeking students at primarily residential four-year colleges.[4]

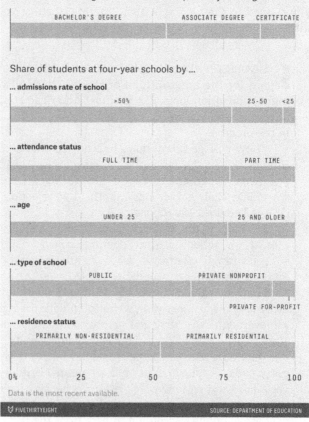

College doesn't always mean leafy campuses

Share of U.S. undergraduates at schools primarily offering ...

BACHELOR'S DEGREE   ASSOCIATE DEGREE   CERTIFICATE

Share of students at four-year schools by ...

... admissions rate of school

>50%   25-50   <25

... attendance status

FULL TIME   PART TIME

... age

UNDER 25   25 AND OLDER

... type of school

PUBLIC   PRIVATE NONPROFIT

PRIVATE FOR-PROFIT

... residence status

PRIMARILY NON-RESIDENTIAL   PRIMARILY RESIDENTIAL

0%   25   50   75   100

Data is the most recent available.

FIVETHIRTYEIGHT   SOURCE: DEPARTMENT OF EDUCATION

Of course, the readerships of the *Atlantic* and *Washington Post* probably don't mirror the U.S. as a whole. Many readers probably did attend selective institutions or have children they are hoping will. It's understandable that media outlets would want to cater to their readers, particularly in stories that aim to give advice to students or their parents.

But it's hard not to suspect that there is also another reason for reporters' focus on elite colleges: At least in major national media outlets, that's where most of them went. There's no definitive data on where reporters went to school, but the newsrooms of influential media outlets in New York and Washington, D.C., are full of graduates from Ivy League or similarly selective colleges. Those who attended public colleges often went to a handful of top research universities such as the University of Michigan or the University of California, Berkeley. FiveThirtyEight is just as bad: The vast majority of our editorial staff, including me, went to elite, selective colleges. (I went to Columbia.)

> **Here's the reality: Most students never have to write a college entrance essay, pad a résumé or sweet-talk a potential letter-writer.**

"Ninety-five percent of the newsroom probably went to private institutions, they went to four-year institutions, and they went to elite institutions," said Jeff Selingo, a longtime higher-education journalist who has a new book focused on giving advice to a broader group of students. "It is exactly the opposite of the experience for the bulk of American students."

It isn't just newsrooms. Hollywood is guilty of this too—think of a movie about college, and it probably took place on a leafy suburban campus. That's true even of movies that aren't set in the real world; when the writers of the Pixar film "Monsters University" wanted a model for their animated campus, they visited Harvard, MIT and Berkeley, according to *The Wall Street Journal*.[5] One result, Selingo said: "We tend to view higher education through the eyes of private higher education," even though nearly two-thirds of U.S. undergraduates[6] attend public institutions.

That myopia has real consequences for education policy. Based on media accounts, it would be easy to think that the biggest issues on U.S. campuses today are the spread of "trigger warnings," the rise of "hookup culture" and the spiraling cost of amenity-filled dorms and rec centers. Meanwhile, issues that matter to a far larger share of students get short shrift.

The media's focus on elite schools draws attention away from state cuts to higher-education funding, for example. Private colleges, which feature disproportionately in media accounts, aren't affected by state

10

budget cuts; top-tier public universities, which have outside resources such as alumni donations, research grants and patent revenue, are much less dependent on public dollars than less selective schools.

Or consider the breathless coverage of the college application game that few students ever play: For most students, or at least most high school graduates, getting into college isn't nearly as big a challenge as getting out. Barely half of first-time, full-time bachelor's degree students graduate within six years; for part-time or community college students, that share is even lower. But it took years for what is known in education jargon as "college completion" to break into mainstream education coverage, perhaps because at selective schools, the vast majority of students graduate on time or close to it.

Even issues that do get attention, such as student debt, are often covered through the lens of elite institutions. Reporters can't resist stories of students with eye-popping debt loads in the six figures. But many of those stories involve people who went to graduate school, most (though not all) of whom will end up making good salaries in the long run. Meanwhile, those who are struggling most to pay off loans are often those with smaller balances who either have degrees that don't help them find jobs (often from for-profit colleges) or who never got a degree in the first place. Nearly one in five Americans age 25 to 34 has some college credits but no degree,[7] and a growing share of them have student debt.

> **[I]t's hard not to suspect that there is also another reason for reporters' focus on elite colleges: At least in major national media outlets, that's where most of them went.**

"The biggest issue is that people can't afford to spend enough time in college to actually finish their darn degrees," said Sara Goldrick-Rab, a sociology professor and education-policy expert at the University of Wisconsin.[8]

15   What few journalists seem to understand, Goldrick-Rab said, is how tenuous a grasp many students have on college. They are working while in school, often juggling multiple jobs that don't readily align with class schedules. They are attending part time, which makes it take longer to graduate and reduces the chances of finishing at all. They are raising children, supporting parents and racking up debt trying to pay for it all.

"One little thing goes awry and it just falls apart," Goldrick-Rab said. "And the consequences of it falling apart when they're taking on all this debt are just so severe."

Students keep taking that risk for a reason: A college degree remains the most likely path to a decent-paying job. They aren't studying literary theory or philosophy; the most popular undergraduate majors in recent years have been business and health-related fields such as nursing.

Yet the public debate over whether college is "worth it," and the related conversation over how to make higher education more affordable, too often focuses on issues that are far removed from the lives of most students: administrative salaries, runaway construction costs, the value of the humanities. Lost in those discussions are the challenges that affect far more students: How to design college schedules to accommodate students who work, as more than half of students do;[9] how to make sure students keep their credits when they transfer, as more than a third of students do at least once; and, of course, how to make college affordable not just for the few who attend Harvard but for the many who attend regional public universities and community colleges.

NOTES

[1]Unless otherwise noted, all data in this article is from the Department of Education's College Scorecard database. Data is the most recent available.

[2]Degree-seeking undergraduates at four-year schools.

[3]Defined as schools offering primarily associate degrees or certificates.

[4]"Primarily residential" colleges are those where at least 25 percent of students live on campus.

[5]Thanks to Selingo for pointing out this anecdote.

[6]At four-year colleges.

[7]According to the Current Population Survey, via IPUMS.

[8]Goldrick-Rab is leaving Wisconsin for Temple University at the end of the academic year.

[9]CPS, via IPUMS.

FOR A SECOND READING

1. In his effort to present a more accurate picture of college life, Casselman cites a number of statistics: "Nearly half of all college students attend community colleges; among those at four-year schools, nearly a quarter attend part time and about the same share are 25 or older. In total, less than a third of U.S. undergraduates are 'traditional' students in the sense that they are full-time, degree-seeking students at primarily residential four-year colleges" (p. 304). How effective do you find Casselman's use of statistics to be? In what ways does such data challenge our preconceptions about what the typical college experience is like? Do you agree with Casselman that challenging these preconceptions is important?

2. Media images about college life, notes Casselman, are becoming "increasingly disconnected from reality" (p. 302). How much do you think this fact matters? In your view, what are the effects of living in a media environment that consistently misrepresents the "reality" of college life? Which effects seem to most concern Casselman?

3. "For most students," writes Casselman, "or at least most high school graduates, getting into college isn't nearly as big a challenge as getting out" (p. 304). To what extent do your own experiences confirm this claim? From your vantage, does remaining enrolled in (and ultimately graduating from) college represent a bigger challenge than being admitted to college in the first place? In your view, what are the main factors contributing to this problem?

PUTTING IT INTO WRITING

4. Cast yourself in the role of a college admissions officer whose job is to devise new standards for admitting applicants to your school. Then write an essay in which you describe and defend what these standards include. How much emphasis do these standards place upon traditional criteria like grades, class rank, and standardized test scores? What alternative criteria for measuring student eligibility do they propose? Why do you feel these standards are correct? What educational goals do they advance?

5. "Here," writes Casselman, is "how the national media usually depicts the admissions process: High school seniors spend months visiting colleges; writing essays; wrangling letters of recommendation; and practicing, taking and retaking an alphabet soup of ACTs, SATs and AP exams" (p. 301). In a 500-word essay, discuss how this description compares to your own experiences with the "admissions process." What tasks did you undertake to prepare yourself for college admission? How are they similar to or different from the tasks Casselman outlines here? And what, finally, would you say these tasks tell us about the true goals of the admissions process?

COMPARING ARGUMENTS

6. In Casselman's view, our overreliance on college rankings "skew[s] the public debate over everything from student debt to the purpose of college in the process" (p. 301). How do you think Frank Bruni (p. 296) would respond to this statement? Do you think Bruni would agree that the broader educational "debate" has become "skewed"? Given his own argument about the dangers and deficiencies of our current ranking system, how do you think Bruni would argue for our educational debate to be changed?

Then and Now: *Encyclopedic Knowledge*

For generations, the classic multivolume encyclopedia has epitomized what it means to be an educated person. Studded with dense descriptions and overviews of countless subjects — from astronomy to anatomy, geography to world history — these leather-bound tomes have long stood as tangible symbols of what we consider legitimate knowledge. Supporting these compendia of information were a number of unspoken assumptions: not only about the things we were expected to know, but also about the proper way we were expected to go about acquiring this knowledge. Widely respected as the arbiter of learning, the encyclopedia drew boundaries around what is and is not a worthwhile subject of study; and even more fundamentally, it conveyed a clear message about who was in charge of setting these boundaries. Legitimate knowledge, these monumental volumes implied, was not something we were allowed to define on our own; this task, rather, remained the purview of those with greater expertise and authority — namely, the experts and editors deemed educated enough to write the encyclopedia.

Neale Cousland/Shutterstock

With the explosion of digital technologies, however, many of these cherished norms have been turned on their head. Case in point: *Wikipedia*. As the latter half of the name implies, this site is designed to function as a comprehensive collection of entries on subjects of importance. On closer inspection, however, it becomes clear that the wiki does a good deal more than simply transpose old practices and old assumptions into a new century. Unlike the traditional encyclopedia, *Wikipedia* sets very different parameters around what constitutes legitimate knowledge. Rather than a collection of facts culled by a cadre of faceless experts, wikis offer themselves as clearinghouses for information to which virtually anyone — regardless of training, background, or expertise — can contribute. The prerogative to weigh in on a given subject — to present information — is not confined to so-called experts; it is an invitation, rather, for collaborative writing about subjects important to culture, revisable almost in real time. The result is not just a more democratic definition of knowledge, but also one that is far more fluid and dynamic — one that is constantly undergoing change as more and more contributors add to the body of information.

But are these changes for the better? To be sure, *Wikipedia* goes a long way toward broadening the range of information and perspectives that are allowed to be included: It makes great strides in reconfiguring research and knowledge sharing as collaborative undertakings, and it's interactive in ways that traditional encyclopedias aren't. But these changes give rise to important questions having to do with credibility and reliability of the information this new technology makes available. Are there adequate standards in place for determining what gets defined as legitimate knowledge? Have we lost a belief in the value of experts and expertise that perhaps we shouldn't have? What are the new norms, the new definitions, of education these sorts of changes have ushered in? Does this exciting new technology actually improve the ways we learn?

KAREN BLEIER/Getty Images

PUTTING IT INTO WRITING

1. How does technology such as *Wikipedia* redefine what it means to conduct research? Does knowing that the information contributed in a *Wikipedia* article comes from many anonymous sources change the way you evaluate its contents? Write a brief evaluation of the pros and cons of using *Wikipedia* versus a more traditional research source.

2. Pull up a *Wikipedia* article for a subject of your choosing that also has an entry in a traditional encyclopedia. Write a comparison of how each source treats the subject. Which is more useful to you, and why? What are the shortcomings of each source? In the end, does either source provide adequate information for research? Why or why not?

AARON HANLON
The Trigger Warning Myth

Few debates on campus these days elicit stronger reactions than those around the use of so-called trigger warnings. For some, the idea that students should be forewarned about class material they may find offensive or harmful reflects an ill-advised impulse to "coddle" them, the worst form of "political correctness." For others, such warnings represent an important effort to balance the educational goals of the classroom with the emotional and psychological needs of the students in it. Wading into this debate, Aaron Hanlon offers an impassioned defense of trigger warnings, arguing that — rather than pamper students — this practice can actually serve as a useful educational tool. Aaron Hanlon is an assistant professor of English at Colby College. This essay appeared in the *New Republic* in 2015.

Before You Read

Have you ever found yourself "triggered" by material you were required to read for class? What policies do you think should be in place for dealing with this possibility?

IN THE ATLANTIC'S LATEST COVER STORY, "THE CODDLING OF THE American Mind," Greg Lukianoff and Jonathan Haidt insinuate that trigger warnings and "vindictive protectiveness" are behind the college mental health crisis. "A movement is arising, undirected and driven largely by students, to scrub campuses clean of words, ideas, and subjects that might cause discomfort or give offense," they write, adding that a "campus culture devoted to policing speech and punishing speakers is likely to engender patterns of thought that are surprisingly similar to those long identified by cognitive behavioral therapists as causes of depression and anxiety. The new protectiveness may be teaching students to think pathologically." Which is just an academic way of saying that politically correct students are driving themselves crazy.

How have trigger warnings, of all things, been elevated to explanatory value akin to academic and professional pressures, increased accessibility to college, familial and broader economic pressures, reduced sleep, sexual assault epidemics, social media image policing, and any number of other factors that experts have identified as serious contributors to mental health problems on college campuses? I don't doubt that emotional coddling can play a negative role in the mental health of college students, and so is worth investigating. But I also think Lukianoff, the head of the Foundation for Individual Rights in Education, and Haidt, a social psychologist at the NYU-Stern School of Business, are granting certain practices of care on college campuses outsized and in some cases misleading roles in the mental health crisis.

I write this as a professor well outside of Haidt's field, from a pedagogical standpoint; which is to say from one of several very different kinds of caregiving roles on a college campus, one concerned primarily with students' intellectual development (as opposed to their general mental health in a clinical context). Our national conversations about trigger warnings and political correctness evince a troubling lack of awareness about what it actually looks like in real life to express sensitivities to college students about their apparently increasing anxieties and traumas. We're still getting trigger warnings wrong.

I never imagined becoming a defender of trigger warnings. This is the first time I've written (or spoken) the word "microaggressions" in recent memory. I have been and continue to be a proponent of the idea that the best way to handle wrongheadedness and hate speech is to address these with corrective speech, to present ideas, rationales, and evidence that overwhelm ignorance and bigotry with a blistering light. Accordingly, when vulgar or emotionally challenging material is part of the subject matter I'm responsible for teaching, or serves an otherwise specific pedagogical purpose, I'm not shy about it.

5   Here's a brief and by no means exhaustive list of things I've carefully selected for college syllabi and deliberately taught in college courses: a pair of poems about impotence and premature ejaculation; a satire about slaughtering human infants and feeding them to "persons of quality and fortune"; a poem that uses the c-word twice in a mere 33 lines, and describes King Charles II in coitus with his mistress with the phrase "his dull, graceless bollocks hang an arse"; a novel in which a wealthy man gets his maid to marry him by kidnapping her and continually cornering her with unwanted sexual advances; a graphic history of the torture methods and other cruelties done to African slaves leading up to the Haitian Revolution; a poem written in the voice of a male domestic servant and attempted rapist contacting his victim from prison.

The items on this list, and many others on my syllabi, could be censored by "social justice warriors" from the left,

> **Our national conversations about trigger warnings and political correctness evince a troubling lack of awareness about what it actually looks like in real life to express sensitivities to college students about their apparently increasing anxieties and traumas.**

310

since many of them could be triggering for students suffering from post-traumatic stress. In another context, however, they could be censored from the right, by people who tell the sexual assault survivor balking at a literary rape scene to "grow up," then turn around and oppose the teaching of sexually explicit material because it's "trash."

Simply put, leaving this stuff off the syllabus because it might be triggering is not an option.

In both cases, censoring this material is a bad idea, and providing context is the best avenue for explaining why. If you read the list above and wonder how or why any serious person would teach such material at a prestigious (and expensive) college, consider the authors behind the list. It includes works by major, canonical authors from antiquity to the eighteenth century, such as Ovid, Aphra Behn, Jonathan Swift, John Wilmot, Samuel Richardson, and Lady Mary Wortley Montagu. It also includes the historian C.L.R. James's *The Black Jacobins*, one of the definitive histories of the Haitian Revolution. Simply put, leaving this stuff off the syllabus because it might be triggering is not an option.

As I've explained elsewhere, however, I use trigger warnings in the classroom as a way of preparing students who may be suffering from post-traumatic stress disorder while also easing the entire class into a discussion of the material. The thinking behind the idea that trigger warnings are a form of censorship is fundamentally illogical: those who offer warnings, at our professional discretion, about potentially triggering material are doing so precisely because we're about to teach it! If we used trigger warnings to say, effectively, "don't read this, it's scary," then there'd be no need to warn in the first place; we'd just leave the material off the syllabus.

It's true that giving a warning runs the risk of students avoiding or 10 disengaging with the material out of fear of being triggered (in my three years of teaching, students have come to office hours to discuss sensitive material, but not one has left class or failed to turn in an assignment because of a trigger warning). If a student disengages, however, a professor still can (and should) follow up in a couple of ways. One is to have a private conversation with the student about the material, away from the pressures of the classroom; another is to take the student's response as an occasion to check in with the student and make sure they have access to campus mental health resources. Few of the media voices catastrophizing trigger warnings seem to understand that professors' interactions with students in the classroom and during office hours are some of the most important ways of catching mental health (or time management, or substance abuse) issues in our students that may need further attention. While the purpose of trigger warnings is not to screen for mental health problems, being attuned to how students are reacting to material, and prompting them to react to the hard stuff, can help us catch problems before they become real catastrophes.

For those of you who are imagining scores of students using professors' trigger warnings disingenuously, as a way to get out of class or a reading assignment, this isn't (for most of us) our first rodeo. Students use deception all the time, but an office hours summons is really all we need to determine whether the student might need help from a mental health professional, or was just trying to game the system. In most cases, however, when you warn students that something might be emotionally challenging or explicit, most of them do exactly what we do when someone tells us to watch out for something lurid: they become even more curious.

Lukianoff and Haidt view trigger warnings as ways of assuming negative outcomes despite the facts of the situation, a form of what they describe as "fortune-telling": "'predicting the future negatively' or seeing potential danger in an everyday situation." Further, for Lukianoff and Haidt, trigger warnings are ways of enabling those who do suffer from PTSD to disengage, counterproductively, from the harsh realities of the world. They view trigger warnings, in other words, as not only a form of censoring what professors can teach, but of censoring students' experience of real life. But trigger warnings don't need to be the end of a difficult conversation; more often they're actually the beginning of one.

Lukianoff and Haidt define trigger warnings as "alerts that professors are expected to issue if something in a course might cause a strong emotional response." Note the syntax of this sentence, which presents trigger warnings not as something professors choose to do in environments that we control, but as something externally imposed upon us ("are expected to issue"). This way of describing trigger warnings is an example of a tactic we see used widely to critique trigger warnings while portraying college students as a bunch of paradoxically terrifying wimps.

> **[T]rigger warnings don't need to be the end of a difficult conversation; more often they're actually the beginning of one.**

Lukianoff and Haidt provide a series of such examples, from the viral Vox essay "I'm a Liberal Professor, and My Liberal Students Terrify Me" to the complaints of Jerry Seinfeld that young people are so threateningly soft that he won't play at college campuses. The implication here is that students are at once too thin-skinned to withstand discussions of Ovid or rape law or gay jokes, and powerful to the extent that their demands for trigger warnings must be heeded by professors, university administrations, and visiting comedians.

15   Between these two extremes—of teachers buckling under students' demands and of teachers coddling oversensitive students—there's the reality of teaching. While a miniscule number of colleges and universities have gone so far as to codify trigger warnings for professors, most trigger

warnings exist as a pedagogical choice that professors make in situations over which we exercise considerable control. (And have existed as such for much longer than the present debate suggests: While "trigger warning" was not part of my vocabulary as an undergraduate, introductory comments like "we're going to spend some time today on lynching images, so prepare yourselves for graphic and difficult material" were indeed.)

Professors give warnings of all sorts that, when not explicitly entangled in the national politics of political correctness, amount less to coddling than to minimizing chances of disengagement with material. "Block off more time this weekend than you usually do, since the reading for Monday is a particularly long one," for instance, is a reasonable way of reducing the number of students who show up unprepared by issuing a warning. "Today we're discussing a poem about rape, so be prepared for some graphic discussion, and come to office hours if you have things to say about the poem that you're not comfortable expressing in class," meanwhile, is a similarly reasonable way of relieving the immediate pressure to perform in class, which stresses out so many students.

Those of us who occasionally use trigger warnings are not as naïve as we're made out to be.

Those of us who occasionally use trigger warnings are not as naïve as we're made out to be; we understand that there is no magical warning that will assuage all anxieties and protect students from all traumas, nor is there a boilerplate trigger warning or trigger warning policy that professors can be reasonably expected to follow formulaically. Rather, trigger warnings are, in practice, just one of a set of tools that professors use with varying degrees of formality to negotiate the give-and-take of classroom interactions. If you take away the media hysteria surrounding trigger warnings, you're left with a mode of conversational priming that we all use: "You might want to sit down for this"; "I'm not sure how to say this, but . . ." It's hardly anti-intellectual or emotionally damaging to anticipate that other people may react to traumatic material with negative emotions, particularly if they suffer from PTSD; it's human to engage others with empathy. It's also human to have emotional responses to life and literature, responses that may come before, but in no way preclude, a dispassionate analysis of a text or situation.

I'm not blind to the problems with trigger warnings and hyperbolic political correctness. The examples Lukianoff and Haidt cite are alarming: Harvard law students asking professors not to use the word "violate"; Brandeis students calling even critical acknowledgment of racial stereotypes of Asian-Americans "microaggressions"; Northwestern professor Laura Kipnis being accused of Title IX violations for an article she wrote for *The Chronicle of Higher Education*. But I'm not convinced that we can lay these problems—and by extension, adverse developments in the mental health of college students—at the feet of trigger warnings.

20   The backlash against trigger warnings is part of a larger iteration of backlash against political correctness, which tells us something important about where the public thinks the power lies. People on the margins may get press for tweeting things like "kill all white men," and the occasional professor may be undeservedly shamed or ousted for running afoul of students with certain P.C. language expectations. In both scenarios, however, the heart of the matter is who holds the authority to choose the best (or worst) course of action. The P.C. backlash and the trigger-warning backlash hold a common fallacy: They see pushback from the margins and mistake it for threats to the most institutionally powerful.

"Kill all white people" is a despicable sentiment, but in practice it's not white people who face the gravest threats of being gunned down by those who wield the authority to do so. Similarly, students can demand trigger warnings or sensitivity trainings, but students remain more vulnerable to institutional power than the professors who assign their grades or the administrators who adjudicate their missteps. And if there exist situations in which professors really are "terrified" by our students, and students are actually lapsing into mental distress because we're too afraid to cross them, then the problem is much bigger than trigger warnings. The problem is mistrusting the experience and authority of professors in our roles as teachers and intellectual caregivers. If we can lose our jobs either for teaching traumatic material or for failing to warn students adequately about it, what's really happening here isn't that we're ruining students by coddling them; we're losing the authority we rely on to be sensitive to students' anxieties without giving into them, to use techniques like trigger warnings judiciously without being forced to use them in some generalized and codified way.

The trigger warning problem isn't actually a trigger warning problem; it's what happens when the messy business of teaching and learning, and the complex challenges to students' mental well-being, become flashpoints in the culture wars. The effect of this entanglement is an exaggerated impression of trigger warnings that draws on the most extreme examples, a tactic that mirrors and plays into the very currents of partisan politics that Lukianoff and Haidt lament as a threat to American democracy. Of course, the authors consider trigger warnings to be "bad for American democracy," too, and call on universities to "officially and strongly discourage" them. Instead of seeking new sources of outrage around trigger warnings, though, we should understand more thoroughly why this particular pedagogical choice, one of so many, has become a national wedge issue. That trigger warnings are rare, and may be of occasional benefit to professors like me who employ them, is too inconvenient a reality for those who are busy waging war on political correctness.

FOR A SECOND READING

1. In making the case for how controversial or offensive material should be taught in the classroom, Hanlon draws a distinction between "censorship" and "context." How persuasive do you find this distinction to be? Do you agree with Hanlon that the best approach for such material is not to censor it but rather to provide a fuller context for it? Why or why not?

2. "The trigger warning problem," writes Hanlon, "isn't actually a trigger warning problem; it's what happens when the messy business of teaching and learning, and the complex challenges to students' mental well-being, become flashpoints in the culture wars. The effect of this entanglement is an exaggerated impression of trigger warnings that draws on the most extreme examples, a tactic that mirrors and plays into [the] currents of partisan politics" (p. 314). Analyze the language Hanlon uses here. Why do you think he characterizes what happens within the classroom as a "messy business"? What point is he trying to make by using terms like "exaggerated," "extreme," and "partisan" to describe the views of trigger warning opponents?

3. In defending the use of trigger warnings, Hanlon writes: "It's hardly anti-intellectual or emotionally damaging to anticipate that other people may react to traumatic material with negative emotions . . . it's human to engage others with empathy" (p. 313). Do you share Hanlon's view? Do you agree that "anticipating" students' "negative emotions" can serve as constructive educational strategy? Why or why not?

PUTTING IT INTO WRITING

4. Hanlon writes: "I have been and continue to be a proponent of the idea that the best way to handle wrongheadedness and hate speech is to address these with corrective speech, to present ideas, rationales, and evidence that overwhelm ignorance and bigotry with a blistering light" (p. 310). Write a description of the classroom rules you would create to ensure that this kind of free and fair exchange could occur. What limits would these rules put on speech that expresses "ignorance" or "bigotry"? What guidelines would they create for how others might respond to such expressions with "corrective speech" of their own? And why, finally, do you think these rules are appropriate?

5. Hanlon writes: "Between [the] two extremes—of teachers buckling under students' demands and of teachers coddling oversensitive students—there's the reality of teaching. While a miniscule

number of colleges and universities have gone so far as to codify trigger warnings for professors, most trigger warnings exist as a pedagogical choice that professors make in situations over which we exercise considerable control" (pp. 312–313). First, describe the particular situations you feel it would be most appropriate for a professor to "exercise" the "choice" to use a trigger warning. Next, explain the reasons behind why you believe this policy would be appropriate and/or helpful in these situations.

COMPARING ARGUMENTS

6. In a similar vein, Ferentz Lafargue (p. 317) weighs in on the debate over safe spaces and microaggressions on college campuses. How does his discussion compare to Hanlon's? Do you think Lafargue would regard Hanlon's defense of trigger warnings to be in line with his own vision of what classroom teaching and learning should look like? In your view, what aspects of Hanlon's essay support or reinforce Lafargue's argument? What aspects challenge or complicate it?

FERENTZ LAFARGUE
Welcome to the "Real World"

Among a growing number of educational observers, we increasingly hear concerns about how "coddled," how insulated from the challenges of the "real world," today's generation of college students is becoming. As proof, these commentators point to the rise of campus policies like those designed to combat "microaggressions" or create "safe spaces." But according to Ferentz Lafargue, the argument against such initiatives is really just a surrogate for addressing a deeper set of questions: about the true purpose of college, the barriers preventing equal access to higher education, and the role of free speech in an increasingly diverse society. Bringing these deeper questions to light, Lafargue makes the case that "pampered" students are less the problem than are the broader demographic challenges that define the world beyond the classroom. Ferentz Lafargue is the director of the Center for Cultural Engagement at Catholic University. He previously served in a similar capacity at Williams College. This essay was published in the *Washington Post* in 2016.

Before You Read

Given your own experiences as a college student, how important do you think it is to create campus "safe spaces"? In your view, what educational goal should this kind of policy promote?

> "The imaginary college student is a character born of someone else's pessimism. It is an easy target, a perverse distillation of all the self-regard and self-absorption ascribed to what's often called the millennial generation. But perhaps it goes both ways, and the reason that college stories have garnered so much attention this year is our general suspicion, within the real world, that the system no longer works."
>
> —Hua Hsu, "The Year of the Imaginary College Student," *The New Yorker*,
> Dec. 31, 2015

IN THE WORK THAT I DO AS A DIVERSITY ADVOCATE IN HIGHER education, I hear often a concern that some of our efforts in pursuit of equity may be doing students a disservice—that we're not preparing them for the "real world."

The implied logic is that if students feel empowered to voice their discontent with microaggressions experienced on campus, then they're not developing the thick skin necessary to deal with the slights they'll see in the workplace, out in the "real world."

Students should "toughen up," and we should stop "coddling" them, we're told.

I've heard these sentiments expressed about the college's efforts to counsel students against donning offensive Halloween costumes, the distribution of a "Pronouns Matter" pamphlet last fall and in more general discussions about what constitutes a "safe space" on campus.

5 To be sure, the real world is full of anti-Semitism, homophobia, sexism and racism. The question is: Do we prepare students to accept the world as it is, or do we prepare them to change it?

Telling students either explicitly or implicitly that they should grin and bear it is the last thing one should do as an educator. Yet that is essentially the gospel that the "wait until the real world" parishioners would have many of us adopt.

The purpose of a college experience isn't to make students feel as if they are in a well-insulated bubble. Just as depictions of a typical college student as a video game-addicted humanities major who uses the pronoun "they" and abides by a strict gluten-free diet disregards the lived experiences of countless students, so too do any allusions that colleges are idyllic enclaves.

Enrolling at Williams for example, does not immediately reshape all students' lives into concentric circles with Frosh Quad at their center. Instead, each student has a Venn diagram-like series of circles of their families, previous neighborhoods, schools and friend groups, all bartering for space among 2,100 other students.

> **To be sure, the real world is full of anti-Semitism, homophobia, sexism and racism. The question is: Do we prepare students to accept the world as it is, or do we prepare them to change it?**

Over the last five years, to help mitigate some of the tensions that are bound to arise from this complex configuration, staff members at the Davis Center have been leading workshops on social identity formation and facilitation as part of the spring and fall training sessions for Junior Advisors. These trainings are complemented by an array of events during First Days that seek to provide the entering class an introduction to the identities and perspectives they are likely to encounter at Williams.

10 Virtually every entering class arrives on campus better versed on issues related to gender, race and sexuality than their predecessors. Challenges posed by trying to keep up with the pace of this ever changing community partly explain why college students are such fraught discursive subjects.

Rapidly shifting demographics, an evolving language of gender and sexual identity so vibrant it would make Hilda Doolittle [a modernist poet known for challenging gender norms] proud, are but just two of the factors pushing colleges through existential dilemmas.

There are broader questions as well, such as: Is college a place for intellectual exploration? Or is it a glorified worker-training program?

We are not immune to these debates here at Williams, and some of our students and their families bear the weight more than others.

Students whose families are facing financial distress often feel guilty about engaging in any pursuit that is not alleviating their family's hardships. The decisions these students are forced to make range from deciding whether to take time off from school to find jobs so they can better support their families to choosing majors based on projected earning expectations immediately after graduation.

Moreover, for some students these debates are about far more than 15 college; they represent yet another variable in trying to understand how and where they fit in society.

Therefore, whether one is suspicious of the merits of college as a whole or cynical about the existence of "safe spaces," the truth of the matter is that "coddled" college students aren't the problem.

The real culprits—on campuses and in the real world—are the persistent effects of homophobia, income inequality, misogyny, poverty, racism, sexism, white supremacy and xenophobia.

When students refuse to accept discrimination on college campuses, they're learning important lessons about how to fight it everywhere.

> *[W]hether one is suspicious of the merits of college as a whole or cynical about the existence of "safe spaces," the truth of the matter is that "coddled" college students aren't the problem.*

FOR A SECOND READING

1. According to Lafargue, many observers characterize today's generation of college students as "coddled," and living within a "well-insulated bubble." Take a moment to analyze this language more specifically. What vision of college students, and college life more generally, do descriptors like these suggest? How accurately does this vision describe you or your own experiences?

2. Speaking about life on the campus where he used to work, Lafargue writes: "[E]ach student has a Venn diagram-like series of circles of their families, previous neighborhoods, schools and friend groups, all bartering for space among 2,100 other students" (p. 318). Why do

you think he makes this observation? How does it serve to advance his larger argument about diversity, free speech, and the educational mission of college? Do you think this observation succeeds in accomplishing this goal? Why or why not?

3. "[F]or some students," Lafargue claims, "these debates [over campus safe spaces] are about far more than college; they represent yet another variable in trying to understand how and where they fit in society" (p. 319). How do you respond to this claim? Does it make sense to you that "debates" over safe spaces or microaggressions can serve as a vehicle for figuring out where students "fit in society"? Why or why not?

PUTTING IT INTO WRITING

4. "Telling students either explicitly or implicitly that they should grin and bear [offensive language or behavior]," writes Lafargue, "is the last thing one should do as an educator" (p. 318). Write a 500-word essay in which you evaluate and respond to this claim. Why does Lafargue believe this particular message is so unacceptable? What does he argue should be an educator's response instead? Do you agree? In your view, is advice to "grin and bear" uncomfortable or offensive behavior antithetical to the goals of education?

5. Lafargue cites some examples from his own campus of initiatives that many educational critics find most objectionable: "[E]fforts to counsel students against donning offensive Halloween costumes, the distribution of a 'Pronouns Matter' pamphlet last fall . . . and general discussions about what constitutes a 'safe space' on campus" (p. 318). Cast yourself in the role of a college administrator. What argument could you make that such initiatives are necessary? What limits or guidelines would you recommend for how these initiatives should be implemented?

COMPARING ARGUMENTS

6. Lafargue concludes his essay by making the following statement: "When students refuse to accept discrimination on college campuses, they're learning important lessons about how to fight it everywhere" (p. 318). How do you think Aaron Hanlon (p. 309) would respond to this statement? Given what he says about trigger warnings, do you think he would endorse Lafargue's contention that college campuses should be at the vanguard of fighting discrimination in the wider society? Why or why not?

Scenes and Un-Scenes: **Looking at Learning**

How do we define what learning looks like? What a good education looks like? Underneath every definition of the ideal school, every vision of the perfect teacher or model student, there lies an even more fundamental vision: of what it means to be truly educated. Think for a moment about all of the different material promoted in our culture that, in one way or another, claims to answer this question. There are all of the advice books, offering parents and educators "expert" instruction on how to enhance kids' learning. There are all of the "enrichment" games, toys, and programs currently on the market. There are all of the TV shows — from *Dora the Explorer* to *Sesame Street* to *Mr. Rogers' Neighborhood* — that model the proper way of "doing school." Whatever its individual purview, each of these can be understood as an effort to script for us the standards and ideals that define "real" education. Each of the following examples invites you to conduct this kind of analysis: to decode the vision of learning, the model of schooling each presents.

Though school environments like the one pictured here are less and less the norm (with the advent of pods and grouping), nonetheless this stereotype of school remains relevant. How many scripts can you spot here regarding teacher authority, student interaction, learning styles, and so on?

Tim Boyle/Getty Images

▲▲ *Much debate on U.S. education focuses not only on what is taught but also on the environment in which it is taught, including concerns about school security. What do images like this make you think about learning environments today? How does this shift the norm from the previous photo?*

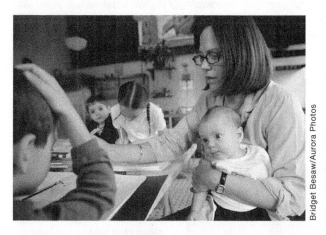

Bridget Besaw/Aurora Photos

▲▲ *We are much more likely today to think of educational environments as diverse. This photo shows a mother homeschooling her children. What strikes you as inherently different about this environment versus those that we more commonly associate with school?*

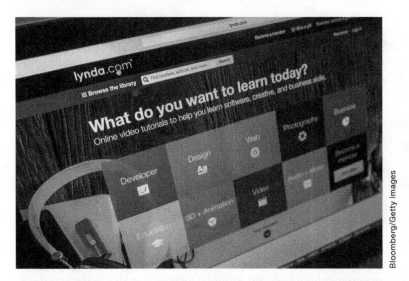

Bloomberg/Getty Images

More and more our education these days is being mediated through computer screens. From *TED Talks* to *Kahn Academy*, massive open online courses (MOOCs) to for-profit online universities, "doing school" is becoming for many an increasingly digital experience. How do you evaluate this shift? Do you find the transition toward digital learning to be an improvement over the more traditional ways of "doing school"? Why or why not?

Leren Lu/Getty Images

Photos like this one show how our culture values learning by even the youngest children before they enter formal schooling. How does this photo present the learning process? Are there any elements of this photo that critics who oppose pushing children into formal learning too soon would alter?

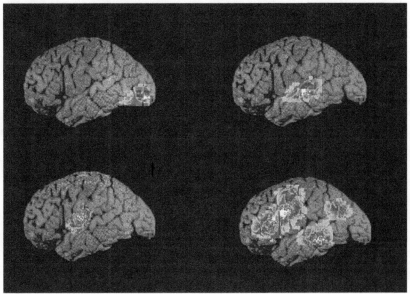

WDCN/Univ. College London/Science Source

▲ *This photo shows activity in the brain during the learning process.*
▲ *Without any knowledge of the environment or context for the*
learning process shown here, how does this photo change your
impression of what learning looks like?

FOR A SECOND READING

1. Which of these images best captures your experiences in school? Which of them would you most want to use as a model for rewriting the scripts by which your experiences as a student unfolded?

2. Do you think any of these depictions promote educational messages that are problematic or dangerous?

3. Are there any educational ideals that you think this collection of images leaves out? If so, what are they? And what, in your view, makes them so valuable?

PUTTING IT INTO WRITING

4. Choose a television show or movie that sketches a portrait of modern school life. How does it depict school? What specific aspects of schooling (e.g., school rules, teacher or student behavior, and so on) get idealized? Which satirized? Write an essay in which you analyze the practices and standards this portrait presents as

the ideal. How do they compare with the images of school or learning shown in this feature?

5.   Make a list of all the different aspects of contemporary education that you think this collection could critique. Then write an essay in which you identify a particular question or issue that does not get raised or referenced in this collection. What is it, and why in your view does it merit particular focus? Can you find an image of this issue that you would include to better balance this set?

COMPARING ARGUMENTS

6.   Choose one of the images above, one whose depiction clearly lays out an alternative model of schooling. Then choose the writer in this chapter whose own critique of conventional education most closely mirrors this model. Write an essay in which you compare and contrast the specific features within each of these alternative visions.

Acting Like a Citizen: **Educational Scripts**

The selections assembled in this chapter make clear how many of our individual choices as students can be scripted for us in advance. But they make equally clear how the act of "choosing for ourselves" allows us to challenge such scripts, or even rewrite them to better serve our own interests. Undertaking such work is at the heart of what it means to "act like a citizen." The following exercises give you an opportunity to do just this, inviting you to consider your own views and values about education, and to apply them to the educational world of which you are a part.

QUIZZING TEACHERS   Prepare an interview questionnaire about attitudes toward teaching and education and ask an instructor, teacher, or education major you know to complete it. Here are some suggested questions: *What do you like most about teaching? Least? What are the biggest challenges you face as an educator? What do you believe is the purpose of education? What do you believe is most important for your students to know?* Feel free to ask any other questions you might think of. When you get his or her answers, write an essay in which you analyze the responses based on what you think are the most common ways we think of education in our culture. How do the answers reflect this common thinking? Where do they differ? Do any of the responses echo the critiques or anxieties of any of the authors in this chapter?

DOING YOUR HOMEWORK   Choose some educational issue or controversy that is currently being publicly debated: the value of standardized testing, the growing cost of higher education, and so on. First, research this issue as thoroughly as you can. What are the key points of disagreement? What questions or issues does it involve? What people, organizations, or interest groups are on each side? If you were asked to pick a side in the debate, which would it be, and why? Then read an article that engages this debate and write a description of your observations and responses.

GRADING THE IMPACT   Choose one of the educational issues discussed by the writers included in this chapter and write a personal essay in which you discuss how this issue has impacted your life as a student. What new insight have you gained by reading further about this issue? How do you view your education differently? If you could, what would you change about your education?

WHO'S HELPED BY RAISING THE MINIMUM WAGE?

WHAT PEOPLE THINK

Teenager

Works part time after school

Lives with parents

Earning extra spending money

THE REALITY

Average age:
35 years old

88% are not teens.
They're 20 or older

**36% are
40 or older**

**56% are
women**

28% have children

**55% work
full time**

On average, they
**earn half of their
family's total income**

Note: Statistics describe civilian workers, ages 16+, that would be affected by an increase in the federal minimum wage to $10.10 over three years, as explained in *Raising the federal minimum wage to $10.10 would give working families, and the overall economy, a much-needed boost.* The median age of affected workers is 31 years old. **Visit epi.org/issues/minimum-wage for more details.**

ECONOMIC POLICY INSTITUTE

This infographic was created by the Economic Policy Institute (EPI), a nonprofit, nonpartisan think tank based in Washington, DC, which focuses on policies designed to serve the needs of low- and middle-income workers. Take a closer look at this text. Then answer the following questions:

➲ How does this infographic invite viewers to think about the challenges confronting the working poor?

➲ To what extent does it challenge cultural norms about income, work, and/or poverty in America?

➲ How would you characterize its message about the minimum wage? In your view, is this infographic advocating for a change in the federal minimum wage policy?

➲ What specific elements in this website would you point to as evidence of this?

5 How We
WORK
What Do Our Jobs Say About Us?

Introduction

RULES AND ROLES/REWARDS AND PUNISHMENTS

Think back to your last job. Perhaps you waited on tables, made cold calls as a telemarketer, or gave guided tours at a museum. Or maybe you worked construction, delivered pizza, or interned at a nonprofit. Whatever the case, it likely came as no surprise that the job you held carried with it clear instructions, regulations, and requirements. Whether white-collar, blue-collar, or no-collar, every job is defined by its own set of rules, laying out in specific detail what we are and are not permitted to do. Usually, for example, we are told up front what tasks we have to perform and how much we're going to get paid to complete them. Other expectations are laid out less overtly: the norms, for instance, about how employees interact with bosses or dress appropriately for their jobs. Whether formal or informal, overt or implied, however, all of these rules share one thing: They are set in stone long before we ever step behind the counter, sit down at a desk, pick up a shovel, or type our first word on the computer.

We adhere to these rules, of course, because we *have* to. Following scripts we had no hand in creating ourselves, we all know, is an expected and nonnegotiable part of the job. And yet while undoubtedly true, this explanation is also incomplete. The rules of work are more than just marching orders we have no choice but to obey simply because we can't think of any alternative. It is more accurate, in fact, to think of these rules as *transactions* or *bargains* in which we choose to adopt a particular role or conform to a particular script in exchange for a payoff that we've decided makes doing so worth it. From the perks or promotions dangled in front of us to the threats of reprimand or dismissal we face, the truth is that our day-to-day lives on the job are shaped less by a set of abstract rules per se than by a set of very tangible rewards and punishments. When we go along with the office mandate to wear "standard business attire" or accede to our supervisor's reminder to "always wear a smile," we're doing so not because we are mindless robots or powerless pawns, but rather because we have made the calculation that such compliance is in our better interest. When reframed in cost/benefit terms, a slightly different set of questions emerges: On what basis do we decide what is and is not in our better interest? When it comes to work, what standards do we use to make our choices? And how do we know whether or not these standards are right?

What is normal?

Pacific Press/Getty Images

What does this image ask you to believe? What are the ideas/values/attitudes it asks you to accept as normal?

SELLING SUCCESS, SCRIPTING FAILURE

As we consider these questions, it's useful to keep in mind that the standards we use to make our decisions about work are partly shaped by the wider pop culture around us. Think back to the number of TV shows and websites, movies, and commercials you've seen over the last few months that convey some type of message about the world of work. It's difficult, for example, to come away from a reality show like *Shark Tank* without thinking that being a corporate CEO is a more worthwhile pursuit than being a nurse, a social worker, or a high school teacher. Whether we embrace this kind of lesson or resist it, whether it accurately reflects our personal values or drastically misrepresents them, it is undeniable that our pop culture plays an important role in shaping the standards by which we are expected to measure the value of work.

Indeed, we may be drawn to pop culture generalizations about work precisely *because* they're stereotypes — because they take a situation that otherwise would feel complicated and messy, and render it disarmingly simple. It's no easy task to figure out what really makes work satisfying, meaningful, or valuable. While commercials depict corporate boardrooms filled with zany pranksters and free-thinking individuals, construction sites populated by truck-driving he-men, and insurance offices staffed with empathetic, dedicated salespeople, we know on some level that these images don't supply us with scripts that adequately explain the true meaning or value of work. Rather than take these messages at face value, our job is to question the kinds of social scripts they create and the cultural norms they reinforce: to ask whether they are helpful or harmful, whether they crowd out other, more valid ways to measure our personal value.

Each of the essays collected here presents readers with some version of this question, inviting us to look more closely at the places where issues of work and questions of self-worth most powerfully intersect. The first two pieces accomplish this goal by taking a closer look at the rules, norms, and scripts that define the world of manual or blue-collar work. Relating his own experiences moving from a white-collar "think tank" position to a job as a motorcycle mechanic, Matthew Crawford challenges the way that employment in the "trades" are devalued in relation to

What is normal?

"I always say: Moms have the toughest job in the world."

Talk-show host and superstar Oprah Winfrey

Do you share this belief? Should we automatically accept it as normal?

What is normal?

"200+ Million Members. Manage Your Professional Identity. Build and Engage with Your Professional Peers."

From the home page of LinkedIn, a professional networking website

What kind of social script does this quotation create? What would it feel like to act out this script in our personal lives?

the work of sitting behind a desk. Mac McClelland, meanwhile, uncovers the darker side of manual work, taking her readers on a guided tour of life in the "modern-day sweatshop" of shipping fulfillment work.

The next pair of selections drills more deeply into the costs and inequities confronting those on the lowest rungs of the socioeconomic ladder. Barbara Ehrenreich chronicles many of the hidden costs — both social and financial — our society imposes on the working poor, while Linda Tirado provides a bracing firsthand account of what it means to survive as a minimumwage worker.

Adopting a contemporary perspective, Emily Badger and Catherine Rampell share their insights about the ways that work is being redefined *for* and *by* the millennial generation. Badger turns a critical eye to the emerging gig economy, posing provocative questions about what happens in a world where "we all become our own bosses." Rampell, meanwhile, urges readers to rethink the myths and stereotypes that have scripted young Americans as the "slacker generation."

What is normal?

"A brand for a company is like a reputation for a person. You earn reputation by trying to do hard things well."

Jeff Bezos, founder of Amazon

Can social scripts be rewritten? Are there alternative norms to those described here?

The final two selections, by Maddie Oatman and Mike Rose, round out this chapter by uncovering some of the embedded, and problematic, social norms that define the world of "service work." Oatman shines a light on some of the race- and class-based assumptions embedded in the practice of restaurant tipping, while Rose argues passionately about (and against) the false assumptions we are taught to make about the intellectual caliber of service work in general.

MATTHEW CRAWFORD
The Case for Working with Your Hands

In our hyperactive, information-based economy, it's easy to assume that any work involving manual skill has become obsolete. According to Matthew B. Crawford, however, ours may well be the moment where precisely such work is most urgently needed. Taking a critical look at current cultural conceits about "knowledge work," he offers a spirited defense of what he calls "working with your hands." Crawford lives in Richmond, Virginia, and is a fellow at the Institute for Advanced Studies in Culture at the University of Virginia. He is the author of the books *Shop Class as Soulcraft: An Inquiry into the Value of Work* (2009) and *The World Beyond Your Head: On Becoming an Individual in an Age of Distraction* (2015). The following essay appeared in the May 21, 2009, issue of the *New York Times Magazine*.

Before You Read

What associations do you bring to the term "manual labor"? Do your views on this topic derive from personal experience? Popular culture? A combination of both?

THE TELEVISION SHOW *DEADLIEST CATCH* DEPICTS COMMERCIAL crab fishermen in the Bering Sea. Another, *Dirty Jobs*, shows all kinds of grueling work; one episode featured a guy who inseminates turkeys for a living. The weird fascination of these shows must lie partly in the fact that such confrontations with material reality have become exotically unfamiliar. Many of us do work that feels more surreal than real. Working in an office, you often find it difficult to see any tangible result from your efforts. What exactly have you accomplished at the end of any given day? Where the chain of cause and effect is opaque and responsibility diffuse, the experience of individual agency can be elusive. *Dilbert, The Office,* and similar portrayals of cubicle life attest to the dark absurdism with which many Americans have come to view their white-collar jobs.

Is there a more "real" alternative (short of inseminating turkeys)?

High-school shop-class programs were widely dismantled in the 1990s as educators prepared students to become "knowledge workers." The imperative of the last 20 years to round up every warm body and send it to college, then to the cubicle, was tied to a vision of the future in which we somehow take leave of material reality and glide about in a pure information economy. This has not come to pass. To begin with, such work often feels more enervating than gliding. More fundamentally, now as ever, somebody has to actually do things: fix our cars, unclog our toilets, build our houses.

When we praise people who do work that is straightforwardly useful, the praise often betrays an assumption that they had no other options. We idealize them as the salt of the earth and emphasize the sacrifice for others their work may entail. Such sacrifice does indeed occur—the hazards faced by a lineman restoring power during a storm come to mind. But what if such work answers as well to a basic human need of the one who does it? I take this to be the suggestion of Marge Piercy's poem "To Be of Use," which concludes with the lines "the pitcher longs for water to carry/and a person for work that is real." Beneath our gratitude for the lineman may rest envy.

5   This seems to be a moment when the useful arts have an especially compelling economic rationale. A car mechanics' trade association reports that repair shops have seen their business jump significantly in the current recession: people aren't buying new cars; they are fixing the ones they have. The current downturn is likely to pass eventually. But there are also systemic changes in the economy, arising from information technology, that have the surprising effect of making the manual trades—plumbing, electrical work, car repair—more attractive as careers. The Princeton economist Alan Blinder argues that the crucial distinction in the emerging labor market is not between those with more or less education, but between those whose services can be delivered over a wire and those who must do their work in person or on site. The latter will find their livelihoods more secure against outsourcing to distant countries. As Blinder puts it, "You can't hammer a nail over the Internet." Nor can the Indians fix your car. Because they are in India.

A gifted young person who chooses to become a mechanic rather than to accumulate academic credentials is viewed as eccentric, if not self-destructive.

If the goal is to earn a living, then, maybe it isn't really true that 18-year-olds need to be imparted with a sense of panic about getting into college (though they certainly need to learn). Some people are hustled off to college, then to the cubicle, against their own inclinations and natural bents, when they would rather be learning to build things or fix things. One shop teacher suggested to me that "in schools, we create artificial learning environments for our children that they know to be contrived and undeserving of their full attention and engagement. Without the opportunity to learn through the hands, the world remains abstract and distant, and the passions for learning will not be engaged."

A gifted young person who chooses to become a mechanic rather than to accumulate academic credentials is viewed as eccentric, if not self-destructive. There is a pervasive anxiety among parents that there is only one track to success for their children. It runs through a series of gates controlled by prestigious institutions. Further, there is wide use of drugs to medicate boys, especially, against their natural tendency toward action, the better to "keep things on track." I taught briefly in a public high school and would have loved to have set up a Ritalin fogger in my classroom. It is a rare person, male or female, who is naturally inclined to sit still for 17 years in school, and then indefinitely at work.

The trades suffer from low prestige, and I believe this is based on a simple mistake. Because the work is dirty, many people assume it is also stupid. This is not my experience. I have a small business as a motorcycle mechanic in Richmond, Virginia, which I started in 2002. I work on Japanese and European motorcycles, mostly older bikes with some "vintage" cachet that makes people willing to spend money on them. I have found the satisfactions of the work to be very much bound up with the intellectual challenges it presents. And yet my decision to go into this line of work is a choice that seems to perplex many people.

After finishing a Ph.D. in political philosophy at the University of Chicago in 2000, I managed to stay on with a one-year postdoctoral fellowship at the university's Committee on Social Thought. The academic job market was utterly bleak. In a state of professional panic, I retreated to a makeshift workshop I set up in the basement of a Hyde Park apartment building, where I spent the winter tearing down an old Honda motorcycle and rebuilding it. The physicality of it, and the clear specificity of what the project required of me, was a balm. Stumped by a starter motor that seemed to check out in every way but wouldn't work, I started asking around at Honda dealerships. Nobody had an answer; finally one service manager told me to call Fred Cousins of Triple O Service. "If anyone can help you, Fred can."

I called Fred, and he invited me to come to his independent motor- 10 cycle-repair shop, tucked discreetly into an unmarked warehouse on Goose Island. He told me to put the motor on a certain bench that was free of clutter. He checked the electrical resistance through the windings, as I had done, to confirm there was no short circuit or broken wire. He spun the shaft that ran through the center of the motor, as I had. No problem: it spun freely. Then he hooked it up to a battery. It moved ever so slightly but wouldn't spin. He grasped the shaft, delicately, with three fingers, and tried to wiggle it side to side. "Too much free play," he said. He suggested that the problem was with the bushing (a thick-walled sleeve of metal) that captured the end of the shaft in the end of the cylindrical motor housing. It was worn, so it wasn't locating the shaft precisely enough. The shaft was free to move too much side to side (perhaps a couple of hundredths of an inch), causing the outer circumference of the rotor to bind on the inner circumference of the motor housing when a current was applied. Fred scrounged around for a Honda motor. He found one with the same bushing, then used a "blind hole bearing puller" to extract it, as well as the one in my motor. Then he gently tapped the new, or rather newer, one into place. The motor worked! Then Fred gave me an impromptu dissertation on the peculiar metallurgy of these Honda starter-motor bushings of the mid-'70s. Here was a scholar.

Over the next six months I spent a lot of time at Fred's shop, learning, and put in only occasional appearances at the university. This was something of a regression: I worked on cars throughout high school and college, and one of my early jobs was at a Porsche repair shop. Now I was rediscovering the intensely absorbing nature of the work, and it got me thinking about possible livelihoods.

As it happened, in the spring I landed a job as executive director of a policy organization in Washington. This felt like a coup. But certain perversities became apparent as I settled into the job. It sometimes required me to reason backward, from desired conclusion to suitable premise. The organization had taken certain positions, and there were some facts it was more fond of than others. As its figurehead, I was making arguments I didn't fully buy myself. Further, my boss seemed intent on retraining me according to a certain cognitive style—that of the corporate world, from which he had recently come. This style demanded that I project an image of rationality but not indulge too much in actual reasoning. As I sat in my K Street office, Fred's life as an independent tradesman gave me an image that I kept coming back to: someone who really knows what he is doing, losing himself in work that is genuinely useful and has a certain integrity to it. He also seemed to be having a lot of fun.

Seeing a motorcycle about to leave my shop under its own power, several days after arriving in the back of a pickup truck, I don't feel tired even though I've been standing on a concrete floor all day. Peering into the portal of his helmet, I think I can make out the edges of a grin on the face of a guy who hasn't ridden his bike in a while. I give him a wave. With one of his hands on the throttle and the other on the clutch, I know he can't wave back. But I can hear his salute in the exuberant "bwaaAAAAP!" of a crisp throttle, gratuitously revved. That sound pleases me, as I know it does him. It's a ventriloquist conversation in one mechanical voice, and the gist of it is "Yeah!"

After five months at the think tank, I'd saved enough money to buy some tools I needed, and I quit and went into business fixing bikes. My shop rate is $40 per hour. Other shops have rates as high as $70 per hour, but I tend to work pretty slowly. Further, only about half the time I spend in the shop ends up being billable (I have no employees; every little chore falls to me), so it usually works out closer to $20 per hour—a modest but decent wage. The business goes up and down; when it is down I have supplemented it with writing. The work is sometimes frustrating, but it is never irrational.

And it frequently requires complex thinking. In fixing motorcycles you come up with several imagined trains of cause and effect for manifest symptoms, and you judge their likelihood before tearing anything down. This imagining relies on a mental library that you develop. An internal combustion engine can work in any number of ways, and different manufacturers have tried different approaches. Each has its own proclivities for failure. You also develop a library of sounds and smells and feels. For example, the backfire of a too-lean fuel mixture is subtly different from an ignition backfire.

As in any learned profession, you just have to know a lot. If the motorcycle is 30 years old, from an obscure maker that went out of business 20 years ago, its tendencies are known mostly through lore. It would probably be impossible to do such work in isolation, without access to a collective historical memory; you have to be embedded in a community of mechanic-antiquarians. These relationships are maintained by telephone, in a network of reciprocal favors that spans the country. My most reliable source, Fred, has such an encyclopedic knowledge of obscure European motorcycles that all I have been able to offer him in exchange is deliveries of obscure European beer.

There is always a risk of introducing new complications when working on old motorcycles, and this enters the diagnostic logic. Measured in likelihood of screw-ups, the cost is not identical for all avenues of inquiry when deciding which hypothesis to pursue. Imagine you're trying to figure out why a bike won't start. The fasteners holding the engine covers on 1970s-era Hondas are Phillips head, and they are almost always rounded out and corroded. Do you really want to check the condition of the starter clutch if each of eight screws will need to be drilled out and extracted, risking damage to the engine case? Such impediments have to be taken into account. The attractiveness of any hypothesis is determined in part by physical circumstances that have no logical connection to the diagnostic problem at hand. The mechanic's proper response to the situation cannot be anticipated by a set of rules or algorithms.

There probably aren't many jobs that can be reduced to rule-following and still be done well. But in many jobs there is an attempt to do just this, and the perversity of it may go unnoticed by those who design the work process. Mechanics face something like this problem in the factory service manuals that we use. These manuals tell you to be systematic in eliminating variables, presenting an idealized image of diagnostic work. But they never take into account the risks of working on old machines. So you put the manual away and consider the facts before you. You do this because ultimately you are responsible to the motorcycle and its owner, not to some procedure.

There probably aren't many jobs that can be reduced to rule-following and still be done well.

Some diagnostic situations contain a lot of variables. Any given symptom may have several possible causes, and further, these causes may interact with one another and therefore be difficult to isolate. In deciding how to proceed, there often comes a point where you have to step back and get a larger gestalt. Have a cigarette and walk around the lift. The gap between theory and practice stretches out in front of you, and this is where it gets interesting. What you need now is the kind of judgment that arises only from experience; hunches rather than rules. For me, at least, there is more real thinking going on in the bike shop than there was in the think tank.

20   Put differently, mechanical work has required me to cultivate different intellectual habits. Further, habits of mind have an ethical dimension that we don't often think about. Good diagnosis requires attentiveness to the machine, almost a conversation with it, rather than assertiveness, as in the position papers produced on K Street. Cognitive psychologists speak of "metacognition," which is the activity of stepping back and thinking about your own thinking. It is what you do when you stop for a moment in your pursuit of a solution, and wonder whether your understanding of the problem is adequate. The slap of worn-out pistons hitting their cylinders can sound a lot like loose valve tappets, so to be a good mechanic you have to be constantly open to the possibility that you may be mistaken. This is a virtue that is at once cognitive and moral. It seems to develop because the mechanic, if he is the sort who goes on to become good at it, internalizes the healthy functioning of the motorcycle as an object of passionate concern. How else can you explain the elation he gets when he identifies the root cause of some problem?

This active concern for the motorcycle is reinforced by the social aspects of the job. As is the case with many independent mechanics, my business is based entirely on word of mouth. I sometimes barter services with machinists and metal fabricators. This has a very different feel than transactions with money; it situates me in a community. The result is that I really don't want to mess up anybody's motorcycle or charge more than a fair price. You often hear people complain about mechanics and other tradespeople whom they take to be dishonest or incompetent. I am sure this is sometimes justified. But it is also true that the mechanic deals with a large element of chance.

I once accidentally dropped a feeler gauge down into the crankcase of a Kawasaki Ninja that was practically brand new, while performing its first scheduled valve adjustment. I escaped a complete tear-down of the motor only through an operation that involved the use of a stethoscope, another pair of trusted hands, and the sort of concentration we associate with a bomb squad. When finally I laid my fingers on that feeler gauge, I felt as if I had cheated death. I don't remember ever feeling so alive as in the hours that followed.

Often as not, however, such crises do not end in redemption. Moments of elation are counterbalanced with failures, and these, too, are vivid, taking place right before your eyes. With stakes that are often high and immediate, the manual trades elicit heedful absorption in work. They are punctuated by moments of pleasure that take place against a darker backdrop: a keen awareness of catastrophe as an always-present possibility. The core experience is one of individual responsibility, supported by face-to-face interactions between tradesman and customer.

Contrast the experience of being a middle manager. This is a stock figure of ridicule, but the sociologist Robert Jackall spent years inhabiting the world of corporate managers, conducting interviews, and he poignantly describes the "moral maze" they feel trapped in. Like the mechanic, the manager faces the possibility of disaster at any time. But in his case these disasters feel arbitrary; they are typically a result of corporate restructurings, not of physics. A manager has to make many decisions for which he is accountable. Unlike an entrepreneur with his own business, however, his decisions can be reversed at any time by someone higher up the food chain (and there is always someone higher up the food chain). It's important for your career that these reversals not look like defeats, and more generally you have to spend a lot of time managing what others think of you. Survival depends on a crucial insight: you can't back down from an argument that you initially made in straightforward language, with moral conviction, without seeming to lose your integrity. So managers learn the art of provisional thinking and feeling, expressed in corporate doublespeak, and cultivate a lack of commitment to their own actions. Nothing is set in concrete the way it is when you are, for example, pouring concrete.

Those who work on the lower rungs of the information-age office 25 hierarchy face their own kinds of unreality, as I learned some time ago. After earning a master's degree in the early 1990s, I had a hard time finding work but eventually landed a job in the Bay Area writing brief summaries of academic journal articles, which were then sold on CD-ROMs to subscribing libraries. When I got the phone call offering me the job, I was excited. I felt I had grabbed hold of the passing world—miraculously, through the mere filament of a classified ad—and reeled myself into its current. My new bosses immediately took up residence in my imagination, where I often surprised them with my hidden depths. As I was shown to my cubicle, I felt a real sense of being honored. It seemed more than spacious enough. It was my desk, where I would think my thoughts—my unique contribution to a common enterprise, in a real company with hundreds of employees. The regularity of the cubicles made me feel I had found a place in the order of things. I was to be a knowledge worker.

But the feel of the job changed on my first day. The company had gotten its start by providing libraries with a subject index of popular magazines like *Sports Illustrated*. Through a series of mergers and acquisitions, it now found itself offering not just indexes but also abstracts (that is, summaries), and of a very different kind of material: scholarly works in the physical and biological sciences, humanities, social sciences, and law. Some of this stuff was simply incomprehensible to anyone but an expert in the particular field covered by the journal. I was reading articles in *Classical Philology* where practically every other word was in Greek. Some of the scientific journals were no less mysterious. Yet the categorical difference between, say, *Sports Illustrated* and *Nature Genetics* seemed not to have impressed itself on the company's decision makers. In some of the titles I was assigned, articles began with an abstract written by the author. But even in such cases I was to write my own. The reason offered was that unless I did so, there would be no "value added" by our product. It was hard to believe I was going to add anything other than error and confusion to such material. But then, I hadn't yet been trained.

My job was structured on the supposition that in writing an abstract of an article there is a method that merely needs to be applied, and that this can be done without understanding the text. I was actually told this by the trainer, Monica, as she stood before a whiteboard, diagramming an abstract. Monica seemed a perfectly sensible person and gave no outward signs of suffering delusions. She didn't insist too much on what she was telling us, and it became clear she was in a position similar to that of a veteran Soviet bureaucrat who must work on two levels at once: reality and official ideology. The official ideology was a bit like the factory service manuals I mentioned before, the ones that offer procedures that mechanics often have to ignore in order to do their jobs.

My starting quota, after finishing a week of training, was 15 articles per day. By my 11th month at the company, my quota was up to 28 articles per day (this was the normal, scheduled increase). I was always sleepy while at work, and I think this exhaustion was because I felt trapped in a contradiction: the fast pace demanded complete focus on the task, yet that pace also made any real concentration impossible. I had to actively suppress my own ability to think, because the more you think, the more the inadequacies in your understanding of an author's argument come into focus. This can only slow you down. To not do justice to an author who had poured himself into the subject at hand felt like violence against what was best in myself.

The quota demanded, then, not just dumbing down but also a bit of moral re-education, the opposite of the kind that occurs in the heedful absorption of mechanical work. I had to suppress my sense of responsibility to the article itself, and to others—to the author, to begin with, as well as to the hapless users of the database, who might naïvely suppose that my abstract reflected the author's work. Such detachment was made easy by the fact there was no immediate consequence for me; I could write any nonsense whatever.

Now, it is probably true that every job entails some kind of mutila- 30
tion. I used to work as an electrician and had my own business doing it for a while. As an electrician you breathe a lot of unknown dust in crawl spaces, your knees get bruised, your neck gets strained from looking up at the ceiling while installing lights or ceiling fans, and you get shocked regularly, sometimes while on a ladder. Your hands are sliced up from twisting wires together, handling junction boxes made out of stamped sheet metal, and cutting metal conduit with a hacksaw. But none of this damage touches the best part of yourself.

You might wonder: Wasn't there any quality control? My supervisor would periodically read a few of my abstracts, and I was sometimes corrected and told not to begin an abstract with a dependent clause. But I was never confronted with an abstract I had written and told that it did not adequately reflect the article. The quality standards were the generic ones of grammar, which could be applied without my supervisor having to read the article at hand. Rather, my supervisor and I both were held to a metric that was conjured by someone remote from the work process—an absentee decision maker armed with a (putatively) profit-maximizing calculus, one that took no account of the intrinsic nature of the job. I wonder whether the resulting perversity really made for maximum profits in the long term. Corporate managers are not, after all, the owners of the businesses they run.

At lunch I had a standing arrangement with two other abstracters. One was from my group, a laconic, disheveled man named Mike whom I liked instantly. He did about as well on his quota as I did on mine, but it didn't seem to bother him too much. The other guy was from beyond the partition, a meticulously groomed Liberian named Henry who said he had worked for the C.I.A. He had to flee Liberia very suddenly one day and soon found himself resettled near the office parks of Foster City, California. Henry wasn't going to sweat the quota. Come 12:30, the three of us would hike to the food court in the mall. This movement was always thrilling. It involved traversing several "campuses," with ponds frequented by oddly real seagulls, then the lunch itself, which I always savored. (Marx writes that under conditions of estranged labor, man "no longer feels himself to be freely active in any but his animal functions.")

Over his burrito, Mike would recount the outrageous things he had written in his abstracts. I could see my own future in such moments of sabotage—the compensating pleasures of a cubicle drone. Always funny and gentle, Mike confided one day that he was doing quite a bit of heroin. On the job. This actually made some sense.

How was it that I, once a proudly self-employed electrician, had ended up among these walking wounded, a "knowledge worker" at a salary of $23,000? I had a master's degree, and it needed to be used. The escalating demand for academic credentials in the job market gives the impression of an ever-more-knowledgeable society, whose members perform cognitive feats their unschooled parents could scarcely conceive of. On paper, my abstracting job, multiplied a millionfold, is precisely what puts the futurologist in a rapture: we are getting to be so smart! Yet my M.A. obscures a more real stupidification of the work I secured with that credential, and a wage to match. When I first got the degree, I felt as if I had been inducted to a certain order of society. But despite the beautiful ties I wore, it turned out to be a more proletarian existence than I had known as an electrician. In that job I had made quite a bit more money. I also felt free and active, rather than confined and stultified.

A good job requires a field of action where you can put your best capacities to work and see an effect in the world. Academic credentials do not guarantee this.

35   Nor can big business or big government—those idols of the right and the left—reliably secure such work for us. Everyone is rightly concerned about economic growth on the one hand or unemployment and wages on the other, but the character of work doesn't figure much in political debate. Labor unions address important concerns like workplace safety and family leave, and management looks for greater efficiency, but on the nature of the job itself, the dominant political and economic paradigms are mute. Yet work forms us, and deforms us, with broad public consequences.

> *A good job requires a field of action where you can put your best capacities to work and see an effect in the world.*

The visceral experience of failure seems to have been edited out of the career trajectories of gifted students. It stands to reason, then, that those who end up making big decisions that affect all of us don't seem to have much sense of their own fallibility, and of how badly things can go wrong even with the best of intentions (like when I dropped that feeler gauge down into the Ninja). In the boardrooms of Wall Street and the corridors of Pennsylvania Avenue, I don't think you'll see a yellow sign that says "Think Safety!" as you do on job sites and in many repair shops, no doubt because those who sit on the swivel chairs tend to live remote from the consequences of the decisions they make. Why not encourage gifted students to learn a trade, if only in the summers, so that their fingers will be crushed once or twice before they go on to run the country?

There is good reason to suppose that responsibility has to be installed in the foundation of your mental equipment—at the level of perception and habit. There is an ethic of paying attention that develops in the trades through hard experience. It inflects your perception of the world and your habitual responses to it. This is due to the immediate feedback you get from material objects and to the fact that the work is typically situated in face-to-face interactions between tradesman and customer.

An economy that is more entrepreneurial, less managerial, would be less subject to the kind of distortions that occur when corporate managers' compensation is tied to the short-term profit of distant shareholders. For most entrepreneurs, profit is at once a more capacious and a more concrete thing than this. It is a calculation in which the intrinsic satisfactions of work count—not least, the exercise of your own powers of reason.

Ultimately it is enlightened self-interest, then, not a harangue about humility or public-spiritedness, that will compel us to take a fresh look at the trades. The good life comes in a variety of forms. This variety has become difficult to see; our field of aspiration has narrowed into certain channels. But the current perplexity in the economy seems to be softening our gaze. Our peripheral vision is perhaps recovering, allowing us to consider the full range of lives worth choosing. For anyone who feels ill suited by disposition to spend his days sitting in an office, the question of what a good job looks like is now wide open.

FOR A SECOND READING

1. What are some of the stereotypes we are taught to associate with "working with your hands"? What are the social scripts that teach us to define and evaluate this type of labor? In your view, are these attitudes accurate or fair? Why or why not?

2. For Crawford, cultural norms around work are intimately entwined with cultural norms around school. "Some people," he writes, "are hustled off to college, then to the cubicle, against their own inclinations and natural bents, when they would rather be learning to build things or fix things" (p. 334). In your view, is Crawford correct? Do you agree that there exists a bias within our educational system against manual labor? And do you share Crawford's sense that this educational script needs to be rewritten? Why or why not?

3. "Ultimately," Crawford writes, "it is enlightened self-interest, then, not a harangue about humility or public-spiritedness, that will compel us to take a fresh look at the trades" (p. 343). Do you agree?

In your view, is it ultimately in our better interests—whether individually or societally—to change our public attitudes toward manual work? If so, how?

PUTTING IT INTO WRITING

4. Part of Crawford's argument in favor of manual work rests on the claims he makes about "knowledge work." In a brief essay, explore what characterizes white-collar or knowledge work. What rules dictate what this kind of labor is supposed to look like and what it is supposed to be for? What specific forms of work does it involve? What skills does it require? Next, explain what, specifically, Crawford finds wanting or problematic about this type of work. Do you agree?

5. Write an essay in which you apply Crawford's analysis to your own experiences with work. How do you define the ideal job? Does this ideal resemble or differ from Crawford's portrait of his own work? Does your ideal confirm or challenge the claims Crawford makes about hands-on versus knowledge work? How or how not?

COMPARING ARGUMENTS

6. Like Crawford, Mac McClelland (p. 345) takes a closer look at the world of manual work. Write an assessment of how these two depictions of such work compare. How does McClelland's exposé about "warehouse wage slavery" differ from Crawford's portrayal of motorcycle repair? What is each writer using her or his depiction to say about the meaning and value of "blue-collar" work?

MAC McCLELLAND
I Was a Warehouse Wage Slave

In the eyes of many pundits and commentators, the rise of online commerce has been a boon for companies and consumers alike. But what about all the anonymous workers who labor behind the scenes to make all of these dazzling new commercial opportunities possible? This is the question journalist Mac McClelland takes up here. Chronicling her experiences working as a "warehouse wage slave" for an online retailer order-fulfillment center, McClelland presents a portrait that dramatically challenges the feel-good narrative of life and work in the age of the Internet. McClelland is a human rights reporter for *Mother Jones* magazine. She is also the author of *For Us Surrender Is Out of the Question: A Story from Burma's Never-Ending War* (2010) and *Irritable Hearts: A PTSD Love Story* (2015). This article appeared in *Mother Jones* in 2012.

Before You Read

How much experience do you have as a consumer ordering items online? How often do you think explicitly about the work and workers responsible for responding to these orders? Do you think anything about your own online shopping behavior would change if you did?

"DON'T TAKE ANYTHING THAT HAPPENS TO YOU THERE PERSONALLY," the woman at the local chamber of commerce says when I tell her that tomorrow I start working at "Amalgamated Product Giant Shipping Worldwide Inc." She winks at me. I stare at her for a second.

"*What?*" I ask. "Why, is somebody going to be mean to me or something?"

She smiles. "Oh, yeah." This town somewhere west of the Mississippi is not big; everyone knows someone or is someone who's worked for Amalgamated. "But look at it from their perspective. They need you to work as fast as possible to push out as much as they can as fast as they can. So they're gonna give you goals, and then you know what? If you make those goals, they're gonna increase the goals. But they'll be yelling at you all the time. It's like the military. They have to break you down so they can turn you into what they want you to be. So they're going to tell you, 'You're not good enough, you're not good enough, you're not good enough,' to make you work harder. Don't say, 'This is the best I can do.' Say, 'I'll try,' even if you know you can't do it. Because if you say, 'This is the best I can do,' they'll let you go. They hire and fire constantly, every day. You'll see people dropping all around you. But don't take it personally and break down or start crying when they yell at you."

Several months prior, I'd reported on an Ohio warehouse where workers shipped products for online retailers under conditions that were surprisingly demoralizing and dehumanizing, even to someone who's spent a lot of time working in warehouses, which I have. And then my editors sat me down. "We want you to go work for Amalgamated Product Giant Shipping Worldwide Inc.," they said. I'd have to give my real name and job history when I applied, and I couldn't lie if asked for any specifics. (I wasn't.) But I'd smudge identifying details of people and the company itself. Anyway, to do otherwise might give people the impression that these conditions apply only to one warehouse or one company. Which they don't.

5   So I fretted about whether I'd have to abort the application process, like if someone asked me why I wanted the job. But no one did. And though I was kind of excited to trot out my warehouse experience, mainly all I needed to get hired was to confirm 20 or 30 times that I had not been to prison.

The application process took place at a staffing office in a run-down city, the kind where there are boarded-up businesses and broken windows downtown and billboards advertising things like "Foreclosure Fridays!" at a local law firm. Six or seven other people apply for jobs along with me. We answer questions at computers grouped in several stations. Have I ever been to prison? the system asks. No? Well, but have I ever been to prison for assault? Burglary? A felony? A misdemeanor? Raping someone? Murdering anybody? Am I sure? There's no point in lying, the computer warns me, because criminal-background checks are run on employees. Additionally, I have to confirm at the next computer station that I can read, by taking a multiple-choice test in which I'm given pictures of several album covers, including Michael Jackson's *Thriller*, and asked what the name of the Michael Jackson album is. At yet another set of computers I'm asked about my work history and character. How do I feel about dangerous activities? Would I say I'm not really into them? Or *really* into them?

In the center of the room, a video plays loudly and continuously on a big screen. Even more than you are hurting the company, a voice-over intones as animated people do things like accidentally oversleep, you are hurting yourself when you are late because you will be penalized on a point system, and when you get too many points, you're fired—unless you're late at any point during your first week, in which case

> *I realize that for whatever relative youth and regular exercise and overachievement complexes I have brought to this job, I will never be able to keep up with the goals I've been given.*

you are instantly fired. Also because when you're late or sick you miss the opportunity to maximize your overtime pay. And working more than eight hours is mandatory. Stretching is also mandatory, since you will either be standing still at a conveyor line for most of your minimum 10-hour shift or walking on concrete or metal stairs. And be careful, because you could seriously hurt yourself. And watch out, because some of your coworkers will be the kind of monsters who will file false workers' comp claims. If you know of someone doing this and you tell on him and he gets convicted, you will be rewarded with $500.

The computers screening us for suitability to pack boxes or paste labels belong to a temporary-staffing agency. The stuff we order from big online retailers lives in large warehouses, owned and operated either by the retailers themselves or by third-party logistics contractors, a.k.a. 3PLs. These companies often fulfill orders for more than one retailer out of a single warehouse. America's largest 3PL, Exel, has 86 million square feet of warehouse in North America; it's a subsidiary of Deutsche Post DHL, which is cute because Deutsche Post is the German post office, which was privatized in the 1990s and bought DHL in 2002, becoming one of the world's biggest corporate employers. The $31 billion "value-added warehousing and distribution" sector of 3PLs is just a fraction of what large 3PLs' parent companies pull in. UPS's logistics division, for example, pulls in more than a half a billion, but it feeds billions of dollars of business to UPS Inc.

Anyhow, regardless of whether the retailer itself or a 3PL contractor houses and processes the stuff you buy, the actual stuff is often handled by people working for yet another company—a temporary-staffing agency. The agency to which I apply is hiring 4,000 drones for this single Amalgamated warehouse between October and December. Four thousand. Before leaving the staffing office, I'm one of them.

I'm assigned a schedule of Sunday through Thursday, 7 a.m. to 5:30 p.m. 10 When additional overtime is necessary, which it will be soon (Christmas!), I should expect to leave at 7 or 7:30 p.m. instead. Eight days after applying, i.e., after my drug test has cleared, I walk through a small, desolate town nearly an hour outside the city where I was hired. This is where the warehouse is, way out here, a long commute for many of my coworkers. I wander off the main road and into the chamber of commerce to kill some afternoon time—though not too much since my first day starts at 5 a.m.—but I end up getting useful job advice.

"Well, what if I do start crying?" I ask the woman who warns me to keep it together no matter how awfully I'm treated. "Are they really going to fire me for that?"

"Yes," she says. "There's 16 other people who want your job. Why would they keep a person who gets emotional, especially in this economy?"

Still, she advises, regardless of how much they push me, don't work so hard that I injure myself. I'm young. I have a long life ahead of me. It's not worth it to do permanent physical damage, she says, which, considering that I got hired at elevensomething dollars an hour, is a bit of an understatement.

As the sun gets lower in the curt November sky, I thank the woman for her help. When I start toward the door, she repeats her "No. 1 rule of survival" one more time.

15   "Leave your pride and your personal life at the door." If there's any way I'm going to last, she says, tomorrow I have to start pretending like I don't have either.

Though it's inconvenient for most employees, the rural location of the Amalgamated Product Giant Shipping Worldwide Inc. warehouse isn't an accident. The town is bisected by a primary interstate, close to a busy airport, serviced by several major highways. There's a lot of rail out here. The town became a station stop on the way to more important places a hundred years ago, and it now feeds part of the massive transit networks used to get consumers anywhere goods from everywhere. Every now and then, a long line of railcars rolls past my hotel and gives my room a good shake. I don't ever get a good look at them, because it's dark outside when I go to work, and dark again when I get back.

> **"Leave your pride and your personal life at the door." If there's any way I'm going to last, she says, tomorrow I have to start pretending like I don't have either.**

Inside Amalgamated, an employee's first day is training day. Though we're not paid to be here until 6, we have been informed that we need to arrive at 5. If we don't show up in time to stand around while they sort out who we are and where they've put our ID badges, we could miss the beginning of training, which would mean termination. "I was up half the night because I was so afraid I was going to be late," a woman in her 60s tells me. I was, too. A minute's tardiness after the first week earns us 0.5 penalty points, an hour's tardiness is worth 1 point, and an absence 1.5; 6 is the number that equals "release." But during the first week even a minute's tardiness gets us fired. When we get lined up so we can be counted a third or fourth time, the woman conducting the roll call recognizes the last name of a young trainee. "Does your dad work here? Or uncle?" she asks. "Grandpa," he says, as another supervisor snaps at the same time, sounding not mean but very stressed out, "We gotta get goin' here."

The culture is intense, an Amalgamated higher-up acknowledges at the beginning of our training. He's speaking to us from a video, one of several videos—about company policies, sexual harassment, etc.—that we watch while we try to keep our eyes open. We don't *want* to be so intense, the higher-up says. But our customers demand it. We are surrounded by signs that state our productivity goals. Other signs proclaim that a good customer experience, to which our goal-meeting is essential, is the key to growth, and growth is the key to lower prices, which leads to a better customer experience. There is no room for inefficiencies. The gal conducting our training reminds us again that we cannot miss any days our first week. There are NO exceptions to this policy. She says to take Brian, for example, who's here with us in training today. Brian already went through this training, but then during his first week his lady had a baby, so he missed a day and he had to be fired. Having to start the application process over could cost a brand-new dad like Brian a couple of weeks' worth of work and pay. Okay? Everybody turn around and look at Brian. Welcome back, Brian. Don't end up like Brian.

Soon, we move on to practical training. Like all workplaces with automated and heavy machinery, this one contains plenty of ways to get hurt, and they are enumerated. There are transition points in the warehouse floor where the footing is uneven, and people trip and sprain ankles. Give forklifts that are raised up several stories to access products a wide berth: "If a pallet falls on you, you won't be working with us anymore." Watch your fingers around the conveyor belts that run waist-high throughout the entire facility. People lose fingers. Or parts of fingers. And about once a year, they tell us, someone in an Amalgamated warehouse gets caught by the hair, and when a conveyor belt catches you by the hair, it doesn't just take your hair with it. It rips out a piece of scalp as well.

If the primary message of one-half of our practical training is Be 20 Careful, the takeaway of the other half is Move As Fast As Humanly Possible. Or superhumanly possible. I have been hired as a picker, which means my job is to find, scan, place in a plastic tote, and send away via conveyor whatever item within the multiple stories of this several-hundred-thousand-square-foot warehouse my scanner tells me to. We are broken into groups and taught how to read the scanner to find the object among some practice shelves. Then we immediately move on to practicing doing it faster, racing each other to fill the orders our scanners dictate, then racing each other to put all the items back.

"Hurry up," a trainer encourages me when he sees me pulling ahead of the others, "and you can put the other items back!" I roll my eyes that my reward for doing a good job is that I get to do more work, but he's got my number: I am exactly the kind of freak this sort of motivation appeals to. I win, and set myself on my prize of the bonus errand.

That afternoon, we are turned loose in the warehouse, scanners in hand. And that's when I realize that for whatever relative youth and regular exercise and overachievement complexes I have brought to this job, I will never be able to keep up with the goals I've been given.

The place is immense. Cold, cavernous. Silent, despite thousands of people quietly doing their picking, or standing along the conveyors quietly packing or box-taping, nothing noisy but the occasional whir of a passing forklift. My scanner tells me in what exact section—there are nine merchandise sections, so sprawling that there's a map attached to my ID badge—of vast shelving systems the item I'm supposed to find resides. It also tells me how many seconds it thinks I should take to get there. Dallas sector, section yellow, row H34, bin 22, level D: wearable blanket. Battery-operated flour sifter. Twenty seconds. I count how many steps it takes me to speed-walk to my destination: 20. At 5-foot-9, I've got a decently long stride, and I only cover the 20 steps *and* locate the exact shelving unit in the allotted time if I don't hesitate for one second or get lost or take a drink of water before heading in the right direction as fast as I can walk or even occasionally jog. Olive-oil mister. Male libido enhancement pills. Rifle strap. Who the fuck buys their paper towels off the internet? Fairy calendar. Neoprene lunch bag. Often as not, I miss my time target.

Plenty of things can hurt my goals. The programs for our scanners are designed with the assumption that we disposable employees don't know what we're doing. Find a Rob Zombie Voodoo Doll in the blue section of the Rockies sector in the third bin of the A-level in row Z42, my scanner tells me. But if I punch into my scanner that it's not there, I have to prove it by scanning every single other item in the bin, though I swear on my life there's no Rob Zombie Voodoo Doll in this pile of 30 individually wrapped and bar-coded batteries that take me quite a while to beep one by one. It could be five minutes before I can move on to, and make it to, and find, my next item. That lapse is supposed to be mere seconds.

25   This week, we newbies need to make 75 percent of our total picking-volume targets. If we don't, we get "counseled." If the people in here who've been around longer than a few weeks don't make their 100 percent, they get counseled. *Why* aren't you making your targets? the supervisors will ask. You *really* need to make your targets.

From the temp agency, Amalgamated has ordered the exact number of humans it should take to fill this week's orders if we work at top capacity. Lots of retailers use temporary help in peak season, and online ones are no exception. But lots of warehousing and distribution centers like this also use temps year-round. The Bureau of Labor Statistics found that more than 15 percent of pickers, packers, movers, and unloaders are temps. They make $3 less an hour on average than permanent workers. And they can be "temporary" for years. There are so many temps in this warehouse that the staffing agency has its own office here. Industry consultants describe the temp-staffing business as "very, very busy." "On fire." Maximizing profits means making sure no employee has a slow day, means having only as many employees as are necessary to get the job done, the number of which can be determined and ordered from a huge pool of on-demand labor literally by the day. Often, temp workers have to call in before shifts to see if they'll get work. Sometimes, they're paid piece rate, according to the number of units they fill or unload or move. Always, they can be let go in an instant, and replaced just as quickly.

Everyone in here is hustling. At the announcement to take one of our two 15-minute breaks, we hustle even harder. We pickers close out the totes we're currently filling and send them away on the conveyor belt, then make our way as fast as we can with the rest of the masses across the long haul of concrete between wherever we are and the break room, but not before passing through metal detectors, for which there is a line—we're required to be screened on our way out, though not on our way in; apparently the concern is that we're sneaking Xbox 360s up under our shirts, not bringing in weapons. If we

> **If the primary message of one-half of our practical training is Be Careful, the takeaway of the other half is Move As Fast As Humanly Possible.**

don't set off the metal detector and have to be taken aside and searched, we can run into the break room and try to find a seat among the rows and rows and long-ass rows of tables. We lose more time if we want to pee—and I do want to pee, and when amid the panic about the time constraints it occurs to me that I don't have my period I toss a fist victoriously into the air—between the actual peeing and the waiting in line to pee in the nearest one of the two bathrooms, which has eight stalls in the ladies' and I'm not sure how many in the men's and serves thousands of people a day. Once I pare this process down as much as possible, by stringing a necktie through my belt loops because I can't find a metal-less replacement for my belt at the local Walmart—and if my underwear or butt-crack slips out, I've been warned, I can get penalized—and by leaving my car keys in the break room after a manager helps me find an admittedly "still risky" hiding place for them because we have no lockers and "things get stolen out of here all the time," I get myself up to seven minutes' worth of break time to inhale as many high-fat and -protein snacks as I can. People who work at Amalgamated are always working this fast. Right now, because it's almost Black Friday, there are just more of us doing it.

Then as quickly as we've come, we all run back. At the end of the 15 minutes, we're supposed to be back at whichever far-flung corner of the warehouse we came from, scanners in hand, working. We run to grab the wheeled carts we put the totes on. We run past each other and if we do say something, we say it as we keep moving. "How's the job market?" a supervisor says, laughing, as several of us newbies run by. "Just kidding!" Ha ha! "I know why you guys are here. That's why I'm here, too!" At another near collision between employees, one wants to know how complaining about not being able to get time off went and the other spits that he was told he was lucky to *have* a job. This is no way to have a conversation, but at least conversations are not forbidden, as they were in the Ohio warehouse I reported on—where I saw a guy get fired for talking, specifically for asking another employee, "Where are you from?" So I'm allowed the extravagance of smiling at a guy who is always so unhappy and saying, "How's it goin'?" And he can respond, "Terrible," as I'm running to the big industrial cage-lift that takes our carts up to the second or third floors, which involves walking under a big metal bar gating the front of it, and which I should really take my time around. Within the last month, three different people have needed stitches in the head after being clocked by these big metal bars, so it's dangerous. Especially the lift in the Dallas sector, whose bar has been installed wrong, so it is extra prone to falling, they tell us. Be careful. Seriously, though. We really need to meet our goals here.

> **At lunch, the most common question is "Why are you here?" like in prison.**

Amalgamated has estimated that we pickers speed-walk an average of 12 miles a day on cold concrete, and the twinge in my legs blurs into the heavy soreness in my feet that complements the pinch in my hips when I crouch to the floor—the pickers' shelving runs from the floor to seven feet high or so—to retrieve an iPad protective case. iPad anti-glare protector. iPad one-hand grip-holder device. Thing that looks like a landline phone handset that plugs into your iPad so you can pretend that rather than talking via iPad you are talking on a phone.

30   I've started cringing every time my scanner shows a code that means the item I need to pick is on the ground, which, in the course of a 10.5-hour shift—much less the mandatory 12-hour shifts everyone is slated to start working next week—is literally hundreds of times a day. "How has OSHA signed off on this?" I've taken to muttering to myself. "*Has* OSHA signed off on this?" ("The thing about ergonomics," OSHA says when I call them later to ask, "is that OSHA doesn't have a standard. Best practices. But no laws.")

At lunch, the most common question is "Why are you here?" like in prison. A guy in his mid-20s says he's from Chicago, came to this state for a full-time job in the city an hour away from here because "Chicago's going down." His other job doesn't pay especially well, so he's here—pulling 10.5-hour shifts and commuting two hours a day—anytime he's not there. One guy says he's a writer; he applies for grants in his time off from the warehouse. A middle-aged lady near me used to be a bookkeeper. She's a peak-season hire, worked here last year during Christmas, too. "What do you do the rest of the year?" I ask. "Collect unemployment!" she says, and laughs the sad laugh you laugh when you're saying something really unfunny. All around us in the break room, mothers frantically call home. "Hi, baby!" you can hear them say; coos to children echo around the walls the moment lunch begins. It's brave of these women to keep their phones in the break room, where theft is so high—they can't keep them in their cars if they want to use them during the day, because we aren't supposed to leave the premises without permission, and they can't take them onto the warehouse floor, because "nothing but the clothes on your backs" is allowed on the warehouse floor (*anything* on your person that Amalgamated sells can be confiscated—"And what does Amalgamated sell?" they asked us in training. "Everything!"). I suppose that if I were responsible for a child, I would have no choice but to risk leaving my phone in here, too. But the mothers make it quick. "How are you doing?" "Is everything okay?" "Did you eat something?" "I love you!" and then they're off the phone and eating as fast as the rest of us. Lunch is 29 minutes and 59 seconds—we've been reminded of this: "Lunch is *not* 30 minutes and 1 second"—that's a penalty-point-earning offense—and that includes the time to get through the metal detectors and use the disgustingly overcrowded bathroom—the suggestion board hosts several pleas that someone do something about that smell—and time to stand in line to clock out and back in. So we chew quickly, and are often still chewing as we run back to our stations.

The days blend into each other. But it's near the end of my third day that I get written up. I sent two of some product down the conveyor line when my scanner was only asking for one; the product was boxed in twos, so I should've opened the box and separated them, but I didn't notice because I was in a hurry. With an hour left in the day, I've already picked 800 items. Despite moving fast enough to get sloppy, my scanner tells me that means I'm fulfilling only 52 percent of my goal. A supervisor who is a genuinely nice person comes by with a clipboard listing my numbers. Like the rest of the supervisors, she tries to create a friendly work environment and doesn't want to enforce the policies that make this job so unpleasant. But her hands are tied. She needs this job, too, so she has no choice but to tell me something I have never been told in 19 years of school or at any of some dozen workplaces. "You're doing really bad," she says.

I'll admit that I did start crying a little. Not at work, thankfully, since that's evidently frowned upon, but later, when I explained to someone over Skype that it hurts, oh, how my body hurts after failing to make my goals despite speed-walking or flat-out jogging and pausing every 20 or 30 seconds to reach on my tiptoes or bend or drop to the floor for 10.5 hours, and isn't it awful that they fired Brian because he had a baby, and, in fact, when I was hired I signed off on something acknowledging that anyone who leaves without at least a week's notice—whether because they're a journalist who will just walk off or because they miss a day for having a baby and are terminated—has their hours paid out not at their hired rate but at the legal minimum. Which in this state, like in lots of states, is about $7 an hour. Thank God that I (unlike Brian, probably) didn't need to pay for opting into Amalgamated's "limited" health insurance program. Because in my 10.5-hour day I'll make about $60 after taxes.

"This is America?" my Skype pal asks, because often I'm abroad.

35   Indeed, and I'm working for a gigantic, immensely profitable company. Or for the staffing company that works for that company, anyway. Which is a nice arrangement, because temporary-staffing agencies keep the stink of unacceptable labor conditions off the companies whose names you know. When temps working at a Walmart warehouse sued for not getting paid for all their hours, and for then getting sent home without pay for complaining, Walmart—not technically their employer—wasn't named as a defendant. (Though Amazon has been named in a similar suit.) Temporary staffers aren't legally entitled to decent health care because they are just short-term

> *Temporary staffers aren't legally entitled to decent health care because they are just short-term "contractors" no matter how long they keep the same job.*

"contractors" no matter how long they keep the same job. They aren't entitled to raises, either, and they don't get vacation and they'd have a hell of a time unionizing and they don't have the privilege of knowing if they'll have work on a particular day or for how long they'll have a job. And that is how you slash prices and deliver products superfast and offer free shipping and still post profits in the millions or billions.

"This really doesn't have to be this awful," I shake my head over Skype. But it is. And this job is just about the only game in town, like it is in lots of towns, and eventually will be in more towns, with US internet retail sales projected to grow 10 percent every year to $279 billion in 2015 and with Amazon, the largest of the online retailers, seeing revenues rise 30 to 40 percent year after year and already having 69 giant warehouses, 17 of which came online in 2011 alone. So butch up, Sally.

"You look way too happy," an Amalgamated supervisor says to me. He has appeared next to me as I work, and in the silence of the vast warehouse, his presence catches me by surprise. His comment, even more so.

"Really?" I ask.

I don't really *feel* happy. By the fourth morning that I drag myself out of bed long before dawn, my self-pity has turned into actual concern. There's a screaming pain running across the back of my shoulders. "You need to take 800 milligrams of Advil a day," a woman in her late 50s or early 60s advised me when we all congregated in the break room before work. When I arrived, I stashed my lunch on a bottom ledge of the cheap metal shelving lining the break room walls, then hesitated before walking away. I cursed myself. I forgot something in the bag, but there was no way to get at it without crouching or bending over, and any extra times of doing that today were times I couldn't really afford. The unhappy-looking guy I always make a point of smiling at told me, as we were hustling to our stations, that this is actually the second time he's worked here: A few weeks back he missed some time for doctors' appointments when his arthritis flared up, and though he had notes for the absences, he was fired; he had to start the application process over again, which cost him an extra week and a half of work. "Zoom zoom! Pick it up! Pickers' pace, guys!" we were prodded this morning. Since we already felt like we were moving pretty fast, I'm quite dispirited, in fact.

"Really?" I ask.   40

"Well," the supervisor qualifies. "Just everybody else is usually really sad or mad by the time they've been working here this long."

It's my 28th hour as an employee.

I probably look happier than I should because I have the extreme luxury of not giving a shit about keeping this job. Nevertheless, I'm tearing around my assigned sector hard enough to keep myself consistently light-headed and a little out of breath. I'm working in books today. "Oh," I smiled to myself when I reached the paper-packed shelves. I love being around books.

Picking books for Amalgamated has a disadvantage over picking baby food or Barbies, however, in that the shelving numbers don't always line up. When my scanner tells me the book I need is on the lowest level in section 28 of a row, section 28 of the eye-level shelf of that row may or may not line up with section 28 of the lowest level. So when I spot eye-level section 28 and squat or kneel on the floor, the section 28 I'm looking for might be five feet to my right or left. Which means I have to stand up and crouch back down again to get there, greatly increasing the number of times I need to stand and crouch/kneel in a day. Or I can crawl. Usually, I crawl. A coworker is choosing the crouch/kneel option. "This gets so tiring after a while," he says when we pass each other. He's 20. It's 9:07 a.m.

45   There are other disadvantages to working in books. In the summer, it's the heat. Lots of the volumes are stored on the second and third floors of this immense cement box; the job descriptions we had to sign off on acknowledged that temperatures can be as low as 60 and higher than 95 degrees, and higher floors tend to be hotter. "They had to get fans because in the summer people were dying in here," one of the supervisors tells us. The fans still blow now even though I'm wearing five shirts. "If you think it's cold in *here*," one of my coworkers told me when she saw me rubbing my arms for warmth one morning, "just hope we don't have a fire drill." They evacuated everyone for one recently, and lots of the fast-moving employees had stripped down to T-shirts. They stood outside, masses of them, shivering for an hour as snow fell on their bare arms.

      In the books sector, in the cold, in the winter dryness, made worse by the fans and all the paper, I jet across the floor in my rubber-soled Adidas, pant legs whooshing against each other, 30 seconds according to my scanner to take 35 steps to get to the right section and row and bin and level and reach for *Diary of a Wimpy Kid* and a hot spark shoots between my hand and the metal shelving. It's not the light static-electric prick I would terrorize my sister with when we got bored in carpeted department stores, but a solid shock, striking enough to make my body learn to fear it. I start inadvertently hesitating every time I approach my target. One of my coworkers races up to a shelving unit and leans in with the top of his body first; his head touches the metal, and the shock knocks him back. "Be careful of your head," he says to me. In the first two hours of my day, I pick 300 items. The majority of them zap me painfully.

      "Please tell me you have suggestions for dealing with the static electricity," I say to a person in charge when the morning break comes. This conversation is going to cost me a couple of my precious few minutes to eat/drink/pee, but I've started to get paranoid that maybe it's not good for my body to exchange an electric charge with metal several hundred times in one day.

      "Oh, are you workin' in books?"

      "Yeah."

50   "No. Sorry." She means this. I feel bad for the supervisors who are trying their damnedest to help us succeed and not be miserable. "They've done everything they can"—"they" are not aware, it would appear, that anti-static coating and matting exist—"to ground things up there but there's nothing you can do."

      I produce a deep frown. But even if she did have suggestions, I probably wouldn't have time to implement them. One suggestion for minimizing work-related pain and strain is to get a stepladder to retrieve any items on shelves above your head rather than getting up on your toes and overreaching. But grabbing one of the stepladders stashed few and far between among the rows of merchandise takes time. Another is to alternate the hand you use to hold and wield your cumbersome scanner. "You'll feel carpal tunnel start to set in," one of the supervisors told me, "so you'll want to change hands." But that, too, he admitted, costs time, since you have to hit the bar code at just the right angle for it to scan, and your dominant hand is way more likely to nail it the first time. Time is not a thing I have to spare. I'm still only at 57 percent of my goal. It's been 10 years since I was a mover and packer for a moving company, and only slightly less since I worked ridiculously long hours as a waitress and housecleaner. My back and knees were younger then, but I'm only 31 and feel pretty confident that if I were doing those jobs again I'd still wake up with soreness like a person who'd worked out too much, not the soreness of a person whose body was staging a revolt. I can break into goal-meeting suicide pace for short bouts, sure, but I can't keep it up for 10.5 hours.

"Do not say that," one of the workampers tells me at break. Workampers are people who drive RVs around the country, from temporary job to temporary job, docking in trailer camps. "We're retired but we can't . . ." another explains to me about himself and his wife, shrugging, "*make* it. And there's no jobs, so we go where the jobs are."

Amalgamated advertises positions on websites workampers frequent. In this warehouse alone, there are hundreds of them.

"Never say that you can't do it," the first workamper emphasizes. "When they ask you why you aren't reaching your goals—"

"Say, 'It's because they're totally unreasonable'?" I suggest.   55

"Say you'll do better, even if you know you can't," she continues, ignoring me. "Say you'll try harder, even if the truth is that you're trying your absolute hardest right now, no matter how many times they tell you you're not doing good enough."

There *are* people who make the goals. One of the trainers does. She works here all year, not just during Christmas. "I hated picking for the first month," she told me sympathetically the other day. "Then you just get used to it." She's one of many hardcore workers here, a labor pool studded with dedicated and solid employees. One of the permanent employees has tried to encourage me by explaining that he *always* makes his goals, and sometimes makes 120 percent of them. When I ask him if that isn't totally exhausting, he says, "Oh yeah. You're gonna be crying for your mommy when today's over." When I ask him if there's any sort of incentive for his overperformance, if he's rewarded in any way, he says occasionally Amalgamated enters him in drawings for company gift cards. For $15 or $20. He shrugs when he admits the size of the bonus. "These days you need it." Anyway, he says, he thinks it's important to have a good attitude and try to do a good job. Even some of the employees who are total failures are still trying really hard. "I heard you're doing good," one of the ladies in my training group says to me. Her eyebrows are heavy with stress. I am still hitting less than 60 percent of my target. Still, that's better than she's doing. "Congratulations," she says, and smiles sadly.

We will be fired if we say we just can't or won't get better, the workamper tells me. But so long as I resign myself to hearing how inadequate I am on a regular basis, I can keep this job. "Do you think this job has to be this terrible?" I ask the workamper.

"Oh, no," she says, and makes a face at me like I've asked a stupid question, which I have. As if Amalgamated couldn't bear to lose a fraction of a percent of profits by employing a few more than the absolute minimum of bodies they have to, or by storing the merchandise at halfway ergonomic heights and angles. But that would cost space, and space costs money, and money is not a thing customers could possibly be expected to hand over for this service without huffily taking their business elsewhere. Charging for shipping does cause high abandonment rates of online orders, though it's not clear whether people wouldn't pay a few bucks for shipping, or a bit more for the products, if they were guaranteed that no low-income workers would be tortured or exploited in the handling of their purchases.

60   "The first step is awareness," an e-commerce specialist will tell me later. There have been trickles of information leaking out of the Internet Order Fulfillment Industrial Complex: an investigation by the Allentown, Pennsylvania, *Morning Call* in which Amazon workers complained of fainting in stifling heat, being disciplined for getting heat exhaustion, and otherwise being "treated like a piece of crap"; a workampers' blog picked up by *Gizmodo*; a *Huffington Post* exposé about the lasting physical damage and wild economic instability temporary warehouse staffers suffer. And workers have filed lawsuits against online retailers, their logistics companies, and their temp agencies over off-the-clock work and other compensation issues, as well as at least one that details working conditions that are all too similar. (That case has been dismissed but is on appeal.) Still, most people really don't know how most internet goods get to them. The e-commerce specialist didn't even know, and she was in charge of choosing the 3PL for her midsize online-retail company. "These decisions are made at a business level and are based on cost," she says. "I never, ever thought about what they're like and how they treat people. Fulfillment centers want to keep clients blissfully ignorant of their conditions." If you called major clothing retailers, she ventured, and asked them "what it was like at the warehouse that ships their sweaters, no one at company headquarters would have any fucking clue."

Further, she said, now that I mentioned it, she has no idea how to go about getting any information on the conditions at the 3PL she herself hired. Nor how to find a responsible one. "A standard has to be created.

Like fair trade or organic certification, where social good is built into the cost. There is a segment of the population"—like the consumers of her company's higher-end product, she felt—"that cares and will pay for it."

If they are aware how inhumane the reality is. But awareness has a long way to go, and logistics doesn't just mean online retail; food packagers and processors, medical suppliers, and factories use mega-3PLs as well. And a whole lot of other industries—hotels, call centers—take advantage of the price controls and plausible deniability that temporary staffing offers.

"Maybe awareness will lead to better working conditions," says Vinod Singhal, a professor of operations management at Georgia Tech. "But . . ." Given the state of the economy, he isn't optimistic.

This is the kind of resignation many of my coworkers have been forced to accept. At the end of break, the workamper and I are starting to fast-walk back to our stations. A guy who's been listening to our conversation butts in. "They can take you for everything you've got," he says. "They know it's your last resort."

At today's pickers' meeting, we are reminded that customers are 65 waiting. We *cannot* move at a "comfortable pace," because if we are comfortable, we will never make our numbers, and customers are not willing to wait. And it's Christmastime. We got 2.7 million orders this week. People need—*need*—these items and they need them right now. So even if you've worked here long enough to be granted time off, you are not allowed to use it until the holidays are over. (And also forget about Election Day, which is today. "What if I want to vote?" I ask a supervisor. "I think you should!" he says. "But if I leave I'll get fired," I say. To which he makes a sad face before saying, "Yeah.") No time off includes those of you who are scheduled to work Thanksgiving. There are two Amalgamated-catered Thanksgiving dinners offered to employees next week, but you can only go to one of them. If you attend one, your employee badge will be branded with a nonremovable sticker so that you cannot also attempt to eat at the other. Anyway, good luck, everybody. Everybody back to work. Quickly!

Speed-walking back to the electro-trauma of the books sector, I wince when I unintentionally imagine the types of Christmas lore that will prevail around my future household. I feel genuinely sorry for any child I might have who ever asks me for anything for Christmas, only to be informed that every time a "Place Order" button rings, a poor person takes four Advil and gets told they suck at their job.

I suppose this is what they were talking about in the radio ad I heard on the way to work, the one that was paid for by a coalition of local businesses, gently begging citizens to buy from them instead of off the internet and warning about the importance of supporting local shops. But if my coworker Brian wants to feed his new baby any of these

24-packs of Plum Organics Apple & Carrot baby food I've been picking, he should probably buy them from Amazon, where they cost only $31.16. In my locally owned grocery store, that's $47.76 worth of sustenance. Even if he finds the time to get in the car to go buy it at a brick-and-mortar Target, where it'd be less convenient but cost about the same as on Amazon, that'd be before sales tax, which physical stores, unlike Amazon, are legally required to charge to help pay for the roads on which Brian's truck, and more to the point Amazon's trucks, drive.

Back in books, I take a sharp shock to my right hand when I grab the book the scanner cramping my left hand demands me to and make some self-righteous promises to myself about continuing to buy food at my more-expensive grocery store, because I can. Because I'm not actually a person who makes $7.25 an hour, not anymore, not one of the 1 in 3 Americans who is now poor or "near poor." For the moment, I'm just playing one.

"Lucky girl," I whisper to myself at the tail of a deep breath, as soon as fresh winter air hits my lungs. It's only lunchtime, but I've breached the warehouse doors without permission. I've picked 500 items this morning, and don't want to get shocked anymore, or hear from the guy with the clipboard what a total disappointment I am. "Lucky girl, lucky girl, lucky girl," I repeat on my way to my car. I told the lady from my training group who's so stressed about her poor performance to tell our supervisor not to look for me—and she grabbed my arm as I turned to leave, looking even more worried than usual, asking if I was sure I knew what I was doing. I don't want our supervisor to waste any time; he's got goals to make, too. He won't miss me, and nobody else will, either. The temp agency is certainly as full of applicants as it was when I went to ask for a job.

70   "Just look around in here if you wanna see how bad it is out there," one of the associates at the temp office said to me, unprompted, when I got hired. It's the first time anyone has ever tried to comfort me *because* I got a job, because he knew, and everyone in this industry that's growing wildfire fast knows, and accepts, that its model by design is mean. He offered me the same kind of solidarity the workers inside the warehouse try to provide each other at every break: *Why are you here? What happened that you have to let people treat you like this?* "We're all in the same boat," he said, after shaking my hand to welcome me aboard. "It's a *really* big boat."

FOR A SECOND READING

1.   What do you make of the phrase "wage slave"? What does the conjunction of these two terms suggest about the larger argument McClelland is trying to make here?

2. "I feel genuinely sorry," McClelland writes, "for any child I might have who ever asks me for anything for Christmas, only to be informed that every time a 'Place Order' button rings, a poor person takes four Advil and gets told they suck at their job" (p. 359). What point is she trying to make here? What kind of connection is she suggesting exists between the customer who places an online order and the worker who labors to fill this order?

3. The number-one piece of advice McClelland receives upon being hired is: "Leave your pride and your personal life at the door" (p. 348). To what extent does this advice capture the broader critique McClelland is advancing here? In what ways does this kind of job strip workers of their "personal" or human qualities?

PUTTING IT INTO WRITING

4. Much of McClelland's critique of warehouse work involves detailing her attempts to follow her employers' draconian rules about efficient time management. "At the end of the 15 minutes, we're supposed to be back at whichever far-flung corner of the warehouse we came from, scanners in hand, working. We run to grab the wheeled carts we put the totes on. We run past each other and if we do say something, we say it as we keep moving" (p. 352). In an essay, identify and analyze the specific critique this passage is designed to convey. To what aspects of warehouse work does a description like this draw your attention? And what sort of criticism of this work does it ask you to consider?

5. Near the end of the essay, McClelland identifies what she believes is the fundamental question underlying all of her interactions with her coworkers: "*Why are you here? What happened that you have to let people treat you like this?*" (p. 360). Based on the portrait of "wage slave" work she presents here, how do you think McClelland would answer her own question? According to this essay, what are some of the key factors that compel workers to seek and keep this kind of job? Do you find this explanation persuasive? Why or why not?

COMPARING ARGUMENTS

6. McClelland chronicles both the physical and the psychological toll the "warehouse" work can exact. How does her account about the psychic cost of such work compare to what Matthew Crawford (p. 333) has to say about the intellectual and emotional satisfactions of motorcycle repair work? What, in your view, accounts for the stark difference in the conclusions about this question each writer draws? What makes the one version of manual work so emotionally trying and the other so emotionally satisfying?

Rewriting the Script: **Working at Wal-Mart**

“ *While Wal-Mart isn't the only big box store criticized for its policies, it has become a symbol for much of what is wrong with employers. Wal-Mart reported a net income of over $11 billion last year — surely plenty of money to remedy some questionable workplace practices — yet stories persist about wage law violations, inadequate health care, exploitation of workers, and the retailer's anti-union stance.”*

WORKPLACE FAIRNESS INSTITUTE, 2013

CHALLENGING THE WAL-MART WORKPLACE

Whether in television commercials or magazine spreads, Internet job sites or help-wanted ads, it is hardly a secret that virtually every job gets hyped in ways calculated to cast it in the best possible light. As many of us know from personal experience, however, sooner or later most such rosy predictions bump up against the kinds of pressures and limitations that these promotions rarely mention. We know, for example, that in the "real world" discrepancies in economic and educational background or barriers of race and class can drastically restrict the opportunities available to people looking for work. Or that when we actually find ourselves in a given job, the interests of employers and the rights of employees are not always in sync. Take, for instance, the controversy surrounding Wal-Mart's employment practices. While it may be commonplace for corporate boosters to describe their workforce as one big, happy family, it is also true that such feel-good language can serve to direct attention away from more serious and pressing discussions — about things like fair wages, hiring discrimination, or unionization. In this case, the gap between the promise and the reality suggests that we may need to rethink the scripts we use to talk about work. Should these scripts be rewritten? And if so, what would these new scripts look like?

IDENTIFY THE SCRIPT: Make a list of the different expectations big retail companies like Wal-Mart have for their workers. What attitudes and behaviors are such workers expected to follow as the norm? Then write a paragraph in which you discuss the ways these expectations are being challenged in the quotation above.

CHALLENGE THE SCRIPT: Write a one-page essay in which you discuss the ways these expectations are being challenged in the quotation above. What aspect of this dominant social script does this quotations critique most effectively? Least effectively? Why? In this essay, evaluate the attitudes toward the workplace this cheer scripts for the typical Wal-Mart employee. Are they reasonable attitudes to expect Wal-Mart workers to adopt? Do these attitudes serve the interests of the Wal-Mart corporation in any particular way? In your view, are these attitudes Wal-Mart workers should be encouraged to adopt? Why or why not?

WRITE YOUR OWN SCRIPT: Based on your assessment of the critique offered by the Workplace Fairness Institute, describe the social script you believe should govern a workplace like Wal-Mart. What kind of regulations would you advocate for how Wal-Mart workers should be compensated? What opportunities for unionizing should such workers be afforded? What policies about workplace safety should prevail?

J. D. Pooley/Getty Images

BARBARA EHRENREICH
How the Poor Are Made to Pay For Their Poverty

We've all heard the complaints that government needs to become leaner, more efficient, more cost effective. But what happens when the brunt of such efforts is borne by those least able to withstand it? Offering a portrait of the unique and punitive costs society imposes upon the working poor, Barbara Ehrenreich asks some hard questions about fairness, responsibility, and social class in America today. Ehrenreich is a writer and political activist who has written for a variety of magazines and newspapers including the *Nation*, the *Atlantic*, *Ms.*, and the *Progressive*. She has published over a dozen books of journalism and social commentary. *Nickel and Dimed: On (Not) Getting By in America* (2002) is an undercover investigation of low-wage jobs, and a chapter of it won Ehrenreich a Sidney Hillman Award for Journalism. Among her other books are *Bait and Switch: The (Futile) Pursuit of the American Dream* (2005) and, most recently, *Living with a Wild God* (2014). The selection below was first published in the *Guardian* in 2012.

Before You Read

Do you think it's fair to talk about the "criminalization of poverty"? In your view, do we live in a world where being poor exposes you to greater risk and greater punishment from law enforcement?

INDIVIDUALLY, THE POOR ARE NOT TOO TEMPTING TO THIEVES, FOR obvious reasons. Mug a banker and you might score a wallet containing a month's rent. Mug a janitor and you will be lucky to get away with bus fare to flee the crime scene. But as *Businessweek* helpfully pointed out in 2007, the poor *in aggregate* provide a juicy target for anyone depraved enough to make a business of stealing from them.

The trick is to rob them in ways that are systematic, impersonal, and almost impossible to trace to individual perpetrators. Employers, for example, can simply program their computers to shave a few dollars off each paycheck, or they can require workers to show up 30 minutes or more before the time clock starts ticking.

Lenders, including major credit companies as well as payday lenders, have taken over the traditional role of the street-corner loan shark, charging the poor insanely high rates of interest. When supplemented with late fees (themselves subject to interest), the resulting effective interest rate can be as high as 600% a year, which is perfectly legal in many states.

It's not just the private sector that's preying on the poor. Local governments are discovering that they can partially make up for declining tax revenues through fines, fees, and other costs imposed on indigent defendants, often for crimes no more dastardly than driving with a suspended license. And if that seems like an inefficient way to make money, given the high cost of locking people up, a growing number of jurisdictions have taken to charging defendants for their court costs and even the price of occupying a jail cell.

The poster case for government persecution of the down-and-out 5 would have to be Edwina Nowlin, a homeless Michigan woman who was jailed in 2009 for failing to pay $104 a month to cover the room-and-board charges for her 16-year-old son's incarceration. When she received a back paycheck, she thought it would allow her to pay for her son's jail stay. Instead, it was confiscated and applied to the cost of her own incarceration.

GOVERNMENT JOINS THE LOOTERS OF THE POOR

You might think that policymakers would take a keen interest in the amounts that are stolen, coerced, or extorted from the poor, but there are no official efforts to track such figures. Instead, we have to

Being poor itself is not yet a crime, but in at least a third of the states, being in debt can now land you in jail.

turn to independent investigators, like Kim Bobo, author of *Wage Theft in America*, who estimates that wage theft nets employers at least $100 billion a year and possibly twice that. As for the profits extracted by the lending industry, Gary Rivlin, who wrote *Broke USA: From Pawnshops to Poverty, Inc—How the Working Poor Became Big Business*, says the poor pay an effective surcharge of about $30 billion a year for the financial products they consume and more than twice that if you include sub-prime credit cards, sub-prime auto loans, and sub-prime mortgages.

These are not, of course, trivial amounts. They are on the same order of magnitude as major public programs for the poor. The government distributes about $55 billion a year, for example, through the largest single cash-transfer program for the poor, the Earned Income Tax Credit; at the same time, employers are siphoning off *twice that amount*, if not more, through wage theft.

And while government generally turns a blind eye to the tens of billions of dollars in exorbitant interest that businesses charge the poor, it is notably chary with public benefits for the poor. Temporary Assistance to Needy Families, for example, our sole remaining nationwide welfare program, gets only $26 billion a year in state and federal funds. The impression is left of a public sector that's totally self-contradictory: on the one hand, offering safety net programs for the poor; on the other, enabling large scale private sector theft from the very people it is supposedly trying to help.

At the local level though, government is increasingly opting to join in the looting. In 2009, a year into the Great Recession, I first started hearing complaints from community organizers about ever more aggressive levels of law enforcement in low-income areas. Flick a cigarette butt and get arrested for littering; empty your pockets for an officer conducting a stop-and-frisk operation and get cuffed for a few flakes of marijuana. Each of these offenses can result, at a minimum, in a three-figure fine.

10   And the number of possible criminal offenses leading to jail and/or fines has been multiplying recklessly. All across the country—from California and Texas to Pennsylvania—counties and municipalities have been toughening laws against truancy and ratcheting up enforcement, sometimes going so far as to handcuff children found on the streets during school hours. In New York City, it's now a crime to put your feet up on a subway seat, even if the rest of the car is empty, and a South Carolina woman spent six days in jail when she was unable to pay a $480 fine for the crime of having a "messy yard." Some cities—most recently, Houston and Philadelphia—have made it a crime to share food with indigent people in public places.

Being poor itself is not yet a crime, but in at least a third of the states, being in debt can now land you in jail. If a creditor like a landlord or credit card company has a court summons issued for you and you fail to show up on your appointed court date, a warrant will be issued for your arrest. And it is easy enough to miss a court summons, which may have been delivered to the wrong address or, in the case of some bottom-feeding bill collectors, simply tossed in the garbage—a practice so common that the industry even has a term for it: "sewer service." In a sequence that National Public Radio reports is "increasingly common," a person is stopped for some minor traffic offense—having a noisy muffler, say, or broken brake light—at which point, the officer discovers the warrant and the unwitting offender is whisked off to jail.

LOCAL GOVERNMENTS AS PREDATORS

Each of these crimes, neo-crimes, and pseudo-crimes carries financial penalties as well as the threat of jail time, but the amount of money thus extracted from the poor is fiendishly hard to pin down. No central agency tracks law enforcement at the local level, and local records can be almost willfully sketchy.

According to one of the few recent nationwide estimates, from the National Association of Criminal Defense Lawyers, 10.5 million misdemeanors were committed in 2006. No one would risk estimating the average financial penalty for a misdemeanor, although the experts

I interviewed all affirmed that the amount is typically in the "hundreds of dollars." If we take an extremely lowball $200 per misdemeanor, and bear in mind that 80–90% of criminal offenses are committed by people who are officially indigent, then local governments are using law enforcement to extract, or attempt to extract, at least $2 billion a year from the poor.

And that is only a small fraction of what governments would like to collect from the poor. Katherine Beckett, a sociologist at the University of Washington, estimates that "deadbeat dads" (and moms) owe $105 billion in back child-support payments, about half of which is owed to state governments as reimbursement for prior welfare payments made to the children. Yes, parents have a moral obligation to their children, but the great majority of child-support debtors are indigent.

Attempts to collect from the already-poor can be vicious and often, 15 one would think, self-defeating. Most states confiscate the drivers' licenses of people owing child support, virtually guaranteeing that they will not be able to work. Michigan just started suspending the drivers' licenses of people who owe money for parking tickets. Las Cruces, New Mexico, just passed a law that punishes people who owe overdue traffic fines by cutting off their water, gas, and sewage.

Once a person falls into the clutches of the criminal justice system, we encounter the kind of slapstick sadism familiar to viewers of *Wipeout*. Many courts impose fees without any determination of whether the offender is able to pay, and the privilege of having a payment plan will itself cost money.

In a study of 15 states, the Brennan Center for Justice at New York University found 14 of them contained jurisdictions that charge a lump-sum "poverty penalty" of up to $300 for those who cannot pay their fees and fines, plus late fees and "collection fees" for those who need to pay over time. If any jail time is imposed, that too may cost money, as the hapless Edwina Nowlin discovered, and the costs of parole and probation are increasingly being passed along to the offender.

The predatory activities of local governments give new meaning to that tired phrase "the cycle of poverty." Poor people are far more likely than the affluent to get into trouble with the law, either by failing to pay parking fines or by incurring the wrath of a private sector creditor like a landlord or a hospital.

Once you have been deemed a criminal, you can pretty much kiss your remaining assets goodbye. Not only will you face the aforementioned court costs, but you'll have a hard time ever finding a job again once you've acquired a criminal record. And then, of course, the poorer you become, the more likely you are to get in fresh trouble with the law, making this less like a "cycle" and more like the waterslide to hell. The further you descend, the faster you fall—until you eventually end up on the streets and get busted for an offense like urinating in public or sleeping on a sidewalk.

20   I could propose all kinds of policies to curb the ongoing predation on the poor. Limits on usury should be reinstated. Theft should be taken seriously even when it's committed by millionaire employers. No one should be incarcerated for debt or squeezed for money they have no chance of getting their hands on. These are no-brainers, and should take precedence over any long term talk about generating jobs or strengthening the safety net.

> **Before we can "do something" for the poor, there are some things we need to stop doing to them.**

Before we can "do something" for the poor, there are some things we need to stop doing to them.

FOR A SECOND READING

1. Ehrenreich uses the concept of thievery to describe such everyday practices as employers deducting extra pay from workers who fail to show up for work early or payday lenders who loan out money at interest rates that can top 600 percent. Do you agree with her characterization? In your view, is it accurate or valid to describe such practices as theft? Why or why not?

2. "Before we can 'do something' for the poor," Ehrenreich writes, "there are some things we need to stop doing to them" (p. 368). How do you understand this distinction? And what larger point is Ehrenreich trying to make by drawing this distinction here?

3. "I could propose," writes Ehrenreich, "all kinds of policies to curb the ongoing predation on the poor. Limits on usury should be reinstated. Theft should be taken seriously even when it's committed by millionaire employers. No one should be incarcerated for debt or squeezed for money they have no chance of getting their hands on" (p. 368). What do you think of the solutions Ehrenreich proposes here? Are they adequate responses to the problems she describes in this essay? Do you think they would make a substantial or meaningful difference? How or how not?

PUTTING IT INTO WRITING

4. "Being poor," writes Ehrenreich, "itself is not yet a crime, but in at least a third of the states, being in debt can now land you in jail. If a creditor like a landlord or credit card company has a court summons issued for you and you fail to show up on your appointed

court date, a warrant will be issued for your arrest" (p. 366). In a short essay, respond to the scenario Ehrenreich lays out here. What larger argument about the challenges and injustices of "being poor" is she using this example to make? And do you find yourself convinced by the evidence she presents here? Why or why not?

5. Here is a partial list of the concepts Ehrenreich uses to describe the way employers, local governments, and creditors treat the working poor: *robbery, persecution, predatory*. In an essay, conduct a close reading of the language Ehrenreich uses. What picture of the plight confronting the working poor do these terms evoke? What critique of employers, government, and creditors does it imply? And how valid do you find this commentary?

COMPARING ARGUMENTS

6. Linda Tirado (p. 370) is another writer who chronicles the challenges confronting the working poor. How does her profile of low-wage service work compare to Ehrenreich's discussion of the working poor? Based on the argument she makes here, which specific aspects of Tirado's essay do you think Ehrenreich would find most persuasive? Why?

LINDA TIRADO
You Get What You Pay For

Politicians and pundits speak endlessly about the problems confronting the poor, but few, if any, do so having actually experienced these problems themselves. Offering just such a firsthand perspective, Linda Tirado gives readers a glimpse of the daily realities and chronic challenges that define life as a member of the "working poor." Linda Tirado has worked a range of low-wage jobs, from fast-food worker to night cook, and has used these experiences to write extensively about issues of poverty in America. She is the author of *Hand to Mouth: Living in Bootstrap America* (2014), from which this selection is taken.

Before You Read

Have you ever held a job in the service industry? How would you characterize the social scripts and cultural norms that define this particular type of job?

AS FAR AS I'M CONCERNED, I EARN MY WAGES WITH MY SCARS. Anything above and beyond that is me doing my employers a favor. And I'm not inclined to do favors for people who treat me poorly. See, we work in insane conditions. Dangerous, even. Most kitchens in the middle of the summer are intolerable, with temperatures well into the triple digits. I've seen people sent to the hospital with heatstroke. A lot of us will run into the freezer for a few minutes until we cool down. I'm not a doctor and I can't say for sure, but I'm fairly certain that going from overheated to a minus-5 environment can't be healthy.

My arms and hands are covered in scars from the fryers. Oil at nearly 400 degrees doesn't tickle when it hits your skin, and you can't avoid the spatter entirely. I've burned my hands because the oven gloves had worn through and the owners were too cheap to spring for another pair. I've sliced my fingers open nearly to the bone when knives have slipped. I've dropped equipment on my feet because it was so busy I didn't have time to wash the grease off my hands. I've hurt myself in more ways than I can count because that was how I got my seven or eight bucks an hour.

Stuff like that is unavoidable; it's the nature of the work. We know and understand that when we take the jobs. Any dangerous job is like that; we're not stupid. The point is more that the risk is devalued—that our injuries, rather than being seen as a sign of our willingness to literally bleed for our employers, are seen as a liability.

The kitchen scars are more dramatic, but the emotional toll of retail is the worst. The conditions are patently impossible. I've been expected to spend three hours per shift stocking in the back, while also being told that the register was never to be left unattended. I've been told to always have coffee ready for customers and that it should always be fresh, and in the same breath been told that I was going through too much coffee. My section of the store is always supposed to be neat, but there's only one of me and over three hundred square feet to cover, and there are shoppers everywhere and not enough racks for all this shit to begin with.

My shoe size actually changed with the quality of the jobs I've had. 5 The better ones let me sit down sometimes. At the not-so-nice ones, I've stood for eight to ten hours, and my feet have gotten so swollen that my shoes don't fit.

The mandatory cheerleading is why I never worked for Walmart. Apparently this has changed now, but during employee meetings, they used to require their people to actually cheer. With pelvic thrusting. (Go watch the YouTube videos. It must be seen to be believed.) In those not long ago days, if you didn't wiggle your ass with sufficient vigor, you'd find yourself on the wrong side of management and then brought to the front to lead the cheer yourself. Sure, give me a W and an A and an L and a squiggly (or I guess now it's an asterisk since they rebranded), and I will happily shove them straight up your ass. Friends of mine will swear that they never got demerits until after they upset management by lacking enthusiasm. (To be fair to Wal*Mart, my friends weren't actually let go because they wouldn't wiggle enough. They can't prove causation. It's just that they didn't start getting demerits until they stopped wiggling.)

At work, I'm often told what words to say, and I will be written up if I deviate from the script or combine two steps to save time. In retail, we must acknowledge a customer who comes within a set radius of us with a certain tone and tenor in our voices. In telemarketing, our every word might be scripted. In fast food, we're typically given three greetings to choose from. At one large fast-food chain (let's call it LFC for short), the choices were these:

1) Welcome to LFC, how can I help you?

2) Welcome to LFC, would you like to try a delicious chicken meal today for only $4.99?

3) Welcome to LFC, what can we make fresh for you today?

The company even sent in undercover customers to make sure we stayed on script.

All of our actions are carefully dictated to us. I assume this is because employers think we have monkey brains and are incapable of making decisions. This means that they're paying me to pretend I'm not me and also that I care about you.

10   And as long as we're on the topic of insane things your bosses can do, you should be aware that you have no legal right to take breaks in America. Go ahead, Google it. Some states mandate breaks. Some farm-work has a federal break mandate. But overall, you've no right to demand a lunch break or a break at all. That's all at the discretion of your employer.

> ### *The kitchen scars are more dramatic, but the emotional toll of retail work is the worst.*

Some people have the luxury of asking themselves whether a job fulfills their career hopes and ambitions. I've got my own metric to gauge the fabulosity of a job: Does that job require me to keep my boss informed of the inner workings of my gastrointestinal system, or am I allowed to go to the bathroom at will? It's physically uncomfortable to hold it forever, and it sucks to stand by for the okay like a dog waiting for someone to open the door. But for me, the indignity of the whole thing is less about the potential bladder infections. It's more what the requirement for that kind of notification reveals about the tone of the place. In my experience, the jobs where the boss regulates your urinary tract also tend to demand a bunch of other degrading stuff.

We all know that a lot of folks think that poor people are lazy and incompetent. They think we get fired from jobs because we don't know how to behave, or we're always late, or we just don't care. But what rich people don't realize is how unbelievably easy it is to get fired. And a lot of times what gets you fired is that you're working more than one job.

Whenever you are working for the kind of place that has a corporate office, you're typically given the fewest possible hours—definitely less than full-time, because then they'd have to pay you benefits. (Full-time is often in the twenty-eight- to thirty-two-hours-a-week range, to boot.) But even though your employer might schedule you for twenty hours a week, you might wind up working ten, or thirty. It depends on how busy it is—when it's slow, they send you home, and when it's busy, they expect you to stay late. They also expect you to be able to come in to cover someone's shift if a co-worker gets sick at the last minute. Basically, they're expecting you to be available to work all the time. Scheduling is impossible.

At one chain, I was required to sign a contract stating that I was an at-will employee, that I would be part-time with no benefits, and that if I took another job without permission, I would be subject to termination because the company expected me to be able to come in whenever they found it necessary. And yes, this is legal in the United States of America.

It's unavoidable; even I have had to admit the impossibility of this 15 system and let people go, one an employee that I actually liked very much. Competent, friendly, good sense of humor. But her other boss simply would not post the schedule far enough in advance for me to give the woman any hours. If the workweek started Monday, the schedule at her other job went up Sunday night. I tried to do my scheduling a week or more in advance, and when I called the other restaurant to discuss the issue, the manager told me that she didn't actually feel any need to change her routines and that it was my problem to deal with. I simply had to let the woman go, because her other boss wanted the availability.

How is that legal, you ask? Well, a huge number of jobs in this country—and a crazy high percentage of the jobs that poor people hold down—are considered at-will. Sometimes you'll sign a paper stating that you understand what that means, sometimes not. It depends on the sophistication and size of the business hiring you. What "at-will" means is that your boss can decide that your eyes are too brown one day and let you go on the spot. As long as they're not in violation of civil rights law, they don't have to give you a reason, and they can decide that anything is a fireable offense. I've been fired because my boss made a mistake on some paperwork. I've been fired because I had the flu. I've been fired because I wouldn't sleep with someone. I've been fired because I *did* sleep with someone. I once saw a stripper fired because she couldn't afford breast implants and the club manager didn't find her natural breasts alluring enough to dance topless for drunken construction workers.

So let's break this down: You're poor, so you desperately need whatever crappy job you can find, and the nature of that crappy job is that you can be fired at any time. Meanwhile, your hours can be cut with no notice, and there's no obligation on the part of your employer to provide severance regardless of why, how, or when they let you go. And we wonder why the poor get poorer?

Of course not every firing is part of an intricate plot by the plutocrats. I've also been fired for calling off work too much ("calling off work," for those unfamiliar with the vernacular, just means that you call your boss to say you're not coming in). Usually I've called off because I was legitimately sick, because I rarely miss work more than I can help. But sometimes it was because my car wouldn't start or because I just couldn't face it. It doesn't matter what you say, and your boss doesn't care; the point is whether you do it too much, not whether your reasons are legit.

I admit it—I've been fired for doing some stupid shit. I've been fired for consistent tardiness because I simply didn't care, and more than once because I gave my boss the finger. And as a manager, I've fired people for being dumbasses—stuff like showing up to work too hung over to stand up straight. Once I had to fire a guy because he went and got knuckle tattoos. I've even fired someone for relentless creepiness. That was the one time I thanked God for at-will states. He wasn't a terrible worker, and there was nothing to point to, but he did brush his groin with his hand once too often while looking at the girls up front.

20   Idiot pranks are risky too. One kid I worked with got bored and built a castle out of cardboard boxes in the parking lot. They fired him a) because it made the company "look unprofessional," and b) for "time theft." I've seen someone get fired, no shit, because he didn't want to wear buttons proclaiming him proficient at cleaning and other menial tasks. I barely made it through the day without mentioning TPS reports. (If you don't know what those are, drop everything and go watch *Office Space* right now.)

I know a lot of people think that I'm supposed to be a good little worker bee and do my part to help move the wheels of capitalism. I just don't see what's in it for me anymore beyond my little paycheck.

Mostly, I've fired people because they didn't care about the things that do matter to me. I've never cared any more for the owners of the companies I've worked for than they have for me, but I will kill myself for my co-workers. A lot of us do that. When we work through fevers and injuries and bone weariness, it's for the money but also because if we don't, we know that we'll be leaving our co-workers holding the bag. However bad the shift is, with a man down, it'll be that much worse on whoever's left. There's a siege mentality in the service industry in particular; you go through hell together. If you tap out and go home, you're leaving your co-workers to deal with more customers with even fewer hands. And that means that they're more likely to get fired themselves—because if customers start complaining about the service, the boss doesn't really care that you're covering for someone who's out sick. So you bet your sweet ass that if you work for me and I see you being deadweight, I'll get rid of you.

All of this is not to cast myself as some kind of paragon of work perfection. I'm a terrible corporate manager, every time I tried it. My employees loved me, but I made a lousy guardian of profit margins. My first loyalty is to my co-workers. Then the customers. And then, in a distant third, the company.

For example, when I found out that some of my employees had themselves a fantastic gig pulling the expired salad and bruised or unusable produce out of the Dumpster and taking it home, I started making sure that the food was disposed of *next to* the trash rather than in it. This, you should know, was highly against the rules on everyone's part.

I figured if I got busted, I'd just say that I was trying to keep track of how much got thrown away to help me order properly the next time. I'm not sure what the company would have done if they'd found out; most companies simply don't want to know about stuff like that because even they don't want to be that harsh, but liability exists. No restaurant can knowingly allow anyone to eat expired food, even if it's obviously still sound. With that said, companies also discourage letting employees eat unservable food because they assume that a worker would have bought food instead of just going without, and heaven knows it's a sin to lose potential profits from workers! Only, most people don't buy their food half-off at their own stores; most people just drink more on hungry shifts when they can't eat. I always figured that my cooks would probably not be doing their best work if they were salivating every time some food finished cooking. And I just couldn't live with myself letting these guys look longingly at the burgers they were flipping as if they were Victorian street urchins lusting after a hot roll in a bakery window.

If one of my people was hungry, I gave them food. I'd send parents 25 home with boxes of expired chicken nuggets for their kids. My bosses, of course, generally hated dealing with me. It's been a pattern. I don't really blame them—their jobs sucked as much as mine did and I was a huge pain in their asses. One of my favorite bosses once told me that he hated having to explain the *why* of everything to me, but I considered it my job to be able to explain the why to the people who reported to me. If hours were getting cut or pay frozen, I damn well was going to give them a reason that made sense. If we were going to lay off a quarter of the staff, I'd better be able to explain it.

I know a lot of people think that I'm supposed to be a good little worker bee and do my part to help move the wheels of capitalism. I just don't see what's in it for me anymore beyond my little paycheck. Think about it this way: At my earning peak, I made approximately nineteen cents a minute before taxes.

So when I go out of my way to work hard, I'm not doing it for my bosses, I'm doing it for my co-workers. There's definitely a mutual covering of asses going on in the lower classes. (Hey, why should the upper classes do all the ass covering?) I've even tracked down babysitters for employees who'd lost their child care and couldn't afford to lose their shift as well. Instead of letting an employee call off work and winding up shorthanded to boot, I called around until I found a cashier who was more than happy to babysit for a few hours for some extra cash. I loaned the cook the money to pay the cashier, and everyone got something they needed. We do shit like that a lot.

We'd never survive otherwise.

FOR A SECOND READING

1. Tirado opens this essay by listing the various injuries she has either witnessed or suffered working in the food-service industry: "burned hands," "sliced fingers," "heatstroke." Why do you think she chooses to begin this way? In your view, does this strategy help Tirado make her larger argument about these types of jobs? If so, how effective do you find this strategy to be?

2. Tirado spends a good deal of time in this essay detailing the ways that the behavior, the wardrobe, even the speech of retail workers are "dictated" and "scripted" by their employers. Why do you think she gives this aspect of retail work so much attention? What does the prevalence of such scripts tell us about the nature of such work?

3. About the experience of being a workplace supervisor, Tirado writes: "My employees loved me, but I made a lousy guardian of profit margins. My first loyalty is to my co-workers. Then the customers. And then, in a distant third, the company" (p. 374). Respond to the list of "loyalties" Tirado enumerates here. Does it reflect the same standards or priorities you would follow? Does it reflect the standards and priorities scripted for the typical service or retail worker?

PUTTING IT INTO WRITING

4. "We all know," writes Tirado, "that a lot of folks think that poor people are lazy and incompetent. They think we get fired from jobs because we don't know how to behave, or we're always late, or we just don't care" (p. 372). In a 500-word essay, explain how the account of service work Tirado presents in this piece can be read as an attempt to refute precisely this view. Where in this essay does Tirado offer evidence that this view of "poor people" is incorrect? What portrait of these workers does Tirado present instead? And how does she use these portraits to make a larger argument about how the general public should actually view "poor people"?

5. Tirado also devotes significant time in this essay detailing the ways in which, and the reasons why, she has been fired from different jobs. Write an essay in which you describe and defend the standards you would use to determine whether or not a service or retail employee should be fired. What actions constitute a fire-able

offense and which do not? Why, in your view, is it fair to draw this particular distinction? And how do your standards compare to the ones used to justify firing Tirado?

COMPARING ARGUMENTS

6. Like Tirado, Barbara Ehrenreich (p. 364) is interested in questioning the fairness of the cultural and financial constraints confronting the working poor. Write an essay in which you compare what each writer has to say about this issue. To what extent does Tirado's account of the "double standards" imposed upon retail workers echo Ehrenreich's critique of the unjust ways the working poor are made to "pay for their own poverty"?

EMILY BADGER

What Happens When We All Become Our Own Bosses

The phrase "sharing economy" conjures a vision of industrious, independent individuals busily exchanging goods and services in efficient, fair-minded, and mutually beneficial collaboration. But the reality, notes journalist Emily Badger, is considerably more complicated. The rise of the "sharing economy," she notes, raises important questions about how work is to be overseen and regulated, and how workers themselves are to be protected and compensated. Emily Badger is a reporter for the *Washington Post* and a frequent contributor to the paper's Wonkblog, which covers urban policy. This essay was published in the *Washington Post* in 2016.

Before You Read

Would you say that the "sharing economy" is an accurate descriptor for the kinds of freelance work where individuals market their services directly to customers? Can you think of a different phrase that might more accurately describe this type of work?

THE "SHARING ECONOMY" HAS EVOKED TWO POSSIBLE FUTURES for what work will look like in the years to come: one dystopian, the other idealistic.

In the first, workers scurry among shopping trips, carpools, minor home repairs and menial errands so that the wealthy don't have to. "Work" will mean piecing together other people's tasks, with no benefits, picking up a few bucks Mechanical Turk-ing in between.

In the second, the sharing economy will free workers of the 9-to-5 drudge, making more of us "micro-entrepreneurs" who set our own hours and incomes. Finally empowered to profit off our own assets and time, we won't need traditional employers.

Arun Sundararajan believes in this second vision—or, at least, the idea that the first is not inevitable, that we might still redesign benefits and labor protections that would leverage the next fundamental shift in the economy for broad good. His case for optimism in his new book, "The Sharing Economy: The End of Employment and the Rise of Crowd-Based Capitalism," is compelling in large part because it comes from a business-school wonk and not a "sharing!" proselytizer devoted to the literal meaning of the word.

5   Sundararajan, a professor at New York University, is more interested in who owns the means of production than how to create *belonging* (Airbnb's buzzword) or *community* (part of Etsy's mission).

We're witnessing the beginning, he argues, of a radical change in how economic activity is organized where "the 'crowd' replaces the corporation at the center of capitalism." And so when you buy something—a dress, a ride to the airport, a vacation rental—you may get it from a marketplace of individuals rather than a big company. And when you earn income, it may come from your own car or home workshop—connected over the Internet to a crowd of consumers—and not an employer's biweekly paycheck.

> *We're witnessing the beginning . . . of a radical change in how economic activity is organized where "the 'crowd' replaces the corporation at the center of capitalism."*

Today, the vast majority of us in the United States work for someone else. The change Sundararajan envisions implies many more of us in the future will work for ourselves, whether as Lyft drivers, or copy-writing freelancers or shop owners. Some of these jobs are not new. But the ease with which individuals can connect to vast markets that would pay for those services will be.

If this sounds like rolling back more than a century of progress from economies of scale—reverting to a world where everyone is a small-time shopkeeper—Sundararajan suggests we can have both in the digital age: millions of small providers *and* scale.

"What gets me excited about the shift that we're seeing now is that it transitions the role of the individual from being a wage receiver to being an owner of that system of production in some small way," he says in an interview. "At the heart of it is an empowering shift."

People who are skeptical of that, he argues, are making an unfair comparison between this new type of work and today's full-time employment. 10

"Full-time employment at scale has been around for decades," he says. "And we've had plenty of time to understand the huge imbalance in bargaining power between the individual and the institution, and to correct it in a wide variety of ways."

In the United States, we've had the rise of labor unions, collective bargaining, minimum-wage laws, workers' comp and unemployment insurance. We've developed a system where benefits like paid leave and health care are largely provided by employers.

Full-time employment, in other words, means something a lot better than could have been the case, Sundararajan argues. And it'll take us time to figure out how to do the same for work in the new crowd-based capitalism. "When we transition to the individual-is-an-owner model," he adds, "you're starting at a better place fundamentally."

Part of his argument is that we shouldn't lament that Uber drivers don't get full-time benefits; we should reconsider why benefits and security come attached only to full-time jobs. The challenge, then, is much harder than making Uber treat its drivers as "employees." It entails dramatically redesigning the safety net and how we classify workers and companies.

15   That might mean finding ways to fund portable benefits that would cover workers who piece together freelance jobs and Instacart runs and Uber rides. It might mean allowing independent workers to collectively bargain with the platforms like Uber and Etsy. It might mean considering something like a universal basic income, which would counteract the insecurity of self-employment and gig work.

Sundararajan also envisions creating "safe harbors" for these platforms to experiment. Today, a company that offers training classes or tax withholdings to gig workers risks tripping over the legal distinction between having "independent contractors" and "employees." So current labor law actively discourages them from offering more benefits to the workers who use their platforms.

Sundararajan is convinced we'll solve these problems, eventually. "We will because individuals aspire to it," he says. "Individuals want stability."

> *Freelance and gig workers make up a small minority of the labor force today. Even if their numbers rise, will they really amass enough power to force broad changes to the safety net?*

But there is plenty of room for skepticism here, too. Freelance and gig workers make up a small minority of the labor force today. Even if their numbers rise, will they really amass enough power to force broad changes to the safety net? Americans spent years waging a bruising national debate over how to reform health care. But even with the Affordable Care Act, we still didn't manage to substantially sever the link between insurance and full-time employment.

Whether these solutions are economically wise or logistically possible or politically realistic are all different questions.

20   Perhaps some will also view Sundararajan's optimism as letting companies like Uber off the hook. They are, after all, making a lot more money off the rise of this new kind of work than the individual owner-workers doing it. Uber would no doubt prefer a solution where society comes up with the safety net so the company doesn't have to (chief executive Travis Kalanick essentially acknowledged this when he praised Obamacare for creating individual insurance markets that allow people to drive for Uber).

Then again, if Sundararajan is right, this new era of work we're shifting into will probably long outlast Uber the company.

FOR A SECOND READING

1. Take a moment to reflect on the title of this essay. What image is evoked in your mind by a world "where we all become our own bosses"? Does this vision of work seem preferable to what currently stands as the cultural norm? Why or why not?

2. Can you envision a world in which we no longer need "traditional employers"? As a worker, is this a world you would prefer to live in? Why or why not?

3. To some, Badger notes, the rise of the sharing economy "sounds like rolling back more than a century of progress" (p. 379). Do you share this view? Does the system of work at the heart of this new economy (i.e., the relative protection afforded to workers, the degree of workplace regulation, the nature of the worker–customer relationships) strike you as antiprogressive? How or how not?

PUTTING IT INTO WRITING

4. Badger considers some of the ways that the rise of the new "sharing economy" might entail a rethinking of the rules, regulations, and norms governing work: "[It] might mean finding ways to fund portable benefits that would cover workers who piece together freelance jobs and Instacart runs and Uber rides. It might mean allowing independent workers to collectively bargain with the platforms like Uber and Etsy. It might mean considering something like a universal basic income, which would counteract the insecurity of self-employment and gig work" (p. 380). In a 500-word essay, analyze and evaluate some of the potential changes Badger outlines here. Do you agree that the rise of a "sharing economy" might necessitate changes in how benefits, bargaining rights, and compensation for these workers are determined? In your view, are such efforts to address the "insecurity" of "gig work" important or necessary? Why or why not?

5. "The sharing economy," writes Badger, "has evoked two possible futures for what work will look like in the years to come: one dystopian, the other idealistic" (p. 378). Given what Badger has to say about the "sharing economy" in this essay, which of these two futures do you think is more likely? What specific points raised in this essay would you point to as evidence to support your view?

COMPARING ARGUMENTS

6. How much of Badger's discussion here reminds you of what
    Catherine Rampell (p. 383) has to say about work and the millennial
    generation? Write a review of Badger's essay from Rampell's point of
    view. To what extent would Rampell find in Badger's account of the
    "sharing economy" support for her own argument about how the
    "slacker" label gets misapplied?

CATHERINE RAMPELL

A Generation of Slackers? Not So Much

According to popular myth, young people today rank among the most entitled, coddled, and laziest in history. But this cultural conceit, says Catherine Rampell, is more the result of generational misunderstanding than it is any accurate assessment of reality. Rebutting stereotypes about America's "slacker generation," Rampell sketches a portrait of work among "millennials" in which commitment, sacrifice, and ambition have not so much disappeared as taken on new forms. Rampell was the founding editor of the Economix blog at the *New York Times*. She currently writes a biweekly opinion column for the *Washington Post*. This article appeared in the *New York Times* in 2011.

Before You Read

How do you respond to the term "slacker"? In your own experience, what type of person is this term typically used to describe or criticize? Have you ever had this term applied to you?

YOU'D THINK THERE WOULD BE A LITTLE SYMPATHY. THIS MONTH, college graduates are jumping into the job market, only to land on their parents' couches: the unemployment rate for 16- to 24-year-olds is a whopping 17.6 percent.

The reaction from many older Americans? This generation had it coming.

Generation Y—or Millennials, the Facebook Generation, or whatever you want to call today's cohort of young people—has been accused of being the laziest generation ever. They feel entitled and are coddled, disrespectful, narcissistic, and impatient, say authors of books like *The Dumbest Generation* and *Generation Me*.

And three in four Americans believe that today's youth are less virtuous and industrious than their elders, a 2009 survey by the Pew Research Center found.

In a sign of humility or docility, young people agree. In that 2009 Pew survey, two-thirds of millennials said older adults were superior to the younger generation when it came to moral values and work ethic. 5

After all, if there's a young person today who's walked 10 miles barefoot through the snow to school, it was probably on an iPhone app.

It's worth remembering that to some extent, these accusations of laziness and narcissism in "kids these days" are nothing new. . . . Even Aristotle and Plato were said to have expressed similar feelings about the slacker youth of their times.

So is this the Laziest Generation? There are signs that its members benefit from lower standards. Technology has certainly made life easier. But there may also be a generation gap; the way young adults work is simply different.

It's worth remembering that to some extent, these accusations of laziness and narcissism in "kids these days" are nothing new—they've been leveled against Generation X, Baby Boomers, and many generations before them. Even Aristotle and Plato were said to have expressed similar feelings about the slacker youth of their times.

But this generation has had it easy in some ways.

10   They can access just about any resource, product, or service anywhere from a mere tap on a touch screen. And as many critics have noted, it's also easier to get A's. The typical grade-point average in college rose to about 3.11 by the middle of the last decade, from 2.52 in the 1950s, according to a recent study by Stuart Rojstaczer, professor emeritus at Duke, and Christopher Healy of Furman University.

College students also spend fewer hours studying each week than did their counterparts in 1961, according to a new working paper by Philip S. Babcock of the University of California, Santa Barbara, and Mindy Marks of the University of California, Riverside. That doesn't mean all this leftover time is spent on PlayStation 3's.

There is ample evidence that young people today are hardworking and productive. The share of college students working full time generally grew from 1985 onward—until the Great Recession knocked many millennials out of the labor force, according to the Labor Department.

And while many college students today—like those of yesterday—get financial help from their parents, 44 percent of students today say that work or personal savings helped finance their higher educations, according to a survey of recent graduates by Rutgers University.

"I don't think this is a generation of slackers," said Carl Van Horn, a labor economist at Rutgers. "This image of the kid who goes off and skis in Colorado, I don't think that's the correct image. Today's young people are very focused on trying to work hard and to get ahead."

15   Defying the narcissism stereotype, community service among young people has exploded. Between 1989 and 2006, the share of teenagers who were volunteering doubled, to 26.4 percent from 13.4 percent, according

to a report by the Corporation for National and Community Service. And the share of incoming college freshmen who say they plan to volunteer is at a record high of 32.1 percent, too, U.C.L.A.'s annual incoming freshman survey found.

Perhaps most important, many of the behaviors that older generations interpret as laziness may actually enhance young people's productivity, say researchers who study Generation Y.

Members of Gen Y, for example, are significantly more likely than Gen X'ers and boomers to say they are more productive working in teams than on their own, according to Don Tapscott, author of *Grown Up Digital: How the Net Generation Is Changing Your World*, a book based on interviews with 11,000 millennials.

> *[M]any of the behaviors that older generations interpret as laziness may actually enhance young people's productivity.*

To older workers, wanting help looks like laziness; to younger workers, the gains that come from teamwork have been learned from the collaborative nature of their childhood activities, which included social networks, crowd-sourcing, and even video games like World of Warcraft that "emphasize cooperative rather than individual competition," Mr. Tapscott says.

Employers also complain about millennials checking Facebook and Twitter on the job, or working with their ear buds in.

Older workers have a strong sense of separate spheres for work and play: the cubicle is for work, and home is for fun. But to millennials, the boundaries between work and play are fuzzier, said Michael D. Hais, co-author of *Millennial Makeover: MySpace, YouTube, and the Future of American Politics*. 20

Think of the corporate cultures at prototypical Gen Y employers like Facebook and Google, he says, where foosball, volleyball courts, and subsidized massages are office fixtures.

The prevailing millennial attitude is that taking breaks for fun at work makes people more, not less, productive. Likewise, they accept that their work will bleed into evenings and weekends.

Some experts also believe that today's young people are better at quickly switching from one task to another, given their exposure to so many stimuli during their childhood and adolescence, said John Della Volpe, the director of polling at Harvard's Institute of Politics. (The jury is still out on that one.)

Of course, these explanations may be unconvincing to older bosses, co-workers, and teachers on the other side of this culture clash. But at least they can take comfort in one fact: someday, millennials will have their own new generation of know-it-all ne'er-do-wells to deal with.

FOR A SECOND READING

1. What do you make of the phrase "slacker generation"? What image does it conjure in your mind? And in your view, does it serve as an accurate descriptor for young people today?

2. As Rampell notes, "Accusations of laziness and narcissism in 'kids these days' are nothing new—they've been leveled against Generation X, Baby Boomers, and many generations before them" (p. 384). How important do you think this observation is? In your view, does it matter that there is historical precedent for today's attitude toward millennials? Does having this historical context give you a different way of thinking about the accusations leveled against young people today?

3. "In a sign of humility or docility," writes Rampell, "two-thirds of millennials said older adults were superior to the younger generation when it came to moral values and work ethic" (p. 383). If you were asked this same question in a poll, how would you respond? Do you share the majority view that there exists a measurable, generational difference where moral values and work ethic are concerned?

PUTTING IT INTO WRITING

4. Much of the pessimism directed toward younger workers these days, Rampell argues, stems from the fact that the norms around work have undergone such dramatic change. While older workers continue to define hard work in terms of such ideals as self-sufficiency and competition, younger workers subscribe to more contemporary values like teamwork and collaboration. Write an essay in which you evaluate the merits of this argument. What do you make of the distinction between older and younger workers Rampell draws here? Do you find her claim about the power of cultural norms to change personal attitudes toward work persuasive? How does this compare to your own view?

5. Rampell lists some of the skills and attitudes she believes young people bring to the workplace: a familiarity with working in teams; a willingness to blur the boundaries between work and play; a capacity to switch easily from one task to another. What do you make of this list? Do you think it itemizes a set of skills that are genuinely valuable? And how accurately does this list reflect your own workplace attitudes and skills? Can you cite an example from your own work experience that either confirms or challenges the accuracy of this list?

COMPARING ARGUMENTS

6. Emily Badger (p. 378) also offers a portrait of employment for young workers. Her essay, however, paints a picture of the sharing economy where the workplace norms and employment pressures are far different from those presented by Rampell here. How do these two depictions of work compare? What are the key differences between them? And do you think Badger's essay challenges or supports Rampell's thesis about the cultural misconceptions surrounding the so-called slacker generation?

Then and Now: **Dressing for Success**

The rules establishing proper workplace attire have changed markedly over the years. But are these changes merely cosmetic? Or do they tell us something about the ways our attitudes toward work, or perhaps even our social or cultural attitudes, have changed as well? To be sure, there is a long and storied history in America of treating workplace wardrobe as a kind of societal barometer. In the case of the 1950s office worker, for example, the "gray flannel suit" came to be widely viewed as a metaphor for the corporate standardization, political conformity, and social conservatism that for many defined American life during this period. For countless commentators, this unadorned and anonymous business uniform not only captured the supposedly faceless, robotic nature of 1950s office work, but it also symbolized a pervasive hostility in mid-century America toward individuality, creativity, and dissent.

When compared to the corporate dress codes that prevail today, it's hard not to feel we've come a long way from this buttoned-down, bygone era. Nowadays the drab uniformity of gray flannel has given way to the more flexible and informal wardrobe norms of so-called business casual — a shift, we are told, that proves how much more liberated, freewheeling, and creative office work has become. No longer the faceless drone of yore, the corporate employee of the twenty-first century (at least according to

J. R. Eyerman/Getty Images

what we see in countless commercials) plies his or her trade in an environment where individuality and diversity are prized, a world in which employees are members of teams, professional colleagues are also personal friends, and creativity rather than conformity is the rule of thumb.

But is this actually true? Does this shift in dress code really prove how much more liberated office life — or life in general — has become?

In answering this question, we might begin by pointing out a paradox: Despite its emphasis on nonconformity and individual choice, business casual is nonetheless still a *style*, a wardrobe standard established for and marketed to us. Just because we get to wear khakis and sandals to the office these days doesn't automatically mean we're now using clothes to express our individuality — particularly when

Larry Williams/Getty Images

we may well have gotten the idea for this outfit by paging through a clothing catalog. Even when an office wardrobe is informal, it isn't necessarily any less of an office uniform. What the rise of business casual may well demonstrate, in fact, is not how nonconformist modern American culture has become, but rather how the terms defining such conformity have simply changed. It certainly seems a stretch to claim that white-collar work is no longer hierarchical or rigidly organized, or that the contemporary business landscape has grown any less "corporate." Perhaps this shift toward casualness is best understood not as a movement beyond conformity but as a compensation for conformity: a style change designed to add a gloss of informality and autonomy to a work world still largely dictated by scripts we ourselves do not write.

PUTTING IT INTO WRITING

1. Write an essay in which you analyze the norms about work being conveyed by the style of dress in these two examples. What, if anything, seems to have changed between the work dress in the 1950s versus today? In your opinion, which of these photographs seems more typical of the concepts of work and career? Why?

2. One of the most visible differences between white-collar and blue-collar work is the difference in dress. How do you think Matthew Crawford (p. 333) would respond to the idea of business-casual dress? In your opinion, does the idea of business casual highlight or diminish the differences between white- and blue-collar work? Why?

MADDIE OATMAN
The Racist, Twisted History of Tipping

Within the restaurant industry, tipping — leaving an extra gratuity for servers in order to recognize and reward them for the service they provide — has long been an assumed and unquestioned norm. But how many of us, asks Maddie Oatman, know the history behind this long-established practice? And how, she further asks, does learning this history challenge our assumptions about food service work more generally? Maddie Oatman is a story editor at *Mother Jones* magazine, where she writes frequently about food, health, and the environment. This essay appeared in *Mother Jones* in 2016.

Before You Read

What guidelines do you follow in deciding whether, or how much, to tip food servers? How much do you think these rules depend on whether or not you have done this type of work yourself?

FRESH OUT OF COLLEGE AND WORKING AS AN UNPAID INTERN FOR A San Francisco nonprofit, I paid the bills by moonlighting at an Indian restaurant in the Pacific Heights neighborhood. My hostess job entailed long stretches of boredom punctuated by a cacophonous frenzy. There were icy glares from impatient diners and reprimands from managers for drifting from my podium, but compared with most restaurant workers, I was sitting pretty: My hourly rate exceeded California's minimum wage, I was tipped out by the servers at the end of each shift, and I even received health care benefits — a city mandate.

Very few of America's 11 million restaurant workers share my story. The federal minimum wage is a paltry $7.25 an hour, but in 18 states servers, bussers, and hosts are paid just $2.13 — less than the price of a Big Mac. This is known as the federal "tipped minimum wage" because, in theory, these food workers will make up the difference in tips. Twenty-five states and DC have their own slightly higher tipped minimums. The remaining seven, including California, guarantee the full state minimum wage to all workers.

> *The origin of the word is unclear—one theory says "tip" is shorthand for "to insure promptness"; another suggests it's from 17th-century thief slang meaning "to give."*

On the surface, tipping seems little more than a reward for astute recommendations and polite, speedy service. But the practice has unsavory roots, as Saru Jayaraman, a labor activist and author of *Forked: A New Standard for American Dining*, told me during a taping of *Bite*, the new food and politics podcast from *Mother Jones*. The origin of the word is unclear—one theory says "tip" is shorthand for "to insure promptness"; another suggests it's from 17th-century thief slang meaning "to give." In any case, European aristocrats popularized the habit of slipping gratuities to their hosts' servants, and by the mid-1800s rich Americans, hoping to flaunt their European sophistication, had brought the practice home.

• • •

Restaurants and rail operators, notably Pullman, embraced tipping primarily, Jayaraman says, because it enabled them to save money by hiring newly freed slaves to work for tips alone. Plenty of Americans frowned upon the practice, and a union-led movement begat bans on tipping in several states. The fervor spread to Europe, too, before fizzling in the United States—by 1926, the state tipping bans had been repealed.

America's first minimum-wage law, passed by Congress in 1938, 5 allowed states to set a lower wage for tipped workers, but it wasn't until the '60s that labor advocates persuaded Congress to adopt a federal

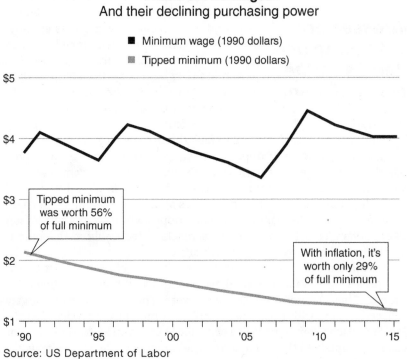

A Tale of Two Wages
And their declining purchasing power

■ Minimum wage (1990 dollars)
▨ Tipped minimum (1990 dollars)

Tipped minimum was worth 56% of full minimum

With inflation, it's worth only 29% of full minimum

'90   '95   '00   '05   '10   '15

Source: US Department of Labor

tipped minimum wage that increased in tandem with the regular minimum wage. In 1996, former Godfather's Pizza CEO Herman Cain, who was then head of the National Restaurant Association, helped convince a Republican-led Congress to decouple the two wages. The tipped minimum has been stuck at $2.13 ever since.

This is why restaurant workers today take home some of the lowest pay offered by any industry. Seven of the 10 worst-paying job categories tracked by the Bureau of Labor Statistics (BLS) are in food services. Real median wages for waiters and waitresses are down 5 percent since 2009; cooks saw a decline of 9 percent.

Sure, we occasionally hear about waiters hauling in $80K at posh urban establishments. Those are the stories that corporate players such as Darden, the notoriously stingy owner of the Olive Garden chain, want you to remember. The restaurant association's website claims the national median take-home pay for tipped servers is $16 to $22 an hour. But those same workers, according to the BLS, made just $9.01 an hour in 2014—poverty wages for a family of four and nowhere near enough to cover rent on the average two-bedroom apartment. (The association says this figure is low because some restaurants report tips improperly.)

America's two-tiered wage system is hardest on women, who make up 71 percent of tipped servers—waitresses are twice as likely to use food stamps as the general population. And while federal law requires employers to make sure their tipped workers earn at least minimum wage *after* tips, that rarely happens—from 2010 to 2012, according to the Department of Labor, 84 percent of restaurants were in violation of federal wage law, "which means the women who put food on the tables in America can't actually afford to feed themselves," Jayaraman says.

> **[W]aitresses are twice as likely to use food stamps as the general population.**

The racist origins of tipping persist, meanwhile, in the take-home wages of nonwhite restaurant workers, who earn 56 percent less than their white colleagues. In one study, researchers at Cornell University and Mississippi College found that customers at an unnamed national chain restaurant—even the black customers—tipped white servers better than black servers. This disparity, the researchers noted, could in theory render the tipped minimum wage unlawful.

10   Jayaraman says she's not advocating the end of tipping, just that it take on a different form. Several celebrated restaurants, including Alice Waters' Chez Panisse and Danny Meyer's The Modern, have largely replaced tipping with higher menu prices or mandatory service charges. San Francisco's Bar Agricole tried it, too, but reverted to tipping after servers complained they were making less money. At least they're working in California, where they'll never take home less than the current $10-an-hour minimum wage, even if every last table stiffs them.

FOR A SECOND READING

1. Oatman highlights the difference between the federal minimum wage ($7.25/hour) and the "tipped minimum wage" ($2.13/hour) paid to food service workers. Why does she emphasize this difference? What larger point about tips and tipping is she trying to make by calling out this difference?

2. Oatman describes the "icy glares from impatient diners and reprimands from managers" (p. 390) she encountered while working as a restaurant hostess. Analyze the language Oatman chooses here. What do terms like "icy," "impatient," and "reprimands" suggest about the kind of work environment Oatman experienced? What larger point about food service work do you think she is making by choosing these kinds of terms?

3. Oatman cites data showing a disparity in the "take-home wages of nonwhite restaurant workers, who earn 56 percent less than their white colleagues" (p. 392). Put yourself in the position of a researcher studying this issue. What is significant about this statistic? What does it tell you about the ongoing legacy of racial discrimination in tipping? And how do you think this legacy should be addressed?

PUTTING IT INTO WRITING

4. "On the surface," Oatman writes, "tipping seems little more than a reward for astute recommendations and polite, speedy service. But the practice has unsavory roots" (p. 390). In a 500-word essay, evaluate Oatman's decision to uncover the "unsavory roots" of tipping. In your view, is this an important story to tell? What lessons does this "hidden history" teach us? And, in your view, are these valuable lessons for us to learn? Why or why not?

5. Certain high-end restaurants, Oatman tells us, "have largely replaced tipping with higher menu prices or mandatory service charges" (p. 392). Write a 500-word essay in which you evaluate the specific policy changes presented here. What are the specific advantages and/or drawbacks of this system? Which of these changes do you support? Why?

COMPARING ARGUMENTS

6. Mike Rose (p. 394) presents his own portrait of food service work. How do you think Oatman would respond to his essay? In your view, does Rose's argument about "blue-collar brilliance" lend further support or credibility to Oatman's call for the rules around "tipping" to be changed? If so, how?

MIKE ROSE
Blue-Collar Brilliance

Among the many stereotypes that shape cultural attitudes toward manual or blue-collar work is the assumption that such work is not intellectually challenging. Working with your head and working with your hands, the social script would have us believe, are fundamentally different, even incompatible, endeavors. Challenging this thinking, noted educator Mike Rose presents us with a portrait of blue-collar work that flouts this narrow view. Rose has spent his career studying literacy and the relationship of working-class Americans to the educational system. His books include *Possible Lives: The Promise of Public Education in America* (1995), *The Mind at Work: Valuing the Intelligence of the American Worker* (2004), *Why School? Reclaiming Education for All of Us* (2009), and *Back to School: Why Everyone Deserves a Second Chance at Education* (2012). He is currently professor of social research methodology at the UCLA Graduate School of Education and Information Studies. This essay originally appeared in the Summer 2009 edition of the *American Scholar.*

Before You Read

Do you think it's valid to draw conclusions about a person's intelligence based upon the job she or he holds? Why or why not?

MY MOTHER, ROSE MERAGLIO ROSE (ROSIE), SHAPED HER ADULT identity as a waitress in coffee shops and family restaurants. When I was growing up in Los Angeles during the 1950s, my father and I would occasionally hang out at the restaurant until her shift ended, and then we'd ride the bus home with her. Sometimes she worked the register and the counter, and we sat there; when she waited booths and tables, we found a booth in the back where the waitresses took their breaks.

There wasn't much for a child to do at the restaurants, and so as the hours stretched out, I watched the cooks and waitresses and listened to what they said. At mealtimes, the pace of the kitchen staff and the din from customers picked up. Weaving in and out around the room, waitresses warned *behind you* in impassive but urgent voices. Standing at the service window facing the kitchen, they called out abbreviated orders. *Fry four on two*, my mother would say as she clipped a check onto the metal wheel. Her tables were *deuces*, *four-tops*, or *six-tops* according to their size; seating areas also were nicknamed. The *racetrack*, for instance, was the fast-turnover front section. Lingo conferred authority and signaled know-how.

Rosie took customers' orders, pencil poised over pad, while fielding questions about the food. She walked full tilt through the room with plates stretching up her left arm and two cups of coffee somehow cradled in her right hand. She stood at a table or booth and removed a plate for this person, another for that person, then another, remembering who had the hamburger, who had the fried shrimp, almost always getting it right. She would haggle with the cook about a returned order and rush by us, saying, *He gave me lip, but I got him.* A minute to flop down in the booth next to my father. *I'm all in,* she'd say, and whisper something about a customer. Gripping the outer edge of the table with one hand, she'd watch the room and note, in the flow of our conversation, who needed a refill, whose order was taking longer to prepare than it should, who was finishing up.

I couldn't have put it in words when I was growing up, but what I observed in my mother's restaurant defined the world of adults, a place where competence was synonymous with physical work. I've since studied the working habits of blue-collar workers and have come to understand how much my mother's kind of work demands of both body and brain. A waitress acquires knowledge and intuition about the ways and the rhythms of the restaurant business. Waiting on seven to nine tables, each with two to six customers, Rosie devised memory strategies so that she could remember who ordered what. And because she knew the average time it took to prepare different dishes, she could monitor an order that was taking too long at the service station.

Like anyone who is effective at physical work, my mother learned to   5
work smart, as she put it, *to make every move count.* She'd sequence and group tasks: What could she do first, then second, then third as she circled through her station? What tasks could be clustered? She did everything on the fly, and when problems arose—technical or human—she solved them within the flow of work, while taking into account the emotional state of her coworkers. Was the manager in a good mood? Did the cook wake up on the wrong side of the bed? If so, how could she make an extra request or effectively return an order?

And then, of course, there were the customers who entered the restaurant with all sorts of needs, from physiological ones, including the emotions that accompany hunger, to a sometimes complicated desire for human contact. Her tip depended on how well she responded to these needs, and so she became adept at reading social cues and managing feelings, both the customers' and her own. No wonder, then, that Rosie was intrigued by psychology. The restaurant became the place where she studied human behavior, puzzling over the problems of her regular customers and refining her ability to deal with people in a difficult world. She took pride in *being among the public,* she'd say. *There isn't a day that goes by in the restaurant that you don't learn something.*

Intelligence is closely associated with formal education, and most people seem to move comfortably from that notion to a belief that work requiring less schooling requires less intelligence. These assumptions run through our cultural history, from the post–Revolutionary War period, when mechanics were characterized by political rivals as illiterate and therefore incapable of participating in government, until today. Generalizations about intelligence, work, and social class deeply affect our assumptions about ourselves and each other, guiding the ways we use our minds to learn, build knowledge, solve problems, and make our way through the world.

Although writers and scholars have often looked at the working class, they have generally focused on the values such workers exhibit rather than on the thought their work requires—a subtle but pervasive omission. Our cultural iconography promotes the muscled arm, sleeve rolled tight against biceps, but no brightness behind the eye, no image that links hand and brain.

One of my mother's brothers, Joe Meraglio, left school in the ninth grade to work for the Pennsylvania Railroad. From there he joined the Navy, returned to the railroad, which was already in decline, and eventually joined his older brother at General Motors, where, over a 33-year career, he moved from working on the assembly line to supervising the paint-and-body department. When I was a young man, Joe took me on a tour of the factory. The floor was loud—in some places deafening—and when I turned a corner or opened a door, the smell of chemicals knocked my head back. The work was repetitive and taxing, and the pace was inhumane.

10   Still, for Joe the shop floor was a school. He learned the most efficient way to use his body by acquiring a set of routines that were quick and preserved energy. Otherwise he never would have survived on the line.

> **Most people seem to move . . . to a belief that work requiring less schooling requires less intelligence.**

As a foreman, Joe constantly faced new problems and became a consummate multi-tasker, evaluating a flurry of demands quickly, parceling out physical and mental resources, keeping a number of ongoing events in his mind, returning to whatever task had been interrupted, and maintaining a cool head under the pressure of grueling production schedules. In the midst of all this, Joe learned more and more about the auto industry, the technological and social dynamics of the shop floor, the machinery and production processes, and the basics of paint chemistry and of plating and baking. With further promotions, he not only solved problems but also began to find problems to solve: Joe initiated the redesign of the nozzle on a paint sprayer, thereby eliminating costly and unhealthy overspray. And he found a way to reduce the energy costs of the baking ovens without affecting the quality of the paint. He lacked formal knowledge of how the machines under his supervision worked, but he had direct experience with them, hands-on knowledge, and was savvy about their quirks and operational capabilities. He could experiment with them.

In addition, Joe learned about budgets and management. Coming off the line as he did, he had a perspective of workers' needs and management's demands, and this led him to think of ways to improve efficiency on the line while relieving some of the stress on the assemblers. He had each worker in a unit learn his or her coworkers' jobs so they could rotate across stations to relieve some of the monotony. He believed that rotation would allow assemblers to get longer and more frequent breaks. It was an easy sell to the people on the line. The union, however, had to approve any modification in job duties, and the managers were wary of the change. Joe had to argue his case on a number of fronts, providing him a kind of rhetorical education.

Eight years ago I began a study of the thought processes involved in work like that of my mother and uncle. I catalogued the cognitive demands of a range of blue-collar and service jobs, from waitressing and hair styling to plumbing and welding. To gain a sense of how knowledge and skill develop, I observed experts as well as novices. From the details of this close examination, I tried to fashion what I called "cognitive biographies" of blue-collar workers. Biographical accounts of the lives of scientists, lawyers, entrepreneurs, and other professionals are rich with detail about the intellectual dimension of their work. But the life stories of working-class people are few and are typically accounts of hardship and courage or the achievements wrought by hard work.

Our culture—in Cartesian fashion—separates the body from the mind, so that, for example, we assume that the use of a tool does not involve abstraction. We reinforce this notion by defining intelligence solely on grades in school and numbers on IQ tests. And we employ social biases pertaining to a person's place on the occupational ladder. The distinctions among blue, pink, and white collars carry with them attributions of character, motivation, and intelligence. Although we rightly acknowledge and amply compensate the play of mind in white-collar and professional work, we diminish or erase it in considerations about other endeavors—physical and service work particularly. We also often ignore the experience of everyday work in administrative deliberations and policymaking.

Here's what we find when we get in close. The plumber seeking 15 leverage in order to work in tight quarters and the hair stylist adroitly handling scissors and comb manage their bodies strategically. Though work-related actions become routine with experience, they were learned at some point through observation, trial and error, and, often, physical or verbal assistance from a coworker or trainer.

The use of tools requires the studied refinement of stance, grip, balance, and fine-motor skills. Workers must also know the characteristics of the material they are engaging—how it reacts to various cutting or compressing devices, to degrees of heat, or to lines of force. Some of these things demand judgment, the weighing of options, the consideration of multiple variables, and, occasionally, the creative use of a tool in an unexpected way.

Carpenters have an eye for length, line, and angle; mechanics troubleshoot by listening; hair stylists are attuned to shape, texture, and motion. Sensory data merge with concept, as when an auto mechanic relies on sound, vibration, and even smell to understand what cannot be observed.

Planning and problem solving have been studied since the earliest days of modern cognitive psychology and are considered core elements in Western definitions of intelligence. To work is to solve problems. The big difference between the psychologist's laboratory and the workplace is that in the former the problems are isolated and in the latter they are embedded in the real-time flow of work with all its messiness and social complexity.

Verbal and mathematical skills drive measures of intelligence in the Western Hemisphere, and many of the kinds of work I studied are thought to require relatively little proficiency in either. Compared to certain kinds of white-collar occupations, that's true. But written symbols flow through physical work.

20   Numbers are rife in most workplaces: on tools and gauges, as measurements, as indicators of pressure or concentration or temperature, as guides to sequence, on ingredient labels, on lists and spreadsheets, as markers of quantity and price. Certain jobs require workers to make, check, and verify calculations, and to collect and interpret data. Basic math can be involved, and some workers develop a good sense of numbers and patterns. Consider, as well, what might be called material mathematics: mathematical functions embodied in materials and actions, as when a carpenter builds a cabinet or a flight of stairs.

A simple mathematical act can extend quickly beyond itself. Measuring, for example, can involve more than recording the dimensions of an object. As I watched a cabinetmaker measure a long strip of wood, he read a number off the tape out loud, looked back over his shoulder to the kitchen wall, turned back to his task, took another measurement, and paused for a moment in thought. He was solving a problem involving the molding, and the measurement was important to his deliberation about structure and appearance.

In the blue-collar workplace, directions, plans, and reference books rely on illustrations, some representational and others, like blueprints, that require training to interpret. Esoteric symbols—visual jargon—depict switches and receptacles, pipe fittings, or types of welds. Workers themselves often make sketches on the job. I frequently observed them grab a pencil to sketch something on a scrap of paper or on a piece of the material they were installing.

Though many kinds of physical work don't require a high literacy level, more reading occurs in the blue-collar workplace than is generally thought, from manuals and catalogs to work orders and invoices, to lists, labels, and forms. With routine tasks, for example, reading is integral to understanding production quotas, learning how to use an instrument, or applying a product. Written notes can initiate action, as in restaurant orders or reports of machine malfunction, or they can serve as memory aids.

True, many uses of writing are abbreviated, routine, and repetitive, and they infrequently require interpretation or analysis. But analytic moments can be part of routine activities, and seemingly basic reading and writing can be cognitively rich. Because workplace language is used in the flow of other activities, we can overlook the remarkable coordination of words, numbers, and drawings required to initiate and direct action.

If we believe everyday work to be mindless, then that will affect the 25 work we create in the future. When we devalue the full range of everyday cognition, we offer limited educational opportunities and fail to make fresh and meaningful instructional connections among disparate kinds of skill and knowledge. If we think that whole categories of people—identified by class or occupation—are not that bright, then we reinforce social separations and cripple our ability to talk across cultural divides.

Affirmation of diverse intelligence is not a retreat to a softhearted definition of the mind. To acknowledge a broader range of intellectual capacity is to take seriously the concept of cognitive variability, to appreciate in all the Rosies and Joes the thought that drives their accomplishments and defines who they are. This is a model of the mind that is worthy of a democratic society.

> *If we think that whole categories of people — identified by class or occupation — are not that bright, then we reinforce social separations.*

FOR A SECOND READING

1. Take a closer look at this essay's title. How do you interpret the phrase "blue-collar brilliance"? To what extent does this phrase challenge or rewrite the norms we are taught to use when thinking about blue-collar work? What alternative vision of such work does a phrase like this suggest?

2. Using his mother's experiences on the job as a kind of case study, Rose presents readers with a list of the particular skills and knowledge that one blue-collar job requires. His mother, Rose tells us, "took customers' orders, pencil poised over pad, while fielding questions about the food. She walked full tilt through the room with plates stretching up her left arm and two cups of coffee somehow cradled in her right hand. She stood at a table or booth and removed a plate for this person, another for that person, then another, remembering who had the hamburger, who had the fried shrimp, almost always getting it right" (p. 394–95). Does this list, in your view, successfully make the case that blue-collar jobs can call on and foster brilliance in workers? Do the skills, talents, and knowledge necessary to perform this job fit your definition of *brilliance*? How or how not?

3. Can you think of an example of blue-collar work that fits Rose's definition of *brilliance*? What kind of job is it? What aptitudes and skills does it require? How are these skills and aptitudes typically viewed?

PUTTING IT INTO WRITING

4. This essay asks you to think about the relationship between blue- and white-collar work. Write an essay in which you compare the particular rules, scripts, roles, and norms that teach us how to think about each of these two categories. How is each type of work typically defined? What tasks, skills, or abilities are we told each conventionally involves? And, perhaps most important, how are we taught to value these types of work differently? In your view, are these value distinctions fair? Accurate? How or how not?

5. What would a job training program look like that values and teaches the skills and abilities Rose showcases in this essay? What type of instruction would it include? What assignments or activities would it involve? Assess how this would differ from the more typical job training program. How do its rules differ? What role does it script for participants? What are the underlying norms it is designed to support? And which do you find preferable? Why?

COMPARING ARGUMENTS

6. Like Rose, Maddie Oatman (p. 390) is also interested in rethinking some of the social norms around restaurant service work. How do you think Oatman would respond to the argument Rose makes here? Do you think she would find support for her own call to challenge the biases built into the history of restaurant tipping in Rose's dissection of "blue-collar brilliance"? How or how not?

Scenes and Un-Scenes: **A Woman's Work**

For decades, if not centuries, Americans have been encouraged not only to draw firm boundaries between men's work and women's work, but also to *value* these kinds of work in very different ways. As many of us know firsthand, gender stereotypes continue to play a prominent role in scripting the ways we are taught to think about and evaluate life on the job. Whether measured in terms of annual income, social prestige, or professional clout, we know, for example, that we are supposed to view being a kindergarten teacher and being a corporate CEO very differently. We know how to assess and rank these respective occupations because our culture has supplied us with a set of ready-made and highly gendered assumptions (for example, about the kind of person who is the most natural fit for the job, about the rewards and respect such a jobholder is allowed to expect, and so on).

But do these assumptions really offer us an accurate guide? Do they frame choices or script norms that actually "work" for us? And if they don't, to what extent can they be challenged or revised? Each of the following images presents us with an image that rewrites stereotypical scripts by which we have been taught to segregate men's work from women's work. What do these acts of revision involve? What particular norms do their portraits of women and work seem to parody or critique? And what new norms do they posit in their place?

Newscom/World History Archive

▲▲ An image initially created as part of a government-led effort during World War II to recruit women into industries that had lost their all-male workforces to overseas fighting, Rosie the Riveter was originally intended to represent the country's short-term employment crisis. One of the most iconic work images of the twentieth century, Rosie the Riveter stands as a pointed rebuke to the ways Americans have traditionally been taught to think about "women's work."

"What do you say, gentlemen—ready for some girltalk?"

Jim Sizemore/Cartoonstock.com

▲▲ *Other cultural texts have built on Rosie's legacy in different ways.*
Unlike its preceding counterparts, this image works much more
clearly to redirect traditional gender stereotypes toward nontraditional
ends. Rather than a sexist shorthand used to marginalize the
contributions of working women, the phrase girltalk — uttered here by a
female executive — gets transformed into a sly joke, one that inverts
conventional gender hierarchies by making men the object of humor.

Michael Ochs Archives/Getty Images

▲▲ *In the 1980 film 9 to 5, three women office workers run their company when, through a series of comic misunderstandings, they end up holding their boss hostage. Over the last few decades, our airwaves have been filled with movies and television shows that attempt the very Rosie-like feat of placing women within positions of workplace authority traditionally occupied by men. However, this sort of role reversal has often been undertaken for comic effect: a way of poking fun at conventional gender norms and gender hierarchies by turning them upside down. In the end, though, how much of the film's comedy rests on the assumption that a woman running a company is inherently funny?*

The Washington Post/Getty Images

In 2016, Hillary Clinton became the first female presidential nominee of a major political party in American history. Is there anything about the composition of this photo, taken at the 2016 Democratic National Convention, that could be said to be reminiscent of the depiction of Rosie the Riveter from the 1940s? In what ways does it differ?

FOR A CLOSER LOOK

1. How does the Rosie the Riveter image seem to define the ideal job? What kinds of work? What particular roles? And to what extent does this definition challenge or rewrite conventional gender stereotypes?

2. How accurately do the images presented in this feature capture or comment on your experiences on the job? Do they convey messages or model norms that would be considered acceptable within the work environments you know personally? How or how not?

3. How valid do you think the distinction between men's work and women's work is in this day and age? Is it a distinction that continues to exert influence in our culture? Does it present a script we are still encouraged to use?

PUTTING IT INTO WRITING

4. Choose the image in this feature that you think most directly reinforces the connection between work and self-worth. Write an essay in which you assess the merits and/or flaws of this depiction. In what ways does this image encourage viewers to forge a connection between their work and their self-worth? What, in your view, are the implications of embracing this message? Of using it as the basis for living one's own life?

5. In addition to the distinction between men's and women's work, the examples here also underscore certain differences between white-collar and blue-collar jobs. What are the scripts in our culture by which we are taught to differentiate these two types of employment? Choose one of the images and write an essay in which you analyze how particular gender stereotypes influence the depiction

of white- or blue-collar work. What gender roles or gender scripts get associated with this kind of work? How does the photo convey them? Does this portrayal seem accurate? Fair? How or how not?

6. Linda Tirado chronicles her experiences working restaurant service jobs often stereotyped as "women's work" (p. 370). How do you think she would respond to the images you have just seen, all of which depict women in stereotypically male-dominated types of work? What images can you think of from popular culture that might be added to the preceding set that would reflect and validate the types of work Tirado profiles?

Acting Like a Citizen: **Working Hard or Hardly Working?**

In the ways they shine a light on our culture's unspoken assumptions about work, the selections in this chapter invite us to think more critically about the specific cultural norms on which our own job or career-related choices are based. In doing so, they equip us with the tools to not only think differently where work is concerned, but to act differently as well. The following exercises give you a chance to utilize these tools even further.

BUILDING THE PERFECT WORK ENVIRONMENT The selections in this chapter cover many different types of jobs, but they also describe, sometimes indirectly, different work *environments*. Write an essay in which you describe the different environments in two or three of these selections. What are the standards of dress or behavior you think these environments condone? What isn't allowed? What type of work environment do you believe is most suited to your personality? Why? What does your ideal "office" (whether or not it's a traditional work-space) look like? What are the standards of conduct you would implement?

EVALUATING SALARIES The U.S. Department of Labor Bureau of Labor Statistics has compiled a list of mean salaries for 800 jobs (www.bls.gov/oes/current/oes_nat.htm). Select several different occupations and see how each one compares in terms of its related salary. Write an essay in which you discuss what salary tells us about the "value" of work. What sorts of skills or training seem to lead to larger salaries? In your opinion, do the higher-earning jobs truly merit their larger salaries? Why or why not? If you could reassign rank to the jobs you've chosen, how would your list compare with the real salaries for those jobs?

PUTTING YOUR BEST FOOT FORWARD Visit your school's Career Services office and ask to see sample résumés. Think about a job or career path that you are interested in pursuing, and use these resources to write a résumé for an entry-level job (or one commensurate with your experience) in this field.

Jeff Kravitz/Getty Images

Photographed at the 2014 Outside Lands Music and Arts Festival in San Francisco, California, this sign promotes the work of Digital Detox, a for-profit organization dedicated to "provid[ing] individuals, families and companies the opportunity to set aside their digital arm [and] gain perspective." As you look at this photo, think about the particular message it is conveying about living in our current digital age. Then answer the following questions:

➲ How do you understand the term "digital detox"? What kind of process do you think this kind of "detox" involves?

➲ Why would someone want to "detox" from the digital world? What aspects of this world, in your view, might be addictive or harmful?

➲ What would it mean to live, even temporarily, in an "analog zone"? How do you think life in this environment would differ from your typical habits and routines?

6 How We
CONNECT
What Forces Help — and Hinder — Our Relationships with Others?

Introduction

"LET'S STAY IN TOUCH"

We hear a lot these days about the virtues of being connected. From commercials touting the latest smart phone app to pundits making pronouncements about our "shrinking planet," we find ourselves at the center of a new world in which the pleasures and pay-offs of "connectedness" are increasingly taken as an indisputable fact of life. But does this new cultural ideal truly live up to its billing? Whether through Google or Facebook, YouTube or Twitter, it's undeniable that we now inhabit a wired environment in which our access to each other has come to feel almost limitless. And yet it is far from clear whether we've fully confronted all the questions these dazzling possibilities raise. In a world where our interactions are increasingly mediated through online technologies, are we becoming less practiced in the art of face-to-face conversation? As we grow ever more accustomed to tracking the daily minutiae of each others' lives, do we find the notion of privacy slipping away? As we spend more and more of the day plugged in, are we losing the capacity to think of ourselves as a community? Living at the center of a world in which we are perpetually in contact, constantly communicating, and boundlessly informed, are we using all our vaunted access to remain *truly* connected?

As we've seen throughout the book, questions like these point toward the ways an established cultural norm can be questioned, challenged, or reimagined. Answering them becomes a means of exercising our own agency, allowing us to ask not just "what does our culture teach us is normal?" but also "how can we define what is normal for ourselves?" When, for example, the nineteenth-century writer Henry David Thoreau decided to forsake the world for a simpler life at Walden Pond, he was offering his own take on the idea of being connected. And while this act of writing did not in itself change the world, it did set forth his own principles for living a happy, meaningful life — principles that have been passed down as beliefs for future generations to discover and contend with. As you develop your own views on the ideal of "connectedness," imagine yourself following in the footsteps of Thoreau, using your own writing to reflect upon, and rewrite, the rules, scripts, and norms you live by.

What is normal?

"I never found the companion that was so companionable as solitude."

Henry David Thoreau, *Walden*

What does this quotation ask you to believe? What are the ideas, values, or attitudes it asks you to accept as normal?

THE PLUGGED-IN WORLD

One way to do this is to reflect on how the notion of "connectedness" has evolved over the years. Think, for example, about what it meant to be connected generations ago. In the era before Twitter, Instagram, and Skype, the task of staying in touch involved very different investments of time and energy. In the nineteenth century, for example, staying in touch involved composing and responding to actual handwritten letters. A couple of decades later, the telephone, an invention that made instantaneous connection an option for millions of people for the first time, made this task far easier. A few years later, mass media such as radio and television put countless Americans into regular daily contact with characters, stories, and viewpoints very different from their own immediate experience. In each case, these technological advances brought equivalent cultural change as well. As innovations like the telephone and television supplied Americans with new ways to connect, they also raised a number of key questions. As we find ourselves increasingly able to stay in touch, where do we draw the line between what can be made public and what should remain private? In a world that affords us more opportunities to speak out on topics of importance, whose voices get to be heard? As communication over great distance has come to replace face-to-face contact, what is happening to our ability to interact as a community?

As technological and social change has continued to remake our world, we find ourselves confronting these same complex cultural questions anew — questions that the selections assembled in this chapter address from a variety of perspectives. Taking aim at the cultural norms surrounding connection, each of these essays showcases the ways individual people negotiate and remake this norm to suit their own purposes.

The first two selections, by Navneet Alang and Mae Wiskin, reflect upon the social and psychological impact of a world in which we find ourselves increasingly dependent on our digital devices. Alang explores implications of turning to these devices for emotional or psychological connection, while Wiskin shares her thoughts on the growing phenomenon of digital "addiction."

Extending this focus, the second pair of writers, Bijan Stephen and Caroline O'Donovan, explore the ways social media can serve as an instrument for either fostering or inhibiting racial equality. Stephen does this by considering the ways social media have helped to facilitate the Black

What is normal?

"**Your world delivered. Connecting to your world, everywhere you live and work.**"

AT&T Slogan

Do you share the attitude this quotation reflects? Should we automatically accept it as normal?

DENIS CHARLET/
Getty Images

What is normal?

"Build resilient communities. We find our humanity—our will to live and our ability to love—in our connections to one another. Be there for your family and friends. And I mean in person. Not just in a message with a heart emoji."

Commencement speech at the University of California Berkeley, by Facebook CEO Sheryl Sandberg, 2016

What kind of social script do these instructions write? What would it feel like to act out this script in our own lives? And can this kind of social script be rewritten?

Lives Matter movement. O'Donovan, meanwhile, examines the complicated role social media have played in efforts to combat racial profiling.

Sherry Turkle and Charles Duhigg pose a different question about the digital world, asking whether our daily online sharing habits have exposed too much of our private information to the inspection and manipulation of others. Turkle takes up this question by looking more closely at the tactics and technologies that comprise the world of "Big Data." Duhigg, on the other hand, tracks the growing efforts of online retailers to monitor and record every move their customers make.

Rounding out our selections, Peter Lovenheim and Matthew Desmond address the issue of connection by investigating the ways the modern experience of "home" and "community" is changing. Lovenheim tells a story that shows just how little we often know about the neighbors who live right next door, while Desmond describes the devastating effect home eviction can have on economically vulnerable families.

NAVNEET ALANG

The Comfort of a Digital Confidante

Given how immersive our online lives have become, is it any wonder that so many of us are turning to our digital devices for greater emotional connection? This is the provocative question Navneet Alang seeks to answer in this essay. What exactly, he asks, are we looking for when we reach for connection online? And when we find it, does it always measure up to what we crave? Navneet Alang is a Toronto-based writer whose work explores the intersections of media, technology, and culture. His essays have appeared in such publications as the *New Republic* and the *Atlantic*. This piece was published in the *Atlantic* in 2015.

Before You Read

What are some of the emotional "comforts" you would say the digital world is able to provide? How do they compare to the kinds of support or connection you find offline?

I'M STILL NOT QUITE SURE WHAT MADE ME THANK ALEXA. I WAS ON vacation in an unfamiliar city and I had just used Amazon's so-called "smart speaker" to check the weather. But after finding out tomorrow called for rain, sitting alone in an empty, quiet apartment, I made a point to express my gratitude to the inanimate black cylinder lying on the kitchen counter. "No problem," it intoned jovially in reply.

In retrospect, I had what was a very strange reaction: a little jolt of pleasure. Perhaps it was because I had mostly spent those two weeks alone, but Alexa's response was close enough to the outline of human communication to elicit a feeling of relief in me. For a moment, I felt a little less lonely.

If I wanted to take my relationship with Alexa to the next level, sharing deeply-held thoughts rather than just thanks, I had options. Secret Keeper, an app for Alexa, lets you whisper a private thought to Alexa, and protect it with a password. Your secret will either be locked away forever, or it can be heard anonymously

> *Alexa's response was close enough to the outline of human communication to elicit a feeling of relief in me. For a moment, I felt a little less lonely.*

So much of human communication is wrapped up this desire: our inarticulate, inevitably futile wish to have another person understand us exactly as we understand ourselves. Alas, that person doesn't exist.

by others. There are of course worries that come with trusting one's skeletons to the cloud. But the appeal of the app is obvious—it lets you get something off your chest. It also suggests that sometimes, who listens isn't important; what matters is simply saying it out loud.

Using technology as a kind of lockbox for what is private is not new. First there were diaries with locks, or messages written onto paper and then stuffed into bottles cast into the ocean. In each there was a kind of yearning to be heard, without suffering the social consequences of disclosure. It's as if what we want isn't a real connection, but the release of an imagined perfect one. If anything, digital technologies have made that impulse more ubiquitous. Apps like Whisper, and the popular site Postsecret, both of which let you post confessions anonymously, add publicity to the mix, letting an unknown audience become a blank repository for our secrets.

5   Even our public-facing or friend-facing social networks are peppered with tweets or Facebook updates with no likes and no responses. These are slightly different from simply depositing a thought into the abyss; we know someone will likely see it. But the orphaned post is often one written more for the writer than the reader. Even if no one responds, it solidifies some vague thought or feeling so we can make sense of it for ourselves.

It is a particularly acute phenomenon on small platforms likely not long for this world. Peach, for example, experienced a brief week or two of hype, and then fell off most people's radars. Stragglers remain, however, and at least in my limited friend list, are often found typing out ideas or sharing gifs that aren't really aimed at anyone in particular—a fact made all the more strange by the fact that Peach's cozy aesthetics and tiny user-base tend to invite emotional, confessional posting. The private anxieties and yearnings of people I barely know are splashed out onto the app's pastel background, frequently eliciting no reaction at all. Yet people continue to post—no doubt because the fact that others are doing the same means the possibility of interaction still looms—but also because the mere fact of expressing a thought has its own purpose.

The rhetoric around social networks has always been, depending on your proclivities, either about connection and socialization, or less charitably, narcissism and presenting a falsely idealized version of yourself to the world. But perhaps it isn't practical communication or an idealized self that drives much of what we do online as much as it is the abstract idea of the unsullied connection. So much of human communication is wrapped up in this desire: our inarticulate, inevitably futile wish to have another person understand us exactly as we understand ourselves. Alas, that person doesn't exist. The aching chasm between one person and another is exactly what generates so much misunderstanding, but also drives everything from making art to talking over coffee for hours, the very gap itself making those rare moments of connection feel like such ecstatic relief. What we want is to be seen in our entirety, and we are always striving to inch closer to that impossible goal.

Perhaps, then, that Instagram shot or confessional tweet isn't always meant to evoke some mythical, pretend version of *ourselves*, but instead seeks to invoke the imagined perfect audience—the non-existent people who will see us exactly as we want to be seen. We are not curating an ideal self, but rather, an ideal Other, a fantasy in which our struggle to become ourselves is met with the utmost empathy.

It also may explain why empty social networks or app that securely tuck away our thoughts are unexpectedly such ideal venues for catharsis. After all, only where no-one truly listens can we ever be perfectly heard. What we want is mutuality—and if that can't exist, then just the outline of it tides us over for just a little longer.

There is inevitably an alluring, risky seductiveness to that empty box online or the tiny black obelisk on a kitchen counter. Sometimes a chirpy response from a digital assistant is just what you need. At other times it is a too-easy substitute for something a little more complex or less predictable than the welcoming blankness of the void. Like everything, the key is balance, a tricky concept that is as subjective as it is dependent upon context. Only we ourselves will know whether expressing ideas into the abyss is good for us, or if we need the pushback of a plain-spoken friend. 10

But what digital technologies do best, to our benefit and detriment, is to act as a canvas for our desires. The promise of the democratizing effect of digital was always predicated on blank spaces waiting to be inscribed upon and seen by others so that, in painting out our thoughts and feelings, we make sense of ourselves. True, typing or screaming into the void can evoke a certain sense of futility, even nihilism. Carried underneath, however, is something deeply human—a wish to be seen, to be heard, to be apprehended as nothing less than who we imagine ourselves to be.

FOR A SECOND READING

1. Alang begins his essay by recounting a moment when he "thanked" his Amazon device for providing him information about the weather. Why do you think Alang chose to open with this

particular anecdote? In what ways does it preview the key concepts or questions he goes on to explore in the rest of the essay? Do you, as a reader, find it to be an effective way to begin? Why or why not?

2. "[P]erhaps," Alang muses, "it isn't practical communication or an idealized self that drives much of what we do online as much as it is the abstract idea of the unsullied connection" (pp. 414–15). How do you respond to this proposition? What vision or model of communication does the term "unsullied connection" suggest to you? And does the prospect of this kind of communication seem appealing? Why or why not?

3. "[W]hat digital technologies do best," Alang declares, "is to act as a canvas for our desires" (p. 415). What do you think Alang is trying to say here about how and why we use digital technologies? Do you agree that these communication tools allow us to express or project "our desires"? Can you think of an example from your own experience that supports or illustrates this point?

PUTTING IT INTO WRITING

4. "Using technology as a kind of lockbox for what is private is not new," Alang writes. "First there were diaries with locks, or messages written onto paper and then stuffed into bottles cast into the ocean. In each there was a kind of yearning to be heard, without suffering the social consequences of disclosure" (p. 414). In a 500-word essay, respond to Alang's statement. Do you agree that our current privacy technology shares much in common with the kinds of "lockbox" options employed by earlier generations? Can you think of some particular ways in which the privacy apps of today are fundamentally different?

5. According to Alang, the fundamental appeal of digital communications technology is that it satisfies our "yearning to be heard" without forcing us to "suff[er] the social consequences of disclosure" (p. 414). Imagine yourself as a social media design specialist. What kind of app would you design to fulfill this goal? What vehicle or outlet for being "heard" would it create for users? What protections against "disclosure" would it include?

COMPARING ARGUMENTS

6. Mae Wiskin (p. 417) is another writer who explores the forms our current dependency on social media can take. Write an essay in which you speculate about how Wiskin might respond to the argument Alang is advancing about the rise of "digital confidantes." Do you think Wiskin would find much commonality between this phenomenon and what she terms the "rise of social media rehab"? How or how not?

MAE WISKIN

Can't Quit the Clicks: The Rise of Social Media Rehab

In our increasingly wired world, it's become a cliché to speak about being "addicted" to our smartphones, laptops, and the like. But the time may have come, argues Mae Wiskin, to begin taking these off-handed remarks a bit more seriously. Taking a closer look at the growing prevalence of digital dependency, Wiskin asks whether we have reached a point where such dependency may now warrant more concerted, even medical, attention. Mae Wiskin received her master's degree from the Parsons School of Design Studies at the New School. She is a contributor to *VICE*, an online media magazine dedicated to exploring arts, culture, and current events. This piece appeared in *VICE* in 2016.

Before You Read

Have you ever found yourself utilizing a particular digital technology (e.g., an app, site, game, etc.) compulsively? If so, what particular aspects or features made it so addictive?

YOU WAKE UP, YOUR EYES STILL CLOSED, AND PAT AROUND THE mattress until you find your phone. It rests beside your head, beaming with notifications. You remain lying down for a few more minutes and begin scrolling, shaking your phone a few times with mild annoyance to force the screen to align with the way you're positioned. Before your feet have even touched the ground, you've already scanned the news, marked priority emails, and checked the weather. You slowly get out of bed and look over at your partner. Too busy playing Candy Crush, he barely acknowledges you.

Social media and smartphones have irreversibly changed the landscape of human connection and fundamentally redefined how people interact with one another. Eighty percent of users check their phones within fifteen minutes of waking up, according to a 2013 study sponsored by Facebook. The same study also found that the average user checks their mobile device every six minutes. Although striking, these statistics are far from extraordinary.

We often joke that we are "addicted" to our phones, but imagine becoming so devoted that you find yourself checking into rehab.

Dr. Hilarie Cash is the Co-Founder and Chief Clinical Officer of the reSTART Center for Digital Technology Sustainability, a center offering rehab and recovery services for those with tech, gaming, and internet addictions. Cash says people can get "high" from technology use, and

We often joke that we are "addicted" to our phones, but imagine becoming so devoted that you find yourself checking into rehab.

they may also experience withdrawal and other symptoms of addiction. But to her, the way to identify an addiction is through asking: "Are there negative consequences to your use? And if so, do you continue in spite of those negative consequences?" According to Cash, sometimes her clients are very much in denial, but people on the outside will see the problem.

5   Over the past few years, mental health professionals and social psychologists have debated over whether "digital" addiction ought to be classified in the same way as substance-related disorders and addictions. The word "addiction" can be applied in many ways, making its boundaries difficult to define. Generally, in order to be considered an addiction, the processes involved must interfere with daily functioning, resulting in social, academic, or occupational impairment.

"So, you know, you have an 18-year-old who is [addicted to] gaming and socially isolated," Cash explains. "He avoids people, has no other interests, or if he has any interests, he's given them up. Well, from the perspective of what constitutes a healthy and balanced life, you need sleep, exercise, and face-to-face social interactions. So not getting any of those things—those are the negative consequences."

Although various technological addictions are still under consideration in the current Diagnostic and Statistical Manual of Mental Disorders, some argue that tech overuse ought to be classified as a subset of behavioral addictions, similar to other nonchemical addictions such as pathological gaming and compulsive shopping. "There needs to be a general category for addiction," says Dr. Cash. "There are so many behavioral addictions out there, like: social media, sex, porn, and gambling. I think it's silly to exclude digital addictions. They are just like any other addiction in that they produce both a sense of euphoria and profound withdrawal. The addiction literature needs to be more inclusive."

Technology addiction rehab centers like the one Dr. Cash directs are popping up all over the country. The reSTART Center markets itself as "a place of rest and renewal for technology users seeking a private, peaceful, and spacious place to confront their digital lives." Her eight to 12-week digital detox program costs upwards of $14,000 and has been running since 2009. When asked about the people currently seeking her help, Dr. Cash says her clients tend to be men between the ages of 18 and 28—there are some women, but very few. "They all tend to be bright, likable people, but again, it all varies. Some people have had full lives before they fell off the rails, while others have only lived an online existence. As you can imagine, treating these people is a lot harder."

Once in the program, clients are cut off from using any form of technology and the center's coaches and therapists work with them to learn how to "reconnect with real life" and deal with any co-occurring mental health conditions. In order to "break the cycle of dependency," reSTART enforces a 45-day abstinence-based structure in which her clients—all of whom also have sponsors—are taught the life skills that may go underdeveloped as a result of excessive technology use.

Clients also live in "tech limited, video game free, democratically   10 self-supporting, and drug free housing," modeled after the Oxford House, a concept for housing spaces for recovery from substance abuse and addiction.

For those who can't afford the hefty price tag at tech rehab spaces like reSTART, outpatient networks are also available. At the end of 2015, Talkspace, a messaging-based online therapy service, developed a "Social Media Dependency Therapy Program," which the company claims is the first program of its kind designed to help people manage their use of and response to Facebook, Instagram, Twitter, and other social platforms. The 12-week program works similarly to other text-based therapy plans in that you can message your remote therapist at any time or place from your phone.

It may seem counterintuitive to use technology in order to limit technological overuse; however, Talkspace addiction specialist, Katherine Glick, defends the program's design. "It's a funny thing using social media to address social media addiction, but everyone uses social media," she says. "It is a staple of our cognitive landscape, and so to use it to our advantage—to use it purposefully and meaningfully—I think just readapts your relationship with it."

For example, one of Glick's specialty areas is food addiction, the recovery process for which she compares to social media addiction. "You abstain from alcohol or drugs and that's great, but you can't abstain from food. So in terms of working with my current addiction clients, it's all about renegotiating their relationship with food and figuring out what functions food has served for you up until this point, whether its comfort or escapism or whatever, and then readapting a healthier, more balanced relationship with food," she says. "I think that we can use technology and social media to our advantage and help people with their compulsive technology use. It's just moving someone from

> *Once in the program, clients are cut off from using any form of technology and the center's coaches and therapists work with them to learn how to "reconnect with real life" and deal with any co-occurring mental health conditions.*

a mindless place to one where they are more mindful about their relationship to technology."

Both tech rehab and social media dependency programs are new and imperfect; nevertheless, ubiquitous computing and smart technologies are likely here to stay. While Dr. Cash and Glick's approaches to technological and social media dependency are dissimilar, they agree that these sorts of disorders are not only on the rise, but will soon need to be legitimized by the American Psychiatric Association.

15   "I predict that digital and internet addiction will be incorporated into the DSM very much like gambling disorder was in 2013," she explains. "More and more treatment facilities are going to be incorporating modalities centered towards technology addiction. I do think that all healthcare systems are moving toward an online model. We are in a technology growth overload and I don't see that stopping anytime soon; I think it's just going to ramp up and continue to increase."

FOR A SECOND READING

1.   "Social media and smartphones," Wiskin states, "have irreversibly changed the landscape of human connection and fundamentally redefined how people interact with one another" (p. 417). To what extent do you share the view Wiskin expresses here? Do you agree that the rise of digital technology has "irreversibly changed" how we connect and interact with each other? If so, how specifically?

2   According to one of the digital "rehab" experts Wiskin quotes in this essay, "people can get 'high' from technology use, and they may also experience withdrawal and other symptoms of addiction" (pp. 417–18). What image of addiction does this statement evoke? What types of high, what forms of withdrawal do you picture as you read it?

3.   One of the key questions Wiskin explores has to do with whether it is valid to classify "digital addiction" in the same way as other substance-related disorders. Where do you stand on this question? In your own view, what are the similarities or parallels that justify treating "digital addiction" in the same way as other disorders? What, conversely, would you identify as important distinctions or differences?

PUTTING IT INTO WRITING

4.   Wiskin writes: "Over the past few years, mental health professionals and social psychologists have debated over whether 'digital' addiction ought to be classified in the same way as substance-related disorders and addictions. The word 'addiction' can be applied in many ways, making its boundaries difficult to define" (p. 418). Put yourself

in the position of a health care professional tasked with the responsibility of defining the phenomenon of "digital addiction." What specific behaviors would you classify as symptoms of this disorder? What particular challenges or problems would you treat as evidence of true addiction? And finally, what treatment would you proscribe for addressing this addiction?

5. To support the idea that digital addiction may constitute an urgent public health problem, Wiskin cites statistics like the following: "Eighty percent of users check their phones within fifteen minutes of waking up, according to a 2013 study sponsored by Facebook. The same study also found that the average user checks their mobile device every six minutes" (p. 417). Write a 500-word essay in which you analyze and evaluate the data Wiskin presents here. What point about social media use do these kinds of statistics illustrate? What particular problem do they highlight? And in your view, do these statistics offer effective support for the argument that "digital addiction" is real? Why or why not?

COMPARING ARGUMENTS

6. Wiskin's discussion of "digital addiction" shares with Navneet Alang's portrait of digital connection (p. 413) a healthy skepticism regarding the benefits and limitations of online technology. How do you think Alang would respond to the addiction treatment programs Wiskin outlines in her piece? Do you think he would view the kinds of online communication and confession her essay describes as "disorders" in need of treatment? Why or why not?

Rewriting the Script: **Political Gridlock**

❝ *Gridlock — you hear a lot about gridlock. Gridlock is not some mysterious fog that just kind of drops down on Washington. Gridlock is not the Democrats and Republicans just both being equally unreasonable. Gridlock is happening, has happened, will happen when politicians . . . decide they will oppose anything that's good for the country just because [another politician] proposes it."*

— FORMER PRESIDENT BARACK OBAMA,
NOVEMBER 4, 2016

No single term more aptly encapsulates the problems in our current political culture than *gridlock*. As countless commentators and pundits have lamented, our model of governance seems to have devolved from one that values the art of compromise into one that practices the scorched-earth tactics of destroying the opponent at all costs. Surveying this dysfunctional scene, many have begun to wonder whether it's possible any longer for policymakers to set aside their differences and forge genuine political connections.

The remarks by former President Obama, delivered on the brink of the 2016 presidential election, represent one attempt to challenge this current and lamentable status quo. He calls out the fact that political gridlock, rather than some natural or immutable phenomenon, is actually the result of deliberate choices made by individual politicians. And by doing so, the

Anadolu Agency/Getty Images

former president offers his audience a bracing reminder that gridlock is a social script — one that can be rewritten if there exists sufficient public will. Taking up such an invitation, however, requires that we understand exactly where gridlock comes from, and why it remains such a potent tactic for politicians on both sides of the aisle. The questions below provide a starting point for doing just this.

IDENTIFY THE SCRIPT: Choose a current political issue that is the subject of polarizing, even paralyzing, political debate (examples include health care or financial reform, environmental legislation, or immigration reform). Write about how this issue gets debated. What groups does this debate pit against each other? What position does each group stake out?

CHALLENGE THE SCRIPT: Next, analyze why you think this particular issue is so polarizing. What specific social or cultural norms does this debate pit against each other? And what factors account for why there exists so little common ground between the opposing sides?

WRITE YOUR OWN SCRIPT: Imagine that you are a political strategist tasked with creating a new model for conducting this particular debate. First, write a description of the specific strategies this effort would entail. What specific aspects of or elements within the current debate would you change in order to bridge the ideological differences this debate currently involves? What specific groups or constituencies would you target? What groups or constituencies would you not target? When you're done, write an assessment of why you made these particular choices. How do you think these strategies would help lead to greater political collaboration and connection?

BIJAN STEPHEN

Get Up, Stand Up: Social Media Helps Black Lives Matter Fight the Power

From selfies to cat videos, it has become fashionable in recent years to deride the world of social media as little more than a repository for trivia. As Bijan Stephen's essay makes clear, however, such a view overlooks the many ways social media can serve as a powerful instrument for social change. Taking a closer look at the uses to which digital platforms have been put by the Black Lives Matter movement, Stephen sketches a portrait of what we might call digital activism. Stephen is an associate editor at the *New Republic*. His writing has appeared in such publications as the *Paris Review*, *n + 1*, and *VICE*. This essay was published in *Wired* magazine in 2015.

Before You Read

How do you understand the relationship between social media and social activism?

IN THE 1960S, IF YOU WERE A CIVIL RIGHTS WORKER STATIONED IN the Deep South and you needed to get some urgent news out to the rest of the world—word of a beating or an activist's arrest or some brewing state of danger—you would likely head straight for a telephone.

From an office or a phone booth in hostile territory, you would place a call to one of the major national civil rights organizations. But you wouldn't do it by dialing a standard long-distance number. That would involve speaking first to a switchboard operator—who was bound to be white and who might block your call. Instead you'd dial the number for something called a Wide Area Telephone Service, or WATS, line.

Like an 800 line, you could dial a WATS number from anywhere in the region and the call would patch directly through to the business or organization that paid for the line—in this case, say, the Student Nonviolent Coordinating Committee.

On the other end of the line, another civil rights worker would be ready to take down your report and all the others pouring in from phones scattered across the South. The terse, action-packed write-ups would then be compiled into mimeographed "WATS reports" mailed out to organization leaders, the media, the Justice Department, lawyers, and other friends of the movement across the country.

5   In other words, it took a lot of infrastructure to live-tweet what was going on in the streets of the Jim Crow South.

Any large social movement is shaped by the technology available to it and tailors its goals, tactics, and rhetoric to the media of its time. On the afternoon of Sunday, March 7, 1965, when voting-rights marchers in Selma, Alabama, were run down by policemen at the Edmund Pettus Bridge, the WATS lines were in heavy use. ("Here come the white hoodlums," an activist said from a corner pay phone at 3:25 pm.) But the technology that was most important to the movement's larger aims was not in activists' hands at all: It was in a set of film canisters being ferried past police blockades on Highway 80 by an ABC News TV crew, racing for the Montgomery airport and heading to New York for an evening broadcast. That night, 48 million Americans would watch the scene in their living rooms, and a few days later Martin Luther King Jr. would lay bare the movement's core media strategy. "We will no longer let them use their clubs on us in the dark corners," he said. "We're going to make them do it in the glaring light of television."

"It was a rare admission," writes media historian Aniko Bodroghkozy. "King and other civil rights organizers seldom acknowledged their own self-conscious use of the mass media." Today's African-American civil rights organizers, by contrast, talk about the tools of mass communication all the time—because their media strategy sessions are largely open to everyone on the Internet.

If you're a civil rights activist in 2015 and you need to get some news out, your first move is to choose a platform. If you want to post a video of a protest or a violent arrest, you put it up on Vine, Instagram, or Periscope. If you want to avoid trolls or snooping authorities and you need to coordinate some kind of action, you might chat privately with other activists on GroupMe. If you want to rapidly mobilize a bunch of people you know and you don't want the whole world clued in, you use SMS or WhatsApp. If you want to mobilize a ton of people you might not know and you do want the whole world to talk about it: Twitter.

And if, God forbid, you find yourself standing in front of the next Michael Brown or Walter Scott, and you know the nation's attention needs to swerve hard to your town, your best bet might be to send a direct message to someone like DeRay Mckesson, one of a handful of activists who sit at the apex of social networks that now run hundreds of thousands strong. "The thing about King or Ella Baker is that they could not just wake up and sit at the breakfast table and talk to a million people," says

> *Harassment, threats, and insults are basic hazards of online activism today, but they are especially pervasive for anyone speaking on the touchy subject of race in America.*

Mckesson, a former school district administrator who has become one of the most visible faces of the movement. "The tools that we have to organize and to resist are fundamentally different than anything that's existed before in black struggle."

• • •

10 #BlackLivesMatter became a hashtag in the summer of 2013, when an Oakland, California, labor organizer named Alicia Garza responded on her Facebook page to the acquittal of George Zimmerman, the man who gunned down Trayvon Martin. Since then it has become the banner under which dozens of disparate organizations, new and old, and millions of individuals, loosely and tightly related, press for change.

Any phenomenon that seizes the nation's attention this much needs a name—headline writers make sure of that. But it is hard to talk about the national Black Lives Matter movement without imparting a false sense of institutional coherence to it. Of course, the civil rights movement of the '60s was itself far from monolithic, but there aren't really analogues to the Southern Christian Leadership Conference or the Student Nonviolent Coordinating Committee in today's activist scene. "It's decentralized but coordinated," says Maurice Mitchell, an organizer with a group called Blackbird. "There are no top-down mandates."

You could look at it this way: The movement of the '60s needed a big institutional structure to make things work—in part because of the limitations of the tech at the time. Now that kind of structure has come to seem vestigial. After Michael Brown was shot dead in Ferguson, Missouri, and the city became a lightning rod for activism, Mckesson says he had a kind of epiphany about movement-building: "We didn't need institutions to do it," he says. Social media could serve as a source of live, raw information. It could summon people to the streets and coordinate their movements in real time. And it could swiftly push back against spurious media narratives with the force of a few thousand retweets.

Of course, some level of institution-building is still crucial, as the movement has realized. And there are downsides to the media environment that today's activists have adapted to. Despite its success in making videos of police violence go viral, social media itself has become another arena where black people are abused. Harassment, threats, and insults are basic hazards of online activism today, but they are especially pervasive for anyone speaking on the touchy subject of race in America. Mckesson, for one, says he has blocked more than 15,000 people from interacting with him on Twitter. He retweets some of the haters. It's occasionally hard to read. (There's a stale, conventional wisdom that says overt racism is largely a thing of the past in America. Whoever says this clearly has not spent much time on Twitter. God help them if they start reading comments on YouTube.)

This might seem like an opportunity: Drawing hate out into the light was, after all, a signature tactic of the civil rights movement. Televised footage of well-dressed white people heckling black children as they walked to school were powerful because they were so public, says Lisa Nakamura, a professor of media and race at the University of Michigan. "But when that happens on Twitter, it's really, really private." Any given tweet might be public, but online threats are disembodied and anonymous. Bystanders don't seem to take them as seriously. Plus, the full experience of receiving a thousand threats may only really be felt by the recipient. Even in the panopticon of social media, mobs aren't all that visible.

And of course, social media is also profoundly susceptible to surveillance. We know now that many leaders of Black Lives Matter have been monitored by federal law enforcement agencies. That has prompted many to start seeking out more secure channels; in nearly all my conversations with activists about how they use different platforms, there was a point when they told me they didn't want to say any more for security reasons. 15

> *I wasn't politically conscious. I didn't have the language to speak about microaggressions, aggression-aggressions, or structural prejudice. I just endured a thing I wasn't totally sure I was enduring.*

Still, this movement, as diffuse and protean as it may seem, has mounted some of the most potent civil rights activism since the '60s. It helped secure the removal of the Confederate flag from the South Carolina capitol. It helped pressure the federal government to investigate police practices in Ferguson and Baltimore. It has successfully pushed Democratic presidential contenders to come forward with policy proposals on the issues that specifically concern black people in America. And an offshoot of the movement, a project called Campaign Zero that was organized in part by Mckesson, has put forward a bunch of specific policy proposals to uproot police violence. A huge reason for all this success is that, perhaps more than any other modern American protest movement, they've figured out how to marshal today's tools.

• • •

The movement has also had another profound but less concrete effect: I believe that Black Lives Matter has changed the visceral experience of being black in America. I see this in the way it has become a community reflex to record interactions with police — a habit that is empowering, even as it highlights black vulnerability. I see it in the rise of a new group of black public intellectuals and in the beginnings of a new political language. And I see it in my own experience.

I grew up in Tyler, Texas, a small city in the eastern part of the state, in the 2000s. I attended the local Catholic high school—not the local public school named after Robert E. Lee, where the majority of the student body was nonwhite. No one called me a nigger, though white friends would sometimes use the slur to refer to other black people; in the next breath, they'd assure me I was different. Despite constantly feeling like I was a token, or that I had to tiptoe around white sensitivities, I couldn't have told you what ailed me. I wasn't politically conscious. I didn't have the language to speak about microaggressions, aggression-aggressions, or structural prejudice. I just endured a thing I wasn't totally sure I was enduring.

But I can still remember the fluorescent lighting of my high school's hallways and the pervasive sense that something was deeply wrong. The air itself felt toxic. I had nightmares about nuclear reactors sending clouds of poison into the sky. On those nights I'd wake up and look through my window at the moon and wonder how long it would be before I could escape.

20   Does it seem strange that I now associate those dreams with racism? That I see the unease I felt then as a species of profound alienation that I wasn't at all able to comprehend, because nothing I'd experienced before had prepared me to understand unthinking hate? This kind of clarity about my own experience has come with time and distance. I can't help but think that if I'd been a few years younger—if my upbringing in Tyler had overlapped with the past two years of digital and intellectual ferment in America—I would have realized far earlier that what I felt wasn't particularly unusual. "All of a sudden," Mckesson says, "you see that there's a community of people who share the same symptoms."

Of course, shared symptoms are not enough. That's why Black Lives Matter appears to be shifting into a new phase. "The movement doesn't win if there's only a small set of people who understand the solutions," Mckesson says. The movement wins when there's a broad understanding that we need a system that doesn't kill people, when a critical mass of citizens can envision what that looks like, and when concrete steps are taken to make it happen. Historians of the 1960s talk about how the media of the time helped establish a "new common sense" about race in America. I think the new common sense being established now is that racism and the struggle against it do not exist somewhere in the distant past; racial activism didn't end after King and the Black Panther Party. Technology has helped make today's struggle feel both different from and continuous with the civil rights era. All the terror and greatness we associate with that moment is right in front of our faces, as near to us as our screens.

FOR A SECOND READING

1. Stephen organizes part of his essay around an historical comparison between the communications tools employed by the civil rights movement in the 1960s and the use of social media by movements like Black Lives Matter today. Why do you think he chooses this organizational strategy? What larger point about social media and social activism does this strategy help Stephen make?

2. As Stephen notes, the opportunity provided by social media to witness and record civil rights violations is counterbalanced by the threat of surveillance: "[I]n nearly all my conversations with activists about how they use different platforms, there was a point when they told me they didn't want to say any more for security reasons" (p. 427). How serious a threat do you think this is? In your view, do the dangers of being monitored by authorities outweigh the benefits of bearing witness? Why or why not?

3. Stephen concludes his essay with the following statement: "Technology has helped make today's struggle feel both different from and continuous with the civil rights era. All the terror and greatness we associate with that moment is right in front of our faces, as near to us as our screens" (pp. 428–29). How do you interpret the tone of this conclusion? Do you read it as a hopeful prediction about the future or a skeptical warning? Why?

PUTTING IT INTO WRITING

4. "Any large social movement," writes Stephen, "is shaped by the technology available to it and tailors its goals, tactics, and rhetoric to the media of its time" (p. 425). Choose a "social movement" you feel is significant and is representative of our current (social, cultural, or political) era. Then write a 500-word essay in describing the media technology you think would be best suited to this movement, and explaining how it could be used to advance this movement's goals.

5. "If you're a civil rights activist [today]," Stephen writes, "and you need to get some news out, your first move is to choose a platform" (p. 425). Choose the particular platform (e.g., e-mail, Instagram, Twitter, Snapchat, etc.). Then write a 250-word essay in which you argue for the ways this platform could be used to foster or facilitate some type of civil rights activism. To what specific uses could this platform be put? What activist goals could they help accomplish?

COMPARING ARGUMENTS

6. Like Stephen, Caroline O'Donovan (p. 431) is also interested in how social media can be leveraged to address civil rights issues. How do you think Stephen would respond to O'Donovan's discussion of Nextdoor.com? Do you think Stephen would point to the example of Nextdoor as proof in support of the argument he makes about social media and civil rights? What particular aspects of this platform would do you think he would focus on? Why?

CAROLINE O'DONOVAN

Nextdoor Rolls Out Product Fix It Hopes Will Stem Racial Profiling

We tend to think of racial prejudice as a personal phenomenon: a set of false and harmful views consciously held and intentionally expressed by bigoted people. But is racial prejudice also something that can be programmed? Is it possible for this type of bias to find its way into technologies we use to interact and communicate? This is the provocative possibility Caroline O'Donovan considers in this essay. Focusing on the operations of Nextdoor .com, a website designed to allow residents to share information about what is happening in their neighborhood, O'Donovan tells the story of what can happen when racial discrimination becomes the unintended consequence of an online algorithm. Caroline O'Donovan is a staff writer at the Nieman Journalism Lab, a website that brings together cutting-edge journalism on a range of social and political topics. O'Donovan has also contributed pieces to *National Public Radio* and *CBS Radio*. This essay appeared in *BuzzFeed* in 2016.

Before You Read

Where do you get information about your neighbors? What kind of information about your neighbors is it most important for you to know? Why?

NEXTDOOR, A LOCATION-BASED SOCIAL NETWORK FOR NEIGHBORS that has more than 10 million registered users, is rolling out a new tool today that the company says has reduced incidents of racial profiling on its network by 75% during tests. In recent years, so many people have used Nextdoor to report things like black men driving cars or Hispanic women knocking on doors as suspicious or even criminal that the site has become known as a hub for racial profiling.

The new tool, an algorithmic form for reporting crime and safety issues, has been in beta for an ever-increasing portion of Nextdoor's 108,000 neighborhood groups since May. This feature, which automatically identifies racially coded terms and prevents users from posting without supplemental descriptors, goes live for all users today.

"The impact of being racially profiled in general is terrible," CEO Nirav Tolia told BuzzFeed News on Tuesday. "It runs counter to the mission of Nextdoor. It's something we feel morally obligated to take seriously."

Racial profiling became an issue for Nextdoor in 2015, when a number of news outlets reported on the frequency of posts about crime or suspicious behavior that mentioned an individual's race, but little or nothing related to actual criminal activity. In many cases, these posts would refer to people of color doing things such as talking on the phone or walking a dog.

5   Tolia said it wasn't the bad press, but the work of civic groups in Oakland that brought the issue to his attention. Nextdoor touts its collaborations with police departments, city governments, and other public agencies. Last fall, Oakland Vice Mayor Annie Campbell Washington encouraged Oakland city departments to stop using the app to communicate with citizens until Nextdoor addressed the issue of racial profiling. By October, Tolia's team was holding working groups with advocacy groups and city officials, and together they came up with a solution.

The idea, which Tolia credits to members of a group called Neighbors for Racial Justice, was to change the way crime and safety issues are reported on Nextdoor. Instead of a blank text box and subject line, it was suggested that Nextdoor design a form that more closely resembles a police report or 911 dispatcher questionnaire. By explicitly requesting details about height, clothing, and age, they would discourage people filing reports from focusing exclusively on the race or ethnicity of the subject.

Nextdoor features a wide variety of post categories — Classifieds, Events, etc. — but it's the Crime and Safety section where people tend to focus on race to the exclusion of other salient details.

Nextdoor features a wide variety of post categories—Classifieds, Events, etc.—but it's the Crime and Safety section where people tend to focus on race to the exclusion of other salient details. As of today, Nextdoor neighbors posting a "crime" or "suspicious behavior" to the site will be warned against allowing an individual's race to color their interpretation of events. And if their post focuses too much on the race or ethnicity of the subject, they'll be prevented from publishing it. "When race is invoked, we create a higher bar," Tolia explained.

For example, try to post about your car windows being smashed, and you'll be prompted with this message:

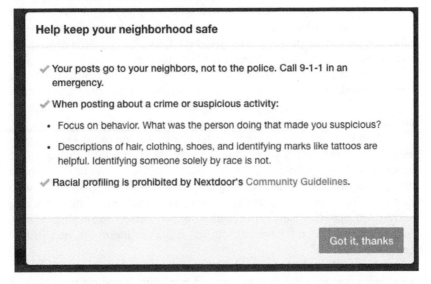

Try to describe someone with just a racial characteristic, and you'll see this prompt, asking you to be more descriptive:

Nextdoor claims this new multi-step system has, so far, reduced instances of racial profiling by 75%. It's also decreased considerably the number of notes about crime and safety. During testing, the number of crime and safety issue reports abandoned before being published rose by 50%. "It's a fairly significant drop-off," said Tolia, "but we believe that, for Nextdoor, quality is more important than quantity."

Vice Mayor Washington said she's "thrilled" with the results Nextdoor has achieved. "I don't think a lot of technology companies would have taken the steps they did, and made significant changes to their platform," she said.

10   When tech companies come under fire for failing to take race issues seriously—Snapchat, Twitter, and Airbnb are examples—critics often assert that, were minorities better represented on the staffs of those companies, the same mistakes might not have been made. But Tolia, who himself identifies as a person of color, said that while he's working actively to diversify Nextdoor's staff, when it comes to racial profiling, "we believe we get the best information from our members, and in this case, our advisers."

But not all of Nextdoor's advisers on the racial profiling project are satisfied with how the process turned out. Two founding members of Neighbors for Racial Justice, Audrey Williams and Shikira Porter, said Nextdoor left them out of the development process after a flurry of early interest. Porter told BuzzFeed News that she continues to see instances of racial profiling in her Nextdoor neighborhood despite the rollout of the form. Nextdoor confirmed that the company has not met with Neighbors for Racial Justice since the test pilot began in April, but said it was made aware of only two instances of racial profiling that had slipped through its algorithms in the last few months.

"We've been doing the work of consultants for them, and they've been taking it as free, pro-bono, volunteer advice from the community," said Williams, who works in digital marketing. "And we've been happy to give it, because it makes our lives better. But over time, it began to feel a bit like exploitation."

Nextdoor will hold a conference call for local stakeholders on Wednesday, but neither Williams nor Porter will be able to attend. Porter said it "didn't feel right" to have Neighbors for Racial Justice attached to a project they felt the organization hadn't been given a chance to sign off on.

"We appreciate working with [Neighbors for Racial Justice] to create these improvements," said Tolia in a follow-up email. "We are encouraged by the progress, but know there is still more work to do."

15   However, it's clear that the contributions of Neighbors for Racial Justice and other local organizations to Nextdoor's efforts were integral to the design and execution of the final product. Some of the copy

Nextdoor ended up using in the form—such as, "Ask yourself, 'Is what I saw actually suspicious, if I take race or ethnicity out of the question?'"—came at the suggestion of Neighbors for Racial Justice.

The new racial profiling form isn't the only change Nextdoor has made in service of tempering racial profiling on its platform. Last November, the company introduced a checkbox that allows users to flag posts for racial profiling. More recently, it's trained the group of in-house customer service representatives that reviews such posts in conflict resolution and "cultural humility" with an eye towards helping users understand why their posts were flagged, and how racial profiling negatively impacts whole communities.

When tech companies come under fire for failing to take race issues seriously — Snapchat, Twitter, and Airbnb are examples — critics often assert that, were minorities better represented on the staffs of those companies, the same mistakes might not have been made.

It's unusual for a tech company to take such an active role in policing its users, or to make an investment in educating them about social and cultural issues. In addition to relying on community members, Nextdoor also hired consultants to help, among other things, define what racial profiling outside of a police setting even is. Debo Adegbile, a civil rights attorney with the NAACP who was nominated for US assistant attorney general by President Obama, and Grande Lum, a race relations expert with the Department of Justice, both worked as advisers to Nextdoor.

Because the new form makes it less likely that users will post to Nextdoor, Tolia said there's a "business cost to doing this." But given the way Airbnb, Twitter, and other tech companies have struggled with issues of race in recent months, it's easy to see Tolia's decision to meet the racial profiling problem head-on not just as morality, but also as good business sense.

"Let's not be fooled," said Audrey Williams of Neighbors for Racial Justice. "It's a win for us, and it's a win for them."

FOR A SECOND READING

1. "Racial profiling," writes O'Donovan, "became an issue for Nextdoor in 2015, when a number of news outlets reported on the frequency of posts about crime or suspicious behavior that mentioned an individual's race, but little or nothing related to actual

criminal activity. In many cases, these posts would refer to people of color doing things such as talking on the phone or walking a dog" (p. 432). What does this passage suggest about the ways this particular app can foster racial prejudice? In your view, does it offer convincing proof of this hypothesis?

2. O'Donovan writes: "When tech companies come under fire for failing to take race issues seriously—Snapchat, Twitter, and Airbnb are examples—critics often assert that, were minorities better represented on the staffs of those companies, the same mistakes might not have been made" (p. 434). How valid do you find this argument to be? Do you agree that the racial biases of apps like "Snapchat, Twitter, and Airbnb" are a reflection of the racial composition of the workforce these social media sites employ?

3. As O'Donovan notes, Nextdoor seeks to promote community safety by allowing neighbors to report "suspicious activity." How do you understand this term? According to your own definition, which "activities" qualify as "suspicious" and which do not? As you reflect on this, do you think racial bias plays any role in how you draw this distinction?

PUTTING IT INTO WRITING

4. Here is how O'Donovan describes one potential solution for addressing the prevalence of racial bias on the Nextdoor site: "Instead of a blank text box and subject line, it was suggested that Nextdoor design a form that more closely resembles a police report or 911 dispatcher questionnaire. By explicitly requesting details about height, clothing, and age, they would discourage people filing reports from focusing exclusively on the race or ethnicity of the subject" (p. 432). In a 500-word essay, evaluate how effective you think these changes would be. Do you agree that designing a form that "resembles a police report" would help eliminate racial bias? Why or why not? Can you think of other "design" strategies that might also accomplish this goal?

5. Another change implemented by Nextdoor, writes O'Donovan, involves creating a group of "in-house customer service representatives" whose job is to help educate the site's users about "how racial profiling negatively impacts whole communities" (p. 435). Imagine yourself as the supervisor tasked with implementing this plan. What kind of training would you require these customer service

representatives to undergo? What specific kinds of information would you mandate be communicated to users?

COMPARING ARGUMENTS

6. O'Donovan's piece raises important questions about the ways that social media can lead or contribute to violations in civil rights. How do you think Bijan Stephen (p. 424) would respond to the effort by Nextdoor to "fix" racial profiling that O'Donovan profiles here? Based on his own argument about how social media can be used to promote civil rights, do you think Stephen would find this "fix" to be sufficient? Why or why not?

Then and Now: **Personal Shopping**

In America, few relationships have undergone as many changes over the years as the one between retailers and consumers. For those living outside of major cities a hundred years ago, for example, the primary lifeline connecting them to the world of purchasable goods was the mail-order catalog. Filled with images and descriptions of every product imaginable — from children's toys and formal clothing, household gadgets to beauty aids — the catalog evoked for millions of nineteenth-century readers a vision of the commercial marketplace as an exotic, mysterious, and faraway world. Today this vision has long since been superceded by a model of shopping in which the distance between seller and buyers has almost entirely collapsed. In place of the mail-order catalog, we now have sites like eBay and Craigslist, online venues that allow people to play the role of consumer and retailer simultaneously — hunting for bargains on the one hand while hawking their own wares to the highest bidder on the other.

Image Courtesy of The Advertising Archives

NICHOLAS KAMM/Getty Images

And yet while today's digital marketplace puts buyers and sellers into far more immediate and intimate contact, it's still an open question whether all this new proximity has entirely dispelled all of the mystery from the shopping experience. True, goods no longer arrive at our doorstep like exotic talismans from a far-off land. And, yes, shoppers in the do-it-yourself world of online retail no longer have to base their purchasing decisions on a catalog's stylized images or idealized portraits. But this doesn't automatically mean that the allure of these products is any less powerful. Even though we've forsaken the mail-order catalog for the personal shopping website, the marketplace may well remain just as inscrutable and mysterious as it ever was.

PUTTING IT INTO WRITING

1. What are some of the social scripts that govern the way people typically shop online? And do you think these scripts are useful or effective? Pick an example of a product that gets marketed online. How is this product marketed to potential customers? What particular strategies does its seller use to persuade customers to "buy into" what is on display? How would you respond if you were among this target audience?

2. What example in our current popular culture comes closest to the Sears & Roebuck catalog? What are the key similarities and differences between them? And which do you find a more effective or persuasive vehicle for selling products? Why?

SHERRY TURKLE

The Public Square

We are used to turning to the web for answers to any question we might have — whether it's about the latest news headlines, an upcoming sale at our favorite store, or tomorrow's weather forecast. But are we fully aware of what our never-ending search for data also asks us to give up? With every "like," "share," or "search" online, notes Sherry Turkle, we are simultaneously creating a public record of who we are — a record that shapes not only how the world views us, but also how we view ourselves. Sherry Turkle is a professor in the Science, Technology, and Society program at the Massachusetts Institute of Technology (MIT). She is the author of numerous books, including: *The Second Self* (1984), *Life on the Screen* (1995), *Evocative Objects* (2007), and *Alone Together* (2011). Her most recent book is called *Reclaiming Conversation: The Power of Talk in a Digital Age* (2015), from which the selection below is excerpted.

Before You Read

Is there a difference between the person you are online and offline? If so, how would you characterize this difference?

LIFE ON OUR NEW DIGITAL LANDSCAPE CHALLENGES US AS CITIZENS. Although the web provides incomparable tools to inform ourselves and mobilize for action, when we are faced with a social problem that troubles us, we are tempted to retreat to what I would call the online real. There, we can choose to see only the people with whom we agree. And to share only the ideas we think our followers want to hear.

There, things are simpler. Or rather, we can make them appear to be. And in that world we have called friction-free, we are used to the feeling of getting things done—generations have now grown up with the pleasures of mastering a game or a "level" and getting to a new screen. This history of easy dispatch is only one way that digital life shapes a new public self. It conditions us to see the world as a collection of crises calling for immediate action. In this context, it is easy to skip necessary conversations. What led to the problem? Who are the stakeholders? What is the situation on the ground? For on the ground there is never a simple fix, only friction, complexity, and history.

When the world of the computer was new, I used the metaphor of a second self to describe what was on our screens, because I observed how people defined themselves in the mirror of the machine. They looked at their computer desktops and felt ownership. The desktop was itself a new way to confirm their identities through the applications they had chosen, the content they had created and curated. This continues, of course. But now there is a parallel and less transparent movement.

Now we know that our life online creates a digital double because we took actions (we don't know which) that are acted on by algorithms (we don't know how). Our life has been "mined" for clues to our desires. But when our screens suggest our desires back to us, they often seem like broken mirrors.

A STATE OF EMERGENCY

Elizabeth, the economics graduate student who struggled with multi-tasking, tells the story of her involvement in online politics. In 2012, online activists—a group called Invisible Children, Inc.—publicized the atrocities of Joseph Kony, head of a militant group with operations in Uganda, South Sudan, the Democratic Republic of Congo, and the Central African Republic. Invisible Children made a thirty-minute video that highlighted Kony's use of child soldiers. The video instructed people to send money in return for signs that had Kony's face on them. On April 20, in a program called "Cover the Night," the signs were to be placed on lawns and in community buildings. The organizers said that this would make Kony "famous" and would exert the moral pressure that would end his reign of terror.

Released on March 5, 2012, by July 2012 the video had over 91 million   5
views on YouTube and over 18 million on Vimeo. In the days following its release, 58 percent of people aged eighteen through twenty-nine said that they had heard about it. Elizabeth was living in the United States when the video came out. She felt connected to the tragedy of the Kony story and became involved in the online movement.

Elizabeth's mother is a lawyer from Nairobi; her father, an American, met her when he was in the Peace Corps. Elizabeth has always felt both tied to Africa and at a distance from it—she always wanted to do more, but never saw an opportunity. The Kony action felt like a chance. She was optimistic about its promise and annoyed, almost uncomprehending, at the skepticism of her African friends, who did not believe that people really cared about what was going in Africa. They distinguished curiosity—enough curiosity to watch a video—from significant concern. And indeed, on the appointed day, few people stepped out into the physical world to put up their signs. Elizabeth sums up what she learned from this experience: "You go on a website, you send in your money—that satisfies your requirement for being in the conversation. You show solidarity with a movement by going online, and then, that's it."

The Kony video itself provides ways to understand the ultimate inaction. The video voice-over states as its premise that social media is a political idea that will change the world:

> Right now there are more people on Facebook than there were on the planet two
> hundred years ago. Humanity's greatest desire is to belong and connect. And

now we hear each other, we see each other . . . we share what we love, and it reminds us what we all have in common. . . . And this connection is changing the way the world works. Governments are trying to keep up . . . now we can taste the freedom.

Freedom to what? The narrator of the video says, "Our goal is to change the conversation of our culture." It encouraged people to feel that they are doing just that when they post a video online, or "like" a cause, or buy a sign. Or go to a Twitter feed—here, it was #StopKony.

There is nothing wrong with doing these things. They build awareness for your cause. But the difference between online support and putting up a real sign on your real lawn is this: With the physical sign you might have had to confront a person in your neighborhood who might have asked, "What are we supposed to do next about Kony? What is your commitment? What is the plan?" (As of this writing, Kony's activities continue and the group that organized the website has dissolved.)

FRIENDSHIP POLITICS: THINGS TO BUY AND CLICK ON

10 The Kony 2012 video describes a "friendship model" for politics: "The people of the world see each other and can protect each other. . . . Arresting Joseph Kony will prove that the world we live in has new rules, that the technology that has brought our planet together is allowing us to respond to the problems of our *friends*." So, this is the new ideal scenario: In the Facebook world, we friend, we share, and those in political power ultimately surrender.

Why should power surrender? According to an artist interviewed in the Kony video, power will be shaken by the simple tools of friendship. He says, referring to the promotional materials and the very sharing of the video, "Here are really simple tools. Go out and rock it."

Elizabeth is chastened. As she sees it now, sharing warm feelings gave people the illusion that they were doing politics. The experience left her thinking that there are no "simple tools"—no things to buy, no links to click on—that can fix a problem as difficult as what Kony represents. The #StopKony action got people talking. But it did not begin to transfer their online "likes" to other actions. Expressions of interest in the physical world—for example, giving a few dollars to a cause when there is a neighborhood charity drive—can also lead to a dissipation of interest when the person who asked for money is no longer at your door. The difference, for Elizabeth, is that the scale of the online declarations (so many millions of likes!) was deceiving. It made her think that something important was happening.

For Elizabeth, the most important lesson of her Kony experience was that the connections you form with people you don't know have significant limitations. They are good for getting people talking but not effective in getting them to do much else. She was intoxicated by the feeling of being part of a vibrant and growing movement. But the website couldn't get people to put real signs on real lawns. It couldn't get people to declare themselves to their physical neighbors.

Wherever we let our gaze fall online, we leave a trace that is now someone else's data.

It was a lesson, although Elizabeth didn't put it in these terms, in what sociologists call the power of strong and weak ties. Weak ties are friends of friends or casual acquaintances. Strong ties are people you know and trust. They are people with whom you are likely to have a long history of face-to-face conversation. So Facebook connections, the kinds of conversations we have online, and in general what we mean by Internet "friending" all draw on the power of weak ties.

There are those who see the conversations of the Internet as a direct 15 source of political change. Mark Pfeifle, a former U.S. national security adviser, wrote after the 2009 uprising in Iran, "Without Twitter, the people of Iran would not have felt empowered and confident to stand up for freedom and democracy," and called for Twitter to be nominated for the Nobel Peace Prize. When the demonstrations in Tehran began, the State Department asked Twitter not to perform scheduled maintenance operations so as not to take such a powerful political tool out of the hands of the protesters. We are, naturally, thrilled by the possibilities of a new, efficient activism.

But what do we forget when we talk through machines? We are tempted to forget the importance of face-to-face conversation, organization, and discipline in political action. We are tempted to forget that political change is often two steps forward and one step back. And that it usually takes a lot of time.

Malcolm Gladwell, writing about the strengths and limitations of social media in politics, contrasts online activism with what was needed during the American civil rights movement and comes to this formulation: If you are in a conversation with someone you don't know well—and these are most of your web contacts—the basic rule is to ask little. As in the Kony 2012 example, web activism works when you are asked to watch a video, give a thumbs-up, or buy a poster. Most recently, a fun gesture—dumping a bucket of ice on your head and asking a friend to do the same (and hopefully send a donation to the ALS Foundation)—has raised over a hundred million dollars for this cause. The power of weak ties is awesome. Quite literally, it inspires awe.

But if you want to take on political authority, says Gladwell, if you want to take those risks, you need ties of deeper trust, deeper history. You will have moved beyond gestures and donations; you will need to reach consensus, set goals, think strategically, and have philosophical direction. Lives will depend on your deliberations. Perhaps your own life. You will need a lot of long conversations.

To make this point, Gladwell tells the story of the 1960 Woolworth's lunch counter sit-in that opened a new chapter in the civil rights movement. It was something that a group of friends had discussed for nearly a month. The first young black man who asked to be served a cup of coffee at the lunch counter "was flanked by his roommate and two good friends from high school." They had the strongest of ties. They needed these to organize against violent opposition, to change tactics, and to stay the course. . . .

20   Politics still needs meetings that are meetings. It still needs conversations that require listening, conversations in which you are prepared to learn that a situation is more complex than you thought. You might want to change your mind. This is what our current political landscape discourages. There is a lot of conversation—both online and off—in which opponents broadcast prepared sound bites. There is a lot of staged conversation. You can avoid challenging conversations on and off the web. The web just makes it easier.

As Elizabeth sees it now, what she did with her friends during the heady days of #StopKony seems to have satisfied many people's requirements for political "action." Yet in her view, nothing got done. Hers is a story about activity at a frantic pace: a response to a crisis, followed by disillusion. . . .

ROOM TO THINK IN A WORLD OF BIG DATA

On our new data landscape, conversations that we traditionally have thought of as private—talking on the phone, sending email and texts—are actually shared with corporations that claim ownership over our data because they have provided us with the tools to communicate. Wherever we let our gaze fall online, we leave a trace that is now someone else's data. Insofar as we soul-search when we search the web and let our minds wander as we wonder what to read, what to buy, what ideas intrigue us, these introspective activities, too, belong to the company that facilitates our search. It mines them for data it finds useful now and saves them for what it might find useful in the future. For all of this information exists independently of us and is in a state, in parts and slices, to be sold to third parties. And outside this world of commercial transactions, we've learned that our government, too, feels that it has a claim on listening in.

Over time, living with an electronic shadow begins to feel so natural that it seems to disappear. Mark Zuckerberg, founder and CEO of Facebook, has said, "Privacy is no longer a relevant social norm." Well, privacy may not be convenient for the social network, but what is intimacy without privacy? What is democracy without privacy? Is there free thought without privacy?

THE WORLD WITHOUT PRIVACY

My grandparents knew how to talk about this. At length. When I was ten, and my grandmother thought I was old enough to understand, she took me to the main public library in Brooklyn, a great, imposing structure at Grand Army Plaza. I already had a library card that I used at our local library, a few minutes' walk from our home. But now we were going to the big library.

My grandmother made a picnic lunch—chicken sandwiches on rye bread and lemonade—and we sat on the concrete-and-wood benches of the Prospect Park parade grounds. The conversation turned to the library "rules." My grandmother wanted me to understand that I could take out any book. But the books I chose would be a secret between me and the library. No one had a right to know the list of books I read. It was like the privacy of our mailbox. Both protected what I would call *mindspace*. It was crucial to why she was so glad to be raising her family in America. 25

My grandmother had explained to me that in the Europe of her parents, the government used the mail to spy on people. Here, it was a protected space. (Clearly, my grandmother was less than informed about the excesses of J. Edgar Hoover, but she had taken comfort from the demise of Senator Joseph McCarthy.) We had talked about the privacy of mailboxes from when I was very young; indeed, as I remember it, the morning ritual of going down to get the mail gave my grandmother a new chance—almost every day—to comment on the reassuring mailboxes.

But the secrecy of my book list was something we didn't talk about until later. She clearly saw it as a more subtle civics lesson: how to explain to a child that no one should ever be able to hold what I read against me. Indeed, no one had the right to know what I was reading.

My grandmother's reverence for the American mailbox and library was her deepest expression of patriotism. And mindspace was central to that patriotism. From my grandparents' perspective, as second-generation Americans in the Brooklyn working class, being able to think and communicate in private meant that you could disagree with your employer and make a private decision about whether you were going to join a union. When making this decision, you would be wise to read union literature in private. Otherwise you might be threatened or fired before you got to your decision. And you needed time to let your ideas jell. You needed privacy to change your mind about important matters.

During the televised confirmation hearings for Supreme Court justice Clarence Thomas, the question came up as to whether Anita Hill's testimony against Thomas would be supported if it could be shown that he was a regular viewer of pornography. Did he regularly check pornography out from his local video store? Hill's lawyers wanted those records to be entered as testimony. I believed Anita Hill; I wanted those video records to support her account of Thomas's vulgarity and harassment. But his advocates argued that video store records and the list of the books one withdraws from a public library should get the same protection. Clarence Thomas had a right to his mindspace. He won that round and I considered it a round that my grandmother would have wanted him to win.

30 We make our technologies and they make and shape us. I learned to be an American citizen at the mailboxes in an apartment lobby in Brooklyn. And my understanding of the mindspace that democracy requires was shaped by how things worked at the public library. I did not know where to take my daughter, now twenty-four, as she grew up with the Internet.

She had to learn that her email is not protected. And although her library books are still private, what she reads online is not. She shows me how she tries to protect her privacy—for example, on social media apps, she never uses her real name but rather multiple other names, a protective habit of a generation that learned to avoid predators on Facebook by not using real names. But she knows that anyone sophisticated and determined would be able to find her. And when it comes to her cell phone, she gives up all privacy for convenience. She wants to use maps, so the GPS on her phone is turned on. This means that her phone leaves a trail of bread crumbs detailing her location. And the system knows her friends, what she searches for, what she reads.

A generation grows up assuming nothing is private and offering faint resistance.

When she was eighteen, my daughter showed me a program called Loopt. Like Find My Friends, it uses the GPS capability of the iPhone to show the location of friends. She thought it seemed creepy but told me that it would be hard to keep it off her phone if all her friends had it. "They would think I had something to hide."

And just recently, because I learned it just recently, I had to tell her that if she tries to protect her privacy by using browser settings designed to hide her identity, it may well activate greater surveillance of her online behavior. These days, the desire for privacy is considered suspicious and limits your ability to have it. This is distressing when I think of the lessons I learned at the public library. Wasn't the need for private mindspace why we protected the library books in the first place?

A generation grows up assuming nothing is private and offering faint resistance. Only a few years ago, a sixteen-year-old tried to reassure me that it somehow didn't matter that her email wasn't private by saying. "Who would care about my little life?" It was not an empowering mantra. And she turned out to be wrong. A lot of people care about her "little life."

SURVEILLANCE CREATES THE DIGITAL DOUBLE

When the Internet was new, we thought of it as a frontier. Historian of technology Evgeny Morozov points out that the advertising tagline for Microsoft's Internet Explorer was "Where do you want to go today?" These days, our online practices put us in a world where the real question is "What do you have to *give* today?" What information about yourself will you offer up today? We exist alongside digital representations of ourselves—digital doubles—that are useful to different parties at different times, or for some, at a time to be determined. The digital self is archived forever.

Gradually, we have come to learn all of this. And in the post-Snowden years, we have learned more—that the calls, locations, and online searches of ordinary Americans are monitored. But almost everything about this process remains as secret as possible, shrouded under the mantle of national security or the claim of proprietary interests. Exactly what is taken? In what form? How long is it kept? What is it used for? What most people have come to understand is that this is out of their hands.

What happens to conversation in these circumstances? One thing I've already noted is that people tend to forget their circumstances. This is one of the great paradoxes of digital conversation: It feels private despite the fact that you are onstage. If you are on Gmail, your email is searched for clues for how to best sell to you, but for the individual, the experience of being on email remains intimate. You face a glowing screen and you feel alone. The experience of digital communication is out of sync with its reality. Online, you are under a kind of surveillance.

THE SELF OF SELF-SURVEILLANCE

Previously, when we thought about surveillance, we thought about the effects of being watched all the time. The English philosopher Jeremy Bentham had a model for it. He called it the panopticon. It is a way to construct a building: You put a guard at the hub of a spoked wheel. Since those who are living in the spokes don't know when the guard is looking at them, they act as if he always is, because he always could be. They put themselves on good behavior, conforming to what they think of as the norm.

It works for prisons; it works for asylums. The French sociologist Michel Foucault took Bentham's image of panopticon surveillance and made it relevant to thinking about being a citizen of the modern state. For Foucault, the task of the modern state is to reduce its need for surveillance by creating a citizenry that is always watching itself. With cameras on most corners, you don't misbehave even if you don't know if a camera is on any particular corner. It might be. This is the self of self-surveillance. And it operates on the digital landscape. If you know that your texts and email are not private, you watch out for what you write. You internalize the censor.

40 Now, participation in the life of the data-gathering web has given "self-surveillance" a new twist. We do more than actively give up information by reporting our preferences or by taking surveys or by filling out forms. *These days, the most important data to those who watch us are the data trails we leave as we go about the business of our daily lives.* We feed databases as we shop, chat, watch movies, and make travel plans. Tracking one's fitness, keeping in touch with friends on social media, using a smartphone—all of these make surveillance and social participation seem like the same thing. Every new service on our smartphone, every new app, potentially offers up a new "species" of data to our online representation. The goal for those who make the apps is to link surveillance with the feeling that we are cared for. If our apps take "care" of us, we are not focused on what they take from us.

In the world as Foucault analyzed it, when you put cameras on street corners, you want people to notice them and build a self that takes surveillance as a given. Knowing that the cameras are there makes you "be good" all by yourself. But in our new data regime, the goal is for everyone to be unaware, or at least to forget in the moment, that surveillance exists. The regime works best if people feel free to "be themselves." That way they can provide "natural data" to the system.

So these days, while I might have only a general sense of where I've spent my day shopping, my iPhone knows, and this means that Apple knows and Google knows—a development I was not thinking about when I was thrilled to discover that, with GPS, my phone could double as an interactive map and I would never have to get lost again.

SHAPED BY THE SYSTEM: LIVING IN THE BUBBLE

Each of us who "feeds" the system ends up being shaped by it, but in a very different way than the person caught in the panopticon. We don't so much conform because we fear the consequences of being caught out in deviant behavior; rather, we conform because what is shown to us online is shaped by our past interests. The system presents us with what it believes we will buy or read or vote for. It places us in a particular world that constrains our sense of what is out there and what is possible.

For any query, search engines curate results based on what they know about you, including your location and what kind of computer you are using. So, if you do a search about the Ukraine and opposition movements don't come up, this may be because an algorithm has decided that you don't want to see them. This means that you won't learn (at least not then) that they exist. Or, by the logic of the algorithm, you may be presented with only certain political advertisements. You may not learn that a candidate who seems "moderate" in national advertising sends anti–gun control advertising to other people, just not to you.

The web promises to make our world bigger. But as it works now, it 45 also narrows our exposure to ideas. We can end up in a bubble in which we hear only the ideas we already know. Or already like. The philosopher Allan Bloom has suggested the cost: "Freedom of the mind requires not only, or not even especially, the absence of legal constraints but the presence of alternative thoughts. The most successful tyranny is not the one that uses force to assure uniformity, but the one that removes awareness of other possibilities."

Once you have a glimmer—and you only need a glimmer—of how this works, you have reason to believe that what the web shows you is a reflection of what you have shown it. So, if anti-abortion advertisements appear on your social media newsfeed, you may well ask what you did to put them there. What did you search or write or read? Little by little, as new things show up on the screen, you watch passively while the web actively constructs its version of you.

Karl Marx described how a simple wooden table, once turned into a commodity, danced to its own ghostlike tune. Marx's table, transcendent, "not only stands with its feet on the ground . . . it stands on its head, and evolves out of its wooden brain, grotesque ideas far more wonderful than 'table-turning' ever was." These days, it is our digital double that dances with a life of its own.

Advertising companies use it to build more targeted marketing campaigns. Insurance companies use it to apportion health benefits. From time to time, we are startled to get a view of who the algorithms that work over our data think we are. Technology writer Sara Watson describes such a moment. One day, Watson receives an invitation, a targeted advertisement, to participate in a study of anorexia in a Boston-area hospital. Watson says, "Ads *seem* trivial. But when they start to question whether I'm eating enough, a line has been crossed."

Watson finds the request to participate in the anorexia study personal and assaultive, because she is stuck with the idea that she made the invitation appear. But how? Is the study targeting women with small grocery bills? Women who buy diet supplements? We are talking through machines to algorithms whose rules we don't understand.

For Watson, what is most disorienting is that she doesn't understand 50 how the algorithm reached its conclusion about her. And how can she challenge a black box? For the algorithms that build up your digital double are written across many different platforms. There is no place where you can "fix" your double. There is no place to make it conform more exactly to how you want to be represented. Watson ends up confused. "It's hard to tell whether the algorithm doesn't know us at all, or if it actually knows us better than we know ourselves." Does the black box know something she doesn't?

In conversations with others over a lifetime, you get to see yourself as others see you. You get to "meet yourself" in new ways. You get to object on the spot if somebody doesn't "get you." Now we are offered a new experience: *We are asked to see ourselves as the collection of things we are told we should want, as the collection of things we are told should interest us.* Is this a tidier version of identity?

Building narratives about oneself takes time, and you never know if they are done or if they are correct. It is easier to see yourself in the mirror of the machine. You have mail.

THINKING IN PUBLIC

Thoreau went to Walden to try to think his own thoughts, to remove himself from living "too thickly"—how he referred to the constant chatter around him in society. These days, we live more "thickly" than Thoreau could ever have imagined, bombarded by the opinions, preferences, and "likes" of others. With the new sensibility of "I share, therefore I am," many are drawn to the premise that thinking together makes for better thinking.

Facebook's Zuckerberg thinks that thinking is a realm where together is always better. If you share what you are thinking and reading and watching, you will be richer for it. He says that he would always "rather go to a movie with [his] friends" because then they can share their experience and opinions. And if his friends can't be there physically, he can still have a richer experience of the movie through online sharing. Neil Richards, a lawyer, cross-examines this idea. Always sharing with friends has a cost.

> It means we'll always choose the movie they'd choose and won't choose the movie we want to see if they'd make fun of it. . . . If we're always with our friends, we're never alone, and we never get to explore ideas for ourselves. Of course, the stakes go beyond movies and extend to reading, to web-surfing, and even thinking.

55 And even thinking. Especially thinking. One student, who was used to blogging as a regular part of her academic program for her master's degree, changed styles when she changed universities and began her doctoral studies. In her new academic program blogging was discouraged. She comments that, looking back, the pressure to continually publish led to her thinking of herself as a brand. She wanted everything she wrote to conform to her confirmed identity. And blogging encouraged her to write about what she could write about best. It discouraged risk taking. Now, writing privately, she feels more curious. Research shows that

people who use social media are less willing to share their opinions if they think their followers and friends might disagree with them. People need private space to develop their ideas.

Generations of Americans took as self-evident the idea that private space was essential to democratic life. My grandmother had a civics lesson ready when she talked about the privacy of my library books. In order to be open to the widest range of ideas, I had to feel protected when making my reading choices. "Crowdsourcing" your reading preferences, says Richards, drives you "to conformity and the mainstream by social pressures." . . .

VAGUE ON THE DETAILS

When I talk to young people, I learn that they are expert at keeping "local" privacy—privacy from each other when they want to keep things within their clique, privacy from parents or teachers who might be monitoring their online accounts; here they use code words, a blizzard of acronyms. But as for how to think about private mindspace on the net, most haven't thought much about it and don't seem to want to. They, like the larger society, are, for the most part, willing to defer thinking about this. We are all helped in this by staying vague on the details.

And the few details we know seem illogical or like half-truths. It is illegal to tap a phone, but it is not illegal to store a search. We are told that our searches are "anonymized," but then, experts tell us that this is not true. Large corporations take our data, which seems to be legal, and the government also wants our data—things such as what we search, whom we text, what we text, whom we call, what we buy.

And it's hard to even learn the rules. I am on the board of the Electronic Freedom Foundation, devoted to privacy rights in digital culture. But it was only in spring 2014 that an email circulated to board members that described how easy it is to provoke the government to put you on a list of those whose email and searches are "fully tracked." For example, you will get on that list if, from outside the United States, you try to use TOR, a method of browsing anonymously online. The same article explained that from within the United States, you will also activate "full tracking" if you try to use alternatives to standard operating systems—for example, if you go to the Linux home page. It would appear that the Linux forum has been declared an "extremist" site.

> *I have felt for a long time, as a mother and a citizen, that in a democracy, we all need to begin with the assumption that everyone has something to "hide," a zone of private action and reflection.*

One of my graduate research assistants has been on that forum 60 because she needed to use annotation software that ran only on Linux.

When she reads the communiqué about Linux and full tracking, she is taken aback, but what she says is, "Theoretically I'm angry but I'm not having an emotional response." According to the source we both read, undisputed by the NSA, the content of her email and searches is surveilled. But still, she says, "Who knows what that means. Is it a person? Is it an algorithm? Is it tracking me by my name or my IP address?"

Confused by the details, she doesn't demand further details. Vague understandings support her sense that looking into this more closely can wait. So does the idea that she will be blocked or perhaps singled out for further surveillance if she tries to get more clarity.

One college senior tells me, with some satisfaction, that he has found a way around some of his concerns about online privacy. His strategy: He uses the "incognito" setting on his web browser. I decide that I'll do the same. I change the settings on my computer and go to bed thinking I have surely taken a step in the right direction. But what step have I taken? I learn that with an "incognito" setting I can protect my computer from recording my search history (so that family members, for example, can't check it), but I haven't slowed down Google or anyone else who might want access to it. And there is the irony that articles on how to protect your privacy online often recommend using TOR, but the NSA considers TOR users suspect and deserving of extra surveillance.

I come to understand that part of what sustains apathy is that people think they are being tracked by algorithms whose power will be checked by humans with good sense if the system finds anything that might actually get them into trouble. But we are in trouble together. Interest in Linux as probable cause for surveillance? We're starting not to take ourselves seriously.

My research assistant says she's not worried about her data trail because she sees the government as benign. They're interested in terrorists, not in her. But I persist. Now that my assistant knows she is subject to tracking because of her activity on the Linux forum, will it have a chilling effect on what she says online? Her answer is no, that she will say what she thinks and fight any attempt to use her thoughts against her "if it should ever come to that." But historically, the moments when "it came to that" have usually been moments when it has been hard or too late to take action.

65   I recall how Lana summed up her thoughts about online privacy: She said she would worry about it "if something bad happens." But we can turn this around and say that something bad has happened. We are challenged to draw the line, sometimes delicate, between "personalization" that seems banal (you buy shoes, so you see ads for shoes) and curation that poses larger questions.

In the 2012 presidential election, Facebook looked at random precincts and got people to go to the polls by telling them that their friends had voted. This political intervention was framed as a study, with the following research question: Can social media affect voter turnout? It can. Internet and law expert Jonathan Zittrain has called the manipulation of votes by social media "digital gerrymandering." It is an unregulated threat. Facebook also did a study, a mood experiment, in which some people were shown posts from happy friends and some people were shown posts from unhappy friends to see if this changed their moods. It did. Social media has the power to shape our political actions and emotional lives. We're accustomed to media manipulation—advertising has always tried to do this. But having unprecedented kinds of information about us—from what medications we take to what time we go to bed—allows for unprecedented interventions and intrusions. What is at stake is a sense of a self in control of itself. And a citizenry that can think for itself.

SNOWDEN CHANGES THE GAME

I have been talking to high school and college students about online privacy for decades. For years, when young people saw the "results" of online data collection, chiefly through the advertisements that appeared on their screens, it was hard for them to see the problem. The fact that a desirable sneaker or the perfect dress popped up didn't seem like a big deal. But in the years since Edward Snowden's revelations about how the government tracks our data, young people are more able to talk about the problems of data mining, in some measure because it has become associated (at least in their minds) with something easier to think about: spying. What Snowden was talking about seemed enough like old-fashioned spying that it gave people a way into a conversation about the more elusive thing: the incursions of everyday tracking.

So, after the Snowden revelations, high school students would begin a conversation about Snowden and then pivot to "Facebook knowing too much." What did Facebook know? What did Facebook keep? And had they really given it permission to do all this?

Or they would begin a conversation by talking about how they were trying to stay away from Facebook, now a symbol of too much online data collection, and then pivot to Snowden. A different set of issues entirely, but Snowden gave them a handle on their general sense of worry. The worry, in essence: How much does the Internet "know" and what is the Internet going to do about it? After Snowden, the helpful ads on their screens had more of a backstory. Someone, many someones, knows a lot more about them than their sneaker preferences.

And yet it is easy for this conversation to slip away from us. Because 70 just as we start to have it, we become infatuated with a new app that asks us to reveal more of ourselves: We could report our moods to see if there are concerns to address. We could track our resting heart rate or the amount of exercise we get each week. So we offer up data to improve ourselves and postpone the conversation about what happens to the data we share. If someday the fact that we were not careful about our diet in our forties is held against us—when it comes to giving us an insurance rate in our fifties—we will have offered up this data freely.

Instead of pursuing the political conversation, we sign up for another app.

Technology companies will say—and they do—that if you don't want to share your data, don't use their services. If you don't want Google to know what you are searching, don't search on Google. When asked to comment on all that Google knows, its executive chairman said, in essence, that "the way to deal is to just be good."

I have felt for a long time, as a mother and as a citizen, that in a democracy, we all need to begin with the assumption that everyone has something to "hide," a zone of private action and reflection, a zone that needs to be protected despite our techno-enthusiasms. You need space for real dissent. A mental space and a technical space (those mailboxes!). It's a private space where people are free to "not be good." To me, this conversation about technology, privacy, and democracy is not Luddite or too late.

FOR A SECOND READING

1. The term Turkle uses to describe the version of ourselves we create online is "digital double." What images or associations does this term evoke? What does it suggest about the power of digital technology to shape how we see and present ourselves?

2. "The web," writes Turkle, "promises to make our world bigger. But as it works now, it also narrows our exposure to ideas. We can end up in a bubble in which we hear only the ideas we already know" (p. 449). Respond to Turkle's statement here. Do you agree that our online interactions can leave us "in a bubble in which we hear only the ideas we already know"? And if so, should this situation be considered a problem? Why or why not?

3. In Turkle's view, privacy is a prerequisite for democracy: "Generations of Americans took as self-evident the idea that private space was essential to democratic life" (p. 451). Do you think this view is still operative today? Do you feel yourself part of a generation that continues to value privacy as a fundamental (civic and personal) right?

PUTTING IT INTO WRITING

4. "These days," writes Turkle, "our online practices put us in a world where the real question is 'What do you have to *give* today?' What information about yourself will you offer up today?" (p. 447). Make a list of the kinds of information about yourself (e.g., interests, hobbies, background, peer group, politics, etc.) you think gets "offered up" when you go online. What sort of profile does this information create? Do you believe this profile is an accurate reflection of who you truly are? Why or why not?

5. Choose an online activity that you think lends itself most easily to surveillance. First describe it. What kind of activity is this? Next put yourself in the position of the entity, agency, or organization you think would be most interested in monitoring this activity. What information would you most want to gather? To what purpose could this information be put?

COMPARING ARGUMENTS

6. How do you think Charles Duhigg (p. 456) would respond to Turkle's discussion of digital surveillance? Do you think he would find Turkle's argument about privacy and democracy in the era of "Big Data" a confirmation or challenge to his thesis about the power of habit? What aspects of Duhigg's discussion in particular make you say so?

CHARLES DUHIGG
How Companies Learn Your Secrets

We hear a lot these days about the dangers posed by government surveillance. Just as extensive, and perhaps even more troubling, however, is the phenomenon of corporate surveillance: the efforts of countless retail companies to monitor, and ultimately manipulate, our personal shopping behavior. What are the implications, asks Charles Duhigg, of living in a world where the stores we patronize may know more about us than we know about ourselves? Charles Duhigg is a staff writer for the *New York Times* and author of *The Power of Habit: Why We Do What We Do in Life and Business* (2013). The essay below appeared in the *New York Times Magazine* in 2012.

Before You Read

How much of your online behavior would you say is dictated by habit?

ANDREW POLE HAD JUST STARTED WORKING AS A STATISTICIAN FOR Target in 2002, when two colleagues from the marketing department stopped by his desk to ask an odd question: "If we wanted to figure out if a customer is pregnant, even if she didn't want us to know, can you do that?"

Pole has a master's degree in statistics and another in economics, and has been obsessed with the intersection of data and human behavior most of his life. His parents were teachers in North Dakota, and while other kids were going to 4-H, Pole was doing algebra and writing computer programs. "The stereotype of a math nerd is true," he told me when I spoke with him last year. "I kind of like going out and evangelizing analytics."

As the marketers explained to Pole—and as Pole later explained to me, back when we were still speaking and before Target told him to stop—new parents are a retailer's holy grail. Most shoppers don't buy everything they need at one store. Instead, they buy groceries at the grocery store and toys at the toy store, and they visit Target only when they need certain items they associate with Target—cleaning supplies, say, or new socks or a six-month supply of toilet paper. But Target sells everything from milk to stuffed animals to lawn furniture to electronics, so one of the company's primary goals is convincing customers that the only store they need is Target. But it's a tough message to get across, even with the most ingenious ad campaigns, because once consumers' shopping habits are ingrained, it's incredibly difficult to change them.

There are, however, some brief periods in a person's life when old routines fall apart and buying habits are suddenly in flux. One of those moments—*the* moment, really—is right around the birth of a child, when parents are exhausted and overwhelmed and their shopping patterns and brand loyalties are up for grabs. But as Target's marketers explained to Pole, timing is everything. Because birth records are usually public, the moment a couple have a new baby, they are almost instantaneously barraged with offers and incentives and advertisements from all sorts of companies. Which means that the key is to reach them earlier, before any other retailers know a baby is on the way. Specifically, the marketers said they wanted to send specially designed ads to women in their second trimester, which is when most expectant mothers begin buying all sorts of new things, like prenatal vitamins and maternity clothing. "Can you give us a list?" the marketers asked.

"We knew that if we could identify them in their second trimester, 5 there's a good chance we could capture them for years," Pole told me. "As soon as we get them buying diapers from us, they're going to start buying everything else too. If you're rushing through the store, looking for bottles, and you pass orange juice, you'll grab a carton. Oh, and there's that new DVD I want. Soon, you'll be buying cereal and paper towels from us, and keep coming back."

The desire to collect information on customers is not new for Target or any other large retailer, of course. For decades, Target has collected vast amounts of data on every person who regularly walks into one of its stores. Whenever possible, Target assigns each shopper a unique code—known internally as the Guest ID number—that keeps tabs on everything they buy. "If you use a credit card or a coupon, or fill out a survey, or mail in a refund, or call the customer help line, or open an e-mail we've sent you or visit our Web site, we'll record it and link it to your Guest ID," Pole said. "We want to know everything we can."

Also linked to your Guest ID is demographic information like your age, whether you are married and have kids, which part of town you live in, how long

Target can buy data about your ethnicity, job history, the magazines you read, if you've ever declared bankruptcy or got divorced, the year you bought (or lost) your house, where you went to college, what kinds of topics you talk about online, whether you prefer certain brands of coffee, paper towels, cereal, or applesauce, your political leanings, reading habits, charitable giving, and the number of cars you own.

it takes you to drive to the store, your estimated salary, whether you've moved recently, what credit cards you carry in your wallet and what Web sites you visit. Target can buy data about your ethnicity, job history, the magazines you read, if you've ever declared bankruptcy or got divorced, the year you bought (or lost) your house, where you went to college, what kinds of topics you talk about online, whether you prefer certain brands of coffee, paper towels, cereal, or applesauce, your political leanings, reading habits, charitable giving, and the number of cars you own. (In a statement, Target declined to identify what demographic information it collects or purchases.) All that information is meaningless, however, without someone to analyze and make sense of it. That's where Andrew Pole and the dozens of other members of Target's Guest Marketing Analytics department come in.

Almost every major retailer, from grocery chains to investment banks to the U.S. Postal Service, has a "predictive analytics" department devoted to understanding not just consumers' shopping habits but also their personal habits, so as to more efficiently market to them. "But Target has always been one of the smartest at this," says Eric Siegel, a consultant and the chairman of a conference called Predictive Analytics World. "We're living through a golden age of behavioral research. It's amazing how much we can figure out about how people think now."

The reason Target can snoop on our shopping habits is that, over the past two decades, the science of habit formation has become a major field of research in neurology and psychology departments at hundreds of major medical centers and universities, as well as inside extremely well financed corporate labs. "It's like an arms race to hire statisticians nowadays," said Andreas Weigend, the former chief scientist at Amazon.com. "Mathematicians are suddenly sexy." As the ability to analyze data has grown more and more fine-grained, the push to understand how daily habits influence our decisions has become one of the most exciting topics in clinical research, even though most of us are hardly aware those patterns exist. One study from Duke University estimated that habits, rather than conscious decision-making, shape 45 percent of the choices we make every day, and recent discoveries have begun to change everything from the way we think about dieting to how doctors conceive treatments for anxiety, depression, and addictions.

> **Researchers have figured out how to stop people from habitually overeating and biting their nails. They can explain why some of us automatically go for a jog every morning and are more productive at work, while others oversleep and procrastinate.**

This research is also transforming our understanding of how habits 10
function across organizations and societies. A football coach named Tony
Dungy propelled one of the worst teams in the N.F.L. to the Super Bowl by
focusing on how his players habitually reacted to on-field cues. Before he
became Treasury secretary, Paul O'Neill overhauled a stumbling conglom-
erate, Alcoa, and turned it into a top performer in the Dow Jones by relent-
lessly attacking one habit—a specific approach to worker safety—which
in turn caused a companywide transformation. The Obama campaign has
hired a habit specialist as its "chief scientist" to figure out how to trigger
new voting patterns among different constituencies.

Researchers have figured out how to stop people from habitually
overeating and biting their nails. They can explain why some of us automatically go for a jog every morning and are more productive at work,
while others oversleep and procrastinate. There is a calculus, it turns out,
for mastering our subconscious urges. For companies like Target, the
exhaustive rendering of our conscious and unconscious patterns into
data sets and algorithms has revolutionized what they know about us
and, therefore, how precisely they can sell.

Inside the brain-and-cognitive-sciences department of the Massachusetts Institute of Technology are what, to the casual observer, look like
dollhouse versions of surgical theaters. There are rooms with tiny scal-
pels, small drills, and miniature saws. Even the operating tables are petite,
as if prepared for 7-year-old surgeons. Inside those shrunken O.R.'s, neu-
rologists cut into the skulls of anesthetized rats, implanting tiny sensors
that record the smallest changes in the activity of their brains.

An M.I.T. neuroscientist named Ann Graybiel told me that she and
her colleagues began exploring habits more than a decade ago by putting
their wired rats into a T-shaped maze with chocolate at one end. The
maze was structured so that each animal was positioned behind a barrier
that opened after a loud click. The first time a rat was placed in the maze,
it would usually wander slowly up and down the center aisle after the
barrier slid away, sniffing in corners and scratching at walls. It appeared
to smell the chocolate but couldn't figure out how to find it. There was no
discernible pattern in the rat's meanderings and no indication it was
working hard to find the treat.

The probes in the rats' heads, however, told a different story. While
each animal wandered through the maze, its brain was working furiously. Every time a rat sniffed the air or scratched a wall, the neurosen-
sors inside the animal's head exploded with activity. As the scientists
repeated the experiment, again and again, the rats eventually stopped
sniffing corners and making wrong turns and began to zip through the
maze with more and more speed. And within their brains, something
unexpected occurred: as each rat learned how to complete the maze

more quickly, its mental activity *decreased*. As the path became more and more automatic—as it became a habit—the rats started thinking less and less.

15   This process, in which the brain converts a sequence of actions into an automatic routine, is called "chunking." There are dozens, if not hundreds, of behavioral chunks we rely on every day. Some are simple: you automatically put toothpaste on your toothbrush before sticking it in your mouth. Some, like making the kids' lunch, are a little more complex. Still others are so complicated that it's remarkable to realize that a habit could have emerged at all.

Take backing your car out of the driveway. When you first learned to drive, that act required a major dose of concentration, and for good reason: it involves peering into the rearview and side mirrors and checking for obstacles, putting your foot on the brake, moving the gearshift into reverse, removing your foot from the brake, estimating the distance between the garage and the street while keeping the wheels aligned, calculating how images in the mirrors translate into actual distances, all while applying differing amounts of pressure to the gas pedal and brake.

Now, you perform that series of actions every time you pull into the street without thinking very much. Your brain has chunked large parts of it. Left to its own devices, the brain will try to make almost any repeated behavior into a habit, because habits allow our minds to conserve effort. But conserving mental energy is tricky, because if our brains power down at the wrong moment, we might fail to notice something important, like a child riding her bike down the sidewalk or a speeding car coming down the street. So we've devised a clever system to determine when to let a habit take over. It's something that happens whenever a chunk of behavior starts or ends—and it helps to explain why habits are so difficult to change once they're formed, despite our best intentions.

To understand this a little more clearly, consider again the chocolate-seeking rats. What Graybiel and her colleagues found was that, as the ability to navigate the maze became habitual, there were two spikes in the rats' brain activity—once at the beginning of the maze, when the rat heard the click right before the barrier slid away, and once at the end, when the rat found the chocolate. Those spikes show when the rats' brains were fully engaged, and the dip in neural activity between the spikes showed when the habit took over. From behind the partition, the rat wasn't sure what waited on the other side, until it heard the click, which it had come to associate with the maze. Once it heard that sound, it knew to use the "maze habit," and its brain activity decreased. Then at the end of the routine, when the reward appeared, the brain shook itself awake again and the chocolate signaled to the rat that this particular habit was worth remembering, and the neurological pathway was carved that much deeper.

The process within our brains that creates habits is a three-step loop. First, there is a cue, a trigger that tells your brain to go into automatic mode and which habit to use. Then there is the routine, which can be physical or mental or emotional. Finally, there is a reward, which helps your brain figure out if this particular loop is worth remembering for the future. Over time, this loop—cue, routine, reward; cue, routine, reward—becomes more and more automatic. The cue and reward become neurologically inter-twined until a sense of craving emerges. What's unique about cues and rewards, however, is how subtle they can be. Neurological studies like the ones in Graybiel's lab have revealed that some cues span just milliseconds. And rewards can range from the obvious (like the sugar rush that a morning doughnut habit provides) to the infinitesimal (like the barely noticeable—but measurable—sense of relief the brain experiences after successfully navigating the driveway). Most cues and rewards, in fact, hap-pen so quickly and are so slight that we are hardly aware of them at all. But our neural systems notice and use them to build automatic behaviors.

Habits aren't destiny—they can be ignored, changed, or replaced. But 20 it's also true that once the loop is established and a habit emerges, your brain stops fully participating in decision-making. So unless you deliber-ately fight a habit—unless you find new cues and rewards—the old pattern will unfold automatically.

"We've done experiments where we trained rats to run down a maze until it was a habit, and then we extinguished the habit by changing the placement of the reward," Graybiel told me. "Then one day, we'll put the reward in the old place and put in the rat and, by golly, the old habit will re-emerge right away. Habits never really disappear."

Luckily, simply understanding how habits work makes them easier to control. Take, for instance, a series of studies conducted a few years ago at Columbia University and the University of Alberta. Researchers wanted to understand how exercise habits emerge. In one project, 256 members of a health-insurance plan were invited to classes stressing the importance of exercise. Half the participants received an extra lesson on the theories of habit formation (the structure of the habit loop) and were asked to identify cues and rewards that might help them develop exercise routines.

The results were dramatic. Over the next four months, those partici-pants who deliberately identified cues and rewards spent twice as much time exercising as their peers. Other studies have yielded similar results. According to another recent paper, if you want to start running in the morning, it's essential that you choose a simple cue (like always putting on your sneakers before breakfast or leaving your running clothes next to your bed) and a clear reward (like a midday treat or even the sense of accom-plishment that comes from ritually recording your miles in a log book).

After a while, your brain will start anticipating that reward—craving the treat or the feeling of accomplishment—and there will be a measurable neurological impulse to lace up your jogging shoes each morning.

Our relationship to e-mail operates on the same principle. When a computer chimes or a smartphone vibrates with a new message, the brain starts anticipating the neurological "pleasure" (even if we don't recognize it as such) that clicking on the e-mail and reading it provides. That expectation, if unsatisfied, can build until you find yourself moved to distraction by the thought of an e-mail sitting there unread—even if you know, rationally, it's most likely not important. On the other hand, once you remove the cue by disabling the buzzing of your phone or the chiming of your computer, the craving is never triggered, and you'll find, over time, that you're able to work productively for long stretches without checking your in-box.

25   Some of the most ambitious habit experiments have been conducted by corporate America. To understand why executives are so entranced by this science, consider how one of the world's largest companies, Procter & Gamble, used habit insights to turn a failing product into one of its biggest sellers. P.&G. is the corporate behemoth behind a whole range of products, from Downy fabric softener to Bounty paper towels to Duracell batteries and dozens of other household brands. In the mid-1990s, P.&G.'s executives began a secret project to create a new product that could eradicate bad smells. P.&G. spent millions developing a colorless, cheap-to-manufacture liquid that could be sprayed on a smoky blouse, stinky couch, old jacket, or stained car interior and make it odorless. In order to market the product—Febreze—the company formed a team that included a former Wall Street mathematician named Drake Stimson and habit specialists, whose job was to make sure the television commercials, which they tested in Phoenix, Salt Lake City, and Boise, Idaho, accentuated the product's cues and rewards just right.

> **Habits aren't destiny — they can be ignored, changed, or replaced.**

The first ad showed a woman complaining about the smoking section of a restaurant. Whenever she eats there, she says, her jacket smells like smoke. A friend tells her that if she uses Febreze, it will eliminate the odor. The cue in the ad is clear: the harsh smell of cigarette smoke. The reward: odor eliminated from clothes. The second ad featured a woman worrying about her dog, Sophie, who always sits on the couch. "Sophie will always smell like Sophie," she says, but with Febreze, "now my furniture doesn't have to." The ads were put in heavy rotation. Then the marketers sat back, anticipating how they would spend their bonuses. A week passed. Then two. A month. Two months. Sales started small and got smaller. Febreze was a dud.

The panicked marketing team canvassed consumers and conducted in-depth interviews to figure out what was going wrong, Stimson recalled. Their first inkling came when they visited a woman's home outside Phoenix. The house was clean and organized. She was something of a neat freak, the woman explained. But when P.&G.'s scientists walked into her living room, where her nine cats spent most of their time, the scent was so overpowering that one of them gagged.

According to Stimson, who led the Febreze team, a researcher asked the woman, "What do you do about the cat smell?"

"It's usually not a problem," she said.

"Do you smell it now?"   30

"No," she said. "Isn't it wonderful? They hardly smell at all!"

A similar scene played out in dozens of other smelly homes. The reason Febreze wasn't selling, the marketers realized, was that people couldn't detect most of the bad smells in their lives. If you live with nine cats, you become desensitized to their scents. If you smoke cigarettes, eventually you don't smell smoke anymore. Even the strongest odors fade with constant exposure. That's why Febreze was a failure. The product's cue—the bad smells that were supposed to trigger daily use—was hidden from the people who needed it the most. And Febreze's reward (an odorless home) was meaningless to someone who couldn't smell offensive scents in the first place.

P.&G. employed a Harvard Business School professor to analyze Febreze's ad campaigns. They collected hours of footage of people cleaning their homes and watched tape after tape, looking for clues that might help them connect Febreze to people's daily habits. When that didn't reveal anything, they went into the field and conducted more interviews. A breakthrough came when they visited a woman in a suburb near Scottsdale, Ariz., who was in her 40s with four children. Her house was clean, though not compulsively tidy, and didn't appear to have any odor problems; there were no pets or smokers. To the surprise of everyone, she loved Febreze.

"I use it every day," she said.

"What smells are you trying to get rid of?" a researcher asked.   35

"I don't really use it for specific smells," the woman said. "I use it for normal cleaning—a couple of sprays when I'm done in a room."

The researchers followed her around as she tidied the house. In the bedroom, she made her bed, tightened the sheet's corners, then sprayed the comforter with Febreze. In the living room, she vacuumed, picked up the children's shoes, straightened the coffee table, then sprayed Febreze on the freshly cleaned carpet.

"It's nice, you know?" she said. "Spraying feels like a little minicelebration when I'm done with a room." At the rate she was going, the team estimated, she would empty a bottle of Febreze every two weeks.

When they got back to P.&G.'s headquarters, the researchers watched their videotapes again. Now they knew what to look for and saw their mistake in scene after scene. Cleaning has its own habit loops that already exist. In one video, when a woman walked into a dirty room (cue), she started sweeping and picking up toys (routine), then she examined the room and smiled when she was done (reward). In another, a woman scowled at her unmade bed (cue), proceeded to straighten the blankets and comforter (routine), and then sighed as she ran her hands over the freshly plumped pillows (reward). P.&G. had been trying to create a whole new habit with Febreze, but what they really needed to do was piggyback on habit loops that were already in place. The marketers needed to position Febreze as something that came at the end of the cleaning ritual, the reward, rather than as a whole new cleaning routine.

40   The company printed new ads showing open windows and gusts of fresh air. More perfume was added to the Febreze formula, so that instead of merely neutralizing odors, the spray had its own distinct scent. Television commercials were filmed of women, having finished their cleaning routine, using Febreze to spritz freshly made beds and just-laundered clothing. Each ad was designed to appeal to the habit loop: when you see a freshly cleaned room (cue), pull out Febreze (routine), and enjoy a smell that says you've done a great job (reward). When you finish making a bed (cue), spritz Febreze (routine), and breathe a sweet, contented sigh (reward). Febreze, the ads implied, was a pleasant treat, not a reminder that your home stinks.

And so Febreze, a product originally conceived as a revolutionary way to destroy odors, became an air freshener used once things are already clean. The Febreze revamp occurred in the summer of 1998. Within two months, sales doubled. A year later, the product brought in $230 million. Since then Febreze has spawned dozens of spinoffs—air fresheners, candles, and laundry detergents—that now account for sales of more than $1 billion a year. Eventually, P.&G. began mentioning to customers that, in addition to smelling sweet, Febreze can actually kill bad odors. Today it's one of the top-selling products in the world.

Andrew Pole was hired by Target to use the same kinds of insights into consumers' habits to expand Target's sales. His assignment was to analyze all the cue-routine-reward loops among shoppers and help the company figure out how to exploit them. Much of his department's work was straightforward: find the customers who have children and send them catalogs that feature toys before Christmas. Look for shoppers who habitually purchase swimsuits in April and send them coupons for sunscreen in July and diet books in December. But Pole's most important assignment was to identify those unique moments in consumers' lives when their shopping habits become particularly flexible and the right advertisement or coupon would cause them to begin spending in new ways.

In the 1980s, a team of researchers led by a U.C.L.A. professor named Alan Andreasen undertook a study of people's most mundane purchases, like soap, toothpaste, trash bags, and toilet paper. They learned that most shoppers paid almost no attention to how they bought these products, that the purchases occurred habitually, without any complex decision-making. Which meant it was hard for marketers, despite their displays and coupons and product promotions, to persuade shoppers to change.

But when some customers were going through a major life event, like graduating from college or getting a new job or moving to a new town, their shopping habits became flexible in ways that were both predictable and potential gold mines for retailers. The study found that when someone marries, he or she is more likely to start buying a new type of coffee. When a couple move into a new house, they're more apt to purchase a different kind of cereal. When they divorce, there's an increased chance they'll start buying different brands of beer.

Consumers going through major life events often don't notice, or   45 care, that their shopping habits have shifted, but retailers notice, and they care quite a bit. At those unique moments, Andreasen wrote, customers are "vulnerable to intervention by marketers." In other words, a precisely timed advertisement, sent to a recent divorcee or new homebuyer, can change someone's shopping patterns for years.

And among life events, none are more important than the arrival of a baby. At that moment, new parents' habits are more flexible than at almost any other time in their adult lives. If companies can identify pregnant shoppers, they can earn millions.

The only problem is that identifying pregnant customers is harder than it sounds. Target has a baby-shower registry, and Pole started there, observing how shopping habits changed as a woman approached her due date, which women on the registry had willingly disclosed. He ran test after test, analyzing the data, and before long some useful patterns emerged. Lotions, for example. Lots of people buy lotion, but one of Pole's colleagues noticed that women on the baby registry were buying larger quantities of unscented lotion around the beginning of their second trimester. Another analyst noted that sometime in the first 20 weeks, pregnant women loaded up on supplements like calcium, magnesium, and zinc. Many shoppers purchase soap and cotton balls, but when someone suddenly starts buying

But Pole's most important assignment was to identify those unique moments in consumers' lives when their shopping habits become particularly flexible and the right advertisement or coupon would cause them to begin spending in new ways.

465

lots of scent-free soap and extra-big bags of cotton balls, in addition to hand sanitizers and washcloths, it signals they could be getting close to their delivery date.

As Pole's computers crawled through the data, he was able to identify about 25 products that, when analyzed together, allowed him to assign each shopper a "pregnancy prediction" score. More important, he could also estimate her due date to within a small window, so Target could send coupons timed to very specific stages of her pregnancy.

One Target employee I spoke to provided a hypothetical example. Take a fictional Target shopper named Jenny Ward, who is 23, lives in Atlanta and in March bought cocoa-butter lotion, a purse large enough to double as a diaper bag, zinc and magnesium supplements, and a bright blue rug. There's, say, an 87 percent chance that she's pregnant and that her delivery date is sometime in late August. What's more, because of the data attached to her Guest ID number, Target knows how to trigger Jenny's habits. They know that if she receives a coupon via e-mail, it will most likely cue her to buy online. They know that if she receives an ad in the mail on Friday, she frequently uses it on a weekend trip to the store. And they know that if they reward her with a printed receipt that entitles her to a free cup of Starbucks coffee, she'll use it when she comes back again.

50 In the past, that knowledge had limited value. After all, Jenny purchased only cleaning supplies at Target, and there were only so many psychological buttons the company could push. But now that she is pregnant, everything is up for grabs. In addition to triggering Jenny's habits to buy more cleaning products, they can also start including offers for an array of products, some more obvious than others, that a woman at her stage of pregnancy might need.

Pole applied his program to every regular female shopper in Target's national database and soon had a list of tens of thousands of women who were most likely pregnant. If they could entice those women or their husbands to visit Target and buy baby-related products, the company's cue-routine-reward calculators could kick in and start pushing them to buy groceries, bathing suits, toys and clothing, as well. When Pole shared his list with the marketers, he said, they were ecstatic. Soon, Pole was getting invited to meetings above his paygrade. Eventually his paygrade went up.

At which point someone asked an important question: How are women going to react when they figure out how much Target knows?

"If we send someone a catalog and say, 'Congratulations on your first child!' and they've never told us they're pregnant, that's going to make some people uncomfortable," Pole told me. "We are very conservative about compliance with all privacy laws. But even if you're following the law, you can do things where people get queasy."

About a year after Pole created his pregnancy-prediction model, a man walked into a Target outside Minneapolis and demanded to see the manager. He was clutching coupons that had been sent to his daughter, and he was angry, according to an employee who participated in the conversation.

"My daughter got this in the mail!" he said. "She's still in high school, 55 and you're sending her coupons for baby clothes and cribs? Are you trying to encourage her to get pregnant?"

The manager didn't have any idea what the man was talking about. He looked at the mailer. Sure enough, it was addressed to the man's daughter and contained advertisements for maternity clothing, nursery furniture, and pictures of smiling infants. The manager apologized and then called a few days later to apologize again.

On the phone, though, the father was somewhat abashed. "I had a talk with my daughter," he said. "It turns out there's been some activities in my house I haven't been completely aware of. She's due in August. I owe you an apology."

When I approached Target to discuss Pole's work, its representatives declined to speak with me. "Our mission is to make Target the preferred shopping destination for our guests by delivering outstanding value, continuous innovation, and exceptional guest experience," the company wrote in a statement. "We've developed a number of research tools that allow us to gain insights into trends and preferences within different demographic segments of our guest population." When I sent Target a complete summary of my reporting, the reply was more terse: "Almost all of your statements contain inaccurate information and publishing them would be misleading to the public. We do not intend to address each statement point by point." The company declined to identify what was inaccurate. They did add, however, that Target "is in compliance with all federal and state laws, including those related to protected health information."

When I offered to fly to Target's headquarters to discuss its concerns, a spokeswoman e-mailed that no one would meet me. When I flew out anyway, I was told I was on a list of prohibited visitors. "I've been instructed not to give you access and to ask you to leave," said a very nice security guard named Alex.

Using data to predict a woman's pregnancy, Target realized soon after 60 Pole perfected his model, could be a public-relations disaster. So the question became: how could they get their advertisements into expectant mothers' hands without making it appear they were spying on them? How do you take advantage of someone's habits without letting them know you're studying their lives?

Before I met Andrew Pole, before I even decided to write a book about the science of habit formation, I had another goal: I wanted to lose weight.

I had got into a bad habit of going to the cafeteria every afternoon and eating a chocolate-chip cookie, which contributed to my gaining a few pounds. Eight, to be precise. I put a Post-it note on my computer reading "NO MORE COOKIES." But every afternoon, I managed to ignore that note, wander to the cafeteria, buy a cookie, and eat it while chatting with colleagues. Tomorrow, I always promised myself, I'll muster the will-power to resist.

Tomorrow, I ate another cookie.

When I started interviewing experts in habit formation, I concluded each interview by asking what I should do. The first step, they said, was to figure out my habit loop. The routine was simple: every afternoon, I walked to the cafeteria, bought a cookie, and ate it while chatting with friends.

65   Next came some less obvious questions: What was the cue? Hunger? Boredom? Low blood sugar? And what was the reward? The taste of the cookie itself? The temporary distraction from my work? The chance to socialize with colleagues?

Rewards are powerful because they satisfy cravings, but we're often not conscious of the urges driving our habits in the first place. So one day, when I felt a cookie impulse, I went outside and took a walk instead. The next day, I went to the cafeteria and bought a coffee. The next, I bought an apple and ate it while chatting with friends. You get the idea. I wanted to test different theories regarding what reward I was really craving. Was it hunger? (In which case the apple should have worked.) Was it the desire for a quick burst of energy? (If so, the coffee should suffice.) Or, as turned out to be the answer, was it that after several hours spent focused on work, I wanted to socialize, to make sure I was up to speed on office gossip, and the cookie was just a convenient excuse? When I walked to a colleague's desk and chatted for a few minutes, it turned out, my cookie urge was gone.

All that was left was identifying the cue.

Deciphering cues is hard, however. Our lives often contain too much information to figure out what is triggering a particular behavior. Do you eat breakfast at a certain time because you're hungry? Or because the morning news is on? Or because your kids have started eating? Experiments have shown that most cues fit into one of five categories: location, time, emotional state, other people, or the immediately preced-ing action. So to figure out the cue for my cookie habit, I wrote down five things the moment the urge hit:

Where are you? (Sitting at my desk.)

What time is it? (3:36 P.M.)

What's your emotional state? (Bored.)

Who else is around? (No one.)

What action preceded the urge? (Answered an e-mail.)

The next day I did the same thing. And the next. Pretty soon, the cue was clear: I always felt an urge to snack around 3:30.

Once I figured out all the parts of the loop, it seemed fairly easy to 70 change my habit. But the psychologists and neuroscientists warned me that, for my new behavior to stick, I needed to abide by the same principle that guided Procter & Gamble in selling Febreze: To shift the routine—to socialize, rather than eat a cookie—I needed to piggyback on an existing habit. So now, every day around 3:30, I stand up, look around the newsroom for someone to talk to, spend 10 minutes gossiping, then go back to my desk. The cue and reward have stayed the same. Only the routine has shifted. It doesn't feel like a decision, any more than the M.I.T. rats made a decision to run through the maze. It's now a habit. I've lost 21 pounds since then (12 of them from changing my cookie ritual).

After Andrew Pole built his pregnancy-prediction model, after he identified thousands of female shoppers who were most likely pregnant, after someone pointed out that some of those women might be a little upset if they received an advertisement making it obvious Target was studying their reproductive status, everyone decided to slow things down.

The marketing department conducted a few tests by choosing a small, random sample of women from Pole's list and mailing them combinations of advertisements to see how they reacted.

"We have the capacity to send every customer an ad booklet, specifically designed for them, that says, 'Here's everything you bought last week and a coupon for it,'" one Target executive told me. "We do that for grocery products all the time." But for pregnant women, Target's goal was selling them baby items they didn't even know they needed yet.

"With the pregnancy products, though, we learned that some women react badly," the executive said. "Then we started mixing in all these ads for things we knew pregnant women would never buy, so the baby ads looked random. We'd put an ad for a lawn mower next to diapers. We'd put a coupon for wineglasses next to infant clothes. That way, it looked like all the products were chosen by chance."

"And we found out that as long as a pregnant woman thinks she 75 hasn't been spied on, she'll use the coupons. She just assumes that everyone else on her block got the same mailer for diapers and cribs. As long as we don't spook her, it works."

In other words, if Target piggybacked on existing habits—the same cues and rewards they already knew got customers to buy cleaning supplies or socks—then they could insert a new routine: buying baby products, as well. There's a cue ("Oh, a coupon for something I need!"), a routine ("Buy! Buy! Buy!"), and a reward ("I can take that off my list"). And once the shopper is inside the store, Target will hit her with cues and rewards to entice her to purchase everything she normally buys somewhere else. As long as Target camouflaged how much it knew, as long as the habit felt familiar, the new behavior took hold.

Soon after the new ad campaign began, Target's Mom and Baby sales exploded. The company doesn't break out figures for specific divisions, but between 2002—when Pole was hired—and 2010, Target's revenues grew from $44 billion to $67 billion. In 2005, the company's president, Gregg Steinhafel, boasted to a room of investors about the company's "heightened focus on items and categories that appeal to specific guest segments such as mom and baby."

Pole was promoted. He has been invited to speak at conferences. "I never expected this would become such a big deal," he told me the last time we spoke.

A few weeks before this article went to press, I flew to Minneapolis to try and speak to Andrew Pole one last time. I hadn't talked to him in more than a year. Back when we were still friendly, I mentioned that my wife was seven months pregnant. We shop at Target, I told him, and had given the company our address so we could start receiving coupons in the mail. As my wife's pregnancy progressed, I noticed a subtle upswing in the number of advertisements for diapers and baby clothes arriving at our house.

80 Pole didn't answer my e-mails or phone calls when I visited Minneapolis. I drove to his large home in a nice suburb, but no one answered the door. On my way back to the hotel, I stopped at a Target to pick up some deodorant, then also bought some T-shirts and a fancy hair gel. On a whim, I threw in some pacifiers, to see how the computers would react. Besides, our baby is now 9 months old. You can't have too many pacifiers.

When I paid, I didn't receive any sudden deals on diapers or formula, to my slight disappointment. It made sense, though: I was shopping in a city I never previously visited, at 9:45 P.M. on a weeknight, buying a random assortment of items. I was using a corporate credit card, and besides the pacifiers, hadn't purchased any of the things that a parent needs. It was clear to Target's computers that I was on a business trip. Pole's prediction calculator took one look at me, ran the numbers, and decided to bide its time. Back home, the offers would eventually come. As Pole told me the last time we spoke: "Just wait. We'll be sending you coupons for things you want before you even know you want them."

FOR A SECOND READING

1. Take a moment to evaluate the title of this essay. How do you react to the prospect of retailers trying to "learn your secrets"? Do you find this possibility surprising? Troubling? Unremarkable? Why?

2. "Habits," writes Duhigg, "aren't destiny—they can be ignored, changed, or replaced. But it's also true that once the loop is established and a habit emerges, your brain stops fully participating in decision-making" (p. 461). How do you respond to this claim? Does your own personal experience reinforce or challenge this belief in the power of habit?

3. Underneath Duhigg's examination of corporate "snooping" is a deeper concern over what might be called corporate manipulation: the effort by retailers to use the personal data they collect to influence the ways we think, feel, and act. In your view, is this a valid concern? Should we be worried that our choices and actions are being scripted in this way? Why or why not?

PUTTING IT INTO WRITING

4. Duhigg connects the issue of corporate surveillance (i.e., how companies gather data about our shopping choices and behaviors) to the broader question of habituation (i.e., the degree to which these choices and behaviors are governed by deeply ingrained habit). Write an essay in which you use your own personal experience to test the validity of this connection. Do you feel that your personal shopping behavior is dictated largely by habit? Can you think of an example of your own that either confirms or refutes this hypothesis? And based on your own shopping behavior, do you think you would make a particularly valuable target for retailers intent on gathering information about their customers? How or how not?

5. Duhigg cites a number of experiments that seem to confirm the role that habituation plays in scripting our daily actions and choices. Create an experiment of your own that, in your view, could be used to measure the power of habit in everyday life. To get yourself started, think about the specific parameters you want to establish. What aspect of everyday life do you want to focus on? What particular behavior do you want to measure? Next speculate about the findings or results you think your experiment would produce.

COMPARING ARGUMENTS

6. Like Duhigg, Sherry Turkle (p. 440) is calling on readers to reassess the cultural norm of privacy. How do these writers' respective examinations of privacy compare? Does each see privacy under threat by the same forces? Does each define privacy in the same way or value it for the same reasons? And finally, which writer's discussion of privacy do you find more compelling? Why?

Scenes and Un-Scenes: *"Hello, Neighbor"*

It has become cliché to bemoan the demise of community in contemporary life. But what exactly do we mean by the term *community*? Ritually invoked by politicians and pundits, commentators and educators, community stands as one of the most frequently lauded, and yet chronically unspecified, ideals in public life — defined as much by what it's not and where it's missing as by anything else. To speak of community is, on some level, to pose the questions "What do we have in common? What interests or sympathies, experiences or background, bind us to one another?" To watch the news and listen to pundits, one is always hearing declarations that the nature of community is changing and, by many accounts, eroding. But do you agree?

How we answer such questions depends in large measure on where we stand. Different vantages generate different notions of community. This, in the broadest sense, is what the images assembled here make clear. Sampling some of the more representative perspectives on community within our culture, these visuals show us the extent to which our definitions of community are determined by our given perspective.

An iconic figure in American pop culture, Mr. Rogers embodied for generations of American children what it means to be part of a community. The gentle invitation with which he opened every show — "Won't you be my neighbor?" — grew over the years into one of the most universally recognized and endlessly imitated phrases in all of television. In its own way, this phrase encapsulated the concept of community that guided the entire show. To be a "neighbor" meant joining a community that placed no restrictions on belonging, a world in which differences of race and class, gender, and age were dissolved in the vision of an all-inclusive neighborhood in which all were recognized as equals. What do you make of this ethic? Does such acceptance and inclusiveness still constitute a norm in our society?

Fotos International/Getty Images

▼▼ *When we think of community, many of us think of the physical space we inhabit. Looking at a community from a distance, how does our idea of it change? How is this space dependent on who lives inside it? Does an image like this say "community" to you? When looking at an aerial image, does community still evoke the same communal ideals?*

Steve Dunwell/Getty Images

▲▲ What happens when community goes online? In the wake of technologies that now allow us to invent, control, or even fabricate our chosen community, we have seen the emergence of an entirely new set of rules and norms around how this ideal can be defined. Virtual relationships, those that exist nowhere except online, now routinely fall within the category of community. But should they? What are the differences between an online and a so-called real-world community? Are communities we create online any less authentic than those we join in our everyday lives?

"NOW THAT WE'VE LEARNED TO TALK, WE'D BETTER ESTABLISH SOME LOCAL COMMUNITY STANDARDS."

◀◀ This cartoon takes a tongue-in-cheek look at the idea of communal living, namely that we collaborate on rules by which we live. But it also skewers this notion. How does it do that? What does this cartoon seem to say about the existence of community standards? Are they good or bad?

475

INSTEAD OF JUST HANGING OUT ON SATURDAYS
I HELP KIDS HANG IN THERE
AT SCHOOL
BECAUSE I DON'T JUST WEAR THE SHIRT, I LIVE IT.
GIVE. ADVOCATE. VOLUNTEER. LIVE UNITED

Michael Cleveland is part of United Way's ongoing work to improve the education, income, and health of our communities. To find out how you can help create opportunities for a better life for all, visit LIVEUNITEDANYTOWN.ORG.

United Way
United Way of Anytown

For many, the term *community* is a rallying cry, a call to tackle and redress a pressing social problem. In this context, *community* denotes less a specific group or place than a program or plan for implementing some type of policy. This United Way campaign is designed to advocate for community involvement in urban areas. What ideas about community are present in this image? Which are missing?

FOR A SECOND READING

1. Which of these images most resembles your notion of community? Why is that?

2. Which of these images seems most foreign to you? How does its depiction of community or community ideals fail to relate to your experience?

3. Do you think any images are missing from this portfolio? What would they be? How would they represent your opinion on the way community is changing?

PUTTING IT INTO WRITING

4. Pick one of the images in this portfolio and write a brief essay in which you evaluate how well it reflects your notion of what community ideals are. Be sure to focus on specific aspects of the image in your critique. What might you change, if anything, about this image to bring it in line with your own experience of community?

5. Do the images in this portfolio represent fundamental changes in the nature of community? Write an essay in which you argue how they do or do not.

6. Peter Lovenheim (p. 478) writes about bygone ideals of community. Write an essay in which you use his definition of *community* to evaluate the images shown in this portfolio. Do any images in particular fit his ideal? Would he find any of them undesirable? Why or why not?

PETER LOVENHEIM
Won't You Be My Neighbor?

In a "wired" age often celebrated for its interactivity and interconnectedness, it may come as a surprise to hear how disconnected from each other so many of us have become. For Peter Lovenheim, this disconnection has become the signature condition of our times. Reflecting on how this has come to be and what it means, he offers some suggestions — at once both unorthodox and commonsensical — about how to ameliorate the loneliness at the heart of modern life. Lovenheim is the author of *In the Neighborhood: The Search for Community on an American Street, One Sleepover at a Time* (2010), the culmination of a project he discusses in the following essay, originally published in the *New York Times* on June 23, 2008. He teaches writing at Rochester Institute of Technology and is also the author of *Portrait of a Burger as a Young Calf: The Story of One Man, Two Cows, and the Feeding of a Nation* (2002).

Before You Read

In your view, do we have a crisis of community in today's culture? If so, what specific factors or forces are contributing to it?

THE ALARM ON MY CELLPHONE RANG AT 5:50 A.M., AND I AWOKE to find myself in a twin bed in a spare room at my neighbor Lou's house.

Lou was 81. His six children were grown and scattered around the country, and he lived alone, two doors down from me. His wife, Edie, had died five years earlier. "When people learn you've lost your wife," he told me, "they all ask the same question. 'How long were you married?' And when you tell them 52 years, they say, 'Isn't that wonderful!' But I tell them no, it isn't. I was just getting to know her."

Lou had said he gets up at six, but after 10 more minutes, I heard nothing from his room down the hall. Had he died? He had a heart ailment, but generally was in good health. With a full head of silver-gray hair, bright hazel-blue eyes, and a broad chest, he walked with the confident bearing of a man who had enjoyed a long and satisfying career as a surgeon.

The previous evening, as I'd left home, the last words I heard before I shut the door had been, "Dad, you're crazy!" from my teenage daughter. Sure, the sight of your 50-year-old father leaving with an overnight bag to sleep at a neighbor's house would embarrass any teenager, but "crazy"? I didn't think so.

5   There's talk today about how as a society we've become fragmented by ethnicity, income, city versus suburb, red state versus blue. But we also divide ourselves with invisible dotted lines. I'm talking about the property

lines that isolate us from the people we are physically closest to: our neighbors.

It was a calamity on my street, in a middle-class suburb of Rochester, several years ago that got me thinking about this. One night, a neighbor shot and killed his wife and then himself; their two middle-school-age children ran screaming into the night. Though the couple had lived on our street for seven years, my wife and I hardly knew them. We'd see them jogging together. Sometimes our children would carpool.

Some of the neighbors attended the funerals and called on relatives. Someone laid a single bunch of yellow flowers at the family's front door, but nothing else was done to mark the loss. Within weeks, the children had moved with their grandparents to another part of town. The only indication that anything had changed was the "For Sale" sign on the lawn.

A family had vanished, yet the impact on our neighborhood was slight. How could that be? Did I live in a community or just in a house on a street surrounded by people whose lives were entirely separate? Few of my neighbors, I later learned, knew others on the street more than casually; many didn't know even the names of those a few doors down.

> *Why is it that in an age of cheap long-distance rates, discount airlines, and the Internet . . . we often don't know the people who live next door?*

According to social scientists, from 1974 to 1998, the frequency with which Americans spent a social evening with neighbors fell by about one-third. Robert Putnam, the author of *Bowling Alone*, a groundbreaking study of the disintegration of the American social fabric, suggests that the decline actually began 20 years earlier, so that neighborhood ties today are less than half as strong as they were in the 1950s.

Why is it that in an age of cheap long-distance rates, discount airlines, and the Internet, when we can create community anywhere, we often don't know the people who live next door?

Maybe my neighbors didn't mind living this way, but I did. I wanted to get to know the people whose houses I passed each day—not just what they do for a living and how many children they have, but the depth of their experience and what kind of people they are.

What would it take, I wondered, to penetrate the barriers between us? I thought about childhood sleepovers and the insight I used to get from waking up inside a friend's home. Would my neighbors let me sleep over and write about their lives from inside their own houses?

A little more than a year after the murder-suicide, I began to telephone my neighbors and send e-mail messages; in some cases, I just walked up to the door and rang the bell. The first one turned me down,

10

479

but then I called Lou. "You can write about me, but it will be boring," he warned. "I have nothing going on in my life—nothing. My life is zero. I don't do anything."

That turned out not to be true. When Lou finally awoke that morning at 6:18, he and I shared breakfast. Then he lay on a couch in his study and, skipping his morning nap, told me about his grandparents' immigration, his Catholic upbringing, his admission to medical school despite anti-Italian quotas, and how he met and courted his wife, built a career, and raised a family.

15   Later, we went to the Y.M.C.A. for his regular workout; he mostly just kibitzed with friends. We ate lunch. He took a nap. We watched the business news. That evening, he made us dinner and talked of friends he'd lost, his concerns for his children's futures, and his own mortality.

Before I left, Lou told me how to get into his house in case of an emergency, and I told him where I hide my spare key. That evening, as I carried my bag home, I felt that in my neighbor's house lived a person I actually knew.

I was privileged to be his friend until he died, just this past spring.

Remarkably, of the 18 or so neighbors I eventually approached about sleeping over, more than half said yes. There was the recently married young couple, both working in business; the real estate agent and her two small children; the pathologist married to a pediatrician who specializes in autism.

Eventually, I met a woman living three doors away, the opposite direction from Lou, who was seriously ill with breast cancer and in need of help. My goal shifted: could we build a supportive community around her—in effect, patch together a real neighborhood? Lou and I and some of the other neighbors ended up taking turns driving her to doctors' appointments and watching her children.

20   Our political leaders speak of crossing party lines to achieve greater unity. Maybe we should all cross the invisible lines between our homes and achieve greater unity in the places we live. Probably we don't need to sleep over; all it might take is to make a phone call, send a note, or ring a bell. Why not try it today?

FOR A SECOND READING

1. For Lovenheim, the relations among the neighbors on his street become a barometer of how "community" has come to be defined in our culture. "Did I live in a community," he asks, "or just in a house on a street surrounded by people whose lives were entirely separate?" (p. 479). Do you share Lovenheim's concerns? In your view, does a belief in the importance of community constitute one of our culture's vanishing norms?

2. How would you define the ideal neighborhood? What kinds of relationships among neighbors would you most like to see? Why did you choose these types of connections?

3. Many of his neighbors, Lovenheim observes, didn't seem to mind living next door to people they barely knew. How do you think you would feel? Would you find this kind of anonymity acceptable? Troubling? Why?

PUTTING IT INTO WRITING

4. "There's talk today," writes Lovenheim, "about how as a society we've become fragmented by ethnicity, income, city versus suburb, red state versus blue. But we also divide ourselves with invisible dotted lines. I'm talking about the property lines that isolate us from the people we are physically closest to: our neighbors" (pp. 478–79). Write an essay in which you respond to this claim. Is Lovenheim correct, in your opinion? Do the physical barriers in our lives divide us from each other as deeply as do social differences in income, age, ethnicity, or gender? How or how not?

5. How well do you know your neighbors? And how well do they, in turn, know you? In a two-page essay, reflect on how much of Lovenheim's argument about neighborliness and community applies to your experiences. Based on your interactions with the people who live in your neighborhood, would you say Lovenheim's insights are valid? In what ways do your experiences either confirm or challenge his insights?

COMPARING ARGUMENTS

6. In many ways, Lovenheim's essay could be read as a response to the crisis of community Matthew Desmond examines (p. 482). Write an essay in which you identify and assess the parallels connecting Lovenheim's examination of neighbors and neighborliness and Desmond's argument about eviction.

MATTHEW DESMOND
Home and Hope

Few concepts are more powerful than the idea of home. As Matthew Desmond observes, home is a source of both social and economic security and personal identity. But what happens, Desmond asks, when our connection to home is severed? When we end up disconnected — both physically and psychologically — from the place that is supposed to secure our safety and anchor our sense of self? Desmond tackles these questions by taking a hard look at the experience of Americans — poor, marginal, and disenfranchised — who find themselves evicted from their homes. Taking stock of the devastation — social, emotional, and economic — wrought by eviction, Desmond makes a powerful case for doing more to help those fellow citizens who find themselves tossed out into the street. Matthew Desmond is the John L. Loeb Associate Professor of the Social Sciences, and the codirector of the Justice and Poverty Project, at Harvard University. He is also the author of *Evicted: Poverty and Profit in the American City* (2016) from which this selection is excerpted.

Before You Read

What does the concept of home mean to you? Do you believe that a connection to home should be considered a basic right?

THE HOME IS THE CENTER OF LIFE. IT IS A REFUGE FROM THE GRIND of work, the pressure of school, and the menace of the streets. We say that at home, we can "be ourselves." Everywhere else, we are someone else. At home, we remove our masks.

The home is the wellspring of personhood. It is where our identity takes root and blossoms, where as children, we imagine, play, and question, and as adolescents, we retreat and try. As we grow older, we hope to settle into a place to raise a family or pursue work. When we try to understand ourselves, we often begin by considering the kind of home in which we were raised.

In languages spoken all over the world, the word for "home" encompasses not just shelter but warmth, safety, family—the womb. The ancient Egyptian hieroglyph for "home" was often used in place of "mother." The Chinese word *jiā* can mean both family and home. "Shelter" comes from two Old English words: *scield* (shield) and *truma* (troop), together forming the image of a family gathering itself within a protective shell.[1] The home remains the primary basis of life. It is where meals are shared, quiet habits formed, dreams confessed, traditions created.

Civic life too begins at home, allowing us to plant roots and take ownership over our community, participate in local politics, and reach out to neighbors in a spirit of solidarity and generosity. "It is difficult to force a man out of himself and get him to take an interest in the affairs of the whole state," Alexis de Tocqueville once observed. "But if it is a question of taking a road past his property, he sees at once that this small public matter has a bearing on his greatest private interests."[2] It is only after we begin to see a street as *our* street, a public park as *our* park, a school as *our* school, that we can become engaged citizens, dedicating our time and resources for worthwhile causes: joining the Neighborhood Watch, volunteering to beautify a playground, or running for school board.

Working on behalf of the common good is the engine of democracy, 5 vital to our communities, cities, states—and, ultimately, the nation. It is "an outflow of the idealism and moralism of the American people," wrote Gunnar Myrdal.[3] Some have called this impulse "love of country" or "patriotism" or the "American spirit." But whatever its name, its foundation is the home. What else is a nation but a patchwork of cities and towns; cities and towns a patchwork of neighborhoods; and neighborhoods a patchwork of homes?

America is supposed to be a place where you can better yourself, your family, and your community. But this is only possible if you have a stable home. When Scott was provided with an affordable apartment through the Guest House's permanent housing program, he was able to stay off heroin, find meaningful work as a resident manager for homeless people, and begin striving for independence.

> *In languages spoken all over the world, the word for "home" encompasses not just shelter but warmth, safety, family — the womb.*

He remains stably housed and sober. And then there are the Hinkstons. After Malik Jr. was born, Patrice and Doreen finally did move to Brownsville, Tennessee, a town of about 10,000. They found a nice three-bedroom place. Out of the rat hole, Patrice earned her GED, impressing her teacher so much that she was named Adult Learner of the Year. Patrice went on to enroll in a local community college, where she took online classes in computers and criminal justice, hoping to one day become a parole officer. She liked to half joke, "I got a lot of friends who are criminal who are going to need my help!"

The persistence and brutality of American poverty can be disheartening, leaving us cynical about solutions. But as Scott and Patrice will tell you, a good home can serve as the sturdiest of footholds. When people have a place to live, they become better parents, workers, and citizens.

If Arleen and Vanetta didn't have to dedicate 70 or 80 percent of their income to rent, they could keep their kids fed and clothed and off the streets. They could settle down in one neighborhood and enroll their children in one school, providing them the opportunity to form long-lasting relationships with friends, role models, and teachers. They could start a savings account or buy their children toys and books, perhaps even a home computer. The time and emotional energy they spent making rent, delaying eviction, or finding another place to live when homeless could instead be spent on things that enriched their lives: community college classes, exercise, finding a good job, maybe a good man too.

But our current state of affairs "reduces to poverty people born for better things."[4] For almost a century, there has been broad consensus in America that families should spend no more than 30 percent of their income on housing.[5] Until recently, most renting families met this goal. But times have changed—in Milwaukee and across America. Every year in this country, people are evicted from their homes not by the tens of thousands or even the hundreds of thousands but by the millions.[6]

10 Until recently, we simply didn't know how immense this problem was, or how serious the consequences, unless we had suffered them ourselves.

America is supposed to be a place where you can better yourself, your family, and your community. But this is only possible if you have a stable home.

For years, social scientists, journalists, and policymakers all but ignored eviction, making it one of the least studied processes affecting the lives of poor families. But new data and methods have allowed us to measure the prevalence of eviction and document its effects. We have learned that eviction is commonplace in poor neighborhoods and that it exacts a heavy toll on families, communities, and children.

Residential stability begets a kind of psychological stability, which allows people to invest in their home and social relationships. It begets school stability, which increases the chances that children will excel and graduate. And it begets community stability, which encourages neighbors to form strong bonds and take care of their block.[7] But poor families enjoy little of that because they are evicted at such high rates. That low-income families move often is well known. Why they do is a question that has puzzled researchers and policymakers because they have overlooked the frequency of eviction in disadvantaged neighborhoods.[8] Between 2009 and 2011, roughly a quarter of all moves undertaken by Milwaukee's poorest renters were involuntary. Once you account for those dislocations (eviction, landlord foreclosure), low-income households move at a similar rate as everyone else.[9] If you study eviction court records in other cities, you arrive at similarly startling numbers. Jackson County, Missouri, which includes half of

Kansas City, saw 19 formal evictions a day between 2009 and 2013. New York City courts saw almost 80 nonpayment evictions a day in 2012. That same year, 1 in 9 occupied rental households in Cleveland, and 1 in 14 in Chicago, were summoned to eviction court.[10] Instability is not inherent to poverty. Poor families move so much because they are forced to.

Along with instability, eviction also causes loss. Families lose not only their home, school, and neighborhood but also their possessions: furniture, clothes, books. It takes a good amount of money and time to establish a home. Eviction can erase all that. Arleen lost everything, Larraine and Scott too. Eviction can cause workers to lose their jobs. The likelihood of being laid off is roughly 15 percent higher for workers who have experienced an eviction. If housing instability leads to employment instability, it is because the stress and consuming nature of being forced from your home wreak havoc on people's work performance.[11] Often, evicted families also lose the opportunity to benefit from public housing because Housing Authorities count evictions and unpaid debt as strikes when reviewing applications. And so people who have the greatest need for housing assistance—the rent-burdened and evicted—are systematically denied it.[12]

This—the loss of your possessions, job, home, and access to government aid—helps explain why eviction has such a pronounced effect on what social scientists call "material hardship," a measure of the texture of scarcity. Material hardship assesses, say, whether families experience hunger or sickness because food or medical care is financially out of reach or go without heat, electricity, or a phone because they can't afford those things. The year after eviction, families experience 20 percent higher levels of material hardship than similar families who were not evicted. They go without food. They endure illness and cold. Evicted families continue to have higher levels of material hardship at least two years after the event.[13]

These families are often compelled to accept substandard housing conditions. In Milwaukee, renters whose previous move was involuntary were 25 percent more likely to experience long-term housing problems than similar renters who moved under less trying circumstances.[14]

And families forced from their homes are pushed into undesirable parts of the city, moving from poor neighborhoods into even poorer ones; from crime-filled areas into still more dangerous ones. Arleen's favorite place was nested in a working-class black neighborhood. After the city condemned it and forced her out, she moved into an apartment complex teeming with drug dealers. Even after controlling for a host of important factors, families who experience a forced move relocate to worse neighborhoods than those who move under less demanding circumstances.[15] Concentrated poverty and violence inflict their own

15

wounds, since neighborhoods determine so much about your life, from the kinds of job opportunities you have to the kinds of schools your children attend.[16]

Then there is the toll eviction takes on a person's spirit. The violence of displacement can drive people to depression and, in extreme cases, even suicide. One in two recently evicted mothers reports multiple symptoms of clinical depression, double the rate of similar mothers who were not forced from their homes. Even after years pass, evicted mothers are less happy, energetic, and optimistic than their peers.[17] When several patients committed suicide in the days leading up to their eviction, a group of psychiatrists published a letter in *Psychiatric Services*, identifying eviction as a "significant precursor of suicide." The letter emphasized that none of the patients were facing homelessness, leading the psychiatrists to attribute the suicides to eviction itself. "Eviction must be considered a traumatic rejection," they wrote, "a denial of one's most basic human needs, and an exquisitely shameful experience." Suicides attributed to evictions and foreclosures doubled between 2005 and 2010, years when housing costs soared.[18]

Eviction even affects the communities that displaced families leave behind. Neighbors who cooperate with and trust one another can make their streets safer and more prosperous. But that takes time. Efforts to establish local cohesion and community investment are thwarted in neighborhoods with high turnover rates. In this way, eviction can unravel the fabric of a community, helping to ensure that neighbors remain strangers and that their collective capacity to combat crime and promote civic engagement remains untapped.[19] Milwaukee neighborhoods with high eviction rates have higher violent crime rates the following year, even after controlling for past crime rates and other relevant factors.[20]

Losing your home and possessions and often your job; being stamped with an eviction record and denied government housing assistance; relocating to degrading housing in poor and dangerous neighborhoods; and suffering from increased material hardship, homelessness, depression, and illness—this is eviction's fallout. Eviction does not simply drop poor families into a dark valley, a trying yet relatively brief detour on life's journey. It fundamentally redirects their way, casting them onto a different, and much more difficult, path. Eviction is a cause, not just a condition, of poverty.

> *[D]o we believe that the right to a decent home is part of what it means to be an American?*

Eviction affects the old and the young, the sick and able-bodied. But for poor women of color and their children, it has become ordinary. Walk into just about any urban housing court in America, and you can see them waiting on hard benches for their cases to be called. Among Milwaukee renters, over 1 in 5 black women report having been evicted in their adult life, compared with 1 in 12 Hispanic women and 1 in 15 white women.[21]

Most evicted households in Milwaukee have children living in them, and across the country, many evicted children end up homeless. The substandard housing and unsafe neighborhoods to which many evicted families must relocate can degrade a child's health, ability to learn, and sense of self-worth.[22] And if eviction has lasting effects on mothers' depression, sapping their energy and happiness, then children will feel that chill too. Parents like Arleen and Vanetta wanted to provide their children with stability, but eviction ruined that, pulling kids in and out of school and batting them from one neighborhood to the next. When these mothers finally did find another place to live, they once again began giving landlords most of their income, leaving little for the kids. Families who spend more on housing spend less on their children.[23] Poor families are living above their means, in apartments they cannot afford. The thing is, those apartments are already at the bottom of the market. Our cities have become unaffordable to our poorest families, and this problem is leaving a deep and jagged scar on the next generation.

All this suffering is shameful and unnecessary. Because it is unnecessary, there is hope. These problems are neither intractable nor eternal. A different kind of society is possible, and powerful solutions are within our collective reach.

But those solutions depend on how we answer a single question: do we believe that the right to a decent home is part of what it means to be an American?

The United States was founded on the noble idea that people have "certain unalienable Rights, that among these are Life, Liberty and the pursuit of Happiness." Each of these three unalienable rights—so essential to the American character that the founders saw them as God-given—requires a stable home.

Life and home are so intertwined that it is almost impossible to think about one without the other. The home offers privacy and personal security. It protects and nurtures. The ideal of liberty has always incorporated not only religious and civil freedoms but also the right to flourish: to make a living however one chooses, to learn and develop new skills. A stable home allows us to strive for self-reliance and personal expression, to seek gainful employment and enjoy individual freedoms.

And happiness? It was there in the smile that flashed across Jori's face when Arleen was able to buy him a new pair of sneakers, in the church hymn Larraine hummed when she was able to cook a nice meal, in the laughter that burst out of the Hinkstons' house after a good prank.

20

25

The pursuit of happiness undeniably includes the pursuit of material well-being: minimally, being able to secure basic necessities. It can be overwhelming to consider how much happiness has been lost, how many capabilities snuffed out, by the swell of poverty in this land and our collective decision not to provide all our citizens with a stable and decent place to live.

We have affirmed provision in old age, twelve years of education, and basic nutrition to be the right of every citizen because we have recognized that human dignity depends on the fulfillment of these fundamental human needs. And it is hard to argue that housing is not a fundamental human need. Decent, affordable housing should be a basic right for everybody in this country. The reason is simple: without stable shelter, everything else falls apart.

NOTES

[1] Lewis Mumford, *The City in History: Its Origins, Its Transformations, and Its Prospects* (New York: MJF Books, 1961), 13; with special thanks to Rowan Flad and Shamus Khan for etymology insights.

[2] Alexis de Tocqueville, *Democracy in America* (New York: Perennial Classics, 2000), 511.

[3] Gunnar Myrdal, *An American Dilemma*, vol. 2, *The Negro Social Structure* (New York: McGraw-Hill Publishers, 1964 [1944]), 810.

[4] Plato, *The Republic* (New York: Penguin Classics, 1987), 312. I have changed "men" to "people."

[5] Mary Schwartz and Ellen Wilson, *Who Can Afford to Live in a Home? A Look at Data from the 2006 American Community Survey* (Washington, DC: US Census Bureau, 2007).

[6] Chester Hartman and David Robinson, "Evictions: The Hidden Housing Problem," *Housing Policy Debate* 14 (2003): 461–501.

[7] Gary Evans, "The Environment of Childhood Poverty," *American Psychologist* 59 (2004): 77–92; Shigehiro Oishi, "The Psychology of Residential Mobility: Implications for the Self, Social Relationships, and Well-Being," *Perspectives on Psychological Science* 5 (2010): 5–21; Robert Sampson, *Great American City: Chicago and the Enduring Neighborhood Effect* (Chicago: University of Chicago Press, 2012).

[8] In fact, one can detect a thick middle-class bias among researchers who assume that moves are deliberate and planned. For a further explanation of the intentionality bias in residential mobility research, see Matthew Desmond and Tracey Shollenberger, "Forced Displacement from Rental Housing: Prevalence and Neighborhood Consequences," *Demography*, forthcoming. On high rates of residential mobility among poor families, see David Ihrke and Carol Faber, *Geographical Mobility: 2005 to 2010* (Washington, DC: United States Census Bureau, 2012); Robin Phinney, "Exploring Residential Mobility Among Low-Income Families," *Social Service Review* 87 (2013): 780–815.

[9] This finding comes from a negative binomial model that estimated the number of moves renters undertook in the previous two years, conditioning on household income, race, education, gender, family status, age, criminal record, and three recent life shocks: job loss, relationship dissolution, and eviction. The analysis found that low incomes predicted higher rates of mobility only before controlling

for involuntary displacement and that, all else equal, renters who experienced a forced move were expected to have a moving rate 1.3 times greater than those who avoided involuntary displacement. See Matthew Desmond, Carl Gershenson, and Barbara Kiviat, "Forced Relocation and Residential Instability Among Urban Renters," *Social Service Review* 89 (2015): 227–62. By "Milwaukee's poorest renters," I mean renting households in the lowest income quartile (with incomes below $12,204). Milwaukee Area Renters Study, 2009–2011.

[10]On Jackson County, Missouri, see Tara Raghuveer, "'We Be Trying': A Multistate Analysis of Eviction and the Affordable Housing Crisis," B.A. thesis (Cambridge, MA: Harvard University, Committee on the Degrees in Social Studies, 2014). In 2012, New York City's Housing Courts processed 28,743 eviction judgments and 217,914 eviction filings for nonpayment. See New York City Rent Guidelines Board, *2013 Income and Affordability Study*, April 4, 2013. Cleveland, a city of approximately 95,702 occupied renter households, saw 11,072 eviction filings in 2012 and 11,031 in 2013—meaning that almost 12 percent of renter households were summoned to eviction court each year. See Northeast Ohio Apartment Association, *Suites* magazine, "Eviction Index," 2012–2013; American Community Survey, 2013. In 2012, an estimated 32,231 evictions were filed in Chicago, which represents 7 percent of the city's rental inventory; see Kay Cleaves, "Cook Eviction Stats Part 5: Are Eviction Filings Increasing?," StrawStickStone.com, February 8, 2013.

[11]Matthew Desmond and Carl Gershenson, "Housing and Employment Insecurity Among the Working Poor," *Social Problems*, forthcoming.

[12]Evictions also help to exacerbate the problem most responsible for their rise by driving up rents. This is plain in cases where landlords evict tenants from rent-regulated units so that they may offer apartments at market rates. But it is also true of normal evictions of families from unregulated units because it is easier to raise the rent on new tenants than old ones. In Milwaukee, a tenant annually pays almost $58 less in rent for every year she has lived in an apartment, all else equal. Turnover facilitates rent hikes, and evictions create turnover. Matthew Desmond and Kristin Perkins, "Are Landlords Overcharging Voucher Holders?," working paper, Harvard University, June 2015. In San Francisco, Ellis Act evictions—often used to convert rent-regulated apartments into condos or market-rate units—increased by 170 percent between March 2010 and February 2013. Marisa Lagos, "San Francisco Evictions Surge, Report Finds," *San Francisco Gate*, November 5, 2013.

[13]Matthew Desmond and Rachel Tolbert Kimbro, "Eviction's Fallout: Housing, Hardship, and Health," *Social Forces* (2015), in press.

[14]Desmond et al., "Forced Relocation and Residential Instability Among Urban Renters."

[15]Technically, the results of lagged dependent variable regression models showed that experiencing a forced move is associated with a standard deviation increase of more than one-third in both neighborhood poverty and crime rates, relative to voluntary moves. Across all models, the most robust and consistent predictors of neighborhood downgrades between moves are race (whether a renter is African American) and move type (whether the move was forced). Desmond and Shollenberger, "Forced Displacement from Rental Housing."

[16]Sampson, *Great American City*; Patrick Sharkey, *Stuck in Place: Urban Neighborhoods and the End of Progress toward Racial Equality* (Chicago: University of Chicago Press, 2013).

[17]This finding is documented in a study called "Eviction's Fallout," coauthored with Rachel Kimbro. In that study, we rely on a dichotomous indicator to measure *depressive symptoms* in mothers. Mothers were asked a series of questions,

focused on experiences in the previous twelve months, based on the Composite International Diagnostic Interview Short Form (CIDI-SF). Respondents were asked whether they had feelings of dysphoria (depression) or anhedonia (inability to enjoy what is usually pleasurable) in the past year that lasted for two weeks or more, and if so, whether the symptoms lasted most of the day and occurred every day of the two-week period. If so, they were asked more specific questions about: (a) losing interest, (b) feeling tired, (c) change in weight, (d) trouble sleeping, (e) trouble concentrating, (f) feeling worthless, and (g) thinking about death. Mothers were classified as probable cases of depression if they endorsed either dysphoria or anhedonia plus two of the other symptoms in the follow-up questions (leading to a CIDI-SF MD score of 3 or higher). Results are robust to varying the cut-point for the depression scale as well as to negative binomial models estimating the number of depressive symptoms respondents reported. See Ronald Kessler et al., "Methodological Studies of the Composite International Diagnostic Interview (CIDI) in the US National Comorbidity Survey (NCS)," *International Journal of Methods in Psychiatric Research* 7 (1998): 33–55.

[18]Michael Serby et al., "Eviction as a Risk Factor for Suicide," *Psychiatric Services* 57 (2006): 273–74. Katherine Fowler et al., "Increase in Suicides Associated with Home Eviction and Foreclosure During the US Housing Crisis: Findings from 16 National Violent Death Reporting System States, 2005–2010," *American Journal of Public Health* 105 (2015): 311–16.

[19]Sampson, *Great American City.*

[20]This result draws on neighborhood-level data for Milwaukee, 2005–2007. Using a lagged-response model, I predicted a neighborhood's violent-crime rate for one year, controlling for violent crime and eviction rates the *previous year* as well as for the percentage of families in poverty, of African Americans in the neighborhood, of the population under eighteen years of age, of residents with less than a high school education, and of households receiving housing assistance. The final model documented a significant association between a neighborhood's violent crime rate and its eviction rate the previous year (B = .155; p < .05). See Matthew Desmond, "Do More Evictions Lead to Higher Crime? Neighborhood Consequences of Forced Displacement," working paper, Harvard University, August 2015.

[21]Milwaukee Area Renters Study, 2009–2011.

[22]United States Conference of Mayors, *Hunger and Homelessness Survey* (Washington, DC: United States Conference of Mayors, 2013); Martha Burt, "Homeless Families, Singles, and Others: Findings from the 1996 National Survey of Homeless Assistance Providers and Clients," *Housing Policy Debate* 12 (2001): 737–80; Maureen Crane and Anthony Warnes, "Evictions and Prolonged Homelessness," *Housing Studies* 15 (2000): 757–73.

On the effects of substandard housing and unsafe neighborhoods on children's health, see Julie Clark and Ade Kearns, "Housing Improvements, Perceived Housing Quality and Psychosocial Benefits from the Home," *Housing Studies* 27 (2012): 915–39; Tama Leventhal and Jeanne Brooks-Gunn, "The Neighborhoods They Live In: The Effects of Neighborhood Residence on Child and Adolescent Outcomes," *Psychological Bulletin* 126 (2000): 309–37.

[23]Joseph Harkness and Sandra Newman, "Housing Affordability and Children's Well-Being: Evidence from the National Survey of America's Families," *Housing Policy Debate* 16 (2005): 223–55; Sandra Newman and Scott Holupka, "Housing Affordability and Investments in Children," *Journal of Housing Economics* 24 (2014): 89–100.

FOR A SECOND READING

1. "Residential stability," notes Desmond, "begets a kind of psychological stability, which allows people to invest in their home and social relationships" (p. 484). Do you agree? In your view, is "residential stability" essential to a healthy emotional and social life? What happens to people when their "residential stability" is not guaranteed?

2. Desmond describes eviction as the "violence of displacement." Why do you think he chooses this particular phrase? What does it suggest to you about nature and effect of eviction on those who experience eviction? Do you think it is a fair way to characterize this experience? Why or why not?

3. The primary experience of eviction, Desmond observes, is loss: "Families lose not only their home, school and neighborhood but also their possessions: furniture, clothes, books" (p. 485). What do you think the effect—social, financial, psychological—of such pervasive loss is? What do you think it would be like to experience this type of loss yourself?

PUTTING IT INTO WRITING

4. As Desmond notes, we are far more likely to take action on issues like homelessness or eviction when we feel a direct sense of involvement and responsibility: "It is only after we begin to see a street as *our* street, a public park as *our* park, a school as *our* school, that we can become engaged citizens, dedicating our time and resources for worthwhile causes" (p. 483). Write an essay in which you respond to this claim. Do you agree that cultivating a sense of shared responsibility is key to taking meaningful social action? If so, what are the forces that prevent us from doing this more often? What changes do you believe are needed to foster a greater sense of shared responsibility?

5. Desmond writes: "The United States was founded on the noble idea that people have 'certain unalienable Rights, that among these are Life, Liberty, and the pursuit of Happiness.' Each of these three unalienable rights—so essential to the American character that the founders saw them as God-given—requires a stable home" (p. 487). In a 500-word essay, make an argument that either supports or challenges the central claim Desmond makes here. In your view, does each of these three "unalienable rights" require a "stable home" in order to be fulfilled? How or how not specifically?

COMPARING ARGUMENTS

6. How do you think Desmond would respond to the "experiment"
    Peter Lovenheim (p. 478) describes in his essay? Do you think
    Lovenheim's decision to temporarily move in with a neighbor
    represents the kind of action Desmond is calling for? Why or
    why not?

Acting Like a Citizen: **Bridging the Divide**

Connection is more than an issue to read about; it is also a value to put into practice. But how do we cultivate more "connectedness" in our daily lives? And what benefits or changes would doing so actually bring? The following exercises provide an opportunity to address just these questions. Calling attention to the some of the ways in which we have grown disconnected, they invite you take action in order to bridge the divide.

DESIGNING YOUR IDEAL COMMUNITY   Write a one-page description of the community in which you live, whether it represents your school, home, church, or other institution. Be as specific as possible about the connections (e.g., social, cultural, professional, etc.) this community make possible. Then write another page in which you evaluate aspects of these types of connections that do not measure up to your own ideal. What aspects about this community would you change to make it fit your ideal of the truly connected community?

BRIDGING THE PARTISAN DIVIDE   Think of a divisive or polarizing social issue that interests you and research groups in your community that advocate for different positions on this issue. What are their goals, and how do they go about achieving them? What are the key differences that define their respective positions? If possible, interview a member of one organization and find out what about this group appeals to him or her. Using all the information you have collected, write an essay in which you propose a plan for how these differences might be overcome.

PERSONAL CONNECTIONS   Write a personal reflection in which you identify and address a particular moment in your life when you felt (physically, socially, culturally) disconnected from the larger world around you. What did this experience of disconnection feel like? What factors caused or contributed to it? How did you respond to this situation? And as you think about it now, do you regard this experience as positive or negative? Why?

Courtesy Wisconsin League of Conservation Voters

This screenshot comes from the Wisconsin League of Conservation Voters, a nonpartisan organization that advocates for the preservation of the state's natural habitats. Take a closer look at this screenshot. Then answer the following questions:

⊃ What messages are being promoted about why conservation is an important issue?

⊃ What strategies does this site use to get viewers to identify with these messages?

⊃ In what particular ways does this site encourage viewers to turn this identification into action?

7 How We

IDENTIFY

Do The Roles We Play Reflect Who We Truly Are?

Introduction

PLAYING ROLES, CHOOSING SELVES

As we've seen throughout the book, there are any number of roles we play in public life — from student to worker, friend to family member, consumer to citizen. And as we've also seen, part of what solidifies our connection to these roles, part of what anchors our sense that they are right for us, are the cultural norms that tell us how proper or natural it is for us to take them on. But cultural norms do not by themselves fully explain *why* we play the roles we do. To fully accept and adopt a role as our own requires that we do some work too. More specifically, it requires that we see ourselves within the roles we play, that we *identify* with the attitudes, assumptions, and actions they script as natural, normal, or right.

This kind of identification doesn't happen automatically. It is a process that involves considerable calculation and evaluation. Our culture may tell us to play a given role, but unless we give our consent, unless we agree to choose it for ourselves, such instruction will go unheeded. To illustrate, let's return to the visual opener of this chapter. Clearly, the Wisconsin League of Conservation Voters is aware that not every viewer will automatically identify as a "conservation voter." In many ways, in fact, their main objective here is to encourage viewers to form just such an identification. They do so in part by choosing their language very carefully. The slogan "*Your* air. *Your* land. *Your* water." implies that taking on the role of "conservation voter" should be considered a natural choice because it involves protecting resources that already belong to them. This strategy is reinforced through the site's use of visuals, which likewise invites viewers to identify (either by recalling their own childhood or reflecting on their responsibility as adults to take care of kids) with the young boy playing on the dock. Of course, how individual viewers respond to these kinds of persuasive tactics is up to them. But that is precisely the point. Even when we recognize that a given role is being scripted for us, it is still our job to figure out whether or not we see ourselves in it.

There is a reason, after all, why the terms "identification" and "identity" are so closely related. Whenever we identify with a given role, whenever we agree to see ourselves in the actions, attitudes, or values being scripted as the norm, we are making a powerful statement about who

What is normal?

kali9/Getty Images

What kind of role does this image construct? What ideas/values/ attitudes does it ask you to identify with?

we are. When, for example, we identify ourselves as a Republican, a Democrat, or an Independent, we are saying something important about our political values. When we identify as a daughter or son, a brother or sister, a mother or father, we are saying something about the importance of family in our lives. When we identify as white or black, Asian or Latinx, we are saying something about the importance of race to our sense of self.

This may seem like an obvious fact, but it raises questions whose answers are more complex than they might at first seem: Are the roles we play a true reflection of who we actually are? Do we live in a culture that allows us the full agency to create our own roles? And if we don't, how do we negotiate those cultural expectations that demand we take on only those roles that are scripted for us? How do we create the cultural leeway to think, choose, and identify for ourselves?

What is normal?

Paul Bradbury/Getty Images

What does it feel like to act out these roles in your own life? Should we automatically identify with them?

In one way or another, each of the selections gathered here endeavors to address just these questions. Our first pair of essays, by Sarah Mirk and Thomas Page McBee, explores how the boundaries defining gender roles and sexual identity are undergoing significant change. Mirk examines the growing trend among teenagers to turn to the web for answers about sexuality, while McBee tells a personal story about what being a transgendered man has taught him about the meaning of masculinity in today's culture.

The next two writers, Rebecca Traister and Jodi Kantor, turn their attention to the subject of marriage, delving into the ways that the social imperatives and legal boundaries around this supposedly timeless institution are being redrawn. Traister chronicles the growing number of single women today, calling out the rise of this demographic group as evidence of a new (social, professional, political) role for women. Kantor, on the other hand, takes stock of the ambivalence with which many in the gay community have greeted the legalization of same-sex marriage.

From very different vantage points, the next two writers, David Brooks and J. D. Vance, take up the broader issue of social or cultural diversity in America. Brooks pushes back against what he sees as the nation's hollow commitment to (racial/social/economic) diversity, seeing within the behavior of contemporary Americans a much stronger drive to associate with people only like themselves. Vance, meanwhile, offers his own portrait of a (racial/social/economic) monoculture, recalling his upbringing in white, working-class Appalachia.

What is normal?

"If I was lying on my deathbed and I had kept this secret and never ever did anything about it, I would be lying there saying, 'You just blew your entire life. You never dealt with yourself.'"

Caitlyn Jenner, discussing her decision to transition to a female, in an interview with Vanity Fair magazine in 2015

Kevin Winter/Getty Images

Can public roles be challenged or changed? Can they be used to promote different or alternative norms?

Garnette Cadogan and Ta-Nehisi Coates round out our selections by taking a deeper look into the state of race relations in America. Cadogan does so by bringing his perspective as a native of Jamaica to his experiences as a "black man" walking the streets of American cities. Complementing this perspective, Coates's essay, framed as a letter to his fifteen-year-old son, reviews the history of violence perpetrated against black bodies in America.

SARAH MIRK

Tuning In: How a Generation Is Schooling Itself on Sexuality

In the annals of school history, sex education has long been a controversial topic. But what happens, asks Sarah Mirk, when such instruction migrates from the classroom to the Internet? Can the web serve as an alternative resource, forum, or sounding board for young people seeking honest answers to their questions about sex? Sarah Mirk is a journalist based in Portland, Oregon. Since 2013, she has served as the online editor of national feminism and pop culture for *Bitch Media*, a nonprofit website devoted to examining issues of gender and culture. This piece was published as one of the website's "Dispatches on Media" in 2016.

Before You Read

Did you ever take a sex education class in school? If so, did you find the education it provided helpful? Why or why not?

AT AGE 25, JACKSON BIRD WAS ALREADY AN ACCOMPLISHED VIDEO creator—his day job is in communications at a nonprofit called the Harry Potter Alliance, which is just as awesome as it sounds. But this video, running 12 minutes long (*Lord of the Rings*–length in YouTube world), was special. After showing pictures of a childhood spent being forced into dresses and girly hairstyles, Bird said, "Figuring out how to continue the balancing act of who I feel I am and who society tells me I should be has become harder and harder . . . I am transgender. Yep, okay, said it on the internet now, so that's that. Can't put that smoke back in the jar."

In turning his coming-out process into a public video—which has now been seen 77,000 times—Bird is part of a movement of young people who are using YouTube as a platform for positive, inclusive sex ed. Whereas previous generations resorted to surreptitiously looking up unfamiliar words in the dictionary, today if you type "What is transgender?" into YouTube, in less than a second you'll have a page of in-depth information: television documentaries about

> *"Figuring out how to continue the balancing act of who I feel I am and who society tells me I should be has become harder and harder."*

499

the lives of trans children, a national magazine's rundown on "transgender 101," and a 14-year-old trans kid from Chino Hills, California, explaining on film why being transgender is not a choice.

In a society where the quality of sex education in schools is hodgepodge at best and shifts depending on political whims, YouTube is a dynamic, democratic space for discussions of gender and sexuality. Since only 24 states require sex ed in schools, YouTube serves a crucial role for young people wanting to find out about everything from condoms to consent.

"A lot of people still have trouble talking about these issues in our country, and seeing someone else talk about them on YouTube is really powerful, it's very affirming," says Lawrence Swiader, vice president of digital media at the National Campaign to Prevent Teen and Unplanned Pregnancy, which runs Bedsider.org, an online birth-control support network geared toward millennial women. On YouTube, Bedsider publishes a "Real Stories" series where people talk about the pros and cons of their birth-control methods. "It makes a big difference for people to see actual humans telling stories about their lives rather than just reading about birth control on a page," says Swiader. "In a split second, you decide whether that person's relatable and whether you're going to take advice from them. That's what makes videos really great, accessible, and powerful." It's not just that YouTube provides information, it's that the information comes from people who viewers can identify with and trust.

5   The morphing media landscape of the past 20 years has splintered audiences—instead of just tuning into MTV, for example, young people now seek out the media they want to watch on all sorts of platforms. That's good because it helps support more voices, but it makes it hard to reach a majority of the populace. So when Bedsider, for example, wants to get the word out about birth control, they partner with mainstream TV shows—they recently got a plug on *Teen Mom 2*—but they also make YouTube videos targeted at specific demographics. On YouTube, Bedsider has the ability to make their own media centering on people who don't often show up on TV, like people of color and nonbinary teens. "YouTube is an unprecedented way to reach audiences that are unrepresented on TV and in mainstream media," says Swiader.

The key to crafting an effective YouTube sex-ed video is to combine extreme brevity with accuracy, nuanced personal insight, and humor. Laci Green, a 26-year-old YouTuber, is arguably the world's most popular sex educator. She's gained a following by approaching sex ed like a friend would, addressing her camera in an upbeat, bubbly way, even when taking on tricky topics. She begins a video about consent with the convivial greeting "Oh hi, babes!" before launching into some serious stuff: "Consent isn't just hot, it's also mandatory. Sexual contact without consent is assault." These aren't videos with big budgets—most of them are filmed in her living room—but they have a big impact. Her YouTube channel, where she posts videos grappling with issues such as sexual assault, female orgasm, and how to put on a condom, has more than 1.5 million subscribers.

As the host of the podcast and YouTube show *Stuff Mom Never Told You*, Cristen Conger, 31, hears from a lot of young people who usually have one big question: Am I normal? There's not a lot of easily accessible, medically accurate information out there about genitalia, so Conger says she fields lots of questions from teens who are worried about whether their clitorises, labia, and penises are too small, too big, or just too "weird." "When I'm thinking about what kind of sex-ed-related videos to make, I think about what kind of videos I wish existed when I was 13, so I would have different answers when dudes in high school complained about blue balls, etc.," says Conger. "That's why I made videos like 'Seven Reasons Why Your Nipples Are Normal' and 'Things You Didn't Know About Your Clitoris.'"

YouTube fills in a lot of gaps that our pop culture leaves wide open, but that doesn't mean it's a replacement for school-based sex education. While hundreds of videos on niche topics are available, you still have to know what to look for. YouTube originally launched when Jackson Bird was a high schooler in rural Texas, but the wealth of information on the site wasn't much help to him then—his exposure to transgender identities had been limited to "half an *Oprah* special." "I didn't have enough correct terminology to even know what to Google about my gender and my sexuality," says Bird, who is now 26. Now he often meets tweens who have worldly vocabularies. "I'll meet 12-year-olds who are like, 'Yeah, I'm nonbinary aromantic,' and I'm like, 'How do you even know these words?!'" Bird often stresses taking it slow when figuring out one's own identity—it's okay not to know exactly how to identify in terms of gender and sexuality, and when teens jump to attach themselves to a label, it can actually wind up boxing them in.

> *[I]t's okay not to know exactly how to identify in terms of gender and sexuality, and when teens jump to attach themselves to a label, it can actually wind up boxing them in.*

It's also important to note that information delivered in school sex-ed classes comes from a place of authority—a teacher and a textbook—which carries a different weight than one person making a video in their bedroom. A healthy foundation of sex ed from a teacher or parent goes a long way to easing the lifelong process of building one's sexual identity.

While YouTube's take-all-kinds approach is its strength, allowing 10 videos from individual teens to share equal space with those created by companies and big nonprofits, that also means bigoted or misleading information can rise to the top. For example, on the first page of search results for "What is transgender?" amid the positive and scientific videos are videos like one headlined "Why Transgender Is Wrong" and a salacious one promising sexy photos of "10 beautiful women who were born as males" that drools over the details of each person's surgeries in a scandalized, gossip-mag tone. And as uplifting as many YouTube sex educators' videos are, their comment sections are often dispiriting, full of the usual slurs and trolls. Some YouTubers turn off comments entirely, but this also nixes positive community interactions. Others actively moderate their comments, deleting all the pond scum, but reading through strangers' tirades takes an emotional toll.

Through all the nasty negativity, YouTube provides a lifeline for a lot of teens and tweens and it feels like a direct point of contact between teenagers and adults who are up for being frank with them on topics lots of people refuse to discuss. That connection builds community, even if there's no one IRL they can talk to honestly. "A lot of kids these day speak with a vocabulary that I didn't have growing up," says Conger. "They are finding each other online, engaging in these communities, and creating entirely new terms that precisely fit what they feel in that moment."

FOR A SECOND READING

1. "It's . . . important to note," Mirk writes, "that information delivered in school sex-ed classes comes from a place of authority—a teacher and a textbook—which carries a different weight than one person making a video in their bedroom" (p. 501). Do you agree with Mirk that this is an important fact to note? In your view, how might the authority of the source of sex-ed information affect the way students respond?

2. In Mirk's estimation, one of the key benefits of an online approach to conversations about sex is the degree of honesty it can foster: "YouTube provides a lifeline for a lot of teens and tweens and it feels like a direct point of contact between teenagers and adults who are up for being frank with them on topics lots of people refuse to discuss" (p. 502). Do you share this view? When it comes to sex education, should "frankness" be a guiding priority? Why or why not?

3. Take a moment to consider the title of this piece. In your view, what does it mean to "tune in" to issues and questions about sexuality? Does Mirk's discussion of online sex education resources provide an adequate illustration of what "tuning in" to sexuality looks like? How or how not?

PUTTING IT INTO WRITING

4. "While YouTube's take-all-kinds approach [to sex ed] is its strength," notes Mirk, "allowing videos from individual teens to share equal space with those created by companies and big nonprofits . . . also means bigoted or misleading information can rise to the top" (pp. 501–2). Write a 500-word essay in which you argue either for or against the advantages of a "YouTube approach" to sex education. If you are arguing in favor, what are the specific advantages or benefits you believe this approach provides? And why do you think they outweigh the potential problems? If you are arguing against, what are the particular problems or challenges this approach raises? And why do you feel they outweigh the potential benefits?

5. Taken together, the examples Mirk cites amount to an instruction manual in how our society's approach to sex education should be reformed. Write an essay in which you offer your thoughts on the same question. How would you evaluate the current state of sex education? What changes in the way issues of sexuality get taught would you advocate? And why?

COMPARING ARGUMENTS

6. Mirk and Thomas Page McBee (p. 504) both approach gender/sexual identity as a fluid category: a construct that can shift and change over time. In a 500-word essay, identify and analyze the parallels between the ways these two essays examine the issue of gender/sexual identity. How does Mirk's discussion of transgender teens compare to McBee's depiction of what it feels like to be a "self-made man"? What are the key similarities and differences?

THOMAS PAGE McBEE
The Truck Stop

What are the qualities and characteristics that define what it means to "be a man"? And what happens when these qualities and characteristics, as well as the gender roles they create, begin to be rethought? These are the questions at the heart of Thomas Page McBee's essay, which tells the story of a trans-gender man's efforts to navigate, and at times overcome, the gender scripts and gender norms of contemporary society. McBee is a trans man and the author of *Man Alive: A True Story of Violence, Forgiveness, and Becoming a Man* (2014). His essays have appeared in the *New York Times*, *Glamour*, and *Salon*. He also writes the "Self-Made Man" column for the *Rumpus*, an online magazine that features writing about art, literature, and culture. The essay below originally appeared as a "Self-Made Man" column in 2012.

Before You Read

What qualities or characteristics would you say "make a man"? What cultural stereotypes does our culture teach us to use to answer this question? Are these stereotypes, in your view, accurate or fair? Why or why not?

I AM IN A PUBLIC RESTROOM OFF 95 IN SOUTHERN MAINE, wondering what makes a man and also if I can muffle my piss stream with balled up toilet paper so as not to draw attention to myself. Will I ever be able to walk into a bathroom and not think about the sound of urine on porcelain? Can I be proud to sit down and have the foreign echoes of my splashing business announce me to the universe as a transman, a crosser of the great divide, a miracle. Can I be a man and a miracle at once?

It's not necessarily time for philosophy, but I have just begun to pass and I am still whisker-less and slight compared to fellow travelers. My biggest concern currently is not spiritual but physical, specifically the physicality of the two huge dudes who walked in right behind me, line-backer in size and head-to-toe in leather and flannel, sort of like Libertarian, less mullet-y versions of Dog the Bounty Hunter. I hurry ahead, trying not to look tweaky, and keep my head up. I am, more and more, shading "guy" in people's first-glance assessments. I am "Sir" and sometimes "Son." I am, finally, never "Ma'am."

I drop trough and try to relax, but the particularly barrel-chested one takes the stall next to me, which stops my stream mid-flow. I see the leather-daddy-ish one in front of the stall on my other side, the zipper of his motorcycle jacket glinting menacingly in the fluorescent light.

This is not good. I've used men's rooms even before taking T without ever an issue, but now bowel-quivering visions of cracked skulls and internal bleeding dance through my head. The floor is tacky with urine and dark with something I'd rather not meditate on; not where I want to faceplant.

When I started hormone therapy eight months ago, I'd already had 5 top surgery. I'd spent most of my young adulthood making old folks working the register at CVS tongue-tied, and I thought knowing how to cock my hat and swagger a little so as to not get my ass kicked while refueling in Wyoming was all I needed to navigate the world of men. I figured I'd mostly stick to my own kind: queers and sensitive straight dudes who made art and knew their rising signs.

But that's not how it turned out. I moved back to New England after years in the woo-woo Bay Area, and suddenly I was a sausage-less guy in a sea of sausage, a dude who knew astrology and wrote lyrical essays and halfway paid attention to the Steelers but only if they're winning. No "think fast," no Sox hat. I am a lover, not a fighter. In high school I chased girls and wrote poetry and went to metal shows with my queer best friend. Now I co-edit a style blog and have a messy pompadour and kind of gay obsession with James Dean. That about catches us up, and now here I am in a restroom off the interstate in southern Maine in desert boots. And glasses.

> **I am, more and more, shading "guy" in people's first-glance assessments. I am "Sir" and sometimes "Son." I am, finally, never "Ma'am"**

I realize that 30 years of blurry insults about my indeterminate gender by drunks outside of bars, rapey newspaper headlines, and some run-ins with a few exceptionally bad seeds (including the one, most memorably, that held a gun to my head a couple of years ago) has made me pretty afraid of dudes. Now that I am one, this is becoming a problem.

I flush the toilet to give myself a minute to think. I could wait them out. I could run (right?) But what if my wife wasn't waiting outside? What if she went to the snack bar? If I made it out alive, I wouldn't even tell her that I was scared, because then she would imagine me getting boot stomped to my face every time we stopped for food and I couldn't let that happen.

As the whoosh subsides, I decide to stay, and just as my thoughts crystallize and the water settles, the dude on my left, in a soothing, breathy falsetto, says, "Alright, I'm going to lift you up, ready?"

And a tiny voice squeaks, "Yeahyeahyeahyeahyeah." 10

I exhale, and almost laugh. There it is. This is what being in the world of men means to me. It means the threat of violence, knife-sharp, ready

I realize that 30 years of blurry insults about my indeterminate gender . . . has made me pretty afraid of dudes. Now that I am one, this is becoming a problem.

to explode in a brushed shoulder at a strange bar. It means head nods from maintenance workers, a whole team of humans welcoming me wherever I go. It means women cross the street away from me at night. And it means that I know nothing, that a man stands guard over his son's stall on my right and another praises his kid's tinkles on my left, and it's heartbreaking, almost, how little we really know about each other.

What does it mean to be a man? To me it means a lot, and nothing at all. It means I'm 30 years old and I love my body. It means that men look at me and see an ally, or a threat. It means that in male spaces I am often apprehensive, that I keep my head down, but lately, when I look up my co-worker has stopped by to get advice on tailoring, or the guy in the stall next to me sings "Good job" unselfconsciously to his child. It means nothing is what it seems, that none of us can look at another and know what's in his pants or his heart, and that surprise is inevitable, but how you react to it is who you are.

FOR A SECOND READING

1. Based on his discussion here, what quality or characteristic do you think McBee would say best defines what it means to be a man? What examples or quotations from the essay would you say best illustrate this?

2. McBee writes: "[N]one of us can look at another and know what's in his pants or his heart, and that surprise is inevitable, but how you react to it is who you are" (p. 506). What do you think McBee is trying to say here about the way we think about gender roles and gender identity? Do you agree that how we react to gender says something fundamental about "who you are"? Why or why not?

3. McBee describes a moment when he discovers how little our cultural assumptions about gender tell us about who we actually are. Do you read this discovery as optimistic and hopeful, or pessimistic and despairing? Why?

PUTTING IT INTO WRITING

4. Spend some time reflecting on the specific language McBee uses to describe himself as a man. How does this language differ from the kind stereotypically associated with manhood? What

specific cultural norms do you think this description is intended to challenge? What larger point about the way we are taught to view manhood do you think this description is designed to convey? Make sure to include quotations from McBee's essay to support your analysis.

5. "This," writes McBee, "is what being in the world of men means to me. It means the threat of violence, knife-sharp, ready to explode in a brushed shoulder at a strange bar. It means head nods from maintenance workers, a whole team of humans welcoming me wherever I go. It means women cross the street away from me at night" (p. 506). In a 500-word essay, analyze the different answers McBee provides here to the question of what it "means to be in the world of men." What does each of these scenarios suggest about what it means to play this particular gender role? What do they suggest about the ways different people react to this role?

COMPARING ARGUMENTS

6. McBee and Sarah Mirk (p. 499) are both interested in how our understanding of gender roles can change through time and experience. Write an essay in which you compare and contrast the ways these two writers explore this question. Do they tell similar or different stories about the ways cultural assumptions or norms about gender can change? What are these similarities and differences specifically?

Rewriting the Script: **Gender as Choice**

❝ *I've always been really interested in secrets — how people find ways of doing things without telling anyone else in order to keep themselves feeling safe in the world. . . . So the trans thing just seemed like a great metaphor for anyone transitioning from who they used to be to who they want to be."*

— JILL SOLOWAY,
CREATOR OF THE AMAZON SERIES,
TRANSPARENT

Amazon/Kobal/REX/Shutterstock

CHOOSING YOUR GENDER

According to long-established social scripts, gender is something fixed and immutable: a foundational element of our identity set in stone from the moment we are born. But it is becoming increasingly apparent that gender — rather than being static and unchanging—can in fact be highly fluid: an aspect of personal identity that can morph or evolve as we ourselves change. It is precisely this view that the quotation above encapsulates. Rather than treat gender as a fixed *identity*, Jill Soloway, the creator of *Transparent*, a show about a transgender parent, treats it as an act of *identification*: a process through which people actively choose "who they want to be." Tellingly, this view of gender is coming to find greater and greater recognition within popular culture, attested by the popularity of shows like *Transparent* and the public transition of former Olympian Bruce Jenner to Caitlyn Jenner. Everywhere we look, it seems, we find evidence that a new set of gender norms is coming to the fore.

IDENTIFY THE SCRIPT: Choose an example from pop culture (e.g., an ad, website, TV show, etc.) that, in your view, promotes a vision of gender as something fixed and static. Describe what this vision of gender looks like. What roles does it proscribe for men and women? In what ways does it present these roles as something immutable or natural?

CHALLENGE THE SCRIPT: Write a brief essay in which you assess the merits and shortcomings of the gender roles this pop culture example promotes. In what ways (if any) do you find the gender boundaries these roles establish to be reasonable or necessary? In what ways (if any) do you find them to be artificial or restrictive? Why?

MAKE YOUR OWN SCRIPT: Create a pop culture text that promotes a vision of gender that most accurately reflects your own view. In a brief essay, describe what this text would look like. What form would it take (e.g., ad, website, tv show, etc.)? What gender norms would it promote? What gender roles would it create?

REBECCA TRAISTER

All The Single Ladies

For centuries, marriage has been considered the natural, indeed inevitable, culmination of a successful life for women. But we now live in an era, notes Rebecca Traister, where this long-dominant cultural mandate is undergoing significant change. These days, Traister observes, more and more American women are choosing to defer or decline marriage altogether — a choice that has dramatically reframed what it means to be "single" in contemporary culture. A former staff writer for the *New Republic*, Rebecca Traister is currently a writer-at-large for *New York Magazine* and a contributing editor at *Elle* magazine. She is also the author of *All The Single Ladies: Unmarried Women and the Rise of an Independent Nation* (2016), from which this selection is excerpted.

Before You Read

Do you think singlehood is still a choice that gets stigmatized for women? If so, what do you think accounts for this bias?

BY THE TIME I WALKED DOWN THE AISLE — OR RATHER, INTO A judge's chambers — I had lived fourteen independent years, early adult years that my mother had spent married. I had made friends and fallen out with friends, had moved in and out of apartments, had been hired, fired, promoted, and quit. I had had roommates I liked and roommates I didn't like and I had lived on my own; I'd been on several forms of birth control and navigated a few serious medical questions; I'd paid my own bills and failed to pay my own bills; I'd fallen in love and fallen out of love and spent five consecutive years with nary a fling. I'd learned my way around new neighborhoods, felt scared and felt completely at home; I'd been heartbroken, afraid, jubilant, and bored. I was a grown-up: a reasonably complicated person. I'd become that person not in the company of any one man, but alongside my friends, my family, my city, my work, and, simply, by myself.

I was not alone.

In fact, in 2009, the proportion of American women who were married dropped below 50 percent.[1] And that median age of first marriage that had remained between twenty and twenty-two from 1890 to 1980?[2] Today, the median age of first marriage for women is around twenty-seven, and much higher than that in many cities. By our mid-thirties, half of my closest girlfriends remained unmarried.

During the years in which I had come of age, American women had pioneered an entirely new kind of adulthood, one that was *not* kicked off by marriage, but by years and, in many cases, whole lives, lived on their own, outside matrimony. Those independent women were no longer aberrations, less stigmatized than ever before. Society had changed, permitting this revolution, but the revolution's beneficiaries were about to change the nation further; remapping the life span of women, redefining marriage and family, reimagining what wifeliness and motherhood entail, and, in short, altering the scope of possibility for over half the country's population.

For the first time in American history, single women (including those 5 who were never married, widowed, divorced, or separated) outnumbered married women. Perhaps even more strikingly, the number of adults younger than thirty-four who had *never* married was up to 46 percent,[3] rising twelve percentage points in less than a decade. For women under thirty, the likelihood of being married had become astonishingly small: Today, only around 20 percent of Americans are wed[4] by age twenty-nine, compared to the nearly 60 percent in 1960. In a statement from the Population Reference Bureau, the fact that the proportion of young adults in the United States that has never been married is now bigger than the percentage that has married was called "a dramatic reversal."[5]

> *Young women today no longer have to wonder, as I did, what unmarried adult life for women might look like, surrounded as we are by examples of exactly this kind of existence.*

For young women, for the first time, it is as normal to be unmarried as it is to be married, even if it doesn't always feel that way.

British journalist Hannah Betts wrote in 2013, "Ask what has changed most about society during my lifetime and I would answer: the evolution from the stigmatised 'spinsters' of my childhood . . . to the notion of the 'singularist,' which is how I would currently define myself at 41."[6]

Young women today no longer have to wonder, as I did, what unmarried adult life for women might look like, surrounded as we are by examples of exactly this kind of existence. Today, the failure to comply with the marriage plot, while a source of frustration and economic hardship for many, does not lead directly to life as a social outcast or to a chloral hydrate prescription.

It is an invitation to wrestle with a whole new set of expectations about what female maturity entails, now that it is not shaped and defined by early marriage.

In 1997, the year that I graduated college, journalist Katie Roiphe 10 wrote about the befuddlement felt by her generation of unmarried women. Four years earlier, Roiphe had published *The Morning After*, a screed against campus date-rape activism rooted firmly in her belief in the sexual agency and independence of college-aged women. However, as Roiphe and her compatriots closed in on thirty, many living unmarried into their second decade of adulthood, she argued that they were feeling the long-term effects of that independence and longing instead for the "felicitous simplicities of the nineteenth-century marriage plot."[7]

> People live together and move out. They sleep together for indefinite periods. They marry later. They travel light. I recently overheard a pretty woman at a party say, not without regret, 'When our mothers were our age, they had husbands instead of cats.' She is one of the many normal, pulled-together people I know inhabiting the prolonged, perplexing strip of adolescence currently provided by this country to its twenty- to thirty-year olds. The romantic sensibility—cats or husbands?—is fragile and confused. We go to parties and occasionally fall into bed with people we don't know well, but we also have well-read paperbacks of Austen's *Mansfield Park* or *Emma* lying open on our night tables: the dream of a more orderly world.

The unmarried state that Roiphe viewed as a kind of disorder was in fact a *new* order, or at least a new normal, in which women's lots in life were not cast based on a single binary (husbands *versus* cats). Instead, women's paths were increasingly marked with options, off-ramps, variations on what had historically been a very constrained theme.

While Roiphe may have felt herself in a prolonged period of adolescence because marriage had not yet come along to mark its end, she was in fact leading a very adult life, with a romantic history, an undergraduate education at Harvard, and a thriving career. The liberating point was that Roiphe's status and that of her cohort didn't hinge on the question of whether they had husbands or cats. It didn't have to, because they had jobs. They had sex lives. They had each other. They inhabited a universe that Jane Austen, for whose "orderly world" Roiphe claimed to pine, could never have imagined: Austen's novels had been as much ambivalent cries *against* the economic and moral strictures of enforced marital identity for women than they were any kind of reassuring blueprint for it.

Contemporary, unmarried life may have felt—to Roiphe and to many single women who continue to come after her—a lot more complicated, confusing and scary than the simpler single option on offer to women of previous generations. But the wholesale revision of what female life might entail is also, by many measures, the invention of independent female adulthood.

THE SINGLE LADIES

The independence can be punishing. Many single women are poor or struggling. Almost 50 percent of the 3.3 million Americans now earning minimum wage or below are unmarried women.[8] Many of them live, often with children, in communities where unemployment, racial and class discrimination, and a drug war that puts many young men in prison combine to make the possibilities of stable marriages scarce, making singlehood less of a freeing choice than a socially conscripted necessity. More than half of unmarried young mothers with children under the age of six are likely to live below the poverty line, a rate that is five times the rate of the corresponding population of married women.[9]

Yes, many single women, across classes and races, would like to marry, or at least form loving, reciprocal, long-term partnerships, but have not found mates who want the same thing, or who can sustain it. Some are lonely.   15

Many women, unmarried into their thirties, living in geographic, religious, and socio-economic corners of the country where early marriage remains a norm, as well as many women who remain single less by choice than by circumstance, into their forties, fifties, and sixties, do not feel as though they are living in a new, singles-dominated world. They feel ostracized, pressured; they are challenged by family and peers.

However, statistically, across the country, these women are not alone. Their numbers are growing by the year. There were 3.9 million more single adult women in 2014 than there were in 2010.[10] Between 2008 and 2011, the rate of new marriage fell by 14 percent for those who had not completed high school and by 10 percent for those with at least a bachelor's degree.[11]

In the course of researching this book, I spoke to scores of American women from different backgrounds and classes and faiths and races about their experiences of living singly.

"We all expected to be married at twenty-six," said Kitty Curtis, a New Jersey hairstylist who is, at twenty-six, not married. "I don't really know anyone who is married," she said. "And the ones I do know, there's a sense that it's weird, strange. It's a foreign idea to be married before thirty." Meaghan Ritchie, a fundamentalist Christian college student from Kentucky, told me that she will not marry before she's at least twenty-two, because she believes that dropping out of college—as her mother did to marry her father—would not be an economically sound idea. Amanda Neville, a thirty-five-year-old New Yorker, flew to Russia to adopt a daughter, who is deaf, within a year of opening a wine store and beginning a new relationship with a boyfriend. Ada Li, a manicurist from China living in Brooklyn, told me that her decision to wait until her late thirties to marry and have a child was what made her life in the United States happy and free.

Single female life is not prescription, but its opposite: liberation.

Some women actively decided against early marriage, in part out of fear that matrimony would put a stop to their ambitions. "The moment I saw that ring," wrote Jessica Bennett, a journalist who turned down a   20 proposal at twenty-four, "I saw dirty dishes and suburbia . . . I saw the career I had hardly started as suddenly out of reach . . . the independence I had barely gained felt stifled. I couldn't breathe." Some are sad to not yet have found mates, like Elliott Holt, a forty-year-old novelist who told me, "I guess I just had no idea, could never have predicted, how intense the loneliness would be at this juncture of my life." And others, including Susana Morris, a thirty-two-year-old English professor in Alabama, are less worried about themselves than they are about how concerned every-one *else* is about them. "What's anxiety provoking is that every time you open a magazine or a book or turn on the television, there's someone telling you there's something wrong with you as a black woman—you're too fat, too loud, don't nobody want to marry you. *That* is anxiety producing!"

These women are not waiting for their real lives to start; they are living their lives, and those lives include as many variations as there are women.

To be clear, the vast increase in the number of single women is to be celebrated not because singleness is in and of itself a better or more desirable state than coupledom. The revolution is in the expansion of options, the lifting of the imperative that for centuries hustled nearly all (non-enslaved) women, regardless of their individual desires, ambitions, circumstances, or the quality of available matches, down a single high-way toward early heterosexual marriage and motherhood. There are now an infinite number of alternate routes open; they wind around combina-tions of love, sex, partnership, parenthood, work, and friendship, at dif-ferent speeds.

Single female life is not prescription, but its opposite: liberation.

This liberation is at the heart of our national promise, but that prom-ise of freedom has often been elusive for many of this country's resi-dents. This makes it all the more important to acknowledge that while the victories of independent life are often emblematized by the country's most privileged women, the war was fought by many Americans who have always had far fewer options to live free: women of color, poor, and working-class women.

NOTES

[1]Mather, Mark and Diana Lavery, "In U.S. Proportion Married at Lowest Recorded Levels," *Population Reference Bureau*, 2010 http://www.prb.org/Publications/Articles/2010/usmarriagedecline.aspx.

[2]According to Robert B. Bernstein at the Census Bureau, in 1979, the median age rose to 22.1.

[3]Mather and Lavery, "In U.S., Proportion Married at Lowest Recorded Levels," 2010.

[4]Cohn, D'vera, Jeffery S. Passel, Wendy Wang and Gretchen Livingston, "Barely Half of U.S. Adults Are Married—A Record Low," Pew Research Center, December 14, 2011, http://www.pewsocialtrends.org/2011/12/14/barely-half-of-u-s-adults-are-married-a-record-low/.

[5]Mather and Lavery, "In U.S., Proportion Married at Lowest Recorded Levels," 2010.

[6]Betts, Hannah, "Being Single by Choice Is Liberating," *The Telegraph*, March 21, 2013.

[7]Roiphe, Katie, *Last Night in Paradise*, via *New York Times* excerpt, 1997, http://www .nytimes.com/books/first/r/roiphe-paradise.html.

[8]Gardner, Page, "Equal Pay Day: Unmarried Women Bear the Brunt of the Pay Gap," The Voter Participation Center, August 13, 2015, http://www.voterparticipation .org/equal-pay-day-2015/.

[9]Mather, Mark and Beth Jarosz, "Women Making Progress in U.S. but Gaps Remain," Population Reference Bureau, 2014, http://www.prb.org/Publications/ Reports/2014/us-inequality-women-progress.aspx.

[10]"America's Families and Living Arrangements: 2014: Adults" (Table 1A), United States Census Bureau, http://www.census.gov/hhes/families/data/cps2014A .html *via* Lake Research Partners, "The Power of Unmarried Women," The Voter Participation Center, March 2012.

[11]Fry, Richard, "No Reversal in the Decline of Marriage," Pew Research Center, November 20, 2012, http://www.pewsocialtrends.org/2012/11/20/ no-reversal-in-decline-of-marriage/#src=prc-newsletter.

FOR A SECOND READING

1. Traister begins this essay by itemizing all the different things she had experienced or accomplished before she got married: "made friends and fallen out with friends"; "had been hired, fired, promoted and quit"; "paid my own bills and failed to pay my own bills"; "learned my way around new neighborhoods, felt scared and completely at home" (p. 510). Why do you think she chooses this organizational strategy? How does a list such as this prepare readers for the argument about marriage and singlehood to follow? Do you find this strategy to be effective? Why or why not?

2. Traister notes the independence that comes from being unmarried can also be punishing: "Almost 50 percent of the 3.3 million Americans now earning minimum wage or below are unmarried women. Many of them live, often with children, in communities where unemployment, racial and class discrimination, and a drug war that puts many young men in prison combine to make the possibilities of stable marriages scarce" (pp. 512–13). How do you interpret this data? What does it tell you about the social, cultural, and economic pressures that confront women when deciding whether or not to marry?

3. As Traister notes, many single women "decided against early marriage, in part fear that matrimony would put a stop to their ambitions" (p. 513). In your view, does this fear reflect a cultural attitude that is still prevalent? Do we still live in an era where the cultural norm pits decisions about marriage and career as mutually exclusive?

PUTTING IT INTO WRITING

4. For Traister, a shift in the cultural expectations for women regarding marriage represents an invaluable opportunity: "It is an invitation to wrestle with a whole new set of expectations about what female maturity entails, now that it is not shaped and defined by early marriage" (p. 511). In a 500-word essay, take up the invitation Traister outlines here. What model of female maturity would you say this shift away from early marriage makes possible? What specific possibilities or expectations (social, professional, political) might this kind of alternative script involve?

5. Traister organizes her discussion of singlehood around statistical data documenting a decline in marriage rates, an increase in the median marrying age for women, and a rise in the overall number of unmarried women in contemporary American society. In an essay (300–500 words), explain how you think this data should be interpreted. What do these statistics suggest to you about the ways cultural norms and social scripts around gender and marriage are changing? In your views, are these changes for the better? Why or why not?

COMPARING ARGUMENTS

6. Traister and Jodi Kantor (p. 517) both focus on cultural moments where entrenched norms around marriage are undergoing significant change. How similar do you find these two stories to be? Does Traister's account of the rise of singlehood involve the same key questions as Kantor's discussion of gay marriage? How or how not?

JODI KANTOR

Historic Day for Gays, but Twinge for Loss of Outsider Culture

The last ten years have witnessed a dramatic shift in public attitudes toward gay marriage, a development that parallels a broader acceptance of gay culture more generally. But does all of this newfound acceptance come with its own costs? This is the question Jodi Kantor explores in this essay. Reviewing all of the recent advances in cultural acceptance of and political rights for gay people, Kantor probes the hidden losses this laudable progress also entails. Jodi Kantor is a *New York Times* correspondent who writes about technology, the workplace, and gender. This article appeared in the *New York Times* in 2015.

Before You Read

Are you surprised to hear that being a cultural "outsider" can carry a certain appeal, even a degree of authority? Can you think of an example from contemporary life that illustrates this?

FROM CAPITOL HILL IN SEATTLE TO DUPONT CIRCLE IN WASHINGTON, gay bars and nightclubs have turned into vitamin stores, frozen yogurt shops and memories. Some of those that remain are filled increasingly with straight patrons, while many former customers say their social lives now revolve around preschools and playgrounds.

Rainbow-hued "Just Be You" messages have been flashing across Chase A.T.M. screens in honor of Pride month, conveying acceptance but also corporate blandness. Directors, filmmakers and artists are talking about moving past themes of sexual orientation, which they say no longer generate as much dramatic energy.

The Supreme Court on Friday expanded same-sex marriage rights across the country, a crowning achievement but also a confounding challenge to a group that has often prided itself on being different. The more victories that accumulate for gay rights, the faster some gay institutions, rituals and markers are fading out. And so just as the gay marriage movement peaks, so does a debate about whether gay identity is dimming, overtaken by its own success.

"What do gay men have in common when they don't have oppression?" asked Andrew Sullivan, one of the intellectual architects of the marriage movement. "I don't know the answer to that yet."

5   John Waters, the film director and patron saint of the American marginal, warned graduates to heed the shift in a recent commencement speech at the Rhode Island School of Design. "Refuse to isolate yourself. Separatism is for losers," he said, adding, "Gay is not enough anymore."

No one is arguing that prejudice has come close to disappearing, especially outside major American cities, as waves of hate crimes, suicides by gay teenagers and workplace discrimination attest. Far from everyone agrees that marriage rights are the apotheosis of liberation. But even many who raced to the altar say they feel loss amid the celebrations, a bittersweet sense that there was something valuable about the creativity and grit with which gay people responded to stigma and persecution.

For decades, they built sanctuaries of their own: neighborhoods and vacation retreats where they could escape after workdays in the closet; bookstores where young people could find their true selves and one another. Symbols like the rainbow flag expressed joy and collective defiance, a response to disapproving families, laws that could lead to arrests for having sex and the presumption that to be lesbian, gay, bisexual or transgender was shameful.

"The thing I miss is the specialness of being gay," said Lisa Kron, who wrote the book and lyrics for "Fun Home," a Broadway musical with a showstopping number sung by a young girl captivated by her first glimpse of a butch woman. "Because the traditional paths were closed, there was a consciousness to our lives, a necessary invention to the way we were going to celebrate and mark family and mark connection. That felt magical and beautiful."

Ms. Kron is 54, and her sentiments seem to resonate among gay people of her generation and older. "People are missing a sense of community, a sense of sharing," said Eric Marcus, 56, the author of "Making Gay History."

10   "There is something wonderful about being part of an oppressed community," Mr. Marcus said. But he warned against too much nostalgia. The most vocal gay rights activists may have celebrated being outsiders, but the vast majority of gay people just wanted "what everyone else had," he said—the ability to fall in love, have families, pursue their careers and "just live their lives."

The more victories that accumulate for gay rights, the faster some gay institutions, rituals and markers are fading out.

Mainstream acceptance does not necessarily cause minority cultures to wither. Other groups have been both buffered and buoyed by greater inclusion. But being gay is different from being a member of an ethnic or religious minority. Many gay children are born into heterosexual families, and same-sex couples often have offspring who are straight. There is less continuity, several gay sociologists said, and there are fewer traditions or holidays that reinforce identity and unite the generations.

The unifying experience for many gay people is not marriage but coming out of the closet. In 1997, as Ellen DeGeneres rehearsed the sitcom scene in which her character came out, she broke into tears every time she rehearsed saying, "I'm gay." She was welling up because of "shame, you know, self-hatred, and all of these feelings that society feeds you to tell you that you're wrong," she said in a later interview.

But many gay people in their teens, 20s and 30s today say the phrase "coming out of the closet" does not apply to them because they were never in one. For Ariel Boone of Oakland, Calif., who began to describe herself as queer in 2008, when she was 18, the time between when she realized her attraction to women and when she started telling others was "maybe 12 hours."

Blaine Edens told her parents in 2013, when she was 22, sharing the news with her father in Arizona and her mother in Montana. They each said, "Yeah, we know. We're sad it took you this long," she said.

For too many artists and writers to count, being gay infused their 15 work with an outsider sensibility, even when they were not explicitly addressing those themes. Their private lives and identity gave them "a cunning and sophisticated way of looking at the world and questioning its normative notions," said Todd Haynes, the director of "Far From Heaven" and the coming film "Carol," based on the lesbian romance novel "The Price of Salt," by Patricia Highsmith.

Curators and art critics said they could not name a recent work about sexual orientation with the impact of Robert Mapplethorpe's provocative portraits from decades ago—or that of Kara Walker's gigantic 2014 sugar sculpture, a commentary on black women, plantations and whiteness, among other themes. In theater, playwrights say there will never be another "The Normal Heart," Larry Kramer's 1985 cri de coeur about AIDS, or "Angels in America," Tony Kushner's 1991 saga about the same topic. On many television shows, gay themes and humor are integrated seamlessly, almost casually, as on "Orange is the New Black" and "Broad City."

> *[E]ven many who raced to the altar say they feel loss amid the celebrations, a bittersweet sense that there was something valuable about the creativity and grit with which gay people responded to stigma and persecution.*

Many gay artists, politicians and celebrities say they prefer life with fewer labels, that they enjoy the freedom of not being put into an identity-politics box or expected to behave a certain way. They "don't feel the responsibility to speak for a community," Dean Daderko, curator of the Contemporary Arts Museum Houston, said in a telephone interview.

When Pete Buttegieg, 33, the mayor of South Bend, Ind., told constituents that he was gay in an op-ed article this month, he emphasized that sexual orientation was "just a part of who I am," along with being a naval reservist and a businessman. His article echoed the one in which Tim Cook, 54, the chief executive of Apple, came out last year. "I'm an engineer, an uncle, a nature lover, a fitness nut, a son of the South, a sports fanatic and many other things," Mr. Cook said.

For decades, the cartoonist Alison Bechdel thrived on the edges of the publishing world, turning her comic strip "Dykes to Watch Out For" into a sociology of lesbian life, its title a joke about supposed menace. Now "Fun Home," which is based on her memoir, is a Broadway hit and winner of the Best Musical Tony. Theatergoers identify with its themes "without any mediating feeling of 'now I'm watching this lesbian character,'" Ms. Kron said. "Sometimes I look at the audience and think, 'Are there any gay people here?'"

20   There are. Beth Malone, who plays the adult Alison, said in an interview that young women sometimes waited for her at the stage door and whispered their plans for coming out, even with an unknowing parent standing a few feet away. This is why gay culture is unlikely to disappear: because there will always be young people discovering they are different from their families, several historians and sociologists said.

They also said that gay culture had a natural successor to which it is bequeathing its boundary-breaking qualities: queer culture, which questions rigid categories like male and female and gay and straight. Over the years, the relationship between the more established gay world and those who consider themselves transgender or queer has been strained at times. Some lesbians accuse transgender men of abandoning feminism, and some people who identify themselves as transgender or queer see gay men and women as too conformist.

Now one may be enabling the other, the societal discussion moving from "Is it O.K. for a man to marry a man?" to "Is gender as fixed as we assume?" In Northampton, Mass., a landmark lesbian community, the shift is visible on the streets. A generation ago, it was bracing to see lesbians with short haircuts strolling around, said Rachel Simmons, a writer and educator who came out in college. Recently, she recalled, she was jogging on the town bike path when a transgender man whipped by, shirt off, mastectomy scars revealed for all to see.

Meanwhile, in Provincetown, Mass., a longtime gay male summer capital, Mr. Sullivan continues to track what he has dubbed "the end of gay culture," which he says erodes a little more each year. Lately, he said in an interview, he has noticed that the old gay bars have become popular sites for heterosexual bachelorette parties, the women showing up in sashes and white veils.

When they do, friends tease him about the consequences of the gay marriage fight he helped ignite. "See what you asked for?" they say.

FOR A SECOND READING

1. Kantor cites a number of examples that demonstrate how gay culture is becoming increasingly mainstream: "gay bars and nightclubs . . . turned into vitamin stores, frozen yogurt shops"; "Rainbow-hued 'Just Be You' messages . . . flashing across Chase A.T.M. screens in honor of Pride month" (p. 517). What do these examples suggest to you about the ways mainstream culture is coming to accept and absorb gay culture? What would you say are the benefits and potential problems of this cultural change?

2. "Mainstream acceptance," writes Kantor, "does not necessarily cause minority cultures to wither. Other groups have been both buffered and buoyed by greater inclusion. But being gay is different from being a member of an ethnic or religious minority" (p. 518). How do you respond to this claim? Do you agree that sexual orientation represents a different type of minority identity than one based on ethnicity or religion? Why or why not?

3. At the heart of Kantor's discussion is what appears to be a contradiction: "The more victories that accumulate for gay rights, the faster some gay institutions, rituals and markers are fading out" (p. 517). Does this cause-and-effect relationship make sense to you? Would you expect that the achievement of gay rights on the one hand would result in the institutions and markers of gay culture to fade out? Why or why not?

PUTTING IT INTO WRITING

4. As public acceptance of gay life and gay culture continues to grow, Kantor notes, the broader societal discussion around issues of sexuality is shifting from questions like "Is it OK for a man to marry a man?" to "Is gender as fixed as we assume?" Write a 500-word essay in which you address this shift. Do you see lines that have traditionally been used to denote gender identity becoming less fixed? Can you think of an example from contemporary culture that illustrates the ways gender is becoming a more fluid category?

5. Kantor is quick to remind readers that growing public acceptance of gay culture does not mean that discrimination and violence

against gay people is no longer an issue: "No one is arguing that prejudice has come close to disappearing, especially outside major American cities, as waves of hate crimes, suicides by gay teenagers and workplace discrimination attest" (p. 518). In a 500-word essay, address the paradox this passage highlights. How do we make sense of the fact that, as gay life is increasingly regarded as part of the cultural mainstream, gay people still find themselves subject to harassment, discrimination, and violence?

COMPARING ARGUMENTS

6. From very different vantages, Kantor and Rebecca Traister (p. 510) ask readers to consider what happens when long-held stigmas toward cultural outsiders (i.e., gay people, unmarried women) begin to disappear. How do their respective arguments compare? Do these writers make similar claims about what happens to a so-called minority community when it finds itself becoming more mainstream? How or how not?

Then and Now: **Saying "I Do"**

For centuries, pundits and moralists of all stripes have celebrated marriage as the bedrock of American society. Throughout most of this history, however, the arbiters of our country's matrimonial norms have tended to define this revered cultural institution in exceedingly narrow (class, racial, and gender) terms. It wasn't until 1967, for example, that the Supreme Court ruled in favor of legalizing interracial marriage, and it was only in 2014, that the Supreme Court recognized the legal right of same-sex couples to marry. While incremental, the shift in the legal and cultural norms around marriage has been profound. Rather than a social obligation to fulfill, we now speak of marriage as a civil right to be exercised, an individual choice to be made.

Planet News Archive/Getty Images

A closer look at the images presented here, however, suggests that, however far-reaching these transformations may be, not everything concerning our thinking about marriage has changed. Even as the boundaries around marriage have been expanded to encompass a far wider and more diverse range of relationships, the basic idea of what marriage is — and is for — has remained remarkably stable. True, the complexion and composition

523

of those now choosing to marry has changed dramatically, but what this choice means, the values and norms it is understood to express, are still largely the same. Regardless of who enters into it, the ideal of marriage still expresses a cultural belief in the importance, for example, of lifelong commitment. It still treats monogamy as a desirable, natural norm. Marriage also continues to symbolize a cultural belief in the importance of family: the assumption that procreation (i.e., having children) is an expected, if not inevitable, aspect of adult life.

So how much has really changed? As it has expanded to include a broader, more representative swath of American society, has the institution of marriage undergone a comparable transformation in social values and cultural norms? And if not, do we think it should?

ArrowStudio/Shutterstock

PUTTING IT INTO WRITING

1. In a brief essay, compare the similarities and differences you note between these two depictions of a wedding ceremony. What definition of marriage does each image present? What ideas or values does each image seem designed to represent? Are these ideas and values similar of different?

2. Rebecca Traister (p. 510) chronicles the rise of singlehood as an emerging cultural norm in American society. In what ways do you think Traister's argument complicates or challenges the marriage norms promoted by the images here? How do you think Traister would react to these images herself?

DAVID BROOKS

People Like Us

In this essay, David Brooks takes up some of the key terms that currently anchor our public discussions of race, prompting us to think about the assumptions we bring to bear on this question. Do we, he asks, really care about diversity? And even more provocatively, should we? Brooks, a prominent voice for conservative politics, has been a columnist at the *New York Times* since 2003. He has also worked at the *Weekly Standard*, *Newsweek*, and the *Atlantic Monthly* and has appeared on NPR's *All Things Considered* and PBS's *NewsHour.* He is the author of the books *Bobos in Paradise: The New Upper Class and How They Got There* (2000), *On Paradise Drive: How We Live Now (and Always Have) in the Future Tense* (2004), *The Social Animal: The Hidden Sources of Love, Character, and Achievement* (2011), and *The Road to Character* (2015). The following essay first appeared in the September 2003 issue of the *Atlantic Monthly.*

Before You Read

Does "diversity" matter to you? If so, how?

MAYBE IT'S TIME TO ADMIT THE OBVIOUS. WE DON'T REALLY CARE about diversity all that much in America, even though we talk about it a great deal. Maybe somewhere in this country there is a truly diverse neighborhood in which a black Pentecostal minister lives next to a white anti-globalization activist, who lives next to an Asian short-order cook, who lives next to a professional golfer, who lives next to a postmodern-literature professor and a cardiovascular surgeon. But I have never been to or heard of that neighborhood. Instead, what I have seen all around the country is people making strenuous efforts to group themselves with people who are basically like themselves.

Human beings are capable of drawing amazingly subtle social distinctions and then shaping their lives around them. In the Washington, D.C., area Democratic lawyers tend to live in suburban Maryland, and Republican lawyers tend to live in suburban Virginia. If you asked a Democratic lawyer to move from her $750,000 house in Bethesda, Maryland, to a $750,000 house in Great Falls, Virginia, she'd look at you as if you had just asked her to buy a pickup truck with a gun rack and to shove chewing tobacco in her kid's mouth. In Manhattan the owner of a $3 million SoHo loft would feel out of place moving into a $3 million Fifth Avenue apartment. A West Hollywood interior decorator would feel dislocated if you asked him to move to Orange County. In Georgia a barista from Athens would probably not fit in serving coffee in Americus.

It is a common complaint that every place is starting to look the same. But in the information age, the late writer James Chapin once told me, every place becomes more like itself. People are less often tied down to factories and mills, and they can search for places to live on the basis of cultural affinity. Once they find a town in which people share their values, they flock there, and reinforce whatever was distinctive about the town in the first place. Once Boulder, Colorado, became known as congenial to politically progressive mountain bikers, half the politically progressive mountain bikers in the country (it seems) moved there; they made the place so culturally pure that it has become practically a parody of itself.

But people love it. Make no mistake—we are increasing our happiness by segmenting off so rigorously. We are finding places where we are comfortable and where we feel we can flourish. But the choices we make toward that end lead to the very opposite of diversity. The United States might be a diverse nation when considered as a whole, but block by block and institution by institution it is a relatively homogeneous nation.

5   When we use the word "diversity" today we usually mean racial integration. But even here our good intentions seem to have run into the brick wall of human nature. Over the past generation reformers have tried heroically, and in many cases successfully, to end housing discrimination. But recent patterns aren't encouraging: according to an analysis of the 2000 census data, the 1990s saw only a slight increase in the racial integration of neighborhoods in the United States. The number of middle-class and upper-middle-class African-American families is rising, but for whatever reasons—racism, psychological comfort—these families tend to congregate in predominantly black neighborhoods.

> **[W]e are increasing our happiness by segmenting off so rigorously.**

In fact, evidence suggests that some neighborhoods become more segregated over time. New suburbs in Arizona and Nevada, for example, start out reasonably well integrated. These neighborhoods don't yet have reputations, so people choose their houses for other, mostly economic reasons. But as neighborhoods age, they develop personalities (that's where the Asians live, and that's where the Hispanics live), and segmentation occurs. It could be that in a few years the new suburbs in the Southwest will be nearly as segregated as the established ones in the Northeast and the Midwest.

Even though race and ethnicity run deep in American society, we should in theory be able to find areas that are at least culturally diverse. But here, too, people show few signs of being truly interested in building diverse communities. If you run a retail company and you're thinking of opening new stores, you can choose among dozens of consulting firms that are quite effective at locating your potential customers. They can do this because people with similar tastes and preferences tend to congregate by ZIP code.

The most famous of these precision marketing firms is Claritas, which breaks down the U.S. population into sixty-two psycho-demographic clusters, based on such factors as how much money people make, what they like to read and watch, and what products they have bought in the past. For example, the "suburban sprawl" cluster is composed of young families making about $41,000 a year and living in fast-growing places such as Burnsville, Minnesota, and Bensalem, Pennsylvania. These people are almost twice as likely as other Americans to have three-way calling. They are two and a half times as likely to buy Light n' Lively Kid Yogurt. Members of the "towns & gowns" cluster are recent college graduates in places such as Berkeley, California, and Gainesville, Florida. They are big consumers of Dove Bars and *Saturday Night Live*. They tend to drive small foreign cars and to read *Rolling Stone* and *Scientific American*.

Looking through the market research, one can sometimes be amazed by how efficiently people cluster—and by how predictable we all are. If you wanted to sell imported wine, obviously you would have to find places where rich people live. But did you know that the sixteen counties with the greatest proportion of imported-wine drinkers are all in the same three metropolitan areas (New York, San Francisco, and Washington, D.C.)? If you tried to open a motor-home dealership in Montgomery County, Pennsylvania, you'd probably go broke, because people in this ring of the Philadelphia suburbs think RVs are kind of uncool. But if you traveled just a short way north, to Monroe County, Pennsylvania, you would find yourself in the fifth motor-home-friendliest county in America.

Geography is not the only way we find ourselves divided from people 10 unlike us. Some of us watch Fox News, while others listen to NPR. Some like David Letterman, and others—typically in less urban neighborhoods—like Jay Leno. Some go to charismatic churches; some go to mainstream churches. Americans tend more and more often to marry people with education levels similar to their own, and to befriend people with backgrounds similar to their own.

My favorite illustration of this latter pattern comes from the first, noncontroversial chapter of *The Bell Curve*. Think of your twelve closest friends, Richard J. Herrnstein and Charles Murray write. If you had chosen them randomly from the American population, the odds that half of your twelve closest friends would be college graduates would be six in a thousand. The odds that half of the twelve would have advanced degrees would be less than one in a million. Have any of your twelve closest friends graduated from Harvard, Stanford, Yale, Princeton, Caltech, MIT, Duke, Dartmouth, Cornell, Columbia, Chicago, or Brown? If you chose your friends randomly from the American population, the odds against your having four or more friends from those schools would be more than a billion to one.

Many of us live in absurdly unlikely groupings, because we have organized our lives that way.

It's striking that the institutions that talk the most about diversity often practice it the least. For example, no group of people sings the diversity anthem more frequently and fervently than administrators at just such elite universities. But elite universities are amazingly undiverse in their values, politics, and mores. Professors in particular are drawn from a rather narrow segment of the population. If faculties reflected the general population, 32 percent of professors would be registered Democrats and 31 percent would be registered Republicans. Forty percent would be evangelical Christians. But a recent study of several universities by the conservative Center for the Study of Popular Culture and the American Enterprise Institute found that roughly 90 percent of those professors in the arts and sciences who had registered with a political party had registered Democratic. Fifty-seven professors at Brown were found on the voter-registration rolls. Of those, fifty-four were Democrats. Of the forty-two professors in the English, history, sociology, and political-science departments, all were Democrats. The results at Harvard, Penn State, Maryland, and the University of California at Santa Barbara were similar to the results at Brown.

What we are looking at here is human nature. People want to be around others who are roughly like themselves. That's called community. It probably would be psychologically difficult for most Brown professors to share an office with someone who was pro-life, a member of the National Rifle Association, or an evangelical Christian. It's likely that hiring committees would subtly—even unconsciously—screen out any such people they encountered. Republicans and evangelical Christians have sensed that they are not welcome at places like Brown, so they don't even consider working there. In fact, any registered Republican who contemplates a career in academia these days is both a hero and a fool. So, in a semi-self-selective pattern, brainy people with generally liberal social mores flow to academia, and brainy people with generally conservative mores flow elsewhere.

People want to be around others who are roughly like themselves. That's called community.

15   The dream of diversity is like the dream of equality. Both are based on ideals we celebrate even as we undermine them daily. (How many times have you seen someone renounce a high-paying job or pull his child from an elite college on the grounds that these things are bad for

equality?) On the one hand, the situation is appalling. It is appalling that Americans know so little about one another. It is appalling that many of us are so narrow-minded that we can't tolerate a few people with ideas significantly different from our own. It's appalling that evangelical Christians are practically absent from entire professions, such as academia, the media, and filmmaking. It's appalling that people should be content to cut themselves off from everyone unlike themselves.

The segmentation of society means that often we don't even have arguments across the political divide. Within their little validating communities, liberals and conservatives circulate half-truths about the supposed awfulness of the other side. These distortions are believed because it feels good to believe them.

On the other hand, there are limits to how diverse any community can or should be. I've come to think that it is not useful to try to hammer diversity into every neighborhood and institution in the United States. Sure, Augusta National should probably admit women, and university sociology departments should probably hire a conservative or two. It would be nice if all neighborhoods had a good mixture of ethnicities. But human nature being what it is, most places and institutions are going to remain culturally homogeneous.

It's probably better to think about diverse lives, not diverse institutions. Human beings, if they are to live well, will have to move through a series of institutions and environments, which may be individually homogeneous but, taken together, will offer diverse experiences. It might also be a good idea to make national service a rite of passage for young people in this country: it would take them out of their narrow neighborhood segment and thrust them in with people unlike themselves. Finally, it's probably important for adults to get out of their own familiar circles. If you live in a coastal, socially liberal neighborhood, maybe you should take out a subscription to the *Door,* the evangelical humor magazine; or maybe you should visit Branson, Missouri. Maybe you should stop in at a megachurch. Sure, it would be superficial familiarity, but it beats the iron curtains that now separate the nation's various cultural zones.

Look around at your daily life. Are you really in touch with the broad diversity of American life? Do you care?

FOR A SECOND READING

1. According to Brooks, our good intentions to create a more racially integrated society have failed because they "have run into the brick wall of human nature" (p. 526). Do you agree? Is segregation in America largely or exclusively a matter of human nature? And what kinds of solutions to this problem does such an understanding imply?

2. What do you make of the title of Brooks's essay? What, in his view, makes choosing "people like us" a preferable option to that of integration?

3. One of the main assumptions behind Brooks's argument is that issues like where we live and whom we associate with are fundamentally matters of personal choice. How accurately do you think his discussion treats the issue of choice? Do we all possess this kind of freedom to choose? And if not, what factors or circumstances undermine this possibility?

PUTTING IT INTO WRITING

4. Brooks ends his essay by challenging his readers: "Look around at your daily life. Are you really in touch with the broad diversity of American life? Do you care?" (p. 529). Write an essay in which you respond directly to Brooks's questions. How does the organization of your life (for example, by community, by living situation, by leisure activities) either support or refute Brooks's argument? In a hypothetical world that reflected an idealized portrait of diversity, what would need to change in the ways your life is structured to bring you in line with the ideal?

5. What kind of reader do you think would respond most favorably to Brooks's argument? In a three- to five-page essay present a detailed portrait of the type of reader you feel would make the ideal audience for this essay. What background, education, or political beliefs would this ideal reader have? What attitudes, values, or worldview? Make sure to explain, using quotes from Brooks's essay, why you define this reader in the ways you do. In what ways does defining this ideal reader strengthen or diminish Brooks's argument?

COMPARING ARGUMENTS

6. To what extent does Brooks's discussion of diversity intersect with J. D. Vance's portrait of "hillbilly" life (p. 531). Write an assessment of the ways these two authors seem to understand the issue of social class. What aspects of social class does each writer highlight? What larger conclusion(s) about the importance of class and class difference does each writer draw? Which conclusion resonates more with you? Why?

J. D. VANCE
Hillbilly Elegy

Our culture is rife with cultural stereotypes — images and depictions of people different from ourselves that emphasize these differences as signs of inferiority. Despite their obvious falseness, cultural stereotypes can nonetheless sometimes exert powerful influence over how we think about and judge people not "like us." Tackling this challenge head on, J. D. Vance takes a deeper dive into the stereotypes that defined his upbringing as a member of rural Appalachia's "hillbilly" class. In the process, he offers a portrait of rural, white, working-class life that alternately challenges and reinforces some of the most powerful stigmas this stereotype evokes.
J. D. Vance is a Kentucky-born writer who is currently a contributing opinion columnist for the *New York Times*. He is also the author of *Hillbilly Elegy: A Memoir of a Family and a Culture in Crisis* (2016), from which the selection below is excerpted.

Before You Read

What does the term "hillbilly" mean to you? What images or associations does it evoke?

DURING THAT TIME, MAMAW AND I STARTED TO TALK ABOUT the problems in our community. Mamaw encouraged me to get a job—she told me that it would be good for me and that I needed to learn the value of a dollar. When her encouragement fell on deaf ears, she then demanded that I get a job, and so I did, as a cashier at Dillman's, a local grocery store.

Working as a cashier turned me into an amateur sociologist. A frenetic stress animated so many of our customers. One of our neighbors would walk in and yell at me for the smallest of transgressions—not smiling at her, or bagging the groceries too heavy one day or too light the next. Some came into the store in a hurry, pacing between aisles, looking frantically for a particular item. But others waded through the aisles deliberately, carefully marking each item off of their list. Some folks purchased a lot of canned and frozen food, while others consistently arrived at the checkout counter with carts piled high with fresh produce. The more harried a customer, the more they purchased precooked or frozen food, the more likely they were to be poor. And I knew they were poor because of the clothes they wore or because they purchased their food with food stamps. After a few months, I came home and asked Mamaw

> *As my job taught me a little more about America's class divide, it also imbued me with a bit of resentment, directed toward both the wealthy and my own kind.*

why only poor people bought baby formula. "Don't rich people have babies, too?" Mamaw had no answers, and it would be many years before I learned that rich folks are considerably more likely to breast-feed their children.

As my job taught me a little more about America's class divide, it also imbued me with a bit of resentment, directed toward both the wealthy and my own kind. The owners of Dillman's were old-fashioned, so they allowed people with good credit to run grocery tabs, some of which surpassed a thousand dollars. I knew that if any of my relatives walked in and ran up a bill of over a thousand dollars, they'd be asked to pay immediately. I hated the feeling that my boss counted my people as less trustworthy than those who took their groceries home in a Cadillac. But I got over it: One day, I told myself, I'll have my own damned tab.

I also learned how people gamed the welfare system. They'd buy two dozen-packs of soda with food stamps and then sell them at a discount for cash. They'd ring up their orders separately, buying food with food stamps, and beer, wine, and cigarettes with cash. They'd regularly go through the checkout line speaking on their cell phones. I could never understand why our lives felt like a struggle while those living off of government largesse enjoyed trinkets that I only dreamed about.

5   Mamaw listened intently to my experiences at Dillman's. We began to view much of our fellow working class with mistrust. Most of us were struggling to get by, but we made do, worked hard, and hoped for a better life. But a large minority was content to live off the dole. Every two weeks, I'd get a small paycheck and notice the line where federal and state income taxes were deducted from my wages. At least as often, our drug-addict neighbor would buy T-bone steaks, which I was too poor to buy for myself but was forced by Uncle Sam to buy for someone else. This was my mind-set when I was seventeen, and though I'm far less angry today than I was then, it was my first indication that the policies of Mamaw's "party of the working man"—the Democrats—weren't all they were cracked up to be.

Political scientists have spent millions of words trying to explain how Appalachia and the South went from staunchly Democratic to staunchly Republican in less than a generation. Some blame race relations and the Democratic Party's embrace of the civil rights movement. Others cite religious faith and the hold that social conservatism has on evangelicals in that region. A big part of the explanation lies in the fact that many in the white working class saw precisely what I did, working at Dillman's. As far back as the 1970s, the white working class began to turn to Richard Nixon because of a perception that, as one man put it, government was "payin' people who are on welfare today doin' nothin'! They're laughin' at our society! And we're all hardworkin' people and we're gettin' laughed at for workin' every day!"[1]

At around that time, our neighbor—one of Mamaw and Papaw's oldest friends—registered the house next to ours for Section 8. Section 8 is a government program that offers low-income residents a voucher to rent housing. Mamaw's friend had little luck renting his property, but when he qualified his house for the Section 8 voucher, he virtually assured that would change. Mamaw saw it as a betrayal, ensuring that "bad" people would move into the neighborhood and drive down property values.

Despite our efforts to draw bright lines between the working and nonworking poor, Mamaw and I recognized that we shared a lot in common with those whom we thought gave our people a bad name. Those Section 8 recipients looked a lot like us. The matriarch of the first family to move in next door was born in Kentucky but moved north at a young age as her parents sought a better life. She'd gotten involved with a couple of men, each of whom had left her with a child but no support. She was nice, and so were her kids. But the drugs and the late-night fighting revealed troubles that too many hillbilly transplants knew too well. Confronted with such a realization of her own family's struggle, Mamaw grew frustrated and angry.

> *Despite our efforts to draw bright lines between the working and nonworking poor, Mamaw and I recognized that we shared a lot in common with those whom we thought gave our people a bad name.*

From that anger sprang Bonnie Vance the social policy expert: "She's a lazy whore, but she wouldn't be if she was forced to get a job"; "I hate those fuckers for giving these people the money to move into our neighborhood." She'd rant against the people we'd see in the grocery store: "I can't understand why people who've worked all their lives scrape by while these deadbeats buy liquor and cell phone coverage with our tax money."

These were bizarre views for my bleeding-heart grandma. And if she blasted the government for doing too much one day, she'd blast it for doing too little the next. The government, after all, was just helping poor people find a place to live, and my grandma loved the idea of anyone helping the poor. She had no philosophical objection to Section 8 vouchers. So the Democrat in her would resurface. She'd rant about the lack of

10

jobs and wonder aloud whether that was why our neighbor couldn't find a good man. In her more compassionate moments, Mamaw asked if it made any sense that our society could afford aircraft carriers but not drug treatment facilities—like Mom's—for everyone. Sometimes she'd criticize the faceless rich, whom she saw as far too unwilling to carry their fair share of the social burden. Mamaw saw every ballot failure of the local school improvement tax (and there were many) as an indictment of our society's failure to provide a quality education to kids like me.

Mamaw's sentiments occupied wildly different parts of the political spectrum. Depending on her mood, Mamaw was a radical conservative or a European-style social Democrat. Because of this, I initially assumed that Mamaw was an unreformed simpleton and that as soon as she opened her mouth about policy or politics, I might as well close my ears. Yet I quickly realized that in Mamaw's contradictions lay great wisdom. I had spent so long just surviving my world, but now that I had a little space to observe it, I began to see the world as Mamaw did. I was scared, confused, angry, and heartbroken. I'd blame large businesses for closing up shop and moving overseas, and then I'd wonder if I might have done the same thing. I'd curse our government for not helping enough, and then I'd wonder if, in its attempts to help, it actually made the problem worse.

Mamaw could spew venom like a Marine Corps drill instructor, but what she saw in our community didn't just piss her off. It broke her heart. Behind the drugs, and the fighting matches, and the financial struggles, these were people with serious problems, and they were hurting. Our neighbors had a kind of desperate sadness in their lives. You'd see it in how the mother would grin but never really smile, or in the jokes that the teenage girl told about her mother "smacking the shit out of her." I knew what awkward humor like this was meant to conceal because I'd used it in the past. Grin and bear it, says the adage. If anyone appreciated this, Mamaw did.

The problems of our community hit close to home. Mom's struggles weren't some isolated incident. They were replicated, replayed, and relived by many of the people who, like us, had moved hundreds of miles in search of a better life. There was no end in sight. Mamaw had thought she escaped the poverty of the hills, but the poverty—emotional, if not financial—had followed her. Something had made her later years eerily similar to her earliest ones. What was happening? What were our neighbor's teenage daughter's prospects? Certainly the odds were against her, with a home life like that. This raised the question: What would happen to me?

I was unable to answer these questions in a way that didn't implicate something deep within the place I called home. What I knew is that other people didn't live like we did. When I visited Uncle Jimmy, I did not wake to the screams of neighbors. In Aunt Wee and Dan's neighborhood, homes were beautiful and lawns well manicured, and police came around to smile and wave but never to load someone's mom or dad in the back of their cruiser.

So I wondered what was different about us—not just me and my   15
family but our neighborhood and our town and everyone from Jackson to Middletown and beyond.

NOTE

[1]Rick Perlstein, *Nixonland: The Rise of a President and the Fracturing of America* (New York: Scribner, 2008).

FOR A SECOND READING

1. Vance devotes a good deal of this essay to examining and analyzing the political views of his grandmother, Mamaw. How would you characterize these views? Do they accord with your assumptions or expectations about white, working-class politics? How or how not?

2. Vance is deeply critical of the welfare system, recalling with bitterness those of his friends and neighbors who "lived off the dole" while he worked for a living. Do you think Vance's critique is fair? Does he characterize the welfare system in ways you think are accurate? How or how not?

3. Vance characterizes the emotional state of his childhood Appalachian community as one of "desperate sadness." How do you respond to this phrase? What does it suggest about the rules, scripts, and norms that govern life in this community?

PUTTING IT INTO WRITING

4. "Working as a cashier," writes Vance, "turned me into an amateur sociologist" (p. 531). To what extent can this same role be applied to Vance's readers? In a 500-word essay, present a "sociological" analysis of the portrait of white, working-class life this essay presents. Which behaviors or attitudes Vance profiles here stand out to you as most noteworthy? What do they suggest to you about the culture of rural Appalachia he attempts to evoke?

5. Vance writes: "Mom's struggles weren't some isolated incident. They were replicated, replayed and relived by many of the people who like us, had moved hundreds of miles in search of a better life. There was no end in sight. . . . What was happening?" (p. 534). How does Vance answer his own question? What kind of explanation does this

essay provide for the cycle of struggle it depicts? What reasons does the essay offer for why this cycle is so difficult to break? Do you find these reasons persuasive? Why or why not?

COMPARING ARGUMENTS

6. Vance shares with David Brooks (p. 525) an interest in exploring the dynamics of homogeneous culture: places where people largely share the same background, attitudes, and experience. How do you think Brooks would respond to Vance's portrait of "hillbilly" life? Do you think he would find in it support of his thesis about Americans' reluctance to embrace diversity? Why or why not?

Scenes and Un-Scenes: *Class Dismissed?*

It has long been a commonplace that Americans are unable, or at least unwilling, to talk directly about social class. Rather than tackle this issue head on, Americans often address social class indirectly, by focusing on other issues. To illustrate, consider today's pop culture. These days, we are far more apt to come across news stories, TV shows, or websites that address racial, ethnic, or gender difference, than we are to encounter ones that offer a frank discussion of social class. If we want to understand how Americans are encouraged to think about class, therefore, we need to dig beneath the surface of what is explicitly shown or said to the unspoken messages that lie underneath these words. This is where we can find the clearest evidence of the norms and scripts designed to teach us about class difference. The examples that follow present you with an opportunity to do just this.

Patrick Wymore/Moviestills/AGE Fotostock

▲ *The hit ABC series* Black-ish *has been lauded as a smart, contemporary depiction of African American life, credited by many for using its light comic touch to address such serious issues as racial profiling, police brutality, and workplace discrimination. Largely overlooked, however, is the degree to which* Black-ish *also serves as a telling index of contemporary America's class ideals as well. Living in a well-appointed, suburban home, filled with all the comforts and possessions that symbolize the good life, the fictional Johnson family illustrates the complex ways that messages about race and class intersect in today's popular culture.*

Bloomberg/Getty Images

▲▲ *In the aftermath of the 2016 presidential campaign, many observers credited the success of Donald Trump to his ability to mobilize and manipulate the anger of working-class voters. During the many months of the campaign, however, Trump and his representatives framed his appeal less in terms of class than in more broadly nationalist terms: as an effort to "Make America Great Again." Embedded within this patriotic encomium, though, were some clearly class-coded messages designed to address the concerns of blue-collar voters anxious about the prospect of shrinking wages and job loss.*

Class appeals have ▶▶ *also long been a hallmark of advertising as well. Here we see an example of how retailers sell the idea of social mobility to their customers, holding forth the "promise" that their "new brand" can deliver middle-class status at a reasonable price.*

JCPENNEY LAUNCHES NEW BRAND PROMISE:

GET YOUR PENNEY'S **WORTH**

538

FOR A SECOND READING

1. Are we always fully aware of the ways media shape our assumptions about social class? What do you think would change if we were to become more aware?

2. In your view, does the social class of the viewer make any difference in what these images show or say? How might people from different social classes draw different conclusions about what these pop culture texts are saying? Why?

3. How typical or representative do you think these examples are? In your view, are they emblematic of the ways Americans are taught to think (or not think) about social class?

PUTTING IT INTO WRITING

4. This collection of images makes clear that cultural messages about social class can be conveyed by what a text says and also by what it does *not* say, by what it shows and also by what it leaves out. Choose one of the images showcased above. Then write a quick assessment of the messages about social class it conveys by virtue of what is omitted. What key elements or aspects of social class are left out? How do these omissions influence the conclusions viewers are encouraged to draw?

5. As discussed earlier in this chapter, identification is often a process in which we learn to read ourselves into the messages and norms promoted by our culture. Choose one of the examples above and write a one-page analysis of how it invites its viewers to identify with the class norms it promotes. What portrait of social class does this image present? What strategies does it use to encourage viewers to read themselves into this portrait?

COMPARING ARGUMENTS

6. J. D. Vance (p. 531) is a writer interested in exploring how the dynamics of social class affect peoples' attitudes and actions. Describe the kind of pop culture text you think Vance would create to capture the world of working-class Appalachia his essay depicts. What form would this text take (e.g., ad, website, TV show, etc.)? What kind of portrait would it present? And what messages (spoken or unspoken) would it convey?

GARNETTE CADOGAN
Black and Blue

We're all likely familiar with the phrase "driving while black," a refrain uttered by countless African Americans who have found themselves stopped and interrogated by the police for minor or nonexistent infractions. But what, asks Garnette Cadogan, about the parallel experience of "walking while black"? What fears, suspicions, and outright hostility do black men in particular confront whenever they walk down the street? Using his own personal experiences as a model, Cadogan tells the story of what he saw and what he learned as a black man navigating public space in America. Cadogan is editor-at-large of *Nonstop Metropolis* and is at work on a book on walking. He is currently a Martin Luther King Jr. Visiting Scholar at the Department of Urban Studies and Planning at the Massachusetts Institute of Technology (MIT), a Visiting Fellow at the Institute for Advanced Studies in Culture at the University of Virginia, and a Visiting Scholar at the Institute for Public Knowledge at New York University. This selection was published in *The Fire This Time* (2016), a collection of essays exploring race in contemporary America, and was first published in *Freeman's: Arrival*.

Before You Read

How do you respond to the phrase, "walking while black"? What does it suggest to you about the state of race relations in America?

> *"My only sin is my skin.*
> *What did I do, to be so black and blue?"*
> >   –Fats Waller, "(What Did I Do to Be So) Black and Blue?"
>
> *"Manhattan's streets I saunter'd, pondering."*
> >   –Walt Whitman, "Manhattan's Streets I Saunter'd, Pondering"

MY LOVE FOR WALKING STARTED IN CHILDHOOD, OUT OF NECESSITY. No thanks to a stepfather with heavy hands, I found every reason to stay away from home and was usually out—at some friend's house or at a street party where no minor should be—until it was too late to get public transportation. So I walked.

The streets of Kingston, Jamaica, in the 1980s were often terrifying—you could, for instance, get killed if a political henchman thought you came from the wrong neighborhood, or even if you wore the wrong color. Wearing orange showed affiliation with one political party and green with the other, and if you were neutral or traveling far from home you chose your colors well. The wrong color in the wrong neighborhood could mean your last day. No wonder, then, that my friends and the rare nocturnal passerby declared me crazy for my long late-night treks that traversed warring political zones. (And sometimes I did pretend to be crazy, shouting non sequiturs when I passed through especially dangerous spots, such as the place where thieves hid on the banks of a storm drain. Predators would ignore or laugh at the kid in his school uniform speaking nonsense.)

I made friends with strangers and went from being a very shy and awkward kid to being an extroverted, awkward one. The beggar, the vendor, the poor laborer—those were experienced wanderers, and they became my nighttime instructors; they knew the streets and delivered lessons on how to navigate and enjoy them. I imagined myself as a Jamaican Tom Sawyer, one moment sauntering down the streets to pick low-hanging mangoes that I could reach from the sidewalk, another moment hanging outside a street party with battling sound systems, each armed with speakers piled to create skyscrapers of heavy bass. These streets weren't frightening. They were full of adventure when they weren't serene. There I'd join forces with a band of merry walkers, who'd miss the last bus by mere minutes, our feet still moving as we put out our thumbs to hitchhike to spots nearer home, making jokes as vehicle after vehicle raced past us. Or I'd get lost in Mittyesque moments, my young mind imagining alternate futures. The streets had their own safety: Unlike at home, there I could be myself without fear of bodily harm. Walking became so regular and familiar that the way home became home.

The streets had their rules, and I loved the challenge of trying to master them. I learned how to be alert to surrounding dangers and nearby delights, and prided myself on recognizing telling details that my peers missed. Kingston was a map of complex, and often bizarre, cultural and political and social activity, and I appointed myself its nighttime cartographer. I'd know how to navigate away from a predatory pace, and to speed up to chat when the cadence of a gait announced friendliness. It was almost always men I saw. A lone woman walking in the middle of the night was as common a sight as Sasquatch; moonlight pedestrianism was too dangerous for her. Sometimes at night as I made my way down from hills above Kingston, I'd have the impression that the city was set on "pause" or in extreme slow motion, as that as I descended I was cutting across Jamaica's deep social divisions. I'd make my way briskly past the mansions in the hills overlooking the city, now transformed into a carpet of dotted lights under a curtain of stars, saunter by middle-class subdivisions hidden behind high walls crowned with barbed wire, and zigzag through neighborhoods of zinc and wooden shacks crammed together and leaning like a tight-knit group of limbo dancers. With my descent came an increase in the vibrancy of street life—except when it didn't; some poor neighborhoods had both the violent gunfights and the eerily deserted streets of the cinematic Wild West. I knew well enough to avoid those even at high noon.

5   I'd begun hoofing it after dark when I was ten years old. By thirteen I was rarely home before midnight, and some nights found me racing against dawn. My mother would often complain, "Mek yuh love street suh? Yuh born a hospital; yuh neva born a street." ("Why do you love the streets so much? You were born in a hospital, not in the streets.")

I left Jamaica in 1996 to attend college in New Orleans, a city I'd heard called "the northernmost Caribbean city." I wanted to discover—on foot, of course—what was Caribbean and what was American about it. Stately mansions on oak-lined streets with streetcars clanging by, and brightly colored houses that made entire blocks look festive; people in resplendent costumes dancing to funky brass bands in the middle of the street; cuisine—and aromas—that mashed up culinary traditions from Africa, Europe, Asia, and the American South; and a juxtaposition of worlds old and new, odd and familiar: Who wouldn't want to explore this?

On my first day in the city, I went walking for a few hours to get a feel for the place and to buy supplies to transform my dormitory room from a prison bunker into a welcoming space. When some university staff members found out what I'd been up to, they warned me to restrict my walking to the places recommended as safe to tourists and the parents of freshmen. They trotted out statistics about New Orleans's crime rate. But Kingston's crime rate dwarfed those numbers, and I decided to ignore these well-meant cautions. A city was waiting to be discovered, and I wouldn't let inconvenient facts get in the way. These American criminals are nothing on Kingston's, I thought. They're no real threat to me.

In this city of exuberant streets, walking became a complex and often oppressive negotiation.

What no one had told me was that I was the one who would be considered a threat.

Within days I noticed that many people on the street seemed apprehensive of me: Some gave me a circumspect glance as they approached, and then crossed the street; others, ahead, would glance behind, register my presence, and then speed up; older white women clutched their bags; young white men nervously greeted me, as if exchanging a salutation for their safety: "What's up, bro?" On one occasion, less than a month after my arrival, I tried to help a man whose wheelchair was stuck in the middle of a crosswalk; he threatened to shoot me in the face, then asked a white pedestrian for help.

10   I wasn't prepared for any of this. I had come from a majority-black country in which no one was wary of me because of my skin color. Now I wasn't sure who was afraid of me. I was especially unprepared for the cops. They regularly stopped and bullied me, asking questions that took

my guilt for granted. I'd never received what many of my African American friends call "The Talk": No parents had told me how to behave when I was stopped by the police, how to be as polite and cooperative as possible, no matter what they said or did to me. So I had to cobble together my own rules of engagement. Thicken my Jamaican accent. Quickly mention my college. "Accidentally" pull out my college identification card when asked for my driver's license.

My survival tactics began well before I left my dorm. I got out of the shower with the police in my head, assembling a cop-proof wardrobe. Light-colored oxford shirt. V-neck sweater. Khaki pants. Chukkas. Sweatshirt or T-shirt with my university insignia. When I walked I regularly had my identity challenged, but I also found ways to assert it. (So I'd dress Ivy League style, but would, later on, add my Jamaican pedigree by wearing Clarks Desert Boots, the footwear of choice of Jamaican street culture.) Yet the all-American sartorial choice of white T-shirt and jeans, which many police officers see as the uniform of black troublemakers, was off-limits to me—at least, if I wanted to have the freedom of movement I desired.

In this city of exuberant streets, walking became a complex and often oppressive negotiation. I would see a white woman walking toward me at night and cross the street to reassure her that she was safe. I would forget something at home but not immediately turn around if someone was behind me, because I discovered that a sudden backtrack could cause alarm. (I had a cardinal rule: Keep a wide perimeter from people who might consider me a danger. If not, danger might visit me.) New Orleans suddenly felt more dangerous than Jamaica. The sidewalk was a minefield, and every hesitation and self-censored compensation reduced my dignity. Despite my best efforts, the streets never felt comfortably safe. Even a simple salutation was suspect.

One night, returning to the house that, eight years after my arrival, I thought I'd earned the right to call my home, I waved to a cop driving by. Moments later, I was against his car in handcuffs. When I later asked him—sheepishly, of course; any other way would have asked for bruises—why he had detained me, he said my greeting had aroused his suspicion. "No one waves to the police," he explained. When I told friends of his response, it was my behavior, not his, that they saw as absurd. "Now why would you do a dumb thing like that?" said one. "You know better than to make nice with police."

A few days after I left on a visit to Kingston, Hurricane Katrina slashed and pummeled New Orleans. I'd gone not because of the storm but because my adoptive grandmother, Pearl, was dying of cancer. I hadn't wandered those streets in eight years, since my last visit, and I returned to them now mostly at night, the time I found best for thinking, praying, crying. I walked to feel less alienated—from myself, struggling with the pain of seeing my grandmother terminally ill; from my home in New Orleans, underwater and seemingly abandoned; from my home country, which now, precisely because of its childhood familiarity, felt foreign to me. I was surprised by how familiar those streets felt. Here was the corner where the fragrance of jerk chicken greeted me, along with the warm tenor and peace-and-love message of Half Pint's "Greetings," broadcast from a small but powerful speaker to at least a half-mile radius. It was as if I had walked into 1986, down to the soundtrack. And there was the wall of the neighborhood shop, adorned with the Rastafarian colors red, gold, and green along with images of local and international heroes Bob Marley, Marcus Garvey, and Haile Selassie. The crew of boys leaning against it and joshing each other were recognizable; different faces, similar stones. I was astonished at how safe the streets felt to me, once again one black body among many, no longer having to anticipate the many ways my presence might instill fear and how to offer some reassuring body language Passing police cars were once again merely passing police cars. Jamaican police could be pretty brutal, but they didn't notice me the way American police did. I could be invisible in Jamaica in a way I can't be invisible in the United States.

15   Walking had returned to me a greater set of possibilities. And why walk, if not to create a new set of possibilities? Following serendipity, I added new routes to the mental maps I had made from constant walking in that city from childhood to young adulthood, traced variations on the old pathways. Serendipity, a mentor once told me, is a secular way of speaking of grace; it's unearned favor. Seen theologically, then, walking is an act of faith. Walking is, after all interrupted falling. We see, we listen, we speak, and we trust that each step we take won't be our last, but will lead us into a richer understanding of the self and the world.

In Jamaica, I felt once again as if the only identity that mattered was my own, not the constricted one that others had constructed for me. I strolled into my better self. I said, along with Kierkegaard, "I have walked myself into my best thoughts."

When I tried to return to New Orleans from Jamaica a month later, there were no flights. I thought about flying to Texas so I could make my way back to my neighborhood as soon as it opened for reoccupancy, but my adoptive aunt, Maxine, who hated the idea of me returning to a hurricane zone before the end of hurricane season, persuaded me to come to stay in New York City instead. (To strengthen her case she sent me an article about Texans who were buying up guns because they were afraid of the influx of black people from New Orleans.)

This wasn't a hard sell: I wanted to be in a place where I could travel by foot and, more crucially, continue to reap the solace of walking at night. And I was eager to follow in the steps of the essayists, poets, and novelists who'd wandered that great city before me—Walt Whitman, Herman

Melville, Alfred Kazin, Elizabeth Hardwick. I had visited the city before, but each trip had felt like a tour in a sports car. I welcomed the chance to stroll. I wanted to walk alongside Whitman's ghost and "descend to the pavements, merge with the crowd, and gaze with them." So I left Kingston, the popular Jamaican farewell echoing in my mind: "Walk good!" *Be safe on your journey, in other words, and all the best in your endeavors.*

I arrived in New York City, ready to lose myself in Whitman's "Manhattan crowds, with their turbulent musical chorus." I marveled at what Jane Jacobs praised as "the ballet of the good city sidewalk" in her old neighborhood, the West Village. I walked up past midtown skyscrapers, releasing their energy as lively people onto the streets, and on into the Upper West Side, with its regal Beaux Arts apartment buildings, stylish residents, and buzzing streets. Onward into Washington Heights, the sidewalks spilled over with an ebullient mix of young and old Jewish and Dominican American residents, past leafy Inwood, with parks whose grades rose to reveal beautiful views of the Hudson River, up to my home in Kingsbridge in the Bronx, with its rows of brick bungalows and apartment buildings nearby Broadway's bustling sidewalks and the peaceful expanse of Van Cortlandt Park. I went to Jackson Heights in Queens to take in people socializing around garden courtyards in Urdu, Korean, Spanish, Russian, and Hindi. And when I wanted a taste of home, I headed to Brooklyn, in Crown Heights, for Jamaican food and music and humor mixed in with the flavor of New York City. The city was my playground.

I explored the city with friends, and then with a woman I'd begun 20 dating. She walked around endlessly with me, taking in New York City's many pleasures. Coffee shops open until predawn; verdant parks with nooks aplenty; food and music from across the globe; quirky neighborhoods with quirkier residents. My impressions of the city took shape during my walks with her.

As with the relationship, those first few months of urban exploration were all romance. The city was beguiling, exhilarating, vibrant. But it wasn't long before reality reminded me I wasn't invulnerable, especially when I walked alone.

One night in the East Village, I was running to dinner when a white man in front of me turned and punched me in the chest with such force that I thought my ribs had braided around my spine. I assumed he was drunk or had mistaken me for an old enemy, but found out soon enough that he'd merely assumed I was a criminal because of my race. When he discovered I wasn't what he imagined, he went on to tell me that his assault was my own fault for

Walking — the simple, monotonous act of placing one foot in front of the other to prevent falling — turns out to be not so simple if you're black.

545

running up behind him. I blew off this incident as an aberration, but the mutual distrust between me and the police was impossible to ignore. It felt elemental. They'd enter a subway platform; I'd notice them. (And I'd notice all the other black men registering their presence as well, while just about everyone else remained oblivious to them.) They'd glare. I'd get nervous and glance. They'd observe me steadily. I'd get uneasy. I'd observe them back, worrying that I looked suspicious. Their suspicions would increase. We'd continue the silent, uneasy dialogue until the subway arrived and separated us at last.

I returned to the old rules I'd set for myself in New Orleans, with elaboration. No running, especially at night; no sudden movements; no hoodies; no objects—especially shiny ones—in hand; no waiting for friends on street corners, lest I be mistaken for a drug dealer; no standing near a corner on the cell phone (same reason). As comfort set in, inevitably I began to break some of those rules, until a night encounter sent me zealously back to them, having learned that anything less than vigilance was carelessness.

After a sumptuous Italian dinner and drinks with friends, I was jogging to the subway at Columbus Circle—I was running late to meet another set of friends at a concert downtown. I heard someone shouting and I looked up to see a police officer approaching with his gun trained on me. "Against the car!" In no time, half a dozen cops were upon me, chucking me against the car and tightly handcuffing me. "Why were you running?" "Where are you going?" "Where are you coming from?" "I said, why were you running?!" Since I couldn't answer everyone at once, I decided to respond first to the one who looked most likely to hit me. I was surrounded by a swarm and tried to focus on just one without inadvertently aggravating the others.

25   It didn't work. As I answered that one, the others got frustrated that I wasn't answering them fast enough and barked at me. One of them, digging through my already-emptied pockets, asked if I had any weapons, the question more an accusation. Another badgered me about where I was coming from, as if on the fifteenth round I'd decide to tell him the truth he imagined. Though I kept saying—calmly, of course, which meant trying to manage a tone that ignored my racing heart and their spittle-filled shouts in my face—that I had just left friends two blocks down the road, who were yes, sir, yes, officer, of course, officer, all still there and could vouch for me, to meet other friends whose text messages on my phone could verify that, it made no difference.

For a black man, to assert your dignity before the police was to risk assault. In fact, the dignity of black people meant less to them, which was why I always felt safer being stopped in front of white witnesses than black witnesses. The cops had less regard for the witness and entreaties of black onlookers, whereas the concern of white witnesses usually registered on them. A black witness asking a question or politely raising an objection could quickly become a fellow detainee. Deference to the police, then, was sine qua non for a safe encounter.

The cops ignored my explanations and my suggestions and continued to snarl at me. All except one of them, a captain. He put his hand on my back, and said to no one in particular, "If he was running for a long time he would have been sweating." He then instructed that the cuffs be removed. He told me that a black man had stabbed someone earlier two or three blocks away and they were searching for him. I noted that I had no blood on me and had told his fellow officers where I'd been and how to check my alibi—unaware that it was even an alibi, as no one had told me why I was being held, and of course, I hadn't dared ask. From what I'd seen, anything beyond passivity would be interpreted as aggression.

The police captain said I could go. None of the cops who detained me thought an apology was necessary. Like the thug who punched me in the East Village, they seemed to think it was my own fault for running.

Humiliated, I tried not to make eye contact with the onlookers on the sidewalk, and I was reluctant to pass them to be on my way. The captain, maybe noticing my shame, offered to give me a ride to the subway station. When he dropped me off and I thanked him for his help, he said, "It's because you were polite that we let you go. If you were acting up it would have been different."

I realized that what I least liked about walking in New York City wasn't merely having to learn new rules of navigation and socialization—every city has its own. It was the arbitrariness of the circumstances that required them, an arbitrariness that made me feel like a child again, that infantilized me. When we first learn to walk, the world around us threatens to crash into us. Every step is risky. We train ourselves to walk without crashing by being attentive to our movements, and extra-attentive to the world around us. As adults we walk without thinking, really. But as a black adult I am often returned to that moment in childhood when I'm just learning to walk. I am once again on high alert, vigilant.

Some days, when I am fed up with being considered a troublemaker upon sight, I joke that the last time a cop was happy to see a black male walking was when that male was a baby taking his first steps. On many walks, I ask white friends to accompany me, just to avoid being treated like a threat. Walks in New York City, that is; in New Orleans, a white woman in my company sometimes attracted more hostility. (And it is not lost on me that my woman friends are those who best understand my plight; they have developed their own vigilance in an environment where they are constantly treated as targets of sexual attention.) Much of my walking is as my friend Rebecca once described it: A pantomime undertaken to avoid the choreography of criminality.

30

Walking while black restricts the experience of walking, renders inaccessible the classic Romantic experience of walking alone. It forces me to be in constant relationship with others, unable to join the New York flaneurs I had read about and hoped to join. Instead of meandering aimlessly in the footsteps of Whitman, Melville, Kazin, and Vivian Gornick, more often I felt that I was tiptoeing in Baldwin's—the Baldwin who wrote, way back in 1960, "Rare, indeed, is the Harlem citizen, from the most circumspect church member to the most shiftless adolescent, who does not have a long tale to tell of police incompetence, injustice, or brutality. I myself have witnessed and endured it more than once." Walking as a black man has made me feel simultaneously more removed from the city, in my awareness that I am perceived as suspect, and more closely connected to it, in the full attentiveness demanded by my vigilance. It has made me walk more purposefully in the city, becoming part of its flow, rather than observing, standing apart.

But it also means that I'm still trying to arrive in a city that isn't quite mine. One definition of home is that it's somewhere we can most be ourselves. And when are we more ourselves but when walking, that natural state in which we repeat one of the first actions we learned? Walking—the simple, monotonous act of placing one foot before the other to prevent falling—turns out not to be so simple if you're black. Walking alone has been anything but monotonous for me; monotony is a luxury.

A foot leaves, a foot lands, and our longing gives it momentum from rest to rest. We long to look, to think, to talk, to get away. But more than anything else, we long to be free. We want the freedom and pleasure of walking without fear—without others' fear—wherever we choose. I've lived in New York City for almost a decade and have not stopped walking its fascinating streets. And I have not stopped longing to find the solace that I found as a kid on the streets of Kingston. Much as coming to know New York City's streets has made it closer to home to me, the city also withholds itself from me via those very streets. I walk them, alternately invisible and too prominent. So I walk caught between memory and forgetting, between memory and forgiveness.

FOR A SECOND READING

1. Take a moment to evaluate the title of this essay. What is the phrase "black and blue" typically used to describe? What image is it generally intended to evoke? How is this different from the way Cadogan is using it here?

2. "The sidewalk," Cadogan writes, "was a minefield, and every hesitation and self-censored compensation reduced my dignity" (p. 543).

Analyze the language Cadogan chooses here. What is he trying to say by comparing a sidewalk to a minefield? What behavior is he trying to describe by using the phrase "self-censored compensation"? And why do you think he ends this sentence by raising the question of his own dignity?

3. Cadogan writes: "Some days, when I'm fed up with being considered a troublemaker upon sight, I joke that the last time a cop was happy to see a black male walking was when that male was a baby taking his first steps" (p. 547). Do you find this joke to be funny? What more serious point is Cadogan trying to make by telling it?

PUTTING IT INTO WRITING

4. "I noticed," writes Cadogan, "that many people on the street seemed apprehensive of me: Some gave me a circumspect glance as they approached, and then crossed the street; others, ahead, would glance behind, register my presence, and then speed up; older white women clutched their bags; young white men nervously greeted me, as if exchanging a salutation for their safety, 'What's up, bro'?" (p. 542). Reflect on the various reactions that Cadogan itemizes here. What do these responses tell us about the particular social scripts that govern how black men in public spaces are viewed? In what ways do you think Cadogan is attempting to rewrite these scripts?

5. Cadogan organizes his essay, in part, around a comparison between the experience of walking the streets in America (New Orleans and New York) and walking the streets in Jamaica (Kingston). In a 500-word essay, evaluate how these two pedestrian portraits compare. What key differences between these two experiences does Cadogan emphasize? How is he using these differences to make a larger argument about what it means to navigate public space as a black man?

COMPARING ARGUMENTS

6. Cadogan and Ta-Nehisi Coates (p. 550) both examine the complex relationship between black men and the police. Taken together, what larger argument about police behavior—and police brutality—do these two essays present? What specific actions, assumptions, and attitudes on the part of the police are these two writers calling out for critique? How persuasive do you find this critique to be? Why?

TA-NEHISI COATES
Between the World and Me

For all the attention devoted to the state of race relations in America, it is still easy to overlook the central, inescapable fact that for countless black citizens, racism is a visceral daily reality. It is this central fact that both initiates and animates the selection below by Ta-Nehisi Coates. Chronicling the countless ways black people experience racism as a threat to or assault upon their bodies, Coates offers a bracing rebuke to the comforting fictions we often use to obscure the harder truths about race in America. Ta-Nehisi Coates is a national correspondent for *The Atlantic* magazine, where he writes about culture, politics, and social issues. He is also a recipient of a MacArthur "genius grant," as well as the author of *The Beautiful Struggle: A Father, Two Sons, and an Unlikely Road to Manhood* (2009), and *Between the World and Me*, which won the National Book Award in 2015. This selection is excerpted from the introduction to *Between the World and Me*.

Before You Read

How comfortable are you talking about the issue of race? Do you think we are encouraged in this culture to speak about this issue honestly and openly?

SON,

Last Sunday the host of a popular news show asked me what it meant to lose my body. The host was broadcasting from Washington, D.C., and I was seated in a remote studio on the far west side of Manhattan. A satellite closed the miles between us, but no machinery could close the gap between her world and the world for which I had been summoned to speak. When the host asked me about my body, her face faded from the screen, and was replaced by a scroll of words, written by me earlier that week.

The host read these words for the audience, and when she finished she turned to the subject of my body, although she did not mention it specifically. But by now I am accustomed to intelligent people asking about the condition of my body without realizing the nature of their request. Specifically, the host wished to know why I felt that white America's progress, or rather the progress of those Americans who believe that they are white, was built on looting and violence. Hearing this, I felt an old and indistinct sadness well up in me. The answer to this question is the record of the believers themselves. The answer is American history.

There is nothing extreme in this statement. Americans deify democracy in a way that allows for a dim awareness that they have, from time to time, stood in defiance of their God. But democracy is a forgiving God and America's heresies—torture, theft, enslavement—are so common among individuals and nations that none can declare themselves immune. In fact, Americans, in a real sense, have never betrayed their God. When Abraham Lincoln declared, in 1863, that the battle of Gettysburg must ensure "that government of the people, by the people, for the people, shall not perish from the earth," he was not merely being aspirational; at the onset of the Civil War, the United States of America had one of the highest rates of suffrage in the world. The question is not whether Lincoln truly meant "government of the people" but what our country has, throughout its history, taken the political term "people" to actually mean. In 1863 it did not mean your mother or your grandmother, and it did not mean you and me. Thus America's problem is not its betrayal of "government of the people," but the means by which "the people" acquired their names.

This leads us to another equally important ideal, one that Americans 5 implicitly accept but to which they make no conscious claim. Americans believe in the reality of "race" as a defined, indubitable feature of the natural world Racism—the need to ascribe bone-deep features to people and then humiliate, reduce, and destroy them inevitably follows from this inalterable condition. In this way, racism is rendered as the innocent daughter of Mother Nature, and one is left to deplore the Middle Passage or the Trail of Tears the way one deplores an earthquake, a tornado, or any other phenomenon that can be cast as beyond the handiwork of men.

> *[B]y now, I am accustomed to intelligent people asking about the condition of my body without realizing the nature of their request.*

But race is the child of racism, not the father. And the process of naming "the people" has never been a matter of genealogy and physiognomy so much as one of hierarchy. Difference in hue and hair is old. But the belief in the preeminence of hue and hair, the notion that these factors can correctly organize a society and that they signify deeper attributes, which are indelible—this is the new idea at the heart of these new people who have been brought up hopelessly, tragically, deceitfully, to believe that they are white.

These new people are, like us, a modern invention. But unlike us, their new name has no real meaning divorced from the machinery of criminal power. The new people were something else before they were

> *Turn into a dark stairwell and your body can be destroyed. The destroyers will rarely be held accountable. Mostly they will receive pensions.*

white — Catholic, Corsican, Welsh, Mennonite, Jewish — and if all our national hopes have any fulfillment, then they will have to be something else again. Perhaps they will truly become American and create a nobler basis for their myths. I cannot call it. As for now, it must be said that the process of washing the disparate tribes white, the elevation of the belief in being white, was not achieved through wine tastings and ice cream socials, but rather through the pillaging of life, liberty, labor, and land; through the flaying of backs; the chaining of limbs; the strangling of dissidents; the destruction of families; the rape of mothers; the sale of children; and various other acts meant, first and foremost to deny you and me the right to secure and govern our own bodies.

The new people are not original in this. Perhaps there has been, at some point in history, some great power whose elevation was exempt from the violent exploitation of other human bodies. If there has been, I have yet to discover it. But this banality of violence can never excuse America, because America makes no claim to the banal. America believes itself exceptional, the greatest and noblest nation ever to exist, a lone champion standing between the white city of democracy and the terrorists, despots, barbarians, and other enemies of civilization. One cannot, at once, claim to be superhuman and then plead mortal error. I propose to take our countrymen's claims of American exceptionalism seriously, which is to say I propose subjecting our country to an exceptional moral standard. This is difficult because there exists, all around us, an apparatus urging us to accept American innocence at face value and not to inquire too much. And it is so easy to look away, to live with the fruits of our history and to ignore the great evil done in all of our names. But you and I have never truly had that luxury. I think you know.

I write you in your fifteenth year. I am writing you because this was the year you saw Eric Garner choked to death for selling cigarettes; because you know now that Renisha McBride was shot for seeking help, that John Crawford was shot down for browsing in a department store. And you have seen men in uniform drive by and murder Tamir Rice, a twelve-year-old child whom they were oath-bound to protect. And you have seen men in the same uniforms pummel Marlene Pinnock, someone's grandmother, on the side of a road. And you know now, if your did not before, that the police departments of your country have been endowed with the authority to destroy your body. It does not matter if the destruction is the result of an unfortunate overreaction. It does not matter if it originates in a misunderstanding. It does not matter if the destruction springs from a foolish policy. Sell cigarettes without the proper authority and your body can be destroyed. Resent the people trying to entrap your body and it can be destroyed. Turn into a dark stairwell and your body can be destroyed. The destroyers will rarely be held accountable. Mostly they will receive pensions. And destruction is merely the superlative form of a dominion whose prerogatives include friskings, detainings, beatings, and humiliations. All of this is common to black people. And all of this is old for black people. No one is held responsible.

There is nothing uniquely evil in these destroyers or even in this moment. The destroyers are merely men enforcing the whims of our country, correctly interpreting its heritage and legacy. It is hard to face this. But all our phrasing—race relations, racial chasm, racial justice, racial profiling, white privilege, even white supremacy—serves to obscure that racism is a visceral experience, that it dislodges brains, blocks airways, rips muscle, extracts organs, cracks bones, breaks teeth. You must never look away from this. You must always remember that the sociology, the history, the economics, the graphs, the charts, the regressions all land, with great violence, upon the body.

That Sunday, with that host, on that news show, I tried to explain this as best I could within the time allotted. But at the end of the segment, the host flashed a widely shared picture of an eleven-year-old black boy tearfully hugging a white police officer. Then she asked me about "hope." And I knew then that I had failed. And I remembered that I had expected to fail. And I wondered again at the indistinct sadness welling up in me. Why exactly was I sad? I came out of the studio and walked for a while. It was a calm December day. Families, believing themselves white, were out on the streets. Infants, raised to be white, were bundled in strollers. And I was sad for these people, much as I was sad for the host and sad for all the people out there watching and reveling in a specious hope. I realized then why I was sad. When the journalist asked me about my body, it was like she was asking me to awaken her from the most gorgeous dream. I have seen that dream all my life. It is perfect houses with nice lawns. It is Memorial Day cookouts, block associations, and driveways. The Dream is treehouses and the Cub Scouts. The Dream smells like peppermint but tastes like strawberry

> **[F]or so long I have wanted to escape into the Dream, to fold my country over my head like a blanket. But this has never been an option because the Dream rests on our backs, the bedding made from our bodies.**

shortcake. And for so long I have wanted to escape into the Dream, to fold my country over my head like a blanket. But this has never been an option because the Dream rests on our backs, the bedding made from our bodies. And knowing this, knowing that the Dream persists by warring with the known world, I was sad for the host, I was sad for all those families, I was sad for my country, but above all, in that moment, I was sad for you.

FOR A SECOND READING

1. Coates organizes this essay as a letter to his teenage son. Why do you think he chooses this particular form to present his argument? Do you find this choice to be effective? Why or why not?

2. "Race," declares Coates, "is the child of racism, not the father" (p. 551). What do you think he means by this? What is Coates saying here about where our ideas of race and racial difference come from? About the kind of cultural power racial thinking exerts over us?

3. Throughout this essay, Coates speaks of "the belief in being white" as a way of describing what it means to be white in America. Why do you think he uses this phrase rather than a more conventional term like "white identity"? What is Coates trying to say here about the nature and basis of white identity?

PUTTING IT INTO WRITING

4. Coates writes: "[T]he elevation of the belief in being white was not achieved through wine tastings and ice cream socials, but rather through the pillaging of life, liberty, labor, and land; through flaying of backs; the chaining of limbs; the strangling of dissidents; the destruction of families; the rape of mothers; the sale of children; and various other acts meant, first and foremost, to deny you and me the right to secure and govern our own bodies" (p. 552). In a 500-word essay, analyze the version of American history Coates evokes here. How would you characterize the story of enslavement this passage presents? What larger point about racial violence and white identity is Coates using this story to make?

5. Coates goes to great lengths to emphasize the ways racism is experienced as violence against black bodies: "[A]ll our phrasing— race relations, racial chasm, racial justice, racial profiling, white privilege, even white supremacy—serves to obscure that racism is a visceral experience, that it dislodges brains, blocks airways, rips muscle, extracts organs, cracks bones, breaks teeth" (p. 553). In a 500-word essay, analyze and evaluate the argument Coates is making here.

Do you agree that the public language typically used to discuss race relations actually obscures more than it illuminates the truth about racism itself? Do you find Coates's visceral description here to be a more accurate and effective way to capture the truth about racism? Why or why not?

COMPARING ARGUMENTS

6. For both Coates and Garnette Cadogan (p. 540), an examination of American racism is inextricably tied to a discussion of the black male body. Discuss the importance of the black male body to the argument each of these writers is making about race and racism in America. In each case, how do these writers make the body a central focus of their discussion? What particular aspects of racist behavior or racist history does the body enable each of these writers to highlight? Which writer, in your view, uses more effective rhetorical strategies to depict and discuss the black male body? Why?

Acting Like a Citizen: **Checking ID**

As noted in the introduction, identification can be a powerful tool for perpetuating and reinforcing cultural norms. When we identify with a role scripted for us, and when we act out this role in our own lives, we are signaling our acceptance of the cultural norms that underlie it. Of course, we have also seen that the flip side of this can be true too. When we identify with (and act out) a public role outside of the mainstream, we are making clear our resistance to prevailing cultural norms. It is in this way, in fact, that identification can be understood as part of what it means to "act like a citizen." When we identify with roles that are at odds with the cultural norms, we are in a sense taking action, creating a new and different set of norms for ourselves. The following exercises give you an opportunity to test out this proposition.

PERSONAL POLITICS   Spend some time scrolling through political campaign ads on the web. What similarities do you notice? What are the most common strategies these ads use to promote their respective candidates or causes? Next, create a campaign ad for a candidate or cause important to you. As you do, think about the type of language, layout, and imagery you want this ad to include. Then, explain in writing why you created this particular type of ad. Why is this candidate or cause important to you? What do you think makes the strategies you employed here especially powerful or persuasive?

READING YOURSELF INTO THE NEWS   As more and more of the news these days reaches us through social media, we find ourselves steered toward stories that reinforce our preexisting assumptions and biases. Choose a social media platform through which you regularly access news. First, describe the types of stories your newsfeed presents. Next, analyze the ways these stories seem designed to appeal to a specific type of reader. What views and/or biases do these news stories reinforce? To what extent do you hold these views and/or biases yourself? And finally, create an alternative newsfeed, one that better reflects who you truly are and what you actually want to know.

SOCIAL ACTION SELFIE Media observers of all stripes routinely bemoan the widespread habit of taking "selfies," deriding this practice as proof that our culture is growing increasingly narcissistic. Push back against this view by creating a selfie that advocates for action to be taken on a larger social or civic issue. What image does your selfie present? What larger issue does it address, and what action does it argue should be taken? Share this selfie with your classmates, and ask them to write a brief response. Do they understand the issue being addressed? Are they persuaded to take action? Why or why not?

Acknowledgments

ACKNOWLEDGMENTS

Pages 390–393

Maddie Oatman, "The Racist, Twisted History of Tipping," from *Mother Jones*, May/June 2016. Copyright © 2016 The Foundation for National Progress. All rights reserved. Used by permission and protected by the Copyright Laws of the United States. The printing, copying, redistribution, or retransmission of this Content without express written permission is prohibited.

Pages 394–400

Mike Rose, "Blue-Collar Brilliance," reprinted from *The American Scholar*, Volume 78, No. 3, Summer 2009. Copyright © 2009 by Mike Rose. Used by permission.

Pages 413–416

Navneet Alang, "The Comfort of a Digital Confidante," *The Atlantic*, August 31, 2016. Copyright © 2016 The Atlantic Media Co., as first published in The Atlantic Magazine. All rights reserved. Distributed by Tribune Content Agency, LLC.

Pages 417–421

Mae Wiskin, "Can't Quit the Clicks: The Rise of Social Media Rehab," *Broadly. Vice*, August 17, 2016. Reprinted by permission of the author.

Pages 424–430

Bijan Stephen, "Get Up, Stand Up: Social Media Helps Black Lives Matter Fight the Power," *Wired,* November 2015. Copyright © 2015 Conde Nast. Used with permission.

Pages 431–437

Caroline O'Donovan, "Nextdoor Rolls Out Product Fix It Hopes Will Stem Racial Profiling," BuzzFeed, August 24, 2016. Reprinted by permission.

Page 440

Sherry Turkle, *Reclaiming Conversation: The Power of Talk in a Digital Age.* Copyright © 2015 by Sherry Turkle. Used by permission of Penguin Press, an imprint of Penguin Publishing Group, a division of Penguin Random House LLC. All rights reserved.

Pages 456–471

Charles Duhigg, "How Companies Learn Your Secrets," from *The New York Times*, February 16, 2012. Copyright © 2012 by The New York Times Company. All rights reserved. Used by permission and protected by the Copyright Laws of the United States. The printing, copying, redistribution, or retransmission of this Content without express written permission is prohibited.

Pages 478–481

Peter Lovenheim, "Won't You Be My Neighbor?" from *The New York Times*, June 23, 2008 issue. Copyright © 2008 by The New York Times. All rights reserved. Used by permission and protected by the Copyright Laws of the United States. The printing, copying, redistribution, or retransmission of this Content without express written permission is prohibited.

Page 482

Matthew Desmond, *Evicted: Poverty and Profit in the American City*. Copyright © 2016 by Matthew Desmond. Used by permission of Crown Books, an imprint of the Crown Publishing Group, a division of Penguin Random House LLC. All rights reserved.

Pages 499–503
Sarah Mirk, "Tuning In: How a New Generation Is Schooling Itself on Sexuality," *Bitch Magazine* Fall Issue, September 28, 2016. Reprinted by permission of Bitch Media.

Page 504
Thomas Page McBee, "Self-Made Man #1: The Truckstop," *The Rumpus*, February 21, 2012. Reprinted by permission of the author.

Pages 510–516
Rebecca Traister, *All the Single Ladies: Unmarried Women and the Rise of an Independent Nation.* Copyright © 2016 by Rebecca Traister. Reprinted by permission of Simon & Schuster

Pages 517–522
Jodi Kantor, "Historic Day for Gays, but Twinge of Loss for an Outsider Culture," from *The New York Times*, June 26, 2015. Copyright © 2015 The New York Times. All rights reserved. Used by permission and protected by the Copyright Laws of the United States. The printing, copying, redistribution, or retransmission of this Content without express written permission is prohibited.

Pages 525–530
David Brooks, "People Like Us," *The Atlantic*, September 2003. Reprinted by permission of the author.

Pages 531–536
J. D. Vance, *Hillbilly Elegy: A Memoir of a Family and Culture in Crisis,* pp. 138–143. Copyright © 2016 by J. D. Vance. Reprinted by permission of HarperCollins Publishers.

Pages 540–549
Garnette Cadogan, "Black and Blue," from *Freeman's Arrival.* Copyright © 2015. Reprinted by permission of the Chris Calhoun Agency on behalf of the author.

Pages 550–555
Ta-Nehisi Coates, excerpt from *Between the World and Me.* Copyright © 2015 by Ta-Nehisi Coates. Used by permission of Spiegel & Grau, an imprint of Random House, a division of Random House LLC. All rights reserved.

Index of Authors and Titles